ENCYCLOPEDIA OF
THE UNITED STATES
IN THE TWENTIETH CENTURY

# Editorial Board

# Encyclopedia of
# The United States
## in the Twentieth Century

Stanley I. Kutler
*Editor in Chief*

Robert Dallek
David A. Hollinger
Thomas K. McCraw
*Associate Editors*

Judith Kirkwood
*Assistant Editor*

## Volume IV

CHARLES SCRIBNER'S SONS
Macmillan Library Reference USA
Simon & Schuster Macmillan
*New York*

SIMON & SCHUSTER AND PRENTICE HALL INTERNATIONAL
*London   Mexico City   New Delhi   Singapore   Sydney   Toronto*

Charles Scribner's Sons
Macmillan Publishing Company
1633 Broadway
New York, New York 10019

Library of Congress Cataloging-in-Publication Data

Encyclopedia of the United States in the twentieth century
    / Stanley I. Kutler, editor in chief; Robert Dallek,
    David A. Hollinger, Thomas K. McCraw, associate
    editors; Judith Kirkwood, assistant editor.

     p.        cm.

    Includes bibliographical references and index.

    ISBN 0-13-210535-7 (set: hc: alk. paper). —
0-13-307190-1 (vol. 1: hc: alk. paper). — 0-13-307208-8
(vol. 2: hc: alk. paper). — 0-13-307216-9 (vol. 3: hc:
alk. paper). — 0-13-307224-X (vol. 4: hc: alk. paper).

    1. United States—Encyclopedias.   I. Kutler, Stanley
I.  E740.7.E53  1996
973′.003–dc20
95-22696                         CIP

    5 7 9 11 13 15 17 19       20 18 16 14 12 10 8 6 4

PRINTED IN THE UNITED STATES OF AMERICA

The paper in this publication meets the requirements of
ANSI/NISO Z39.48-1992 (Permanence of Paper)

# Contents

# Contents of Other Volumes

# CONTENTS OF OTHER VOLUMES

# CONTENTS OF OTHER VOLUMES

# Alphabetical Table of Contents

# ALPHABETICAL TABLE OF CONTENTS

# Common Abbreviations Used in This Work

| | | | |
|---|---|---|---|
| Ala. | Alabama | Me. | Maine |
| Ariz. | Arizona | Mich. | Michigan |
| Ark. | Arkansas | Minn. | Minnesota |
| Art. | Article | Miss. | Mississippi |
| b. | born | Mo. | Missouri |
| c. | *circa*, about, approximately | Mont. | Montana |
| Calif. | California | n. | note |
| cf. | *confer*, compare | N.C. | North Carolina |
| chap. | chapter (plural, chaps.) | n.d. | no date |
| Cong. | Congress | N.D. | North Dakota |
| Colo. | Colorado | Neb. | Nebraska |
| Conn. | Connecticut | Nev. | Nevada |
| d. | died | N.H. | New Hampshire |
| D | Democrat, Democratic | N.J. | New Jersey |
| D.C. | District of Columbia | N.Mex. | New Mexico |
| Del. | Delaware | no. | number (plural, nos.) |
| diss. | dissertation | n.p. | no place |
| ed. | editor (plural, eds); edition | n.s. | new series |
| e.g. | *exempli gratia*, for example | N.Y. | New York |
| enl. | enlarged | Okla. | Oklahoma |
| esp. | especially | Oreg. | Oregon |
| et al. | *et alii*, and others | p. | page (plural, pp.) |
| etc. | *et cetera*, and so forth | Pa. | Pennsylvania |
| exp. | expanded | P.L. | Public Law |
| f. | and following (plural, ff.) | pt. | part (plural, pts.) |
| Fla. | Florida | R | Republican |
| Ga. | Georgia | Rep. | Representative |
| ibid. | *ibidem*, in the same place (as the one immediately preceding) | rev. | revised |
| | | R.I. | Rhode Island |
| Ida. | Idaho | S.C. | South Carolina |
| i.e. | *id est*, that is | S.D. | South Dakota |
| Ill. | Illinois | sec. | section (plural, secs.) |
| Ind. | Indiana | Sen. | Senator |
| Kan. | Kansas | ser. | series |
| Ky. | Kentucky | ses. | session |
| La. | Louisiana | supp. | supplement |
| M.A. | Master of Arts | Tenn. | Tennessee |
| Mass. | Massachusetts | Tex. | Texas |
| Md. | Maryland | UN | United Nations |

# COMMON ABBREVIATIONS USED IN THIS WORK

| | | | | |
|---|---|---|---|---|
| U.S. | United States | | Vt. | Vermont |
| U.S.S.R. | Union of Soviet Socialist Republics | | Wash. | Washington |
| v. | versus | | Wis. | Wisconsin |
| Va. | Virginia | | W.Va. | West Virginia |
| vol. | volume (plural, vols.) | | Wyo. | Wyoming |

ENCYCLOPEDIA OF
THE UNITED STATES
IN THE TWENTIETH CENTURY

# Part 6

# CULTURE

# INTRODUCTION

## *David A. Hollinger*

At the start of the twentieth century "culture" was an idea of how people "ought to behave but did not." These words of the historian Henry F. May catch the meaning of culture when it was understood to be a set of wholesome ideals embodied in the best of "popular" as well as "fine" arts and philosophies.

This highly normative sense of culture was gradually displaced by a more descriptive, anthropological perspective that withheld judgment of other people's behavior. According to this more expansive and generous notion, virtually the totality of human creativity and behavior counted as culture, regardless of whether it was taken to be uplifting to the beholder. Even politics, scientific knowledge, and economic behavior were sometimes said to partake of culture.

Yet distinctions needed to be made, or the concept of culture would lose its utility to distinguish anything at all. In recent years this notoriously problematic word has served most often as a means of identifying a loosely bounded sphere of human endeavor in which people are understood to be less constrained by physical, economic, and social conditions. Culture, in this view, is the sphere in which people show their distinctive humanity the most clearly, and construct their own *meanings* for the world they encounter.

In this common understanding, culture is a broad category that embraces religion and recreation as well as literature, philosophy, and a multitude of popular and refined arts. These are the topics addressed in this part of the Encyclopedia. Yet a number of the topics addressed elsewhere in this work have a strong cultural content.

The traditional distinction between "elite" and "popular" culture helps to define many topics within cultural history. Part 6 opens with two articles of especially broad scope, each designed to present prominent features of the development of "elite" and "popular" culture, respectively, and to lay the groundwork for many of the other articles in this section.

"Literary Culture," by David A. Hollinger, traces the movements in critical taste surrounding the production and reception of literary art, especially as these movements interact with the political enthusiasms and social tensions of the successive decades of this century. This article connects with a number of the other articles in this section, including "Philosophy" by David J. Depew and "Patronage of the Arts" by Katherine D. McCarthy.

The second opening essay, "Mass Media and Popular Culture" by Ronald G. Walters, deals with the content, technology, and political economy of profit-making performances in a great variety of genres of entertainment, including vaudeville, film, radio, television, and magazines. This essay, too, connects closely with several other articles, especially Peter Levine's "Sports," Nancy Rexford's "Clothing and Appearance," and Randy Roberts's "Leisure and Recreation."

But the distinction between "elite" and "popular" culture should not be drawn too sharply. Indeed it is properly blurred in many of the articles in this section, including "Architecture" by Robert Twombly and "Visual Arts" by George H. Roeder, Jr. So, too, is this distinction appropriately blurred in relation to the cultural creativity that takes place within religiously and ethno-racially defined communities.

Communities of this kind are highly relevant to much of the cultural life of Americans in the twentieth century. The articles on African American cultural movements by Kenneth W. Warren and Judaism and Jewish culture by Deborah Dash Moore address two of the most sharply defined and historically conspicuous of these communities. The varieties of Protestantism, Catholicism, and nontraditional religions are dealt with in other essays of the same genre by Richard Wightman Fox, Patrick W. Carey, and Catherine L. Albanese, respectively.

But this Encyclopedia approaches the multicultural character of the United States less through a study of groups than through a recognition of the role groups play in arenas of culture that transcend particular communities of descent. Richard Crawford's article on music, for example, traces the contributions to an American musical tradition inspired by a number of different, specific ethno-racial communities. The United States is more than a collection of ethno-racial and religious groups, and its cultural life is more than a series of discrete, descent-defined traditions. The process by which ethno-racial communities are formed, and transformed, could well be a topic within this part, but the editors found these topics to be important enough to merit two extended articles in Part 1, "Race" and "Ethnicity and Immigration."

Part 6 concludes with two articles on schools, the major institutions of cultural transferral in modern, industrialized societies. Carl F. Kaestle's "Elementary and Secondary Education" addresses the shifting dy-namics of schooling for children, while Hugh Hawkins's "The University" traces the development of higher education in relation to the increasing demands that American society has placed on its colleges and universities as the century has gone forward.

Studies of culture have been prominent in the historiography of the 1970s to the 1990s. An encyclopedia of this type published in 1976 would have emphasized social history, in keeping with the preoccupations of scholars of that era. In 1956, political and diplomatic history would have dominated the pages of a work of this kind. Historians of neither of these earlier eras would have devoted nearly as much space to the history of culture as does this Encyclopedia of 1996. In this respect, as in many others, this Encyclopedia reflects the current engagements of the historical profession and tries to harvest the profession's recent work.

# LITERARY CULTURE

## David A. Hollinger

In 1900, Americans who talked about literature, or tried to write it, knew what it was. Literature consisted chiefly of poems, plays, essays, novels, and short stories. Some artfully designed diaries, letters, and old-fashioned, narrative histories could also count, as could biographies and autobiographies. Americans of 1900 were also resolved about the tasks literature was expected to perform. It was to direct attention to higher things, especially to the ideals that could inform proper conduct. Look only upon the good, the true, and the beautiful, it was said, not upon the evil, the false, and the ugly. The established literary doctrines of 1900 were idealization, uplift, and refinement. A more "realistic" encounter with social, economic, and psychological complexities was promoted with equal resolution by a few scattered, dissenting voices, including some of the period's most eloquent. Many of these realists, however, were also moralists who believed that literature's honest exposure of unjust and sordid social realities might inspire men and women of good will to act effectively and morally in the world.

Nine decades later, the prevailing literary culture was quite different. Genre-blurring, boundary-crossing, and canon-revision were prominent occupations of a generation of literary intellectuals acutely aware of the socially constructed status of the categories once taken to be natural. Some teachers and scholars of American literature scrutinized political tracts, philosophical treatises, films, and a great range of folk and commercially popular artifacts with the same methodological sobriety traditionally brought to Shakespeare and Henry James. Literary doctrines were defined less sharply, and constituted a less coherent presence in the intellectual discourse of the society than had been the case a century before. The popular label for the tastes and expectations of the 1990s was a term that itself stood for a principled suspicion of coherence and integration: "postmodernism." The autonomy and agency of the human subject was in doubt, and texts exposing these humanistic conceits were often praised as postmodernist. Just what else postmodernism entailed, and whether it was even a good thing, were matters for an earnest debate that overlapped episodically with discussion of another issue: should works of literature be valued only for their perceived aesthetic merit, or also for their good social effects? This issue was far from new, but was now engaged with unprecedented intensity in relation to several specific social goals, including the appreciation of human diversity and the critical exploration of the distribution of power along lines of gender, race, ethnicity, and class.

The historical path from the prevailing literary culture of 1900 to that of the 1990s was anything but straight and singular. Literature is a site of contestation, as is implied by the conflicts between uplifters and realists and between postmodernists and their critics; it is not a single torch to be passed from Victorians to moderns, and then from moderns to postmoderns. Yet these familiar labels and much-heralded transitions do call attention to an important, if simple truth. Literature and the critical discussion surrounding it often do display distinctive sensibilities and help to constitute some of the major intellectual movements of a given time and place. "Literary culture," a term broader than the sum of anyone's list of literature's genres, denotes this involvement of literature in movements that sweep across many arts and disciplines, often connect with politics and religion, and promote particular tastes and expectations. "Victorianism" and "modernism" are literary cultures in this sense.

The distinction between a period's "literature" and its "literary culture" can be illustrated with the case of Sinclair Lewis, the first American to win the Nobel Prize for literature. Many constructions of American literature of the 1920s offered in the final quarter of the twentieth century do not include Lewis, because his works, however moving they may have been to readers of two or three generations ago, are no longer considered interesting. But Lewis has not been erased from the literary culture of the 1920s. The latter is a distribution of cultural power then in effect, and still visible in the historical record. Hence Lewis remains an inescapably major figure in any historical treatment of the literary culture of the 1920s, but can be a minor figure in a history of literature written from the viewpoint of the critical tastes—the literary culture—of the 1990s.

What specific literary cultures have flourished in the United States in the twentieth century? What are the preeminent examples of literary art, critical commentary, educational practice, and political conduct associated with each of these cultures? What accounts for the rise and decline of these cultures in relation to one another? These are the central questions to which this article is addressed. This article also calls attention to major points of disjunction between the literary culture of a given era, on the one hand, and on the other, specific works undervalued at the time but much appreciated in the context of literary cultures of later decades.

## VICTORIANISM AND ITS CRITICS

The literary culture that emphasized idealization, uplift, and refinement was first identified and named by people who did not like it. These critics of the 1910s and 1920s called it "genteel," or "Puritan." Its own adherents did not see it as distinctive, however, and for that reason they called it, simply, "Culture," with the capital letter indicating its universal authority. By incanting this word, they confidently invoked principles more specific than they realized. Scholars of more recent times have called these principles "Victorian," a term less invidious than genteel, and more historically accurate than Puritan.

Several features of this particular literary culture render the England-centered label, Victorian, highly appropriate. This set of tastes and expectations was overwhelmingly Anglophilic. Its American adherents espoused, in a fashion somewhat more cheerful than was the norm in England, the moral intensity and the petty-bourgeois values of thrift, diligence, and individualism often called Victorian. The reticence about sexuality to which Queen Victoria gave her name was also evident. The most treasured part of the acknowledged canon was the same body of English texts recognized as great in England. This canon featured Milton and Shakespeare, but made room for a number of nineteenth-century poets and novelists, including Alfred Lord Tennyson and William Makepeace Thackeray. Charles Dickens, too, was revered, although the anxiety about industrial society

found in his work by later readers was generally ignored amid confidence in the progress of modern civilization. The supervisors of this literary culture, again following their English mentors, gave generous attention to classics of other modern European languages, including Cervantes in Spanish and Goethe in German, but were suspicious of recent and contemporary continental literature. Greek and Latin literature continued to command deference, but on terms set long since by classicists in England. Victorian, then, this literary culture certainly was. Yet the original, more polemical labels also help us to understand it.

What led H. L. Mencken and others to call it Puritan was its ethnosocial base in New England, and the decidedly Protestant character of its moralism. To be sure, Puritanism as a specific variation on Calvinist religion was long extinct, but the men and women who most conspicuously preached idealization, uplift, and refinement were of New England Protestant descent. They and their followers understood American literature to be almost entirely the work of New England authors. This understanding was displayed in Edmund Clarence Stedman's *An American Anthology 1787–1900* (1900), the first acclaimed collection of poems written by residents of the United States, and in Stedman's earlier, multigenre collection, the *Library of American Literature* (10 vols., 1888–1890).

Stedman was a leader in a generation of men of letters that consolidated a canon of American literature, consisting chiefly of works produced in the middle years of the nineteenth century by Henry Wadsworth Longfellow, James Fenimore Cooper, John Greenleaf Whittier, James Russell Lowell, Washington Irving, Oliver Wendell Holmes, Ralph Waldo Emerson, and William Cullen Bryant. Even within the range of the New England tradition, this list was later to seem selective. Stedman and his contemporaries paid little attention to Herman Melville, who until the 1920s was most often mentioned as an author of sea stories for boys. Nathaniel Hawthorne, Margaret Fuller, Edgar Allan Poe, and Henry David Thoreau were seen as minor figures, not remotely of the stature they would attain in the 1940s and 1950s when they, along with Melville, Emerson, and the distinctly non-New England Walt Whitman, became the basis for the notion of an "American renaissance."

By the time this notion flourished, the American writers most admired at the century's turn were, with the exception of Emerson, patronized as school authors. Their works were indeed required reading in public and private elementary and high schools throughout the United States until well into the twentieth century. The memorizing of Byrant's "Thanatopsis" (1817), of Lowell's "The Present Crisis" (1844), and of long selections from Longfellow's romantic wilderness epic, "The Song of Hiawatha" (1855), enabled this particular literary culture to sink its roots so deeply that generation after generation of intellectuals seemed never able to get it fully out of their systems, however much they fought it. As late as the 1950s *Mad* magazine could still take sufficiently for granted a youthful audience's familiarity with "Hiawatha" to subject it to playful parody: "In the bar called Gitchy Goomy, Where they drink the Giggle Water, There sits Melvin Furd, the Shoe Clerk."

One of Longfellow's nostalgic and didactic lyrics, "The Village Blacksmith" (1842), is an especially compact embodiment of the principles espoused by Stedman, George E. Woodbury, Hamilton Wright Mabie, and a host of other turn-of-the-century prescribers of public taste. The idealized shoer-of-horses is "a mighty man," whose hammer hits the anvil with a "measured beat" emitting sounds akin to those of "a sexton ringing the village bell." The "sweat" on our laborer's "brow" is "honest," and provides a lesson in rudimentary political economy: he can look "the whole world in the face, For he owes not any man." This didacticism is made explicit when Longfellow says "Thanks, thanks to thee, my worthy friend," for the lessons "thou hast taught," which include the value of hard work and persistence— "Each morning sees some task begin, Each evening sees its close"— and the need to achieve one's fortunes "at the flaming forge of life." On Sunday this epitome of American masculine strength shows his refinement. He "hears the parson pray and preach," and hears his daughter sing in the church choir, reminding him of "her mother's voice, Singing in Paradise!" Thus his strength is chaste, his uplifting character fully accessible to children, like those who, "running home from school," love to watch the blacksmith at work, and to "hear the bellows roar."

The child's perspective was vital. That nothing should appear in literature that could not be safely placed in the hands of a young girl was a principle defended even by so liberal a critic as William Dean Howells. The recognized dean of American letters had fought throughout the 1880s and 1890s against many of the limits of his tradition, cautioning against a gentility too precious to engage the social pathologies of industrial society. That this author of so blunt a novel of urban, capitalist life as *The Hazard of New Fortunes* (1890), patron of such realist writers as Mark

Twain, Hamlin Garland, and Stephen Crane, remained willing to confine literature to topics and language he thought suitable for the most innocent members of society is a telling sign of the intensity of Victorian reticence in 1900. In that year, when Theodore Dreiser's *Sister Carrie* suggested that a young woman confronting the new industrial conditions might have good reason to choose to sell her body, Howells, like his more "puritanical" colleagues, was appalled.

Works like *Sister Carrie* gave currency to Ambrose Bierce's sardonic definition of realism as "the art of depicting life as it is seen by toads." Dreiser's matter-of-fact account of social degradation beyond the reforming powers of the Christian conscience placed him well outside the established literary culture. But if *Sister Carrie* gave realism a new dimension, it did so by stretching in a "naturalistic" direction conventions of realistic representation that had already been developed by Howells, Garland, Crane, and Twain, among others. In 1900, realism was a recognized movement challenging the gentility associated with the school authors, and looking beyond Thackeray to a different set of models from the European continent: Émile Zola, Henrik Ibsen, and Gustave Flaubert. In place of the autonomous values idealized in the genteel texts, the realists were inclined, as Eric J. Sundquist has phrased it, to interpret the power of values as itself "a function of the many pressures of the economic and social market."

At the core of the proclaimed sensibility of realism was a determination to face reality directly, in an almost scientific fashion, substituting an ethic of truth-telling for an ethic of idealization, uplift, and refinement. "We must ask ourselves before we ask anything else" about a work of literature, insisted Howells, "Is it true?—true to the motives, the impulses, the principles that shape the life of actual men and women?" If the world about which Howells wanted the truth was somewhat more cheerful and encouraging of the human spirit than was the reality glimpsed by the average toad, Howells's ideal of truth-telling was nevertheless a direct response to what he saw as the excessively saccharine ideal of looking only on the good, the true, and the beautiful. Howells had to contend with zealots like Thomas DeWitt Talmage, who insisted that the reading of a single book that challenged Christian ideals could destroy a soul, just as "the scratch of a pin" could cause "lockjaw."

The realist revolt had gender, regional, and religious dimensions essential to an understanding of its historical significance. Realists routinely vilified the old tradition as effeminate. In fact, the realm of "polite letters" had been one of very few arenas in which women of late-nineteenth-century America had been able to pursue publicly a life of intellect. Careers in science, philosophy, and theology as well as law and politics were even more thoroughly closed to women. Socially prominent women such as Harriet Beecher Stowe and Louisa May Alcott managed to become best-selling authors in this milieu. While not quite the equals in critical acclaim of the classic school authors, these New England women were respected figures in Victorian literary culture. Realism was in part a masculinist project, informed by stereotypical notions of male hardness and of female proclivities for the fanciful and the frivolous. The men who made the realist movement were indeed men, and tended to be pompous about it. They also came from such out-of-the-way places as Wisconsin (Garland), Missouri (Twain), and California (Frank Norris), and thus brought to realism a regional diversity lacking in the vision of American literature advanced by Stedman and his friends. Howells himself had grown up in Ohio, then considered part of the West. These realists were, moreover, markedly more secular than were most of their Victorian counterparts. Lowell had invoked "the Great Avenger" keeping watch over humanity's "death-grapple in the darkness," but this reassuring presence was hard to find amid the wheatfields and railroads of Norris's *The Octopus* (1901), or behind the sun that looked down on Henry Fleming in Crane's *The Red Badge of Courage* (1895), or in the satanic hero of Twain's "The Mysterious Stranger."

When Twain's nihilistic account of the devil entertaining children was published posthumously in 1916, it was, in a remarkable triumph of the genteel tradition, greeted as a splendid story for little girls and boys. Twain, originally a "humorist," had been accepted as a man of letters before the turn of the century, but in the process many of the people doing the accepting had screened out as humor the depressed, jagged, and contradictory themes that have since engaged more sophisticated readers of *The Adventures of Huckleberry Finn* (1885) and *A Connecticut Yankee in King Arthur's Court* (1889). As has been demonstrated by Henry Nash Smith, Twain used a vernacular voice to bring into literature a range of experience and feeling alien to the school authors, whom Twain alternately worshiped and hated. Twain owed much of his acceptance to the mediating efforts of his close friend, Howells, who called him "the Lincoln of our literature." As this accolade implied, it was Twain, a realist idiosyncratically absorbed by

Victorians and later idolized in all American literary cultures, who came to occupy in the American language an informal office still held today in the Russian language by Pushkin, in the Italian by Dante, and in the English by Shakespeare: the office of the national poet, the writer who did more than any other to bring the national language to its most complete powers.

When Twain died in 1910 at the age of seventy-five, he was not surrounded by young realists taking over the American literary scene. Quite the contrary. One of the most remarkable facts in the historical demography of American literature is the sudden eclipse of realism through the deaths and quasi-retirements of its rising, young talents. Harold Frederic died two years after the publication in 1896 of his important realistic novel, *The Damnation of Theron Ware*, and both Norris and Crane died just after the turn of the century. Jack London, despite his youth, was in ill-health and died within a few years. Dreiser wrote nothing for a decade after the suppression of *Sister Carrie*. Garland had lost the realistic edge of his early fiction and was complacently writing his memoirs. Muckraking novels, of which Upton Sinclair's *The Jungle* (1906) was the most notorious, were counted more as reform efforts than as literature. Howells, born in 1837, had long since become the ornament of a literary establishment that downplayed his socially radical tendencies. Even the few women who had gained attention for strong writing in a realistic mode were not major factors at this time. The underappreciated Kate Chopin, whose *The Awakening* (1899) had been banned in her native Saint Louis and after 1906 was not reprinted until the 1950s, died in 1904. Charlotte Perkins Gilman, later hailed for *The Yellow Wall-Paper* (1892), a tale of madness that served to indict the gender-biased therapies of the day, was then known primarily as an economic theorist and social reformer. Edith Wharton moved to Paris two years after *The House of Mirth* (1905) had detailed a civilized woman's realization that beneath the facade of genteel conventions there operated a sexual economy imprisoning and virtually commodifying the women of polite society.

These destinies of individual realists, taken with Twain's death, left literature in the hands of a doctrinal old guard. The Victorian literary culture was more fully dominant during the decade prior to World War I than it had been at any time during the previous fifteen years. Prominent among the best-sellers of 1913 was Eleanor Hodgman Porter's indefatigably cheerful *Pollyanna*. Among the American writers who enjoyed great critical acclaim in the mid-1910s, the one whose work most tested the prevailing expectations for literature was James Branch Cabell. But the depth of Cabell's skepticism was concealed from many readers by his humor and irony.

Henry James survived until 1916, when he died a British subject, having resided primarily in England since the 1870s. The extent to which this exceptionally accomplished novelist—a brother of the philosopher William James—was an American, a realist, and a Victorian have all been debated earnestly. These uncertainties about James bespeak the protean character of his art, and they remind us, helpfully, of the limitations of literary cultures as frameworks for addressing in any detail the work of any individual artist of genius. Yet the work and reputation of Henry James is highly relevant to an understanding of the concerns that animated many Victorians and realists.

James had contempt for the Victorian literary culture as displayed in most of the American magazines of the era. He believed that the ideals of uplift, idealization, and refinement too often licensed an uncritical acceptance of morally naive, aesthetically stultifying work. His precise account of the social and psychological states of his characters was more realist than genteel, but he never exulted in bringing his readers face to face with dirt, as did some of the other realists, who—Twain among them—thought James too aristocratically aloof from the grubby realities in which they more often dealt. At the same time, James found a warm reception from Howells, and from the most discerning, least rigidly moralistic of the Victorians. William Crary Brownell, the only Victorian-genteel-Puritan critic other than Charles Eliot Norton whose writings inspire respect today, offered a lucid and probing appreciation of James's fiction in *American Prose Masters* (1909).

James's fiction itself provided the era's richest exploration of a tension between cosmopolitan and provincial impulses that, like James's artistic ideology and practice, cut across the realist-Victorian divide. This tension propelled Frederic's *Damnation of Theron Ware*, in which a young minister tries to find his way amid the attractions and repulsions of fin de siècle aesthetic, scientific, and religious complexities as available even in a small town in upstate New York. In James, this tension took the form of a career-long meditation on the cultural relationship of the United States to Europe. Americans traveling in Europe confronted their own American provinciality even in James's early fiction, in the 1870s and 1880s; but the complexity of this confrontation increased in the series of monumental books James produced shortly

after the turn of the century. "Live all you can," pleads the hero of *The Ambassadors* (1903), Lambert Strether, who engineers his own growth in worldliness by passively opening himself to the experience of Paris. In this novel and in two others, *The Golden Bowl* (1904) and *Wings of the Dove* (1902), and in *The American Scene* (1907), James's personal survey of America as he saw it after an absence of twenty-one years, James constructed the most nuanced, multidimensional account ever written of the terms on which European sophistication challenged, but was in some respects defeated by, American provinciality.

By the time James died in England, many Americans were caught up the preparedness movement in anticipation of entry into the war that had been underway in Europe for two years. This movement merits attention here because it played a brief, but pivotal role in the process by which the genteel tradition was finally weakened to the point that strikingly different principles could triumph in the 1920s. England's cause won the early and vehement support of many of the defenders of the established, highly Anglophilic culture. The absoluteness of this commitment to England, and the extravagant moralizing that often came with it, widened the gulf between these "custodians of culture," as Henry F. May has called them, and a group of younger writers based largely in New York's Greenwich Village. These dissidents, of whom John Reed, Emma Goldman, Max Eastman, Amy Lowell, and Randolph Bourne became the most widely known, were exploring abstract art, radical politics, experimental poetry, Freudian psychology, the philosophy of Nietzsche, and a variety of other initiatives resisted by the "custodians." Some of the latter actually welcomed the war as a means of suppressing silly, bohemian enthusiasms infecting youth throughout the North Atlantic West. Barrett Wendell, a professor of literature at Harvard University, declared the war a tonic for societies on the verge of moral and aesthetic decadence.

In this overheated atmosphere the heralds of the new became more iconoclastic, and the defenders of the old more rigid and shrill. Even Brownell, in *Standards* (1917), came close to matching the image of the stuffy, authoritarian critic retailed by Bourne and Mencken. Bourne was the strongest of the Greenwich Village dissenters. Amid this escalating, dialectical conflict between well-placed conservatives and a tiny but vocal avant-garde, Bourne wrote a series of antiwar, anti-Victorian essays in *Seven Arts*, a little magazine that folded under political pressure after American entry into the war. These essays set the stage for what would happen in the wake of the

Versailles Conference. Once the moral superiority of the Allied cause came to be seen as a fraud, the intellectuals who had massively invested their cultural capital in that cause were impoverished, while those, like Bourne, who been more skeptical found their credibility as public moralists incalculably increased. Although Bourne himself died as the war ended, his legacy was felt in the decade that followed.

## ANTI-VICTORIANS, LEFTISTS, AND SOUTHERNERS

In keeping with this dialectical conflict of the 1910s, the literary culture of the 1920s developed largely as a continuation of the reaction against Victorianism. The repudiation of the "sissy school of letters" in the name of a more robust and autonomous art became an almost sacred, and increasingly triumphant, calling. During the 1910s Mencken had railed in relative isolation against the Puritan-genteel culture, but when it was in ruins in 1919 and 1920 his attacks on its "timorous flaccidity" and "amiable hollowness" won the popular following that made his slashing prose a lasting emblem for the 1920s. Emblematic, too, were the fiercely anti-idealistic novels of Ernest Hemingway. In *The Sun Also Rises* (1926), set in Paris with a cast of American and British expatriates explicitly presented as a lost generation, Hemingway constructed modernity in the form of a friendship between a nymphomaniac and a veteran who had lost his sexual potency as a result of a wound suffered in the war. Again in *A Farewell to Arms* (1929), Hemingway offered a stoic hero who, bearing injuries and disillusion, made his lonely way through a world that plainly did not work. James Russell Lowell had urged young men to master fate, but fate, for Hemingway, had the last word. It was no coincidence that readers were simultaneously discovering *Moby-Dick* (1851), in which Lowell's contemporary, Melville, used an enigmatic white whale to bring down to size New England's extravagant confidence in human capabilities.

Many novelist contemporaries of Hemingway rode the crest of anti-Victorianism, including Sherwood Anderson, whose *Winesburg, Ohio* (1919) turned on its head the images of small-town life perpetuated by Longfellow's "Village Blacksmith," and, above all, Sinclair Lewis. *Main Street* (1920) detailed the deprivations of Carol Kennicott, a sensitive young woman trapped in a midwestern, small-town milieu subjected to additional satire in Lewis's *Babbitt* (1922). In response to the charge that these works offered nothing positive, Lewis wrote his most

critically acclaimed work, *Arrowsmith* (1925), which upheld the ethical ideals of pure science as an antidote to the philistinism, avarice, and general mediocrity Lewis believed characterized virtually every aspect of American life. Yet Lewis made scientific disinterestedness a virtually unattainable ideal, with the result that the power of this novel, too, was primarily in its scathing critique of officialdoms ranging from local businessmen's clubs to university administrators. A half-century later, Lewis was seen as a provincial writer of juvenile tastes whose fiction had involuntarily reproduced the conventionally wholesome side of the midwestern values he had labored to renounce. "Lewis's men are boys at heart," observed Alfred Kazin. Lewis's name was dropped from most lists of important American authors. But in his own time Lewis was made a giant by the market for antigentility, however shrill and shallow. Lewis's stature was reinforced when he was awarded the Pulitzer Prize for *Arrowsmith*, an honor he declined in a blaze of antiestablishment bravado. He linked the Pulitzer judges to the "the inquisition of earnest literary ladies" the misogynist Lewis believed compelled American authors "to become safe, polite, obedient, and sterile." Lewis continued this screed in 1930, when, as the first American to win the Nobel Prize for literature, he accepted with a speech in Stockholm denouncing American critics for appreciating Longfellow and for having listened too attentively to Howells.

In their affirmations of varieties of grit, Hemingway and Lewis bore some similarity to the realists of a quarter-century before. But another major novelist of the 1920s was less thoroughly consumed by the need to bloody his immediate cultural forebears. F. Scott Fitzgerald produced fiction equidistant from both the old realism and the old Victorianism, and aloof from the preoccupations of Mencken. Fitzgerald began as the writer of light stories for the *Saturday Evening Post* in which an attractive young man offered token resistance to convention before providing the reader with the reassuring lesson that the new generation will not be so terribly different from the old. In these soft, pleasant stories, which are not without an element of uplift, as Robert Sklar has shown, the hero's cleverness and charm eventually won the girl and the worldly success for which she was a symbol. Fitzgerald developed a more critical edge in *This Side of Paradise* (1920), but then, under the influence of the muckraking-realist classic, *The Jungle*, he produced a very different book, *The Great Gatsby* (1925). Here, Fitzgerald's romantic hero was redefined, and mocked, in relation to the hardness and corruption of urban, industrial society. The charming young man got neither the girl nor improved social standing, but was still to be loved as a poignant symbol for an American dream now lost.

Fitzgerald achieved this effect by telling two stories simultaneously. One updates "The Village Blacksmith" by celebrating the individual's capacities for self-creation and advancement, and the other updates the realist insistence on an honest look at a social order in which wealth and class, not diligent labor or clever maneuvering, determine one's fate. In the first story, a young man from North Dakota named James Gatz overcomes one material obstacle after another to make himself into Jay Gatsby, a Long Island millionaire. Gatsby wins the loyalty of the earthly and moralistic Nick Carraway, a character designed as a vehicle for the reader's prescribed appreciation for the virtues of traditional, small-town life. After the plutocracy closes ranks against Gatsby, then defeats and kills him, Carraway becomes, as Frederick J. Hoffman has said, "the guardian of Gatsby's illusion," and makes the reader love Gatsby in defeat. The triumph of the plutocracy is shown to be spiritually hollow. Against the grain of this myth-appreciating, idealist narrative cuts a second, demystifying-realist narrative based on what the reader is to accept as the facts of life. The agents of this second story are the realities to which Gatsby and other American dreamers are oblivious. Chief among these realities is the power of wealth and social standing, which crushes the bounder, whose dream of advancement is worth no more than the "obscene word" scrawled on the white steps of Gatsby's mansion by "some boy with a piece of brick." But this potentially climactic note of Hemingwayan disillusion is ultimately suppressed by the rival, mystifying narrative. Fitzgerald will not allow the obscene word to stand as Gatsby's benediction; he sends Carraway to erase it, drawing a shoe "raspingly across the stone." At the end we are unsure what the narrator Carraway will do with the rest of his life, but we know that bearing witness to Gatsby's "heightened sensitivity to the promises of life" (a point of the first narrative) is for Nick a more compelling mission than exposing in the public interest the illusory character of the American dream of upward mobility (a point of the second).

Fitzgerald's elaborate symbolism and his carefully qualified enchantment with a hero created out of a "Platonic conception of himself" were eventually taken as marks of a modernist sensibility. Not until the 1940s did a consistent pattern of tastes come to be associated with the word *modernism,* and to be institutionalized in magazines and in universities. At that time there was in place a modernist literary culture comparable in authority and coherence to the Victorian literary culture of the early years of the century. One striking feature of that literary culture demands attention here, while *The Great Gatsby* and other works of the 1920s are in close view: mid-century modernism's canon consisted almost entirely of works written between 1890 and 1930.

The selections later critics made from the 1920s, however, were indeed selective. The novels of Hemingway and Fitzgerald were included, but most of the authors were Europeans—James Joyce, Thomas Mann, and Marcel Proust are examples—who gradually built up a critical following until they came to occupy a position similar to that occupied at the turn of the century by Milton and Shakespeare. Prominent in this modernist canon, too, were works by Americans who had expatriated to Europe and had enjoyed only a limited following in the United States during the 1920s, when Fitzgerald and the returned expatriate Hemingway were already popular. These long-term expatriates included Gertrude Stein of Oakland, California, Ezra Pound of Idaho, and, above all, the great poet and critical essayist, T. S. Eliot of Saint Louis. Decisively excluded from the modernist canon were Mencken and Lewis, whose preoccupation with the ancient Victorians and whose lack of subtlety were by then seen as tedious failings of spirit. The poems of Edna St. Vincent Millay, popularly understood in the 1920s as pensive commentaries on "flaming youth," were dismissed as too light. Of the homespun sentimentalist Edgar A. Guest, a poet of enormous popularity in the 1920s, it was often said in the 1940s, "I'd rather be laid to rest than read a poem by Edgar Guest." Dismissed, too, was Willa Cather, whose *My Ántonia* (1918) and *Death Comes for the Archbishop* (1927) were seen as defenses of aesthetic and religious tradition at best, and, at worst, as romantic exercises in nostalgia. Not until the 1970s would Cather achieve a critical reputation to match the popular following her novels enjoyed when she published them. Cather was recovered through the claim, advanced with great ingenuity by Phyllis Rose and other critics, that Cather had been modernist all along. The 1920s are thus a vital inventory of potential ingredients for modernist literary culture, but the ingredients eventually selected stand to the modern tradition—as it came to be called—in the same relation that the school authors stand in relation to the genteel tradition.

A helpful signpost amid these complexities in the great transition from Victorian to modern is a book of 1931 written by Fitzgerald's Princeton classmate, Edmund Wilson. When Wilson wrote *Axel's Castle: A Study in the Imaginative Literature of 1870 to 1930*, he was both trying to define an element in the sensibility destined to be called modernist and searching for a way to make literature relevant to a society suddenly suffering from an acute economic depression. A revolution had been made by French writers, Wilson argued, and was manifest in the poems of Paul Valéry and the fiction of Proust. This French-centered symbolist movement embraced an individual conception of life, rather than a social one. It attempted to convey "unique personal feelings" through "a complicated association of ideas represented by a medley of metaphors." Wilson thought "English and American criticism" too often "at a loss" when trying to deal with this sharpened aestheticism. Wilson tried to explain this aestheticism, and to show that it had influenced some English poetry and fiction, too. To demonstrate this, Wilson included chapters on Joyce, William Butler Yeats, and two American expatriates, Eliot and Stein. *Axel's Castle* was thus an indictment of American critics of the 1920s for having provincially undervalued the era's most interesting innovations. This book did more than any other single work by an American to prepare the way for the modernist canon that was consolidated in the 1940s. But *Axel's Castle* also did something else. It expressed politically significant reservations about this modernist-symbolist sensibility.

Symbolist heroes "would rather drop out of the common life than have to struggle to make themselves a place in it," Wilson complained. "Indifferent to action and unconcerned with the group," these admittedly dazzling literary works were socially and politically barren. Insofar as they criticized society, they did so as a mere exercise: Proust exemplified "the pure intelligence playing luminously all about but not driven by the motor power of any hope and not directed by any creative imagination for the possibilities of human life." Such writers "will no longer serve as guides," said Wilson, looking into the Depression as an editor of the *New Republic*, the most distinguished Left-oriented journal in the country. In its pages Wilson had just urged liberals to "take communism away from the Communists" and to apply some of its basic insights to the United States. Although Wilson never joined the Communist party, he supported its candidates in the election of 1932 and read deeply in Marxism throughout the 1930s. At that decade's end, he published *To the Finland Station: A History of European Socialism to 1917* (1940), a guarded but sympathetic account of intellectual and

political steps culminating in Lenin's arrival at Saint Petersburg's Finland Railway Station in 1917. Thus Wilson was not only a discerning commentator on the literary culture of the 1920s and a prophet of the modernist synthesis that dominated the 1940s and 1950s; he was also a leading figure in the short-lived, but wave-making literary culture of the Left. Another of the *New Republic*'s literary editors, Malcolm Cowley, wrote one of that culture's most influential artifacts. In *Exile's Return: A Narrative of Ideas* (1934), Cowley recounted the exploits and ideologies of American expatriates in Paris, and justified the return of most of these exiles—himself above all—in terms of the inadequacy of individualist aestheticism and the imperative of artists to engage with the real world. Hence the salient return was twofold, from Paris back to the United States, and from indulgence in rarified mental states back to social responsibilities. "The religion of art is dead," Cowley proclaimed; "the inner world" so exquisitely nourished by the "lost generation" had become "enfeebled as a result of its isolation." But "the outer world" is "strong and colorful" and demands the attention of artists. Cowley believed that writers were inevitably caught up in a worldwide class struggle, and that by denying this reality any writer risked serving interests he or she might regret. Cowley wanted writers to actively choose "the worker's side," which he believed would both aid the cause of social justice and "make them better artists." For Cowley, the side of the worker was usually the side of the Communist party, although he, like Wilson, stopped short of joining that organization. He sometimes declared himself a "Stalinist" in the pages of the *New Republic*, most notoriously in 1937 when essentially defending the Moscow trials against the charges—later established as true—that these trials had been rigged by Stalin, and that the confessions of the accused had been obtained through torture.

Writers more strictly loyal than Cowley to the Communist party took the lead in trying to develop a "proletarian realism" responsive to the needs and interests of workers. Michael Gold formulated the most strict and widely quoted conception of this realism, which required that all literary works have a "social theme" and eschew the "precious silly little agonies" favored by bourgeois writers. "We know that the manure heap is the hope of the future," Gold explained, and "we know" that the reinforcing of "revolutionary élan" rather than the cultivation of "pessimism" is the role that literature can play in the class struggle. Gold applied these principles in *Jews without Money* (1930), an account of immigrant Jewish ghetto life culminating in a political rally converting the hero to communism. Most of the fiction, drama, and poetry praised in the 1930s as successful examples of proletarian realism attracted little attention in later decades. The movement was often mocked as an effort, in Daniel Aaron's phrase, to produce a "Shakespeare in overalls." But the genre of semifictional reportage was developed with skill. Some examples of this hyperrealistic genre were later remembered as the strongest writing generated under the aegis of communism. Meridel Le Sueur designed "I Was Marching" (1934) as a moment-by-moment, first-person narrative of a Minneapolis strike during which Le Sueur claimed to have been led by immediate realities to overcome bourgeois inhibitions and to join striking workers in a protest march.

Work less formulaic than Le Sueur's, even if suffused with sympathy for the victims of capitalist exploitation, had trouble winning the approval of Communists. Even James T. Farrell, whose *Young Lonigan* (1932), *The Young Manhood of Studs Lonigan* (1934), and *Judgment Day* (1935) were among the most consciously Marxist pieces of fiction written in the United States, found the party's literary attitudes much too restrictive. Farrell left the Communist party and became an increasingly savage critic of both its literary tastes and its domestic and international politics. Farrell found a new political home in the tiny but intellectually intense movement of the followers of the exiled Bolshevik Leon Trotsky. Farrell's Lonigan trilogy, however, survived both his Stalinist and his Trotskyist phases, and endured as the decade's most ambitious effort to revitalize the highly deterministic, naturalist variation on realism pioneered by Dreiser and Norris three decades before.

Two other major novelists who made the communist leadership uncomfortable illustrate the range of work carried out under the inspiration of the Left during the 1930s. John Steinbeck's fiction explored, in the specific social and economic setting of California agricultural labor, a variety of dilemmas apparently general to human life. Neither *In Dubious Battle* (1936) nor *Of Mice and Men* (1937) brought its worker-characters to the unambiguous political resolution prescribed by leftist convention. *In Dubious Battle* even explored doubts about the morality of the manipulation of workers by organizers. Yet Steinbeck's generous depiction of the spirit of people victimized by the Depression won the approval of a larger public. *The Grapes of Wrath* (1939), Steinbeck's epic of migration from the Dust Bowl to California, bears to the leftist literary culture of the 1930s somewhat the same relation born by Lewis's novels to the

anti-Victorian impulse of the 1920s: hailed enthusiastically in their own time, these monuments of contemporary taste failed to impress later critics. The opposite is true of a second famous example of "leftist" literature of the 1930s, Henry Roth's *Call It Sleep* (1934). By the 1960s this novel of an immigrant boy's confused search for safety and coherence in a multilingual, cruel, contradiction-filled slum was routinely counted as one of the finest works of fiction produced in twentieth-century America, but when published it was embraced neither by the public that rallied to Steinbeck nor by the Communists, of whom Roth himself was then one. Too complicated in its social and psychological analysis to translate into the clear-cut politics required by proletarian realism, *Call It Sleep* was also too gloomy and devoid of sentimentality to reach Steinbeck's constituency.

Arguments over leftist literature and politics were the occasion for a major transition in the ethnic demography of American literary culture. The debates over Stalinism "created the American intellectual class as we know it," Lionel Trilling said in the 1960s. These debates took place just at the time when the first large wave of descendants of Jewish immigrants from the eastern European migration of 1880–1924 completed American educations and began to engage critically with American intellectual life. The issues were cast on a world scale and were oriented in large part to the Soviet Union, from whose territories many of the Jewish immigrants had come; hence the sons and daughters of the immigrants were less "outside" the discourse than when the issue was that of perpetuating or revising the sensibility of the school authors. Debating the merits of Stalin's regime, and of Marxism's implications for literature, put the Jewish intellectuals on a more equal footing with Mayflower descendants and grandchildren of Civil War veterans. These new quarrels established ties of amity and of antagonism that served to integrate, into a single discursive community, intellectuals from a variety of backgrounds. This process applied to a very limited extent to African American writers, who remained victims of a prejudice more severe than that directed against Jews. Not until near the end of the twentieth century did African American and Anglo-Protestant intellectuals interact on remotely the scale that Jews and Anglo-Protestants did beginning in the 1930s. Some intellectuals of Catholic origin, including Farrell and the playwright Eugene O'Neill, were involved in this process, but their numbers were small until about 1960.

The prominence of Jews in this process of ethnic diversification was not simply a function of numbers.

Many of the Jewish intellectuals had been involved in an antiprovincial movement more intense than the comparable one among Catholics. The constraints of traditional Jewish social and religious life had been placed under severe pressure by the *haskalah*, an Enlightenment-like movement within eastern European Jewry that exploded into new, more radically secular forms in the American environment. This struggle of young Jewish writers against the limitations of the *shtetl* and the *yeshiva*, helped to shape Gold and Roth, and was a prominent theme in the autobiography of a leading communist writer, Joseph Freeman, in *An American Testament* (1936). This Jewish antiprovincial movement merged with the antiprovincial movement of Anglo-Protestants. Cowley and Wilson continued, during the 1930s, the Anglo-Protestant reaction against provincialism that had earlier animated Frederic, James, Wharton, Anderson, Lewis, Mencken, Bourne, Pound and a host of others. Bourne and Pound had written the most explicit manifestos for this revolt. In "Provincialism the Enemy" (1917), Pound endorsed the use of "human diversity" by James and a variety of European writers to bring local conceits under critical scrutiny. In "Transnational America" (1916), Bourne celebrated massive immigration as a means of deprovincializing the United States and of creating a truly cosmopolitan culture. The ethnic composition of the editorial board of *Partisan Review* at the end of the 1930s was an emblem for the coming together of the two social types: Philip Rahv and William Phillips were Jews of East European origin, while Dwight Macdonald and F. W. Dupee were from old Anglo-Protestant families. The fifth of the founding editors, Mary McCarthy was, appropriately enough, representative of the gender, religious, and regional minorities in the intelligentsia: she was a woman, a lapsed Catholic, and a product of the Pacific Coast.

*Partisan Review* had begun in 1934 as a literary magazine on the Stalinist side of the cultural politics of the era, but after 1937, when it was reorganized as a forum for anti-Stalinist radicalism, it became important in the early careers of many of the most influential of the Jewish intellectuals of the mid-century decades. These included Lionel Trilling, Meyer Schapiro, Harold Rosenberg, and Sidney Hook. In the pages of this little magazine, cosmopolitanism became all the more prominent a doctrine in American literary culture; here the two major antiprovincial revolts, each of which could make use of the other to correct the perceived failings of its own heritage, could be seen engaging with each other.

Not everyone in the 1930s found cosmopolitanism an attractive ideal, and not everyone of Anglo-Protestant origin welcomed writers of Jewish origin. Militant provincialism defined *I'll Take My Stand* (1930), a collection of essays written by "Twelve Southerners" who became known as "the Nashville Agrarians." Nashville was the home of Vanderbilt University, with which several of these authors were affiliated. Their social ideal centered around the self-sufficient farm family, to which they contrasted the urban, industrial life of modernity in general and of the northern states in particular. John Crowe Ransom, who coordinated the editing and publishing of *I'll Take My Stand*, compared the American South to Scotland, a virtuous, backward province proudly aloof from the hustle and bustle of commerce and enterprise. The point of a wise life was not to expand one's experience in the wider world, nor to get to know people different from oneself; rather, the point was to concentrate life in a bounded and particular province, and there to reinforce inherited religious and social orthodoxies. Ransom and his friends constructed as their roots what was, to historians, an astonishing romanticization of antebellum South as a society in which cultured gentlemen practiced the arts and, when working, did so with an aristocratic spirit of leisure: "it is my thesis," said Ransom, "that their labor itself was leisurely." Slavery was "monstrous enough in theory," Ransom added, "but, more often than not, humane in practice." Robert Penn Warren wrote the chapter of *I'll Take My Stand* devoted to race relations, "The Briar Patch." Warren stopped short of idealizing the life of black sharecroppers, but did not find urbanization and contact with the North to be in their best interests. "The Negro" would best prosper, and might eventually shed his "genial irresponsibility," if he continued, under a Jim Crow system acceptable to Warren, "to sit under his own vine and figtree." Warren, Ransom, the poet Allen Tate and others involved in the Agrarian enterprise gradually went their separate ways, but in the early and middle years of the 1930s they attracted attention as an extreme right-wing counterpart of the Communists on the left.

Among those who admired the Nashville Agrarians was Eliot, who invoked them when in Virginia to deliver the lectures published as *After Strange Gods* (1934). Although the expatriate Eliot was in some ways an exemplar of cosmopolitanism, what he most appreciated about Virginia was its racial and religious homogeneity, which he compared to the happily tribal character of his ancestral New England. "You have here" in the South, Eliot said, an element of valuable tradition "almost effaced" in parts of the North by "the influx of foreign populations." Echoing the Agrarian critique of the secular, liberal ideas associated with John Dewey and other northern intellectuals of the era, Eliot condemned "a spirit of excessive tolerance," and defended local particularisms against the critical perspectives of outsiders. "Reasons of race and religion," he emphasized, "make any large number of free-thinking Jews undesirable." *I'll Take My Stand* itself was not a vehicle for overt anti-Semitism. A decade later Eliot was frequently celebrated by Delmore Schwartz and other Jewish intellectuals as an "international hero" who, by exploring new territories of the soul, had vindicated cosmopolitanism and modernism. But *After Strange Gods* is a reminder of the range of opinions set forth in the literary polemics of the 1930s.

These polemics were avoided by one major American writer of that decade who identified deeply with the South, and whose works would quickly find their way into the modernist canon along with Eliot's—William Faulkner. Superficially, Faulkner's intense preoccupation with particular families living through generations in a particular county would seem to indicate an ideological kinship with the Agrarians. So, too, would Faulkner's decision to spend most of his life in rural Mississippi, and his carefully displayed persona as a backwoods farmer writing alone with only the Bible and Shakespeare on his desk. But Faulkner was anything but a provincial in social fact and in cultural ideology, and his vision of southern society was antithetical to that of the Agrarians.

In the late 1910s and early 1920s the young Faulkner travelled widely and immersed himself in the avant-garde French and English literature addressed by Wilson in *Axel's Castle*. "His exposure to modernist culture was so extensive," Daniel J. Singal has insisted, "that by the time he started his own writing in earnest about 1927 Faulkner was perched on the furthest reaches of the literary frontier, with nothing left to assimilate." Although many contemporary readers found Faulkner's *The Sound and the Fury* (1929) obscure, this fractured narrative, telling an apparently single story through the minds of four people (one of whom is insane), was quickly recognized by some critics as an innovation to be shelved next to the novels of Joyce and Proust. In *As I Lay Dying* (1930) and *Light in August* (1932), Faulkner continued the meditation, begun in the earlier novel, on the way southern experience was rooted in a complex history of interlocking acts, almost none of which owed anything to actual Cavalier inheritance,

aristocratic manners, or yeoman virtue. To such provincial and innocent notions of southern society Faulkner gave the lie most resoundingly in *Absalom, Absalom!* (1936), which told in terms of avarice, incest, murder, and miscegenation the story of a wealthy and respected antebellum planter and his children. The planter, Thomas Sutpen, was actually an overseer's son who had experienced his most acute moment of self-recognition when turned away as a youth from a Tidewater Virginia mansion by a house slave who knew his family as trash. Faulkner depicted the muscular rise and bloody decline of the Sutpen family as the outcomes of a multiplicity of human agencies played out in a dense temporal and social field.

## MODERNISM TRIUMPHANT

Ten years later, Faulkner's most devoted champion among critics was none other than Cowley, the former Stalinist. This fact can serve as an emblem for the range and depth of the transformations registered in American literary culture between the late 1930s and the late 1940s. By 1946, when Cowley's *The Portable Faulkner* promoted Faulkner's reputation with stunning effect, the leftist literary culture of which Cowley had been the illustrious center was gone. In 1946, too, the ex-Agrarian Warren published *All the King's Men*, a novel set in a South that looked more like Faulkner's than like the one presented in *I'll Take My Stand*. The arch-Agrarian Ransom, in the meantime, had abandoned agrarianism, moved to the North, and taken the lead in developing a technically precise style of literary criticism ideally suited to the study of the difficult, forbidding texts then winning wider recognition as a unique, modernist canon. "The poem has a calculated complexity," Ransom said worshipfully of a Wallace Stevens poem, "and its technical competence is so high that to study it . . . is to be happy." The appreciative study of these complicated works, moreover, was being pursued at the same moment in virtually all the leading literary quarterlies by many of the Jewish and Anglo-Protestant intellectuals who had earlier engaged each other over the political issues of the previous decade. The finest novel to come out of World War II, James Gould Cozzens's *Guard of Honor* (1948), was an antiutopian narrative of duty and circumstance. The notion that the United States itself had produced a literature of its own that was actually of great interest—still resisted in most academic departments of English in the 1930s—had become widely accepted under the influence of

F. O. Matthiessen's *American Renaissance: Art and Expression in the Age of Emerson and Whitman* (1941) and Alfred Kazin's *On Native Grounds: A Study of American Prose Literature* (1942).

This series of simultaneous transformations owed much to disillusion with agrarianism and Marxism, and to the awareness of how vulnerable to Hitler the world had shown itself to be. The Nashville idea of holding back the industrial revolution had proved a fantasy once its adherents tried to develop it beyond the manipulation of literary images. The onetime defenders of this program, having withdrawn their spiritual capital from a failing enterprise, invested now in the often austere, enigmatic scriptures of modernism. The same process of reallocating cultural resources took place among the much more numerous cohort that had spent the 1930s hoping that one variety or another of socialism—if not Stalinist, then Trotskyist, or perhaps even a more social democratic type—might carry the future, and literature with it. The socially conscious reservations about Proust and his fellows that Wilson had expressed in *Axel's Castle* seemed less compelling in the 1940s, while Wilson's respect for the artistry of those authors seemed more justified than ever. Stalin's prodigious crimes, harder and harder to deny or to ignore, tainted socialist programs of virtually all sorts, and the muddle-through, bourgeois democracy of Franklin D. Roosevelt had survived the Depression once expected to kill it. Suspicions of utopian projects were also sharpened by the recognition that Germany, one of the world's most advanced societies, had yielded so monstrous an evil as the Third Reich. Perhaps the world was indeed as intractable, ironic, and defiantly irrational a place as had been glimpsed in the pages of some of the artists whose reputations were then growing rapidly in the United States: Franz Kafka, Joseph Conrad, Fyodor Dostoyevsky, and Faulkner.

To this sense of diminished human capabilities was added a sense of increased responsibilities, at least for Americans. World War II had catapulted the United States to a position of unprecedented world power. Accepting the "burden of responsibility for world power" was a matter of extensive public reflection, to which both the work of the theologian Reinhold Niebuhr, and Warren's *All the King's Men* proved to be popular contributions. The elaborate escape from innocence carried out by the symbolically named hero, Jack Burden, entailed acceptance of humble responsibility for tasks the magnitude and complexity of which defied simple-minded distinctions between good and evil. Burden's growth is registered by his perspective on a corrupt, dema-

gogic, but reasonably effective southern governor modelled loosely on Huey Long and Mussolini, both of whom Warren had observed during residencies in Louisiana and Italy. The governor's aphorisms about the necessity of using evil means to accomplish good ends reverberate through *All the King's Men* with the force of the devil's lines in Milton's *Paradise Lost*. Amid references to Machiavelli, Warren used the wisdom of the tough-minded governor to expose the naïveté of the strict moralists who protect their ideals by failing to accept the "awful responsibility" for action in "the cauldron of the world." The governor who built roads and hospitals atop the careers of blackmailed opponents is not forgiven for his iniquity, but a pensive Burden warns at the end that one should not judge too harshly the crimes of men who carry the burden of command. The problem of evil engaged Warren from the perspective of evil's agents, not its victims; *All the King's Men* was a novel for the bombers of Hiroshima, not the bombed. It provided spiritual consolations for people at the top, eager to think of themselves as possessed of the worldly wisdom of the corrupt governor while using power with a humility and restraint he lacked. Warren also conveyed an antiutopian sense of the embeddedness of all moral action in particular, limiting historical circumstances.

The era's premier novelist of circumstance and duty was Cozzens, who addressed moral dilemmas in the context of established institutions and practices. While Warren reached the virtuous middle way between jaded passivity and clean-slate utopianism by making his hero scrutinize a dramatic, transgressive, violent individual, Cozzens got there by working his way through the most tightly ordered and prosaic of institutions: the church, the law, and the army. This he did with some distinction in *Men and Brethren* (1936) and *The Just and the Unjust* (1942), but it was in Cozzens's army novel, *Guard of Honor*, that he achieved the most eloquent sympathy for the intelligent, sagacious, middle-aged men who understand the way the world works. They keep it working by picking up after the impetuous, vain people who threaten a system's ability to deliver the services for which it is designed. The hierarchy of command and the multitude of military regulations serve as a metaphor for the limitations that circumstances invariably place on human action. Colonel Ross, the officer who must figure out how to prevent a crisis that could damage the operation of a Florida base while dealing with black officers prejudicially denied access to an officer's club, is the chief hero because Ross understands better than anyone else the complex of circumstances that limit his choices and locate his duty. Ross finds a way to pacify the black officers, whom he knows to be in the right, while outmaneuvering a small group of white officers who rush to the side of their black colleagues, oblivious to the cost in 1943 of pressing too hard for racial equality on a southern base. Yet Cozzens humbles even Ross, at the end, by bringing the thoughtful colonel to the realization that his own rationalist and pragmatic virtues must be supplemented by those of other, differently endowed officers, and that the contribution he can make to the war effort is too tiny to warrant more than a second's self-congratulation.

The call to take up a burden of responsibility in a world of formidable complexity was heard even by literary critics. In 1948, R. P. Blackmur, in a voice of sober resolution not so different from that of Warren's Jack Burden and Cozzens's Colonel Ross, outlined "A Burden for Critics" in the *Hudson Review.* The literary critic, explained Blackmur, now occupied a position rather like that of Augustine in the setting of the fall of Rome. A known civilization was in ruins, and there loomed the task of making sense of life without the familiar supports. Augustine met this challenge by carrying out a technically rigorous reading of the ancient scriptures, issuing in *The City of God*, but in the middle of the twentieth century—with the whole "Graeco-Christian world" in disarray amid industrialization and repeated wars—there was nothing to rely upon but "the masterpieces of our time." It was the job of literary critics to scrutinize these human artifacts, thereby to "discover what our culture is." What were these masterpieces? Blackmur alluded confidently to "the poetry of Eliot, Yeats, Valéry, Rilke," to "the novels of Joyce, Gide, Hemingway, Proust, Mann, Kafka," to "the plays of Shaw, Pirandello, O'Neill," and to their analogues in music, painting, and sculpture. Here, then, was the modern canon, installed at last in its legendary form as secular scripture.

Although the modernist literary culture became most thoroughly institutionalized just as science-generated technology had achieved a host of imposing breakthroughs, of which the atomic bomb and television were among the most dramatic, this culture was aloof from science and dismissive of its cultural potential. "Almost the whole job of culture" had been "dumped into the hands of the writer," Blackmur insisted, because of the failure of other intellectual modes to produce anything beyond machines and methods. Hence the keepers of the modern canon attributed extraordinary significance to the work of the artist heroes who had created its texts.

In "The Myth of the Modern Myth" (1947), Donald A. Stauffer presented Yeats as almost a secular Christ. Yeats's poetry amounted to a "lonely sacrifice of self . . . not forgetful of the people, but for their sake." Yeats's gift to the species was a potentially enabling "myth" of individual freedom, formulated the most forcefully in regard to his own person. "Yeats's greatest mythical creation" may have been "himself," Stauffer reflected, and "time alone will tell whether or not through his life," Yeats has become "a heartening hero, a myth 'for the common people, for all time to come.' " This hopeful prospect Stauffer contrasted symbolically to a more probable future: the "rough beast" of twentieth-century life slouching toward Bethlehem in Yeats's poem of 1921, "The Second Coming."

No one doubted that Yeats's poems were among the greatest of modernist works, but clarifying the textual borders of modernism proved a major preoccupation throughout the mid-century decades. The canon was of course an informal construction, expanded by showing the similarities between the obvious modernists and the newly recognized modernists. In introducing *The Viking Portable Conrad* (1947), Morton Dauwen Zabel identified, as a theme of Conrad's, "the plight of the man on whom life closes down inexorably, divesting him of the supports and illusory protection of friendship, social privilege, or love." And this was exactly a concern of "Ibsen, James, Mann, Gide, and Kafka," and to some extent of Joyce and Hemingway. The "hero of modern fiction," Zabel explained, "is the man marked by apartness and alienation," the man encountered in Conrad and, yes, in James, Mann, Joyce, and Kafka. Zabel systematically bolstered his basic points about Conrad with comparisons to previously canonized authors. Conrad, as a coworker with the others, is thus a figure with whom the reader is to identify: Conrad, concluded Zabel, was permanently and securely "one of us."

Discussions of canonical modernism from the 1940s through the 1960s most often took the form of a critical appreciation of a single artist-hero in relation to the notion of the modern. Alongside proliferating studies of easily recognized modernists such as D. H. Lawrence and Virginia Woolf, it was announced that various romantics, Victorians, and realists were "modern in feeling." To try to define modernism as such was understood to be a naive and literal-minded project, appropriate, perhaps, for the baroque or for Puritanism, but reductive when attempted in relation to modern literature. If you could not figure out what modernism was, you probably did not belong in the conversation. In that respect, the modern was to this literary culture what Culture had been to the Victorians: a very general but portentous presence that was in no great need of definition. Yet there were, in fact, a number of rather different, working touchstones for modernism invoked by commentators when addressing various texts. Zabel's "apartness and alienation" was only one of these. A wholesale suspicion of middle-class society and a certain "sympathy for the abyss" helped Trilling identify modernism. A particular sense of the "function of metaphor" made the seventeenth-century poet, John Donne, something of a modernist, observed Cleanth Brooks. A timeless synchronicity was singled out by Joseph Frank, who announced that the "peculiarly modern quality" of modern poems and novels was their "continual juxtaposition between aspects of the past and the present so that both are fused into one comprehensive view," transforming, in effect, the historical imagination "into myth."

Mythmaking, indeed, was consistently valued by proponents of modernism, amid whatever other virtues they attributed to the canonical texts. Insofar as the modernist literary culture of mid-twentieth century America had a single master narrative, it was that of the self-sufficient, infinitely resourceful artist who, faced with the spiritual wasteland attendant upon science, technology, and industry, eschewed the naive, mimetic ideal of the realists, and created out of the self a distinctly modern culture. Given the apparent failure of religious, scientific, and political communities to provide sustaining structures of meaning in a society characterized by constant upheaval and displacement, one must rely on the generative capabilities of individual artist-heroes. "Make it new," cried Pound. Artifice, as Hugh Kenner has argued, was a key ideal in modernism, especially as made in America by poets as different as Wallace Stevens and William Carlos Williams, whose contrivances with words Kenner compares to the invention flown by the Wright Brothers at Kitty Hawk. "The author's work," Stevens once said about his own poetry, "suggests the possibility of a supreme fiction, recognized as a fiction, in which men could propose to themselves a fulfillment." Fitzgerald was protective of Gatsby's capability for artifice, while acknowledging that the world was too awful to enable this particular supreme fiction to triumph.

Artifice was certainly a central virtue in the collected European texts of which Blackmur and his colleagues made scriptures. "Old father, old artificer, stand me now and ever in good stead," incants the

subject in Joyce's *A Portrait of the Artist as a Young Man*, before going off to "forge" his race's "uncreated conscience" in "the smithy" of his own subjectivity. Yeats called upon the soul to become "its own betrayer, its own deliverer, the mirror turned lamp." According to Oscar Wilde, the "first duty in life is to become as artificial as possible." Scattered throughout the modern canon are assertions such as these, upholding strategies of artifice as the best way to cope with the disappointments and contradictions of contemporary civilization. Nietzsche, whose place in the canon was secured in the early 1950s, held that life in the wake of the "death of God" should be lived as an art. Wilson, in *Axel's Castle*, had identified this theme in the French symbolists: Rimbaud performed his life "as if it were a great play," and Villiers de l'Isle-Adam was fascinated by a hero who preferred his own magnificent fantasies to fulfillments through human interaction. If Wilson's original judgment on artifice as a strategy for dealing with the predicaments of modern life was more skeptical than that of his successors, his sense of the characteristic modernist strategy had been acute.

Wilson's unease had much in common with the long-suppressed concerns given expression in 1961 by Trilling, the most widely known and respected of the intellectuals caught up in the mystique of canonical modernism. "On the Teaching of Modern Literature" reflected on a career of living with, writing about, and teaching the texts that dominated the mid-century decades. Trilling professed to recant nothing, and insisted that the literature of modernism was the most "intensely spiritual" of all literatures, unsurpassed "in power and magnificence." Trilling implied that this particular literature was so very, very special that people might need protection from it, and that it might need protection from them. These texts needed to be protected from the popularization and vulgarization that is a risk of trying to teach them in a college course, as though it were just another literature of just another period. But the reader, too, may need protection against the antisocial bias and the psychologically terrifying properties of these books. These works were not "pyramids or triumphal arches, they were manifestly contrived to be not static and commemorative but mobile and aggressive, and one does not describe a . . . howitzer or a tank without estimating how much damage it can do." Just how literally were we to take the sympathy for "the Abyss" that one can find in Mann and in Conrad, in Nietzsche and in Dostoyevsky? When a Columbia University undergraduate asked Trilling, in all seriousness, how one might "generalize"

Mann's idea of "the educative value of illness, so that it would be applicable not to a particular individual, Hans Castorp, but to young people at large," was it Mann or the student who needed to be protected? The investment Trilling had made in the modern canon was simply prodigious, and for this reason the texts had to be kept at a certain distance, relevant to daily life in an intimate way, but not too intimate. "I do not venture to call" modern literature "actually religious," said Trilling with characteristic caution, "but it certainly has the special intensity of concern with the spiritual life which Hegel noted when he spoke of the great modern phenomenon of the secularization of spirituality." It was in speaking of the modern texts that Trilling invoked W. H. Auden's reverently passive notion of a reader being read by a book. Trilling called for no retreat from modernism, but, in the earnest, burden-shouldering spirit of Blackmur and Warren, reminded his academic colleagues that for "many students no ideas that they will encounter in any college discipline will equal in force and sanction the ideas conveyed to them by modern literature."

In this conflicted memoir of his teaching experiences, Trilling mentioned no American authors, with the exception of the permanent expatriate Eliot. Although a number of American writers were by then counted as canonical moderns, the omission is a reminder of the autonomous status that "American literature" had attained. Modernism was not only an international movement, but a chronological and stylistic episode in the story of American literature as taught in college courses and displayed in both popular and professional histories. If Faulkner and Stevens did not get their due in Trilling's course on modern literature, they received it elsewhere. That elsewhere was a discursive space rapidly enlarging throughout the 1940s, 1950s, and early 1960s. The notion of a distinctly American literature of real value had been growing during the 1920s and 1930s, but it was Matthiessen's *American Renaissance* that did the most to persuade a generation that in the shadow of the school authors there had labored a group of writers demanding respect even from readers steeped in Joyce and Eliot. To be sure, Melville, Whitman, and Emerson were not quite modernists, but their artistic achievements had a greatness all their own, and their wrestling with the fate of a uniquely democratic society gave their efforts a more heroic feel in the age of democracy's defense against Hitler and Stalin. The founding in 1951 and rapid expansion of the American Studies Association registered and promoted an appreciation for American cultural con-

tributions that were sometimes exploited in Cold War politics, but that were understood to deserve attention simply because of their connection with a relatively successful democratic society that had survived authoritarian challenges from the left and the right. Kazin noted that the experience of "national self-discovery was largely shaped by the sudden emergence of America as the repository of Western culture." The migration of intellectuals from Hitler's Europe reinforced "the pride of helping to breed a new cosmopolitan culture," explained Kazin, and provided a "healthy stimulus" for a more searching exploration of the indigenous literature of the United States.

Writers who completed novels, poems, and plays in the United States during the heyday of modernism sometimes complained that their work was ignored. In "An Age of Criticism" (1952) Randall Jarrell, who knew that literary culture was dominated by critics celebrating works written before 1930, offered his own label for the epoch. At that very moment Hemingway's *The Old Man and the Sea* (1952) was being discussed, but Hemingway had won his following in the 1920s. Hemingway and Faulkner continued to command respect until their deaths in 1961 and 1962, but few readers believed that the later work of either was as interesting as the early novels that had first made their reputations. Creative work after 1930 was more often recognized in poetry than in the novel.

Modernism's four leading American poets were all survivors, like Hemingway and Faulkner, from the innovative 1920s. Stevens's stature continued to increase during the decade before his death in 1955, but not simply on the basis of "Sunday Morning" (1915) and other early classics. Stevens's claim to being the greatest of twentieth-century American poets—an assertion often made on his behalf at century's end, as well as at mid-century—was based in large part on *The Man with the Blue Guitar* (1937) and *Notes toward a Supreme Fiction* (1942), but also on the basis of the even later work appearing in *Collected Poems* (1954). Williams was a prominent, experimental poet of the 1920s, but became the best known for *Paterson* (1946–1958), a five-volume epic poem addressed to his native New Jersey not long before his death in 1963. The expatriated Eliot was a commanding presence until his death in 1965, but with the major exception of *Four Quartets* (1943) the poetry, as well as the criticism for which he was most admired, had been written in the 1910s and 1920s. The last of these four distinguished survivors, Pound, was a unique figure in modernism.

A mentor in the craft of poetry to even so founding a father of modernism as Eliot, and himself the author of "Hugh Selwyn Mauberley" (1920), Pound was truly a legend throughout the decades of modernist hegemony. Yet during his expatriation he had become a bona fide fascist and an increasingly crude anti-Semite. About politics he was often impetuous and ignorant; Gertrude Stein said of him that he was a "village explainer, excellent if you were a village but if not, not." On Italian radio during World War II, he defended the Axis cause in broadcasts addressed to invading American troops. Captured at war's end and returned to the United States in anticipation of a trial for treason, Pound was diagnosed as insane and spent thirteen years in St. Elizabeth's Hospital in Washington, D.C. During this time he completed his *Pisan Cantos* (1946), for which he was awarded the Bollingen Prize in 1948 by representatives of a literary establishment eager to assert the apolitical character of poetry. Pound's insanity was a ruse, as Stanley Kutler has shown, by which sympathetic doctors enabled Pound to avoid criminal prosecution until he returned to Italy in 1958 where, upon deplaning, he raised his arm in the fascist salute.

Pound died in 1972 in Venice, his political past still a matter of controversy but his poems, especially those of the 1940s and before, more widely and enthusiastically acclaimed than ever. Kenner, his greatest champion, offered in *The Pound Era* (1971) a reinterpretation of the whole of modern American poetry as centering on Pound, rather than on Stevens or Eliot. Critics who appreciated Eliot, Stevens, Pound, and Williams were often suspicious of another formidable poet of the same generation, Robert Frost, who died in 1963, two years after reading one of his poems at the inauguration of President John F. Kennedy. Frost, who won three Pulitzer Prizes from the 1920s through the 1940s, wrote poems which today are understood to have a "dark side" but were long regarded by critics as too accessible and too wholesome to be profound.

Yet some altogether new talents managed to emerge, even in the hegemonic old age of Hemingway and Faulkner and the great canonical poets. Among these were Norman Mailer, whose naturalistic combat novel, *The Naked and the Dead* (1948), was the first in a long series of best-sellers Mailer produced during the following forty years. Another new novelist of note was Saul Bellow, who, especially in *The Adventures of Augie March* (1953) and *Herzog* (1964), developed themes from Jewish experience that resonated well with modernist, cosmopolitan predilections. Jews have learned to live between

worlds and are thus "experts in incongruity," Mark Schechner observed when pointing out that Bellow, before practicing his art in the United States, had been born into a Yiddish-speaking family that had emigrated from Russia to French-speaking Quebec. "As immigrant, émigré, displaced person or holder of dual citizenship," the Jew has turned "the hyphen in his identity into the cutting edge of a sharp sensibility." In *The Adventures of Augie March* Bellow merged this intense, urban sensibility with Mark Twain and produced a hero quickly seen as "a Jewish Huck Finn" confronting with resolution a problematic world he did not make.

The link between new authors and the established canon was even clearer in the case of Ralph Ellison. Ellison's *Invisible Man* (1952) was a work of careful craftsmanship, segments of which were modelled on Dostoyevsky, Mann, Eliot, and Joyce. The text was also filled with veiled allusions to Emerson and his contemporaries; Ellison named a black brothel "The Golden Day," a phrase associated with New England in the age of Emerson. While thus appropriating and reworking the prevailing literary culture's most highly valued techniques and icons, Ellison also retrieved and reconfigured elements of a distinctive tradition of African American writing. Especially did Ellison employ tropes from the works of Richard Wright, who had left the United States for Mexico, and ultimately for Paris—where he lived until his death in 1960—shortly after Ellison had made his acquaintance at the end of the 1930s. Wright's *Native Son* (1940) had been the only novel by an African American, prior to *Invisible Man*, to obtain widespread critical acclaim beyond the circles of African American intellectuals. Ellison was also familiar with the less widely appreciated works of Harlem writers of the 1920s and 1930s.

In *Invisible Man*, a nameless black man narrates his own search for identity amid one after another of the classic experiences of black people in the United States in the twentieth century. Ellison gave extensive attention to the hypocrisies of white philanthropists associated with Negro colleges, to black nationalism, and to the exploitation of blacks by the Communist party, which he disguised as "the Brotherhood." By depicting the ostensibly prejudice-free Communists as no more capable of seeing a black man squarely than were other cohorts of white people—agents all of the anonymous hero's "invisibility"—Ellison touched and reinforced the anti-Stalinism still felt intensely by intellectuals angered over the treacheries of the 1930s. Although *Invisible Man* has often been read as an intricate contrivance of static, timeless symbols, it was a fiercely contemporary work, speaking with extraordinary intensity to a host of political and literary preoccupations of its historical moment.

If Ellison's craft and tone were decidedly literary in the grand manner, yet another new voice emerging at the same moment was vernacular. J. D. Salinger's *Catcher in the Rye* (1951) was narrated in the colloquial idiom of a confused and angry teenager. Salinger made Holden Caulfield's attacks on "phonies" so convincing that the entire realm of adult authority seemed called into question. The combination of this subversive effect and Salinger's use of four-letter words in a book read enthusiastically by junior high school students produced endless controversies in local school boards. *Catcher in the Rye* was still banned from some libraries four decades after it was published. But the depth of Holden's cynicism proves to be a function of extravagant expectations, figured in the title: Holden's defining fantasy is of standing at the edge of the world and catching people as they fall off. Holden learns that just because he cannot do that—and cannot erase every obscene graffito he fears will unnerve his younger sister—it does not follow that more modest callings are unworthy. This recognition comes to him as he restrains himself from rushing overprotectively to keep his sister from reaching for the gold ring on a merry-go-round. Yet it is this sister's vulnerability that saves Holden from self-destruction. When she threatens to follow him as a runaway, mirroring his own foolishness, he addresses her as a surrogate parent and accepts a measure of responsibility for her, and indirectly for himself. How much he has learned is thrown into doubt, however, by the fact that Holden is writing from a mental hospital. The reader is left to wonder how capable Holden is of returning to society and acting upon the wisdom he has heard from the teacher he most trusts: "The mark of the immature man is that he wants to die nobly for a cause, while the mark of the mature man is that he wants to live humbly for one."

This sentiment was not so far from those to which Cozzens and Warren were committed, and thus partook of the mood of almost triumphant downsizing and measured resignation that many of the great canonical modernists, too, were understood to vindicate. "We sometimes congratulate ourselves austerely," commented R. W. B. Lewis on behalf of American intellectuals in 1955, "for having settled, like adults or Europeans, upon a course of prolonged but tolerable hopelessness" which we call "the human condition." Lewis made these remarks of gentle, collective self-deprecation at the end of *The American Adam: Innocence, Tragedy, and Tradition in the Nineteenth Century*, which scrutinized the writers of the American Renaissance from a viewpoint shaped by canonical modernism. But while judging most of the nineteenth-century writers negatively for their innocent hopes, for their failure to have seen the complexities subsequently grasped by Kafka and Conrad, Lewis warned that the conventional wisdom of modernism was in danger of becoming just that: conventional. If the strong, autonomous, "plain old Adam" of Emersonian myth was well rejected, in its place we have "the American as Laocoön," the "figure struggling to stand upright amid the most violent cross-currents," bound by a multitude of constraints "in an age of containment." This new picture, warned Lewis, "remains curiously frozen in outline," and threatens to decline "into a cult of original sin." As examples of sound resistance to this danger Lewis cited *Catcher in the Rye, Invisible Man*, and *The Adventures of Augie March*. All were more Laocoönian than Adamic in mode, but in all three "the hero is willing, with marvelously inadequate equipment, to take on as much of the world as is available to him, without ever submitting to any of the world's determining categories."

## THE STRUGGLE TO EXPRESS AND DEFINE A POSTMODERN SENSIBILITY

If Lewis found fault with the prevailing literary culture of 1955, he did so from within. The very Adamic-Laocoönian dichotomy employed by Lewis was deeply constitutive of the modernism eventually reconsidered, and sometimes renounced, in a historic transition broadly comparable to that from Victorianism to modernism. Just as the modernist literary culture of the mid-century decades had been gradually constructed out of bits and pieces of art produced in the 1910s and 1920s, themselves generated in large part by discontents with an inherited set of tastes and expectations for literature, so, too, did what was called postmodernist in the 1980s and 1990s incorporate texts from the 1960s and even from the 1950s that appeared to challenge canonical modernism. And just as the people most concerned to consolidate modernism as a force in the culture had looked back to previous European movements to recruit Dostoyevsky from the 1860s and Flaubert from the 1850s, the people most concerned to strengthen postmodernism turned back to the 1930s to retrieve the young Samuel Beckett and Jean-Paul Sartre, and ultimately rummaged through the whole of the modern canon to identify texts, like Nietzsche's, that could be said to be postmodern in feeling. Yet this transition from the modern to the postmodern—the second of the greatly touted events in the history of American literary culture in the twentieth century—was even less clean-cut than the first, and the results (as visible from the mid-1990s) much more difficult to discern. A convenient place to begin is a novel of 1961 considerably more "subversive" than *Catcher in the Rye*. The vision of life developed in Joseph Heller's *Catch-22* can be construed as one that Holden Caulfield might accept were Holden to conclude that his teacher's maxim about "maturity" was an absurd joke.

Heller's protagonist, Lieutenant Yossarian, is a fighter pilot participating in the bombing of Italy during World War II. The base from which Yossarian flies, on an island in the Mediterranean, amounts to an infinite series of contradictions, one of which gives the novel its name. Whenever you want to do something that a normal, sensible person might desire, there is a "catch," as in catch number 22: anyone who does not want to fly missions is obviously possessed of healthy instincts of self-preservation, so cannot be exempted from duty on account of failing mental health. The corruptions, vanities, and blindnesses of the officers serve to wholly discredit the pieties they mouth to Yossarian about his "responsibilities." *Catch-22* systematically turns on its head virtually every device for the stoic and realistic acceptance of military organization deployed in Cozzens's *Guard of Honor*, also set on an air base in 1943. *Catch-22* is no good-natured burlesque of the inconveniences of military life, but a relentless exercise in gallows humor—alternately madcap and surrealistic—that leaves behind both Adam and Laocoön. It is inconceivable that so absurdist a treatment of the effort to liberate Europe from the Nazis could have been received in the United States in 1943. Heller even laughs at the inability of canonical modernism to speak to Yossarian's dilemmas; he allows the name "T. S. Eliot" to be thrown back and forth in a series of hilarious exchanges between ignorant officers who misconstrue the prank of an educated enlisted man with the invoking of a secret military code.

The appeal of *Catch-22* increased during the Vietnam era, along with a number of other, highly varied works of the late 1950s and early 1960s that were later seen as marks of a struggle to get something new into literature. Or, as these innovations were sometimes described, the struggle was to rid literature of "meaning": the modernists had exaggerated the power of art to provide meaning for people caught in the predicaments of modernity, and the point now was to bring literature down to size and to recognize a hollowness in contemporary life that even the sometimes stark scriptures of modernism inadvertently concealed. In *The End of the Road* (1958) John Barth sketched an antihero devoid of individuality and of ego, defined by an aimlessness antithetical to Holden Caulfield's: Holden's cynical escapes derived in part from his ability to feel too much, but Barth's Jacob Horner cannot feel much of anything. Vladimir Nabokov's *Pnin* (1957) explored the self-contained world of a narcissistic professor who believed that "the cranium is a space-traveller's helmet." A "cosmonaut of inner space" was in turn the self-representation of the "beat" writer, William Burroughs, who explored the "junk" of contemporary life in *Naked Lunch* (1959). Burroughs's "transgressive experiments" are "unstable, violent and often obscene texts," Richard Ruland and Malcolm Bradbury have observed, defending the "free play of consciousness" against "a world of oppressive and authoritarian forces." One especially purposeful and elaborate effort to break through to a new sensibility was Ken Kesey's *Sometimes a Great Notion* (1964), an epic tale of a logging family in Oregon. But Kesey, even while privileging the drug-induced perceptions of the central character, Leland Stamper, imitated the art of Twain, Melville, Hemingway, and Faulkner. The result was a text captured, to a large extent, by the literary culture Kesey sought to transcend. A more convincing breakthrough was made in *V* (1963), by Thomas Pynchon, who set out to describe "the despairing belief," as Josephine Hendin has characterized it, "that the way to reduce anger and pain is to . . . model one's self on those smoothly functioning feedback mechanisms bequeathed to our time by cyberneticists." Pynchon's hero wants a machinelike woman whose "problems" one could "look up in a maintenance manual," and then "remove or replace" as needed. Donald Barthelme's *Snow White* (1967) consisted of an intricate series of word games in which the disintegration of language and the disintegration of human relationships proceed apace.

While these innovations in fiction were being carried out, there took place simultaneously an unprecedented outpouring of critical and historical writings about modernism in general. After a quarter-century in which no one seemed troubled by the diffuse and multitudinous character of modernism, the literary quarterlies were filled with essays of sober reconsideration, of which Trilling's "On the Teaching of Modern Literature" was the most searching and by far the most widely quoted. Yet constructions of the modern varied one from the other no less than in the past. Two of the most thorough students of the problem, Richard Ellman and Charles Feidelson, Jr., frankly threw up their hands: "the modern awaits definition," they proclaimed in introducing their 953-page anthology, *The Modern Tradition* (1965), which they organized around a series of discrete, autonomous themes. One point did find its way into many of the reconsiderations: modernism, whatever it had been, was probably over. Some took the mere fact that modernism was being characterized historically to imply that its creativity was played out.

This broadly based reconsideration of the modern canon and its significance was rarely defensive in the early 1960s. It paid little attention to the writings of Barth or Burroughs, and was more a stock-taking project by the supervisors of a presumably successful project than a reaction to outside attacks. Yet, this reconsideration was enlivened by the more specific and more critical debates generated by C. P. Snow's *The Two Cultures* (1959). Although this contentious lecture by a British novelist and one-time scientist was sometimes taken as merely a lament that scientists and humanists had lost the ability to talk with each other, Snow's central line of argument was a pointed attack on one specific literary culture: that of the modern canon. Snow reviewed Dostoyevsky's reactionary politics, and the fascist and protofascist politics of some of the great modern poets, claiming all the while that scientific intellectuals, whatever their aesthetic deficiencies, were at least progressive in their values, and were committed to trying to feed the world through increased knowledge and attendant technological and economic development. Snow's quotations from D. H. Lawrence to the effect that the flogging of lazy seamen was spiritually beneficial were said by modernism's many respondents to be misleading, but the Snow-centered debates of the early 1960s diminished the dignity and self-assurance of the canon's keepers in the United States as well as Great Britain.

The dignity and self-assurance of many establishments was diminished in the 1960s, especially in relation to the movements against racial discrimination and against the Vietnam War. It would be a mistake to assign to these political upheavals strong causal force in the emergence, during the late 1960s and early 1970s, of a discourse about a postmodernist breakthrough. These political upheavals had more direct influences on efforts to bring multiculturalist and feminist initiatives into literary culture. A greater sensitivity to gender and to ethnoracial distinctions

did eventually become major claims of many self-styled postmodernists, but the relations between feminism, multiculturalism, and postmodernism have proven too complex to be dumped into a single "it-was-the-60s" account. Hence the relevance of the political movements of the 1960s to the early discussions of postmodernism is quite modest.

The early claims for the emergence of a postmodernist sensibility made by Irving Howe, Leslie Fiedler, Susan Sontag, Ihab Hassan, and others in the late 1960s and early 1970s paid less attention to campus radicalism than to recent fiction, and to such apparent analogs in other arts as the music of John Cage and the architectural ideology of Robert Venturi. Barth, Pynchon, and Barthelme were mentioned repeatedly as signs of something new in fiction, although the character of the novelty was not always clear. In this early discourse about postmodernism, two quite different sensibilities were invoked: the first was cooler and less agonistic than modernism, and the other was more anarchic and filled with Dionysian energy. Proponents of both could agree that the prevailing literary culture had become too stuffy and academic. Sontag alluded to a "hypertrophy of the intellect," and praised avant-garde artists as "brokers in madness." Fiedler insisted that the keepers of the modern canon were not much different from their Victorian predecessors. He condemned "the finicky canons of the genteel tradition and the culture religion of modernism, from which Eliot thought he had escaped—but to which, in fact, he only succeeded in giving a High Anglican tone." The new sensibility Fiedler welcomed was also opposed, he explained, to Marxists, those "last ditch defenders of rationality" who, like the priests of modernist religion, were "intrinsically hostile to an age of myth and passion, fantasy, and sentimentality." These claims about the coming of postmodernism were sometimes contested. In "The Myth of the Postmodernist Breakthrough" (1973), Gerald Graff argued that much of what was being called postmodernist was merely the pretentious sharpening of the most antirationalist themes in the romantic and modernist movements.

Two points about these early discussions of postmodernism require underscoring in order that the developments of the remainder of the century make sense. First, epistemology was rarely mentioned. Second, the modernism to which postmodernism was an apparent successor was understood to be the modernism of the great artists of the late nineteenth and earlier twentieth centuries. By the middle of the 1980s, however, modernism was as often as not associated with "the Enlightenment project" coded with the names of Descartes and Kant, and postmodernism with the critique of that project carried out by the French philosophers Michel Foucault, François Lyotard, and to some extent Jacques Derrida. But the earlier, more strictly literary sense of the issues was not lost. What had happened between the early 1970s and the mid-1980s was an opening up of American literary culture to "theory," and exactly at a time when theoretical issues in the humanities and social sciences were being reshaped by French thinkers preoccupied with the perceived deficiencies of Enlightenment-derived ideas about language and human knowing. This absorption of French-centered theory created some confusions that can be minimized by attending here to the process by which the discourse about the modern-postmodern divide was transformed. Understanding that process makes it more possible, in turn, to comprehend the simultaneous flowering of feminist and multiculturalist initiatives within American literary culture in the 1970s, 1980s, and 1990s.

The term *postmodernism* emerged more or less independently in a variety of contexts, including international politics and architecture, but two of the word's incubators were of special importance to American literary culture. One was the reaction against canonical modernism on the part of several American intellectuals of the late 1960s and early 1970s, as described above. The postmodernism addressed in this setting was understood to be a sensibility embodied in works of literature and other arts. The second salient setting for the concept of postmodernism was a movement of French thinkers initially flagged by the label *poststructuralism*. Oriented not to works of art and literature, but to very general ideas about the nature and capabilities of the human subject, poststructuralism was a critical reconsideration of the *structuralism* that had been a prominent feature of French intellectual life during the 1950s and 1960s. At issue between the old structuralists and the new poststructuralists was the extent to which theories could be expected to characterize with any real warrant the totality of any object of study. While the structuralists, of whom Claude Lévi-Strauss was among the most famous, were said to embody a rationalist confidence inherited from the Enlightenment, the poststructuralists stressed the irreducible plurality of objects. Rather than trying to grasp the "essence" of a thing, or to provide an empirically "true" scientific or historical account of it, scholars and scientists should seek to comprehend and elaborate "difference." All thinking is fragmentary and incomplete, in this view, and the thinking subject

itself is not so much an autonomous agent but a field through which trajectories of language pass. This poststructuralist movement intensified rapidly after 1968, when an abortive political revolution in France led many French intellectuals to reconsider their basic principles.

How did this poststructuralist movement become a new postmodernism, and how did it come to exert such influence in the United States? As the poststructuralist movement expanded its scope of interests, its engagements proceeded steadily beyond the pre-1968 structuralists and focused increasingly on larger movements in Western thought of which the structuralists were understood to be the culmination. In France, the notion of the modern was associated with Descartes and the Enlightenment. Hence the "post-" in poststructuralism became a "post" also to this French construction of modernism. The appearance in English of Lyotard's *The Postmodern Condition* (1984) increased sharply the frequency with which a whole cast of French theorists were called postmodernists. Ironically, these French postmodernists drew inspiration from Nietzsche and Martin Heidegger, by then known in the United States as modernists. Nietzsche, in particular, had often been described as the first, or paradigmatic modernist, and was a key figure in, for example, Trilling's Columbia course on modern literature. Yet this new, French way of defining the modern-postmodern divide spread rapidly. During the second half of the 1980s a multitude of books and articles, written by Americans eager to confront the global political and intellectual movements in which literature was involved, reinterpreted many of the canonical modernists as modifiers, rather than true challengers, of the Enlightenment. John Feteke referred to "the positivist-modernist tradition," which would have been an oxymoron to most American men and women of letters of thirty years before. David Harvey's widely discussed *The Condition of Postmodernity* (1989) attributed to the canonical modernists a "new conception" of the Enlightenment challenged only, Harvey argued, since the early 1970s. The canonical modernists who had participated in heroic "mythmaking" were suddenly found to be, like the Victorian positivists and scientific realists, insufficiently appreciative of the ultimately mythical character of all representations.

The most striking feature of the postmodernist debates of the 1980s, from a historical perspective, was the appropriation for postmodernism of those elements of late-nineteenth- and early-twentieth-century thought which had been the most critical of the Enlightenment, and which had been treated by the American literary culture of the mid-twentieth century as basic to modernism. The adulation of Nietzsche as the chief founder of postmodernism was only the most vivid example of this syndrome. William James, a theorist who had long been understood to be the philosophical equivalent of Proust, Joyce, and Stein, was suddenly counted as an exception to modernism's alleged insensitivity to the difficulties of representing the external world without the mediations of language. Even Henry James was said to have developed, in his later work, a sensibility of "nonidentity" that partook of the postmodernist insight into the fluid and dispersed character of the individual human subject. These appropriations had the fire-stealing effect of evacuating the historical moment of 1890–1930, and devaluing the achievements treated so reverently by the generation of Blackmur and Trilling. The modernists of the old canon turned out to be transitional figures who thought they had made a great break—"on or about December 1910 human character changed," Woolf had been repeatedly cited for saying—but did not. A great break there was, to be sure, but it was made by postmodernists, not modernists. Hence the postmodernists developed a vision of intellectual history according to which an Enlightenment tradition that assumed representation to be unproblematic had proceeded with only timid challenges until they, the postmodernists, had faced up to the issue. Whatever the merits of this new narrative, it diminished the spiritual authority of the modernist canon and transmogrified the 1890–1930 epoch from an age of unparalleled innovation and courage into a helpful prologue to Foucault, and, ultimately, to the innovations in architecture, literature, graphics, and other arts hailed as the century neared its close.

In what might be seen as a final twist to this linguistic story, in which the words *modern* and *postmodern* are defined and redefined, there emerged in the late 1980s and early 1990s a group of intellectuals willing to defend both the Enlightenment and the modern canon against the deprecations of the postmodernists. Harvey's *Condition of Postmodernity* performed this maneuver from a Marxist perspective. "Postmodernism," complained Harvey, actually celebrates "the activity of masking and cover-up, and the fetishism of locality, place, or social grouping, while denying the kind of meta-theory which can grasp the political-economic processes" that affect people worldwide. In "Why Modernism Still Matters" (1992), Marshall Berman attacked postmodernism as "a sensible retirement community, a nice place to stay cool." Berman embraced a modernism he construed to include Mill and Marx as well as Stein and Stevens, and, in the immediate present, to include both Salman Rushdie—who wrote irreverently about the Islamic religion—and the "millions of people" who in the Europe of 1989 "learned that they had the capacity to make their own history."

This exciting and enabling lesson some Americans thought they had learned in the 1960s. Berman's oppositional voice is thus a convenient point at which to turn back to the political environment that provided such a fertile ground for feminist and multiculturalist initiatives. Although literary culture was not high on the list of items originally targeted for reform or revolution by the movements of the 1960s, in the 1970s literary culture was widely perceived as an arena in which were present some of the evils identified and engaged in the 1960s, and there more easily diminished, perhaps, than in the social-structural and political-economic realms where the movements of 1960s were first nested. Prejudice against women and against nonwhites had been registered and reinforced, if not actually fomented, in a literary culture created and maintained by people who were, in fact, predominantly white men.

## MULTICULTURALISM, FEMINISM, AND THE QUESTION OF NEW SCHOOL AUTHORS

In the context of this recognition, an ever-growing number of writers, critics, teachers, and scholars engaged in a panorama of efforts to discover and critically assess contemporary and historical literary works by women, African Americans, Native Americans, Latinos, and Asian Americans. This diversification of American letters, past and present, was accompanied by two closely related projects: the exploration and appreciation of literatures from outside the cultural borders of the North Atlantic West, and the analysis of the inherited American and European canons in terms of the gender and ethnoracial biases that could be found in the literature itself and that appeared to have influenced the evaluation of these works as "great." Not everyone who participated in these projects found postmodernist ideas attractive, but many did. The decentering strategies of postmodernism—suspicious of totalities, and committed to the elaboration of difference—were compatible with efforts to get outside of mainstream literature and to explore artifacts of highly particular ethnoracial communities.

The literature of one ethnoracial community, especially, was explored and developed with great vigor and widespread public notice: that of African Americans. The novelist and critic James Baldwin was the most active and widely known black author during the 1960s, and helped to stimulate the recognition of the quality and importance of a tradition of black writing in the United States. Works by Langston Hughes, Countee Cullen, Jean Toomer, and Zora Neale Hurston were rediscovered and extensively discussed in relation to those of Wright and Ellison, and in relation to the writings of contemporary African American authors, including Ishmael Reed, Alice Walker, Amiri Baraka, and Toni Morrison. W. E. B. Du Bois, who had been largely forgotten when he died in Africa as an expatriate the day Martin Luther King, Jr., delivered his "I Have a Dream" speech in 1963, was rescued from undeserved obscurity. Du Bois's *The Souls of Black Folk* (1903) was recognized as a major contribution to American letters, and his career became one of the most studied of the careers of all twentieth-century American intellectuals. The scholarly engagement with African American literature was led by Nathan Huggins, Nathan A. Scott, Jr., Henry Louis Gates, Jr., and Houston A. Baker, Jr.

The comparable engagements with Native American, Asian American, and Latino literatures were more contemporary in focus as a result of differing historical demographies. African Americans had constituted a substantial segment of the population of the United States from the time of the nation's founding. A number of individual black intellectual and political leaders, such as Frederick Douglass and Booker T. Washington, were known to Americans of all colors. Black Americans, moreover, had profoundly affected the self-image of the white majority. An enduring reminder of the centrality of this black-white engagement to American intellectual and literary history is the greatest work of the "national poet," Twain's *Adventures of Huckleberry Finn*. Native Americans, or "Indians," also figured large in the literary imagination of the white majority, but not until well into the twentieth century did Native American authors themselves produce an English-language literature of significant proportions destined to be recognized in the context of multiculturalism as a distinctive contribution to American letters. Duane Niatum's two anthologies of Native American Poetry, *Carriers of the Dream Wheel* (1975) and *Harper's Anthology of 20th Century Native American Poetry* (1988), along with the critical writings of N. Scott Momaday and Arnold Krupat, were instrumental in calling attention to Native American literary creativity. Asian American literature became a significant referent point in American literary culture only at the very end of the century, in relation to a sharp increase in the Asian American population following a change in immigration laws in 1965. Although Jade Snow Wong's *Fifth Chinese Daughter* (1945) had been a popular school text for several decades, and was credited with diminishing prejudice against Chinese Americans, the first Asian American author to win widespread critical acclaim was Maxine Hong Kingston, for *The Woman Warrior* (1975) and *China Men* (1980).

One additional body of literature defined in ethnoracial terms was growing with particular rapidity and public notice as the century drew near its end: Chicano literature. José Antonio Villarreal's *Pocho* (1959) had established the Chicano novel as a genre, but Villarreal's sympathy for assimilation cut against the grain of the movement for a more self-consciously Mexican American culture. This movement, which gathered force in the 1960s and 1970s in the Southwest, promoted the continued use of the Spanish language and the maintenance of intimate connections with Mexico and the rest of Latin America. By the 1980s, however, Chicano literature included voices with a great variety of political agendas and aesthetic sensibilities. The novelist and critic, Americo Paredes, addressed the special characteristics of "border writing." Lorna Dee Cervantes's *Emplumada* (1981) and Gary Soto's *Black Hair* (1985) brought new attention to Chicana and Chicano poetry. Richard Rodriguez's autobiography, *Hunger of Memory* (1981), defended assimilation and generated extensive discussion over what sort of writing was authentically Chicano. Rodriguez himself, although the most famous Chicano author in the United States, was critical of the very process of ethnoracial labeling and cooperated, indirectly, with the effort of some curators of a separate Chicano literary tradition to treat him as an exile from the ethnoracial community. "Identity" emerged as the central problematic in Chicano writing, and was the focus of an extensive and increasingly sophisticated critical literature represented by Ramon Saldívar's *Chicano Narratives: The Dialectics of Difference* (1990) and by the essays of José Limon.

The ethnoracial literary initiatives that flourished in the wake of the 1960s were all sustained, in part, by a dynamic of victimization. In this they contrasted with the loosely comparable initiative involving Jewish American writers that was most noticed in the 1950s and 1960s. Characters in the fiction produced by these writers were often victims of one kind or another, or brooded upon the problem of victimization, but the work of these writers as a group was rarely presented as a reaction against the exclusion of Jewish writers from American literary culture, or as a response to anti-Semitism in American society at large. Insofar as these feelings of neglect-now-remedied did figure in the Jewish American writing of the 1950s, 1960s, they did so in relation to themes that were specifically Jewish: Jews had already won critical acclaim for literary work in every genre, but now Bellow, Bernard Malamud, and Philip Roth developed the ethnic novel focusing on Jewish experience as such. Yet even these self-consciously Jewish novels, ranging from Bellow's *Adventures of Augie March* to Roth's sexually and psychoanalytically preoccupied *Portnoy's Complaint* (1969), carried a sense of triumph that reflected the social history of Jews in America. These writings were ethnic, moreover, in a sense not so different from that in which the novels of Lewis and Fitzgerald were ethnic novels of the Anglo-Protestant Midwest, and those of Carson McCullers and Walker Percy were ethnic novels of the Anglo-Protestant South. Hence it made sense for Fiedler, speaking not as a postmodernist but as a commentator upon this new ethnic literature, to refer to "the great take-over by Jewish American writers" of a task "inherited from certain Gentile predecessors, urban Anglo-Saxons and midwestern provincials of North European origin," the task of "dreaming aloud the dreams of the whole American people." Some writers from other ethnoracial groups were comfortable with this largely assimilationist version of ethnicity, but others were not.

The gap between Jewish American writing and that of the other ethnoracial communities was deepened by the widespread acceptance, during the 1980s and 1990s, of an ethnoracial pentagon according to which Jews were classified along with Anglo-Protestants and white Catholics as Euro-Americans. In this view, a Euro-American bloc constituted the bulk of American society, the remainder of which consisted of African American, Asian American, Native American, and Latino blocs. Not everyone was happy with this demographic structure's downplaying of distinctions between Japanese Americans and Chinese Americans, or between Chicanos and Puerto Ricans, or between Jews and Anglo-Protestants. But it was on the basis of this mythical, pentagonal structure that multiculturalism was most often formulated, and that literary culture was consequently segmented.

Feminist initiatives had an even more far-reaching set of effects on American literary culture. The gender distinction was everywhere that men and women were, and for some people could be felt with

greater immediacy than could ethnoracial distinctions. Therefore, the entirety of literature and the principles used to shape it and judge it fell even more obviously within the purview of feminist investigations and critiques than within the scope of ethnoracially defined inquiries. The immediate roots of the feminism that grew so rapidly in the wake of 1960s were situated, moreover, in soil that was partly cultural as well as socioeconomic. Three years before the founding of the National Organization for Women in 1966, a book by one of its chief founders, Betty Friedan, had indicted the educational and social-scientific establishments for perpetuating narrow and disabling images of womanhood. *The Feminine Mystique* (1963) was only one of many sources of the feminist movement, but it injected at the start a strong element of cultural consciousness that was quickly and energetically directed at the prevailing literary culture.

Modernism's heroic artificers tended to be clusters of stereotypically masculine virtues, after all; perhaps it was no coincidence that so very few female writers had been valued in a literary culture dominated by this particular taste. Pound and Eliot had put in place "intellectual, impersonal, experimental, and concrete" ideals for poetry that served, Elaine Showalter pointed out, to marginalize female poets of contrary sensibilities. Nina Baym criticized a gendered narrowness in conventional constructions of the American novel. Classic fiction from James Fenimore Cooper through Melville and Hawthorne, Twain and Howells, and Hemingway and Fitzgerald told the story of individuals who exist "in some meaningful sense prior to, and apart from, societies in which they happen to find themselves." This frame of men-against-each-other-and-the-elements, especially in wilderness or in war, is difficult enough for women writers to enter, but when they do enter it, Baym complained, the critical reception is largely prejudicial. When women writers "cast the main character as a woman," as was done by Wharton and Cather, their work was read "not as a woman's versions of the myth," but as a story "of the frustration of female nature." Talk of the American Adam even at its most illuminating had been just that, Adamic, and thus highly gendered.

This sense of the matter strengthened the impulse to look toward neglected women authors who had pursued a variety of agendas, some close to the concerns of male authors but some not. Once the search began, there were plenty to be found, especially among white women. In American society, after all, there were more white females than ethnic minorities of any variety, and a great percentage had the advantages of an excellent education and a measure of social support for careers in the arts. These women produced innumerable novels, poems, plays, and essays waiting to be rediscovered and revaluated. The result was that American literary culture of the 1980s and 1990s gave more attention to women authors and to gender as a category of analysis than at any previous time in American history.

The literature of 1900 or of 1925 as constructed from these new engagements began to look quite different from the literary cultures of each period. Chopin's *The Awakening* and Gilman's *The Yellow Wall-Paper* began to be counted as important contributions to the literature of the turn-of-the-century era. Many works, like these, that focused on the experiences and perspectives of women as women were taken seriously for the first time. Gilman's feminist utopian novel, *Herland*, which had published serially in 1915, appeared as a book for the first time in 1979. The novels of Cather, Wharton, and Ellen Glasgow were now found worthy of critical engagements earlier reserved for their male contemporaries. A Martin Scorsese film based on Wharton's *Age of Innocence* helped to make this novel of 1920 one of the fiction hits of 1993. The bona fide modernist poets Marianne Moore and Djuna Barnes emerged from the shadows cast for so long by Pound, Eliot, Stevens, and Williams. The poems and autobiographical sketches of Anne Sexton and Sylvia Plath, both of whom committed suicide, became a substantial field for the exploration of the constraints confronting creative women in the society and culture of the United States in the mid-century decades. Biographical studies of the deeply troubled Plath proliferated to the point that these biographies themselves became the subject of an extensive article in the *New Yorker* in 1993 by one of the nation's most renowned journalists, Janet Malcolm.

Just what constituted American literature from the viewpoint of the prevailing literary culture of 1990 was made clear in the *Heath Anthology of American Literature*, published in that year under the general editorship of Paul Lauter. Here the results of feminism and multiculturalism were brought together by design in a an elaborate project of canon-revision publicly endorsed by many leaders of the Modern Language Association, the chief professional organization for professors of literature. The *Heath Anthology*'s connection to postmodernism was less obvious, but many of the editors, promoters, and reviewers of this work had absorbed several insights that had come to be associated with postmodernism: that lit-

erary categories were constructed, that value-systems were contingent, that canons were dependent upon the priorities of canonmakers, and that canons play a role in the sustaining of particular civic orientations.

In order to meet the goals of diversity and inclusion, Lauter and his associates reprinted not only works in the standard literary genres written by women and by inhabitants of all five segments of the ethnoracial pentagon. The editors also reprinted ballads, travel narratives, folk tales, and a variety of translations from languages other than English, including poems written in Chinese on the walls of the immigrant-receiving center on Angel Island in San Francisco Bay. Anglo-Protestants were decentered, in the process, but the acknowledged cores of the American Renaissance and of classical modernism were preserved. Some of the school authors remained, but even so stalwart a figure in that old company as James Russell Lowell was dropped altogether.

The *Heath Anthology* appeared at a time when professors and editors, as a vocational-professional cohort in the United States, were as conscious as they had ever been of the social significance of routine curricular decisions. In the context of this pedagogical-civic responsibility, more forthrightly acknowledged than by critics of the generation of Matthiessen and Trilling, the *Heath Anthology* necessarily partook of an effort to provide, without apology, a new set of school authors for America, free from the biases of the original set. Lauter was candid about the sociopolitical as well as the aesthetic principles that inform the *Heath Anthology*, and about the work's function in a field of power. In justifying the exclusion of antebellum white southern writing, for example, Lauter explained that these works "consistently display gross racial stereotypes and long-discredited apologies for the slave system. . . . The victors, it is said, write history; perhaps, too, they establish the terms on which culture continues."

Yet it would be a mistake to infer that the *Heath Anthology* is cynical in its basic outlook. On the contrary, this ambitious and successful project in diversification betrays a robust idealism rarely found within the literary cultures that had prevailed in the United States since prior to World War I. Not everyone who contributed to the recognition and appreciation of the diversity of American authorship exaggerated the power of changed reading lists to improve society, of course, but the reception accorded the *Heath Anthology* in the age of "power/knowledge" does reveal a streak of high confidence in the civic value of the right texts. Hence the distance between the orientation of 1900 and that of 1990 might not be quite as great as it first appears. The Lowell sainted by the genteel tradition might well have admired the wholesome resolve surrounding the *Heath Anthology*, and, while himself exiting its canon, could encourage its supporters—mere professors and editors facing a panorama of formidable injustices—with a line he had written to inspire beleaguered abolitionists in 1844: "how weak an arm may turn the iron helm of fate."

SEE ALSO African American Cultural Movements; Judaism and Jewish Culture; Mass Media and Popular Culture (all in this volume).

## BIBLIOGRAPHY

The most up-to-date scholarship and theoretical argumentation concerning virtually all of the episodes, texts, and careers mentioned in this article can be found in studies published in the three leading journals in the field: *American Literary History, American Literature,* and *American Quarterly.* The first of these, which began publication only in 1989, has quickly become the leading forum for theoretically self-conscious, cross-disciplinary work on the political, socioeconomic, and cultural contexts of literary activity in every genre. *American Literary History* is an especially reliable point of access to controversies concerning canon-revision, multiculturalism, feminism, and literatures defined in ethnoracial terms.

Helpful treatments of the literature and literary cultures of the United States in the twentieth century can be found in separate articles within a number of multiauthored reference works, one of the finest of which is Emory Elliott, ed., *The Columbia Literary History of the United States* (1988). Of the many one-volume narratives of the historical development of American literature as a whole, one with an especially incisive discussion of the major twentieth-century movements is Richard Ruland and Malcolm Bradbury, *From Puritanism to Postmodernism: A History of American Literature* (1991).

The most crisp and authoritative account of the Victorian literary culture and the challenges made to it in the 1910s is Henry F. May, *The End of American Innocence: A Study of the First Years of Our Time, 1912–1917* (1959). The best book on Mark Twain's relation to the Victorian and realist literary cultures is Henry Nash Smith, *Mark Twain: The Development of a Writer* (1962). An excellent collection of studies of realism is Eric J. Sundquist, ed., *American Realism: New Essays* (1982). Three other, highly contrasting studies of the early twentieth century are Peter Conn, *The Divided Mind: Ideology and Imagination in America, 1898–1917* (1983); June Howard, *Form and History in American Literary Naturalism* (1985); and Walter Benn Michaels, *The Gold Standard and the Logic of Naturalism* (1987). A striking interpretation of Henry James in a broad cultural context is Ross Posnock, *The Trial of Curiosity: Henry James, William James, and the Challenge of Modernity* (1991).

The most helpful single book on the literary culture of the 1920s remains Frederick J. Hoffman, *The Twenties: American Writing in the Postwar Decade* (1962). The most convincing and comprehensive interpretation of F. Scott Fitzgerald is Robert Sklar, *F. Scott Fitzgerald: The Last Laocoön* (1967). For the writers of the 1920s who came to be known as modernists, the best work is Hugh Kenner, *A Homemade World* (1975). Several excellent essays, especially those by Phyllis Rose and Bruce Robbins, distinguish Robert Kiely, ed., *Modernism Reconsidered* (1983); but the best starting point for the study of literary modernism in America is now Daniel J. Singal, ed., *Modernist Culture in America* (1991).

Singal is also the author of the most carefully researched study of southern literary intellectuals from James Branch Cabell to Robert Penn Warren, *The War Within: From Victorian to Modernist Thought in the South, 1919–1945* (1982). The finest study of the literary Left remains Daniel Aaron, *Writers on the Left: Episodes in American Literary Communism* (1961). The coming together of Jewish and Anglo-Protestant intellectuals is a theme in David A. Hollinger, *In the American Province: Studies in the History and Historiography of Ideas* (1985); and Terry A. Cooney, *The Rise of the New York Intellectuals: Partisan Review and Its Circle, 1934–1945* (1986). Richard Ruland's *The Rediscovery of American Literature: Premises of Critical Taste, 1900–1940* (1967) is a valuable account of arguments over critical doctrine. Two influential, mid-century careers are explored in Mark Krupnick, *Lionel Trilling and the Fate of Cultural Criticism* (1986); and William E. Cain, *F. O. Matthiessen and the Politics of Criticism*

(1988). A historical overview of literary scholarship as an academic profession is offered by Gerald Graff, *Professing Literature: An Institutional History* (1987).

A valuable collection of ambitious articles on a variety of movements and initiatives in the period between World War II and the end of the 1970s is Daniel Hoffman, ed., *Harvard Guide to Contemporary American Writing* (1979). Thomas Hill Schaub's *American Fiction in the Cold War* (1991) is a cogent, provocative analysis.

A central work in the discussion of ethnic literatures is Werner Sollors, *Beyond Ethnicity: Consent and Descent in American Culture* (1986). Excellent bibliographies and commentaries on ethnic literature can be found in Paul Lauter, ed., *The Heath Anthology of American Literature* (1990). Although not limited to the United States, Sandra M. Gilbert and Susan Gubar, *No Man's Land: The Place of the Woman Writer in the Twentieth Century* (1988) is an indispensable work on gender and modern literature. Another useful study is Rachel Blau DuPlessis, *Writing Beyond the Ending: Narrative Strategies of Twentieth-Century Women Writers* (1985).

In the highly contested terrain of the modernist-postmodernist divide, three representative and helpful books are Ingeborg Hoestery, ed., *Zeitgeist in Babel: The Post-Modernist Controversy* (1991); Scott Lash and Jonathan Friedman, eds., *Modernity and Identity* (1992); and Brian McHale, *Constructing Postmodernism* (1992). A spirited attack is mounted by Christopher Norris, *What's Wrong with Postmodernism?* (1990). A loud introduction to poststructuralist theory, intended for historians, is Kenneth Cmiel, "Poststructural Theory," in *Encyclopedia of American Social History* (1993). A journal that regularly publishes strong defenses of postmodernist ideas is *boundary 2*. A solid indicator of many features of the literary culture of the 1980s and 1990s is Frank Lentricchia and Thomas McLaughlin, eds., *Critical Terms for Literary Study* (1990).

# THE MASS MEDIA AND POPULAR CULTURE

*Ronald G. Walters*

In 1988, Americans exported approximately $844 million in television programming to Western Europe. That amounted to 270,000 hours of viewing. The same year, Japan purchased $318 million of U.S.-produced programming, up 20 percent from the year before. In the twilight of the century, *Mr. Ed*—a show starring a talking horse—penetrated markets that American automobiles could not. Although the power of the United States may have declined in other respects in the course of the twentieth century, its ability to make and market words, images, and sounds remained formidable.

Scholars and critics have argued about what is "mass" and what is "popular" for much of this century. For purposes of this essay *popular culture* refers to performances for profit, conveyed through specialized, often technologically sophisticated modes of production (the mass media), usually characterized by a clear distinction between audiences and performers, and designed to be consumed rather than preserved. Although imperfect, that definition locates twentieth-century American popular culture within a capitalist, consumer-oriented system without making it a simple reflection of that system. It says nothing about the pleasures audiences derive from listening and viewing, but directs attention to the crucial link between mass media and popular culture.

Four major lines of inquiry are particularly significant for tracing the history of that link. The first examines the economic and political structures that shaped and produced American mass media and popular culture. The second explores the forms and content of popular culture and their relation to technological, economic, and cultural innovation. The third traces changes in the sites where information and entertainment are produced and consumed. The fourth focuses on the meanings audiences took from, or projected onto, popular culture. This article follows these four lines of inquiry through the histories of different media in the twentieth century, around

which it is organized. Behind that story, however, lies the nineteenth century.

## THE RISE OF COMMERCIAL POPULAR CULTURE

Between 1800 and 1900, a revolution in entertainment occurred as significant as the electronic one that followed. Eighteenth-century America was distinguished in the Western world by a relative lack of commercial popular culture and, indeed, by hostility to it, mostly rooted in religion and primarily rooted in New England. As late as 1763 there was no theater north of New York, no play written by an American produced in North America, and no American-born professional actor. Commercial performances were sparse, expensive, and mostly confined to cities and larger towns.

Change began just before 1800 and continued through the nineteenth century. Theater, the primary form of commercial entertainment in the early nineteenth century, ceased to be almost exclusively urban and the preserve of elites. Larger theaters meant lower ticket prices in the cities. Touring companies followed lines of trade—roads, rivers, canals, and, later, railroads—to take live shows into the hinterland.

Easier access to commercial popular entertainment coincided with an expansion of choices. Eighteenth-century audiences had few kinds of performances available to them. By the time of the Civil War, American audiences had a wide variety, including concerts, Shakespeare, opera, and minstrel shows. By the end of the nineteenth century, the choices were staggering: they encompassed vaudeville, burlesque, phonograph records, concerts, ethnic theater, minstrel shows, "legitimate" stage, circuses, Wild West shows, and movies. In October 1899, a brilliant young man named Guglielmo Marconi made headlines in the United States by wireless transmission of news about a yacht race. Radio, and, ultimately, television were on their way. In the course of a century, Americans moved from impoverishment to a wealth of commercial popular culture.

By 1900, Americans had also become among the most innovative people in the Western world in creating and reshaping forms of entertainment. The minstrel show, Coney Island, the musical, ragtime, the phonograph, and the Wild West show marked the beginning of what, by the end of the twentieth century, became worldwide power in the production of popular culture. A direct line connects the small early-nineteenth-century theatrical troupes that brought Shakespeare by flatboat to Ohio River towns and the electronic networks that radiate American sitcoms across the earth.

In addition to a dramatic increase in the accessibility and variety of popular culture, the nineteenth century foreshadowed the twentieth in other significant respects. It marked the emergence of outsiders—Jews, gays, Italian Americans, Irish Americans, and African Americans, among them—as major creative forces in "mainstream" culture. From the racist appropriation of African American dance and song on the minstrel stage, to the pre–Civil War popularity of Irish music and Jewish musicians, through the birth of Hollywood film and down to the present, much of what was central in American popular culture came from groups pushed to the edge of society by prejudice.

Perhaps because of their connections to alternative traditions, or perhaps because they often played to multilingual immigrant audiences, nineteenth-century entertainers presided over a stylistic shift of considerable significance for the twentieth. It was a move from more verbal to more visual styles of popular culture. Although the change was uneven and incomplete before 1900, it occurred in a variety of ways and places, from the slapstick comedy of minstrel shows and vaudeville to the post–Civil War rise of plays in which spectacle and special effects substituted for plot. Even before the motion picture, American popular culture communicated through images.

Nineteenth-century commercial entertainment also cast the die for the twentieth in economic organization. Popular culture remained too diverse and loosely organized to resemble an "industry" in the sense that oil and steel were industries dominated by giant corporations by 1900. And there was nothing remotely comparable to present-day, highly diversified entertainment conglomerates like Time Warner, or multinational ones like Sony Corporation. American popular culture, nonetheless, had already begun to follow the path of other economic enterprises by becoming increasingly national in scope and consolidated in structure. One sign was formation of the Syndicate in 1896, which exercised considerable power over American theatrical productions through its control over bookings. One estimate held that by 1904 the Syndicate had over five hundred theaters, including most major ones in New York, within its orbit. Similar consolidation occurred in vaudeville and in music publishing, as regional centers like Chicago, Boston, Philadelphia, and Baltimore yielded to the power of New York's Tin Pan Alley. In the twentieth century, film and radio recapitulated the movement from fragmentation and competition to geographic and economic consolidation, but with greater rapidity and higher stakes.

In its more centralized, highly capitalized, and less regional form, late-nineteenth-century popular culture pioneered the consumer ethic of the twentieth. Music provides the best example. In the antebellum period, Thomas Moore's *Irish Melodies,* the first volume of which appeared in 1808, was among the most popular collections of American music. Bound in book form, it passed from generation to generation. By the late nineteenth century, the song-publishing industry depended on sheet music being a commodity that Americans used and discarded. Popular culture led the way into the brave new twentieth-century world of disposability and consumption.

The nineteenth century prepared Americans for the twentieth-century revolution in popular culture in a final respect worth noting. The work of a number of scholars, especially Lawrence Levine and Paul DiMaggio, demonstrates that a strong distinction between "high" and "low" cultures emerged in America only in the last half of the nineteenth century. Without denying differences in taste, Levine argues that prior to the Civil War there was a wide range of shared culture that transcended lines of class, race, region, gender, and ethnicity. Shakespeare and opera attracted large audiences and mingled freely with amusements that later generations would dismiss as "popular." In such a world, it made sense for P. T. Barnum to celebrate Shakespeare's three hundredth birthday in 1864 with a grand event that included "three albino children" and a "musically educated seal."

For understanding the twentieth century, however, the primary problem is to explain why a cultural hierarchy emerged, what sustained it, and whose interests it served. An appealing answer is that elites erected it as a way of distancing themselves from an increasingly heterogeneous urban working class, whose cultural "inferiority" thereby defined their own "superiority." Yet, if cultural labeling was designed to set boundaries, it created permeable ones that enabled some people to rise through learning, skill, and taste, rather than by family or wealth. Elites themselves occasionally opened such bastions of "art" as museums and symphonies to the masses. The view that the hierarchy of taste came downward from elites also neglects other groups involved in the production of culture. The distinction between highbrow and lowbrow rested on the emergence of professional critics, performers, artists, conservatories, universities, and entrepreneurs, each with a measure of power in shaping and maintaining it. Lowbrow culture, moreover, was not foisted on passive consumers. Twentieth, as well as nineteenth-century popular culture offered important things to audiences: cultural breathing room, heroes and heroines, chances to imagine alternative identities, opportunities for sociability, and sources of meaning—in sum, pleasures.

## FROM STAGE TO SCREEN

In 1900, the pleasures of commercial popular culture typically came from live performances. A person of modest means, living in a city, might select from Shakespeare, musicals, ethnic plays, and bawdy shows at the local burlesque house, among other options. Theaters, moreover, were not the only sites of live performances. There were outdoor events like Wild West shows, circuses under the big top, or amusement parks—Coney Island was their epitome—in which audiences both participated and became part of the show. In smaller towns and in the countryside, the options were fewer, but it was the rare American who lacked at least occasional access to live performances of some sort. Of all the choices at the turn of the century, vaudeville was king.

Superficially, vaudeville resembled its contemporary, the English music hall, and its predecessor, the minstrel show, each of which similarly depended on an assortment of short acts strung together to make an evening's entertainment. But vaudeville's real roots were not in England or in minstrelsy; they were in the ethnic hodge-podge of New York City, and in saloons, some of which featured live performances after the Civil War. A part of vaudeville's importance for American commercial popular culture lies in its success in moving beyond those origins by reaching out from the city to the hinterland, from the multiethnic working class to middle-class and rural Americans, and from the mostly male world of the saloon to theaters, some quite lavish, catering to men and women, young and old.

Variety was the essence of vaudeville. Although theater managers differed on what comprised a proper bill, some things were common to the majority of vaudeville shows. The acts were brief, usually around fifteen minutes, and there were a large number of them. A booking agent claimed in 1916 that the secret was to have nine in a sequence that built from a nearly wordless "dumb act" to occupy patrons while late arrivals found their seats, through the eighth, which featured the star, to the concluding one, mostly visual like the first and designed to send the audience home happy. (Some regarded the latter less charitably as a mediocre "chaser" to encourage audiences to leave.) Such a bill might include animal acts like "Burke's Juggling Dogs," dancers, singers, comics, magicians like the great Houdini, impressionists and female impersonators, acrobats, and even celebrities. Babe Ruth, Jack Dempsey, and the famous deaf-mute Helen Keller all appeared in vaudeville.

The diversity of a vaudeville bill both broadened its appeal and foreshadowed characteristics of later popular culture. Although songs and verbal comedy had a prominent place, vaudeville was highly visual, appropriately so for a form that began with largely immigrant audiences for whom English might well be a second language. It thereby unwittingly helped prepare some of the comic and story-telling techniques for the medium that would bring about its demise: film. Vaudeville was also notable for its discontinuity. Serious acts and animal acts and slapstick comedy existed as discrete units—quarter-hour bits—with no attempt to connect them. Later critics who bemoaned television's jarring juxtapositions—quick cuts, for example, from stories of mayhem to cheery commercials—could look back to vaudeville for a moment when popular culture abandoned the unities of plot and theme important in legitimate theater and novels.

In common with the sheet-music industry, vaudeville began with scattered individuals and ended with control concentrated in a few hands, mostly in New York City. In its formative years it was the creature of entrepreneurs and entertainers like Tony Pastor, whose theaters, beginning with his first in 1865, radiated out of New York's Bowery toward uptown semi-respectability by the 1880s. By the end of the nineteenth century, however, power rested with booking agencies capable of organizing the complex process of bringing thousands of theater managers and performers together in orderly fashion. Of these none was greater than the Keith-Albee organization, whose United Booking Office of

America incorporated in 1906 and was dominant in the East by World War I, both for booking acts and for its ownership of a chain of theaters. In 1927 it combined with the Orpheum circuit, which played a similarly powerful role, mostly in the West. Small-time and local vaudeville never entirely disappeared, nor did competing circuits, but the money and action were with big booking agencies. Blacklisting by E. F. Albee, who controlled the Keith-Albee empire for a decade after 1918, could devastate the career of a performer who sought greener pastures. Harpo Marx considered him "more powerful than the president of the United States."

Whatever the ill consequences of the great booking agencies for performers, vaudeville spread across the country after 1900 and reached into small towns very different from the large cities in which it originated. Even before the advent of movies and radio, it formed a loose national entertainment network along which performers moved tirelessly. The men and women who brought vaudeville to the hinterland, however, were anything but stereotypical middle Americans. Reminiscing about his colleagues, one performer recalled "There were Arab tumblers, there were Hungarian teeterboard performers, Spanish dancers, there were Negro dancers, there were Jew comics. . . . There were Catholics and there were Hindus." His list omitted the smattering of African American stars like Bert Williams and Ethel Waters, who once remarked that "we found ourselves applauded by the ofays [whites] in the theater and insulted by them on the streets." For many on the margins of American life, vaudeville—like later forms of show business and professional sports—was one of the few opportunities for fame and fortune. "Where else," asked Minnie Marx, whose sons were once vaudeville's most expensive act, "can people who don't know anything make so much money?"

Immigrants, racial differences, and ethnicity gave vaudeville a creative energy, reservoirs of cultural innovation, and a disrespect for conventional pieties and formalities of language. At one moment a performer like Sophie Tucker could play on maudlin sentiments about motherhood; at the next she could cater to white racist stereotypes about blacks; and at the next she could sing a song like "Angle Worm Wiggle," raunchy enough to provoke a raid by the Chicago police. Vaudeville simultaneously affirmed, challenged, and ignored middle-class values, much to the delight of middle-class, as well as immigrant, audiences. Its messages were as mixed as its format and the ethnicities of its performers.

Variety and energy, however, were not enough to save vaudeville from the movies. The new medium first appeared in the 1890s, as vaudeville was booming. A common response was to show a movie as part of a vaudeville bill. The short running time of early films, coupled with their novelty, made a good fit between the two media, at least until around 1906 when movies began to find a home and audience of their own. Because the big-time circuits and booking organizations had a near monopoly of the best performers, small-time vaudeville operators found films especially useful. Two of their number, William Fox and Marcus Loew, parlayed an opportunistic mix of vaudeville and film into creation of major Hollywood studios.

Although a Keith theater was one of the first to show a film in 1896, Albee threatened to reduce the salaries of, or blacklist, performers who appeared in movies. Even he failed to keep vaudeville dominant. In 1928, Joseph P. Kennedy, father of a future president, bought into the combined Keith-Albee-Orpheum company to secure its theaters for films. The result was a corporation, Radio-Keith-Orpheum (R.K.O.), involved in radio, movies, and, eventually, television. A combination of high costs, the Depression, and audience preferences reduced vaudeville to a shadow and sent Albee into retirement. In November 1932, the Palace in New York, the greatest of all vaudeville theaters since 1913, switched to films. Its first feature starred Eddie Cantor, ex-vaudevillian.

In killing vaudeville, movies hardly ended live performance as an important mode of popular culture. It persists in theater, concerts, sports, stock-car racing, rodeos, and countless other forms. The relationship between audience and performer did, nonetheless, change with the advent of film and other electronic media. They removed the spectator from direct contact with the performer and eliminated the spontaneity and improvisation that occurred in theater, vaudeville, and in certain kinds of music, notably jazz. In addition, the overwhelming power of the electronic media tended, by the last half of the twentieth century, to make many live performances subordinate to other media. Rock groups toured to promote albums; movie and television stars appeared in theatrical productions or in "concert" to bolster careers or to generate a taped performance for the home-video market. One of the more successful rock-concert tours of 1992 played to approximately 800,000 fans, less than a fifth of the number who purchased just one participating group's then-current album. The primary purpose of this tour—Lollapalooza '92—was to introduce the public to "alternative" groups and to sell compact discs. With the demise of vaudeville, live entertainment became—except in certain areas—a junior partner in an interconnected world of popular culture, mostly governed by the electronic media. Before that could happen, movies had to find an audience.

By 1903, use of movies as part of vaudeville bills stalled, and other then-current venues—notably amusement parks and traveling exhibitions—were no more promising if film was to be anything more than a novelty act. Although some movie-only theaters existed from the beginning, the sudden appearance of the nickelodeon in 1905 marked the next stage in the exhibition of films. Admission was cheap: the five-cent ticket gave the nickelodeon its name at a time when vaudeville shows cost anywhere from fifteen cents to $1.25. The theaters were gaudy on the outside, with electric lights, posters, signs, and phonograph music playing. Even if the interior was spartan and the product on the screen crude, the lure was irresistible, as well as affordable, for millions of Americans. By 1910 there were perhaps as many as ten thousand nickelodeons in America. *Variety,* the show business bible, claimed that none had existed six years earlier.

Impressive as the nickelodeon boom was, it misled commentators who saw its rowdy, ethnically mixed working-class patrons in New York as emblematic of early film audiences. Vaudeville had already introduced some middle-class men and women to movies. Films, moreover, were shown in settings other than nickelodeons (including churches), and in cities and small towns with populations far different from New York's. By 1911 the trend was toward theaters with higher admissions, aimed at a more affluent and better-behaved audience, including women and families. Four years later the nickelodeon boom was over and shortly thereafter American cities began to sprout movie palaces seating two thousand or more patrons in luxury and pampering them with such amenities as air-conditioning. In the 1920s and 1930s, these theaters, although fairly few in number, sold more tickets than all smaller theaters combined. Within twenty years, movies had shuffled off the vaudeville stage, out of store-front nickelodeons, and into fantasy-kingdoms of their own.

Although the nickelodeon era barely spanned the decade between 1905 and 1915, it coincided with a time when audiences learned how to see movies and filmmakers learned how to make them. Tales abound of people—mostly from the non-Western world—who could not interpret what appeared on the screen when first exposed to movies. American audiences, already familiar with highly visual forms of popular culture, had few such problems. Patrons of early film often commented on the "realistic" or "life-like" appearance of black-and-white images that strike late-twentieth-century viewers as primitive. Audiences reportedly flinched at scenes of crashing surf and reacted with shock at a close-up in Edwin S. Porter's *The Great Train Robbery* (1903) in which an outlaw suddenly pointed a gun at the audience.

Even if Americans brought a high level of visual sophistication to early movies, directors took time to appreciate how differently film worked from previous media. It allowed abrupt shifts of perspective impossible on the stage—Porter's audiences may well have been as terrified by his quick switch to a close shot as by the image of a gun. The medium's potentially complex narrative strategies were also not obvious to the first movie-makers, who often did little more than film vaudeville acts, melodramas, comedy bits, or scenes of current interest. Even Porter, who mastered a variety of basic cinematic techniques, failed to take much advantage of them. His successors in Europe and in America, however, had begun to learn the languages of film before the nickelodeon era ended. Through editing, camera work, and the juxtaposition of images from different times, places, and points of view, directors like D. W. Griffith told stories in ways distinctive to film. His epic of Reconstruction, *Birth of a Nation* (1915), raised film to new heights of cinematic skill while sending it to depths of antiblack racism.

Other important characteristics of American film emerged during the nickelodeon era. Beginning in 1911 multireel feature films (first imported from Europe) replaced short subjects suitable for vaudeville bills. Stars appeared: men and women who commanded high salaries, and whose private lives, as well as screen presence, attracted millions of fans. In 1919 three of them—Charlie Chaplin, Mary Pickford, and Douglas Fairbanks—joined forces with Griffith to form their own distribution company, United Artists. Resolution of an antitrust suit in 1915 ended a chaotic period of disputes over patents and distribution practices. And in 1907 the Selig Company began the march of film production toward the Los Angeles area, where the combination of good weather, varied scenery, and an attractive labor market were close to ideal.

Before the nickelodeon was gone, and while vaudeville was in full flower, the Hollywood era was dawning. A small number of studios predominated and mass production prevailed. In technological matters, Hollywood proved innovative in its commitment to sound, animation (raised to high standards by Walt Disney's studio in the 1930s), color, special effects, and even in failed efforts like its three-dimensional, or 3-D, movies in the 1950s. In stylistic matters, however, Hollywood was generally conservative. Its films commonly fell into one or the other of several genres—the western, the screwball comedy, the women's film, science fiction, mysteries, musicals, costume drama, and so forth. Critics bemoaned their predictability; industry cynics satirized the banality of the medium that paid their salaries, and a small number of writers, actors, producers, and directors found creativity within Hollywood formulas. Meanwhile, fans eagerly awaited the next hit product from America's dream factory.

It is less clear what films did for, and to, the mass audience they created. Part of the problem is that Hollywood catered to many different tastes, even as the studios sought the largest possible audience. An average filmviewer in 1932 and 1933, for instance, might well see a tough-guy gangster picture featuring the likes of James Cagney or Edward G. Robinson, Mae West's suggestive *She Done Him Wrong* (1933), a Charlie Chan potboiler mystery, the powerful indictment of injustice in *I Am a Fugitive from a Chain Gang* (1932), and the gaudy fluff of *Goldiggers of 1933*. With such variety, it is difficult to know *what* audiences saw, let alone how they interpreted movies.

Further compounding the problem is the fact that Hollywood itself changed—the films of the 1960s were not like the films of the 1930s—and that movies, in common with all other forms of popular culture, often worked best when they were most open to multiple interpretations. The screwball comedies of the late 1930s, for example, featured strong women characters, often with independent careers, sometimes divorced or otherwise morally a bit off-center, in playful combat with male characters. Was the message one of female independence? Or of dependence, because conventional love won in the end? Or was it one of mutual dependence because male and female characters were incomplete without each other?

Openness and ambiguity are not necessarily weaknesses—they characterize *King Lear* and *Moby-Dick* as well as the screwball comedy. In Hollywood film, however, they derived less from the complex view of the human condition that Shakespeare and Melville brought to their craft than from an unwillingness to offend customers. Only exceptional movies tackled difficult social problems, and those that did generally sought comfortable resolution. Similarly, Hollywood commonly reinforced, rather than challenged, racial and ethnic prejudices. It was more

symbolic than the industry intended when the first Academy Award won by an African American actor went to Hattie McDaniel for her role as a stereotypical mammy in *Gone with the Wind* (1939). The movie's producer earlier forbade McDaniel from attending its premiere in segregated Atlanta. Hollywood did little better with gender stereotypes, although an occasional actress like Katharine Hepburn projected unconventional intelligence and independence.

For viewers, however, the point of movies frequently was not to be challenged but rather to find fantasy and escape. A son of poor Jewish immigrants in Chicago, for example, told an interviewer in 1929 that westerns were his haven from abuse by neighborhood bullies. He even built a fish-barrel horse to help him play out a movie-bred dream life in which he starred. For him and millions of others, Hollywood films were a source of images, styles, and alternatives. Movies were also a collective experience, a common bond that sometimes transcended lines of ethnicity and class. Chicana cannery workers in California, for instance, recalled movie stars as a major topic of conversation with Russian-Jewish coworkers in the 1930s and 1940s. Beginning in the 1920s, fan magazines and gossip columns gave Americans a sense of intimacy with movie-colony favorites. Advertising and merchandising based on stars' endorsements further connected the movies with everyday life. Until the 1950s, no other source of commercial popular culture held such sway over Americans, even if the nature and extent of film's influence is difficult to trace with precision.

The mid-1940s, however, were both a high point and the beginning of a time of troubles for the movies. After serious financial difficulties between 1929 and 1933, the major studios came out of the Depression and World War II with profitability intact, thanks in part to innovations in marketing like the double bill, give-aways, and, of course, popcorn. Between 1941 and 1946, Paramount's earnings rose from $10 million to $44 million. Movie attendance peaked in the latter year and the earnings of the other "big five" studios ranged from $12 million for RKO to $22 million for Twentieth Century–Fox. The plunge in movie-going was swift thereafter and, contrary to some accounts, initially had little to do with television: there were only about 14,000 sets in use in 1947, when the slump began. Movie revenues, which dropped less than attendance figures, declined almost 25 per cent in a decade. The prime audience for films, better-educated people of at least modest means, chose to spend savings accumulated during

World War II on houses, especially suburban ones, and on childraising, rather than the cinema. For them, going to the movies became difficult and a luxury. Free entertainment in the home was ideal. As film attendance shrunk after 1946, radio advertising revenues rose to a peak in 1953, at which point television began to have an impact. By then, the mass audience film had created for moving images no longer needed the movie theater.

The invisible hand of economic demand may have been the real cause of Hollywood's postwar woes, but two events in the late 1940s stood as dramatic symbols of the industry's problems. Each spoke less to the relationship between movies and their audience than to the vexing one between commercial popular culture and the modern American state. The first was a House Committee on Un-American Activities (HUAC) investigation of alleged communist infiltration in Hollywood in 1947. The second was a 1948 Supreme Court decision in a decade-old antitrust suit commonly known as the *Paramount* case. The former represented an attempt at political control over the content of popular culture, the latter an effort to regulate the industry's economic structure.

When film left vaudeville houses, it frequently moved into ill-ventilated buildings posing considerable fire hazards, especially given the potentially deadly combination of volatile film stock and hot projectors. Among the early legislation concerning movies were fire-safety laws. More often than not, however, it was the moral, not the health, implications of movies that distressed reformers, from religious conservatives to Progressives who saw state power as a positive force for good. The original battlegrounds were local, with citizens' groups pressing for licensing laws and other legislation to place theaters under police and governmental supervision. Some jurisdictions also imposed local censorship. Even so, glimpses of bare breasts, tales of illicit love, and blatantly sexual, violent, and criminal behavior were good box office throughout the 1910s and 1920s. Vamps and Latin lovers defied local watchdogs.

Regulation at the national level loomed the 1930s. Confronted with sex and drug scandals, as well as pressure from procensorship groups, in 1922 the film industry created a trade organization, the Motion Picture Producers and Distributors Association (MPPDA). Following the precedent of professional baseball, which made a similar move after a World Series fixing scandal in 1919, the MPPDA appointed as its head a public figure with valuable political connections, Will Hays, Warren G. Har-

ding's postmaster general. He proved to be an effective front man as Hollywood sought to improve its image, standardize practices, and avoid regulation.

Sound, introduced in 1927 by Warner Brothers' *The Jazz Singer,* presented new opportunities for cinematic misbehavior. The film industry promulgated a Production Code in 1930, which extended and made more formal guidelines Hays's office had promoted since 1925. Even though Protestants and women's groups had long pressed for censorship, the Code reflected the Catholic Church's growing importance in advocating "decency" in film. It was largely the handiwork of a Jesuit priest and a lay Catholic trade-industry publisher, Martin Quigley.

Enforcement was lax and temptations were great as revenues plunged with the Depression. Indecency sold tickets. In 1934 the Catholic Church supplanted previous tactics, which sought local, state, and federal censorship, with a new weapon: the boycott. It created the Legion of Decency to campaign against attendance at films designated immoral. The Legion quickly claimed that 11 million people, Protestants and Jews among them, signed its pledge to stay away from unwholesome movies. The industry's response was once again to promise self-regulation in the form of the Production Code Administration (PCA), run by an Irish American Catholic, Joseph Breen. Henceforth, movies had to pass PCA muster prior to distribution. They could contain a certain amount of naughtiness, as long as virtue won in the end. They could not treat forbidden topics, such as miscegenation or homosexuality, or use profanity. The Code compromised careers, including the highly successful one of Mae West, whose stock in trade was joyful, unrepentant female sexuality—indecent by Breen Office standards.

Shortly after World War II, Congress added a new wrinkle to the saga of censorship. Prior to the war, a recently created House Committee on Un-American Activities and a Senate subcommittee raised allegations of communist influence in Hollywood, charges tainted by anti-Semitism directed at Jews prominent in the film industry. The accusations came to little, and shortly afterward Hollywood marched loyally to war. Jack Warner, of Warner Brothers, became a lieutenant colonel (he wanted to be a general) and leading figures like director Frank Capra signed up to make propaganda films. (Hedging its bets, Hollywood continued to produce movies at almost the prewar rate and combined wartime fare with genre potboilers.)

Congressional investigations resumed in 1947, following both a banner box office year and labor disputes in which some Hollywood producers, Walt Disney and Louis B. Mayer of MGM among them, thought they detected communist influences. They were among the friendly industry witnesses when HUAC came to town. In the course of its investigations, the Committee—including future president Richard M. Nixon—found little communist propaganda or much else that was un-American in movies. Its mission therefore shifted to ensuring that studios fired and refused to employ radicals. Some in the industry supported and cooperated with HUAC, including another future president, Ronald Reagan, and a future senator from California, George Murphy. Others watched careers dissolve because of minor political indiscretions, irresponsible accusations, or affiliation with radical groups. A few people were defiant. The most famous were the Hollywood Ten, most of whom were screenwriters, convicted and sentenced to prison for contempt of Congress for refusal to cooperate with the Committee.

HUAC stalled in 1949, but hearings resumed in 1951, with further blacklisting of actors, writers, directors, and other industry figures. One effect was to drive a number of creative men and women from the center of Hollywood life; another was to reinforce a tone of darkness and gloom that gave a post–World War II genre its name: *film noir*. In the science-fiction classic *Invasion of the Body Snatchers* (1956) for example, much of the horror came from the fact that "they," the invaders, were virtually indistinguishable from normal people, as communist spies presumably were from loyal Americans. Suspicion, uncertainty, and betrayal characterized what appeared on the screen as well as the industry itself. Meanwhile, box-office receipts continued to slide from their 1946 peak. At the end of World War II, weekly attendance at movies was approximately 90 million; it fell to roughly 20 million in 1990.

HUAC was not responsible for Hollywood's doldrums, creative or financial, and it was not the first, or last, effort to censor popular culture. Indeed, while such efforts flourished, Congress was also engaged in investigating comic books and television for their corrupting influence on America's morals. HUAC's innovation was to add political criteria and personal beliefs to the list of standards Hollywood imposed on itself.

There was irony in HUAC's timing. In May 1952, before the Committee finished with Hollywood, the Supreme Court handed down its first ruling on movie censorship in thirty-seven years. The previous decision declared film was a "business, pure and simple . . . not to be regarded as part of the press of the country." The 1952 decision, *Burstyn* v. *Wilson*, characterized motion pictures differently, as "a significant medium for the communication of ideas" and therefore afforded protection under the First Amendment. As HUAC and Hollywood closed the door to radicals, the Supreme Court opened it for filmmakers to move into previously forbidden areas.

*Burstyn* v. *Wilson* placed local censorship boards under strict procedural guidelines and left only one substantive criterion for banning a film: obscenity. Unpopular ideas, or behavior offensive to particular religious groups, no longer were sufficient cause for censorship. In 1956 the Production Code changed to reflect the Court's ruling. The problem, of course, was to define obscenity. The Court grappled with that in 1957 and ruled that the test for obscenity was "whether to the average person, applying contemporary community standards, the dominant theme of the material taken as a whole appeals to the prurient interest." Sexuality and nudity, by themselves, were not inherently obscene. Over the next two decades a deeply divided Supreme Court produced a series of rulings that were not entirely clear or consistent.

The film industry responded with the customary promise of self-regulation. Following the failure of serious films like *The Pawnbroker* (1965), *Alfie* (1966), and *Who's Afraid of Virginia Woolf?* (1966) to meet Production Code standards, the industry adopted a "Suggested for Mature Audiences" (SMA) label in 1966, acknowledging that the age of viewers might matter. In 1968 the industry created a full-scale rating system under which Production Code staff assigned films a letter designation according to appropriateness for audience members of various ages. The chief criterion was erotic content, although violence and profanity were also taken into account. The rating system was imprecise and contested, but it affected a film's success at the box office. A dreaded "X" rating (no one under seventeen admitted) was poison.

With modification, the rating system endured into the 1990s as a monument to movie-industry efforts to avoid external regulation and to make films for a national audience with differing local standards. By the 1960s, however, the chief problem facing filmmakers was not the threat of censorship. It was how to make money.

In business practices, as with the content of its films, the movie industry was largely successful in avoiding government regulation, up to a point. That point was 1948. Prior to the *Paramount* decision of that year, moviemakers had sought vertical integration—controlling all aspects of film from production through distribution. The first such attempt was the

Motion Picture Patents Company (MPPC), which emerged out of a swirl of litigation over patents, much of it fostered by Thomas A. Edison. By 1908, confusion and lawyers threatened the industry itself. Edison, Biograph, and Eastman Kodak resolved the problem by pooling patents in a "Plan to Reorganize the Motion Picture Business of the United States." It was collusive; it encompassed virtually every aspect of the production and distribution process; it brought a measure of rationality and order to the industry. It failed.

Companies outside the MPPC—the independents—pursued the market aggressively and with success. Between 1909 and 1913, houses showing their films increased from roughly 2,500 to 8,306; in the same period MPPC-licensed houses grew from over 4,000 to 6,877. Although it fostered important technological and business innovations, the MPPC was losing in the marketplace before 1915, when a district court judge in Pennsylvania declared it illegal under the Sherman Antitrust Act.

The next effort at economic integration of the film industry was more successful. It began with the grander theaters that replaced the nickelodeon. Skillful entrepreneurs like Marcus Loew and, especially Chicago-based Balaban and Katz, realized that movies could be marketed more profitably through chains of theaters, just as other commodities in the 1920s were marketed through chain stores. Reaching for a national audience, Balaban and Katz merged with Famous Players–Lasky, the world's largest movie company, in 1925. Thus arose Paramount Pictures. By the 1930s five major companies—Paramount, Warner Brothers, Loew's/MGM, Fox, and RKO—owned important chains of theaters and produced films. They dominated the industry, along with three smaller studios: Universal and Columbia, which also both made and distributed movies, and United Artists, which distributed films for independent producers. Although the major studios made only about 60 percent of the industry's films, theirs were usually the top features in quality and had, thanks to the studios' distribution networks, the best bookings. At their height, the eight major studios took in about 95 percent of all revenue from national film rentals and their own theaters took almost 70 percent of the box-office receipts.

The major studios also cooperated. They loaned talent, including stars, to one another and they distributed each other's films in markets where there was no direct competition. It was a comfortable system and, according to the *Paramount* decision, illegal. In a complex ruling, the Court prohibited a number

of movie-industry business practices and ordered a partial separation of the production of movies from their distribution.

The ruling was not a complete disaster, however distasteful it may have been to the major studios. The little three benefitted by having greater opportunities for high-class distribution of their films. United Artists did especially well. The decision also paved the way for art houses, which flourished in the 1950s and 1960s, and smaller, independent theaters (which, in turn, made enforcement of the Production Code more difficult). Coupled with the peculiarities of tax laws, *Paramount* also encouraged high-priced talent to form independent production companies. Economic concentration remained in film distribution—ten companies monopolized film rentals in 1954, and ten companies (including a few different ones) monopolized them in 1972—but the old system under which a handful of studios dominated output, distribution, and talent was eroding, thanks to competition from other media and governmental intervention the industry had previously dodged.

Beleaguered by HUAC, the *Paramount* case, and declining attendance, Hollywood searched for new gimmicks—such as 3-D and wide-screen movies—and old markets, notably European ones closed during World War II. It usually found success when it did what competing media, especially television, could not, such as producing mature, violent, and sexual films like the stylish, Depression-era gangster movie, *Bonnie and Clyde* (1967) or outsized, lavishly produced ones like the Rodgers and Hammerstein extravaganza, *The Sound of Music* (1965). In the 1970s a younger generation of directors and producers, notably Steven Spielberg and George Lucas, took visual wizardry well beyond anything television could conjure in a series of hits stretching from the shark saga *Jaws* (1975) to the 1993 dinosaur blockbuster *Jurassic Park*. Ironically, some of the best, notably *Star Wars* (1977) and *Raiders of the Lost Ark* (1981), were homages to old, cheaply made Hollywood movies.

Before success returned, however, the industry went through a painful adjustment. Studio heads aged, lost their grip, and watched a rise in independent production and a decline in the number of American movies made each year. The major studios dabbled in television and sold their film libraries and the valuable California real estate that had been the seat of their empires. The film business was always risky—and remains so—but by 1972 the major companies had mostly retrenched and found a profitable formula. In both content and economic strategy, the film industry, however, looked very different in the

1970s, 1980s, and 1990s than it had in earlier decades. The product itself diminished in quantity—in 1940 the major distributors released 363 movies and in 1990 they released 140—and ranged from small personal films to glitzy, big-budget spectaculars. The subject matter, the ability to tell stories through images, and the special effects were light years beyond American cinema of the 1930s, as well as beyond the old Production Code.

As early as the 1960s, however, movies lost their central place and became part of a much larger—sometimes competitive, often interconnected—world of popular culture. The studios sought other sources of revenue and were absorbed into bigger corporations. Paramount became part of Gulf + Western in 1966 (re-emerging as Paramount Communications, Inc. in 1989). A year later, Transamerica Corporation purchased United Artists. Two years afterward, both Warner Brothers and MGM likewise became part of diversified corporations. The case of Warner is especially instructive. As Warner Communications in the 1970s, it was involved in the record industry, music publishing, production of films and video, publishing (including *Mad* magazine), cable television, toy manufacturing, a computer company, cosmetics, a professional soccer club, and the Franklin Mint. Warner films became the basis of Warner television series; Warner cartoon characters and Warner books became Warner movies, with Warner soundtracks and Warner-licensed products. With another merger in 1989 it became Time Warner, the world's largest communications corporation. The vertical integration of the studio system gave way to something equally as sinister in the minds of those who believed competition best served the public: by the 1970s movies were mostly embedded in such highly diversified corporations, and tied to such a wide array of other products, that any kind of control other than that of the marketplace would prove difficult.

Even as the old studios transmuted into entertainment machines, film continued as a significant medium and movie theaters—diminished in size and number, and reduced from grand palaces to cramped multiplexes in shopping malls—continued as an important venue for popular culture. But much had changed since the vaudeville era: by 1990 popular culture came in a greater variety of forms, it was more visual and less dependent on live performances, it was highly interconnected economically and in content, and the number of sites for consuming it was much larger than in 1900. Movies played a major role in some of these changes; radio and television bear heavy responsibility for others.

## FROM RADIO TO TELEVISION AND BEYOND

The century-long process of bringing reproduced sound into the home began with the phonograph and, at about the same time, the player piano. Radio continued the process and television added images. With the advent of cable, video games, compact discs, laser discs, video recorders, and computer technologies, the end is nowhere in sight. For American popular culture, however, the shift from live to reproduced performances, and from the theater to the home as a primary site of commercial entertainment, was momentous. The shift also followed, with variations, a pattern similar to that of the film industry and the print media. To bring technological innovations like the phonograph, radio, and television to national markets required large concentrations of capital, occasional collusion within the industry, and delicate relations between it and the government. The end result, however, was not to create a uniform "mass" culture, but to increase the choices available to audiences.

With the phonograph, as with motion pictures and radio, the pioneers were slow to grasp the new medium's potential as entertainment. The gap between Eadweard Muybridge's experiments with motion photography in California in the 1870s and commercial movies was close to twenty years. The span of time separating Thomas A. Edison's 1877 patent on a "talking machine" was similar. His phonograph both recorded and played back on wax cylinders and he envisioned it as mechanical stenographer for businesses. By the early 1890s phonographs began making their way into homes and by World War I Edison's wax cylinders were giving way to prerecorded discs. Phonograph production increased 400 percent over a five-year span, reaching about 2 million units in 1919. By 1921 the industry was selling about 100 million records a year. Development of electronic technology in 1924 improved the quality and sonic range of recorded sound. What had begun in its inventor's mind as a piece of office equipment brought into American homes everything from marches and comedy routines to popular songs, complex dance music, and great artists like Enrico Caruso.

The high price of records helped ensure that they had a social role and were not purely for personal enjoyment. "Race" records of the 1920s, for example, were aimed at a black audience that could ill-afford the seventy-five cents they cost. For African Americans—whose average family income in parts of the South was below $300 a year—they were party music, or were played for religious gatherings, just as white youth shared records to try the latest dance steps. It was only after World War II, with the invention of high fidelity recordings, headphones, and the personal stereo, that the notion of recorded music as a private experience became possible. Before that happened, sound technology went through several revolutions and a major disaster.

The industry's crash was deep. Between 1927 and 1932 annual record sales plunged from 104 million to 6 million units. Brighter days lay in the future, especially after World War II. By 1948, Columbia Records, a subsidiary of CBS, perfected the 33$^1/_3$ rpm microgroove vinyl record, which made the long-playing album possible. In the meantime RCA introduced the 45 rpm single record and players to handle it. Following a period of confusion, each format found its niche, and the public replaced old 78 rpm machines with ones that played all three kinds of recording. In the 1950s, stars like Elvis Presley sold hit singles by the millions. In the early 1970s, Carole King's album, *Tapestry,* sold 14 million copies, more than double the total sale of records for 1932. Introduction of eight-track and cassette audiotapes in the 1970s, and the compact disc in 1982, in turn made the phonograph record obsolete. Although the industry had its troubles, the grim days of 1932 were long forgotten by 1990, when approximately five thousand companies in the United States produced recordings, with six of them (only one American-owned) dominating the market. Collectively, they shipped about 800 million recordings and generated over $7 billion in revenue. By that time, however, the industry had learned to live with one of the causes of its misery in the late 1920s and 1930s, radio.

Like the phonograph, radio was not born with entertainment in mind. Like the movies, its development required resolution of patent disputes and the end of intense, often chaotic, competition. The key figures in early radio were a multinational lot. They included Guglielmo Marconi, son of a wealthy Italian landowner and a Scotch-Irish mother from the Jameson family of distillers. His wireless telegraph riveted American public attention in 1899 and confirmed that messages could be sent through the air, albeit in the form of Morse code. Also among the pioneers were Reginald Aubrey Fessenden, a Canadian; Lee De Forest, raised in the post–Civil War South as the son of a Yankee missionary and educator; and David Sarnoff, a Russian Jewish immigrant. Fessenden and De Forest's innovations were technological: to the former went credit for the first transmission of voice and sound on Christmas Eve 1906; the latter claimed

to have "discovered an invisible Empire of the Air." What he actually perfected in 1907 was a glass tube that detected radio waves. With the work of Marconi, Fessenden, and others, transmission improved; with De Forest reception improved and the technology for radio began to fall into place. The question was, what to do with it? Sarnoff helped find the answer.

It was no accident that Marconi's wireless telegraph first proved attractive in Britain, where a corporation formed in 1897 to develop the young man's invention. Ships held the island nation's commerce and empire together. For them, wireless communication was invaluable. Indeed, Marconi came to the United States in 1899 primarily to negotiate with the Navy. In addition to its obvious military and commercial applications, radio fascinated a host of amateurs and tinkerers who began to crowd the airwaves. A 1910 House of Representatives report warned that "If the use of wireless is not to be regulated, it may in the future result in disaster."

Two years later, it did. In 1912, failure to receive distress signals from the luxury ocean liner *Titanic* in a clear and timely manner prevented ships in the area from rescuing as many drowning passengers and crew as might have been saved. The legislation that resulted required licenses for transmitters and divided the airwaves to prevent interference, with separate bands for amateurs, the Navy, and the American Marconi Company. The airwaves became a form of property, subject to government regulation, shared uneasily by the military, commercial interests, and amateur experimenters, who comprised the majority of the 8,500 licensed transmitter operators on the eve of World War I.

As the United States entered the war in 1917, the federal government banned all private broadcasting and placed radio transmission under control of the Navy in order to prevent spying and interference with military communications. America had its first monopoly of the airwaves and it was held by the military. There were efforts to continue it in peacetime.

In 1918, Congress considered legislation that would, in the words of a prime supporter, "secure for all time to the Navy Department the control of radio in the United States." The bill died, and with it the prospect that in America the state might monopolize the airways as governments did in Europe. The idea of a monopoly, however, lived. With encouragement from the Navy, the Radio Corporation of America (RCA) emerged in October 1919, out of resources provided by General Electric, American Marconi (whose assets had been expropriated during the war), AT&T, and United Fruit. Its first commercial manager was David Sarnoff; he would become president in

1930 at age thirty-eight. RCA controlled about two thousand crucial patents as well as important international communications facilities.

As early as 1916 Sarnoff articulated a vision of the new medium that transcended military uses and went beyond the experiments of the amateurs. He foresaw it as "a 'household utility' in the same sense as the piano or phonograph," bringing music into the home, along with lectures, news, and baseball scores. He concluded that sale of receivers and transmitters for such broadcasts would "yield a handsome profit." He was right, although several years and a world war ahead of the times.

In 1920, Westinghouse, a manufacturer of receivers, used a rooftop shack radio station in Pittsburgh with the call letters KDKA to transmit presidential-election returns. Although not the first broadcast, the event marked the beginnings of regular broadcasting and led to a small network of Westinghouse stations. It also brought an invitation to join RCA, which promoted broadcasting to sell transmitters and receivers made by its constituent companies. The problem was that, as a monopoly, RCA did not monopolize very effectively, thanks to amateurs and small-scale operators. In 1922 the corporation accounted for less than a fifth of the $60 million in sales of radio receivers. AT&T's Western Electric transmitters—to be used exclusively under the RCA agreement—served only about 6 percent of the first six hundred stations licensed by 1923. By 1924 groups that comprised RCA were feuding and facing a Federal Trade Commission investigation of their business practices.

Under internal and external pressure, the parties renegotiated their arrangements. Out of this came the National Broadcasting Company (NBC), in 1926. By the beginning of 1927 NBC had the first two national radio networks, called the red and the blue, in operation. Their parent corporation, the revamped RCA, announced that it took this step "in the interest of the listening public." Before it did so, however, other developments helped shape the industry. In 1923, broadcasters reached an agreement with the American Society of Composers, Authors, and Publishers (ASCAP) that resolved conflicts over use of copyrighted music on the air. In 1922, AT&T solved the problem of who would pay for broadcasts by inventing the commercial. Secretary of Commerce Herbert Hoover warned, "It is inconceivable that we should allow so great a possibility for service, for news, for entertainment, for education to be drowned in advertising chatter."

In 1927, Congress put in place much of the structure that governed broadcasting for decades. It passed the Radio Act, establishing a Federal Radio Commission (FRC) to bring greater regularity into the licens-ing process. The act also denied private ownership of the airwaves and granted broadcast licenses subject to periodic renewal and to "public interest, convenience or necessity." It further prohibited awarding licenses to persons or corporations engaging in unfair or monopolistic practices. In 1934, Congress, under Roosevelt administration prodding, supplanted the FRC with a Federal Communications Commission (FCC) and included transmission by telephone under its jurisdiction. Shortly after its creation, Sarnoff pressed for rulings favorable to a new medium RCA was testing: television.

By 1927, several things were clear about radio. The airwaves would be open for commercial development and would not remain a state monopoly. Large corporations would squeeze amateurs off to the margins of the spectrum without being fully able to achieve the kind of vertical monopoly RCA sought and that the MPPC had tried to achieve in film. These corporations could, however, create linkages between media. That mostly lay in the future in 1927, although the near future in the case of RCA, which within five years was involved in the movie and music industries while developing television, producing radio shows, and marketing radio receivers. Most apparent in 1927 was a public demand for radio—approximately 6 million sets were in use and over 500 stations in operation.

Also in 1927, a competitor confronted NBC. It was the ancestor of the Columbia Broadcasting System (CBS), put on sound footing in 1929 when a young tobacco entrepreneur named William Paley negotiated a financial arrangement with Paramount Pictures. Although CBS struggled to catch up with NBC in the 1930s, Paley proved innovative in business practices and programming, using, for example, unsold air time to expand the network's news operations. In 1943, RCA, under a government order to ensure greater competition, sold its NBC blue network, which became the American Broadcasting Company (ABC). There would be lesser networks, but these three would dominate the network era in radio and oversee the development of television.

While it flourished, network radio captivated the American public. By 1933 about half the nation's homes had receivers; two years later the figure was closer to 70 percent. A *Fortune* magazine survey in 1938 showed listening to radio as the favorite pastime of Americans, slightly ahead of film and well ahead of reading. The choices facing listeners were considerable—from sports to opera, there was something for everyone. Musical shows, whether classical, dance, or popular, did well. Until 1948, radio had the advantage over the phonograph of being able to play longer works without a break. Audiences thrilled to mysteries such as *The Shadow* and *The Whistler* and dramas like *The Lux Radio Theater.* The latter, begun in 1934, bridged media by having film director Cecil B. DeMille as host and Hollywood stars as guests in radio versions of popular movies. Radio even created forms that television copied—notably, the soap opera (including the long-running *Ma Perkins*) and game shows like Groucho Marx's *You Bet Your Life.*

Comedy did especially well on radio. It was necessarily very different from the highly visual slapstick of vaudeville and silent movies, even though ex-vaudevillians like Groucho Marx, Jack Benny, Edgar Bergen, George Burns and Gracie Allen, and Fred Allen made the transition. Many entered the medium in the early 1930s and stayed until ratings evaporated in the 1950s. (Some made the next transition, into television.) No single style prevailed. Radio humor encompassed the mordant, clever wit of Fred Allen, the twisted logic of Gracie Allen, the homey foibles of *Fibber McGee and Molly,* and the impeccable timing of Jack Benny, whose pauses were often funnier than other comedians' jokes.

Among the most popular and troubling radio comedies was *Amos 'n' Andy,* which by 1932 counted about a third of the nation's population as its audience. It began on NBC's blue network in 1929, moved to CBS in 1948, and featured two whites, Freeman Gosden and Charles Correll, playing a variety of African American characters in dialect. They sometimes enhanced the similarity to the old minstrel show tradition by appearing in publicity photographs in blackface. Although defenders (African Americans among them) pointed out that the characters were sympathetic, varied, and included professionals as well as no-goods, racial humor was less palatable in the 1950s than it had been in the 1930s. When the show moved to television in 1951, with black actors replacing Gosden and Correll, the National Association for the Advancement of Colored People protested and the show left the air permanently in 1953.

Some of radio's finest hours came when it brought Americans together, rather than separating them, by doing what no previous medium could: connecting them, in their homes, to history as it happened. Among politicians, Franklin Delano Roosevelt grasped clearly the potential in radio's combination of immediacy and intimacy. His fireside chats began with his presidency in 1933 and enabled him to reach a majority of American households with a directness and familiarity previously unavailable to a national public figure. Roosevelt's talks, however, were political speeches in new clothing.

Radio also carried news. Movies, of course, similarly brought current events to Americans, beginning with footage of the Spanish-American War, and continuing through newsreels (sometimes shown in separate theaters) in the 1930s and 1940s. No matter how powerful the visual effect of movie news might be, it was already days or weeks old. Newspapers were on the stands earlier—and radio could broadcast on the spot. By World War II, the medium had developed able reporters and commentators, as well as a track record of covering dramatic stories as they unfolded, from the sinking of the *Titanic* to the explosion and crash of the German airship *Hindenburg* on its arrival in the United States in 1937. The following year, CBS instituted a world news format, with short-wave reports from around the globe. Soon after, radio brought American listeners live reports from distant battlefields across the Atlantic and Pacific, like Edward R. Murrow's dramatic broadcasts from London under siege by German bombers in 1940. After U.S. entry into the war, American troops, in turn, listened to programming from home, courtesy of the Armed Forces Radio Service, created in 1942. For the first time the world was interconnected electronically. Murrow was among those who envisioned a glorious future for the medium. "We've seen what radio can do for the nation in war," he exclaimed in 1945, "Now let's go back to show what we can do in peace!"

The record of the networks belied Murrow's optimism. Radio's achievements were genuine, but they came at the expense of other possibilities. The economic power, political clout, and control over patents of a giant like RCA pushed amateurs and inventors, important in early radio, to the sidelines. Public and special interest programming also suffered from network power. In the 1920s, it was possible to imagine a much less commercial, more educational and political, medium. In 1926 in Chicago, WCFL became "the first labor station in the country." As late as 1933, Congress seriously considered proposals from religious, educational, and labor groups to reserve a quarter of all station licenses for nonprofit broadcasting. The result might well have been a different medium. Concern about regulation by the FCC spurred the networks to increase the amount of informational programming, but it often lacked courage and always comprised a small fraction of all network productions: 6 percent in the winter of 1938–1939, according to one estimate, and only 18 percent even in the war years 1943–1944. For the networks, economic strategy was primary, in spite of the sense of mission Murrow and others brought to their work. Corporate leaders cared more for profits than for public service or for the medium itself.

The networks came out of the Depression with rising income, and profitability continued for a few years after World War II, thanks to suburban lifestyles and a baby boom that placed a premium on inexpensive home entertainment. In 1929, the combined revenue for CBS and NBC was $19 million. In 1940, the figure was $91.6 million. After World War II, however, the networks saw a better future, and it was television. The CBS annual report for 1948 commented on "the strength and stability of the AM structure, which enabled [the network] to support the necessary TV programming experimentation and development." What this meant in practical terms was apparent to a number of former CBS employees: cutbacks had begun in radio operations, although revenues were increasing, in order to subsidize television.

The networks starved radio to feed the infant medium, but there is no evidence they foisted it on an unwilling public. Given the choice, audiences preferred the flickering screen. The fate of Bob Hope's radio show tells the story: between 1949 and 1951 the ratings almost halved; in 1953 they more than halved again. The next year Hope's TV show placed in the top ten. The amount of time Americans spent listening to radio remained relatively stable from 1931 to 1950 at roughly four hours per day per household. In the latter year, television viewing per household slightly surpassed it. Five years later, the hours of television viewing rose slightly while those spent listening to the radio fell by almost half.

Figures that measure household listenership, nonetheless, obscure how radio survived, which was by targeting special markets rather than the whole family. Technology helped in this specialization. After World War II, transistors replaced the bulky glass tubes on which radio had depended since De Forest's day. Smaller, more effective, and cheaper, they resulted in tiny, battery-powered radios that could be carried anywhere. The first Japanese transistor radio marketed in the United States, a Sony, appeared in 1957. By 1959, 6 million of them, or half Japan's radio production, entered the country, mostly in the form of miniature, shirt-pocket models. Inexpensive and portable, they took radio listening out of the home and America out of the business of making portable radios.

Lower price and greater mobility meant that radio need not be a family activity as it was in the 1930s. Different people could listen in different places: in the kitchen, at the beach, in the car, or in a teenager's room. As networks lost their mass radio audience, the transistor opened possibilities for reaching diverse audiences, among them adolescents, whose enthusiasm for rock 'n' roll fueled an increase in record album sales of over 250 percent between 1955 and 1959 and created a market for Top-40 format radio stations. Other specialty formats soon appeared: country and western, easy listening, classical, sports, hard rock, alternative music, and talk radio among them. The time when a show like *Amos 'n' Andy* could hold a sizeable portion of the American public entranced was gone.

The new radio market became segmented, and, at the local level, it was profitable. By 1956, advertising expenditures for network shows dropped to less than a third of what they had been in 1946, from $200 million to $60 million. In the same period, advertising revenues for local programming more than doubled, from $157 million to $346 million. By 1990, they would reach $6.615 billion, compared to $495 million for the remaining network productions. In virtually the same period—from 1946 to 1991—the total number of radio stations increased more than tenfold, from 1,005 to 10,830.

In reaching a new, fragmented radio audience, the transistor and diverse programming provided a piece of the solution. FM broadcasting provided another. When it finally reached the market in significant fashion in the 1960s, the impact was considerable. By 1966 there were 1,714 FM stations where there had been 57 in 1946. By the 1980s, FM stations surpassed AM in number. To some extent this represented an increase in educational, nonprofit radio (about a quarter of FM stations fall into that category). But it also reflected the superior sound quality of FM, its pioneering use of stereo broadcasting, and the strategy of focusing programming on special groups. FM, especially stereo, was perfect for people who cared about their music, whether it was album-oriented rock (a form that emerged in the 1960s), country, or classical.

In surviving the end of the network era, radio appears an exception to the rule of increasing concentration of control that applies to other media. The exception is only partial. Radio stations link to one another and to other media, especially television, through interlocking ownership. Moreover, although the old networks are shells, advertising revenues for network programs shot up from $105 million in 1976 to $423 million in 1986, still a fraction of the money going to spot and local advertising on radio, but a formidable increase nonetheless. In addition, by the 1980s, there was a reinvention of network radio by other means. Standardization, for instance, reappeared with consultants who advised stations on formats and on music playlists. Beginning in the 1960s, they made local radio sound a great deal less local. Easy listening in Omaha became interchangeable with easy listening in Oakland. AM radio, unable to compete with FM in music programming, relearned how to talk and fostered yet another kind of national radio, this time through syndicated shows rather than networks. By the late 1980s the AM airwaves were filled with national interview and call-in programs dealing with everything from finances, to politics, to sports, to sex and health. Men and women scattered throughout the country cast their questions, anger, opinions, hopes, and frustrations into the ether in an electronic network of individuals.

By the 1990s, the number of radio stations remained relatively constant since a jump in the mid-1970s. The number of hours spent listening to the radio increased by 50 percent between 1960 and 1990. Radio had reached a plateau, thanks to identifying many audiences rather than seeking one, to its portability, and to recognizing that interaction, not passivity, is deeply embedded in popular culture. Whether or not television, the medium it helped raise, faced as comfortable a future was less clear.

Television existed in the imagination long before it entered American homes. No sooner had Alexander Graham Bell demonstrated the telephone in 1876 than writers and artists began to depict the transmission of images by wire. The word *television* appeared in a 1907 *Scientific American* article. The 1927 Radio Act encompassed it by covering "any intelligence, message, signal, power, picture or communication of any nature transferred by electrical energy." The year of its passage, Secretary of Commerce Herbert Hoover stepped before the camera in an experimental telecast.

The history of television marks clear differences between its development and film and radio. It was a technology called into being by large-scale corporations, rather than a medium that came to concentrate in them. Moreover, it was born with popular culture in mind, in contrast to film and radio, which existed before entrepreneurs learned to exploit their commercial possibilities. Early enthusiasts, like David Sarnoff, never doubted that television could make money by amusing Americans. The real questions were "Who would make the money?" "When?" and "How?"

Because television, like radio, required use of the airwaves and thus fell under federal regulation, the answers were political and legal, as well as economic and technological. In 1930 the Justice Department began proceedings that, in 1932, forced GE, Westinghouse, and AT&T to end many of the interlocking relationships that had produced RCA. The principals in the case dodged litigation and in 1933 RCA emerged with a seemingly bright future. Ensconced in properly imperial new headquarters in New York's Radio City, it became an independent corporation with NBC as its subsidiary while remaining the dominant force in broadcasting and aggressively committed

to developing the new medium, for which it held many patents. David Sarnoff announced in 1935 that RCA would commit a million dollars to television research. Although experimental telecasts of various sorts took place throughout the 1930s, NBC's grand public event came with the New York World's Fair of 1939, which President Franklin Roosevelt formally opened in an April telecast (he was preceded by a trial run of *Amos 'n' Andy* in blackface). Fairgoers stared at a limited schedule of programming—which, within a month, included the first televised baseball game—and at RCA television sets, ready for market. CBS and DuMont Laboratories began experimental transmissions shortly afterward. The medium was on its way, with RCA far in the lead.

War and the FCC intervened. In 1940 the latter downgraded the status of television broadcasting from "limited" to "experimental," only to shift direction the next year by approving commercial broadcasting while cutting the hours of operation from fifteen to four. Such changes, along with other difficulties, drove all but six of twenty-three stations off the air. In the meantime, radio (especially CBS's news operation) flourished through its reporting of World War II; military mobilization fostered significant developments in communications; and the FCC created a third network (ABC) by forcing NBC to sell one of its two.

An end to hostilities abroad reopened them at home over television. In 1945, the FCC issued licenses once again and reallocated the broadcast spectrum in a way that handicapped FM radio while encouraging television. It was a victory for RCA. Another came in 1947 when the FCC deferred ruling on standards for color television. That was a costly defeat for CBS, possessor of an experimental color system superior to RCA's, but incompatible with existing noncolor broadcast standards. Eight months later, the FCC chair resigned to assume a vice presidential post at NBC.

Even when the commission attempted to encourage competition, it usually ended up aiding NBC and CBS, as when it suspended issuing new licenses for television stations between 1948 and 1952 and sought to promote ultra high frequency (UHF) broadcasting to increase the number of channels available. The result was not to help the struggling smaller networks, ABC and DuMont, but to push them to a part of the spectrum many viewers could not receive and few advertisers found attractive.

While lawyers, inventors, and the FCC defined the economic and technological structure of television, Americans bought sets. The proportion of homes owning television receivers rose from 0.4 percent in 1948 to 23.5 percent in 1951. The figure grew to about 34 percent the next year, when AT&T finished laying the coaxial cable upon which network telecasting depended. By 1956, televisions were in nearly 65 percent of American homes. At the end of the decade, 90 percent had them. Within a few years, the problem facing the networks was not one of creating a mass audience but of finding the programming to keep it.

Many of the first television shows borrowed their stars and format from radio. Some established performers, like Jack Benny, made the move easily and successfully. His comedy show lasted fourteen years on television. Groucho Marx did almost as well, with an eleven-year run of the video version of his radio quiz show, *You Bet Your Life*. Other performers, notably Fred Allen and Amos 'n' Andy, found the new medium uncongenial. Some careers took off spectacularly. David Garroway moved through radio to a local Chicago television show before finding network stardom on NBC's *Today* show. Similarly, the enormous success of *I Love Lucy* dwarfed Lucille Ball's earlier work in film and radio.

Probably no performer benefited more from the new medium than Milton Berle. A comedian best known for theft of other performers' material, he struck gold with his *Texaco Star Theater*. Unhindered by good taste, Berle for a time lived up to his nickname, "Mr. Television." Although his popularity rested on the visual nature of the medium (dressing in drag was not effective on radio), his program points to the derivative nature of early television. The format was the familiar variety show, a combination of radio with pictures and vaudeville revived. The form was flexible and durable—Ed Sullivan's show began in 1948, the same year as Berle's, and lasted until 1971—but it was also unoriginal and seldom used the medium's visual potential creatively.

As American television developed its own style in the 1950s, the structure of the industry evolved rapidly. One shift was geographic: at the beginning of the decade virtually all prime-time television came from New York and was broadcast live. By 1960, most programming came from Hollywood and on film. Among the casualties were live television drama anthology series, of which there were fourteen in the 1955–1956 season. In the minds of many critics, they brought some of the best talent and brightest moments to home viewers. Only one survived in 1960. Other changes were equally significant for the industry. FCC decisions provided room for two strong networks, NBC and CBS, and a weaker one. ABC bested DuMont for the third position and the latter ceased operations in 1955. Between then and the emergence of Fox Broad-

casting in 1986, and the rise of cable in the same decade, network television was a three-player game, with CBS leading in viewership for nearly a quarter-century beginning in 1953.

ABC struggled many years to match its rivals in affiliated stations and in talent; but one of its successes in 1954 pointed toward new possibilities. In that year ABC joined forces with Walt Disney to produce a television series. The marriage was one of convenience—Disney was eager for publicity and capital for his risky new venture, the Disneyland amusement park. The step, nonetheless, signaled a wary entente between television and Hollywood at a time when nothing seemed to lure audiences back to movie theaters. The studios' longstanding interest in television had been frustrated by 1950 by the Supreme Court and the FCC, which blocked their efforts to purchase station licenses. Disney's move, however, suggested a different kind of collaboration in which Hollywood productions, old and new, might appear on television. Peace between media could be more profitable than war. A year later, in 1955, RKO ceased film production and became the first studio to sell its movie library for television syndication. Warner Brothers followed in 1956 and Paramount held out until 1958. Columbia and MGM preferred to lease. By 1957, 71 percent of the shows on television were made in Hollywood (as opposed to 40 percent the year before), whether in the form of old movies or new series made for television, whether made by the studios or by independent producers drawing on movie-colony resources. In 1964, NBC took the next step by commissioning Universal to produce three made-for-television movies. The first, too violent to be shown on television, starred Ronald Reagan as a heavy.

The shift from live to film, and New York to Hollywood, did nothing to weaken the networks' power. If anything, they gained a greater measure of control over two important groups: the advertisers who paid their bills and independent producers. In the early years of the medium, as in radio, sponsors approached the networks with shows they wished to put on the air. By the late 1950s, the high cost of commercial time on network television made it virtually impossible for a single advertiser to afford a whole show. While that diminished the power of individual sponsors to influence programming, a series of media scandals in 1958 and 1959 helped strengthen the networks' hands against independent producers. Congressional investigations produced unsavory stories of rigged television quiz shows and payola to radio disk jockeys to promote certain records. The networks' response was the familiar promise to regulate themselves. Whether or not the quality of programming improved is open to question. Network interest in achieving greater control over what went on the air, however, increased. Most of the fixed quiz shows came from independent producers who dealt primarily with sponsors or their advertising agencies. By the middle of the 1960s, they remained a vital source of television shows—responsible for about 71 percent of the offerings—but they generally worked with network programmers and a network financial contribution. While the networks abdicated some creative responsibility to Hollywood by showing more movies in the 1960s, they were highly involved in the television series that remained.

The rapid development of television between 1952 and the mid-1960s left the medium in much the form it had for two decades. The broadcast day divided into the morning, with shows like NBC's *Today,* which long outlived David Garroway and his chimpanzee costar, J. Fred Muggs; daytime, where soap operas ruled; the news hour; prime time, with the largest audiences and fiercest competition; and late night, where a succession of hosts from Steve Allen and Jack Paar through Johnny Carson dominated. The week was also segmented, with the daylight hours of Saturday and Sunday reserved for children's cartoons, sports, and religious and public affairs programming. Dramatic events like the assassination of John F. Kennedy upset the routine, but the structure was relatively stable.

Within that structure, programs changed rapidly, but fell into fairly standard categories, most with antecedents in radio. The situation comedy, or sitcom, was an early and enduring staple. Doctors had recurring vogues, beginning in the early 1960s with ABC's *Ben Casey* (1961–1966) and NBC's *Dr. Kildare,* as did lawyers, with *Perry Mason* (1957–1966) as founding father. Police officers and detectives were hardy perennials: *Dragnet* carried over from radio and, beginning in 1959, *The Untouchables* brought a rare ratings success to ABC and a new level of violence to the home screen. Westerns also had their day, mostly in the late 1950s and early 1960s, when *Cheyenne, Wagon Train, Have Gun Will Travel, Gunsmoke, Rifleman, Wyatt Earp, Frontier Justice,* and *Maverick* dominated the ratings. Sports, televised virtually from the beginning, reached a milestone in 1968, when ABC instituted comprehensive coverage of the Olympics and in 1970, when the same network moved into prime time with *Monday Night Football.*

There were good reasons for producing shows that fit formulae: they were easy to put together and they made money. The networks, after all, were not selling programs, even their own. They were selling audiences to advertisers. Caution paid because what counted in the marketplace was the size and type of audience for particular shows. The measures of success were ratings, first developed for radio and increasingly refined to enable networks and sponsors to know precisely who watched, for how long, and what products they were likely to buy. A rare show could survive low ratings and the product on the screen mattered less than attracting advertising dollars.

In spite of its commercial, generally conservative nature, network television had moments of creativity. In later decades, critics and fans looked back nostalgically on the 1950s "golden age" live dramas and the comedy of Jackie Gleason's *Honeymooners* or *I Love Lucy.* More innovative were the shows of Sid Caesar and Ernie Kovacs, who explored the visual possibilities of television comedy. Although the medium shied away from controversial issues, it occasionally had an edge. Between 1967 and 1969, Tom and Dick Smothers hosted a variety show that included anti–Vietnam War political satire and other controversial subjects, to the dismay of CBS executives. Beginning in 1971, *All in the Family,* the first of several topically-oriented situation comedies produced by Norman Lear, dealt with difficult subjects like bigotry, rape, abortion, and impotence. For seven years, beginning in 1970, *The Mary Tyler Moore Show* featured a single woman with a career who was interested in sex and not necessarily in marriage. In 1977 the ABC miniseries *Roots* attracted an extraordinary audience with a saga of an African American family. By the 1980s and 1990s the newly formed Fox network pushed the limits of acceptability and a number of well-established Hollywood directors took television seriously enough to try their hands at it. They included Steven Spielberg and David Lynch, as well as Academy Award winners Barry Levinson and Oliver Stone. A list of programs in which the medium showed originality, integrity, and courage, nonetheless, would be vastly shorter than a list of programs lacking any of those characteristics.

If entertainment was network television's reason for being, news was its claim to credibility. In some respects, the distinction between entertainment and news was always a fine one. For decades, local television reporters cheerfully alternated between happy talk and tragic stories of violence. A network news anchor of the 1950s, John Cameron Swayze, served as pitchman for watches and appeared on game shows. Barbara Walters, who in 1976 became the first woman anchor of a regular network newscast, achieved greater success in the 1980s through interviews with a mix of world leaders and celebrities. By 1990, the three network newscasts averaged sixty minutes a month covering entertainment-world stories, up 50 percent from two years earlier.

In an important respect, however, the entertainment and the news-and-information aspects of television diverged. After the 1950s, the most popular shows—even those with live audiences—were on film and videotape; some even began to explore the visual possibilities of those media. Television news and information shows also relied on film and videotape; but especially after the launch of the Telstar I communications satellite in 1962 they took advantage of the immediacy of live television by bringing events around the world into the home as they happened. The power of pictures enabled television to assert, as radio could not, that it showed the unvarnished truth. The fact that the claim was untenable did nothing to diminish its force.

The two major networks entered the television news business from the beginning of commercial broadcasting with fifteen-minute evening shows, sometimes without film of the events being reported, sometimes drawing on outside vendors for footage. By the early 1950s, the networks had their own film crews and featured reports from remote correspondents, a technique used earlier in radio. In 1963, NBC, then CBS, went to a half-hour news format, to the dismay of one broadcaster, who complained that "We lose audiences every time we have to put that stuff in place of entertainment." Except for more sophisticated communications techniques, and better satellite linkages, there would be few innovations in news coverage until Ted Turner's around-the-clock Cable News Network (CNN) in 1980.

In addition to regular newscasts, television conveyed information about current affairs in two other important forms: through news specials and documentaries on the one hand, and coverage of live events on the other. Edward R. Murrow, and his colleague Fred W. Friendly, set a high standard for documentary reporting when they moved from radio to television with *See It Now.* The series began in 1951 and hit its stride in 1953 with the first of several shows dealing with McCarthyism. They placed *See It Now* at the center of controversy and Murrow and Friendly at the head of a small group of broadcasters exploring the documentary possibilities of the medium. Improvements in videocamera technology enabled even more imaginative reporting by the time Murrow left the air to head the United States Information Agency in 1961. In the 1960–1961 season both NBC's and CBS's news divisions produced a number of impressive programs treating such topics as rural poverty, westward expansion (including material from Native Ameri-

cans), racism, illegal gambling, American foreign policy, and Portuguese imperialism in Angola.

Documentaries and news specials rarely received such prominence in later years, although they never disappeared from programming and even became a regular feature, thanks to news magazines like the long-lived *Sixty Minutes* and to ABC's *Nightline.* At their best, such shows took stands and explored issues at length, rather than in sixty-second reports. At their worst, they degenerated into voyeurism and focused (as did the evening news) on individuals rather than abstract social, political, and economic forces.

Some of the networks' most powerful hours came when they showed history as it happened. CBS, NBC, and ABC covered live events as early as the HUAC hearings on alleged subversive activity in Hollywood in 1947, a time when there were few television sets. The 1950s and 1960s provided dramatic moments, captured by television cameras with unmatched intensity and immediacy: the civil rights movement, the 1959 kitchen debate in Moscow between Soviet premier Nikita Khrushchev and Vice President Richard Nixon, the Cuban Missile Crisis of 1961, the death of John F. Kennedy in 1963 (including the killing of his assassin, Lee Harvey Oswald, carried live on NBC), the student movement of the 1960s, urban rioting between 1965 and 1968, and, above all, the Vietnam War. Satellite transmission opened the whole world to instantaneous coverage. The 1991 Persian Gulf War both highlighted television's potential and raised serious concerns about it. Live reports came to American households from an Iraqi capital under attack by American airplanes and missiles while an American advertising agency fabricated "news" reports for Kuwaiti clients, reporters complained of censorship, military officials grumbled about press interference, and the Secretary of Defense acknowledged that some of his information came from watching CNN. The line between shaping and reporting events, like that between news and entertainment, was sometimes indistinct.

Political figures found television's capabilities a mixed blessing. A few counted themselves as casualties of the medium. Senate hearings in 1954, carried in their entirety by ABC to make up for its lack of daytime programming, helped discredit Senator Joseph McCarthy's hunt for communist subversion. At times Richard Nixon and Lyndon Johnson also claimed to have been hurt by television. But many politicians—including Nixon and Johnson—also used it for their own ends. An unlikely pioneer was Dwight Eisenhower's austere secretary of state, John Foster Dulles, who, in 1954, hired a media consultant and managed television appearances and reporters with considerable skill. Eisenhower's successor, the photogenic John F. Kennedy, initiated live press conferences, at which he excelled, and found the television camera to be a political ally. As early as 1948, both major parties selected the site for their nominating conventions, Philadelphia, because it had the best access to network television connections.

From that moment on, few people in public life doubted that television was a force with which to reckon. Scholars, politicians, and media critics from all points along the political spectrum credit or blame it for such things as the 1960 defeat of Richard Nixon, the 1968 triumph of Richard Nixon, the 1973 resignation of Richard Nixon, Lyndon Johnson's decision not to seek a second term, the civil rights movement's successes, the New Left's failures, misinforming Americans about Vietnam, making Americans aware of the depth of involvement in Vietnam, the defeat of Gerald Ford in 1976, and the entire presidency of Ronald Reagan.

Whether or not the medium had the power friends and foes attribute to it is another matter. Television is far from the only source of information available to Americans and its reporting is frequently ambiguous (or balanced, bland, or superficial, depending on one's perspective). A number of studies show that it had less impact than imagined in some cases. Even so, television—in both its news and entertainment programming—seemed important enough to provoke periodic attempts to control or reshape the medium. Congress mounted two notable investigations before commercial broadcasting passed its twentieth birthday. The first came in 1959, with the exposure of fixed game shows. The second, presided over by Senator Thomas J. Dodd of Connecticut, started as an investigation into juvenile delinquency, but by mid-1961 turned to violence on television. It was the beginning of a long tradition of hand-wringing over the presumed harmful effects of televised sex and mayhem on young viewers. The Dodd investigations sputtered, in part because of the senator's cozy relationship with media executives, and led to minor changes in programming and major promises of self-regulation. Rumblings from Congress and the FCC in 1974 produced similar results, notably adoption by the National Association of Broadcasters of a CBS-proposed viewing policy that designated the two hours before children's bedtime as "family time," free of most sex and violence. In 1976 a federal judge ruled against family time as a violation of the First Amendment. When his decision was overturned three years later, neither the networks nor the FCC had any inclination to reinstate

family time. The executive who suggested the idea had been fired. Hearings and legislation aimed at curbing television's excesses continued to appear with little impact, including proposals in the 1990s to require a computer chip enabling parents to block reception of offensive shows.

In the early 1960s, one of the most cogent critics of television promised to arouse the FCC from its normal proindustry lethargy and reconstruct the medium. He was Newton Minnow, John F. Kennedy's choice to head the commission in 1961. His first speech before broadcasters included the phrase for which he became famous. Television, he declared, was a "vast wasteland." In an obvious threat, he reminded his audience that "There is nothing permanent or sacred about a broadcast license." Minnow's proposals included loosening network control over their affiliates' programming and promoting the growth of noncommercial television stations, whose numbers reached one hundred in 1965. With support for public television from the Carnegie and Ford Foundations, President Johnson in 1967 encouraged Congress to create the Corporation for Public Broadcasting, parent of the Public Broadcasting System (PBS). Its accomplishments—such as the landmark children's show, *Sesame Street*—were real, as was its dependence on British-made series and its starvation diet of federal appropriations, grants, and viewer donations. By then, however, Minnow was long gone, having left the FCC in 1963. In February of that year, the two most highly rated television shows were *Beverly Hillbillies* and the *Andy Griffith Show*. The industry survived a visionary.

At the height of their power, however, the networks, like the movie studios before them, found themselves beleaguered. The real enemy was not Newton Minnow. It was television itself, in the form of Community Antenna Television (CATV), commonly known as cable.

The first cable systems were designed to provide clear signals to subscribers in remote areas. By 1970 there were 2,500 of them, enough to cause anxiety within the networks. Although restricted by the FCC, cable systems began to produce programming of their own and thereby opened an opportunity for other media corporations to enter broadcasting. Among the first was Time Inc., the publishing giant, which began Home Box Office (HBO) in 1972, a cable operation it expanded in 1975 by leasing a communication satellite for nationwide distribution of its offerings. A 1977 court decision compelled the FCC to end many restrictions on cable television. There followed a scramble to create cable services to reach specialized audiences. Some of these, such as the Playboy Channel, showed programs unacceptable on network television; others offered classic films and educational programming or sports; at least one, Music Television (MTV), mixed media and introduced visual techniques that influenced mainstream television and movies.

Between 1980 and 1990, the number of American households with cable service rose from under 20 to 53 million, or about 60 percent of the total number of homes. During the same decade, the three major networks' share of the prime-time viewing audience fell from about 85 percent to under 65 percent. Three years later, cable was so well entrenched that the networks had come to terms with it and CBS became the last to drop demands that cable companies make major payments to carry its shows.

A striking effect of cable television was to give the audience a greater role in the process of being entertained. In addition to offering more channels, cable increased viewer participation through public-access channels open to local groups, through the call-in format that helped AM radio find its niche after the 1960s, and through marketing techniques such as home shopping. Cable also became a medium for interactive video through which viewers could seek information, play games, and even become part of a program. In pointing toward increased audience involvement in shaping entertainment, cable was joined by other technologies in the 1970s and 1980s. Development of remote control made channel changing easy, to the chagrin of advertisers. The video cassette recorder (VCR), first introduced in 1976, had greater impact because it permitted recording and editing and made it possible to rent or buy thousands of movies for viewing on demand. Thanks to uncertainties over which format would prevail and over copyright restrictions on video recordings, the VCR was slow to find its market. In 1981 only 3 percent of U.S. homes had one, but nine years later slightly over 70 percent had one or more.

If anything, the realm of choice in home video is likely to grow. In 1993, Tele-Communications, Inc., the cable-industry leader, embarked on a project estimated to cost $1.9 billion to replace its existing copper wire network with a fiber optic system that by 1994 would bring over 500 channels to subscribers, including interactive educational ones and data services, for only a "modest" increase in cost to subscribers. Also in 1993, a court, addressing an issue as old as radio, ruled that telephone companies could carry video signals on their lines. Whether the decision stands on appeal, and whatever its impact might be on cable companies, it was one indication among many that the diversity of entertainment and information available to Americans in their homes will expand and continue in the direction of greater interaction between audiences and media. By the 1990s, the major television networks, so successful in building upon an older technology, radio, were squeezed on one side by rising costs for such programming staples as professional sports, and on the other by newer video technologies offering viewers greater freedom in making their own popular culture.

The revolution begun in the late nineteenth century, when the phonograph and player piano brought mechanically reproduced entertainment into the home, resulted in the creation of huge industries, dominated by a small number of corporations, often with interests in several media and—political climate permitting—in several stages of the production and distribution of entertainment. Another result was a linking of forms of entertainment, with music, radio, sports, movies, and television interpenetrating in complicated and shifting ways. At least two other developments were ironic: having moved entertainment into the home, the electronic revolution moved it out again by making radio and television portable; and having linked the world through radio, television, and satellite communications, the media fragmented it into ever smaller, more individual communities of taste, each serviced by some portion of the market.

The existence of choice, nonetheless, was small comfort to critics who feared what audiences might be learning from popular culture, especially television. Certainly, consumption was among the lessons taught. A Federal Trade Commission report in 1979 estimated that "The average child sees 20,000 commercials a year, or about 3 hours of TV advertising a week." Even more chilling was the prospect that an active audience could be a violent and amoral one. Newton Minnow commemorated the thirtieth anniversary of his "vast wasteland" speech by noting a recent study claiming that children reaching age eighteen would see over 25,000 murders depicted on television. "In 1961, I worried that my children would not benefit much from television," he added, "today I worry that my grandchildren will actually be harmed by it."

A revolution had occurred—visual, intense, and sweeping. It was not clear who lost.

## THE PERSISTENCE OF PRINT

Marshall McLuhan, sometime literary scholar and 1960s media guru, once heralded the dawn of "an age for which the meaning of print culture is becoming as alien as the meaning of manuscript culture was to the eighteenth century." The obituary was premature. The written word persisted as a vehicle of popular culture throughout the twentieth century, both in mass media that carried over from the nineteenth century—newspapers, magazines, and books—and in new forms, notably the comic book. It is, nonetheless, tempting to imagine (as McLuhan did) a zero-sum game in which the published word declines as electronic media rise. It is equally easy, at least for cultural critics of twentieth-century life, to imagine a degradation of intelligence as reading gives way to the thirty-second sound bite. Reality was more complex, ambiguous, and interesting. What and how Americans read certainly changed over the twentieth century, as did the industries that produced the printed word. But parallels and convergences with the histories of electronic media are as significant as the differences McLuhan conjured between the world of print and the world of television.

Although critics bemoaned literal and cultural illiteracy, Americans read in impressive quantity throughout the twentieth century. The number of periodicals in the United States doubled between 1936 and 1990. The number of new books published annually rose from 4,490 in 1900 to nearly 31,000 in 1990 (roughly triple the figure for 1956). While comic books may not be the best marker of literacy, their sales also continued to increase throughout the 1980s. Only in the case of newspapers do the numbers show decline. Between 1900 and 1990 the number of daily newspapers fell from 2,154 to 1,611. Weekly papers dropped by 50 percent in the same period. By 1990 only 2.3 percent of American cities had two or more daily newspapers under separate ownership, down from almost 39 percent in 1923. A 1982 survey revealed that the United States had about half the number of newspapers sold per thousand households as Sweden and fewer than Hong Kong. If there was a war between the printed word and the electronic media, newspapers were the chief casualties.

In 1900, magazines could lay claim to having been America's first national mass-circulation print medium. Just prior to the Civil War *Harper's Monthly* had a circulation of approximately 200,000, which, according to an historian of American journalism, placed "it far ahead of any other monthly magazine in the world." At the turn of the century, readers of periodicals had a considerable range from which to select: there were those featuring political exposés, fashion, gossip, poetry and literature; or, for less elevated tastes, sensational and mildly risqué ones. The range broadened in the twentieth century. In 1923,

a giant of American journalism, Henry Luce, created *Time,* the first news magazine. Its function, according to Luce's biographer, was to serve "people willing to spend a half-hour to avoid being entirely uninformed." Over the decades *Time* faced competition, notably *Newsweek* and *U.S. News & World Report,* while being joined in the Luce empire by magazines aimed at different, sometimes overlapping, audiences: *Fortune* (begun in 1930, just after the stock market crash), *Life* (purchased and revamped by Luce in 1936 and selling a million copies per week a year later), *Money, Sports Illustrated,* and *People.* For those whose tastes ran in other directions, the off-color periodical rose to semirespectability with *Playboy* in 1953 and a host of followers, some of which went on to challenge obscenity law.

For magazine, newspaper, and book publishers, however, success in the twentieth century required adaptations in style, content, and economic organization to a market for information and entertainment increasingly shaped by radio, film, and television. Some of the adjustment was to a progressively more visual culture, a process begun before movies appeared and for which, ironically, print media such as sheet music, newspapers, and periodicals prepared the way. A number of nineteenth-century American magazines were lavishly illustrated and attempts to create a visually oriented newspaper went back at least as early as the New York *Daily Graphic,* begun in 1873. With the development of half-tone printing in the 1890s, and the ability to reproduce photographs after the turn of the century, American journalism traded in images well before newsreels and television brought the world into the nation's theaters and, eventually, living rooms.

Two magazines were particular successful in telling stories briefly and with images: *Reader's Digest* and *Life. Reader's Digest,* founded in 1922, provided quick and easy summaries of articles, just as radio and newsreels would soon do for the news. In the same decade important magazines like *Century* magazine and *Harper's* began to drop illustrations, but in the 1930s Henry Luce's *Life* took on the movies by featuring compelling photographs and waging a war of images that it would lose in 1972 to television and to altered reading habits. Newspapers tried mixing photo and print journalism, and experimenting with visually attractive formats, a tactic that reached a peak in 1982, when the Gannett chain began the nationally distributed *USA Today.* By 1990, only the *Wall Street Journal* surpassed it in circulation. With stories seldom exceeding six hundred words, lavish use of color, charts, graphs, and other visual aids,

*USA Today* attracted readers fluent in the visual language of film and television.

Perhaps the ultimate adaptation of print to images was the comic book. Although experimentation with similar publications went back two decades earlier, the comic book emerged as a distinct form in 1934 in *Famous Funnies,* which, for 10 cents offered Depression-era readers the further adventures of newspaper comic strip characters. By 1938, over 2,500,000 comic books a month were being sold and they had begun to develop their own casts of characters. Cowboys, caped crusaders, men of steel, assorted superheroes, and the occasional educational comic book fought for the dimes of Americans. (In 1942 one enterprising publisher began a successful seven-issue series entitled *Picture Stories from the Bible,* the first cover of which featured a fist fight in front of a pyramid.) More than any other print medium, the comic book grasped the visual essence of the new world of popular culture.

Print media adapted to film, radio, and television in content as well as in form. The press quickly learned that movie stars sold papers, especially during a series of unseemly scandals in the 1920s. As early as 1911, however, journals such as *Motion Picture World* and *Moving Picture Story* magazine catered to fans with information about films and stars and with popular scenarios reworked into short stories. By 1922, over a dozen magazines like *Photoplay* conveyed movie-industry gossip to hundreds of thousands of fans, an increasing proportion of them young women. After the advent of television, the relationships between media became ever more tangled. Radio, movie, and TV stars became comic-book characters. Comic-book characters became movie and television heroes. Novels became films and films became novels. Television shows arose with no other purpose than to talk about television shows, movies, and popular music. Autobiographies of stars made the best-seller lists. Books by and about stars became movies or television miniseries. Print journalists appeared on television. Television and movies were a standard subject of print journalism. Appropriately enough, one of the magazine success stories of the 1960s was *TV Guide.* The result was an interlocked set of images and cultural references—not a true mass culture because it contained considerable room for diversity, but a widely shared one nonetheless, and one that bridged the divide McLuhan imagined between the culture of print and the culture of images.

In economic structure, twentieth-century print media followed much the same course as the film, radio, and television industries—increasing concentration in large corporations, although with space for smaller operators and innovators. At first glance, book publishing appears to defy the pattern. By the 1990s, the authoritative guide *Books in Print* listed over 25,000 publishers. A fairer estimate of presses issuing at least a book a year reduces the figure to roughly 2,500, still a considerable number. Of those publishing houses, however, six accounted for over half the gross revenues. In retailing, a similar movement toward concentration emerged by the end of the century, with large bookstore chains emerging in the 1970s and 1980s and joining organizations such as Book-of-the-Month Club (1926) and Literary Guild (1927) in the national mass marketing of popular books. At the same time, a small number of authors dominated sales: Tom Clancy, Stephen King, and Danielle Steel accounted for fifteen of the top twenty-five best-sellers of the 1980s.

Concentration appeared in other print media as well. One analyst, Ben H. Bagdikian, noted that during the 1980s the field of magazine publishing was reduced from twenty to three predominant corporations—Time Warner, News Corp. Ltd., and Hearst. Over the same period, he found a comparable decline in the number of corporations controlling major American newspapers from twenty to fourteen, continuing a tendency toward chain ownership begun decades earlier. In 1900, such chains accounted for approximately 10 percent of newspaper circulation; by 1990, they accounted for 82 percent.

The extent and consequences of such consolidation, however, are not clear-cut. In comparison with other nations, for instance, the United States' concentration of newspaper publishing in fourteen companies scarcely looks like a monopoly. Small book publishers continued to make money in a market dominated by half a dozen large houses. Even in book retailing the figures were ambiguous. From 1972 to 1982, a period in which chains made major gains, the number of book stores almost doubled. The larger chains accounted for a lesser fraction of the increase than did small operators.

Magazine publishing illustrates the complexity of change. On the surface, statistics appear to tell the familiar tale of concentration. About thirty consumer magazines, or 5.4 percent of the total number, had almost half the total circulation in 1990. The market, nonetheless, was not dominated by large-circulation, general-interest magazines such as those that ruled in the 1940s and into the 1960s. *Collier's, Saturday Evening Post, Life,* and *Look* disappeared, some later to be reborn in different, much reduced, guise. In

1990 *Reader's Digest* and *TV Guide* were rated number two and three among the top magazines in circulation; but they were far outdistanced by a periodical that symbolized what happened to the industry. It was *Modern Maturity,* published by the American Association of Retired Persons and aimed at a specific audience, Americans over fifty. The greatest number of magazines, including some of the most financially successful, similarly addressed particular interest groups. One survey of 1990 industry figures revealed ten magazines with circulations under 100,000 (and as low as 21,000) that each generated total revenues of over $15 million. Even in an era of giant media corporations, there was room at the bottom, as well as at the top, for publications focusing on particular lifestyles, occupations, and interests. Computer hackers, sports fans, dirt bikers, interior decorators, the young, the elderly, mercenary soldiers, home gardeners, and hundreds of other enthusiasts had magazines awaiting, some published by media conglomerates, some not.

There were similar niches in book publishing, where a wide range of presses continued to exist in spite of the towering sales figures of the major houses and the blockbuster best sellers they produced. The comic-book industry, where a few firms also came to dominate, likewise never closed the door to a strange array of independents, whose imaginations encompassed everything from the pornographic to the visionary, sometimes simultaneously. Superman, Batman, and Wonder Woman may have ruled the metropolises of the medium, but there was vitality in a subterranean world that included 1960s underground comics—which challenged dominant values—and serious-minded successors in the 1970s, 1980s, and 1990s. By the last decade of the twentieth century, it was conceivable that the niches in publishing might grow wider, in spite of the rise of giant media corporations, as computer technologies, especially desktop publishing and electronic networks, made it cheaper, easier, and faster to put words and images on paper and on video screens.

Whether or not new technologies will ultimately increase access to the world of print or make it irrelevant, the print media were battlegrounds in twentieth-century America. The task of suppressing radical, sexual, and violent literature long engaged religious and other private groups, professional organizations (notably librarians), state and national politicians, and, of course, the Supreme Court, especially in the string of decisions after 1956 dealing with obscenity. Governmental censorship of print media was more difficult than censorship of radio or television because of traditional First Amendment protection and the absence of regulation of print comparable to that of the airwaves. In one particular instance, however, political controversy over a print medium followed a trajectory that imitated the movie industry's self-censorship and anticipated congressional concern over television violence and rock music lyrics later in the century.

Comic books became the focal point of unwanted public attention in the 1950s, especially after publication in 1954 of Dr. Frederic Wertham's *Seduction of the Innocent,* which put into book form the author's longstanding fears about the ill effects of comic books on children. A psychiatrist, Dr. Wertham had both clinical experience and a European émigré's dour view of American popular culture. Although out of sympathy with some who appropriated his views, he nonetheless gained considerable influence through both his book and his testimony before a Senate Judiciary Subcommittee that in 1953 began investigating the causes of juvenile delinquency. As an analyst of comics, Wertham sometimes made claims as lurid as his subject. Batman and Robin, he asserted, had a lifestyle "like the wish dream of two homosexuals living together." Wonder Woman and Black Cat were their "lesbian counterpart."

Whatever the sexual orientation of superheroes, Wertham was correct in pointing to an enormous amount of mayhem and carnage in comic books. And he was persuasive to a significant number of Americans in portraying the effect on children as a kind of subversion from within, comparable to communist subversion, in which traditional values withered under the impact of powerful words and images. Facing state and federal regulation, publishers followed the film industry and instituted self-policing through their own Comics Code Authority, which prohibited most of what had previously horrified critics and entranced youthful readers. One of the sassier comics, *Mad,* begun in 1952, escaped the code by becoming a "magazine."

For all the furor about comics' violence and sexual and satirical content, however, their significance may have been as much in challenging the boundary between "popular" and "art," just as they challenged the one between "print" and "visual" cultures. From 1941 to 1962 *Classic Comics* (*Classics Illustrated* after 1947) ignored the distinction with 169 adaptations of "great" literature in cartoon format. Comic-book styles of illustration, along with advertising, provided the visual language for Pop artists in the 1960s, as they defied conventional aesthetics and attacked the notion that art is eternal and removed from everyday life. By the 1970s, the comic book itself gained serious consideration by critics, thanks in part to underground artists like Robert Crumb, who prepared the way for a new generation of cartoonists who found the form liberating. Their achievements included such works as Jack Jackson's revisionist account of southwestern history in *Los Tejanos* (1982) and the autobiographical musings of Harvey Pekar, who portrayed everyday life in stories that were, in the words of Crumb, his sometime collaborator, "so staggeringly mundane as to border on the exotic!" Even more impressive were the two volumes of Art Spiegelman's *Maus*, which told through cartoon characters the wrenching story of a Holocaust survivor and his son coming to terms with the past and each other. The first in the series received a 1987 National Book Critics Circle Award nomination for biography. The second appeared with an endorsement from intellectual superstar Umberto Eco. It won a Pulitzer Prize in 1992. The relationships between words and images, popular culture, art, and mass media had become tangled indeed when a comic book received an award honoring a pioneer of sensational journalism, given for literary achievement.

## MAKING SENSE: INTERPRETATIONS OF MASS MEDIA AND POPULAR CULTURE

From the beginning, the new mass media of the twentieth century were criticized by reformers who anguished over their potentially corrupting effects on morals. That was predictable in view of a tradition of suspicion of popular, secular amusements that dates back to the Puritans. More striking is how slow the media were to receive sustained scholarly analysis. Moviegoing is a case in point. For the first twenty-five years of film, the only major work to address it in systematic fashion was *The Photoplay: A Psychological Study,* by Hugo Münsterberg, a Harvard psychologist who died in 1916, the year of its publication. In spite of intellectual merit, the book's reputation suffered from World War I anti-German backlash and slipped into such obscurity that by 1960 the then-authoritative work, Siegfried Kracauer's *Theory of Film,* paid no attention to Münsterberg.

The situation changed dramatically over the course of the twentieth century. Critics continued to anguish over the corrupting effects of popular culture (often using mass media to do so); but by the 1990s, each medium had a substantial scholarly literature devoted to it and major universities dedicated departments, programs, and centers to the analysis of mass communications. When media scholar Douglas Gomery recently catalogued work in the field, he listed ten distinct approaches: pioneering syntheses, biographical, economic, technical, cultural/aesthetic, social, intellectual, legal, international, and political. There are other ways of categorizing studies of mass media and popular culture (by medium or by theoretical orientation, for example), but the essential point is that Gomery's thoughtful list is more likely to expand, rather than contract, in the future. Serious scholarly analysis of mass media and popular culture, largely absent in the opening years of the twentieth century, became a growth industry by its close.

The richness and diversity of writings on various aspects of the subject make a brief survey impossible. Some approaches, however, are particularly worth mention, either because of their influence or because of what they reveal about the problems and prospects for understanding the rise of mass media and commercial popular culture in twentieth-century America.

In 1928, the leader of a procensorship organization, Rev. William H. Short, persuaded a foundation, the Payne Study and Experiment Fund, to support a massive study of the effects of film, especially on youth. Between 1929 and 1933, researchers, including prominent University of Chicago sociologists, produced mountains of data, eleven books, and a popular summary written by Henry James Forman, carrying the ominous title, *Our Movie-Made Children.* Research techniques ranged from using electrodes to measure the responses of subjects as they watched movies to detailed interviews. The implications of the Payne Fund Studies were clear to Forman. Movies, he declared, were "a gigantic educational system with an instruction possibly more successful than the present text-book variety." The power of film was enormous and mostly bad.

The data were less straightforward. For example, interviews conducted by Herbert Blumer, a sociologist, told more complicated stories. For many of those questioned, movies were a bond of companionship and a source of conversation with friends. For a few, movies were disturbing or increased their sense of inadequacy, especially when they compared themselves to glamorous stars. Others, however, found validation for their own nonconformity, like a young woman who took the plucky, athletic heroine of a popular serial as a model. Informants were considerably more ambiguous about the meaning of Moviegoing than were those who studied them, including Blumer who, contrary to his own data, insisted that film gains "such a strong grip" on the young fan "that even his effort to rid himself of it by reasoning with himself may prove of little avail."

Not long after, the conclusion of the Payne Fund Studies, a more sophisticated and enduring form of empirical research on the media arrived with Paul Lazarsfeld, who left his native Austria and settled in America in 1935, one of many refugee intellectuals to influence the study of popular culture. Bringing with him both a deep concern for the power of propaganda and a tradition of empirical studies of human behavior, his influential work, such as that on radio in the 1930s, gave rigor to the analysis of audience demographics and the effects of media. Lazarsfeld's research also yielded results and techniques of more than academic interest. Broadcasters and advertisers were as eager as he—for different reasons—to learn what kinds of people liked what programs and, more important, what encouraged them to consume. Empirical research on media even attracted government attention during World War II, as it employed social science to gauge the effects of propaganda and to boost home-front morale.

Lazarsfeld himself never became a captive of the entertainment industry and the government. He produced a large body of important scholarship, including some in the 1940s and 1950s that broke with notions of a "mass culture" by suggesting how personal relationships affected the messages people drew from the media. Along with his colleague, Robert K. Merton, he also expressed concern that mass media "not only continue to affirm the *status quo* but, in the same measure, they fail to raise essential questions about the structure of society." And yet, Lazarsfeld's considerable influence inside and outside academia, no less than the Payne Fund Studies, pointed to awkward possibilities when social science lent its legitimacy and skills to other agendas, whether those of reformers, advertisers, or the state. Media studies could, as Lazarsfeld once warned, become "administrative research," in which case the question became "on whose behalf?"

A highly critical, and much less empirical perspective on mass media and popular culture also came to the United States in the 1930s, borne by a group of Lazarsfeld's fellow refugees from Nazism, usually called the Frankfurt School after the Frankfurt Institute of Social Research from which they had come. As with Lazarsfeld, they were haunted by memories of Hitler's propaganda machine. Their perspective, however, was closer to Marxism than to marketing and was as self-consciously theoretical as Lazarsfeld's was empirical. (One of their number, T. W. Adorno,

worked briefly and unhappily for the Columbia University Office of Radio Research, run by Lazarsfeld). Leading figures of the Frankfurt School, notably Max Horkheimer, Leo Lowenthal, and, especially, Adorno, rejected narrowly construed social-scientific research on the effects of popular culture in favor of a sweeping approach that looked for connections between mass media, politics, and consciousness. For the most part, they did not like what they heard and saw.

For four decades after their arrival in America, Frankfurt intellectuals produced dazzling studies of culture, ranging from classical antiquity to such modern forms as Hollywood film and jazz. What drove these works was not love for popular culture—Frankfurt cultural preferences were for modernist or classical art—but a critique of advanced capitalism, which they believed produced a mass society. Behind the liberal facade of American culture, they found conformity, alienation, and protofascism. At times, their assault on mass media was unrelenting and joyless to the point of self-satire. One of the best statements of Adorno and Horkheimer's ideas, for example, came in an essay on "the culture industry," first published in German in 1944, in which they used violence in cartoons to illustrate the repressive force of capitalism. Those staples of Saturday matinees, they wrote, "hammer into every brain the old lesson that continuous friction, the breaking down of all individual resistance, is the condition of life in this society." Scholars raised on Donald Duck, Bugs Bunny, and Roadrunner found that critique inadequate.

Horkheimer and Adorno returned to West Germany after World War II, leaving Herbert Marcuse as one of the chief American spokesmen for the Frankfurt School. Marcuse's view of popular culture—seemingly more benign than that of Adorno and Horkheimer—gained vogue in the 1960s, as did Walter Benjamin's, especially through his 1930s essay, "The Work of Art in the Age of Mechanical Reproduction." An uneasy ally of the Frankfurt School, Benjamin found a potential for liberation in commercial popular culture that Horkheimer and Adorno denied. Other analyses, as well as events, revealed flaws in the Frankfurt School's views, but by the 1950s, its notions of mass culture and the culture industry persisted, sometimes divorced from its critical posture toward capitalism.

Yet even some of those who accepted the concept of a mass culture came to find it problematic, as the career of Dwight Macdonald, who claimed to have invented the term, illustrates. His first writings on the subject in the 1930s radical journal *Partisan Review* differed from the Frankfurt School in some respects, although similarly portraying the mass media as instruments of capitalist domination. By 1962, his essay, "Masscult & Midcult," yielded to attacks on the notion of a "mass culture" mounted by scholars like Daniel Bell and David Riesman. Like them, Macdonald came to believe that there was no single mass audience, but rather a series of audiences defined by taste and patterns of consumption, far more selective in interpreting the messages of the media than the Frankfurt School granted. Mass culture had become "cultures."

Dwight Macdonald's changes of mind to the contrary, as late as the 1990s, scholars of various political persuasions shared the Frankfurt School's belief in the manipulative, stultifying nature of popular culture, if not the school's distaste for capitalism. Horkheimer, Adorno, and their colleagues remained exemplary for articulating the idea that popular culture flows downward, from the imperatives of capitalism to a largely passive and undifferentiated audience whose "real" interests it obscures.

Thanks to two Canadian scholars, Harold Innis and Marshall McLuhan, a different perspective on popular culture gained currency in the 1960s. An economic historian and Canadian nationalist troubled by the United States' financial and cultural power, Innis produced his major works on media in the last decade of his life. At the time of his death in 1952, they were difficult, incomplete, and sweeping. In them, Innis classified civilizations by their dominant forms of communication and monopolies of knowledge. His, however, was not a theory of progress. He abhorred American cultural imperialism and lamented that mass media conquered space at the expense of a sense of time and history.

A younger contemporary, Marshall McLuhan, claimed discipleship while shifting toward a more psychological approach than Innis's. Beginning his career as a literary scholar, McLuhan assimilated a variety of influences into what became a challenging, inconsistent view of mass media. Best known for his phrase, "the medium is the message," McLuhan focused on the formal qualities of modes of communication, most systematically in *The Gutenberg Galaxy* (1968). When he did so, he rejoiced that the dominance of the printed word was—so he thought—coming to an end. McLuhan believed that the instantaneous and visual nature of electronic communications, especially television, would create a "global village" reminiscent of what he imagined as a primitive age of human wholeness. *How,* not *what,* we communicate would transform the world.

McLuhan was not uniformly cheerful at the prospect. He once declared "we should do ourselves a considerable kindness if we closed down TV operations for a few years." But his words of warning were fewer, and received less attention, than his celebratory ones. He further muddied his ideas, as well as his reputation, by glib aphorisms and by playing to the mass media he purported to analyze with intellectual detachment. He enjoyed a vogue in the advertising industry, made television appearances, and published a corporate newsletter. A string of verbal excesses cast suspicion on the seriousness of his work.

It was unfortunate that McLuhan made it easy to discredit his views. What he grasped, like Innis before him, was the need for analysis, grounded in history, of the importance of changes in forms of communication. In highlighting the ability of modern mass media to transcend time and space through images, Innis and McLuhan also glimpsed the need to analyze the peculiar mix of disconnectedness and connectedness in popular culture. On the one hand, the media tell stories in bits and pieces, instantaneously and disconnectedly. On the other hand, they link people into communities of the imagination that rest on a shared set of images and cultural references. As one analyst put it, "consumers of electronic mass media can experience a common heritage with people they have never seen." McLuhan's focus on the medium may have been overly dismissive of the message, not to mention the audience and the economic structures that sustained the media, but he was correct in emphasizing the importance of understanding how particular forms of communication shape thought and feeling and transcend national boundaries.

In the post-McLuhan, post-Vietnam, post-1960s universe, popular culture and mass media received scrutiny from an extraordinary number of perspectives. Feminist theory produced sharply honed critiques of media representations of gender, violence, and sexuality. African American and "postcolonial" theorists insisted that race, gender, and ethnicity are constructed by culture, shaped by power, and not innate. They powerfully demonstrated that suppressed voices have different stories to tell from the mainstream media version. Poststructuralism and postmodernism challenged, among other things, conventional beliefs about texts, meaning, power, and cultural hierarchies.

Much of the most influential theoretical work on popular culture in the 1980s and early 1990s, however, engaged and sometimes combined these various influences under the rubric of "cultural studies." The term derives from pioneering work in Britain under the aegis of the University of Birmingham

Centre for Contemporary Cultural Studies, founded in 1963. What the term means is another matter. A sympathetic scholar, Richard Johnson, characterized it as "the investigation of how our individual 'subjectivities' are socially constructed." Definitions could be multiplied and genealogies traced—cultural studies in Britain and the United States had somewhat different intellectual roots and emphases. Rather than stand for a single position, however, cultural studies signified crucial intellectual moves in the study of mass media, popular culture, and, especially, audiences.

Cultural studies expanded the notion of a text to include virtually everything human-made and rejected cultural hierarchies of high and low, popular and art. The latter, proponents argued, are socially and culturally constructed ways of creating and sustaining class, racial, gender, and other inequalities. Advocates of cultural studies also dismissed the Frankfurt School belief that cultural power flows monolithically from the top down and McLuhan's claim that form itself is what matters. They saw meaning arising out of negotiations between audiences and texts. Advanced capitalism may produce films, television shows, records, and popular novels; viewers, listeners, and readers, nonetheless—in the cultural studies mode of analysis—escape domination and control by interpreting and reworking what they see and hear. There are multiple meanings, rather than one, in popular texts.

Such analyses were open to objections from several quarters. The rejection of cultural hierarchies struck conservatives as abdicating aesthetic and moral responsibility. Cultural-studies scholars themselves were not always clear on how far audience resistance could go and on how "progressive" the politics of popular culture could be. Cultural studies also showed signs of its own historical limitations: its theories were products of the late-twentieth-century world of transnational media and advanced capitalism that they sought to analyze. Whether or not they could be projected back in time, or to cultures lacking mass media, remained open questions. Such problems aside, cultural studies marked an intellectual advance in understanding popular culture by recasting questions of taste and cultural hierarchy, as well as ones of power, representation, and interpretation, and by placing the audience at the center of analysis.

Although rooted in particular agendas, perspectives, and historical moments, the best works on twentieth-century mass media and popular culture have persistently raised a few key questions: who makes meaning in popular culture—does it flow from the top down, as the Frankfurt School would have it, or arise out of negotiations between audiences and texts, as in the cultural-studies view? Or is meaning mediated by a long series of groups, processes, and structures that stretch from the point at which a performance is produced to the point at which someone receives it? Is the power of popular culture in its forms, as McLuhan claimed, or does content matter (as procensorship groups believe)? Are the media controlled by a small number of corporations and individuals, serving their own interests and those of advanced capitalism, or is popular culture a realm of choice in which audiences increasingly make their own culture out of the array spread before them? If, after nearly a century of theoretical and empirical work, the answers are few, the questions are sharper.

## THE SHOW GOES ON

On one level, the story of the mass media and popular culture seems straightforward, familiar, and broadly characteristic of modern American history. It is a tale of economic consolidation into large-scale national corporations, of entrepreneurs seeking vertical integration of their industries, of technological innovation, of government regulation (sometimes avoided, sometimes manipulated by industry), and, eventually, of the rise of diversified, transnational corporations. Ben H. Bagdikian declared that between publication of the first edition of his book, *The Media Monopoly,* in 1983 and the fourth edition nine years later, "Ownership of most of the major media has been consolidated in fewer and fewer corporate hands, from fifty national and multinational corporations . . . to twenty." The story—the first line of inquiry announced at the beginning of this essay—could be told of any number of twentieth-century American industries.

To say nothing more would be to leave out the spirit of popular culture—its gaudiness, moments of creativity, hours of banality, energy, mindlessness, wit, disrespect, affirmations, and denials. It would also be to leave out the points when even the economic and political story line became more complicated. Technology, for example, was foe as well as friend to media giants from the Keith-Albee vaudeville circuit through newspaper publishing, Hollywood studios, radio networks, television, and cable. In every instance, technological innovation opened opportunities for new players while dealing serious blows to established ones. Political intervention, although usually minimal and benign, similarly reshaped media industries, from the legislation and FCC decisions that allocated the airwaves through Supreme Court rulings, through the as-yet undetermined effects of the Cable Television Act of 1992. Like the original RCA, some corporations in Bagdikian's present-day "media monopoly" owed their existence to political choices and their profitability to new technologies. Such foundations can shift.

Even granting, however, that most media—in common with other American industries—are dominated by a few large corporations, the extent, stability, and consequences of their hegemony are not at all clear. In areas such as publishing, the record industry, comic books, and radio there is still considerable room for small operators. The media empires themselves, moreover, occasionally showed signs of internal strain. The fate of film companies since the 1960s frequently depended on a single motion picture and even the largest and most diversified media conglomerates had the potential for collapse. The 1989 merger that produced Time Warner, for example, also left a staggering debt of over $11 billion that led the corporation to "strategic alliances," including those with Japanese investors.

In one respect, nonetheless, corporations like Time Warner have succeeded in creating a new sort of monopoly, different from the ones Hollywood studios and RCA sought in movies, radio, and television. Rather than integrate a single medium from production through distribution, conglomerates link different media through ownership of cable networks and systems, amusement parks, book publishers, sports teams, record companies, and radio and television stations. There is a strong incentive to make each "product" reinforce others in the company inventory. Time Warner's book, record, and film divisions, for example, all released works based on the movie, *Listen Up: The Lives of Quincy Jones* (1990). The corporation also became a partner with Jones in an entertainment company. In spite of such cases, however, there is no guarantee that corporations like Time Warner ever can speak in a single voice—they are too diverse with too many constituencies. One of the ironies of media conglomerates is that they achieve economic consolidation because of a proliferation of options and the scattering of audiences into communities of taste.

The other lines of inquiry pursued in this essay— relating to form, content, production, consumption, and meaning—present a similarly mixed picture of change and ambiguous consequences. Contrary to critics' opinions, visual culture did not destroy the printed word and mass media did not produce a mass culture. By the 1990s, choice, not uniformity,

characterized popular culture: consumers had numerous alternatives, as well as the ability to make their own popular culture, figuratively through the act of interpretation and literally through use of audio tapes, videocams, and other readily available technologies. Middle-class men and women assembling home videotapes, or African American teenagers creating street music by "sampling" albums, may not pose an economic challenge to giant media corporations; but they are part of a dramatic increase in the number of places where popular culture is made and they contradict dire predictions of a passive, homogeneous audience.

Changes over the course of the twentieth century led not to a single mass culture but to creation of two worlds of popular culture. The first is widely shared and interconnected. It consists, in America, of a broadly consumed milieu of forms and images—the most popular television shows, movies, and records, as well as best-selling books and closely followed sporting events. In it, references from one form are so well-known that they have meaning in another. Television shows, including network newscasts, focus on films, musicians, and popular authors. Movies incorporate television personalities. African American rap musicians denounce white culture by evoking John Wayne and Elvis Presley with assurance that their audiences will know what they reject. There are reminders, sometimes wrenching, that this realm of popular culture is now global, thanks to the worldwide distribution of American entertainment, as when an Associated Press photograph in 1993 showed a small Bosnian girl, victim of a bloody war over ethnic and religious differences, clutching a Mickey Mouse doll on her way to a refugee camp. At such moments, American popular culture is the closest thing to a mass culture produced in the twentieth century.

There is the second world of popular culture. Its realms are smaller, thrive on the openness and ambiguity of popular culture, and rest on differences in interpretation and social perspective. They come in forms that speak to particular audiences—such as country music—or address specific experiences, such as the pains of adolescence. They come when audiences make their own meaning, as when African American moviegoers root for the Indians or a young woman sees female sexuality and independence in a star who is an object of lust for her brother and a sign of moral decay for her parents.

Popular culture and its vehicle, the mass media, is all these things: widely shared and specific to particular groups, global and local, a mass-produced commodity and continually reworked by audiences, simple in surface messages and ambiguous in deeper meanings, a disposable consumer good and a continual source of pleasure and identity. It is also a form of power that simultaneously spans the globe and penetrates individual consciousness.

SEE ALSO Leisure and Recreation; Sports; Music; The Visual Arts; Architecture; Literary Culture; African American Cultural Movements; Judaism and Jewish Culture (all in this volume); Consumption (volume III).

## BIBLIOGRAPHY

Several works cover a broad range of media and varieties of popular culture. Robert C. Toll, *The Entertainment Machine: American Show Business in the Twentieth Century* (1982), is a useful overview. Daniel J. Czitrom, *Media and the American Mind: From Morse to McLuhan* (1971) surveys media, and how Americans have attempted to understand them. The essays in Tania Modleski, ed., *Studies in Entertainment: Critical Approaches to Mass Culture* (1986), cover a variety of forms in theoretically sophisticated fashion. Books that treat the post–World War II period in particularly valuable fashion are James L. Baughman, *The Republic of Mass Culture: Journalism, Filmmaking, and Broadcasting in America since 1941* (1992); Todd Gitlin, *The Whole World Is Watching: Mass Media in the Making and Unmaking of the New Left* (1980); and Stephen J. Whitfield, *The Culture of the Cold War* (1991). Gina Dent, ed., *Black Popular Culture: A Project by Michele Wallace* (1992), is a powerful reminder that race matters in popular culture.

The nineteenth-century background and vaudeville are the subject of Lawrence W. Levine, *Highbrow/Lowbrow: The Emergence of Cultural Hierarchy in America* (1988); John E. DiMeglio, *Vaudeville U.S.A.* (1973); and Robert W. Snyder, *The Voice of the City: Vaudeville and Popular Culture in New York* (1989). Also see W. Russell Neuman, *The Future of the Mass Audience* (1991).

The literature on film is vast, and growing at an exponential rate. My own view of early cinema owes much to Kathryn Helgesen Fuller, *Shadowland: American Audiences and the Movie-Going Experience in the Silent Film Era* (forthcoming). Robert Allen and Douglas Gomery, *Film History: Theory and Practice* (1985), Miriam Hansen, *Babel and Babylon: Spectatorship in American Silent Film* (1991), and Charles Musser, *The Emergence of Cinema: The American Screen to 1907* (1990), are also useful for understanding the first decades. There are numerous, readily available books treating the Hollywood studio years, among them: Tino Balio, ed., *The American Film Industry,* revised ed. (1985); David Bordwell, Janet Staiger, and Kristin Thompson, *The Classical Hollywood Cinema: Film Style and Mode of Production to 1960,* (1985); Douglas Gomery, *Shared Pleasures: A History of Movie Presentation in the United States* (1992); Thomas Schatz, *The Genius of the System: Hollywood Filmmaking in the Studio Era* (1988); and Robert Sklar, *Movie-Made America: A Cultural History of American Movies* (1975).

The technology and the political decisions that shaped radio are well treated in Hugh G. J. Aitken, *The Continuous Wave: Technology and American Radio, 1900–1932* (1985); and Susan J. Douglas, *Inventing American Broadcasting: 1899–1922* (1987). Radio comedy has been the subject of important analysis in Melvin Patrick Ely, *The Adventures of Amos 'n' Andy: A Social History of an American Phenomenon* (1991); and Arthur Frank Wertheim, *Radio Comedy* (1979). Tom Lewis, *Empire of the Air: The Men Who Made Radio* (1991), is a readable account of early radio.

Erik Barnouw is a towering figure in the history of broadcasting. His *Tube of Plenty: The Evolution of American Television,* 2d rev. ed. (1990) is an important condensation of his major works. Tino Balio, ed., *Hollywood in the Age of Television* (1990), likewise gives a significant overview of the development of television and its relation to other media. John E. O'Connor, ed., *American History American Television* (1983), contains useful, if somewhat dated, essays. Lisa A. Lewis, *Gender, Politics, and MTV* (1990), Ellen Seiter, Hans Borchers, Gabriele Kreutzner, Eva-Maria Warth, eds., *Remote Control: Television, Audiences, and Cultural Power* (1989), Lynn Spigel, *Make Room for TV: Television and the Family Ideal in Postwar America* (1992), and Lynn Spigel and Denise Mann, eds., *Private Screenings: Television and the Female Consumer* (1992), are more current and theoretical, as is John Fiske, *Television Culture* (1987). Todd Gitlin,

*Inside Prime Time* (1983), and Mark Crispin Miller, *Boxed In: The Culture of TV* (1989), are critical analyses of network television from different perspectives.

Print culture is the subject of a great deal of interest in recent years. An influential collection is Cathy N. Davidson, ed., *Reading in America: Literature and Social History* (1989). I am also much influenced by Janice Radway, *Reading the Romance: Women, Patriarchy, and Popular Literature* (1984). Michael Schudson, *Discovering the News: A Social History of American Newspapers* (1978), is a helpful survey. On comic books, see the glossy survey by Ron Goulart, *Over Fifty Years of American Comic Books* (1991); and, for alternative artists, Joseph Witek, *Comic Books as History: The Narrative Art of Jack Jackson, Art Spiegelman, and Harvey Pekar* (1989). Joan Shelley Rubin, *The Making of Middlebrow Culture* (1992), treats one kind of attempt to "elevate" American reading tastes.

Critics of the media are legion. Ben H. Bagdikian, *The Media Monopoly,* 4th ed. (1992), is particularly useful for providing information on the economic concentration of media. James B. Twitchell, *Carnival Culture: The Trashing of Taste in America* (1992), and Neil Postman, *Amusing Ourselves to Death* (1986), are witty, forceful attacks on popular culture.

For cogent summaries of theoretical debates about popular culture, see Ben Agger, *Cultural Studies as Critical Theory* (1992); Simon During, ed., *The Cultural Studies Reader* (1993); Patrick Brantlinger, *Caruso's Footprints: Cultural Studies in Britain and America* (1990); and Chandra Mukerji and Michael Schudson, eds., *Rethinking Popular Culture: Contemporary Perspectives in Popular Culture* (1989).

# PROTESTANTISM

*Richard Wightman Fox*

When H. Richard Niebuhr wrote his article "Protestantism" for the *Encyclopedia of the Social Sciences* in 1934, he began by noting the bedeviling challenge he faced. How could he make sense of a phenomenon so dispersed that even in its geographically limited American form it included, on the one hand, high-church Lutherans and Episcopalians, and on the other, low-church Quakers and Baptists? Protestantism had "no common doctrinal basis," and though many Protestant groups stressed "simplicity in worship, the right of private judgment in matters of belief and conscience, and the principle of voluntary association," many others did not. Protestantism in its essence was centrifugal, spinning off new sects in a never-ending crusade to honor and embody the true "Word of God." Protestantism was so diverse that its only common thread, in Niebuhr's view, was a negative one: anti-Catholicism.

The task confronting the author of an article on American Protestantism at the end of the twentieth century is perhaps more daunting still, since even that negative source of unity has dissipated. Liberal Protestants are now more likely to make social, political, and moral alliances with liberal Catholics than they are with theologically conservative Protestants, and the latter do the same with theologically conservative Catholics. Both Protestantism and Catholicism are split into culturally and religiously warring factions.

Protestantism in the United States has fragmented into a kaleidoscope of groups whose rancorous infighting would have astonished Richard Niebuhr in the early twentieth century, a time already marked by serious disagreement between "modernists" and "fundamentalists." Not only are liberals and conservatives still battling over a whole range of social and theological issues, but profound differences have emerged within the liberal and conservative camps. The virulence of the conflict between the liberals and conservatives ironically may stem in part from each side's desire to shore up its threatened inner unity by centering attention on a dire outside threat.

It is also true, however, that fights among Protestants in the United States have always leaned toward vehemence for the basic reason that these religious debates tend to ignite explosive questions of national mission and identity. Unlike Catholics, who can look to Rome for a sense of stable identity, or Jews, who can (at least symbolically) look to Jerusalem, Protestants in the United States can only look to America itself. Differences of opinion among Protestants about religious matters also draw upon still-powerful regional animosities, especially between North and South. Disagreements about even minor matters can easily degenerate into vengeful accusations about who is the truer American, who is more devoted to the "original" stance of the "Founding Fathers," who is more loyal to the Bible or to the Constitution.

In the 1990s, the churches, seminaries, denominations, and interdenominational agencies of American Protestantism—like such broader institutions as universities, professions, and political parties—are crossed and crisscrossed by ideological fault lines. Since the late 1960s, a vast unsettling in American habits, practices, and commitments has occurred, and that unsettling has shaken Protestantism to its foundations. A major realignment of Protestant forces has taken place. Conservative Protestants, calling themselves variously evangelicals, fundamentalists, Pentecostals, charismatics, or born-again Christians, have since the 1970s become much more powerful both within Protestantism and in the broader social and political arenas. The liberals, meanwhile, have seen their numbers plummet and their broad cultural influence erode, a development that correlates very closely with the decline of secular liberalism as a national political force in the United States during the Nixon, Carter, Reagan, and Bush presidencies.

It is also true, however, that some liberal ideas and practices have had a substantial impact upon the rising forces of religious traditionalism, so that contemporary evangelicals are much more "modern," and in some ways more like liberals, than were their conservative forebears. Today's conservatives are much less likely to separate themselves from a contaminating world, much more likely to adjust themselves to, or make avid use of, secular values or methods. And it is true that religious and secular liberalism, though losing adherents over all, remains strong in universities, professions, and mass media, much to the dismay of conservatives, who have launched a culture war against persistent bastions of liberal strength. Much of the stridency of current public arguments over cultural and political priorities springs from this campaign by conservative Christians to dislodge secular and religious liberals ("secular humanists" in the evangelicals' shorthand) from their positions of cultural power. It is only reasonable, they believe, to redistribute cultural power so that it corresponds to the actual movement of church membership and political sentiment away from liberal denominations and political groups.

One key question of the early 1990s was whether the election of President Bill Clinton would help bolster the liberal ramparts against conservative attack. There is no doubt that his election sparked the conservative Christian community to feats of organizational zeal to rival those it undertook in the late 1970s, especially in Jerry Falwell's Moral Majority. Pat Robertson's Christian Coalition is poised to assume that leadership role for the Christian Right at the first opportunity. Since Clinton's centrist campaign focused on economic "growth" rather than on the economic "justice" dear to liberals, it is unclear to what extent, if any, secular and religious liberal ranks will expand or even stabilize against further erosion during and after his administration.

Whatever their disagreements, and however monumental the shifts of power and identity among American Protestants, the overall importance of Protestantism in American life remains incontestable. True, the Protestant portion of the American population has declined over the twentieth century, from three-quarters or more in 1900 to about 70 percent in 1950 and 58 percent in 1990. The Catholic part of the population has risen dramatically, thanks both to its higher birthrate and to the immigration of southern and eastern Europeans before World War I, and Latinos in recent years. By 1950, Catholics made up about 20 percent of the population, and by 1990 they were at about 27 percent and growing.

Yet a decline in relative numbers does not necessarily amount to an equal decline in influence. Protestantism may still hold disproportionate cultural power, especially if, as seems clear, Catholicism has itself over the last half-century embraced an increasingly accommodationist posture toward the adjoining Protestant culture. Moreover, intra-Protestant conflict is not necessarily a sign of overall cultural weakness. It may instead be a vigorous dispute about which Protestant ideas and values should dominate major organs of opinion and prestigious centers of learning and decision making.

American Protestants of all stripes historically have tended to agree on their privileged responsibility to preserve, protect, and defend the God-given mission of this Novus Ordo Seclorum. Until our own day Protestants have remained, for all their ebbing numbers, securely in charge of articulating the broader American civil religion. As Will Herberg argued in the 1950s in *Protestant, Catholic, Jew,* Catholics and Jews have been admitted to that dialogue to the degree that they have accepted Protestant assumptions, especially the bedrock conviction that the United States has been called to an exceptional destiny as moral exemplar and righteous beacon to the world. The question that remains to be answered is whether today's culture wars are being fought on post-Protestant terrain. To the extent that the liberal phalanx of multiculturalists, feminists, and minority-group advocates—many of them liberal Protestants—has abandoned the historic Protestant consensus on America's unique mission, this generation has inaugurated a new religious era.

Recent statistical surveys, especially George Gallup, Jr., and Jim Castelli's *The People's Religion* (1989), allow us to grasp in some detail the composition of contemporary Protestantism, the faith embraced by 58 percent of Americans. Baptists now constitute about 20 percent of the American population, Methodists 9 percent, Lutherans 5 percent, and the Episcopalians, Presbyterians, United Church of Christ (including the former Congregationalists), and Disciples of Christ (Christian Church) 2 percent each. Another 15 percent of the population identifies itself as Protestant but belongs to a smaller denomination or to none in particular. (In addition to the 27 percent of the population that is Catholic, 2 percent is Jewish, 2 percent is Mormon, 2 percent adheres to other non-Protestant faiths, and 9 percent claims no religious affiliation.)

The South is the most Protestant section of the country: 77 percent of southerners are Protestant; 42 percent of southerners are Baptists. By contrast, only 32 percent of New Englanders are Protestant, while 52 percent are Catholic. African Americans are solidly Protestant: 77 percent of American blacks are Protestant (52 percent are Baptist), and 11 percent are Catholic. Latinos, while still heavily Catholic

(74 percent), are entering evangelical Protestant churches at the rate of about 60,000 per year. That increase, however, does not offset the rise in the Hispanic Catholic population through birth and immigration, nor does it counter the losses the Protestant churches are suffering overall. Already less than half (49 percent) of Americans between the ages of eighteen and twenty-nine are Protestant, a fact probably attributable to the defection of young adults from the mainline liberal denominations in which they grew up. If that tide continues, it will combine with lower Protestant birthrates to make Protestantism a minority religion in America sometime during the twenty-first century.

Over the last generation Protestant belief, measured statistically, has become less "liberal," more "evangelical." Although belief in the literal truth of every word in the Bible appears to be dropping somewhat as educational levels increase (31 percent of Americans were literalists in 1988, compared to 34 percent in 1985), there has been a sizable rise in the percentage of Americans who claim a personal commitment to Jesus (66 percent in 1988, up from 60 percent in 1978; among Protestants, 77 percent in 1988, up from 70 percent in 1978). There has been a similar jump in the percentage of those who claim that Jesus is the Son of God (84 percent in 1988, compared to 78 percent in 1978; among Protestants, 92 percent in 1988 compared to 84 percent in 1978). About one-half of Protestants now say they are "born-again," and just over 41 percent say they have had a "religious experience." Furthermore, 12 percent of Protestants (and 22 percent of born-again Christians) are "Pentecostals" (or "charismatics") who claim special gifts of the spirit, such as healing and speaking in tongues. Eighty-five percent of all charismatics are Protestants, and 41 percent are southerners. Pentecostal churches such as the Assemblies of God, along with noncharismatic but strongly evangelical churches such as the Southern Baptists, have continued to gain new members even as overall Protestant numbers sag.

It is the sharp downturn in liberal Protestant church membership since the late 1960s that accounts for much of the recent decline in the Protestant percentage of the population. Between that time and the late 1980s, according to Erling Jorstad, the Episcopalians lost 28 percent of their members, the Presbyterians 25 percent, the United Church of Christ (mostly Congregationalists) 20 percent, the United Methodists 18 percent. The Disciples of Christ (Christian Church) not only lost members but suffered a schism in which conservative (mostly southern) churches left the denomination; its overall loss over two decades was 43 percent. This massive decline occurred during a period in which nearly 50 million people were added to the American population, further aggravating the percentage loss. It would not be far wrong to summarize the development of the twentieth-century American Protestant churches in this fashion: before 1950 the liberal churches reigned (though evangelicals were quietly organizing all the while); after 1950 the liberal churches tottered, and about 1970 they began to crumble. Yet it must be remembered that liberal Protestantism may retain substantial, disproportionate cultural influence even as its numbers shrink.

## THE EMERGENCE OF LIBERAL PROTESTANTISM

Liberal Protestantism is a discrete historical phenomenon, but it is very difficult to define its precise boundaries. Since the early nineteenth century it has been a potent institutional, ideological, and cultural phenomenon that closely resembles and often overlaps considerably with other historical ideas and movements, such as secular liberal, republican, and scientific faiths. But in a rough way we can identify its distinctive features and see it as an independent historical force.

By 1900 liberal Protestantism had reached its apogee, after nearly a century of steady growth. Its beginnings can be traced to the Unitarian revolt against orthodox Calvinism in the early nineteenth century, a revolt centered in Boston and soon institutionalized at Harvard University. Unitarianism was strong among the commercial and educated classes who wished to stress the rational and predictable nature of human life. They had had enough of what they considered the gloom and doom of their Puritan forebears' Calvinism, which understood God's awesome sovereignty as the essential tenet of faith. For the Calvinists, God's action was autonomous, unanswerable, and man's fate predestined: salvation was for those sinners whom God chose, and no human efforts could influence God's plan. The Unitarians found this relentless insistence on God's unalterable will unreasonable, and argued for the power of individual human beings to transcend sin and embody love. Human nature was good at its core, they held, and the human world was a place of growing enlightenment. It was also a place of legitimate fulfillment: people ought to learn to enjoy natural beauty and social pleasures rather than seeing them as temptations calling the Christian away from the earnest pursuit of godly virtue.

The Unitarian faith in human powers has remained a central commitment in liberal Protestantism. So has the campaign to reduce the distance between the natural and the supernatural, to make the transcendent immanent. Liberal Protestants have tended to baptize the natural and human spheres, to see them as sites of the sacred. Along with secular liberals they have applauded the progress of human society, and they have often interpreted that progress as the gradual realization of God's kingdom on earth. Liberal Protestants have frequently been inclined to imagine human life, at its fullest, to be free of conflict. Contrary to orthodox Calvinism, religious liberals have held that neither the human self nor human society is, in principle, a locus of division, contention, or deception. No classical Christian doctrine has been more repellant to liberal Protestants than that of original sin, a doctrine that many evangelical Protestants still hold dear.

Like secular nineteenth-century liberals, liberal Protestants stressed the potency of individual human beings to master their environment and grow in knowledge and virtue. But secular liberals took for granted that individualism meant struggle: social life might be peaceful in the end, but collective tranquility was the paradoxical product of individual conflict in the marketplace of commerce and ideas. The English philosopher Herbert Spencer and the American economist and sociologist William Graham Sumner believed that individual character was forged in battle. Religious liberals tried to have their individualist cake and eat it too by supposing that marketplace endeavor need not undermine genial fellowship. They banished the tension between individual and community by attributing social conflict to such temporary impediments as lingering superstition and insufficient good will.

By the late nineteenth century, liberal sentiments and beliefs had become predominant in the mainline northern Protestant churches. After vigorous internal debates, Congregationalists, Presbyterians, Methodists, Episcopalians, and even many Lutherans and northern Baptists, had come to adopt a liberal viewpoint. Their perspective embraced all the central features of the antebellum religious liberals' standpoint, but late-nineteenth-century social, political, and intellectual developments gave their liberalism a new stamp. It can be summarized schematically by laying out four of its most fundamental commitments.

First, liberal Protestants responded to the industrialization of the United States by developing a Social Gospel. Like other middle-class Americans, liberals in the churches were aghast at the sufferings of farmers and workers during the industrial slowdowns and depressions of the 1850s, 1870s, and 1890s. They were also worried about the immigration of so many non-Protestants—Catholics and Jews—who came to constitute a huge proportion of the industrial labor force. The United States, in the eyes of liberal and traditionalist Protestants alike, had a special mission to embody God's will on earth, and the nation appeared to be losing its unique character: it was experiencing the same economic crises that were racking European societies, and its increasingly polyglot population called into question its capacity to stand forevermore as God's unique beacon.

Industrialization and immigration provoked liberal Protestants to try to reform society, to put "social salvation" on a par with or even ahead of individual salvation. Even many of those religious liberals (probably a majority) who resisted the Social Gospeler label as too radical still departed from the traditional preoccupation with the piety and salvation of individuals, and saw Jesus as the leader of a social movement designed to transform the world. Social Gospelers went further, taking a leading role in advocating greater government regulation and professional management of social and economic life, on the German model, and in seeing scientifically trained experts as mediators between the warring parties of labor and capital. Such renowned figures as Washington Gladden, a Congregationalist pastor, and Richard Ely, a University of Wisconsin economist and leading layman, provided a religious response to the new industrial world. But they did more: they supplied a new theory of society and a new religious practice that helped justify as well as reform the rising industrial order of large-scale corporate capitalism.

To understand these basic historical developments we must see religion not just as a subsidiary social force that responded to more central phenomena such as the economy. Liberal Protestants played a fundamental role in devising a new legitimation for the emergent institutional order to which all Americans had to learn to respond.

Social Gospelers at their most effusive imagined that American society was not only reformable but could come in time to approximate the Kingdom of God. Figures such as Walter Rauschenbusch, the most important Social Gospel thinker, and George Herron, a radical socialist preacher, contributed significantly to the broader Progressive movement of the late nineteenth and early twentieth centuries. Liberal Protestant writers such as George A. Gordon at the turn of the century believed there was no limit to the progress in love and justice that American society could achieve. Less grandiose but equally militant, thousands of reformers all over the country took heart from Jesus' teachings and from the new social science to devote themselves to social transformation. Women were as engaged as men: from Jane Addams at Hull House in Chicago in the late nineteenth century to Jessie Daniel Ames's antilynching campaign in the South in the early twentieth, women not only supported but led major movements to fight for justice and to restructure American institutions.

The second feature of late-nineteenth-century liberal Protestantism was its commitment to world missions. From the 1880s until World War I, liberals were so confident about the prospects for social and moral progress around the globe that they invested enormous resources in missionary work. By 1900 there were about five thousand Protestant missionaries working overseas, and by 1915 there were about nine thousand. Some were more focused on spiritual conversion, others on social (especially medical) work or teaching, but liberal missionary endeavor in general was marked by an evangelical urgency, an obedience to Jesus' command to preach his message to all nations. Evangelization, however, was a paradoxical process: many missionaries discovered other world religions in the course of preaching their own. By the early twentieth century, the missionary field had split into two parts, with the more conservative evangelicals persisting in the campaign to convert the heathen, and the more liberal missionaries laboring to improve living conditions and educational levels. In some instances the liberals came close to embracing a culturally relativist position, according to which each religion had its own valid approach to the divine.

At a time when the dominant bourgeois ideology confined American women by and large either to the home or to worldly work that corresponded to their allegedly domestic and spiritual natures, missionary activity abroad attracted thousands of female participants and supporters. A women's foreign mission movement rose up alongside the previously established denominational agencies. By the early twentieth century, more than 3 million women were dues-paying members of the female missionary societies, and thousands of talented women had served in demanding positions overseas. In this period, foreign missionary enterprise may have been the most taxing and responsible work available to American women. There is no doubt that women exercised considerable power in the missionary enterprise—too much, in the view of the male denominational officers who, beginning in the early twentieth century, took measures to rein it in.

The third feature of late-nineteenth-century liberal Protestantism was its commitment to science. Liberal Protestants believed that no scientific truth could be contrary to God's truth. They therefore took pride in their critical approach to Bible study, in which they distinguished between the essential truths of the Bible and the particular cultural forms in which those truths were expressed. Accused of a dangerous relativism by their traditionalist opponents, liberals insisted that scientific analysis of the Bible was indispensable for grasping the truth in its purity. They did not always recognize how thin the line was between reading the Bible critically—translating basic truths from one cultural language to another—and subjecting biblical ideas to the supposedly superior judgment of enlightened modern man. Traditionalists wanted so badly to resist the elevation of modernist assumptions to the status of self-evident truth that they sometimes needlessly rejected all efforts at cultural translation—efforts that alone could make sense of the many timebound and contradictory assertions in the Bible.

Liberals were very receptive to evolutionary theories, though not all liberals immediately embraced Darwin's particular conclusions about natural selection. Whatever they thought of Darwin, they had no fear of scientific research, which could never, in their view, call into question the truths of religious faith. It was because of their deep commitment to scientific expertise that religious liberals put so much effort into the creation of universities and professions in the late nineteenth century. Scholarly research and professional expertise would be good for America—it would supply disinterested ideas and leadership at a time of what many believed was degenerative class warfare—as well as good for religion. Liberal Protestant energies and ideas were an indispensable component of the vast expansion and reorganization of knowledge production in late-nineteenth-century America. Presidents of the newly created research universities, such as Daniel Coit Gilman at Johns Hopkins University and William Rainey Harper at the University of Chicago, interpreted the founding of their institutions as victories for the (liberal Protestant) religious as well as secular enterprise—thereby attracting support and funding from such leading laymen as liberal Baptist John D. Rockefeller, who single-handedly bankrolled the new University of Chicago.

Protestant liberals were so cheerfully wedded to scientific research because in their view it could never touch or taint the essence of faith. Their way of formulating that faith constituted the fourth general feature of late-nineteenth-century liberal Protestantism. Their bedrock conviction was that the Christian faith was a revelation, in Jesus, of divine personality. They believed that Christians could come in their own lives to embody personality, and that society itself could become infused with it. God came to be seen much less as a stern Father standing in cold-eyed judgment upon the eternal fate of each person's soul, much more as a tender companion on life's way. Biographies of Jesus proliferated: he was portrayed not as an effeminate, retiring figure, but as a potent, manly model, the vital, sensitive, loving brother of humanity. In its preoccupation with the human personality of Jesus, late-nineteenth-century liberal Protestantism sought to remasculinize a faith that many churchmen believed had succumbed to a flowery, feminine sentimentality.

*Personality* is a key term for understanding late-nineteenth-century Protestant liberalism and its legacy to the twentieth century. Of course twentieth-century Americans have become preoccupied with cultivating their personalities for greater satisfaction or success in life, as such popular writers as Ralph Waldo Trine, *In Tune with the Infinite* (1897), Dale Carnegie, *How to Win Friends and Influence People* (1926), and Norman Vincent Peale, *The Power of Positive Thinking* (1952) have successively and profitably recommended. This insistently secular and therapeutic success literature does bear some resemblance, and has some historical connection, to the liberal Protestant fixation on cultivating personality. Indeed, in order to explain the curious paradox that American society is at once profoundly religious but also deeply secular, one must note that the liberal Protestant cherishing of personality has given a decisive cultural boost to the secular manipulation of personal "appearance."

But the religious pursuit of personality is much broader and richer than the secular one. It did turn liberal Christians away from other-worldly salvation and toward this-worldly fulfillment, but it did not simply draft religion into service in the campaign to feel good or attain success. Centering faith on the cultivation of personality was the way that liberal Protestants tried to distinguish religious liberalism from its secular Enlightenment counterpart, while nevertheless enthusiastically endorsing the Enlightenment's scientific enterprise. Personality was the vital core of human life, the place of "spirit" where unpredictable encounters with God took place. Personality was what distinguished human beings from the other animals that, according to modern scientific research, resembled human beings much more closely than formerly believed. And the perfect realization of personality in Jesus was what distinguished Christianity from those other world religions which, in the most relativistic liberal view, provided quite admirable and even sufficient pathways to the divine.

In the thought of Walter Rauschenbusch, the most important liberal Protestant thinker between the turn of the century and World War I, personality was an ethical, theological, and even political concept, the center of Christian life and belief as well as the key to Progressive social transformation. Rauschenbusch managed to preach a gospel that remained individual even as it embraced social salvation, and he maintained an evangelical commitment to the life of prayer and personal piety as he proclaimed his trust in science and even in socialism. Cultivating personality for Rauschenbusch meant practicing humility and sacrifice of self—not in solitude, but in the dynamic embrace of community. The good Christian was the citizen who knew how to subordinate self-interest to communal growth. The good society would follow not just upon a restructuring of economic institutions and a spread of education and good will, but a conversion to personality, in which individuals in society would respect one another the way that friends in personal relationships do. Rauschenbusch's commitment to personality was mirrored by that of many other Christian and secular Progressives of the day, including such well-known figures as John Dewey and Randolph Bourne. In their determination to transform self as well as society, they differed from the later structural social reformers of the New Deal era and harkened back to the antebellum revivalism of such evangelists as Charles Grandison Finney.

Rauschenbusch's left-leaning liberalism, and liberal Protestantism in general prior to World War I, was still evangelical in its devotion to prayer, to the Bible, to transforming the lives of non-Christians, and to reconstructing personal as well as social life. The enormous power of liberal Protestantism in the nineteenth and early twentieth centuries stemmed from this joining of evangelical and scientific reform energies. Strong differences of opinion between left liberals like Rauschenbusch (who resembled Socialists such as Eugene Debs in his focus on empowering the working class), centrists like Washington Gladden and Richard T. Ely (who stressed the primary role of the caring government in transforming self and society), and right-leaning liberals such as Josiah Strong (who thought immigration restriction was the most pressing reform because of the dilution of Anglo-Saxon cultural and political power) could be papered over by their common enthusiasm for social rebuilding and their shared evangelical fervor. Northern Protestantism, they all agreed, would naturally take the lead in reforming America. Prayer and scientific study could be mobilized to restore the nation to its preeminent place in the world.

At the start of the twentieth century, liberal Protestantism could celebrate its power in the churches and its undisputed sway in American culture. As long as Americans maintained their consensus that social progress was either proceeding apace or was only temporarily blocked by social and ideological contingencies, liberal Protestantism was bound to preserve its paramount place in the religious arena, and—given the historic role of Protestantism in defining the national mission—in the broader public culture. But if events conspired to challenge Americans' commitment to a Progressive view of history and society, the supremacy of liberal Protestantism would be seriously threatened.

World War I was the first of a series of twentieth-century blows to the widespread Progressive view of society; World War II in the 1940s, Vietnam in the 1960s, and the demise of world socialism in the 1980s further dismantled it. The First World War was a battle domestically as well as in Europe: there was a great deal of pacifist and even pro-German sentiment in America, especially among Irish Catholics and among those Protestants whose churches did not stem historically from British Protestantism. Bitter feuding erupted in 1914 between prowar and antiwar forces, a division largely overcome in 1917 in the wave of prowar feeling created by German submarine warfare. But a deep split remained in Progressive ranks, secular and religious. The war vastly increased the power of the national state, and remade liberalism into a single-minded faith in scientific, state-administered reform. As a result, many former Progressives, following the example of Randolph Bourne, turned further left toward radical critiques of both liberalism and the state. Some religious liberals followed suit, including the young ministers Norman Thomas, Reinhold Niebuhr, and Harry F. Ward, all of whom would come to prominence first in the Christian Left in the 1920s, then in the broader socialist Left in the 1930s.

Most liberal Protestants probably preserved their faith in social progress during and after the war, since the vastly enlarged federal government of the wartime years offered an edifice capable of undergirding major social innovations. But postwar liberals in the churches tended to give up the bedrock liberal Protestant beliefs in personality, in evangelization, in a transformation that was individual as well as social. Piety, prayer, and missionary activity of the spiritual sort tended after the war to be ceded to more conservative evangelicals. In a decisive historical shift that illuminates the entire sweep of Protestant history in twentieth-century America, liberal Protestantism after World War I came to look more and more like secular liberalism. Faith in the reconstruction of society persisted for many religious and secular liberals, but it was a faith that separated them all much more completely than ever before from Bible-centered evangelism.

The full meaning of the famous Scopes trial of 1925 emerges clearly when we keep in mind the transformation in liberalism that had just taken place. The trial has passed into popular culture as H. L. Mencken in the 1920s and the play *Inherit the Wind* (1955) interpreted it: the enlightened, scientific forces of the modern, urban world, defended by Clarence Darrow and the ACLU, beating back the archaic pieties of old-time religion, represented by William Jennings Bryan and assorted southern rednecks. Of course Darrow "lost," according to this view, because the teacher Scopes was found guilty and the teaching of evolution was banned from Tennessee schools. But liberal modernism ironically "won" anyway, since fundamentalism was supposedly made to look ridiculous and therefore stumbled off the historical stage in disgrace. There is some truth in this standard view, but focusing on whether it was the liberals or the fundamentalists who won obscures the crucial fact that the trial represented the final victory of secular modernist liberalism over the evangelical liberalism that had sparked progressive reform for a full century. A revealing sign of the completeness of that victory is that liberals have by now all but forgotten that William Jennings Bryan was himself, even as late as 1925, an evangelical liberal, not a fundamentalist conservative. His goal in the Scopes trial, as Garry Wills has reminded us in *Under God* (1990), was not to resist science, but to resist the complete secularization of American culture. As Wills notes, "The Scopes trial, comic in its circus aspect, left behind it something tragic: it sealed off from each other, in mutual incomprehension, forces that had hitherto worked together in American history. Bryan's career had been a sign of the possible integration of progressive politics and evangelical moralism." Liberalism ceded piety and evangelicalism to the Right, a development of historic proportions that was not stemmed (and then only partially and temporarily) until the emergence of the nonviolent civil rights movement between 1955 and 1965.

## THE EMERGENCE OF CONSERVATIVE PROTESTANTISM

Even in the late nineteenth century, when an evangelically oriented liberalism dominated American Protestantism and American public culture, there were palpable signs of conservative Protestant dissent. To the extent that they pondered eschatological matters at all, liberal Protestants were for the most part postmillennialist in their contention that the Second Coming of Christ would follow rather than precede the one-thousand-year reign of peace spoken of in the book of Revelation. Post-millennialism made sense to liberals committed to remaking American society: their earnest reform activities, from temperance and antislavery in the early nineteenth century to slum rebuilding and government regulation of business in the late nineteenth, could all be grasped as contributions to the millennial enterprise. But a small group of premillennialists found all this commotion about transforming the world beside the point. Christ's Second Coming would occur before the millennium, they insisted, and it might happen any day.

The liberal standpoint, according to the premillennialists, amounted to a new version of the old heresy of salvation by good works, not by faith. Liberals put too much trust in the world, and failed to grasp the necessity of separating themselves from it. In fact, many liberals believed that they were distancing themselves from the world in the very act of targeting and combating its vices. But the conservatives' judgment on the world was far more alarmist and renunciatory. All entangling alliances with the world must be cut. In the mid-nineteenth century such crusading evangelists as John Darby of the Plymouth Brethren and the adventist William Miller pushed the premillennial position. The Seventh-Day Adventist Ellen White and the famed evangelist Dwight Moody, among others, continued to preach the doctrine in the late nineteenth century. Christians should prepare for the end, they agreed, not make worldly reform their end.

In the early twentieth century this premillennial sentiment combined with biblical literalism and other antimodern attitudes to create, in conscious opposition to the liberal establishment, a full-blown Christian conservatism. The conservatives faulted liberal Protestantism for capitulating to secular, naturalistic habits of mind, for embracing a corrosive individualism that was relativistic in its approach to truth and hedonistic in its approach to morals. Conservatives sought to bolster intellectual certainty in an age of doubt, moral purity in an age of experimentation. Throughout the twentieth century this conservative campaign has been a basic fact of American life, although liberal Americans have frequently ignored it and therefore underestimated its cultural strength. In the 1990s it is conservative American Protestantism that is growing, keeping pace with and in some cases surpassing Catholic growth rates not only inside, but outside the United States, where (especially in Latin America) evangelical missionaries are converting thousands of Catholics to a more emotional, more declamatory faith.

Despite their common opposition over the last century to liberal and modern thoughts and practices, conservative Christians differ so much from one another that it is sometimes difficult to see them as part of a single movement. Moreover, since the 1970s some conservatives have adopted so many modern techniques of organization and have taken so avidly to certain basic liberal assumptions—that the world is indeed to be reformed, that worldly power and prestige are to be sought and celebrated—that for all their evangelical fervor they seem at times closer in spirit to their contemporary liberal opponents than to their own premillennialist forerunners.

Since the early twentieth century, conservative evangelicals have tended to circle around two basic poles, fundamentalist and Pentecostal. But definitions are fuzzy and many evangelicals over the last generation would more vaguely describe themselves as born-again Christians—those who have had a second saving experience (after baptism). Sizable and rapidly growing sects like the premillennialist Seventh-Day Adventists and Jehovah's Witnesses, which join with many fundamentalists and Pentecostals in putting eschatology, the doctrine of last things, at the heart of the faith, diverge markedly from most Christian conservatives in a variety of theological, political, and cultural commitments. The Adventists' Saturday worship, and the Witnesses' refusal to bear arms for any government, are alone sufficient to keep both groups outside the twentieth-century conservative evangelical consensus.

Sharing premillennial and antimodern origins, fundamentalists and Pentecostals diverge both in their religious style and their ecclesiastical heritage. Fundamentalists tend to stress the intellectual, doctrinal dimension of faith, while Pentecostals (also called charismatics, especially when they are members of traditionally mainstream denominations) emphasize the experiential, emotional side of faith. Differences between the two groups have often been vehement, never more so than in the last decades of the twentieth century: both groups put so much stock in the literal truth of the Bible that they readily anathematize those who, with equal insistence, broadcast alternative understandings of the biblical text.

Fundamentalists typically come out of Presbyterian, Baptist, or independent backgrounds and trace their roots to orthodox Calvinist resistance to liberal intellectual developments in the late nineteenth and early twentieth centuries; Pentecostals often trace theirs to the nineteenth-century Holiness movements, especially potent in Methodism, that preached sanctification, the flooding of the heart by the Holy Spirit. With their Holiness roots Pentecostals are more likely to be Arminians—holding that Christians, by voluntarily embracing the Holy Spirit, can contribute potently to their own salvation—than the fundamentalists, many of whom continue to contend, following Calvin, that human efforts to influence God's preordained plan are unavailing.

The term *fundamentalism* was apparently first used in 1920 as a label for those who defended "the Fundamentals," doctrines that orthodox Christians thought they must defend at all costs. Since at least 1875 Christian conservatives had been gathering at summer Bible conferences in order to buttress traditional faith and practice. Soon thereafter they began setting up Bible institutes as educational alternatives to established colleges and seminaries. The institutes could train evangelists unbesmirched by the liberal critical-historical interpretive methods that increasingly dominated the denominational seminaries. The Moody Bible Institute in Chicago founded in 1889 and the Bible Institute of Los Angeles founded in 1908 were two of the most significant in their national impact. It was the founders of the Los Angeles institute who between 1909 and 1915 published a twelve-volume series entitled *The Fundamentals,* a wide-ranging, thoughtful, and even scholarly discussion of biblical, theological, and ethical questions. As Nancy Ammerman has pointed out, *The Fundamentals* was not a fire-eating conservative manifesto. On a subject as controversial as socialism, for example, one essay contended that the "church leaves its members free to adopt or reject socialism as they may deem wise."

But the fear that certain fundamentals were in jeopardy was widespread, leading some traditionalists to codify them. In 1909 Cyrus Scofield tried to defend the Bible itself by publishing his monumental *Scofield Reference Bible,* which explained the precise meaning of each scriptural passage. Scofield, like many Christian conservatives since the late nineteenth century, was a dispensationalist who followed John Nelson Darby's division of human history into seven stages, or dispensations. The Scofield Bible helped spread that viewpoint to millions of twentieth-century readers. In each stage of history, according to the dispensationalists, God inaugurated a new relationship with humanity, and each stage ended in disaster: the Fall, the Flood, the Tower of Babel, the captivity in Egypt, the Crucifixion. The present church age was the sixth stage, and because of the corruption of the churches that stage would end in a great tribulation, a seven-year sequence of calamitous and disintegrative developments. (Twentieth-century fundamentalists have split on the question whether the tribulation will be preceded by a rapture in which God's chosen ones will suddenly be taken from their earthly lives to be with God.) The seventh and last dispensation will be the millennium, when Jesus will return with the raptured saints for a thousand-year reign followed by the Last Judgment. For most of the twentieth century, premillennial dispensationalism has been a basic tenet of the creed of many conservative Protestants and most fundamentalists.

It is easy for liberals to dismiss such ideas as wild inventions of those ignorant of the cultural construction of reality and the historical embeddedness and mutability of scriptural texts. But it is worth noting that dispensationalism was itself an interpretive innovation designed to save biblical literalism by historicizing it: practices apparently justified in one part of the Bible (slavery or polygamy, for instance) need not be valid universally, but only within one or more dispensations. One could be a literalist, therefore, without taking all biblical prescriptions as eternally mandatory.

Certainly dispensationalism was often a willful leap, a quest for certainty at all costs: if the modern world permitted and promoted doubt about eternal truths or solid moral stances, then the Bible would be a rock in the storm, always available for sure answers, a guidebook to who we are, where we are going, and when (or at least under what circumstances) the end will come. But in its most scholarly manifestations, as in the work produced at the Dallas Theological Seminary, founded in 1924, dispensationalism was actually a middle-ground position between absolutist literalism and liberal historicism. It sparked serious biblical scholarship that has continued to this day at Dallas, and other conservative institutions which have abandoned dispensationalism entirely, such as the Fuller Theological Seminary in Pasadena.

Shortly after the publication of the *Scofield Reference Bible,* and concurrent with the appearance of the twelve-volume *Fundamentals,* a debate within the northern Presbyterian church over the defense of traditional doctrine led to another act of codification. To counter liberal developments within the church, traditionalists successfully enacted a plan to endorse five essential doctrines of the Christian faith. They were not the only essential Christian doctrines, but they were beliefs that liberals, in the conservative view, had been far too eager to jettison in their desire to be modern. The five tenets became foundational for much later fundamentalism: biblical inerrancy, the virgin birth, the substitutionary atonement (Jesus literally saving humanity from sin by sacrificing himself), the bodily resurrection, and the authenticity of miracles. During and after World War I, the five doctrines became a pointed symbol of the larger struggle over which party—the modernists or the fundamentalists—would control the church.

The liberal party pressed for doctrinal latitude, and often, in effect, for putting ethical questions ahead of theological ones altogether. Harry Emerson Fosdick, a liberal Baptist who had become a renowned guest preacher at First Presbyterian in New York, articulated the liberal Protestant consensus: the gospel had to be related to the concerns and feelings of modern human beings; what mattered was not theological nicety or the repetition of traditional maxims, but the healing transformation of people's lives. Conservative Presbyterians had him removed from the New York pulpit, but that action only provoked a liberal counterattack, culminating in the Auburn Affirmation of 1924. That declaration of over a thousand churchpeople rejected both biblical literalism and the official status of the five doctrinal tenets.

Conservative Presbyterians, led intellectually by Princeton Seminary professor J. Gresham Machen, tried to withstand the liberal wave. In his 1923 volume *Christianity and Liberalism,* Machen argued that liberalism was a new religion, distinct from traditional Christianity. Liberals, as he ironically put it, were free to found a new religion if they wished, but they ought first to leave the established church. The liberals' dismissal of miracles in the New Testament drew his particular ire. It was they, the naturalistic modernists, he claimed, who were being unscientific: in their worship of the up-to-date, they peremptorily ruled miracles to lie outside the realm of rational possibility. A truly open-minded and liberal viewpoint would make no such categorical judgment. It was they, not the traditionalists, who had succumbed to ideological rigidity, and in doing so they had reduced Jesus to a mere moral exemplar. "The sage of Nazareth may satisfy those who have never faced the problem of evil in their own lives," he wrote, but those acquainted with "the thralldom of sin" would regard the reduction of Jesus to ideal human being as a "cruel mockery."

But by the end of the 1920s, partly because of the publicity surrounding the Scopes Trial in 1925, Machen's orthodoxy had lost the denominational battle. Machen left Princeton in 1929 to found Westminster Seminary in Philadelphia, and traditionalists then left the church altogether to establish the Orthodox Presbyterian Church. Control of the northern mainline Protestant denominations—Presbyterians, Episcopalians, Congregationalists, Methodists, Baptists, Disciples, and (some) Lutherans—was safely in the hands of the liberals. Fundamentalists retreated to alternative seminaries and Bible institutes, but contrary to the complacent expectation of many liberals, they did not meekly accept defeat as a judgment upon the worth of their cause. They redoubled their efforts to outflank the liberals by building up their power at the local level, and by embracing the new technology of radio. When fundamentalists reemerged as a powerful force in the 1950s, liberals, who assumed that their adversaries had died out like some kind of primitive species, were caught by surprise.

While the defenders of traditional doctrine in the twentieth century gravitated to the fundamentalist camp, another conservative group devoted to intense religious experience gathered around the Pentecostal pole. Pentecostals shared the fundamentalists' antimodernism, but they shared the liberals' distaste for elaborately refined, propositional religion. What set them apart from both groups was their determination to make their faith an active site of signs and wonders. Miracles had not come to an end in the age of the New Testament, as many fundamentalists held; they were interventions of the Holy Spirit even in the everyday life of the twentieth century.

The first eruption of Pentecostalism in its twentieth-century form was probably at the Azusa Street revival in Los Angeles in 1906, where the holiness minister William Seymour preached a special baptism by the Holy Spirit, a baptism marked by the outward sign of speaking in tongues. Such leading Pentecostal ministers as Charles Mason (Church of God in

Christ) got their start at Azusa. Women ministers became prominent in the Pentecostal movement, perhaps because women had traditionally been associated with the realms of intense emotion and healing. Renowned early-twentieth-century evangelists like Aimee Semple McPherson, founder of the International Church of the Foursquare Gospel (1927), and Alma White, head of the Pillar of Fire Church (1917), were followed in the mid-twentieth century by the famous faith healer Kathryn Kuhlman and many lesser-known female preachers.

The Pentecostals, like the fundamentalists, sought to transcend the skeptical, pragmatic mindset that by the early twentieth century was coming to dominate liberal cosmopolitan culture, religious and secular. Liberals put a premium on experimentation: openness to new modes of behavior, new forms of belief, and new techniques of social management. Conservative Christians, whether emphasizing intense experience with the Pentecostals or tried-and-true belief with the fundamentalists, thought the liberal mindset was sapping American culture by undermining strong belief of any sort. Secular antimodernists like Joseph Wood Krutch, author of *The Modern Temper* (1929) and secular modernists like Walter Lippmann, author of *A Preface to Morals* (1929), adopted the very same position; Lippmann took pains to praise Machen's *Christianity and Liberalism* as a telling critique of liberalism.

But secular critics such as Krutch and Lippmann stopped at diagnosis. They did not follow the conservative Christians into an embrace of traditional faith. That path was closed to intellectuals seeking national influence in politics and culture. Conservative Christians took the quest for certain knowledge and vital experience to the limit: they refused to accept a disenchanted world in which human beings were cut off from the replenishing springs of the spirit. They insisted on a world in which a real God engaged human beings in real tests with eternal stakes. Where liberals tended to seek their salvation in social transformation and in the self-possession of psychological growth, conservatives held out for battles of cosmic significance and possession of the self by a spirit from beyond. By tending to make God immanent, and in some cases making God symbolic or mythic rather than actual, liberals ceded transcendence and life-or-death encounters to the conservatives, as they also ceded personal piety, evangelization, and revivalism. It stood to reason that masses of Christians in search of a resoundingly transformative faith would, over the course of the twentieth century, abandon what they considered the thin religion of the liberals and

migrate into the fundamentalist and Pentecostal branches of Protestant conservatism—and into the extra-Protestant but thoroughly traditionalist communities of the Adventists, the Jehovah's Witnesses, the Mormons, and other fast-growing evangelical sects.

## LIBERALISM AND ITS NIEBUHRIAN CRITICS, 1920s TO 1950s

Christian and secular conservatives were not the only critics of liberal Protestantism in the 1920s. At the very moment when liberal Christians were applauding their victories in denominational battles (and their apparent victory at the Scopes Trial), a young band of radical dissenters emerged in the liberal churches themselves. Reinhold Niebuhr, since 1915 a politically active preacher in Detroit, soon became their acknowledged leader. A charismatic preacher, tireless organizer, gifted polemicist and thinker, Niebuhr turned first (in the late 1920s) to radical politics, then (in the 1930s) to an Augustinian theology, in an effort to challenge and transform liberal religion. After he moved in 1928 to a professorship at Union Theological Seminary in New York, a longtime bastion of liberal Protestantism, he also became an influential figure in the secular New York and national Left. From the 1940s to the 1960s he was a famous leader in liberal politics and religion.

In the 1920s, liberals did not expect such a powerful revolt from within their own ranks. As they swept aside fundamentalist challenges in the churches, they looked forward to savoring their hegemony in the religious sphere and to spreading love and enlightenment throughout the world. In the wake of the world war, the pacifist movement gained many liberal Protestant adherents—including Charles Clayton Morrison, influential editor of the *Christian Century*—who joined secular liberals like John Dewey in embracing the international outlawry-of-war movement. Other religious liberals, such as the Baptist philanthropist John D. Rockefeller, Jr., took up again the old liberal Protestant mission to spark reconciliation between business and labor through morally concerned expertise. Rockefeller's Institute for Social and Religious Research was one of many agencies that promoted the longstanding progressive quest for a linkage between spiritual endeavor and scientific research. Among the institute's many projects was Robert and Helen Lynds' famous 1929 sociological study, *Middletown,* originally billed as a survey of the spiritual resources of an average American community.

Niebuhr and his retinue of disciples found the moralism of liberal reform quaint and its scientific methods inadequate. By the late 1920s they indicted liberalism for its complacency about social injustice and—echoing the conservative critique of Machen and others—its failure to take seriously the place of sin and evil in personal and social life. Niebuhr lambasted liberalism for its gradualism, its sentimentality, its preoccupation with individual therapeutic growth, its willingness to preach ideals alone instead of decisive action. Following the economic collapse of the early 1930s, Niebuhrians in the Fellowship of Socialist Christians and in the Socialist Party of America (Niebuhr ran for public office twice, unsuccessfully, on the Socialist ticket) denounced capitalism as well as the tepid liberalism of the churches. His classic 1932 volume *Moral Man and Immoral Society* bitterly rejected the liberal tradition of the secular John Dewey as well as that of the established denominations: religious and nonreligious liberals alike, he argued, were blindly preaching the spread of good will, education, and love as social ideals when sinful human beings were bent on self-aggrandizement and social institutions were crashing in ruins.

The Niebuhrian critique of liberalism was in fact an American variant of a widespread development in early-twentieth-century Protestantism. In the wake of the devastation of World War I, the Swiss theologian Karl Barth issued his path-breaking *Epistle to the Romans,* which began to influence young theologians like H. Richard Niebuhr, Reinhold's brother, even before its translation into English in the 1930s. Barth, himself a modernist in his endorsement of critical-historical scholarly methods, blasted liberal squeamishness about a God of thunder and might, and the liberal tendency to emphasize humanity's natural capacity to know God. God, said Barth, was the sovereign who kept his own counsel and made himself known (darkly) only through his chosen revelation. The center of Christian faith was not (as the liberals tended to make it) the veneration of human potential and the imitation of Jesus—the holy embodiment of selfless personality—but the confession of sin and the submission to God's judgment.

Richard Niebuhr welcomed Barth's general perspective because it offered strong resistance to what he considered the subjectivizing and psychologizing of Christianity in liberal Protestantism. Psychology, he wrote in 1927, "has substituted religious experience for revelation, auto-suggestion for communion with God in prayer and mysticism, sublimation of the instincts for devotion, reflexes for the soul, and group consciousness or the ideal wish-fulfillment for

God." Unlike the fundamentalists, Richard Niebuhr (following Barth) had no interest in enforcing obedience to cherished propositional truths, much less in ferreting out once and for all the literal meaning of each scriptural text. His goal was a return to Jonathan Edwards's conviction that God was great and his will unanswerable, and that the Christian's vocation, above all, was repentance.

Richard Niebuhr was a much more devoted humanist than Barth—he studied and valued the human sciences for the light they shed on human nature and society and, indeed, on the encounter between human beings and God—but most American radical critics of liberal religion did not go even as far as he did toward Barth's viewpoint. Reinhold Niebuhr's selective use of Barth was much more typical in its preservation of the older liberal fixation on the reform of society and the valorization of the natural and the secular. Niebuhr's achievement was to stress with Barth the absolute transcendence of God and the sinfulness of human beings, but to use the idea of God's transcendence prophetically and politically as a weapon against sinful social structures.

Following Rauschenbusch and the Social Gospel, Reinhold Niebuhr insisted that God's judgment was not only upon individuals, but upon classes and societies. The Christian vocation was an actively social repentance that tried, in the face of the sure knowledge that final success would never be achieved, to build God's kingdom on earth through ever broader enactments of justice. The human world of political responsibility and social reconstruction was the proper locus of Christian faith; Christianity was a leaven capable of liberating the potential that, in spite of sin, lay always available in human selves and societies. Niebuhr's monumental two-volume work, *The Nature and Destiny of Man* (1941–1943), gave emphatic expression to what Niebuhr considered the central paradox of the Christian faith: human beings were both fumbling sinners and creatures made to excel because they were made in the image of God.

In retrospect, one can see Reinhold Niebuhr's rescue mission—his campaign to save liberal religion by radicalizing it—as a quest with very mixed results. Niebuhr's relentless exposure of the limitations of liberalism helped prepare the way for its decline in the final third of the twentieth century, from its dual position as dominant Protestant faith and centerpiece of America's own public, or civil, religion. If religious liberalism was so prone to sentimentality and complacency, Niebuhr's readers and listeners were forced to ask, why wasn't pure secularism of equal worth morally and politically? Niebuhr might argue that secular naturalism lost sight of the full paradox of human life, but he himself many times made known his personal preference for secular politics over the pious pronouncements of the churchpeople.

Certainly Niebuhr did not single-handedly propel liberalism into its late-century downward spiral, but his withering attack, at the very least, put liberals seriously on the defensive. By belittling both the old liberal devotion to personality and the foundational liberal faith in gradual improvement through science and education, Niebuhr set the foundations of liberal religion to shaking, and his own mortar and trowel could not repair the widening cracks. Preaching a doctrine of original sin might not slow down his own personal campaign to reform society, but it might lead others to conclude either that stoic withdrawal made as much sense as activism, or that activism under secular auspices was less encumbered by pretentious or gratuitous wrappings. Niebuhr left an ideological vacuum into which, after 1950, conservative Christians would rush.

## THE CONSERVATIVE REVIVAL IN THE 1950s

World War II further weakened the historic liberal faith in human progress that World War I had already seriously damaged. Niebuhr's liberal realism still tried to accommodate the notion of indeterminate if not inevitable progress. But since it also drew on traditional conservativism in harping on the tragic limits circumscribing human existence, many observers rightly saw it as a drawing back from the Depression-era insistence on extending justice and equality. As Cold War fears of subversion and the atom bomb increasingly colored public discourse, liberals joined the general celebration and defense of the American way of life—representative democracy might not be perfect, but it was the best option available—and called for resistance to communism around the world.

Between 1925 and 1950, conservative Christians were barely noticed by the national press, and therefore contributed little to national debates about politics, religion, and culture. Whether conservatives had been excluded from the public arena, or had voluntarily withdrawn from it under the barrage of mockery to which they were subjected during and after Scopes, they had nevertheless continued to organize at the local and regional levels. The national press, itself dominated by liberals, did not pursue them into the provinces. Bible institutes continued to multiply, and the Moody Bible Institute grew during the 1930s into a virtual national headquarters of the fundamen-

talist movement. Independent evangelists like Fort Worth's Frank Norris, who set up the World Baptist Fellowship in 1931 and the Bible Baptist Seminary in 1939, and Dallas's John Rice, radio preacher and editor of the monthly *Sword of the Lord* starting in 1934, reached vast audiences. Separatist fundamentalists such as Norris, who regarded even the very conservative Southern Baptist Convention as too tolerant of modernism, and Carl McIntire, who walked out of Machen's secessionist Orthodox Presbyterian Church in 1937 to found the Bible Presbyterian Church, kept up the pressure against creeping accommodation to liberal practices or thoughts. McIntire organized the American Council of Christian Churches in 1941 as an alternative to the liberal Federal Council of Churches (which in 1950 became the National Council of Churches), and in 1942 the National Association of Evangelicals brought together nonseparatist fundamentalists from such institutions as the Dallas Theological Seminary, Wheaton College in Illinois, and the Moody Bible Institute.

The availability of local radio transmission by the mid-1920s was a godsend for conservatives lacking access to national organs of opinion, including the new national radio networks. NBC radio gave the Federal Council of Churches exclusive control of the religious programming that it offered as a "public service," and the council lined up strictly liberal fare. Harry Emerson Fosdick's *National Vespers* ran from 1927 to 1946, and attracted millions of listeners. Conservatives competed diligently by producing local and syndicated broadcasts of their own. Everett Parker's study of Chicago radio in 1941 found that fundamentalists controlled 61 percent of the seventy-seven religious programs offered each week on Chicago's seventeen radio stations.

Many liberal clergymen disparaged radio preaching as entertainment, since it put a premium on dramatic effect and simply encapsulated messages. Conservatives had no such scruples: to them the Bible message was simple and could be stated forcefully and plainly. Radio allowed them to reach huge audiences, including those poorer, less urban, less highly educated listeners who may have been relatively impervious to written appeals. The Moody Bible Institute's own station put out the most professionally skilled transmissions, which followed the old Moody-Sankey revivals in blending music and preaching. The Los Angeles Pentecostalist Aimee Semple McPherson was on the air as early as 1924, and applauded radio for allowing her to acquire an auditory flock of hundreds of thousands. Charles Fuller's *Old Fashioned Revival Hour* from California became a cultural staple of the depression decade of the 1930s, when thirty stations carried it on the Mutual Broadcasting System, and by the middle of World War II it was heard on more than a thousand stations nationwide. The National Religious Broadcasters was founded in 1944 to push the interests of the evangelical radio enterprise.

The radio preacher who after 1950 brought conservative Christianity back into mainstream American culture was Billy Graham. A graduate of the Florida Bible Institute and of Wheaton College in Illinois, he began his radio career on Chicago's WCFL in 1943. He traveled in the mid-1940s as the chief preacher of Youth for Christ, and during the late forties, thanks to his highly publicized Los Angeles revival, was discovered by the national press. His Sunday night radio show, *The Hour of Decision,* started in 1950 on ABC and generated ever larger audiences for his urban revivals.

Graham was a fundamentalist that many liberals found palatable, not only because with his tailored suits and elegant articulation he looked and sounded modern, but because he offered them an olive branch. Contrary to separatist practice, Graham sought to cooperate with local churches during and after his revivals. Separatists like Carl McIntire were incensed, and in 1956 they dissociated themselves from his work. Their boycott only increased Graham's standing with liberals in the mainstream denominations. When he came to New York for a massive show of evangelical force in 1957, no less a liberal figure than Henry Van Dusen, president of Union Theological Seminary, joined the welcoming committee. When Reinhold Niebuhr protested Van Dusen's support, Van Dusen replied that while Graham might not speak the language of the professors, he certainly spoke that of the people, who needed the gospel wrapped in easily grasped packages.

A further sign of the wide respectability of Graham, and of moderate fundamentalism, was Graham's golfing and consulting relationship with a long series of American presidents. From Harry Truman to Bill Clinton, Graham has been a regular White House visitor, and with Richard Nixon he became a virtual White House minister. In the last two decades of the century, he has taken pains to become more prophetic, less priestly, in relation to presidential power, expressing, for example, deep misgivings in the 1980s about the nuclear arms race. Through a half-century of evangelism, however, his conservative message has remained remarkably unchanged. Human beings are sinners in need of the saving grace of Jesus Christ; the devil truly exists and tempts peo-ple to stray from the path of virtue; heaven and hell are real places that await the saved and the damned. What so plainly distinguishes Graham from the liberal Protestantism of the twentieth century is precisely his evangelistic zeal, his belief that carrying the Gospel message of repentance and salvation to the far corners of the earth is a matter of utmost urgency.

## THE CRESTING OF LIBERAL PROTESTANTISM IN THE 1960s

One reason why the liberal churches found it easy to tolerate the work of successful evangelicals like Billy Graham in the 1950s was that liberal religion was expanding too. A culture-wide religious revival, stimulated not only by anxieties about the bomb but by a general postwar desire for the restoration of tradition and normalcy, was filling all the churches with ever larger baby-boom families. Liberals could watch the rising tide of evangelicalism with relative equanimity, especially since the liberal denominations were attracting many former evangelicals whose incomes and educational levels had risen markedly after World War II, and who sought the greater social status still associated with the mainstream churches.

But the liberal Protestant churches were not just sites of status and complacency. By the early 1960s social idealism again took root among secular and religious liberals, many of whom became active in the civil rights movement that had developed in the South since the mid-1950s. Liberal idealism in the 1960s could not possibly recover the unbounded optimism that marked much progressive thought before the devastation of the two world wars, but a steely ethic of responsibility, earlier worked out by Reinhold Niebuhr, underlay the new quest to combat poverty and equalize opportunity. Liberals not only embraced the civil rights movement, but generally bore witness to the spiritual potential of what the northern Baptist minister Harvey Cox called, in his very influential 1965 book of the same name, the secular city.

Following Niebuhr and the martyred German theologian Dietrich Bonhoeffer, Cox called for a liberal religion that eschewed religiosity in favor of a critical immersion in the world. The enthusiasm with which liberals gathered under the secular banner was reflected in the flurry of interest in death-of-God theologians such as Anglican Bishop John Robinson, whose book *Honest to God* attracted much publicity in the mid-1960s. The turn away from God-talk to a secularized social ethics did not mean that liberals had abandoned all concern for individual salvation. Liberal psychotherapeutic literature became a staple of religious as well as secular bookshelves. The theologian Paul Tillich, an erudite liberal émigré from Nazi Germany, became a culture hero with such popular works as *The Courage to Be* (1952), which combined an openness to psychiatric and existentialist perspectives with traditional themes of the Christian cure of souls.

In the civil rights movement, African American liberal Protestants revealed that their Baptist faith, unlike twentieth-century northern liberal religion, still combined a vibrant evangelical piety with the quest for social justice. The movement was locally based in the black churches, and it was out of their collective life that a gifted national leader, Martin Luther King, Jr., emerged. Trained at Morehouse College, Crozer Seminary, and Boston University School of Theology, King could easily have pursued an academic career. Instead he chose the Baptist ministry in which his father and both of his grandfathers had labored. Soon after accepting his first church in Montgomery, Alabama, he was chosen (in 1955) to head the boycott of the city's segregated buses, and for the next thirteen years, until his assassination in 1968, he was a moral, religious, and political force of national stature.

King's crucial contribution to Christian ethics and to American political practice was his doctrine of nonviolent resistance, derived from Mohandas Gandhi and Jesus. Suffering was redemptive if it took place within a supportive community and if the sufferer was resolute in forgiving those who caused it. The courage of the charismatic leader willing to sacrifice his life for the deliverance of the people and unwilling to succumb to bitterness or resentment drew out the courage in others and sparked enduring hope for social transformation. Liberal Protestantism had always preached love as the cardinal principle of the Christian life, but King and the southern black churches joined the preaching of love to the practice of suffering and solidarity, prayer and forgiveness, vastly enriching the liberal Protestant tradition of the twentieth century.

The evangelical and social vigor of the black churches between 1955 and 1968 may have had the ironic effect of pointing up the staid decorum of the white liberal churches in the North, thereby weakening the churches' hold on their younger members, whose departure explains much of the sharp falling off of membership beginning in the late 1960s. But by the mid-1960s the black churches themselves faced a crisis that split the larger liberal movement and further eroded the morale of the liberal churches.

The civil rights movement's success by 1965 in guaranteeing equal access to voting and public accommodations forced liberals to confront more intractable problems: discrimination in employment and housing and cross-generational poverty. Yet at the very moment that those problems might have been addressed, urban riots in the North gave rise to calls for black power and even violence (if only in self-defense) that undermined King's leadership. And the escalation of the Vietnam War both diverted federal funds from social programs and divided the liberal community, religious and secular, into hostile camps of hawks and doves. King chose opposition to the war and to the Johnson administration, and his broad cultural and political influence ebbed dramatically.

Vietnam had an enormously debilitating impact on liberals because they had come to rest their hopes for social progress on the timely intervention of the federal government to enforce justice and redistribute opportunity. Liberals depended on the state to impose a national and cosmopolitan vision of order and freedom. But Vietnam provoked distrust and hatred for the very state on which they depended. It was liberal faith in the beneficence of the state that had allowed such social-religious prophets as Reinhold Niebuhr in the 1930s and 1940s and Martin Luther King, Jr., in the 1950s and 1960s to become cultural heroes of the liberal movement. Prophets could call for justice to roll down like waters and righteousness like an everflowing stream, and policymakers could then translate the call into social policy. But with the withering of liberal confidence in the state in the 1970s and 1980s, the liberal movement ceased calling up religious prophets to positions of national leadership.

Charismatic leaders have continued to be available in the liberal religious community—William Sloane Coffin, Jr., formerly minister of New York's Riverside Church and chaplain at Yale University, Robert McAfee Brown, former President of Union Theological Seminary and Professor of Theology at Stanford University and Berkeley's Graduate Theological Union, Cornel West of Princeton's Afro-American Studies Department, to mention only three—but their influence has been restricted since the liberal movement is so fragmented. In the early 1990s Coffin headed the antinuclear group SANE, Brown centered his work in Latin American-based liberation theology, and West focused his energies in the struggles of the black community and the debates of the academic Left.

These men could not assume the kinds of leadership roles in the liberal community that would have been open to them a generation earlier, because that community was profoundly divided by gender. Many liberal women no longer felt fully represented by male leaders, however charismatic they may be. They produced their own theological spokeswomen—thinkers as varied as Carol Christ, Beverly Harrison, and Carter Heyward—and their own church activists and, increasingly, ministers. Women students constituted the majority of the students at leading liberal seminaries. The cohesiveness of liberal Protestantism up through the mid-1960s could not be recaptured, since it was based on a well-cemented structure of gendered authority that disintegrated after 1970.

Some liberals believed that this fragmentation and divisiveness ironically offered a valuable opportunity to abandon the inherited liberal notion that progress is measured by the spread of a cosmopolitan, uniform culture. Post-liberal thinkers such as George Lindbeck and Stanley Hauerwas in effect generalized from the experience of the civil rights movement: local or confessional loyalties and traditions should be encouraged, not transcended. Cultural tradition rooted in historic communities, they argued, is the foundation for a vibrant collective life of any sort.

## AMERICAN PROTESTANTISM AT CENTURY'S END

Even a casual observer of American Protestantism in the 1990s would note the sharp public rifts between liberals and conservatives over such issues as abortion, gay rights, women's access to the ministry, respect for animals and the natural environment, and third-world liberation. Equally obvious are the tensions that mark the inner life of each group, with, for example, liberals awkwardly tiptoeing around race and gender issues, and conservative televangelists battling for the loyalty of a broadcast audience soured by disclosures of thievery and immorality on the part of such former favorites as Jim Bakker and Jimmy Swaggart.

There was, however, a much deeper level of disarray in end-of-the-century American Protestantism that did not immediately meet the eye. Liberals, for their part, were beset not just by a fragmenting of their concerns into separate movements—feminism, liberation theology, environmentalism, and so on—but by a deepening dilemma concerning two of the most basic liberal (secular as well as religious) convictions: the notion that historical progress has occurred in the past and can in principle be expected to take place in the future, and the idea that America is God's

specially chosen instrument. Conservatives, for their part, were laden with the contradictory tasks of standing up for America's unique mission, endorsing the general notion of historical progress (without which a strong sense of American mission appears to falter), and, yet also voicing the traditional anti-progressive sentiment that in the tragic arena of human events, as Lord Acton put it, all things, given enough time, go badly.

Liberal doubts about future progress and about America's mission were first expressed in the wake of the slaughter of World War I. But World War II, while further eroding any notion of the goodness of human nature or the social efficacy of love and good will, nevertheless resurrected the old consensus about the particular chosenness of the United States for world leadership. It also prompted liberals to hope for progress through worldwide modernization. The monumental importance of the Vietnam War is that it shattered that restored faith. A telling instance of that historic moment was Martin Luther King's conscience-stricken speech at Riverside Church in New York in 1967, when he proclaimed that far from being uniquely blessed, America was "the greatest purveyor of violence in the world today."

In the years after King's speech, liberals remained dubious about the moral stature of the American nation. One of the main attractions of liberation theology for religious progressives has been that it puts the moral locus of political action in base communities well outside the United States. It is conceivable that in the aftermath of the collapse of world socialism in the 1980s, liberal Americans will recover a sense of America's historical uniqueness and special responsibility and even beneficence. But it seems equally likely that the dismantling of the Soviet Union and the demise of the Soviet paradigm—justice and eventual equality through state control—will only further bury the idea of historical progress, to which the notion of American uniqueness has for two centuries been closely linked. Liberals may in fact have been losing a central conviction that withstood the world wars and Vietnam: the Hegelian view that whatever the prospects for the future transformation of society, history in the past moved from narrower to wider enactments of freedom. The French Revolution (however perverted by Robespierre), the American Civil War (however compromised by Reconstruction), and the Russian Revolution (however corrupted by Stalin) were huge leaps forward for humanity. But the passing of world socialism in the 1980s forced a reconsideration of the entire progressive paradigm.

If religious and secular liberals continue to lose faith in America's special mission, in the notion of past as well as future social progress, and in the idea of common culture, then a post-Protestant society will increasingly emerge in the United States. Conservative Christians will certainly keep struggling to restore trust in America's uniqueness, to rekindle the doctrine of progress (through private enterprise, if not government action), and to create a common culture (whether a Christian America or a nation of Protestants, Catholics, and Jews wedded to certain Western documents and traditions). But a withdrawal from the former cultural consensus by liberal Protestants and secularists would decisively alter American society.

Conservative Christians managed to mobilize huge financial resources and volunteer energy in such organizations as Jerry Falwell's Moral Majority and Pat Robertson's Christian Coalition because liberal Protestants ceded nationalism and patriotism, as well as evangelism and revivalism, to them. But the conservatives' often frantic flag-worship, their strained tirades against secular humanism and nonnuclear families, and their occasional veiled appeals to racial purity, signaled an uncertainty even in their own camp about prospects for the future. The implication of some conservative Christian rhetoric was that American culture is already so far sunken into dissipation that it is unredeemable. The very premillennialist sensibility that fundamentalists such as Falwell and Pentecostals such as Robertson chose to downplay in their embrace of modern media politics may increasingly appeal to their constituents and undermine their authority.

Ever since the Puritan settlement of New England, American Protestants have in spite of all their differences agreed that Protestantism would be custodian of the American civil religion, of the underlying American public theology. In the 1990s there is much evidence that liberals are pulling out of this consensus, but there is also some indication that liberals long to preserve the inherited framework. The success of such books as *The Naked Public Square* (1984) by Richard Neuhaus and *Habits of the Heart* (1985) by Robert Bellah et al., is testimony to a deep and widespread desire for the renewal of Protestant-based public theology. Both Neuhaus and the Bellah group tried to conceive of a common culture with a Christian basis but which was non-exclusive, open to dialogue. Neuhaus's vision of culture requires belief in a transcendent God as a foundation for morality, while Bellah's requires only the recovery of a Biblical language that would permit people—in the face of America's relentless individualism—to express yearnings for communal attachment. Both Neuhaus and Bellah offered a vision of culture in which what is common is precisely the asking of questions, an open-ended debate about the character of the common culture itself. Especially in Bellah's account, this procedural view of the common culture surrenders a good deal of ground to secularism.

Since even the explicitly religious cultural visions of liberal Protestant writers like Robert Bellah come so close to being secular visions, there is good reason to suppose that conservative Protestants will, in the twenty-first century, be left alone to carry the banner and the memory of Protestant civil religion. Liberal theologians may increasingly cultivate the separate strands of their own denominational, ethnic, and gendered traditions, and liberal churchpeople may move in opposing directions, some centering themselves in secular social endeavor, others displaying increasing sympathy for Catholicism as a model of tradition-based authority (Richard Neuhaus's recent conversion to Catholicism is a striking sign of the times). The disorientations of contemporary liberal Protestantism and the strains of contemporary conservative Protestantism suggest that America is entering a new epoch of decentered cultural pluralism.

If this analysis is on the mark, American Protestants in the next century may find the work of Reinhold Niebuhr especially relevant. In the 1940s and 1950s Niebuhr sketched, in effect, a fallback position for those prepared to abandon the idea of a common civil religion. He outlined the paradoxical position that public culture should be both secular and religious. Having since the 1930s feared the fanaticism that religions, whether God-fearing or atheistic (like communism), often brought into the public sphere, he insisted that the political and cultural worlds be fundamentally secular, open, protected from domination by any particular viewpoint or faith. (If secularism itself became a crusading faith, it too would have to be resisted: school prayer, he thought, might be admissible on grounds of encouraging a full diversity of viewpoints in education.)

But in Niebuhr's view a public sphere untouched by religion would degenerate into moral and political passivity. Democracy needed prophecy if it was to avoid falling victim to mere technological efficiency or therapeutic adjustment. Prophecy meant cultivating judgment, both critical public scrutiny of social institutions in light of the goal of justice, and divine judgment, through the instrument of the prophetic voice, of the sinful pretensions of human action. A sharp sense of human fallibility and God's mercy would not undermine moral striving, he argued, but would buoy up believers for social struggles that must be carried out over many generations. Significantly, Niebuhr did not stress the Christian character of prophecy so much as its Judeo-Christian sources. The Jewish and Christian religious experience was normative not in the sense that America needed more religious observance in the churches and synagogues, but in the sense that Judaism and Christianity disclosed the right relation between religion and polity.

Civil religion for Niebuhr meant cultural openness to judgment and cultural commitment to justice, not common belief in a particular religious or philosophical tradition. Cultural pluralism had pushed so deeply into American society that it was anachronistic to dream of a common, homogeneous system of beliefs. "We are merely a vast horde of people let loose on a continent with little to unify us by way of common cultural, moral, and religious traditions," he wrote in *Harpers* in 1932. And it was not enough, in his view, to propose liberal dialogue as a new, procedural form of cultural consensus. Justice and judgment, structural transformation combined with repentance, were the only bases for a strong, enduring community.

SEE ALSO Catholicism; Judaism and Jewish Culture; Nontraditional Religions (all in this volume).

## BIBLIOGRAPHY

The starting point for students of twentieth-century American Protestantism is Sydney E. Ahlstrom, *A Religious History of the American People* (1972), which covers the entire sweep of mainstream religion in the American past. William R. Hutchison's *The Modernist Impulse in American Protestantism* (1976, 1992), is the standard work on mainline liberal Protestantism from the mid-nineteenth to the early twentieth centuries, and it should be supplemented by Robert Handy, *Undermined Establishment: Church-State Relations in America, 1880–1920* (1991); and Hutchison's edited collection, *Between the Times: The Travail of the Protestant Establishment in America, 1900–1960* (1989), which treats the established churches in their final decades of uncontested dominance. Martin E. Marty's ongoing multivolume survey, Modern American Religion, Volumes 1 and 2: The Irony of It All, 1893–1919 (1986), and *The Noise of Conflict, 1919–1941* (1991), provides brisk treatments of the main developments.

The best surveys of conservative Protestantism in twentieth-century America are by George Marsden: *Fundamentalism and American Culture: The Shaping of Twentieth-Century Evangelicalism, 1870–1925* (1980), and *Reforming Fundamentalism: Fuller Seminary and the New Evangelicalism* (1987). Nancy T. Ammerman's essay, "North American Protestant Fundamentalism," in Martin E. Marty and R. Scott Appleby, eds., *Fundamentalisms Observed* (1991), is also excellent. On Pentecostalism the literature is still thin, but a probing introduction is Grant Wacker's essay, "Pentecostalism," in Charles H. Lippy and Peter W. Williams, eds., *Encyclopedia of the American Religious Experience,* vol. 2 (1989).

Significant works on the current state of American Protestant religion include Roger Finke and Rodney Stark, *The Churching of America, 1776–1990: Winners and Losers in Our Religious Economy* (1992); James Davison Hunter, *Evangelicalism: The Coming Generation* (1987); Erling Jorstad, *Holding Fast/Pressing On: Religion in America in the 1980s* (1990); Robert Wuthnow, *The Restructuring of American Religion: Society and Faith Since World War II* (1990); Wade Clark Roof, *A Generation of Seekers* (1993); and Roof and William McKinney, *American Mainline Religion: Its Changing Shape and Future* (1987). Important statistical studies of Protestant belief in contemporary America are George Gallup, Jr., and Jim Castelli, *The People's Religion: American Faith in the 90's* (1989); and Andrew M. Greeley, *Religious Change in America* (1989).

On the development of liberal Protestantism in twentieth-century America, Robert Moats Miller, *Harry Emerson Fosdick* (1985), and Richard Wightman Fox, *Reinhold Niebuhr: A Biography* (1985), should be consulted. On the connection between liberalism and women's missionary work, see Patricia R. Hill, *The World Their Household: The American Woman's Foreign Mission Movement and Cultural Transformation, 1870–1920* (1985). The cresting of liberal Protestantism in the civil rights movement is well treated in Taylor Branch, *Parting the Waters: America in the King Years, 1954–1963* (1989). On the black church in general, C. Eric Lincoln and Lawrence Mamiya, *The Black Church in the African American Experience* (1990), is indispensable.

Liberation theology is well analyzed in Philip Berryman, *Liberation Theology* (1987); and feminist theology can be sampled in the work of one of its leading practitioners, Carter Heyward, *Touching Our Strength: The Erotic as Power and the Love of God* (1989). On postliberal theology, one can start with Stanley Hauerwas, *Character and the Christian Life* (1989); and George Lindbeck, *The Nature of Doctrine: Religion and Theology in a Post-Liberal Age* (1984). The continuing preoccupation of American Protestants with the question of civil religion and communal moral and religious norms is provocatively addressed in Robert Bellah et al., *Habits of the Heart: Individualism and Commitment in American Life* (1985); and Richard Neuhaus, *The Naked Public Square* (1984).

Probing studies of evangelical religion in twenti-eth-century America include Randall Balmer, *Mine Eyes Have Seen the Glory: A Journey into the Evangelical Subculture in America* (1989); Paul Boyer, *When Time Shall Be No More: Prophecy Belief in Modern American Culture* (1992); and David Edwin Harrell, Jr., *All Things Are Possible: The Healing and Charismatic Revivals in Modern America* (1975). A still engaging statement of evangelical faith is J. Gresham Machen, *Christianity and Liberalism* (1923, 1985). On the regional character of Protestant religion in the South, a valuable source is Samuel S. Hill, ed., *Varieties of Southern Religious Experience* (1988).

Among the many provocative general studies of Protestant religion in relation to twentieth-century American culture are Will Herberg, *Protestant, Catholic, Jew* (1955); George Armstrong Kelly, *Politics and Religious Consciousness in America* (1984); and Garry Wills, *Under God: Religion and American Politics* (1991).

# CATHOLICISM

*Patrick W. Carey*

During the twentieth century, Roman Catholicism in America gradually emerged from its parochial and ethnic centers into full participation in mainstream political and cultural life. Built on successive layers of immigration, it had to adapt not only to the New World's rapid accommodations to industrialization and urbanization but to the diversity of its multiethnic population. At the same time that it was becoming Americanized, it retained its basic structure and its communion with Rome.

At the beginning of the twentieth century, Roman Catholicism understood itself as a creedal, sacramental, and hierarchical tradition of Christianity that emphasized those elements that set it apart from Protestant Christianity. In its basic trinitarian beliefs, which it shared with most Protestants, it followed the Niceno-Constantinopolitan Creed (381 CE) that Catholics recited each time they celebrated the Eucharist. Unlike most Protestants, Catholics also accepted the dogmatic definitions of the church's twenty ecumenical councils (those from the first Council of Nicaea in 325 to the first Vatican Council of 1869–1870). Catholicism was sacramental not only in its belief that grace and salvation came to human beings through visible signs and symbolic actions but also in its acceptance of seven (rather than two as with most Protestants) sacraments of the church. Catholics asserted, furthermore, that their beliefs, practices, and ecclesial structures were grounded in the public revelation of God in Christ, communicated through a scripture and tradition that was authentically interpreted by the magisterium (i.e., teaching office) of the hierarchical church. Since the First Vatican Council, which defined papal primacy and infallibility, moreover, Catholics tended to emphasize the infallible teaching office of the pope when as head of the church he explicitly defined matters of faith and morals. The Catholic emphasis upon an ecclesiastical magisterium clearly separated Catholics from Protestants, who believed that the Bible alone was the authentic criterion of all Christian belief and practice.

In the United States, as in most countries where Catholics lived, the church was organized geographically into parishes, dioceses, and archdioceses. Parishes were of two types in the early twentieth century: the territorial parish, which was limited by geographical boundaries served by a pastor, and the national parish, which was created to serve a particular ethnic community and was not limited to strict geographical boundaries. Pastors served under the authority of a diocesan bishop and various diocesan bishops of a particular geographical territory like New York State were united together under an archbishop who had authority to convoke provincial synods for ecclesiastical legislation and discipline within an archdiocese.

National councils of bishops and archbishops met periodically during the nineteenth century to legislate for the church throughout the country. In the twentieth century the practice of conciliar legislation ceased to exist and was replaced after World War I with an annual meeting of the nation's bishops, a meeting that frequently produced pastoral letters and position papers on various ecclesiastical and civil matters.

Throughout the nineteenth and twentieth centuries, the American church was also served by over five hundred religious orders of men and women, such as Jesuits, Franciscans, Benedictines, and Dominicans, which created and staffed hundreds of parishes, parish schools, colleges, hospitals, orphanages, and other social institutions that served American Catholic peoples.

Although a small number of Catholics had settled in America prior to Independence—as early as 1776, there were 25,000 out of a population of 4.5 million—it was not until the 1830s and 1840s that large contingents of Irish and German Catholics began immigrating. They were followed by massive immigrations from southern and eastern Europe. By 1900, different sources estimate between 10.5 and 12 million Catholics, about 15 percent of the American population. By 1990, according to the *Official Catho-*

*lic Directory* the Catholic population had increased to 57 million, about 23 percent of the total U.S. population, and other surveys indicated that as many as 67 million Americans, or 26 percent of the population, identified themselves as Catholic.

The first twenty to thirty years of twentieth-century American Catholicism were a story of institution-building for the sake of ethnic and religious survival, internal and external ecclesiastical conflicts among various national forms of Catholic life and experience, and gradual Americanization of the new immigrants through the very institutions they established to preserve their identities. In addition to dissension from within as Irish Catholics criticized Italian Catholics, or German Catholics protested Polish Catholic practices and so on, Catholic rituals and beliefs such as confession and the cult of the saints were viewed as foreign and sometimes pagan by the predominant Protestant culture.

Continuing the immigrant tradition of the late nineteenth and early twentieth centuries, by the late twentieth century 20 percent of the American Catholic population was composed of recent Hispanic, Vietnamese, and other East Asian refugee immigrants. Yet the vast majority of American Catholics were socially, politically, and economically ensconced within the middle class and considerably removed from the immigrant matrix of their religious and cultural lives. The ecclesiastical reforms of the Second Vatican Council and the challenges of social and cultural transformations in American society during the 1960s brought about an intense struggle within the church to preserve its religious identity and continuity and to call into question practices and moral positions on such issues as contraception, abortion, and marriage in the priesthood that had previously been largely unchallenged within the church. Addressing these and other major issues of continuity and change remains the challenge for the twenty-first century.

## ETHNIC TRADITIONS IN THE CATHOLIC POPULATION

In 1900, Catholics constituted about 25 percent of the total population of the Northeast and 12 percent of the Midwest (see table 1 for figures on regions and populations). Before the waves of immigration in the 1880s and 1890s, Catholic immigrants had been predominantly Irish and German. By the 1900s, they had developed such institutional support systems as their own schools and foreign-language parishes (336 by 1900) that enabled them to preserve their religious and ethnic identities while they gradually adjusted to American ways.

Between 1900 and 1920, the Catholic community absorbed about 3.5 million new members: 1,077,000 from Italy; 858,000 from Poland; 792,000 from Austria-Hungary; 320,000 from Mexico; and only 80,000 and 46,500 from Ireland and Germany, respectively. Thus the urban dioceses and churches in particular were preoccupied during the first thirty years of the new century with building institutions and communities to accommodate these groups, in addition to Lithuanians, Czechs, Slovaks, Rusins (Ruthenians), Ukrainians, Magyars, Slovenes, Croatians, Spaniards, French, and others. Catholicism not only expanded significantly, but was transformed by the diversity of the new ethnic traditions. The new immigrants increased Catholicism's foreign cultural and religious character as they brought with them an entire new gallery of patron saints, styles of worship, piety, architecture, forms of institutional and organizational arrangements, and religious sensitivities.

New immigration was slowed significantly by World War I and especially by the immigrant restriction quotas of the 1920s. In 1921 and 1924 Congress created legislation that drastically reduced the quotas of immigrants. The 1924 legislation, for example, restricted the number of immigrants from southern

## Table 1.   GEOGRAPHICAL DISTRIBUTION OF CATHOLICS

| Region | 1900 | | 1990 | |
| --- | --- | --- | --- | --- |
| | Percent of all Catholics | Percent of Region's Population | Percent of all Catholics | Percent of Region's Population |
| Northeast | 50 | 25 | 37 | 38 |
| Midwest | 32 | 12 | 24 | 22 |
| South Central | 7.8 | 5.6 | 10.8 | 14 |
| Southeast | 3 | 4 | 5.7 | 7 |
| Pacific | 3 | 17 | 15 | 21 |
| Intermountain | 2 | 17 | 3 | 15 |

ᵃ The Intermountain region extends from Montana and Idaho to New Mexico and Arizona.

and eastern Europe to 2 percent of the number of its nationals who had resided in the United States at the time of the 1890 census. After World War II, and especially after 1960 when these severe congressional immigrant restrictions had been gradually diminished, however, the Catholic population significantly increased with new Hispanic immigration, and gradually increased with the numbers of Southeast Asians. By 1990, Gallup polls estimated that between 11 and 15 million American Catholics were of Hispanic descent, representing 16 to 20 percent of the Catholic population in the United States. Since many of the Hispanics tend to be younger than the rest of the Catholic population, their presence in American Catholicism will be decisive in the twenty-first century. Their numbers have undoubtedly made an impact on the geographical distribution of Catholicism, for although 37 percent of Catholics reside in the Northeast and 24 percent in the Midwest, the numbers in the South and West have increased due to migration from Mexico and Cuba (see table 1). By 1990, some dioceses and archdioceses were predominantly Hispanic, particularly in southern California and the Southwest. More than 63 percent of the Catholic population in the archdiocese of Miami was of Cuban descent or origins. New York, Chicago, Detroit, and Milwaukee also had significant numbers of Hispanic Catholics.

Like the Catholic immigrants of the nineteenth century, those of the first half of the twentieth century struggled to adjust to American economic, social, and political conditions, while preserving their language, culture, and the particularity of their religious and social traditions. They believed that "language saves faith" and used their native languages in their religious music, pious devotions, and in the confessional. Between l900 and 1940, the peak year for the development of ethnic institutions, the new immigrants built 1,769 foreign-language parishes, 1,043 parish schools, and numerous other ethnic-based organizations to preserve their religious and ethnic solidarity, thereby separating themselves from their English-speaking Protestant and Catholic neighbors and from their fellow Catholics of other nationalities. Implicit in the construction of these institutions was the belief that one need not totally assimilate Anglo culture to be an American, nor accept a single cultural expression of the faith to be Catholic.

Although many first-generation immigrants resisted rapid Americanization, their children and grandchildren would gradually become Americanized through the very institutions they had established

to perpetuate their own cultures. The insistence on preserving their own traditions, however, enabled them to integrate into American society on their own ethnic and Catholic terms. Thus the immigrants were able to make a cultural contribution to American and Catholic life, enriching both. After 1940, as the second and third generations of the new immigrants became increasingly Americanized and moved to the suburbs, the number of ethnic parishes declined, following the pattern established in the older German Catholic communities.

Behind these developments of ethnic religious and cultural institutions was a perspective on religion at odds with certain elements of modernity that the new immigrants found in American society. For many immigrants, religion was communal, concretely cultural, and emotional; it was not predominantly individual, private, intellectual, abstract, and completely voluntary as in some American Protestant and Americanized Catholic religious institutions. Religion was supposed to be an integral part of one's total life. Attempts to maintain Old World institutional practices of local autonomy and/or folk forms of Catholicism periodically clashed with the aims of American church leaders and the sensitivities of Americanized Catholics who had developed voluntary patterns of religious life.

The 1.6 million Italian Catholics, for example, who came to and remained in the United States between 1880 and 1920 brought with them peasant forms of Catholicism (syncretic forms of Catholic belief and ancient pagan practices) and a generally opulent and ostentatious integration of religion and everyday life (which was particularly manifested in the annual festa to the Madonna or some particular saint) that Irish and other Americanized Catholics criticized as insufficiently Catholic at best or pagan at worst. Unlike the Irish, Italian Catholics had little emotional attachment to the clergy or the institutional church, preferring their own folk forms of religion; furthermore, unlike many other immigrant groups, they brought few priests with them, providing problems for the development of Italian religious solidarity. They had no prior experience of contributing financially to the church, as had the Irish. And many Italians were "birds of passage," with every intention of returning to Italy once they had made their fortunes. These differences provoked conflicts within the American Catholic church, and hostilities between Italians and the Americanized or Irish Catholics continued until World War II in many urban areas. Gradually, though, the Italians became Americanized and a large percentage identified with the institutional church through their ethnic parishes and organizations.

Internal and external conflicts marked the Polish Catholic experience in the early twentieth century. From 1880 to 1920, 1.1 million Polish Catholics settled in the United States. The Polish had their own forms of folk Catholicism, but unlike Italians they sought full representation and participation in the institutional church and brought with them a proportionate number of parish clergy, women religious (i.e., members of women's religious orders and congregations; nuns and sisters), and religious-order priests to provide for a continuity of religious and ethnic solidarity. Like earlier German immigrants the Polish leadership called for representation in the hierarchy and for respect for their own religious traditions. Americanized bishops, whether of Irish or German descent, resisted Polish attempts to gain representation because they feared an ecclesiastical nationalism that would break the bonds of unity they had been trying to create since the middle of the nineteenth century. A number of so-called Polish church wars erupted in the late 1890s and early 1900s over the Polish desire for local lay control over parishes. In a few parishes in Pennsylvania, Illinois, Michigan, and Wisconsin, among other places, the ecclesiastical schisms eventually produced a new, independent denomination, the National Polish Catholic Church, reflecting the serious tensions resulting from the clash of different cultural and institutional forms of Catholicism.

Eastern rite Catholic Rusins or Ruthenians—a Slavic people from southern Russia, Galicia and Bukowina in Austria, and northeastern Hungary—in Minneapolis and Saint Paul, too, clashed with their archbishop, John Ireland, over local parish autonomy and their pastor's right to marry, which was a part of Eastern rite discipline. The archbishop's inability to accept the diversity of Catholic rites and practices and the Rusins' resistance to episcopal authority eventually created another schism within the Church. Rather than bow to the authority of the local bishop, the Rusins left Catholicism and joined the Russian Orthodox Church.

Perhaps one thing that the new immigrants and Americanized Catholics had in common was a resistance to accepting African American Catholics into their midst. In the late eighteenth century, African American slaves comprised about 20 percent of the total Catholic population (15,000) in Maryland. Since then, however, they have constituted only an extremely small portion of the Catholic population, which has always had a numerically insignificant presence in the Deep South, where, until the early twentieth century, almost 90 percent of African Americans lived. In the early 1900s, it was estimated that there were about 200,000 African American Catholics in the United States, located primarily in Maryland and the south central region of the country. By 1928, there were 121 parishes (and thirty-five to fifty mission stations) exclusively for African American Catholics throughout the United States. It was prejudice as much as geographical distribution, however, that prevented African American Catholics from enrolling in Catholic seminaries (and other Catholic schools) in the early 1900s. The lack of a significant number of African American Catholic clergy before World War II restricted their representation in the church; after World War II, that increased rapidly when they moved in large numbers to urban areas where Catholics were concentrated and schools and institutions were desegregated, either by law or voluntarily. By 1990, about 2 million African Americans constituted more than 3 percent of the total Catholic population.

During the first years of the twentieth century a host of local ethnic, black, and fraternal societies and professional organizations began to band together into national institutions to make visible their religious solidarity and to address issues of social justice and ecclesiastical life of the Progressive Era.

## PROGRESSIVE-ERA CONSOLIDATION

In the midst of, and perhaps as a result of, massive immigrations during the late nineteenth century a major battle had erupted within American Catholicism over the degree to which the church could or should be accommodated to American ways. That ecclesiastical controversy came to an end in 1899, when Pope Leo XIII's encyclical *Testem Benevolentiae* condemned what he and other Europeans called the heresy of Americanism, that is, a set of three heterodox tendencies: an excessive accommodationism, a spirit of religious subjectivism, and a new form of ecclesiastical localism. He feared in particular that some in the American church wanted a national church that was different from the church of Rome. The encyclical pleased conservatives within the hierarchy because they believed that there were in fact dangerous tendencies of capitulation within American Catholicism that needed to be checked. It cooled the liberals' campaign to develop and export an American-style Catholicism and it frustrated them because they saw the papal charges as creations of misguided Europeans who did not understand the dynamics of American and Catholic life. The condemnation influenced the direction of the hierarchy in their theoretical approach to Americanization, but the episcopal and clerical use of American means and methods for maintaining and propagating the Catholic tradition necessarily involved the Catholic church in the historical forces that led intentionally and unintentionally toward greater and greater degrees of Americanization during the twentieth century.

After the encyclical, Americanization was evident first of all in various Catholic appropriations of the Progressive Era's search for order and its propensity toward consolidation. The National Catholic efforts toward ecclesiastical centralization, however, were as Roman as they were American during the early twentieth century. Ever since the definition of papal infallibility in 1870, Rome had called for greater and greater Roman centralization in the administration of ecclesiastical affairs. In the United States, the Catholic movement toward ecclesiastical consolidation was manifested in the national confederation of local ethnic, black, and fraternal societies, in the creation of new professional organizations, in the rise of big city managerial bishops, and in the establishment of a national coordinating office for the American Catholic hierarchy. The organizations of the American Federation of Catholic Societies (1901, a union of various ethnic, but in fact primarily Irish and German, benevolent and mutual-aid societies), the Catholic Education Association (1904), the National Conference of Catholic Charities (1910), the Catholic Press Association (1911), the Catholic Hospital Association (1915), the Federated Colored Catholics of the United States (1917), the national Catholic War Council (1917, in 1919 changed to Welfare Conference), and the American Catholic Historical Association (1919) created a national sense of Catholic solidarity and purpose among middle-class laity and clergy in responding to social and professional issues that demanded nationally organized movements.

Many of the new organizations adopted a characteristically modern principle of professional associationism in their attempts to improve performance, develop intercommunication, and provide a means for nationally coordinated activities, and reflected a new Catholic progressivism. Middle-class Catholic lay leaders, clerical professors, and pioneer labor priests sought to reinforce the Christian fabric of American society by combining a perspective on social justice and the common good derived from the encyclicals of Leo XIII with progressive moral, social, and legislative reforms.

In the realm of intellectual life, Progressive-minded labor clergy like Peter Dietz, professional sociologists like Father William Kerby of the Catholic University, and social theorists and ethicists like John A. Ryan of Saint Paul also engaged some working-class Catholics as well as intellectuals in various social reform movements and thinking—particularly in the area of a just distribution of economic goods. Combining the natural law tradition of Pope Leo XIII's encyclical on the conditions of labor, *Rerum Novarum* (1891), and the scientific analysis of sociology and economics, Kerby and Ryan in particular developed a Catholic perspective on the structural social ills in American society, a Catholic vision on the goals of social reforms, and programs for the implementation of such a vision. Ryan's "Program of Social Reconstruction," which the national hierarchy adopted as its own in 1919, was the most significant form of Catholic progressivism, advocating a more equitable distribution of economic benefits in American society.

Within large urban dioceses, the first half of the twentieth century witnessed the rise and development of a new episcopal style that was Roman and antimodernist in its intellectual orientation, American in its loyalties to the country's progressive constitutional values, and modernist in its consolidating administrative practices. Like corporate leaders in American big business, big labor, and big government, these big-city bishops, as Edward R. Kantowicz has argued in *Corporation Sole,* "brought order, centralization, and businesslike administration to their previously chaotic dioceses." Using standards of efficiency, rational control, and pragmatic effect that were characteristic signs of modernity and the rising corporate structures in American society, the bishops tried to standardize all parish and diocesan matters and bring various diocesan institutions under the administrative regulation of new diocesan bureaucratic offices, establishing control over the previously ethnically based and semiautonomous parishes and other local ecclesiastical structures.

These new corporate executive bishops were highly visible in their leadership styles, bringing a new respect to the American church. Building big institutions, staging massive public ceremonies, hiring prestigious first-class legal firms, consulting with successful business managers while cultivating their friendship, using the publicity gimmicks of Madison Avenue advertising firms to raise money to finance their building campaigns were all tactics employed by these bishops to create an image of the church that was both Catholic and American. New bishops like William O'Connell of Boston, George William Mundelein of Chicago, John Farley of New York, and John Joseph Glennon of Saint Louis also worked diligently to Americanize the immigrants through schools, hospitals, pious confraternities, and diocesan building campaigns. When they died, they received national media attention rarely accorded their nineteenth-century predecessors.

The episcopal vision and practical implementation of diocesan consolidation, centralization, and control was as American as it was Roman in the early twentieth century, but it was not always realized in fact. These big-city bishops often did not have the power or charisma to fulfill their episcopal designs and authority. Throughout the twentieth century, they confronted currents of localism and local control over large segments of Catholic life. The persistence of ethnic traditions and of the local autonomy of strong-willed pastors, college presidents, superiors of women religious, hospital administrators, and social-agency leaders periodically frustrated the episcopal will and at times made the centralizing tendencies ineffective and practically impotent.

During World War I, the American bishops consolidated various national Catholic societies and fraternities in a new episcopally supervised national institution, the National Catholic War Council (NCWC). The NCWC attempted to coordinate Catholic responses to the American war effort and to develop a united national Catholic voice—similar to the Protestants' Federal (later National) Council of Churches of Christ (1908)—one capable of asserting Catholic interests in public life. After the war, the bishops organized the National Catholic Welfare Council (1919) as a more permanent national episcopal body to assist in the postwar reconstruction of American society, to meet the ongoing needs of American Catholicism at the national level, to serve as a watchdog over federal programs and legislation that affected Catholic interests, and to provide organized lobbying efforts in the United States Congress.

Although by the year 1920 American Catholicism showed a few signs of emerging into national public life, it was still a predominantly immigrant institution that lacked any significant impact on American cultural and political institutions. In the next twenty-five years increasing numbers of Catholics would become active participants in the political and cultural areas while simultaneously feeling some sense of alienation from the culture.

## FROM ALIENATION TO ACTIVISM, 1920 TO 1945

By the early 1920s, American Catholics were confident that they were an essential part of the American experience. The cultural and social changes associated with the "roaring twenties," the Depression of the 1930s, and the development of totalitarianism and religious intolerance in Russia, Mexico, Spain, and Germany, however, made Catholics aware of their continued alienation from aspects of modern American life. Conflicts of the 1920s, including the struggle over the justification of Prohibition, the new immigrant restriction quotas of 1921 and 1924, the Scopes trial of 1925, the Oregon legislative attempt to eliminate private and parochial schools in 1925, and Alfred E. Smith's political defeat in 1928, reinforced the fact that the United States was still predominantly white Anglo-Saxon and Protestant in its culture, and that Catholics had to struggle to define themselves in terms that preserved their religious identity. Whether Catholics faced opposition from the general xenophobia of the Ku Klux Klan and other nativist groups, as they did in Oregon's legislation to prohibit parochial schools, or from the secular and Protestant presses, as they did in the 1928 presidential campaign, they were reminded that their schools were un-American, that their minds were enslaved (because subject to authority) and at war with the modern, liberated mind, and that their church-state positions were antithetical to American constitutional provisions for religious liberty and separation of church and state. Catholicism was perceived by many as alien to American liberties and dangerous to domestic peace. These charges intensified a Catholic sense of alienation from American culture, but simultaneously stimulated a Catholic crusade to Christianize culture.

In the midst of these experiences of alienation, Catholics initiated a major revival of Catholic life that was manifested in an organized intellectual retrieval of the thought of Thomas Aquinas, a movement to reform liturgical life, new forms of social activism, more widespread participation in American political life, and more active concern for issues of international politics that affected Catholic interests. These movements aimed, as Arnold Sparr has demonstrated, to promote Catholicism, defend it from its detractors, and to redeem an increasingly secularized culture. Many of the new initiatives shared the view that Catholicism itself could become the primary agent in the modern world for the restoration and maintenance of a "Christian civilization," as the 1919 episcopal pastoral argued, because it had an inner strength, a belief in the supernatural reality of divine revelation, an emphasis upon the dignity of human nature with the concomitant stress upon the value of the human person and reasonable liberty, and a confidence in the powers of reason. Although Catholic leaders manifested a new confidence, they also revealed continued anxieties about the loss of Catholic identity in the process of Americanization and in the progress of secularization.

The self-conscious revival was evident in the publication of *Commonweal* (1924– ), an independent lay periodical that endeavored to promote Catholic commentary and reflection on American cultural and political developments, and in an organized intellectual return to Thomism that was manifested in the establishment of the *Modern Schoolman* (1925– ), the first *ex-professo* neo-scholastic journal in the English-speaking world, *Thought* (1926– ), *The New Scholasticism* (1927– ), the *Thomist* (1939– ), and the American Catholic Philosophical Society (1926– ). By the end of the 1920s, a self-conscious philosophical movement was well organized and underway. Thereafter various forms of neo-Thomism, all seeking intellectual order, captured the world of articulate American Catholics and became institutionalized in the large number of Catholic colleges and universities between the 1930s and the 1960s.

The liturgical movement was another major Catholic revival of the 1920s. It sought to combat the twin evils of individualism and totalitarian socialism in American society and to emphasize the personal and social integrity along with the unity of the Catholic tradition as it was available in the church's public worship. The liturgical movement, organized by Virgil Michel, a Benedictine monk of St. John's Abbey in Collegeville, Minnesota, sought to restore the concept of the Mystical Body of Christ as the central Catholic doctrine that simultaneously upheld the dignity and worth of the human person and the communal context of all reality, the sense of spiritual interiority, organic communion, and the priesthood of all believers—dimensions that had been diminished by an individualism that was characteristic of Catholic devotional piety as well as the modern mind. The key indigenous element of the American Catholic liturgical movement was its association of public liturgy and social justice, that is, the belief that the liturgy raised social consciousness to motivate Catholics to work for social justice in the world.

Throughout the 1920s and 1930s, moreover, various forms of social Catholicism developed in response to a renewed emphasis Pope Leo XIII's *Rerum Novarum* (1891) and Pope Pius XI's *Quadragesimo Anno* (1931) placed upon social justice and the Catholic responsibility to transform the world. Thomas Wyatt Turner, a Catholic African American biologist at Howard University, organized the Committee against the Extension of Race Prejudice in the Church in 1917 (which became the Federated Colored Catholics of the United States in 1925). Stressing African American solidarity in the church and calling upon the hierarchy to eliminate race prejudice and segregation of Catholic institutions, Turner's minority movement succeeded in providing a forum for African American Catholics to articulate their concerns until 1958 when loss of membership ended the movement. In 1933, two white Jesuit participants, John LaFarge and William Markoe, split the movement and transformed it by stressing interracial justice over racial solidarity. These two transitional movements were signs of the rising African American Catholic consciousness that had its origins under Daniel Rudd in the late-nineteenth-century African American Catholic lay congresses and would be succeeded in the late 1950s and throughout the 1960s by various Catholic clerical and lay African American civil and ecclesiastical rights movements.

The Great Depression reawakened the Catholic sense of economic justice, stimulating new proposals and movements. Under the leadership of John A. Ryan, the NCWC's Social Action Department continued to articulate the national Catholic perspectives on justice in the marketplace. Robert Lucey, as a priest in Los Angeles and as a bishop in Amarillo and San Antonio, advocated for a just wage, especially for Mexican Americans in the Southwest. Young clerical "labor priests" like Peter Dietz and Francis Haas supported and tried to Christianize the labor unions. Lay social activists Dorothy Day and Peter Maurin of the Catholic Worker movement developed a form of Catholic personalism that was institutionalized in numerous houses of hospitality across the country and that influenced a whole generation of young Catholics who became the foundation of what Mel Piehl has called Catholic radicalism. The liturgical movement and the German Central Verein continued to emphasize its social solidarism. Father Charles Coughlin of Detroit became a forceful and severe social critic and populist polemicist through the new medium of the radio. The Jesuits developed a number of schools of social service for training social workers in the principles and practices of justice. And the National Rural Life Conference became an advocate of rural values and challenged the government's agricultural policies. Although these individuals and movements differed among themselves in selectively appropriating principles from the papal encyclicals and in adapting them to the American economic order, they shared a common search for a middle ground between laissez-faire capitalism and socialism, upholding simultaneously individual rights and concern for the common good in the industrial order.

During the early part of the twentieth century, moreover, Catholics became increasingly involved in national and international politics, and by the end of World War II they had moved into significant positions of influence in the federal government and national politics. Since the late nineteenth century, Americanized Catholics, especially the Irish, had been increasingly involved in large urban and state political machines and had won numerous elective offices. Franklin Delano Roosevelt, moreover, acknowledged the growing political significance of the Catholic vote and as president placed such prominent Catholics as James A. Farley, Thomas Corcoran, Joseph Kennedy, and Father Francis Haas in key administrative positions, appointed Frank Murphy to the United States Supreme Court, and generally courted Catholic favor. On the other hand, such prominent ecclesiastical leaders as John A. Ryan, Archbishop Robert Lucey, and Cardinal George William Mundelein accepted much of the New Deal legislation and presented it to Catholics as American implementations of the papal social encyclicals. Catholics voted in large majorities to support Roosevelt's four terms, and their votes, as some studies have indicated, were 27 to 31 percent higher than Protestant votes for FDR. The New Deal years raised Catholics to a new level of political influence which indicated a transformation of the American political attitude toward the church as well as of the church's disposition toward the government.

Catholics also emerged into the arena of international politics during the 1920s and 1930s. Articulate lay and clerical leaders as well as a host of Catholic pious practices protested against international communism, European fascism, and the Mexican persecution of the church. New developments on the international political scene reinforced Catholic fears about the disintegration of Western Christian culture, but the Catholic community, though it had increasing political clout, did not mount a political campaign to influence American foreign policy in those countries where they believed Catholic rights in particular were being violated. Political divisions within the Catholic community and a long-standing self-imposed American prohibition against the church's involvement in politics prevented any specifically Catholic political activities. Catholics were divided among themselves on whether communism or fascism represented the greater threat, but they were united in their view that the political, like the economic, order should steer a middle path between secular individualism and totalitarianism, whether communist or fascist.

Literary campaigns against religious persecutions in Russia, Mexico, Spain, and Germany were motivated by Catholic self-interests but also by an American sense of justice and religious liberty. The struggles against these persecutions reinforced Catholic support for the American constitutional order and laid a solid foundation for an international perspective in the Catholic community that had been developing since the days of Americanism, demonstrating that Catholic concerns were not solely parochial. But, the protests also revealed that distinctive Catholic international interests were not widely shared in the American political community, thus reinforcing the minority status of their own concerns.

The Catholic struggle against socialism and communism as ideological and historical forces antithetical to Christianity was rooted in papal teachings from Pius IX's *Qui Pluribus* (1846) to Pius XI's *Divini Redemptoris* (1937). Whether influenced more by the apocalyptic or by the social justice dimensions of the papal opposition, most Catholics were decidedly anticommunists long before the campaigns of the Joseph McCarthy era. A number of published books and pamphlets, national episcopal statements, Sunday sermons, and forms of Catholic piety were oriented to the divine overthrow of diabolical communism. The 1917 Marian apparitions at Fatima, Portugal, had fostered, among other things, the practice of praying the rosary for world peace and for the consecration of Russia to Mary's immaculate heart. Marian devotions, which had been revived and had multiplied during the middle of the nineteenth century, became by 1920 clearly associated with anticommunism and the conversion of Russia. New Marian pious societies (e.g., the Blue Army of Mary, Legion of Mary, the Militia of the Immaculate Conception) were also organized during the 1920s and 1930s and became a significant part of the popular anticommunist Catholic culture. In 1930, moreover, Pius XI officially sanctioned prayers to be recited after Mass for the conversion of Russia. By 1940, Catholics, whether Americanized or in ethnic communities, had developed a tradition of anticommunism that was integrated into their literature, pious practices, and official liturgical celebrations.

Not all Catholic anticommunists were motivated

by the apocalyptic religious crusade. Some (e.g., the Catholic Workers, the *Commonweal* Catholics, John A. Ryan and other social theorists, Father Francis Haas, and Bishop Robert Lucey of Amarillo) saw the communist critique of unrestrained and individualistic capitalism as valid but sought to combat the appeal of that critique by promoting alternative Christian visions and practices of social justice. These two forms of Catholic anticommunism, the religious crusade and the social justice crusade, would continue throughout the 1950s.

Liberals in the American press, American communists, and a host of other Americans interpreted American Catholic opposition to communism in Russia, Mexico, and especially in Spain either as hysteria or as a Catholic preference for fascist regimes. No doubt some American Catholics, like Father Charles Coughlin and Patrick Scanlan, the editor of the Brooklyn *Tablet,* provided substance for such a charge. And, indeed, Catholic opposition to communism did not always take into account the deplorable unjust social conditions that gave rise to communism in the first place. For more perceptive Catholics like Father Fulton Sheen, however, fascism was only the logical and historical consequence of communism and both ideological systems were totalitarian in their denials of human liberties and their idolatry of the state or the classless society. Catholics like Sheen, moreover, saw their anticommunism as a form of democratic Americanism, but the identification of anticommunism and Americanism would not become a significant part of the larger American culture until the post–World War II era.

During the Spanish Civil War, American Catholics were united in their opposition to the Popular Front's anticlerical and hostile attacks upon the Spanish church, but they were divided among themselves on the means to preserve the church and its institutions and on their support for opposing sides in the war. A 1938 poll revealed that 39 percent of Catholics favored Franco, 30 percent were pro-Loyalist and 31 percent were neutral. Many, perhaps most of the American bishops, most of the diocesan newspapers, and many of the leading Catholic journals of public opinion were pro-Franco, viewing Franco as the strongest support for religion and Catholicism. Dorothy Day, *The Catholic Worker, Commonweal* (after 1937), and a minority of other Catholics protested against Franco's fascism because for them Franco was as totalitarian and ruthless as the Popular Front. These American Catholics protested that support for religious liberty for Spanish Catholics should be closely tied to equally adamant support for social justice in

Spain, and they did not believe that Franco would bring about the social reforms necessary to restore peace and justice in Spain. For consistent pacifists like Day, moreover, the church should condemn violence on all sides and not identify itself with military means to win the peace.

Support for Benito Mussolini and Italian fascism, too, was somewhat divided in the Catholic community, although there appears to have been more support for Mussolini than for Franco. A 1937 opinion poll demonstrated that when given the hypothetical option of choosing between fascism and communism, 61 percent of all Americans favored fascism. A similar poll in 1939, however, showed that that support had fallen to 54 percent, but 66 percent of Catholics in the survey favored fascism over communism. Most Catholic journals of public opinion favored Mussolini and Italian fascism because they saw Mussolini as a pragmatic supporter of Catholicism and a forceful opponent of atheistic communism. Francis Duffy, James Cox, John A. Ryan, and especially the Paulist James Gillis, editor of the *Catholic World,* however, opposed Mussolini and Italian fascism because they rejected his assault upon political liberties and his violent undemocratic procedures. After Pope Pius XI's encyclical *Non abbiamo bisogno* (1931)—an attack upon fascist "statolatry" and fascist assaults upon Catholic Action in Italy—James Gillis charged that American Catholic journals had "soft pedaled" the encyclical and had been blind to fascist injustices and totalitarianism. But the American Catholic opposition to Italian fascism was not as widespread as was the support.

By 1936, the focus of Catholic attention shifted away from Russia, Mexico, and Spain toward Adolf Hitler and German National Socialism. A papal concordat with Nazi Germany in 1933 justified Catholic support for the Third Reich, but violations of the concordat and papal protests in 1935 and Pope Pius XI's *Mit brennender Sorge* (1937), condemning persecutions of Catholics and the Nazi divinization of race, awakened American Catholic opposition to the Reich's denials of religious liberties for Catholics and of basic human rights. The Knights of Columbus in 1938, Bishop Robert Lucey in 1940, the national American hierarchy in 1941, and a few isolated individuals throughout the late 1930s and early 1940s also protested against the inhuman Nazi treatment of the Jewish people, but those voices were not heeded within the general American Catholic community. The popular anti-Semitic demagoguery of Father Charles Coughlin in the late 1930s muffled the effectiveness of any protests.

Despite their growing interests in international affairs during the 1920s and 1930s, American Catholics, like many other Americans, remained isolationists even in view of Hitler's rising power, ambitious designs, and military aggression toward Poland, Czechoslovakia, and Austria. Once Pearl Harbor was bombed in 1941, however, isolationism quickly dissipated. Except for Dorothy Day and some of the pacifists at the *Catholic Worker*, most Catholics united with President Roosevelt in the war with Nazi Germany and the Axis forces. Although more restrained than in the support they gave during World War I, the American bishops placed Catholic institutions and personnel at the President's disposal for service to the country.

Catholic participation in the war manifested patriotism, laid the foundation for a postwar internationalism within American Catholicism, and completed the process of Americanizing the new immigrants. For many Catholics, participation in the war was also the culmination of the previous two decades of Catholic literary and philosophical assault upon totalitarianism (whether in its fascist or communist forms) and another demonstration that fundamental American beliefs and ideals were consistent with the Catholic struggle against the diabolic forces that were tearing asunder the fabric of Western Christian culture. Although a few Catholics protested against the barbaric force of the atom bomb and earlier indiscriminate bombings of European cities to win the war, most celebrated the victory and the survival of Christian culture. But the postwar settlements with communist Russia made Catholics extremely anxious and skeptical about the possibilities of a lasting world peace.

## COLD WAR CATHOLICISM, 1945–1965

The twenty-year period after World War II was one of unprecedented economic growth in the United States, worldwide American economic and political influence, and a statistical resurgence of religious activity in the midst of Cold War anxieties over communism. Like many other religious denominations American Catholicism took advantage of the expanding wealth and built new churches, schools, and other large religious institutions—some of which had been delayed during the previous fifteen years by the Depression and the war. Many Catholics, especially the national hierarchy, were convinced that their numerical strength and growing affluence gave them an exceptional opportunity for moral leadership in American society, but some other Americans perceived the increasing Catholic moral crusades as fundamental threats to American democratic liberties. Although confident, institutionally and numerically strong, and active in promoting an American Christian culture, Catholics were also coming out of their ethnic enclaves, moving rapidly up the social and economic ladder of success, engaging each other in internal ideological battles, and calling for some moderate reforms in American Catholic attitudes and practices. The postwar years began with Catholic anxieties about the twin evils of worldwide communism and secularism, and ended with a confidence that Catholicism had finally made it in American society and in the world community with President John Fitzgerald Kennedy's election and Pope John XXIII's ecumenical council.

Between 1945 and 1965, American Catholicism experienced phenomenal growth, unmatched during the previous twenty years and not repeated after 1965. The total Catholic population increased by 90 percent, from 23.9 million in 1945 to 45.6 million in 1965. The number of bishops and archbishops increased by 58 percent, clergy by 52 percent, women religious by 30 percent, and seminarians by 127 percent. As enrollments in Catholic elementary and secondary schools increased by 3.1 million (more than 120 percent), and—primarily because of the GI bill—in Catholic colleges and universities by a whopping 300 percent, 3,005 new Catholic elementary and high schools, and 94 new colleges were built. Although the schools expanded rapidly to meet the increasing Catholic population, still they enrolled perhaps no more than 50 percent of Catholic youth in primary and secondary education and a significantly smaller percentage in higher education. American Catholics also contributed, through Catholic Relief Services and the Society for the Propagation of the Faith, over $1.35 billion to aid the world's poor and to support missionary activity around the world. This growth and the tremendous financial outlay manifested something not only of the nation's prosperity but also of the general American support for religion and voluntary social services.

The national episcopal pastorals in the postwar period focused Catholic attention upon building up a Christian culture and civilization in the United States and the Western world—a task made particularly urgent by the rapidly rising forces of secularism and worldwide communism. Secularism, the "practical exclusion of God from human thinking and living," the bishops wrote in 1947, accounted for the rise of fascism, Nazism, and communism. Secularism, and its virulent manifestation in worldwide communism, was evident, the bishops repeatedly charged, in the family (where divorce, birth control, and economic injustices threatened to destroy its unity and stability), the entertainment industry (where materialistic values and sexual promiscuity were being promoted), education (which was increasingly divorced from religious and Christian values), the economic order (where either laissez-faire capitalism or totalitarian socialism were destroying the individual's and the family's rights to decent and frugal living), American courts (where religion was being radically separated from the educational institutions of American culture), and the political order (where individual rights were being smashed by totalitarian communism or where political and legal enactments were divorced from fundamental human and Christian values). These threats were a "menace to our Christian and American way of living," the bishops charged in their 1948 pastoral. The connection between Christianity and America was in the realm of fundamental values, not in the realm of the historical and current practices, but the connection itself revealed how closely the bishops had identified the two.

During the postwar period, American Catholics fostered a number of old and new institutions to maintain a Christian culture in America. To promote successful Christian marriages and wholesome Catholic homes, the NCWC established the Family Life Bureau (1931), Chicago Catholics developed the Cana Conference (1943) and the Christian Family Movement (1945) spread across the country. Catholics also mounted a moral crusade against indecency and immorality, particularly in the entertainment industry and in modern literature. In 1934, the American bishops had established the Legion of Decency to provide Catholics with moral ratings of movies; annually during a Sunday mass active Catholics took a pledge of decency to avoid prohibited movies. Many big-city bishops, too, saw themselves as moral watchdogs, periodically condemning movies, forbidding Catholics under pain of sin from seeing them, and calling for boycotts of theaters which showed them. These and other forms of censorship had as their positive aim the promotion of Christian civilization, but the aggressive and authoritarian tactics that were sometimes used seriously discredited this manifestation of "Catholic Action" in the eyes of some non-Catholics and a few articulate Catholic leaders.

The struggle against secularism came out most forcefully in the battles over education. According to many Catholic leaders, prevailing philosophies of education, debates over federal aid to education, and Supreme Court decisions revealed an increasing secularization of modern American education from the primary to the university levels. Numerous Catholic educators believed that John Dewey's pragmatic secularism had influenced generations of public school teachers and created a threat to the Christian cultural education of America's youth. National episcopal pastorals in 1944 and 1955, moreover, tried to tie federal aid to education (for health, safety, and welfare) to all needy children without regard to color, origin, or creed, and, to be equitable, to children in any school that met the requirements of compulsory education.

The continuing highly visible participation of the institutional church in American cultural affairs, the aggressive episcopal appeals for aid, and the Supreme Court decision in *Everson* v. *Board of Education* (1947), allowing New Jersey to use tax funds to pay for bus transportation of children attending Catholic schools, provoked the establishment in 1948 of Protestants and Other Americans United for the Separation of Church and State (POAU) and the publication of Paul Blanshard's *American Freedom and Catholic Power* (1949). What some Catholics saw as an attempt to influence and Christianize culture, others like POAU and Blanshard interpreted as manifestations of traditional Catholic control over culture and as fundamental threats to the American constitutional separation of church and state.

Criticisms by POAU and Blanshard of the political and cultural aggressiveness of Catholicism and the Supreme Court's increasingly secularist interpretations of the First Amendment (making separation of church and state an absolute and reducing religious influence to the privacy of individual conscience and irrelevance in public life) intensified the split between Catholics and some Protestants. It provoked serious questions about the relationship of the Catholic church to the state and American society that demanded more intellectual response than had been previously provided. The postwar question of the church's proper role in society also arose from a new perception of the need for intercreedal cooperation to rebuild war-torn Europe and to work together for the common good in American society. Such cooperation, however, was hardly possible given the great suspicion many had about Catholic understanding of church-state relations and Catholic totalitarian designs on culture. Out of these experiences of conflict over aggressive forms of Catholic action, of the need for intercreedal cooperation, and of the Catholic desire to counter cultural secularism would come a new intellectual struggle to define more adequately the Catholic understanding of church-state relations and to stimulate deeper Catholic reflection on the mode of the church's influence in the public forum.

In response to new postwar conditions, John Courtney Murray, S.J., took up the challenge to rethink Catholic understanding of the church-state issue. The problem he faced was compounded by nineteenth- and early-twentieth-century papal teachings which held that church and state, although distinct and separate in their ends, belonged ideally in some kind of harmonious institutional union—a view contrary to Western political consciousness and institutional developments of the past two centuries, and one that explicitly denied the value of constitutional religious liberty and separation of church and state. Murray's investigations of historical Catholic sources on church-state issues and of Western and American constitutional philosophy and developments led him to develop a Catholic understanding of religious liberty and church-state separation as morally justifiable on the grounds that it served the public good, the ultimate end of good law. This position, moreover, he considered to be consistent with the development of the Catholic tradition itself.

Murray also constructed an American interpretation of the First Amendment that challenged the secularist perspective, upholding simultaneously religious liberty, the historical manifestation of it in separation of church and state, the principle of the superiority of the spiritual to the temporal, and the responsibility of Catholics and other religious persons and communities to exercise some influence upon the nation's public life. Religious liberty and separation for him did not mean the privatization of religion, nor were they matters of religious dogma; they were articles of civil peace and harmony, grounded in the natural moral law.

Murray's support for American constitutional arrangements and his criticisms of some of the traditional Catholic views on the ideal relationship between church and state were condemned in the United States by Joseph Clifford Fenton and Francis J. Connell, C.SS.R., Catholic theologians at the Catholic University of America, and by Cardinal Alfredo Ottaviani, head of the Roman congregation responsible for overseeing Catholic doctrine. Murray's position became so controversial that his Roman Jesuit superiors silenced him in 1954. More open circumstances in church during the late 1950s, shortly after Pope John XXIII announced the Second Vatican Council and during the presidential campaign of 1960, gave Murray the opportunity to publish *We Hold These Truths,* a collection of essays on his understanding of religious liberty and his advocacy of

an American dialogue on the moral issues facing society. Murray eventually contributed to the writing of the Council's declaration on religious liberty *Dignitatis Humanae* (1965), vindicating his preconciliar positions and pushing the universal church into an acknowledgement of religious liberty. In the post–Vatican II period other American Catholics would take up and develop a Catholic understanding of the church's proper role in the democratic public forum.

With the exception of John C. Murray, postwar Catholic scholarship was fairly arid. In 1955, Msgr. John Tracy Ellis, historian at the Catholic University of America, published a widely read and influential critique of American Catholic intellectual life. He argued that the immigrant condition of American Catholicism, among other things, had been, but could no longer be, responsible for intellectual narrowness and even anti-intellectualism in American Catholic higher education. By 1962, during the Second Vatican Council, the nation's bishops reiterated in their pastoral of that year the same complaint, acknowledging that despite tremendous growth and prosperity the American Catholic church could not boast of numerous saints, profound scholars, and brilliant writers—a charge that outsiders had been making for years.

Catholic colleges and universities, as well as Catholic primary and secondary schools, were conceived of as bulwarks against secularism and naturalism in education. The institutions of higher learning, however, did not provide serious intellectual arguments against secularism nor did they encourage or support research and published scholarship. The phenomenal postwar institutional expansion of Catholic colleges and universities, many of which doubled in enrollments in the late 1940s, left little time, financial resources, or energy for developing a Christian educational alternative to naturalism in education. Most university administrators concentrated upon building up their institutions and their professional schools to meet the increasing demands and simply let the Christian character of the institution, which they presupposed, take care of itself. In the process, though, they did provide hundreds of thousands of second- and third-generation Catholic immigrants with the intellectual tools and skills needed to prosper in an increasingly specialized and technological American society. State colleges and universities, too, educated millions of Catholics who did not choose—or could not afford—a Catholic education. Higher education for numerous second- and third-generation immigrant Catholics, made possible by the GI bill, and cheap home mortgages provided the impetus for the social and economic mobility of Catholics, for the assimilation of the ethnic and Catholic population into American society, and for the rapid Catholic movement into the suburbs.

To a large extent, almost all disciplines in Catholic higher education were, as Philip Gleason has shown, "dependent on religion for their value orientation." The principal end of Catholic higher education was conceived of in terms of a religious orientation to the world and all the disciplines were generally supposed to participate in fostering that shared vision. Even though many professors appropriated the methodologies and principles of their secular partners they saw something distinctively Catholic in their approaches to their own disciplines. Since the early 1930s, for example, sociologists were attempting to create what Paul Hanly Furfey called a "supernatural sociology" and what many others simply called a "Catholic sociology." What happened in sociology was also happening in many other disciplines. By the late 1950s and early 1960s, however, there was a significant movement toward more autonomy in the disciplines, a movement that would gain ground rapidly in the post–Vatican II era with the positive celebration of secularity and autonomy on Catholic campuses.

From the Potomac to the Pacific, Catholics like many other Americans, were in the midst of a postwar religious revival that was evident in almost all the measurable indexes of religious participation. About 74 percent of all Catholics, for example, attended church weekly by 1958; contributions to religious causes were demonstrated by the large building programs, rising enrollments in Catholic schools, and voluntary foreign and missionary aid programs. The religious revival, however, came in for some severe criticism by the mid 1950s. The American Catholic bishops, for example, questioned whether statistics alone were indicative of real religious life and they charged that the so-called revival did not have much of an influence upon the nation's culture. Will Herberg and others criticized the revival as a form of American sociability, a religious way of being American, a religion without any serious content or commitment. There is, no doubt, some justification for the criticisms of the superficiality of American religious life in general and Catholic piety in particular. The high levels of religious participation and the variety of forms of postwar Catholic piety, however, are significant for what they tell us about the transformation of Catholicism in response to anxieties of the era.

Catholic piety moved simultaneously in different directions. The center of spirituality for most Catholics remained the sacramental and devotional life at the local parish. The postwar period also created numerous new forms of spirituality (e.g., Father Patrick Peyton's Family Rosary Crusade, Father James Keller's Christopher movement, Bishop Fulton J. Sheen's television program *Life Is Worth Living*) that tried to provide religious security and peace in an age of cold war anxiety and anomie. The new movements accommodated themselves to the continuing process of Americanization, the growing identification of the Catholic population with middle-class culture, the American values of individualism, and the techniques of the mass media. A few Catholics (e.g., Carol Jackson, Joseph and Sally Cunneen) criticized these new forms of piety because they reinforced a bourgeois mentality and forfeited any sense of the sacramental, truly personal, communal, and activist traditions of Catholic spirituality. The Cistercian monk Thomas Merton's *The Seven Storey Mountain* (1948) and his many other widely read publications called Catholics, increasingly involved in American technological and organized corporate culture, to a form of holiness that integrated contemplation and action.

Another spiritual movement, one indicative of a new kind of internationalism in postwar Catholicism, was the revived interest in what was called missionary consciousness. The new initiative was the result of the fundamental threat of world communism, the United States' rise as a world superpower, the visible and active participation of major church leaders like Cardinal Francis Spellman in postwar service to American armed forces throughout the world, and the concerted effort among church leaders, missionaries, popular magazines, and Fulton Sheen's leadership in the Society for the Propagation of the Faith to promote missionary zeal among the American Catholic people. Widely publicized accounts of the church's persecution and stories of the trials of church leaders and missionaries behind the Iron Curtain became regular features in popular Catholic magazines and diocesan newspapers. Parish and school programs to rescue "pagan babies," prayers for missionaries and the conversion of Russia, and numerous fund drives to assist missionaries in their work of social amelioration and evangelism were all part of a massive postwar campaign to create "mission mindedness" among the American Catholic population. The new movement also produced numerous new vocations to the foreign missions and various religious orders sent these young men and women religious into the foreign mission field. For the first time, too, lay Catholics joined these missionary endeavors, the best known by far being the young Doctor Tom Dooley, whose medical work in Laos between 1956 and 1961 made him one of the heroes of the American Catholic imagination. The spirituality of missionary zeal transcended ecclesiastical and national localism and isolationism and brought many Catholics into a growing sense of the catholic nature of their Christianity.

Social Catholicism, too, flourished during the postwar years continuing the path established in the prewar years. The Catholic struggle for labor was popularized in the 1954 Hollywood film *On the Waterfront,* with Karl Malden representing the forceful clerical advocate and friend of labor and justice. Many Catholic labor priests like George Higgins were social activists more interested in communicating and putting into effect previous papal social teachings (emphasizing the democratization of wealth and opportunity in the United States) than they were in developing Catholic social thought. Social Catholics, though, did move into new areas in the postwar period. Urban social activists like Daniel Cantwell and John Egan in Chicago represented those clergy who addressed urban and state legislative bodies on the problems of urban renewal, relocation, housing for the poor, racism, and a host of other issues. A few parish clergy in Chicago, moreover, cooperated with Saul D. Alinsky's "Back of the Yards" movement, organizing laborers and city dwellers to obtain political clout for their neighborhoods. Lay leaders (e.g., Ann Harrigan, Patrick and Patty Crowley, Edward Marciniak, Frank Delany, and John Cogley), too, established institutions, movements, and magazines to promote a socially sensitive urban Catholic population.

These movements took place as large numbers of Catholics left the cities for the suburbs to establish Catholic parishes that lacked the ethnic or extended family bonds that had earlier provided cohesiveness. Some Catholics left the urban areas because of the general prosperity of the times; others because of the large migration of African Americans into their neighborhoods. Racial prejudices, ecclesiastical policies of segregation, and the systematic discrimination in society at large combined to produce overt Catholic racism, African American Catholic protests, and private episcopal reprimands and orders to reverse particular standing racial practices within local parishes. For the most part, American Catholics were slow to meet the pressing problems created by racism in the postwar period. Some local and national actions, however, revealed the gradual rise of Catholic consciousness on the race issue.

Saint Louis's Archbishop Joseph Ritter and Washington's Archbishop Patrick O'Boyle in 1947 and 1948, and San Antonio's Archbishop Lucey and Raleigh's Bishop Vincent Waters in 1954 (prior to *Brown v. Board of Education*) ordered Catholic schools integrated despite loud protests from certain white Catholics in their dioceses. In 1955, after the Supreme Court decision, New Orleans's Archbishop Joseph Francis Rummel ordered Catholic schools there integrated and in 1962 excommunicated those Catholics who publicly defied his order. As a national body the American bishops had called for racial peace and harmony in 1943, in the midst of the Detroit racial riots, but it was not until 1958 that American bishops published a pastoral letter exclusively devoted to the topic of religion and race. That pastoral, "Discrimination and Christian Conscience," forcefully asserted that "the heart of the race question is moral and religious." Racial prejudice in church and society was morally and spiritually damaging to the victims as well as to the perpetrators. By the time of Martin Luther King, Jr.'s 1963 March on Washington and the 1965 march from Selma to Montgomery, numerous Catholic laity, clergy, and women religious were visibly involved in the struggle for African Americans' civil rights. By the early 1960s, the church's official attitude to racism was clear, even though large numbers of Catholics perhaps continued to harbor racial prejudices and to exercise discriminatory practices.

Catholics continued to be involved in national politics. By 1965, twelve Catholic senators and ninety-one representatives served in the United States Congress, a representation in proportion to their numbers in society. Although it is extremely difficult to isolate the so-called religious motivational factor in voting patterns, polling evidence demonstrates that a majority of Catholics, for whatever reasons, voted for Democratic presidential candidates from FDR to Lyndon B. Johnson. As Catholics moved up the social and economic ladder in the 1950s, though, some shifted their political allegiance to the Republican party. This was evident in the elections of 1952 and 1956 when Catholics contributed about 45 percent and 49 percent of their votes to Dwight David Eisenhower. The shift in Catholic voting patterns indicated that something more than religious allegiance was at work in the factors that motivated Catholic political decisions and helped to belie the idea that there was a Catholic voting bloc in the country.

The 1946 elections of Senator Joseph McCarthy of Wisconsin and Congressman John Fitzgerald Kennedy of Massachusetts, and the 1948 election of Congressman Eugene Joseph McCarthy of Minnesota (senator, 1958–1970) demonstrated something of the variety and split in the political allegiances and perspectives among postwar American Catholics. For Senator Joseph McCarthy, as well as for Kennedy, religion was a private and sacramental affair, and politics was largely pragmatic. They showed little interest in the intellectual content of their faith or inclination to probe the political dimensions or implications of their own religious tradition. McCarthy's crusade against communism in the early 1950s certainly reflected something of the pre- and postwar Catholic culture in which he was raised, but his anticommunism was based primarily upon appeals to the American political, rather than to the Catholic, tradition.

Within the context of McCarthyism, a new Catholic intellectual conservative movement emerged. Although such Catholic political conservatives as William F. Buckley, Jr., Russell Kirk, Frederick Wilhelmsen, Thomas Molnar, L. Brent Bozell, and Arnold Lunn shared McCarthy's anticommunism and his fears of the socialist tendencies of the welfare state, they did not always share his political tactics. Shortly after the Senate censured McCarthy, conservative Catholic intellectuals joined Protestant and Jewish political conservatives to establish the *National Review* (1955) and *Modern Age* (1956). Although not specifically Catholic journals, they became the mouthpieces for the revival and dissemination of conservative thought. The new conservatives took a tough stand against "liberals" whom they considered soft on totalitarian communism and attacked them because they lacked fixed and transcendent values by which to judge political questions, relying almost exclusively upon democratic procedural, as opposed to substantive, issues. For the new conservatives, religion and the Catholic church in particular were the dominant forces against nineteenth-century liberalism and the primary instruments for preserving the dignity and spirituality of the human person. Although they criticized all forms of philosophical relativism and were skeptical about the classical capitalist vision of infinite progress, they believed in the American form of laissez-faire economics. They, too, accepted the teachings upon private property and the principle of subsidiarity in papal social encyclicals, but they criticized papal teachings for their lack of concrete knowledge of the benefits of a democratic capitalism.

Congressman Eugene McCarthy represented a different kind of Catholic politician. Unlike Joseph McCarthy and Kennedy, he was a Catholic intellec-

tual, well versed in the tradition of the papal encyclicals, having taught courses in Catholic social and political thought at St. Thomas College and St. John's University in Minnesota. Although he distinguished between religion and politics, he did not separate the two into independent compartments of his life. His Catholicism, too, was not the Catholicism of novenas, rosaries, and parish bingos, but the Catholicism of the Mystical Body, the liturgical movement, the rural life movement, and the social justice tradition of natural law. Religion was not politics, but politics was a part of one's religious and moral responsibility to provide for individual liberty and the common good. The two McCarthys represent extremes in relating religion to politics; most Catholic politicians were probably somewhere on the spectrum between them.

Eugene McCarthy's position was akin to that of a number of Catholics who called themselves "liberal Catholics." Lay and clerical leaders, including Joseph and Sally Cunneen, John Cogley, Edward Skillen, James O'Gara, William Clancy, and George Higgins, associated with *Commonweal* and *Cross Currents* magazines and involved themselves in a number of social and internal ecclesiastical reform movements during the 1950s. They accepted the Catholic doctrinal tradition, the papal encyclicals on social justice, the dynamics of the liturgical reform movement and the mystical body understanding of the church; but they were critical of what they perceived to be a partisan and sectarian spirit in American Catholicism. Most of them wanted to create a self-conscious dialogue with other members of American society in an attempt to resolve social problems. They emphasized, like other liberals, basic constitutional liberties and an American respect for individual integrity and initiative in the democratic political processes. Like the new conservatives, they were anticommunists for religious as well as political reasons, but their anticommunism stemmed more from the papal encyclicals on social justice than from the more explicitly and directly ideological anticommunist papal encyclicals.

For the political liberals the best means for overcoming communism was the promotion of legislative social programs designed to end hunger, disease, deficient housing, and other social and economic ills, all of which were ultimately responsible for the rise of communism and socialism. Unlike the new conservatives, they were much more skeptical of the benefits of democratic capitalism and repeatedly called for legislative reforms that more equitably distributed the wealth of the country. The political liberals, too, were adamantly opposed to Joseph Mc-

Carthy's methods, which they believed violated democratic procedures and threatened the common good in American society. As procedural rather than dogmatic liberals, they fought equally against communism, McCarthyism, and the coercive pressure tactics Catholic church leaders periodically resorted to in order to influence social and cultural values. Very much like John Courtney Murray, they wanted Catholics to support freedom and democratic procedures, to be tolerant and civil in public debates, and to use solidly grounded argumentation to secure a political consensus in society. Because they accepted Catholic doctrine and theology, they were suspect among their liberal political friends; because they sided with the liberals on political procedural questions, they were suspect among conservative Catholics.

John F. Kennedy represented a third type of Catholic politician. A sacramental Catholic like others, he shared Joseph McCarthy's approach to the relation of religion and politics and the liberal Catholics' approach to social issues and democratic procedures. Unlike the liberal Catholics and even some new conservatives, however, Kennedy understood religion as a purely private affair. A year prior to the presidential campaign of 1960, Kennedy told a *Look* reporter: "Whatever one's religion in his private life may be, for the officeholder, nothing takes precedence over his oath to uphold the Constitution and all its parts—including the First Amendment and the strict separation of church and state." Some liberal Protestants as well as liberal Catholics and the new conservatives thought that interview revealed Kennedy as disturbingly secular. Some conservative Protestants, however, were more disturbed by Kennedy's Catholicism than by his supposed secularism. Realizing the potential negative impact of his Catholicism, Kennedy quickly reaffirmed his *Look* interview at a meeting of the Ministerial Association of Greater Houston in September of 1960 and went on to win the presidency by a very narrow margin.

Despite some difficulties with Kennedy's supposed secularism, the vast majority of Catholics voted for him and saw in his win a symbolic victory for American Catholics, erasing as it did the bitter memory of Al Smith's defeat. Postwar Catholics who were gradually moving into business, professional life, and politics in ever greater numbers had one final barrier to their full civic participation eliminated for them. The victory, though, may also have symbolized that religion, not just Catholicism, was no longer a matter of much consequence in American political life, or it may have reflected a more widespread Catholic capitulation to the secular dynamic in politics in order to make it in American society. Whatever the election meant, it is clear that it was the culmination of an era of growing Catholic confidence and transition.

The Second Vatican Council (1962–1965), convoked almost simultaneously with Kennedy's advancement to the presidency, produced a dynamic shift in Catholic consciousness that emphasized the historical dimension of Christian existence and Catholic life, the communal over the institutional nature of the church, the value of legitimate diversity within the church, a spirit of accommodation to the particularity of cultures, freedom and religious liberty, an ecumenical openness to Protestants and other religions, and a dialogical relationship with modernity and modern patterns of thought. To some extent the Council confidently put an end to the confrontational or defensive attitude of much of the post-Tridentine era (1565–1960) and reflected themes that had been here and there articulated in postwar European and American Catholicism. The Council fostered a spirit of renewal, reform, and change—a fundamental shift for those American Catholics who were accustomed to thinking of the church's irreformable nature and its unchanging practices. The Council Fathers also initiated a number of specific internal ecclesiastical reforms and changes that would be implemented in an American cultural, social, and political context that was in the midst of a radical and revolutionary upheaval that included the death of President Kennedy (1963), the civil rights movement, the rising American involvement in Vietnam and the protest movements against it, the sexual revolution and the women's liberation movement.

## REFORM, PLURALISM, AND CONFLICT, 1965–1990

The American Catholic community, perhaps more than any other religious community, experienced the hurricane winds of social and religious reforms and upheavals that blew across the country in the 1960s and early 1970s. During the first decade after the council, a diversity of ecclesiastical reforms, new ways of thinking, new attitudinal adjustments, internal rebellions, conflicts and divisions, closings of numerous institutions, and a dramatic decline in denominational identification shook and transformed an American Catholic community whose most recent experience and memory was one of relative institutional stability, unity and phenomenal growth. These internal ecclesiastical transformations took place at a time of revolutionary change in American political and cultural life, a circumstance that magnified the impact of Vatican II's religious reforms and produced a period of unprecedented turmoil. By the late 1970s and early 1980s, some Catholics, like many others in American society were calling for stabilization and conservation in the political order and for a spiritual revival in the ecclesial realm.

Most of the conciliar reforms took place between 1964 and 1970. The most visible, tangible, significant, and pervasive signs that things were changing in Catholicism occurred in the liturgical reforms. In the immediate past liturgy had come to symbolize the universal and unchanging nature of the Catholic church. Now the church itself was demonstrating that things once considered permanent were changeable. Liturgical reforms were followed by changes in pious practices, ecclesiastical governance, and Catholic lifestyles. Many signs of the preconciliar sectarian identity (e.g., meatless Fridays, Lenten fasting and abstinence, the practice of auricular confession, the wearing of clerical collars and nuns' habits) were also either officially eliminated and modified, or simply disappeared from practice. Changing lifestyles among some clergy and women religious, moreover, became evident in their donning of secular dress, their assumption of new roles in church and society, their public involvement in peace and racial justice marches, and, most disturbingly, in isolated but highly publicized scandals over clerical pedophilia and other abuses of celibacy.

From pope to local priest, furthermore, there was a new openness to Protestants and other religions, and many Catholic lay persons at the local parish and diocesan levels participated in what were called living-room dialogues with members of other Christian traditions during the 1960s and early 1970s. These transformations were of no small account especially for a people in a sacramental tradition who were very conscious of visible signs. Removing the signs of separation and emphasizing the integration of religion and life reflected Vatican II's call for the church's involvement in the modern world and certainly influenced the Catholic imagination. Whether Catholics appreciated or repudiated the changes, they all developed a new Catholic consciousness about the historically conditioned and changeable nature of many things Catholic and became significantly aware that change itself was an issue in the postconciliar period.

In the midst of simultaneous social and religious tensions and transformations, the Catholic church, like many other American institutions during the 1960s and early 1970s, suffered for the first time in its history a massive loss of membership, decline in the statistics of institutional participation and identification, and a weakening of authority or influence over significant areas of moral life.

Gallup and other survey polls have over the past thirty years demonstrated the dramatic weakening of Catholic institutional identification. According to a 1988 poll, about 15 million of the 67 million Americans who identify themselves as Catholic were either lapsed, alienated, or unchurched. Some surveys indicate, too, that about 17 percent of those who were baptized Catholic between 1945 and 1982 had turned to another denomination. Weekly attendance at Mass, moreover, declined about 20 percent from 1963 to 1971, monthly confessions about 18 percent, and, between 1965 and 1988, the number of clergy shrank by more than 8 percent (primarily because 10,000 or more left the priesthood and an 85 percent decrease in the number of seminarians), and the number of women religious fell by 40 percent. Because of the want of clergy and religious, increased costs, lower birthrates, geographical mobility, internal discontent, lack of episcopal and clerical support, and a variety of other reasons, the number of Catholic primary and secondary schools plunged by 32 percent and the number of students by 60 percent between 1965 and 1988. Revolutionary declines took place at a time when the Catholic people were, according to sociologist Andrew M. Greeley's analysis in *The American Catholic: A Social Portrait* (1977), receiving college educations in large numbers, increasingly moving into the professional and business class, becoming economically prosperous, and enjoying a social mobility that solidly identified them with the American middle class. The decline may reflect dissatisfaction with ecclesiastical changes and internal conflicts, social mobility, a weakening of ethnic and family solidarity, and loss of faith and/or ecclesiastical credibility; it may also manifest a general disaffection with American institutions during the period.

Post–Vatican II American Catholicism went through an unprecedented period of polarization, conflict, and indeed acrimony as different factions in the church fought with one another over a variety of ecclesiastical, moral, political, and cultural issues. Division and conflict, of course, were a part of the much longer history of Christianity. What was particularly new for those whose experience of Catholicism was confined to the relatively halcyon days of the immediate past was not only the widespread and public but also the substantive character of the ecclesial conflicts.

The council had opened up the church to criticism and reform and during the postconciliar period it seemed that very little in the church's tradition, from the positioning of the altar to moral and doctrinal issues, was free from at least someone's question or criticism. Those Catholics who supported long held values and institutions were in a position of defense; presumption was no longer on the side of tradition and the church's teaching office, as it had been generally in the preconciliar period. The change of language from "fallen-away Catholic" to "alienated Catholic" indicated where many Catholics placed the blame for the loss of church membership. Some talked of the "old church" or of "ghetto Catholicism" as if there were very little continuity between pre- and postconciliar Catholic institutions and experiences. The postconciliar battle was over the definition of precisely what was and was not continuous and changeable within the Catholic tradition—and it is that character of the battle which helps to explain so much of the acrimony and bitterness that accompanied it.

Five issues were particularly divisive: the nature, extent, and exercise of ecclesiastical authority; the Catholic identity of colleges and universities; social justice; sexual morality and abortion; and the role of religion in politics. The issue of authority became a primary bone of contention and was particularly, although not exclusively, tied to the perceptions of the papacy. Since the Second Vatican Council there have been at least two major images of the papacy. One is that of the warm, open, and dialogical papacy, manifested in Pope John XXIII's personality, in Pope Paul VI's ecumenical travels to Jerusalem to embrace Athanagoras I, the Orthodox Ecumenical Patriarch of Constantinople, in 1964 and to the United Nations to speak for universal peace in 1965, and in Pope John Paul II's missionary trips to numerous countries (including two whirlwind tours of the United States in 1978 and 1987) speaking on behalf of peace, justice, and traditional Catholic moral values. Pope John Paul II's trips, in particular, demonstrated symbolically the council's call for the church's involvement in and dialogue with the world, but they also perhaps desacralized or demystified the papacy in the American Catholic imagination.

The second image was that of an authoritarian and anti-American papacy that wanted to control people's private lives and manage local ecclesiastical affairs. A series of postconciliar Vatican actions helped to create and to intensify tensions between Rome and the American church and to undermine ecclesiastical authority in the minds of large numbers of American Catholics. In 1966, Cardinal Alfredo Ottaviani, prefect of the Vatican's Congregation for Doctrine, sent the American bishops a confidential letter investigating unauthorized ecclesiastical reforms and liturgical experimentations, revealing a Roman fear that American church authorities were losing control of reforms. The letter produced a tension between collegial-minded bishops and the Vatican. This Vatican overture was followed by a papal ban on artificial contraception in 1968, the disciplining of prochoice American nuns in 1984, the investigations of Seattle's Archbishop Raymond Hunthausen's suspected maladministration of his diocese in 1985, the removal of Father Charles Curran's right to teach Catholic theology at the Catholic University of America in 1986 because of his dissent from papal teachings on contraception, and recurring discord between the Vatican and some American bishops over the authority and role of the national episcopal conference. Power struggles in local dioceses between old-style monarchical bishops and reform-minded priests, women religious, and laity were also a part of the conflicts between members of a church that was slowly and painfully coming to terms with some democratic procedures within an institution that was and continued to be hierarchical in nature.

American Catholic colleges and universities, whose enrollments increased by 46 percent between 1965 and 1988, experienced internal conflicts not only over participatory democratic governance, but also over academic freedom, and the relationship of internal governance to the external supervision of the church's magisterium. At the heart of these issues was the recurring postconciliar problem of Catholic identity, and the key issue relative to Catholic identity—a question that was symbolic of the wider search in postconciliar Catholicism—was whether the teaching office of the Catholic church was effectively present in Catholic institutions of higher education through the individual's conscience or through more formal juridical ties. In 1967, representatives of ten Catholic institutions of higher education—under the leadership of Fathers Theodore Hesburgh, C.S.C., and Robert J. Henle, S.J., presidents respectively of the University of Notre Dame and Georgetown University—signed a document, called the Land O'Lakes Statement, in which they agreed that Catholic colleges, like others in American society, "must have a true autonomy and academic freedom in the face of authority of whatever kind, lay or clerical, external to the academic community itself." Some interpreted this statement as a legitimate declaration of independence from Vatican and episcopal interference and others saw it as a capitulation to standards of academic freedom that were grounded in Enlightenment presuppositions about freedom and truth.

By the 1990s, most Catholic colleges and universities had established lay boards of trustees, had some faculty participation in governance, and asserted the right of academic freedom, but the issue of Catholic identity continued to be discussed on a number of campuses and there was, as Philip Gleason pointed out, no working consensus among the faculty on what it meant, in intellectual terms, to be a Catholic and on how the faith should influence one's scholarship. The Catholic universities' desire for prestige and prominence as research and scholarly institutions, and the recurring criticisms of failures to be such, were also symbolic of wider concerns in the postconciliar community that retained something of the preconciliar sense of cultural inferiority.

A third source of internal conflict, but also a defining characteristic of the postconciliar church, was the search for social justice (e.g., over issues of war and peace, world poverty, American international aid and other foreign policy questions, the American economy, race, and women's liberation). Although the emphasis upon social justice continued the preconciliar movements in American Catholicism, there were also a number of postconciliar differences: the focus upon justice within the church as well as in the society; the emphasis upon social liberation and a preferential option for the poor over the stress upon natural law economic rights or upon the economic development of peoples; and human rights perceived in explicitly inclusive terms and in terms of sexual, cultural, and personal empowerments rather than simple immunities. In these emphases postconciliar American Catholic social thought has been modified by its encounter with various liberation movements in North and South America.

The Catholic peace movement of the 1960s and early 1970s, under the leadership of Fathers Daniel and Philip Berrigan (and with the participation of more than 230 Catholic Left activists across the country), represented a new symbolic and prophetic style and a shift in Catholic approaches to social justice—from rational discussion leading to political consensus (à la John Courtney Murray) to passionate witness to gospel values. In a variety of ways the Catholic Left, unlike the older American civil disobedience tradition, emphasized visible (e.g., burning draft cards in defiance of federal legislation, pouring blood on draft records, raiding corporate headquarters of major industries that supplied the tools of war) over verbal protests and, in an age of television, the Catholic

protesters came into their own. These Catholics, moreover, had no compulsion to demonstrate their Americanism as had earlier American Catholic advocates of justice. Their morality of conscience, the higher law, and prophetic witness, although not self-critical or open to the ambiguity of the human situation, was a new departure in American Catholic attempts to promote justice. The protests against Vietnam generally ended up in civil court cases. The Catonsville trial of 1968 became an international news event, a focal point for rallying the antiwar movement, and the subject of a book, a play, a television documentary, and a movie. This was high drama. American Catholics in general, however, did not favor the war protesters' tactics, even when 58 percent of them by 1970, according to a Gallup poll, were against the war in Vietnam.

From 1966 to 1990, moreover, the national body of bishops, various religious orders of women and men, and a host of other Catholic groups focused attention upon national and international responsibility for justice in the world. Hunger in Nigeria-Biafra, human rights in Chile and Brazil, apartheid in South Africa, religious liberty in Eastern Europe, military violence in El Salvador, Namibia, and Nicaragua were among the subjects not only of numerous national episcopal pastorals, but also of episcopal lobbying efforts before Congress. The John Courtney Murray style of rational democratic persuasion continued, but in the postconciliar period it was more widespread in the American Catholic community and much more politically activist in orientation. The most extensive, significant, and widely discussed of the American episcopal pastorals—*The Challenge of Peace* (1983) and *Economic Justice for All* (1986)—exemplified and epitomized the postconciliar concerns of the official church to demonstrate the interrelated practical, political, and social implications of Christian life and thought. Although these teaching statements were not necessarily indicative or representative of actual and popular Catholic practices and perceptions, they did indicate the ideals to which the church aspired, and opinion polls showed that a large majority of American Catholics supported them.

The issue of racial solidarity and justice within the African American Catholic community arose with particular vehemence in 1968 after the assassination of Dr. Martin Luther King, Jr. African American Catholic clergy (of whom there were about 150), nuns, seminarians, and laity formed national organizations that year to protest, as the Black Catholic Clergy Caucus did, against the Catholic church as a "white racist institution" and to call for major attitudinal and institutional changes within the church. For some time African Americans had been calling for more representation in the hierarchy. In 1966, Harold Perry, S.V.D., was named an auxiliary bishop of New Orleans, the first African American to be named a bishop in the twentieth century and only the second since the middle of the nineteenth. By 1988, there were thirteen African American bishops, and one of them, Eugene Marino, was named Archbishop of Atlanta, the first African American Catholic archbishop in the nation's history. Emphasis upon justice, participation and representation, the value of African American culture, and the need for Catholic schools for African Americans came to the fore with renewed vigor in the 1960s. That the movement within the church was not entirely successful is measured to some extent by the 1989 withdrawal of Washington, D.C.'s charismatic Father George Stallings from the Catholic church and his subsequent establishment of the independent and separatist African American Catholic Church.

The same issues that influenced the African American community rose up in the Hispanic Catholic community. The Hispanic community was the fastest growing immigrant group within postconciliar Catholicism, representing by the late 1980s almost 20 percent (circa more than 13 million) of the total Catholic population and the majority of the Catholic population in some sections of the country. Much like the early-twentieth-century Italian immigrants, the newer Hispanics had low incomes (only 20 percent in 1978 had incomes above $15,000 per year), lacked adequate education and skills to compete in society, carried with them particular communal and family traditions and values that clashed with a voluntaristic, technological, urban, and competitive American society. Many, particularly those from Mexico, moreover, came to the United States without a numerous native clergy to serve them.

Like the African Americans, Hispanic clergy, nuns, and lay people in the late 1960s and early 1970s formed a number of national Hispanic ecclesiastical organizations to voice the concerns of Hispanics and the need for greater sensitivity on the part of the Americanized Catholic church to their particular culture. The push for recognition and representation had some results by 1970, when the first contemporary Hispanic, Patricio Flores, was ordained a bishop and later appointed archbishop of San Antonio. In 1983, the national bishops published a pastoral, "The Hispanic Presence," calling attention to the gifts of Hispanic culture and articulating the challenges of

the Hispanic ministry. By 1988, twenty more Hispanic bishops had been ordained, more than half of whom were immigrants. The challenge of ministering to the Hispanic Catholic was complicated by the fact, as surveys showed, that large numbers of Hispanic Catholics continued to be alienated from the institutional church and did not find the Americanized style of Catholicism a very familiar or comfortable one. They found more satisfying the affective, personal, familial, communal, and devotional Catholicism that has been so much a part of their culture than the sanitized (or puritanized) form of Catholic life that has been developing in the United States since World War II.

The struggle for justice for women in society and church was also part of the new consciousness of the period as women themselves became the primary voices in the movement for emancipation from traditional cultural, legal, political, ecclesiastical, and theological barriers. From congressional passage of the Equal Rights Amendment (1972) to its final failure to win ratification in the states (1982), prominent Catholics were found on both sides of the issue, even though eventually a majority of Catholics, according to opinion polls, favored ratification.

Within the church, women religious took a lead in reforming their own institutions according to more democratic procedures than in the past, and took on a host of new roles within the church and the society, demonstrating in very particular ways the influence of the women's liberation movement and of Vatican II. Such reforms did not go unchallenged within the religious orders nor in the episcopacy, as bishops here and there either exercised their veto power over the reforms or simply tried to reverse the reforms. In 1965, for example, half of the Glenmary Sisters left the order to form a lay community when Cincinnati's Archbishop Karl Alter vetoed the sisters' reforms. In 1968, 400 of the 450 Sisters of the Immaculate Heart of Mary did the same when Los Angeles' Cardinal James McIntyre rejected their chapter decisions.

The emptying of convents from the late 1960s to the 1990s was the result of a combination of such factors as the general atmosphere of change and reform in church and society, the women's liberation movement which challenged and criticized the historical structures of church and state as patriarchal, the higher educations of women religious (by 1980, 85 percent of them had college educations and 68 percent of these had advanced degrees), and an increasing emphasis upon freedom, diversity, and self-development. Sisters became involved in a host of new roles in church and society as they increasingly emphasized respect for individual talents and charisms. In the process many left behind teaching and nursing (their primary functions in the immediate past). In the midst of change the sense of a cooperate mission gradually declined and was replaced by a sense of personal mission. This kind of individualism contributed to the decline of convent life and of a sense of shared purpose.

Like earlier and later generations of immigrants, moreover, many of the sisters and feminist lay women called for greater participation and representation in the church. They sought in particular the abolition of celibacy as a requirement for ordination, a married clergy, and ordination of women. Opinion polls revealed that Catholics had become increasingly favorable to women priests, from 29 percent in 1974 to 47 percent in 1985. Despite this growing popular support for ordination of women, Rome steadfastly refused to consider the ordination of women, believing such an innovation was not only contrary to ecclesiastical discipline but also to a Catholic theology of the ministry that asserted that women were incapable of "imaging Christ" as priests because Christ became incarnate as a man.

The fourth area of internal conflict, and perhaps the one that received the greatest amount of public attention, was over a variety of moral and lifestyle issues that seriously challenged official Catholic church teachings. Artificial contraception, premarital sex, abortion, and homosexuality became increasingly accepted by the population at large but created ardent divisions both within the church and society. Some social scientists, like Andrew Greeley, have argued that ecclesiastical authority in general, the church's entire ethic on sexuality, and participation and membership in the church was seriously damaged by Pope Paul VI's encyclical *Humanae Vitae* (1968), which, against the majority advice of his own international advisory commission, condemned artificial contraception as immoral. Whether the encyclical or the general cultural revolution caused the collapse of many Catholic sexual moral values seems to me open to question, but polls demonstrate that there is no doubt about the general relaxation of the official sexual ethic within American Catholicism since the late 1960s.

Public as well as private resistance to and dissent from the encyclical was immediate. Six hundred theologians from throughout the country, under the leadership of Catholic University's Father Charles Curran, protested publicly against the teaching, holding that in some circumstances couples could legiti-

mately and responsibly use contraceptives to preserve and foster their marriages. Some Washington, D.C., clergy who joined the protests were immediately suspended from their clerical duties, and Curran was removed from his teaching position at the Catholic University in 1986, eighteen years after the event. Among married couples, polls showed, large numbers of Catholics simply ignored the papal ban. A 1977 poll indicated that 73 percent of Catholics believed that they should be allowed to practice artificial means of birth control. Whatever the effects the encyclical may have had upon subsequent developments in American Catholicism, there is no doubt that Catholic practices and official Catholic teachings were in conflict in this area. But, such a conflict was not entirely new. Catholics did not always follow the church's teachings in the areas of economic justice, racial discrimination, and sexual ethics in the past. What was important about the issue of contraception is that the church's theologians as well as the laity publicly protested against the teachings themselves and many voted on them by walking out of the church.

The issue of homosexuality divided Catholics, particularly after the Stonewall riot between police and homosexuals in New York City (1969) when the issue came increasingly to public attention. Official church teaching, based upon an interpretation of biblical proscriptions and natural law, prohibited homosexual activity, but increasingly in the 1970s theologians and bishops came to distinguish between homosexual orientations, which were not always freely chosen and therefore were considered amoral, and homosexual activities, which were considered immoral. Only an isolated Catholic theologian here and there (e.g., the Jesuit J. J. McNeill) challenged the church's teaching on homosexual activity, but since the late 1970s Dignity, a Catholic homosexual group established in 1969, publicly opposed Vatican declarations against homosexual activity, intensifying conflicts within the church. By 1982, survey polls demonstrated, 46 percent of the Catholic population rejected homosexuality as an alternate lifestyle (compared to 58 percent of the Protestant population), but they also point out that Catholics have become increasingly tolerant of legalized homosexual relations between consenting adults, support equal job opportunities, and believe that homosexuals can be good Christians or Jews. Although some in the Catholic community saw AIDS (acquired immunodeficiency syndrome), which emerged in the 1980s because of the apparent increase in homosexual activity and drug use, as a divine retribution for sin, the

United States Catholic Conference (USCC) bishops have focused upon pastoral care as well as medical and social services for the victims of AIDS.

Since the late 1960s and the 1973 Supreme Court decision in *Roe* v. *Wade,* abortion became one of the most controversial social issues in American society, and American Catholics in particular have been divided over the issue. Theologians are divided among themselves on the morality of abortion, and, although a 1984 poll indicated that 65 percent of the Catholic population opposed abortion-on-demand, there was a significant percentage of Catholics who rejected the church's official teaching against abortion and who favored the 1973 decision. The abortion issue stirred up much controversy within the church during the 1984 presidential campaign when a group of Catholics, including some nuns and clergy, published an ad in the *New York Times* in support of free choice and legalized abortions and called for an episcopal recognition of the Catholic's right to dissent from the episcopally designated public policy implications of Catholic moral teachings. Later the nuns who signed the ad were disciplined. The whole issue of abortion, like so many issues of the period, again became associated with the issues of freedom and authority, ecclesiastical discipline, and the relation of faith to action and public policy.

Almost every issue of the period related faith to justice in the political order. The old debates of the 1940s and 1950s over religious liberty and separation of church and state gave way to the more general question of religion's role in the political process and in helping to influence governmental policies. The American bishops in particular focused upon four political issues that had moral implications: nuclear strategy, the United States' policy in Central America, equity in the economy, and abortion. Through pastoral letters, published statements and resolutions, testimonies before congressional hearings, and encouragement of parish educational programs, the bishops and their advisers at the USCC in Washington, D.C., tried to focus national attention on the moral dimensions of governmental decisions. Perhaps no other group in the country had linked together these particular issues as part of a campaign to stir up a national moral debate and to influence government. Although the bishops have denied any partisan politics, they have taken sides periodically upon a variety of specific policy choices without indicating that their positions should end the debate. They have endorsed, for example, "no first use" of nuclear weapons, job training programs, restrictive amendments on abortion, withdrawal of military aid

to Central America, and continued negotiations instead of a declaration of war in the Persian Gulf. Such specific positions have been taken not in order to dictate policy choices but to engage in the democratic political process from a moral and religious perspective. This position is radically different from the position of nineteenth-century and pre–Vatican II twentieth-century bishops who abhorred any involvement of Catholicism in American politics even when there were issues like slavery that had moral as well as political dimensions.

The Catholic politician's responsibilities in the democratic political process became an issue in the 1984 presidential campaign (and has remained one here and there ever since) when the Democratic vice presidential candidate, Geraldine Ferraro, although personally opposed to abortion, asserted that she could be a good Catholic and still support the pro-choice position on abortion, and implied that the Catholic position on abortion was not monolithic because Catholics themselves held different views. New York's Cardinal John O'Connor criticized her for separating personal conscience from political responsibility and charged that she was misleading people on the Catholic view of abortion. The battle over the issue raged throughout the campaign. Two other Catholic politicians, New York's Democratic Governor Mario M. Cuomo and Illinois Republican U.S. Representative Henry Hyde, got into the debate. Cuomo, following John Courtney Murray's position, held that in the United States law was built upon consensus and since none existed on abortion, the church should not seek legal remedies for moral problems where there was no consensus. Hyde asserted that it was clearly insufficient for a Catholic public official to hold that his or her personal conscientious objection to abortion ended the matter. For Hyde, law was not simply a matter of public consensus, but was educative, leading people to justice and equity in society. Whether the law should be reflective or creative of a consensus in society, whether politicians should represent the society's prevailing sense of right or teach justice, and whether the abortion issue was one of private and personal morality or a matter of public justice and morality were serious questions which divided opinion in the church and society.

In the midst of unprecedented decline and internal conflict, there arose a number of new movements to revive Catholic spirituality. In May 1976, a *Time* cover story, "U.S. Catholicism: A Church Divided," noted that despite changes and conflict the American Catholic people were displaying a "remarkable tenacity" and showing a "spiritual second wind that suggests that U.S. Catholicism might even be on the verge of a new period of vigor." By 1988, the pollsters George Gallup, Jr., and Jim Castelli argued that Catholics were in the middle of a religious revival. Vatican II and the 1960s spawned conflict and decline, but also gave birth to a new spiritual vitality and new forms of participation.

Although devotional Catholicism continued to characterize the spirituality of many older Catholics and many of the newer immigrants during the postconciliar period, it was gradually replaced by a variety of new forms that emphasized the sacramental, communal, and active dimensions that were thought to be grounded in public liturgy, the Bible, and the personal experiences of modern Catholics. The ecumenical openness of Vatican II, moreover, encouraged some Catholics to look into forms of spirituality outside of the Catholic tradition. The Catholic charismatic movement, having its origins in 1967 and affecting millions of American Catholics by the late 1980s, was the result of personal lay Catholic contact with classical Pentecostals. Like the Pentecostals, Catholic charismatics focused attention upon the personal and communal gifts of the Holy Spirit, especially spirit baptism, emphasizing in a highly technological and activist age the supernatural intervention into history. The charismatic movement was ecumenical, primarily lay in leadership and orientation, evangelistic in motivation, and focused upon internal experience and exotic forms of communal prayer and demonstrations of spiritual power. The movement was particularly Catholic, though, in its sacramental and liturgical orientation, and in its identification with the church's teaching office.

On the local parish level a host of new programs began to develop after the council, including Bible reading groups, living room ecumenical prayer and discussion groups, sacramental preparation classes for parents as well as children, participation in parish councils, involvement in meal programs and other forms of social service, leadership in evangelistic programs for alienated Catholics, and a revitalized public celebration of the liturgy. Although there was no uniform development of spiritual life in the parishes or systematic attempt to revitalize parishes in the immediate wake of the council, there were changes and experimentations. By 1976, however, the Archdiocese of Newark, New Jersey, initiated a national program called RENEW to revitalize parish life. This pastoral program focused upon organizing small groups of laity within parishes that met for three years in their own homes and neighborhoods to pray

together and to discuss biblical readings and social activities appropriate for Christians living in the world. By 1990, RENEW had taken place in ninety-six dioceses and in about one-half of all parishes in the United States. The relatively short-term commitment proved effective in attracting numerous Catholics to participate in the program. The overall effects of this movement, however, have not been studied.

Catholic publishing houses, particularly Paulist Press, produced highly marketable and widely distributed books on the spiritual life from the 1960s to 1990s, and their continued publication indicates something of the renewal of interest in things of the spirit. Even serious classics have found an American audience, as the popularity of Paulist Press's Classics of Western Spirituality and Sources of American Spirituality demonstrate. Numerous other published studies of spirituality also demonstrated that those interested in the spiritual dimension of the Catholic tradition appear to be vital.

Although there are a number of complaints about the institutional church's failures to meet the religious needs of many American Catholics, programs like RENEW, a stabilized (53 percent) weekly Mass attendance by the mid 1970s, widespread participation in prayer meetings, more involvement in church life at the parish and diocesan levels, a significant increase in Bible reading, and a large increment in the purchasing and reading of books on spirituality are some of the indicators of a religious revival. Internal disagreements and conflicts have not, Gallup and Castelli have pointed out in their analysis of polls, changed a sense of belonging to the church. In fact, a 1987 poll found that Catholics have more "confidence in their church than in any other institution," with 85 percent saying that their lifetime experiences in Catholicism have been "overall positive."

Despite the "overall positive" perspectives, there have been since the late 1960s varying interpretations of postconciliar American Catholicism. A minority of American Catholics, usually called Traditionalists, following Father Gommar De Pauw and the French Archbishop Marcel Lefebvre, rejected as invalid the postconciliar liturgical reforms and considered many of the other reforming tendencies within American Catholicism to be heretical. *The Wanderer* Catholics, Catholics United for the Faith, and a number of other ultraconservative Catholic organizations accepted conciliar documents and Vatican-initiated reforms, but repudiated the liberal interpretations of Vatican II and censured a resurgence of modernism in the church. Conservative intellectuals like James Hitchcock, too, began to criticize the disintegration within American Catholicism in the early and mid-1970s and charged that a liberal Catholic leadership in the church had capitulated to modernity by collapsing the distinction between the natural and the supernatural and that liberal bishops and clergy had abdicated their authority within the church in favor of a democratic majoritarianism that was guided more by the mores in society than by the tradition of the church. The Roman leadership of Pope John Paul II and Cardinal Joseph Ratzinger since the late 1970s has also sought to reinforce traditional Catholic values and to reverse the signs of deterioration and disagreement in the church, a movement which some interpreted as reactionary.

The predominant view of post–Vatican II developments was much more favorable to the consequences of reform, change and pluralism. Reform-minded lay and clerical leaders have celebrated the church's dialogue with modernity and appreciated the focus upon the church's active support for issues of social justice. Liberal-minded accommodationists have sought to follow the trajectory of Vatican II in a number of new directions that have departed from the church's earlier tradition (e.g., married priests, ordination of women, and support for moral issues that contradict the church's current teachings). By 1975, however, there occurred a rift in the liberal wing of the church that reinforced a more conservative mood in the church and society at large. That year, Protestant, Catholic, and Jewish theologians created the so-called Hartford Appeal, which called for a recovery of the sacred in the religious traditions and charged that some contemporary theological projects were false and debilitating to the church's life and work. These moderate reformist liberals believed that some in the churches had too easily adapted themselves to the intellectual and attitudinal fashions of a nonbelieving world and could no longer see the distinctive differences between the modern world and the Christian or Jewish traditions.

Religion and culture were integrally related in the American experience of Catholicism throughout the twentieth century. Whether they were Americanized in their feelings and practices or whether they retained their ethnic sensibilities, Catholics believed that their religion could be preserved only in specific cultural expressions. During the first third of the century, Catholicism took many different cultural shapes as immigrants fostered their own ethnic traditions and expressions of Catholicism and as other Catholics adopted American incarnations of their religion. The numerous churches they built for their religious and communal needs, the schools they de-veloped to preserve their languages and introduce their children to skills and American ways, the social agencies they created to help the needy in their communities were responsible for transmitting a strong sense of divine transcendence, order, continuity, and service in large segments of American life.

The immigrant traditions that survived well into the post–World War II period provided a source of local or feudal autonomy and a dizzying diversity within an American church that increasingly emphasized a unity institutionalized through diocesan and national centralized forms of government. As the immigrant traditions were gradually modified through the process of Americanization, the communal diversity of the immigrant traditions was also gradually replaced by a homogenized middle-class individualism that only emerged in full force in American Catholicism after the Second Vatican Council and the cultural revolutions of the 1960s. During the last third of the twentieth century this Americanized middle-class individualism manifested itself particularly in a selective approach to Catholic beliefs and practices—preserving something of the ecclesial diversity of the past, but also significantly clashing with the communal tradition of the immigrant cultural expressions of diversity.

World War II was a watershed in the process of Americanization as more and more Catholics moved into new middle-class suburban communities, shedding something of their ethnic identity, while the churches also moved into the suburbs and adapted to a middle-class American version of Catholicism. The Second Vatican Council and the revolutions of the 1960s, however, brought numbers of Catholics into conflict with both American and Catholic values that were so closely merged during the post-World War II era. Within this context large numbers of middle-class American Catholics incorporated the American tradition of open dissent to many things Catholic as well as American. African American and Hispanic Catholics, too, like earlier immigrants, dissented from elements within the American and Catholic traditions, but from a position of racial and ethnic solidarity and not from a tradition of individualism as was becoming increasingly the case in middle-class Catholicism.

The social, religious, and ideological transformation of American Catholics have made middle-class Catholics more like Protestants at the end of the century than at the beginning. Although middle-class Catholics were significantly influenced by the American tradition of voluntarism in religion, their middle-class individualism continued to be shaped by a religious tradition that was predominantly creedal, sacramental, ecclesial, and institutionally bound together by an episcopal and papal magisterial structure. This ecclesial context continued to provide a distinctive shape to the Catholic experience of individualism in the United States and distinguished Catholicism from the more evangelical, revivalistic, independent, and free church traditions that characterized much of American Protestantism.

At the beginning of the twentieth century, Catholicism played an insignificant role in national life and Catholic contributions to American culture were given little attention. Particularly since the end of World War II, Catholicism increasingly came to the fore of public attention in the United States whenever the media examined the religious issue in American life. Even distinctively Catholic issues at the end of the twentieth century were no longer, as they were at the beginning of the century, purely parochial concerns little noticed by the media, the politicians, and the analysts of public life. Catholic concerns, too, have become more and more identified over the century with the primary issues of justice and morality in American life. Internal controversies, major institutional and attitudinal changes, social and economic mobility, and the phenomenal twentieth-century increase in the Catholic population made

Catholicism a central part of the American religious scene, upstaging in dramatic and symbolic events during the late twentieth century the Protestant traditions that had the major shaping influence upon American cultural and religious life.

During the last third of the twentieth century, American Catholicism experienced unprecedented upheaval. The revolutions of the 1960s helped many to perceive or reinterpret the plural dimensions of their own American and Catholic traditions: the values of freedom, reform, and change; the necessity of diversity and cultural particularity; the new forms of participation and representation—centrifugal forces that made the unity of the tradition problematic on the ideological as well as the practical level. On the other hand, the institutional structures and the traditional affinities for ecclesial unity, cohesion, and continuity reasserted themselves and since the late 1970s were coupled with the conservative and conserving forces in church and society—centripetal forces that made freedom and diversity problematic on the ideological as well as practical level. The struggle to bring these two forces into communion was a new project in the late twentieth century, but it was part of a much longer tradition in Western society to deal with the problem of the one and the many.

SEE ALSO Protestantism; Judaism and Jewish Culture; Nontraditional Religions (all in this volume); Ethnicity and Immigration (volume I).

## BIBLIOGRAPHY

John Tracy Ellis and Robert Trisco, eds., *A Guide to American Catholic History* (2d ed., rev. and enl., 1982), have produced the standard and most useful annotated guide to bibliographical sources on American Catholicism. John Tracy Ellis, ed., *Documents of American Catholic History,* 3 vols. (1987), supplies a number of extremely valuable primary documents on American Catholicism that are not easily accessible. Hugh J. Nolan, ed., *Pastoral Letters of the United States Catholic Bishops,* 5 vols. (1984–1989), provides an extremely valuable source not only for analyzing the development of the national episcopal mind during the twentieth century, but also for reflecting many of the concerns that first emerged in lay and clerical intellectual and social movements.

A number of demographic and other statistical studies of American Catholicism are readily available.

The *Official Catholic Directory* (1900–1990), although not a reliable scientific instrument for determining population statistics, is currently the most useful source for judging Catholic geographical distribution, institutional developments, and population growth. Gerald Schaughnessy, *Has the Immigrant Kept the Faith? A Study of Immigration and Catholic Growth in the United States, 1790–1920* (1925), provides the most scientific statistical account of the demographics of American Catholics, although it is flawed in many particulars. Andrew M. Greeley's *The American Catholic: A Social Portrait* (1977), gives a sociological analysis of the upward social mobility of American Catholics since World War II. Greeley, *American Catholics since the Council: An Unauthorized Report* (1985), summarizes much of the data collected by the National Opinion Research Center on American Catholic opinions, practices, and institutional affiliations. George Gallup, Jr., and Jim Castelli, *The American Catholic People: Their Beliefs, Practices, and Values* (1987), summarizes and analyzes the statistical data taken from survey polls on American Catholics since the 1960s.

A number of general, diocesan, and regional parish histories are useful. John Tracy Ellis, *American Catholicism* (2d rev. ed., 1969), provides a general history of Catholicism particularly within the context of American political movements and demonstrates the pre–Vatican II progressive concern for reform. James Hennesey, *American Catholics: A History of the Roman Catholic Community in the United States* (1981), provides an excellent detailed historical examination of social and institutional developments in various geographical areas of the country. Jay P. Dolan's *The American Catholic Experience: A History from Colonial Times to the Present* (1985) is a widely acclaimed interpretive social history of American Catholicism that provides a creative analysis of the particularity of the immigrant traditions. Dolan, moreover, has edited *The American Catholic Parish: A History from 1850 to the Present*, 2 vols. (1987), which also reflects the new emphasis upon social history and demonstrates the regional and ethnic variations in parish life and structures. Steven Avella's *This Confident Church: Catholic Leadership and Life in Chicago, 1940–1965* (1992) concentrates upon the social transformation of Catholicism during the episcopates of Cardinals Samuel Stritch and Albert Meyer in the nation's largest diocese. Philip Gleason's *Keeping the Faith: American Catholicism Past and Present* (1987) is the best single interpretive volume on American Catholicism, analyzing in particular the inherent conflicts between continuity and change, unity and diversity, within the American Catholic experience.

A number of historical and social studies have focused upon the church's structures and leadership roles. Gerald P. Fogarty, ed., *Patterns of Episcopal Leadership* (1989), has gathered a collection of independently authored historical essays on changing models of episcopal governance in interaction with American social and political values. Edward R. Kantowicz, *Corporation Sole: Cardinal Mundelein and Chicago Catholicism* (1983), offers a creative historical analysis of pre–World War II twentieth-century Chicago Catholicism and the emergence of a new consolidating style of episcopal leadership. Joseph M. Shite's *The Diocesan Seminary in the United States: A History from the 1780s to the Present* (1989) is the first comprehensive study of the diocesan clergy's spiritual formation and theological education. James K. Kenneally, *The History of American Catholic Women* (1990), provides a narrative of the various roles of lay and religious women in American Catholicism, their own internal conflicts over their roles, and their emergence into new positions within the church in the twentieth century. Maria Augusta Neal, *From Nuns to Sisters: An Expanding Vocation* (1990), gives a sociological-historical analysis of the changing roles of sisters in twentieth-century American Catholicism.

The study of immigrants and black Catholics has produced a number of good studies in the last third of the twentieth century. Dolores Liptak, *Immigrants and their Church* (1989), presents a balanced historical view of the internal conflicts over immigrant desires to preserve their cultures and episcopal desires to incorporate the new immigrants into patterns of ecclesiastical life that had been significantly Americanized. Randall M. Miller and Thomas D. Marsik, ed., *Immigrants and Religion in Urban America* (1977), brings together a collection of insightful essays on the varieties of immigrant cultural Catholicisms that marked the dominant tradition in the United States until at least the 1940s. James S. Olson, *Catholic Immigrants in America* (1987), gives a brief description of immigrant variety in American Catholicism and analyzes the issues of consolidation, modernization, acculturation, and assimilation. Anthony J. Kuzniewski, *Faith and Fatherland: The Polish Church War in Wisconsin, 1896–1918* (1980), narrates the emergence of Polish self-assertiveness within the church and the conflicts that surrounded Polish calls for representation and participation. Moises Sandoval, *On the Move: A History of the Hispanic Church in the United States* (1990), gives a brief historical development of Hispanic Catholicism that concentrates upon the post-1960 period. Cyprian Davis, *The History of Black Catholics in the United States* (1990), has written the only comprehensive historical analysis of African American Catholicism, one that draws particular attention to significant lay leaders within the community and the long struggle for justice within the church.

Intellectual and social historians have studied the significance of various forms of Catholic piety. Joseph P. Chinnici's *Living Stones: The History and Structure of Catholic Spiritual Life in the United States* (1989) is a first-rate comprehensive study of the changing historical patterns of Catholic spirituality. Robert Anthony Orsi's *The Madonna of 115th Street: Faith and Community in Italian Harlem, 1880–1950* (1985) is the best single social and cultural analysis of the popular religion and spirituality of an immigrant group.

Examinations of social Catholicism and intellectual history have received increasing attention in the last third of the twentieth century. David O'Brien, *Public Catholicism* (1989), analyzes various historical models of the Catholic involvement with social, economic, and political issues from the late eighteenth to the late twentieth centuries. Patricia McNeal's *Harder Than War: Catholic Peacemaking in Twentieth-Century America* (1992) is the first comprehensive history of Catholic movements. Mel Piehl, *Breaking Bread: The Catholic Worker and the Origin of Catholic Radicalism in America* (1982), provides an excellent examination of the Catholic Worker movement's blending of radical and conservative social ideas that formed the basis for many of the radical Catholic protest movements of the 1960s. William M. Halsey, *The Survival of American Innocence: Catholicism in an Era of Disillusionment, 1920–1940* (1980), analyzes the neo-Thomist intellectual optimism and cultural Americanism that emerged in the early twentieth century and tended to become institutionalized in Catholic structures and in the Catholic imagination. Arnold Sparr, *To Promote, Defend, and Redeem: The Catholic Literary Revival and the Cultural Transformation of American Catholicism, 1920–1960* (1990), offers a provocative analysis of the social aims and functions of pre–Vatican II American Catholic intellectual life. Margaret Mary Reher's *Catholic Intellectual Life in America: A Historical Study of Persons and Movements* (1989) is the only comprehensive study of the development of American Catholic religious thought.

# NONTRADITIONAL RELIGIONS

## Catherine L. Albanese

The Atlantic seaboard colonies that became the United States of America were overwhelmingly Protestant in religion. As the new nation grew, that situation began to change: before 1850 Roman Catholicism had become the largest American denomination, and by the 1880s the small Jewish population was swelling with the immigration of huge numbers of European Jews. By the middle of the twentieth century, Protestant, Catholic, and Jew had become a familiar trinity.

In that context, the designation "nontraditional religion" is a broad and encompassing one, a huge conceptual catch-all for everything from unorganized religious expression to a flotilla of organized religions that, from the point of view of the mainstream, are not traditional *in the United States*. This qualifier is important, for many religions that are considered nontraditional here are *very* traditional in other places in the world. On the other hand, in the last decades of the century there was an efflorescence of "new spirituality" marked by eclecticism and religious combining.

In one sign of the times, a 1992 article in the *New Age Journal* profiled a readership that, in response to a survey, identified itself as mostly Christian or Jewish in background but at the moment of the query involved in a plethora of alternative spiritualities. Fully 95 percent had gone outside of the religions of their childhood to explore spiritual alternatives, and only 30 percent maintained a connection with their early faith tradition. Meanwhile, sociologist Phillip E. Hammond, in a study of religious regionalism, identified a "third disestablishment" in American religion. With the first disestablishment the legal one provided by the First Amendment to the Constitution and the second the loss of Protestant hegemony in the period between the two world wars, Hammond saw a third disestablishment intimately bound to what he called the rise of "personal autonomy" since the 1960s.

For Hammond's sociological colleague Wade Clark Roof especially, it was the "baby-boom" generation that provided the most dramatic evidence of religious change. Those born from 1946 to 1962 were marked in their independence from the churches. Not only was the dropout rate huge (those remaining outside the church or synagogue for at least two years constituted over 60 percent of the sample), but those who chose to return to more or less traditional organized religions did so on their own often-eclectic terms. Even further, some 60 percent of those who dropped out did not return at all. Given this end-of-century religious climate, it is important to gain historical perspective.

## THE BACKGROUND: MAINSTREAM AND OTHER STREAMS

Unchurched America is hardly a new phenomenon. Even during the church-building years of the nineteenth century, unorganized and unchurched religion flourished. The evangelical revivals are often cited for their role in building religious institutions, but religious enthusiasm fostered, in many cases, varieties of "do-it-yourself" Christianity. Just as important, if less well documented, popular occultism and metaphysical beliefs were also widespread. Inherited notions of witchcraft and astrology were predicated on the religious idea of correspondence, according to which the world and human society reflected larger, overarching patterns in the cosmos. Supported by the maxim "as above, so below," folk practitioners acted out long-accepted—if mostly unselfconsciously held—theologies of connection. Such theologies were based on natural laws that were seen as ruling the universe. Magical work sought to manipulate nature and/or events by using objects or acts that corresponded in some way to what (person, object, place, and so forth) they wished to affect. In rural settings, people planted by the astrological "signs" and executed a series of other farming tasks according to the same guides.

With the arrival in America after 1836 of demonstrations of animal magnetism or mesmerism, experimentation with mind-body relationships became a popular fad, and with the new interest came metaphysical speculation regarding the flow of "tides" or energies in the universe that were required for health and happiness. Metaphors of blockage and obstruction began to prevail in some circles in the explanations given for illness. The cure of bodies easily slipped over into the domain of the cure of souls, and the early beginnings of mind-cure and the metaphysical religious tradition could be discerned. After the Civil War, these metaphysical beginnings would take shape in the development of Christian Science and New Thought, with its surviving twentieth-century denominations like Unity, the Church of Religious Science, and the Church of Divine Science.

Much earlier in the nineteenth century, though, the religious views of the eighteenth-century Swedish seer Immanuel Swedenborg made their way among both ordinary and elite Americans. Swedenborg's learned discourses were grounded in the idea of correspondence. His reports of mystical journeys typically conflated matter and spirit in their descriptions of exceedingly sensuous landscapes in heaven and hell. And his theology of the divine influx and of the Divine Human blurred the line between the supernatural world of Christianity and an earthly one.

Swedenborgian theory formed and shaped an "occult" Ralph Waldo Emerson— addressing mysterious connections between nature, mind, and spirit— and Swedenborgian theory also significantly affected the popular religious climate of the times. In this context, in addition to Christian Science and New Thought, the nineteenth century saw the emergence of a series of indigenous religious movements with occult and/or metaphysical roots. Mormonism was a case in point. With its roots intertwined with the folk magic of upstate New York, Mormonism began a saga of growth that eventually distanced it from its origins. But Joseph Smith, who founded Mormonism, was a dowser who engaged in "money-digging"; and from one perspective, the golden plates that he claimed to discover and that were said to contain the Book of Mormon were another instance of buried treasure.

Even given the astounding early success of Mormonism from the 1830s, however, spiritualism was, for most people of the time, the most spectacular of the nineteenth-century indigenous religious movements. After 1848 and the reported communications of the teenage Fox sisters (Maggie and Kate) with the spirit of a murdered peddler buried in the cellar of their upstate New York home, spiritualism spread, seemingly like wildfire. Mainstream Protestants in middle-of-the-road cities like Cleveland, Ohio, felt threatened by a spiritualist onslaught, while liberals, like the Quakers in upstate New York, nurtured and encouraged its growth.

Allying themselves with contemporary interest in science, spiritualists delighted in demonstrating for learned inquisitors the presence of the spirits. In spiritualist thinking, the phenomenon of spirit manifestation in physical form could be verified in scientific terms, for believers saw the spirits as refined material beings. Moreover, identifying themselves with the reform movements of mid-century, like antislavery and women's rights, spiritualists signaled that, in America, occult and metaphysical concerns did not necessarily preclude social action. Later, by the closing years of the twentieth century, that stance would be paralleled by the environmental and related concerns of many in the New Age movement.

In the late nineteenth century, however, spiritualism itself changed with the times, and by 1875 the Theosophical Society came into existence as a spiritualist reform movement. Founded by the unconventional Russian immigrant Madame Helena Blavatsky and the American lawyer and former government official Colonel Henry Olcott, along with William Q. Judge and others, the Theosophical Society at first sought to uncover and study occult laws of nature. Members of the society, like participants in the spiritualist movement from which they emerged, saw no conflict between their endeavors and those of science, and indeed, from their point of view, what they were doing was extending its domains. Drawing mostly upper- and upper-middle-class members, the Theosophical Society would have a profound influence, through its lineage of teachers, on the growth of a new spirituality in the twentieth century.

Meanwhile, on the other side of the religious divide, evangelicalism sparked the birth of new and— important here—millennial religious movements in the antebellum years of the nineteenth century and beyond. Among the leading examples was the Millerite movement, followers of one William Miller who, based on his study of scripture, became convinced that the Second Coming of Christ and the end of the world would occur in 1843 and then—after correction to his calculations—in 1844. But other popular forms of millennialism also flourished, especially in a form called premillennial dispensationalism, brought from England. With considerable interest in the dispensations, or ages, into which Biblical time was divided, many agreed that Jesus would come before the millennium, or endtime—hence the designation "premillennial." In this climate, a number of adventist religions grew, and some of the beginnings of popular Protestant fundamentalism could be found.

Protestantism spawned new religious movements from its liberal side as well, notably in the arrival of Unitarianism and Universalism. Both antebellum developments, the two movements grew strong in New England and shared a number of theological ideas—the goodness of God and humanity and the universal nature of salvation. In the twentieth century (1962), they would come together as the Unitarian-Universalist Association. By that time, the new denomination would be flourishing as a home for nontraditional and combinatory religious thought and practice. By this century's end, non-Christian humanists and rationalists (products of movements earlier in the century) would pursue their beliefs within the association alongside neopagans, who worshiped nature and the Goddess.

The first notable Eastern religious presence to the United States came at the end of the nineteenth century. As Asian religions made their way in this country, they took form in both *export* and *ethnic* manifestations. Export religions involved non-Asian American converts from different religious backgrounds. Ethnic religions were part of the heritage of the national groups that brought them. In their export versions, Asian religious philosophies were spread in elite, and to some extent also in popular, circles by the New England transcendentalists as early as the 1840s. After the Civil War, an emerging interest in comparative religions could be found among scholars, and the Theosophical Society after 1878 especially promoted its own (eclectic and occult) version of Eastern religious ideas, for example, intertwining the concepts of karma and reincarnation.

Then, in 1893, the World's Parliament of Religions, held in conjunction with the Chicago Columbian Exposition of that year, which drew over 27 million people to its exhibits, brought Eastern teachers to the United States. The press gave the speakers at the parliament relatively wide coverage, and the public was introduced to a lesson in comparative religions that was generally favorable to the Asians. After the Columbian World's Fair, a number of these visitors traveled in the states to promote their views, and a few new religious movements for American converts to Asian religions—most notably, the Vedanta Society—remained as legacies.

For Californians and other westerners, the ethnic versions of Asian religions were probably more noticeable. As early as the 1840s, Chinese immigrants appeared on the West Coast. Temples arose in San Francisco's Chinatown by the middle of the next decade, mingling elements of Buddhism, Taoism, and Confucianism. The Japanese brought Buddhism to Hawaii in 1889 and to California a decade later. With few South Asians in the United States at the time, the appearance of ethnic forms of Hinduism would have to await the twentieth century and, indeed, the passage of a new immigration law in 1965, which would greatly expand the entry quota for South Asians.

The ethnic religions attracted the inquiring interest of few, however, due in part to prejudice against, and persecution of, the Asian peoples. The Chinese, who had come to the West Coast mostly as railroad construction workers, suffered hostility, physical violence, and a government policy of exclusion. In an even starker history for the Japanese, legislation restricted their presence, prohibited their citizenship, and later, during World War II, forcibly evacuated them to internment camps. Given the early suspicion, open hatred, and exclusion, it is remarkable that export versions of Asian religions proved as attractive to turn-of-the-century and later non-Asian Americans as they did.

On another front, the general arrival of ethnic Muslims in the United States began toward the end of the nineteenth century. Their numbers were initially small, and among them the largest group was Arabs who came from Syria and what is now Lebanon. Generally, religious practice was not strong, and the relatively small size of the immigrant community militated against a flourishing ethnic religion. Nor were there compelling reasons for non-Arab conversions. It would be in the twentieth century that, with new sources of immigration and new American immigration laws, Islam came into its own as a vital ethnic religion and that it also flourished, especially among African Americans, as an export religion. Even so, by the dawn of the twentieth century, all the elements were present that would determine the future of nontraditional religions in America; and for astute observers, the beginnings of a crumbling mainstream could be witnessed.

## OLDER AMERICAN NEW RELIGIONS

Erosion came slowly, however. By the 1920s late-nineteenth-century changes in evangelical Protestantism brought the birth of a full-fledged fundamentalism. Bringing together premillennial dispensationalism with a rationalism that regarded the Bible as a book of "scientific" facts, fundamentalists brought revival and holiness traditions into a new brand of militant religious antimodernism. In this context fundamentalists identified a short list of traditional beliefs that became the litmus test of orthodoxy. The short list of "fundamentals" varied from statement to statement, but in all of the forms in which the fundamentals were announced, they brought, ironically, a new and nontraditional Protestantism, with a more strident insistence on radical supernaturalism and absolute surety expressed in terms of the literal fulfillment of Biblical prophecy. And significantly, dispensationalism continued to flourish in their midst.

If their movement was, from the historic mainstream Christian perspective of the nation, nontraditional, fundamentalists still maintained strong ties to the mainstream in the Protestant legacy they shared. More independent in its stance, however, was Mormonism. The Latter-day Saints made dramatic shifts as they moved out of the nineteenth century and away from their folk magical roots. They had trekked to the Great Salt Desert from Nauvoo, Illinois, after their founder, Joseph Smith, was shot to death in 1844. In the western desert, under Brigham Young, they formed their theocratic Kingdom of Deseret, and, harnessing agricultural science to business initiative and religious resolve, made the desert blossom. Following a distinctive semicommunal way of life expressed most dramatically, by mainstream standards, in the practice of polygamy, they framed a theological position and ritual accompaniment that marked their difference from Protestant America. Their doctrine of continuing revelation through the church presidency forged them as a resilient religious organization, able to change with the needs of the times.

By the 1890s, the times invited an official end to polygamy to promote the statehood of Utah, after Supreme Court decisions (*Reynolds* v. *United States* in 1879 and *Davis* v. *Beason* in 1890) that attacked Mormon sexual practice. But before it ended officially, the practice of polygamy told implicitly of a church that embraced the restorationism that united a series of nineteenth-century Protestant churches. Mormons went well beyond these Protestant churches, however, seeking to restore the church of the New Testament, and more, the religious culture of the Old. Seen in this context, their polygamous ideal was a radical call to renewal for a new Nation of Israel.

Even after the end-of-century changes that transformed Mormonism, any careful examination finds an enduring legacy from the past. The Swedenborgian conflation of spirit and matter lives on in a theology of materialism. In Mormon teaching, the next world will in many respects resemble this one, and humans will reign with God as material, and even sexual, beings. Meanwhile, Mormon "temple work" uses ritual to bring baptism to ancestors who are regarded as unredeemed. And temple work also aspires to link married couples "for time and eternity."

The Mormon affirmation that families will endure in heaven has likewise encouraged an emphasis on family and community on earth. By the late twentieth century, Mormonism could boast of astonishing success in recruitment, with a membership in the United States alone of well over 4 million, marking it as a leading American denomination. It had linked that success not to the promulgation of an esoteric theology, but to a hearty endorsement of family values. Joining to buttress the family-based community were a mission program that was evangelical in style and the strong encouragement of a disciplined way of life. And the Mormon formula seemed to lead to public prominence and success, with church members identifiable as leaders in business and government. Like the founders of the nation, for whom membership in Freemasonic lodges meant, not occult and esoteric practice, but a social bond with peers and a pathway to success, Mormons used their esoteric past to enhance their more mainstream present.

Those who more thoroughly inherited the occult and metaphysical preference of the nineteenth century could less easily be identified with the mainstream. Still, spiritualism, theosophy, Christian Science, and New Thought continued as viable alternatives in the twentieth century. Generally speaking, each acquired an orthodoxy of its own and assumed organizational form in denominational or denominationlike bodies, many of them—as in the mainstream denominations—the result of separating from other religious bodies.

Within the spiritualist camp, the medium, who communicated with the spirit world, functioned at the center of ritual and life. Two kinds of mediumship—mental and physical—were now standard. In mental mediumship, with the medium in a trance state, formalized practices could be easily recognized by the twentieth century. The medium typically engaged in billet reading by responding to questions submitted on small pieces of paper and directed to a spirit. Or the medium practiced psychometry, in which she (the medium was more often than not a woman) aimed to get in touch with vibrations of a physical object and so learn all she could about people (now dead) who had touched it in the past. Again, the medium prophesied by reading auras, bands of light of different colors believed to emanate from the human body. These auras were thought to record the life history of a person, enabling a spirit to make predictions.

In physical mediumship, spirits were held to acquire material form at a seance (the ritual meeting at which the medium attempted to contact the spirits). Here accounts of spirits tipping over tables and sending objects flying through the air were rife. In automatic writing, spirits were said to use the hand of the medium to write their message, and in independent writing to write, without any material guidance, on paper. On some occasions, spirits reportedly made an object disappear in one place and rematerialize in a second. In another standard practice, they were said to use specially constructed trumpets to speak to people at a seance. Even more standard, in the twentieth century, became the elaborate system of spirit guides identified as manifesting themselves at a seance to aid the medium and others present. Indian chiefs and spirit doctors were popular in these roles, Indian chiefs often as gate keepers, who would keep unwanted spirits away, and spirit doctors as lecturers or advisers on spiritual subjects. Moreover, as in the nineteenth century, mediums sometimes claimed healing gifts through a force thought to flow from their fingers.

The spiritualists, thus, succeeded in developing a full ceremonial range for their seances. They were not so successful in guaranteeing an orthodoxy in their organization. From their nineteenth-century beginnings they resisted structure and splintered into small groups around different mediums or groups of mediums. After the foundation of the Theosophical Society, some took a decidedly theosophical turn in their incorporation of a variety of nontraditional beliefs and practices, especially centering on concepts of karma and reincarnation. Others maintained closer ties to Christianity, and in 1893, the National Spiritualist Association of Churches came into existence with a membership made up mostly of those who had been Christians. Yet, although the National Spiritualist Association of Churches drew on Christian doctrine and in 1930 condemned reincarnation, it still declined to identify itself as specifically Christian. Those who did formed other bodies, the most significant being the Christian Spiritual Church. Begun in 1907, the church still holds to its Confession of Faith that links the authority of the Bible to beliefs regarding spirit communication.

Today the National Spiritualist Association of Churches is the largest of the spiritualist organizations as well as the oldest. Reporting 127 member congregations in 1988, it is clearly neither strong nor universal. The number of Americans who are spiritualists can only be guessed; and, in the best estimate, there are probably between 1,000 and 2,000 churches overall. Moreover, most of the other occult and metaphysical groups reflected the spiritualist difficulty with organization. With their teaching about the unity of matter and spirit, blending of religion with an occult form of science, reform activism, and openness to believers from any background, they were people without boundaries.

The twentieth-century saga of theosophy is a good illustration of these themes. By 1930 there were roughly 50,000 theosophists in forty countries, 10,000 of them in the United States. Yet the society was beset by factionalism even before the death of its founders, and in 1895 William Judge led a huge portion of the American membership in forming the independent Theosophical Society in America. Other schisms followed, and it was evident that theosophists were willing to pursue their quests wherever they would lead.

Divergent though their paths might be, theosophists shared a synthetic style that offered institutional models for mingling ideas and practices culled from many traditions. In fact, the Theosophical Society provided the first organized conduit for the introduction of Asian religious thought to Anglo-America. From the late 1870s, Hinduism and Buddhism began to figure heavily in the thinking of the society, after Madame Blavatsky claimed that she was receiving teaching messages from individuals she called the Mahatmas. These, according to Blavatsky, were members of a select brotherhood who, while still human, had evolved to degrees of perfection beyond those normally reached by others. Usually dwelling in Tibet, they were thought to possess abilities to materialize at will or to communicate through letters that also materialized instantly at their behest.

More than any other American group, theosophists promoted concepts of karma and reincarnation and blended them with the teaching of Western adepts of the occult. Even further, theosophists absorbed plentifully from the popular transcendentalism, Swedenborgianism, mesmerism, and spiritualism that were the legacy of the nineteenth century. And, like the spiritualists, theosophists united metaphysics with what they regarded as the latest reports of science. They championed belief in the lost continents of Atlantis and Lemuria, the existence of the latter supported by nineteenth-century biologists; and they rewrote Darwinian evolution into a theory of the evolution of seven "root" races, the fifth of which included the Aryans. Increasingly, expectation grew among theosophists that one of the Mahatmas, or "masters," would come to earth as a savior figure who was a "world teacher" for humanity. The presence of the master, they said, would inaugurate a "new age." Indeed, so insistent did they become concerning the master who would bring the new age that by the second decade of the twentieth century they claimed his existence in a young Indian boy, Jiddu Krishnamurti. Until 1929, when Krishnamurti denied that he was the world teacher and struck out on his own, theosophists promoted their messianic belief.

The theosophical harvest of belief and practice, with all its organizational weakness, was destined to have an effect on nontraditional America that far exceeded its institutional moorings or size. In fact, in one way the organizational weakness of theosophy became its greatest strength. Theosophists managed to generate perhaps several hundred small organizations that continued their ideas—and any number of individual teachers who, by their presence and publications, served as magnets to attract numerous small followings. With their family resemblances, these could later coalesce in a diffuse, but still powerful, presence in the New Age movement of the late twentieth century.

Paralleling the declarations of nineteenth-century spiritualist mediums who engaged in automatic writing and appeared on public stages as trance speakers, theosophists spoke of receiving the words that a series of masters delivered. Moreover, they felt free to innovate, and in this climate the numbers of masters multiplied. So it was, for example, that by the middle of the 1950s, in the wake of a series of sightings of unidentified flying objects (UFOs) that had begun in 1947, some theosophists regarded the masters as space commanders who were "transmitting" their messages through "channels," that is, through claimed human contactees.

If the theosophical lineage had produced teachers who could reify the farther reaches of space, the late-nineteenth-century legacy of Christian Science was different. Founded in 1879 by Mary Baker Eddy, a New Englander who had encountered spiritualism, mesmerism, and, at least indirectly, Swedenborgianism, Christian Science reflected its cultural context. All three of the earlier movements had taught a kind

of "soft" monism in which there was a materialist gloss on the invisible world. Eddy took the model and, in effect, inverted it. In the new religion she promulgated with the publication of her textbook *Science and Health* in 1875, she taught a monism in which all that was ultimately real was spirit or Mind.

But Eddy's strong Calvinist roots in the Congregational church were as much a part of her context as the metaphysical world. And so, with a personal history of years of chronic illness, she came to believe and to teach the possibility of personal healing through the revelation of Jesus Christ. She urged that this revelation was a practical ideal for others to imitate by bringing to light the perfection of their true (and spiritual) natures, instead of accepting the limitations of the false world of matter.

Hence, Christian Science taught a broad understanding of Christian revelation, expounded a metaphysical system to help modern people understand it, and practiced healing as a logical outcome of its beliefs about Christ and the world. The "science" of the new religion's self-designation, especially as evidenced in its language of "demonstration" (that is, healing) was a function of the same culture in which, earlier, spiritualists had invited scientific scrutiny of seance phenomena. In keeping with the self-consciously scientific framework, Eddy continually referred to members of her organization as "students" and conceived her role as that of teacher. In 1881, just two years after the official incorporation of the church, she received a charter for the Massachusetts Metaphysical College, in which she trained future Christian Science practitioners, or healers.

The National Christian Science Association followed as an organization in 1886, but not long afterward, Eddy's dissatisfaction with innovation in Christian Science ranks led her to take steps to consolidate and regulate her new teaching. She gave up the charter of the college in 1889, and in 1892 dissolved the association. At the same time, she reorganized the Boston church, which she controlled, urging Christian Scientists throughout the country to apply for membership in what she called the Mother Church.

Thus began a process of joint membership in which most Christian Scientists belonged to both a local organization and the Mother Church in Boston. Here a self-perpetuating board of directors assumed a power that lived on after the death of Eddy in 1910, while in the branch churches, pastors were replaced by readers appointed for three-year terms. Worship under the guidance of the readers did not involve the traditional preaching office but, instead, the reading of assigned passages from the Bible and

*Science and Health*, its sanctioned interpretation. In practice, thus, revelation had been given only in the scriptural understanding that Eddy taught, while other readings were forbidden. Under these circumstances, the Christian Science organization became a model of technical efficiency.

It was likewise a decidedly feminine organization, not only in leadership but also in membership. Many of those who joined Eddy were women in midlife and of middle-class status (although, to be sure, there were also many—and prominent—men in the church). The appeal of Eddy's movement for these women was its invitation to a purposeful life that could be lived *alone*. Meanwhile, the denial of the primacy of the social world that the new religion involved was implicitly a rebuttal to the male orientation of public space in an America that had denied the floor to women and their concerns.

By the late twentieth century, however, the earlier feminization of Christian Science had been eclipsed by other factors, and its appeal, even for women, seemed limited. Small (with most of its roughly 3,000 churches in the United States), without an ordained ministry or published membership statistics, Christian Science appeared to be declining. Moreover, by the 1990s, there were noticeable tensions and rifts between at least two factions regarding the future direction of the church. A dominant leadership in its governance structure promoted the work of the *Christian Science Monitor* (founded by Eddy in 1908 to offer a healing approach to social issues) and parallel media ventures. Others, among them leading theologians within the movement, took a more traditionalist stance that turned more to spiritual healing and practice.

Whatever the final resolution of these issues, Christian Science, more than any other single organization, had made its mark on American culture regarding the seriousness of spiritual healing. Its record of court challenges in this regard was noteworthy, and it provided an early model for an alternative healing movement that grew profusely, seemingly from every direction, by the last decades of the twentieth century. In the era of its own beginnings, moreover, its claims for spiritual healing were taken up in a larger mind-cure movement that culminated in the birth of New Thought. Indeed, the histories of Christian Science and New Thought were so entwined that it is difficult to separate them. At a crucial point in her life, in 1862, Eddy had sought the assistance of Phineas P. Quimby, a celebrated mental healer who began to help and to teach her. Quimby also taught the early leaders of New Thought who came to Boston to announce their gospel of mind cure.

Quimby, who had formerly practiced mesmerism and styled himself a "magnetic doctor" (for "animal magnetism"), had become convinced of the power of thought in creating illness and health. Probably under Swedenborgian influence, he had absorbed the idea of correspondence between human beings, whom he understood as spiritual in nature, and a divine Mind. The breakthrough to healing, for him, came through an awakening within the mind of the patient of a sense of divine relationship, and Quimby identified the means to the awakening with a wisdom or science he called the Christ.

Whatever debt Eddy owed to Quimby's ideas, she had molded them in a Calvinist direction. It was Warren Felt Evans who first systematized them for the early mind-cure movement. A former Methodist minister and later a Swedenborgian, he was healed of chronic illness by Quimby and in turn became a healer. In 1869, he produced his first book, *The Mental Cure*, in which he argued that disease was the result of a loss of mental balance that, in turn, affected the body. As Evans developed his views, he posited a Christ Principle as an emanation from a One that was present within every person. Union with this Christ Principle, the divine spark within, said Evans, brought wholeness and health. Still further, he declared that when the basic harmony was disturbed and union with the divine force was interrupted, another individual—a doctor—could help. In that relationship and the healing act, Evans stressed above all the power of suggestion. Likewise, he spoke of the power of conscious affirmation, and it was his thinking that turned later New Thought toward the practice in which the sick person affirmed health in deliberate internal statements at the same time that disease was mentally banished as error.

Mary Baker Eddy's *Science and Health* had attracted readers who also read Evans. Those who were uncomfortable with Eddy's authoritarianism and who left her organization became among the most widely influential of the early New Thought teachers. There is, for example, the case of Emma Curtis Hopkins, who struck out on her own to found a Christian Science seminary in Chicago. More eclectic and mystical than Eddy, with her speaking and writing she taught a generation of future New Thought leaders from Ernest Holmes, who founded Religious Science, to Charles and Myrtle Fillmore, who initiated Unity, and Malinda E. Cramer and Mona L. Brooks, who began Divine Science.

Even earlier, in 1882, Julius and Annetta Dresser,

both former Quimby students, had begun to practice mental healing in Boston. Within a decade, mind cure or "mental science" was coming to be known as New Thought, a way of thinking that was distinguished from older theology, even though people in the movement for the most part did not see themselves forming a separate church. Still, in the mid-1890s, the Church of the Higher Life was organized in Boston, and even more important, the Metaphysical Club was formed in 1895, becoming the center for the movement's national and international development.

By the turn of the century, there was an International Metaphysical League, and it's members were teaching (like Mary Baker Eddy) the universal fatherhood and motherhood of God. Meanwhile, prosperity thinking had joined healing in the teachings of the movement, and worldly wealth and success had come to be seen as expected outcomes for those who did not impede or block the flow of a divine Supply. From 1915, International New Thought Congresses were held annually, bringing together the many diverse groups who worked under the banner of New Thought. An organization called the International New Thought Alliance continued to provide leadership through the twentieth century, while the Unity School of Christianity, with its vast publishing enterprises–including the small and ubiquitous monthly pamphlet *Daily Word*—and its ministerial training program, became probably the best known of New Thought institutions. Other New Thought denominations, such as Divine Science, based in Denver, and Religious Science, headquartered in Los Angeles, helped to spread belief.

Yet New Thought's ambivalence about existing in separate churches proved a continuing theme, and it made its biggest mark through its publishing, with many of its books best sellers in the "self-help" market. Ralph Waldo Trine's *In Tune with the Infinite* (1897), for example, sold well over 2 million copies and continues to be reprinted regularly. Even more, New Thought influenced liberal Protestantism so that many who were part of the mainstream absorbed its ideas and values and began to spread them. Norman Vincent Peale, with his *Power of Positive Thinking* (1952), brought mental healing and the success ethic to millions of people outside the movement, while his other books and magazines also fostered the trend. Indeed, Peale was only the most well-known of a series of writers who brought Americans a similar message. New Thought shared its fundamental assumptions with the occult tradition; but, in the end, its individualism, optimism, and affirmations of health and prosperity dissolved the mystery that surrounded occultism and blended it unobtrusively with mainstream American culture. In this regard, probably more than any other religious movement, New Thought became the precursor for a New Age movement that by the 1990s was dissolving into a more generic "new spirituality."

## EASTERN RELIGIONS IN ETHNIC AND EXPORT FORMS

Throughout the nineteenth century, Eastern religions in the United States were growing in number and in size. Closest to the Protestant and Roman Catholic mainstream was Eastern Orthodoxy. Orthodoxy had come to Alaska from Russia in the eighteenth century and had moved, by 1872, to San Francisco. By the end of the nineteenth century, Russian Orthodoxy officially entered New York, with a rapidly increasing Russian immigration to America. Indeed, in the decade from 1906 to 1916, Orthodox church membership grew fivefold, from 20,000 to 100,000 people.

In the new century, however, Russian Orthodox presence in America was exceeded by the numbers who belonged to the Greek Orthodox church, the result of large-scale immigration beginning at the end of the previous century. Membership in the Greek church swelled, until in the 1970s it reached a figure close to 2 million. By then, the Russian church could claim over 1 million members as well as an intellectual leadership that made it the most prominent theological voice of the Orthodox in America. Nor were the two churches the only representatives of Orthodoxy, for another million or so Orthodox people belonged to various separate national churches—among them Albanian, Bulgarian, Romanian, Serbian, Syrian, and Ukrainian. Thus, the Orthodox community in the United States was close in size to the American Jewish presence. And despite some notable exceptions in the cases of small groups and individual converts, for the most part Orthodoxy took shape in the United States as an ethnic more than export community.

Joining all the representatives of this most "Western" of Eastern traditions were a series of ideas and practices that separated them from both the Roman Catholic and Reformation churches. Indeed, as one student of Orthodoxy has explained, not only were the religious answers different from those of the Western churches but even the questions were. In Orthodoxy, the local community was the church, and religious organization was achieved in a series of self-governing, mostly national churches. Communities such as these were united by their adherence to a common tradition in belief inherited through scripture, through the writings of esteemed authorities, and through word-of-mouth teaching. Thought to lead back to the time of Jesus and to include the teaching of seven ecumenical ("worldwide") church councils, the last of them in the eighth century, Orthodoxy meant, literally, "right, or correct, worship" and the beliefs on which it rested.

With the primacy of worship underscored in its very name, the Orthodox became renowned for the splendor of their services. With their center in the Divine Liturgy (a parallel to the Western Roman Catholic Mass), these services were held in churches constructed to imitate, in their beauty, the heaven of Orthodox belief. Images were held in high repute, and these icons and their veneration became so important that an iconic theology dominated Orthodox thinking. For this theology, sacred images and objects were windows into another world, places for contact with what was considered divine. By extension, human beings were seen as icons of God, and there was less emphasis on sin in Eastern Orthodoxy than in Roman Catholicism or in Protestantism. It followed that turning within to find God in acts of religious contemplation was encouraged. But the most important icon for the Orthodox was Jesus Christ, seen as the image of God's glory and light, as the being in whom the divine had entered the human world to transform it. Hence, the Orthodox portrayed Jesus as a divine king and victor over the forces of evil and minimized depictions of the sufferings of a crucified Christ.

In America, as in other cultures to which Orthodoxy had come, it blended with prevailing ideas and values even as it insisted on its independence from them. Thus, Orthodoxy continued to be a religion of both mystical contemplation and ethnic solidarity. The solidarity, however, was more characteristic of the immigrant generation, and as immigration decreased so did Orthodox allegiance. By the late twentieth century, Orthodoxy was still "other" from the vantage point of the religious mainstream, but second- and third-generation children of the immigrants had grown away from their heritage. Nor did the Orthodox fail to adapt to new times and circumstances. Many of them reformed their liturgies to bring them closer to the cultural style of a Protestant mainstream. English came into use in services, often alternating with various national languages spoken in the different churches. The calendar of feasts and holy days, which had followed ancient Eastern practice, was altered to bring it into conformity with the Western Christian calendar. In many churches, seats were introduced so that people would not have to stand during the Divine Liturgy; and often instruments and mixed choirs were used–different from older Orthodox practice.

American relocation often led, too, to confused jurisdictional claims for these essentially national churches. Disputes frequently erupted and sometimes became long and bitter, since about a dozen or so Orthodox groups had competing claims. By the 1970s there were at least three separate branches of Russian Orthodoxy in the United States (the legacy of the early-century Russian Revolution), three groups of Ukrainian Orthodox church members, and two groups of Syrian Orthodox adherents. Throughout the century small splinter churches were formed by those who sought to make their religion more universal and more American.

Beyond these churches, other Eastern Christians remained outside the Orthodox umbrella but, organized in different national churches and practicing distinctive rites, were linked in communion with the Roman Catholic pope and were known as Uniates. Finally, still other Eastern Christians–those who had separated from the main body of Christendom even before the traditionally dated Orthodox-Western break in the eleventh century–could also be found in twentieth-century America. The most noteworthy examples here were members of the Armenian Apostolic Church and of the Coptic Church.

Close to Eastern Orthodox lands of origin and in some cases overlapping them were the homelands of Islamic peoples. A Middle Eastern religion both geographically and theologically, Islam shares many of the basic ideas of Jews and Christians, but it is also very different. In twentieth-century America, it has been essentially a religion of "otherness," even though, close to this century's end, the changes in the immigration law multiplied the numbers of Muslim immigrants and, among African Americans, the major faction of the former Nation of Islam had edged its way toward Islamic Orthodoxy. In 1992, there were 1,900 Muslim mosques in the United States and 2,400 Muslim institutions.

The general arrival of Muslims from abroad to the United States began toward the end of the nineteenth century. Syrian and Lebanese Arab Muslims, although mostly from an agricultural background, quickly adjusted to city life. They concentrated their settlements in industrial centers such as New York, Chicago, and Detroit, where they peddled dry goods, operated small businesses, or engaged in unskilled labor. Generally, they were economically successful.

In addition to the Arabs, however, other Muslims immigrated to the United States. Among the Europeans, over 3,000 Muslims from Poland, of Tatar origin, settled in New York. And after World War II, when significant numbers of Muslim immigrants began to arrive, they included Albanians and Yugoslavs. Among South Asians, initial immigration had come earlier. A large number of Indian Muslims immigrated to California agricultural sites in 1906, most of them associated with the mission-minded Ahmadiyya Movement in Islam, a reinterpretation of the Islamic tradition begun in India in 1889 by Mirza Ghulam Ahmad. Later, after the Immigration Act of 1965 and the abolition of the old quota system, more and more Indian and Pakistani Muslims immigrated.

By the 1980s, Muslim immigrants in America came from more than sixty countries. Arabs, Middle Easterners, Europeans, and South Asians had been joined by Central and South Americans and even Indians from Fiji. Arabs and Iranians constituted the largest immigrant communities, followed, after 1965, by impressive numbers of Pakistanis and Asian Indians. Like Eastern Orthodoxy, American Islam was an ethnic religion, reflecting the national origins of its immigrant constituencies.

However, Islam had always thought of itself as a universal religion with a message for all people, and there were converts in America and the presence of Islam in export form. Individuals from Protestant, Catholic, Jewish, and Mormon backgrounds came to Islam mostly through marriage. Meanwhile, African Americans were attracted by the Islamic message of universal community and equality among all races. They heard willingly the Muslim tradition that a daughter of Muhammad, the founder of Islam, had married a black man. Some African Americans were drawn to the Indian Ahmadiyya Movement, with its message of universal peace and unity, and to various Muslim organizations. The major African-American presence, however, was in the Nation of Islam that became, sequentially, the World Community of al-Islam in the West, the American Muslim Mission, and then simply the Muslim American community.

Begun in the 1930s as a decidedly heterodox version of Islam, under its second leader, Elijah Muhammad (born Elijah Poole), the Nation of Islam prospered as a militant separatist and nationalistic religious movement that taught black superiority and white moral bankruptcy. Even during the lifetime of Elijah Muhammad, however, there was a variant interpretation of the Nation of Islam. Malcolm X (born Malcolm Little), one of Elijah Muhammad's most trusted lieutenants, gradually came to see the message of Islam as universal human solidarity and broke with the movement in 1964.

Malcolm X was shot to death in 1965 by members of the parent Nation of Islam, but a decade later, some of his ideas flourished. After the death of Elijah Muhammad in 1975, his son Wallace D. Muhammad assumed control of the organization. Educated in Egypt and an Arabic speaker, it was the younger Muhammad who broke with black separatism, radically decentralized the movement, and moved it toward orthodox Islam. Perhaps 100,000 of the Nation's former members followed him, although, to be sure, there were countermovements (the most notable under Minister Louis Farrakhan). Warith (as he had changed his name) Muhammad resigned as official leader of what had now become an essentially congregational structure and reshaped his role as an independent Muslim lecturer and member of the World Council of Masajid with its headquarters in Mecca. Likewise, he acted as official distributor of Arab-donated missionary funds to Muslim organizations in the United States. And in an appointment that was for ritual reasons more honorific, world Islamic leaders designated him to certify American Muslims for participation in the Islamic annual pilgrimage to Mecca.

By the end of the 1980s, African Americans constituted probably 1 million out of the 6 million orthodox Muslims in the nation, and converts to Islam were for the most part black. In the 1990s, Islam in its ethnic and export forms could be found in almost every American town of any size. Muslims were present noticeably in eastern and midwestern industrial and commercial centers and in West Coast cities. With a continuing flow of immigrants, a high birthrate, and consistent attractiveness to converts, American Islam grew faster than statisticians could document. Indeed, if current estimates of numbers of followers of the Muslim tradition are correct, Islam in America may be second only to Christianity in adherents.

As a religion, Islam was the product of the reports of visions and voice revelations of the merchant Muhammad in the seventh-century Arabian desert. Its message was one of radical monotheism: Muhammad was God's (Allah's) Prophet but not, significantly, his equal or his son. Yet Islam was the spiritual relative of Christianity as well as of Judaism, and Muslims saw their faith as the culmination and completion of the teachings of Judaism and Christianity. And with their so-called Five Pillars of religious practice, they emphatically declared that action was central to religion. Formal prayer confessing Allah and his prophet Muhammad was essential, and this was required five times daily, almsgiving enjoined, an annual fast prescribed during the Islamic month of Ramadan, and a pilgrimage to Mecca (the Muslim holy city in present-day Saudi Arabia) urged at least once during a person's lifetime.

Muslim observance of *sunna*, or customs, supplemented the teachings of the Qur'an, and the largest division of the Muslim community, the Sunni Muslims, took their name therefrom. Sunni were historically countered in their claims to Islamic orthodoxy by Shiite Muslims, who quarreled with the Sunni version of early Muslim history and placed authority in imams, religious leaders who functioned as living lawgivers. Beyond these two major divisions, the Sufis, the mystics of Islam, formed a third. Engaging sometimes in austere practices of self-denial and at other times in forms of song and dance that gained them renown, they formed religious communities, or orders, that, by the late twentieth century, inspired groups in the New Age movement.

As the twentieth century began, however, Muslims feared the contact with Anglo-America more than they merged their cultural forms with it. Indeed, the fear of losing Islam was an important factor delaying immigration to this nation. And the early fear was well-founded. Without a critical mass of immigrants, observance of the Five Pillars for the most part fell away: prayer five times daily in a culture not organized to support it became a near-impossible requirement. Fasting during the month of Ramadan, avoidance of pork products, and employment of required ritual slaughter practices for animals intended as food—none of these were easy demands. Even American banking practices, based on interest received or paid, threatened traditional Muslim beliefs that forbade the taking of interest. The foreignness of Islam was painful to many of the young, who were being educated in American public schools and now looked at their religious history from the vantage point of the American mainstream. Perhaps 80 to 90 percent of second- and third-generation Muslims went "unmosqued."

Yet the loss was not total. Like so many other newcomers, ethnic Muslims tended to live together in communities that were modeled on their relationships in their countries of origin. Often, in a city neighborhood members of almost an entire Syrian village would live within blocks of one another, renting apartments in huge buildings acquired by one wealthy villager among them. It was true that tensions sometimes grew between Sunni and Shiite Muslims, with Sunnis building mosques (akin to Christian churches and Jewish synagogues) and Shiites preferring "national clubs." Frequently, though, their situation led Muslims to ignore the differences of the past in their common affirmation of Islam. Moreover, since Islam had been a religion of community and of law, the mosque and its religious service had never been central.

So in America mosques were built only slowly, the first major one at Highland Park (Detroit), Michigan, in 1919. The new mosques were also decidedly Americanized. No longer simply houses of prayer, they became Islamic centers, multiple-purpose buildings that, for example, innovated by founding "Sunday" schools for Muslim children. Often such Sunday morning schools were followed by services at noon, which replaced the Friday observances of traditional Islam. With the American Islamic emphasis on the education of children, too, women gained a role of increasing prominence relative to their position in the past.

Meanwhile, Islamic organization began to acquire a national dimension. One sign of a growing presence and unity was the Islamic Center in Washington, D.C., the result of cooperation between Islamic governments abroad and Muslims in the United States, with the cornerstone of its mosque laid in 1949. By 1952, the Federation of Islamic Associations, under the leadership of second-generation American Muslims mostly of Lebanese ancestry, provided an organizational umbrella for increasing cooperation among Muslims. Still more important was the formation, in 1963, of the Muslim Students Association, which aimed not only to preserve Muslim identity and religious activity among students but also to work toward the establishment of pan-Islamic religious community in the nation. Fourteen years later, in 1977, the Islamic Conference in America was formed with the support of the Muslim World League, with its headquarters in Mecca. The new organization provided advice about Islamic law and its application, assisted mosques in obtaining imams, or prayer leaders, and monitored the media to encourage the presentation of Islam in a favorable light. Then, in 1981, the Muslim Students Association gave its blessing to the creation of the Islamic Society of North America, an organization to foster unity among Muslims from different ethnic groups and to carry forward a mission to non-Muslims.

With the influx of immigrants after 1965, and especially with the increases of the 1980s, a new religious day began to dawn for the Muslim community. The solidarity brought by numbers also brought renewed devotion and dedication, as the multiplication of new mosques suggested. And although Muslims tended to be relatively unpoliticized within the context of American religion, there were growing signs that the large Muslim community was beginning to take lessons from its Protestant, Catholic, and Jewish neighbors. It remains for the twenty-first century, however, to judge whether Muslims will gain a public voice and effectiveness equal to their numbers.

Other Middle Eastern religions did not wait for the twenty-first century before arriving. Religions such as Zoroastrianism (the ancient monotheistic faith of Persia with its radical bifurcation of good and evil) and Baha'i (a new religious movement that proclaimed itself the completion of Islam and all previous religions) also came to America with immigration. Zoroastrianism's main bearers were Parsees, from India, who appeared in recent times. Ten Zoroastrian Associations were present in the country in 1984, and the ethnic Zoroastrian community was recognizable, although small. In export version, too, American converts knew it, if mostly only indirectly, through the Indian spiritual master Meher Baba, who was born a Zoroastrian and in adulthood taught a message of divine love as an avatar, or manifestation of God. The presence of Baha'i, however, was substantially older, with the first Lebanese converts' arrival in America in 1892. Chicago, and its northern suburb Wilmette along Lake Michigan, became especially prominent in what became a multiethnic and interracial movement, and it continued to flourish. By the late 1980s there were some 110,000 Baha'is in the nation organized in 1,700 local assemblies.

If Middle Eastern religions were generally late arrivals on the American scene, so, too, was the major religion of South Asia. India's multifaceted religious system, known to the West as Hinduism, caught the eye of the general public especially in 1893 at the World's Parliament of Religions. The formal gathering brought Swami Vivekananda, among other Asian religious leaders, to Chicago. Success at the parliament was the beginning, for Vivekananda, of a mission that spread the religious philosophy of Vedanta in the United States, and through his work Vedanta Societies sprang up in various places. Then in the 1920s came another in a series of Hindu missionary efforts. As a new arrival from India, Paramahansa Yogananda brought the teachings of yoga to Americans. His Self-Realization Fellowship became the first of the yogic movements that continued and,

in popularized form, were absorbed into American culture. By the 1960s and 1970s, Hindu devotionalism appealed to some among a new generation of Americans in search of religious meaning. And by the late 1960s and 1970s, too, more and more Asian Indian immigrants were bringing ethnic Hinduism to America and beginning an important religious shift toward Hinduism as inherited tradition.

The religious forms collected under the catch-all and Western-inspired term *Hinduism* are too numerous to be detailed here. Uniting them, however, were a series of themes. With Indian speculation about the cosmos a prominent feature, philosophic Hinduism tended to see the world as one reality and the appearance of separation as an illusion. The vast, impersonal force that was posited behind the material world was addressed as Brahman. Still more, corresponding to the all-power of Brahman in the universe, Hindus saw what they called the Atman, a spark of sacred power within each individual that signaled the inner presence of Brahman. In the mystery at the center of the mystical belief of the "realized" Hindu, Atman *was* Brahman.

The monism of this belief was disputed by other Hindus who taught a dualism of spirit and matter, of God and individual souls. Among its ramifications, such dualism encouraged a religious landscape peopled with numbers of Gods and Goddesses, the focus for any number of devotional followings. Indeed, worship of divine beings formed the first of the three major ways that religious commitments were expressed in traditional Hinduism.

In the way of devotion, or *bhakti*, the hospitality ritual of *puja* formed the basis of religious practice, as the deity special to each family was, in statue form, greeted, bathed, perfumed, clothed and fed. On the other hand, in the second way—that of action, or *karma*—the caste system of ancient India was reinforced by the religious prescription to live according to the law of one's caste. To follow the injunction fully meant performing one's caste duty for its own sake, without regard to results or satisfaction gained. Finally, in the third way—the path of knowledge, or *jnana*—Hindu thought enjoined the cultivation of inner states of mind under the guidance of religious teachers. Through them, various techniques for physical and mental control meant to lead to higher states of awareness were transmitted.

When Vedanta came to the United States at the end of the nineteenth century, it brought India's most widespread form of monistic religious philosophy to Americans. Swami Vivekananda had been drawn to the Indian mystic and religious leader Ramakrishna, and after his death shaped the Ramakrishna legacy as an international movement committed to the mystical ideal but also to action in the world. Beginning in 1896 with the Vedanta Society he founded in New York, Vivekananda presented lectures on Vedanta philosophy and offered sessions devoted to the classics of Indian religious literature. The way of devotion came to be represented, too, in temple services that included hymn, scripture, prayer, and sermon and in religious practices in private shrines in members' homes.

Vedanta continued through the twentieth century as a small (in the early 1990s fewer than 3,500 members) yet stable presence. At first it appealed to upper- and middle-class Americans and those from other cultures who had developed an enthusiasm for Eastern spirituality. Later, it came to appeal to Asian Indian immigrants as well. Teaching that the real nature of humanity was divine and that it was each person's duty to develop the Godhead within, Vedanta promoted ideas that blended with liberal Protestant teaching about the immanence of God and goodness of human nature. It offered the option of monastic vows and upheld a mystical ideal, emphasizing that truth was universal and so agreeing with the mood of many who sought a common center amidst the pluralism of sects and denominations.

All the same, the increasing popularity of Hinduism in the United States lay with newer movements that stressed yoga. The man who introduced yoga to the nation, as was noted, was Paramahansa Yogananda. He had come to the United States to attend the International Congress of Religious Liberals, held under Unitarian auspices in Boston in 1920, and then remained in America for thirty years. More than Vivekananda, he employed American techniques of gaining publicity to spread his message, beginning a practice that later Hindu gurus in America would also use.

With yoga (the word means "union") understood as teaching and practice aimed at bringing personal integration and an experience of the oneness of all things in Brahman, Yogananda offered Americans a coherent religious philosophy. In the Self-Realization Fellowship that he founded, he taught the physical exercises called *hatha yoga* that led to breath and body control and prepared the way for meditative experience. But beyond classical yogic teaching, Yogananda promoted *kriya yoga*. This system placed emphasis on awakening a *kundalini* energy thought to lie at the base of the spine and on directing the energy upward to the crown. Such a process, Yogananda taught, would bring energy and integration

to seven *chakras*, or energy centers, in the body. Through use of the mind in attempted movement of energy in coordination with forms of breathing and vocal repetition, the yogic practitioner hoped to reach a superconscious, or mystical, state.

Yogananda told Americans that there was scientific precision to yogic philosophy, he used Western psychological concepts to explain it, and he also introduced Christian ideas in conjunction with his teaching. By the 1960s, perhaps 200,000 people belonged to his Self-Realization Fellowship, and by the early 1970s the movement had forty-four centers in the United States and included both lay members and monastics.

Indeed, from the 1960s to the 1990s, yoga groups and teachers were common features on the American cultural landscape, and in this atmosphere of widely diffused interest in hatha yoga, the appeal of meditation likewise grew. The mood of public interest was cultivated especially by Transcendental Meditation, the movement founded by the Maharishi Mahesh Yogi. The Maharishi, who introduced his teaching to the West in 1959, capitalized on publicity even more than Yogananda had done. Like Yogananda, he underlined the scientific aspects of his teaching, providing data that claimed Transcendental Meditation (TM) lowered blood pressure, relieved stress, increased intelligence, and even reduced crime in areas in which a significant proportion of the population was meditating. And finally, like the classical aspects of Yogananda's teaching, his was a popularized form of Vedanta religious philosophy.

Transcendental Meditation was based squarely on the teachings of the Indian spiritual books, the Upanishads, as interpreted by the Vedanta school. But it stressed that it was a simple and natural technique that anyone could practice with striking results. The product of an India at home with many gods, it felt comfortable existing in tandem with other religions, and it welcomed adherents who were also members of other organized religious groups. In fact, in its public presentations frequently it denied that it was a religion at all. Although the denial became problematic in 1979, when a United States court of appeals ruled TM to be a religion and therefore unlawful in a public school curriculum, Transcendental Meditation continued to teach that it was a form of knowledge—"the science of creative intelligence"— and consequent practice. In fact, in 1974, the World Plan Executive, its general governing organization, founded Maharishi International University at the former site of Parsons College in Fairfield, Iowa. The university began to confer both bachelor's and master's degrees and became an American hub for the world movement.

By the 1990s over a million people had taken the basic TM course that introduced meditation practice. But a million people did not continue to meditate, and estimates of how many do so have been as low as the tens of thousands. In recent years, after interest in the basic course dropped in the mid-1970s, a meditation course that aimed to teach the practitioner to levitate was introduced. But the new course created publicity that was often negative, and it did not solve the problem of rekindling strong public interest in TM. Still, the movement did not disappear and in a small way continued as an expression of *jnana* yogic practice on American soil.

American society also saw one prominent example of *bhakti* in the late twentieth century. The International Society for Krishna Consciousness (ISKCON) became familiar at many airports where its members, sometimes dressed in colorful pink and yellow robes, offered flowers and solicited donations. Founded in 1965 by A. C. Bhaktivedanta Swami Prabhupada, Krishna Consciousness was based on the teachings of a dualistic sixteenth-century sect established by Chaitanya Mahaprabhu. At the center of the old and new devotional movements was Krishna, a Hindu deity and supreme personal God for his followers. Rejecting the traditional polytheism of popular Hinduism, members of the Chaitanya sect and the Hare Krishna movement (the popular name for ISKCON) were Krishna monotheists. And they hailed Chaitanya Mahaprabhu as an incarnation of Vishnu.

Emphasizing the boundaries that separated its members from the rest of the world, Krishna Consciousness demanded a total surrender to Krishna. This surrender was made visible in the monastic lifestyle of members, who rose before 4:00 A.M., practiced vegetarianism, and spent their days in work and prayer as they danced and continually repeated the "Hare Krishna" chant. The sound vibrations, they claimed, brought an experience of transcendental consciousness. Celibacy was preferred in the movement's ideology, and marriage occurred only under the direction of the spiritual leader, with sexual intercourse exclusively for the production of children. While in recent years members of the society have begun to modify the strictness of some of these practices, community continues to be a strong requirement.

Since the 1970s and the death of its founder, ISKCON has seen a decline, especially in its American convert membership. Although Bhaktivedanta

was said to have initiated 5,000 disciples personally, only about 1,000 remained after his death. By the late 1980s, though, there were more than sixty temples belonging to the movement in the United States, generally in cities. Probably 2,500 resided in the temples, and several thousand more came for worship. Beginning in the 1970s, the devotees who took the place of the former American converts were Asian Indian immigrants. In other words, ISKCON began to move from being an export form of Hinduism to one that incorporated both export and ethnic elements. In fact, Asian Indians provided what was probably the difference between mild decline and virtual extinction. They brought not only membership but also financial support and a degree of public respectability that had previously mostly eluded the movement.

Other forms of export Hinduism thrived in late-twentieth-century America. It was a season of religious expansion, and the steady attractiveness of South Asian religious movements persisted, if less spectacularly than in the 1960s. Groups like Divine Light Mission (headed by Guru Maharaj Ji), the Siddhya Yoga movement (Swami Muktananda Paramahansa and later the female Gurumayi Chidvilasananda), Integral Yoga (Swami Satchidananda), the Rajneesh Foundation International (Bhagwan Rajneesh), and the Sri Aurobindo Society (Sri Aurobindo), to name but a few, have endured despite internal problems and even scandals in some of the movements. But after the new United States immigration law of 1965, another story began to unfold—that of South Asian immigrants practicing ethnic forms of Hinduism under new circumstances.

South Asian participation in ISKCON and in the Vedanta Society already suggests one way in which the immigrants made the transition between past and present. But there were other ways, and amalgamation with export Hinduism has not been the preferred pattern. The changed immigration law brought so rapid an increase in the number of Asian Indian immigrants that ethnic Hindus were able to begin to form their own religious institutions. In 1982 alone, for example, more Asian Indians entered the country than in all the years before 1960. The 1980 census recorded over 387,000 Asian Indian immigrants, while estimates at mid-decade suggested that between 525,000 and 800,000 were permanent residents of the United States. Not only was there a dramatic increase in numbers, but the class background of the new immigrants, who overwhelmingly were professionals with a high level of education, encouraged religious organization. These ethnic

Hindus desired to transmit Indian culture to their children, and they decried American materialism and what they saw as decadent American values. With numbers, financial ability, and cultural and moral concern to spur them, the Asian Indians began to create an American efflorescence of their traditional religion.

There were, to be sure, problems in their venture, one of the largest being the heterogeneity in the Asian Indian population itself. With sixteen major languages in India and a series of regional cultures and devotions, no one pattern of Hinduism could speak for all the immigrants. Yet despite the differences and often because of them, what began to emerge was a temple Hinduism in which the construction of large and impressive shrines became the focus for local American Hindu communities. By 1986 there were some forty Hindu temples in the nation, and every community of 100 or more families seemed to be planning a temple or building one. Generally, the temples could be distinguished by their architecture, their gods, and their ritual practice as South Indian, North Indian, ecumenical (meant to have a broad appeal), or sectarian (dedicated to worship as carried on in one Hindu sect). Constructing the temple became an act of Asian Indian community, requiring strong financial commitment and work to iron out differences. Thus, whatever their designation, most of the Indian temples expressed some degree of ecumenicity.

Temples were cultural centers as much as strictly ritual centers, preserving languages, arts, and practices from the ethnic past. They provided an unusually clear example of how the stuff of everyday life was imbedded in religion. Still more, the temples were adaptive mechanisms, supporting the religious expansionism of new South Asian Americans by enabling them to bring their past into an American present. Often prosperous, the temples were sources of identity and pride for Asian Indians. And for mainstream Americans, they signaled a continuing ability to absorb religious diversity in a new contact situation.

In the case of Buddhism, the pattern was to some extent similar. But Buddhism, perhaps more than Hinduism, emphasized methods for the pursuit of transcendence in America. Ethnic Buddhism came to the United States with Chinese and, especially, Japanese immigrants of the late nineteenth century. The predominant form was Jodo Shinshu, a branch of Pure Land Buddhism that flourished in the regions from which the immigrants came. But the late nineteenth century also saw wide publicity for export

Buddhism in America, the result of the Buddhist presence at the World's Parliament of Religions and particularly the Buddhism of Zen master Soyen Shaku. In general, while the first and ethnic form of Buddhism led initially to a "church" religion, the second, mostly convert (export) form led to meditation. A third form, which enjoyed a spurt of growth in the 1960s and 1970s, was Nichiren Shoshu. This was a missionary type of Japanese Buddhism that was popular in America among both Japanese-Americans and mainstream converts.

These and other manifestations of Buddhism looked to Siddhartha Gautama, Buddhism's founder from the sixth century B.C., not as a prophet, but as an exemplar of how to live. Called the Buddha—the "enlightened" or "awakened" one—according to tradition he left a prosperous life as a member of the warrior (ruling) caste of India to seek an answer to the problem of suffering and death. Tradition has it, too, that he sought help from various spiritual masters without success, all the while practicing great austerities and becoming physically weak. Finally, tradition records, he ended his life of rigorous asceticism and began to meditate for himself, and it was then that he broke through to enlightenment. From that time, say the accounts, he spent his days preaching and teaching others how they, too, might come to this state.

Thus, from the first, Buddhism stressed religious knowledge. Compressed into a formula, the substance of the knowledge was taught as the Four Noble Truths: that human suffering had a cause; that the cause of suffering was desire; that there was a way to end suffering; and that the way to end it was to end desire, living in nonattachment to persons, places, or things. But the Four Noble Truths were meant to converge in one moment of enlightenment when *nirvana*—or unconditioned reality—was experienced. As in Hinduism, the Buddhist message was empirical.

Moreover, marking the Buddhist teaching as empirical and practical, the Four Noble Truths led to the Noble Eightfold Path. Named also the Middle Path, it was conceived as a way of balance that would avoid extremes of asceticism and self-indulgence as well as all one-sided views and acts. Instead, Buddhists were enjoined to practice "right" views and intentions, leading to "right" speech, action, livelihood, and effort, and ultimately "right" mindfulness and concentration.

By the third century B.C., two major schools of Buddhist interpretation developed, with a third developing considerably later. Theravada, which became the Buddhism of Southeast Asia, taught that it carried on the original instruction of the Buddha. Here the emphasis was on the individual who, as a solitary spiritual hero, would turn within and quench desire completely. In this form of Buddhism, the historical Buddha was revered for his exemplary character and his teaching, but he was never considered divine by the Theravada elite. Indeed, the Theravada form was atheistic; there was simply no god at all, and the goal was the experience of enlightenment, of pure nonattachment in nirvana.

A second major school of Buddhism, Mahayana, became the Buddhism of China and Japan. The larger of the two schools, Mahayana stressed the importance of the community and promoted the ideal of the *bodhisattva*, one who—on the verge of experiencing nirvana—postponed it indefinitely in order to serve others out of compassion for them. Accounts of the compassion of Siddhartha Gautama, the historical Buddha, were especially recalled as exemplary, and Buddhahood was understood as a quality that others, too, could possess. Thus, Mahayana theology countered the atheism of the Theravada school with an intrinsic polytheism.

In time a third large school, called Vajrayana, grew from Buddhist, Hindu, and other popular religious roots to become the Buddhism, most notably, of Tibet. This form of Buddhism saw the many Buddhas of Mahayana as so many visualizations of human passions. In a process of symbolic manipulation, Vajrayana Buddhists aimed to transform these inner forces into visible and audible beings as a method of coming to terms with each force and experiencing a mystical oneness within. By dramatizing the process in a series of secret initiations and magical techniques, Vajrayana Buddhists hoped to achieve practical control.

Each of these three major forms of Buddhism took shape in many sects and schools of interpretation. Many focused on a specific Buddhist sutra, or writing, making it central to devotion and life. In twentieth-century America, a variety of the sects came to be represented, and some achieved far more of a presence than others.

As in the case of Hinduism, there had been a period of preparation in American culture for the arrival of Buddhism. The New England transcendentalists were in general interested in the wisdom of the East, and by the second half of the nineteenth century a small and elite group of non-Asian American Buddhist sympathizers and adherents could be found. Henry Olcott of the Theosophical Society aided the Buddhist cause both overseas and in the United States, writing a Buddhist catechism that

went through forty editions in his lifetime. His associate, Helena Blavatsky, included Buddhist teaching in her occult works, and her references to Mahatmas identified them as Tibetans familiar with the practices of Vajrayana Buddhism. Both Olcott and Blavatsky formally became Buddhists.

As was noted earlier, ethnic Buddhism was no stranger to nineteenth-century America either. But the Buddhism of the first Chinese immigrants was eclipsed by the work of Jodo Shinshu missionaries who brought to Hawaii and then the mainland the message of the Nishi Hongwanji movement, one of the 170 or so sects of Japanese Buddhism. Like all Mahayana Buddhism of the Pure Land type that it represented, Jodo Shinshu taught faith in a Buddha being called Amida Buddha, who established the Western Kingdom called the Pure Land in fulfillment of his previous bodhisattva vows. Believers claimed that it was now therefore possible, through trust in Amida and devotion to him, to enter the Pure Land after death and there experience enlightenment. Thus, Pure Land Buddhism put the "other-power" of Amida in place of the "self-power" that Theravada and other meditation forms of Buddhism taught. Of all the forms of Buddhism, it probably most resembled Christianity with its God of compassion who, through faith in Jesus, was held to bring believers to an eternal life in paradise.

Because of this resemblance to Christianity, Pure Land seemed most likely of the various Japanese sects to accommodate itself to American culture. Its history in the United States showed how much it did so. From 1899 to 1944 it was largely organized by the Nishi Hongwanji sect as the North American Buddhist Mission, and after that date it became the Buddhist Churches of America. Its membership grew until, in the 1980s, about 100,000 people were affiliated in some 100 churches.

As this account already suggests, from the first, language and style proved to be difficulties for Buddhism in America. There were no "churches" of Buddhism in Japan, and community worship did not take place in Buddhist shrines, save on special occasions. Hence, use of the term "church" in a Buddhist context was clearly a concession to American ears. Similarly, Buddhist churches in America began to call their overseers "bishops," another concession to American Christianity. There were adaptations in worship as well, as Buddhist churches began Sunday services and Sunday schools. Although some worried that these changes might compromise the character of Buddhism, most accepted them as the inevitable result of Americanization.

The second form of Buddhism in America, stressing meditation, was represented most notably in Japanese Zen and Tibetan varieties. Zen originated in China as Ch'an Buddhism and later flourished in Japan as a combination of Mahayana religious philosophy and Theravada meditation techniques. There, as in China, one school (Rinzai Zen) taught that enlightenment was a sudden event, triggered by unusual circumstances that shocked a person out of ordinary awareness. Its practice centered on meditation using *koans*, riddles or verbal puzzles meant to baffle the ordinary working mind. By pondering a koan, believers held, the mind's grasp would be broken and enlightenment would come. The other school (Soto Zen) taught that enlightenment was gradual. Soto Zen practice centered on "just sitting," meditation in which the goal was to quiet the mind and to empty it of all thought.

It was Rinzai Zen that Soyen Shaku introduced at the World's Parliament of Religions in Chicago. His disciple Daisetz Teitaro Suzuki did more than any other person to spread Rinzai Zen in America. From 1897 to 1909, Suzuki worked as an editor for Open Court Publishing Company in La Salle, Illinois. After returning to Japan, he wrote prolifically in English about Buddhism, and his many books were widely read in America. When he came back to the United States in the 1950s, he spoke frequently at universities, including one series of lectures at Columbia. Suzuki aided the communication of Zen to non-Asian Americans by stressing themes that agreed with philosophic existentialism. At the same time, he tended to overlook the discipline and ritual attached to the Zen monastic tradition and to disregard its social setting in Japan.

In the late 1950s, a group of San Francisco artists and writers that included Allen Ginsberg, Jack Kerouac, and, with qualifications, Alan Watts and Gary Snyder, combined the interpretations of Suzuki with other elements to form an eclectic "Beat Zen." As a group, they drew on the side of Rinzai teaching that stressed the suddenness of enlightenment and made it into an exaltation of emotional release. Thus, Beat Zen pursued liberation at the expense of the ascetic meditation practices that were part of the Rinzai tradition.

However, both Watts and Snyder went further. Watts, a prolific author, was an important popularizer of Zen, using Western scientific and psychological categories in order to present it. He romantically portrayed Zen as a new way of life, emphasizing its "otherness," its revolution—by Western standards—in inner awareness. Snyder moved beyond the romanticism of Watts. With a background in anthropology and literature, an extensive knowledge of Native American religions, and ecological concerns, he wrote poetry that expressed themes of interdependence among all creatures. He went to Japan to study Zen, learning the language in order to do so and going through a period of monastic training. More than the others, Snyder brought the two sides of Zen—its meditative discipline and its spontaneity—together.

Meanwhile, the more formal and traditional practice of Zen grew with the introduction of Zen centers in California and New York by Sokatsu Shaku Roshi. Soto Zen also took up residence when in 1962 Shunryu Suzuki established the San Francisco Zen Center, the largest of the American Zen centers. From here and other places, monasteries were organized where individuals might spend either short or extended periods away from society. Finally, in the United States, the Rinzai and Soto lineages were united in a third form of Zen, spread especially by Philip Kapleau's book *The Three Pillars of Zen* (1965). Kapleau had visited Japan as a reporter in 1946 and less than a decade later studied there under Sogaku Harada, who sought the unification of Zen. In 1966, Kapleau opened the Zen Meditation Center in Rochester, New York, where he applied ideas from his book as a teacher. Different in his emphasis from Suzuki and Watts, Kapleau underlined the importance of the traditional practice of sitting meditation as well as the relationship between master and student. Even further, he worked to make Zen American, using English, adapting rituals, and wearing Western clothes during meditation.

Most American Zen adherents in the middle and late twentieth century were young, middle-class people, well-educated and white. They were, in short, converts from mainstream America. Many of the same things could be said about those drawn to Tibetan Buddhism. Brought to the United States by monks fleeing after the Chinese Communist takeover of Tibet, this form of Buddhism became noticeable after 1965. Through the presence of Tibetans on university faculties and the establishment of meditation centers, knowledge of Tibetan Buddhism spread. The esotericism of its teachings and the cloak of symbolism that surrounded them did not deter converts. Moreover Tibetan Buddhist masters, or *rinpoches*, expressed their teaching for Americans in the language of humanistic psychology, pointing to continuities between Tibetan Vajrayana thought and practice and modern American beliefs. Especially under Tarthang Tulku in Berkeley, California, and

Chogyam Trungpa in Boulder, Colorado, Tibetan Buddhism brought Americans another form of religious practice stressing meditation.

Finally, in Nichiren Shoshu, an evangelical form of Buddhism came to America. Its membership grew rapidly after its first appearance in the nation in 1960, and by 1983 it was claimed that it could count here as many as 200,000 to 250,000 members. Still, more conservative estimates suggested that 30,000 or fewer was a likelier figure, and in the 1980s, in general, the movement suffered a sharp decline. Perhaps the most interesting aspect of the membership, though, was its composition. At first, most adherents came from Japanese ancestry, and the few mainstream Americans who joined tended to be men who married Japanese women. Moreover, membership was predominantly middle class, with many followers involved in small businesses. Yet by 1967, almost all (95 percent) of the new converts were non-Asian, while in the East and Midwest, most adherents had no connections with Japan. They were younger, less well established, and more diverse. In fact, more than any other Buddhist group, Nichiren Shoshu drew Hispanics and blacks as well as whites. More than any other Buddhist group, too, it drew working-class as well as college-educated converts.

Nichiren, with its roots in thirteenth-century Japan, taught the centrality of a particular Buddhist holy book, the Lotus Sutra of the Mystical Law. It enjoined chanting praise to the Lotus Sutra, which expounded a vision of the fundamental laws of nature. By turning to the Lotus Sutra, it was said, believers would find their Buddha-nature within and attain happiness, prosperity, and peace. Aggressive from the first in the proclamation of this message, the Nichiren movement was reborn in twentieth-century Japan in the Soka Gakkai organization, a lay group convinced that they should use "forceful persuasion" to convert the world. Hence, Nichiren Shoshu came to the United States as a missionary movement, the most enthusiastic of the export forms of Buddhism in the days of its greatest success.

By the late 1980s and the time when it had declined, however, new processes of change were afoot. The American immigration law of 1965 and a volatile political climate brought new waves of Asian immigrants to the United States, as we have seen. These new immigrants made ethnic Buddhism a stronger presence, and they substantially altered the way mainstream Americans began to perceive the religion. Estimates were made, for example, of 600,000 Vietnamese, the majority of them Buddhists and many of them in Southern California; of 220,000

Laotians, with temples in Los Angeles, Chicago, and Washington, D.C.; of 160,000 Cambodians, with forty-one temples in the nation; and of over 100,000 Thais, with 40,000 of them in Los Angeles alone. By 1987 the appointment of the first Buddhist chaplain to the United States armed forces signaled a Buddhism coming of age. The same year, the establishment of the American Buddhist Congress provided another sign. Formed to explain Buddhism and Buddhists to non-Asian Americans and to articulate a Buddhist community opinion on public policy issues, the congress promised to make Buddhism a visible public presence in a pluralist American society.

## LATE-TWENTIETH-CENTURY NEW RELIGIONS

Buddhism, like Hinduism and other Asian religions, had taken a giant step toward coming of age in the 1960s with the changed immigration law. But the decade of the 1960s was a watershed, too, for new religious movements that arose in the United States. The visible presence of Eastern teachers helped to generate a new contact situation that provided the catalyst for religious change. Moreover, the era of civil rights and the unpopular Vietnam War unleashed a basic questioning of establishments that spread to religion. In this climate, the demographic and sociological changes of the decade made the religious past less serviceable for many. And perhaps the general mood of experiment—so much a part of the religious legacy—encouraged radical departures from the familiar and the embrace of religious novelty.

Beyond these favorable conditions, in the last third of the twentieth century there was a coherent tradition in America from which to construct new religions. Still more, many had been prepared by the heritage of American culture to turn toward self and universe in their quest for religious certainty. A habit of privileging nature—present most prominently in conservation and national park movements as well in a glorification of landscape in art and literature—held its store of religious and mystical content. Religious introspection had been exalted by Puritan, Unitarian, and New England transcendentalist alike; and Protestantism, in general, supported the importance of religious knowledge. Meanwhile, liberal Protestantism stressed the presence of God everywhere and, in teaching that human nature was good, underlined American optimism about it. Even further, liberal Protestantism's diffuseness and permissiveness provided a model of living comfortably without tight organization. Linked to the changes that the 1960s brought, the inherited religious culture could help to foster religious innovation. In this context, it seemed, nearly everyone had an occult or metaphysical belief somewhere on their mental horizon.

Hence, new religious movements—many times short-lived but intense—became a hallmark of the decade, even as they continued through the 1970s and 1980s into the 1990s. Often collectively described as countercultural, these movements are more correctly understood as exaggerating certain tendencies within American culture so that the movements themselves came to appear as alien. The cult movements—to use the sociological label that distinguishes them from the established denominations and the older sects—often encouraged members to break ties with families and friends in order to follow a new way of life more totally. They demanded seemingly everything, and converts were willing to surrender to these demands because they considered them ultimately for their own benefit. At times they turned inward in what seemed destructive ways. In forms like—to cite the most notorious early example—the Jonestown of the Reverend Jim Jones with its collective suicide in Guyana in 1978—they brought confrontation with the law.

As much and more to the point here, these groups—both the destructive ones and others more benign—broke so radically from the normative religiosity of the culture that they claimed, typically, to offer a new revelation to followers. Orthodox Christian or Jewish elements all but disappeared in the belief systems of such groups. Added to the announcement of new revelation was often a sociological structure that depended on a charismatic leader whose presence became vital to the movement's continuance. In this context, the separation that was built into the religious life-style became a self-conscious mechanism to support strongly inflected difference in belief and ideology.

From the occult and metaphysical side of the culture, two of the clearest examples of such movements were neopaganism and scientific-technological new religions. In neopaganism, the assumptions of earlier American occultism were self-consciously present. For believers, the law of correspondence operated to elevate the natural world. It was the macrocosm to which human beings should conform their lives, and neopaganism, or witchcraft, taught reverence for nature as the power of fertility and life. Through the use of ritual, neopagans in witchcraft covens sought to create harmony for members and others with the order of the natural world. Ritual, in this religious schema, was a magical means to assure the operation of nature, and witches believed that they had discovered the key to its powers, which they could turn to its advantage.

Meanwhile, the sexual themes that resonated through the message sometimes assumed an explicit and activist form in feminist covens. Members of groups that called themselves "Dianic," these neopagans emphasized the Goddess and identified, as well, with the women's movement, especially as a spirituality movement. They also excluded men from their ceremonies. (Another form of Dianic witchcraft gave special honor to the feminine and its mysteries as well but did not exclude men.) Beginning in the 1970s, Z Budapest's Susan B. Anthony Coven in Los Angeles has been one prominent example of the feminist Dianic tradition; so has the Craft as it continues to be preached and practiced by the well-known Starhawk.

Even as neopaganism exalted nature and natural themes, scientific-technological cult movements linked science with occultism in ways that repeated the blend of religion with science that was part of ancient Western occultism. For example, UFO cults (already glimpsed earlier through the phenomenon of channeling) took their cue from unexplained flying objects in the space age. Members of these groups saw visitors from outer space as higher and more perfect beings who wanted to teach willing human beings a deeper knowledge that would transform their lives. And the journeys that numbers of "contactees" claimed to make in alien spaceships seemed a technological gloss on the old shamanic theme of flying to a distant place and returning with saving knowledge for self and others.

In another often-cited instance, Scientology—founded by L. Ron Hubbard—used an electrical device called an E-meter to help in spiritual quests. The E-meter, said to measure resistance, or tension, within subjects when they responded to different questions, was meant to help them become "Clear" (like the "clear" button on a calculator). Thus, continuing into the present, Scientologists believed that consciousness could be liberated so that it could control matter, energy, space, and time. Their goal was total freedom, and their means—as in all the scientific-technological movements—was the pursuit of knowledge as a form of power.

But native occultism and metaphysics were not alone in producing new religions. With religious options as available as the foods on a supermarket shelf, it seemed inevitable that religious tendencies from different cultures would be brought together in the atmosphere of ferment and creativity that was the legacy of the 1960s. And even as an abundant catalog of new religious movements stressed the bonding of intense community life in small groups, the mood of religious combination spilled over their boundaries to become a general cultural atmosphere. In the environment of a post-1960s America, religious experiment and expansion—long a part of the American tradition—grew even more noticeable than in the past. Do-it-yourself religion appeared seemingly everywhere, and one influential study by Robert N. Bellah and other sociologists referred, memorably, to the religion of "Sheilaism"—the private religious world constructed by one interviewee.

It was in this context that, as the 1970s progressed, more and more references were heard to what enthusiasts and skeptics alike were calling a "New Age" movement. Although behind the movement stood the entire nineteenth-century metaphysical legacy and although various theories of immediate origin may be cited, one way that the movement congealed was through a series of English "light" groups. These informal communities were made up of individuals who came together intending to "channel" spiritual light to the world and to discuss theosophical writings about the advent of a New Age. Light groups spread from England to this country, and by the early 1970s they were part of an international network that expected the imminent dawn of a new era. Meanwhile, by 1971, the *East-West Journal,* begun that year in Boston under macrobiotic auspices, became a vehicle for the spread of New Age ideas.

The changes in the American immigration law likewise facilitated the influx of Asian teachings, with the teachers now present to advance their views. At the same time, a holistic health movement began to gain momentum, and Native American spirituality became increasingly attractive. Humanistic and transpersonal psychologies flourished, blending with Eastern forms of introspection and old Protestant models of perfectionism and self-culture to encourage attention to the project of self-fashioning.

Science, too, seemed to authorize a radically new vision, for in the new physics of quantum mechanics light had been discovered to be both a particle and a wave. Scientific light merged, for many, with mystical light; particles became shorthand for "matter" and waves, for "spirit." The heritage of Swedenborgianism, mesmerism, transcendentalism, and spiritualism—with their "soft" monistic theology of the continuum between matter and spirit—found rebirth in a new vision that, for proponents, was scientifically true.

Still another parascientific support came from astrology, which for many functioned as symbolic science. Those who subscribed to its tenets believed that the qualities shaping human character and destiny were written large on a sky "map" formed by the patterned configuration of the stars. Even further, in astrological thinking the stars symbolized not only the life paths of individuals but also the quality of time in general, and an astrological dispensationalism came to prevail that transposed the premillennial dispensationalism of Protestant fundamentalists to another key. Astrologers claimed to read the coming of different eras in the stars, and many taught that the Age of Aquarius—an early designation for the New Age—would soon be dawning. A symbol for the consciousness that New Agers believed would replace old and outworn beliefs, the Age of Aquarius was understood as the time when the sun would enter the constellation of Aquarius on the day of the spring equinox. Although, to be sure, in strict astrological reckoning the Age of Aquarius would arrive some 300 years after the last decades of the twentieth century, the concept—and attendant mood of expectation—became an important ingredient in the New Age synthesis.

If astrology signaled collective processes in the heavens that would affect entire human populations, on earth new social and ethical concerns condensed around an environmental movement that, along with the politics of feminism and peace, provided a common action focus for the movement. Healing and reconciliation of self meant regeneration and rebirth for the planet for those who embraced New Age ideas. And in this climate, many Americans—after the decade of the 1960s and the Vietnam War era—found themselves ready for such individual healing and social regeneration. Feeling less certain of old verities and less secure about their own moral compass and direction, these Americans proved more open to new and combinatory spiritual teachings.

A movement grew, at first quietly and without mainstream media attention, through a mostly informal network of communication. Bulletin boards in natural food stores, yoga centers, and alternative healing clinics; word-of-mouth messages from chiropractors, massage therapists, and acupuncturists; local directories of people, goods, and services; multiplying numbers of small, often newsprint periodicals—all helped to announce the New Age. Teachers appeared, and seminars and weekend workshops attracted students. Movement leaders began to gain followings, and New Agers increasingly found one another.

As participants discovered their mutuality and came together to form the emerging New Age synthesis, self-consciousness among them increased. The self-consciousness was reflected in the designation "New Age," which came to stand for the general collection of beliefs and behaviors within the movement. In fact, though, not every person who identified with the name "New Age" shared every belief or engaged in every behavior that characterized the movement as a whole. Rather, individuals appropriated different elements from the common fund, so that New Agers expressed diversity and fluidity in their membership. All the same, late-twentieth-century New Agers could be roughly divided into two camps. On one side were those thinkers with environmental, transformational, and holistic-health agendas; on the other, those acting ritualists who immersed themselves in New Age practices such as channeling and work with crystals. Of course, the distinction is, strictly speaking, somewhat artificial, and the lines blurred in real life. Thinkers became environmental activists, transformational therapists, and working healers; ritualists often brought searching introspective and elaborated mystical agendas to their symbolic action. Participants easily crossed over and functioned in both camps. Still, noticing tendencies toward the speculative or ritualist sides of the movement can help to characterize it more clearly.

Given differing tendencies and variations in the synthesis, however, if the New Age functioned as religion in the late twentieth century it should be possible to identify within it certain common elements that all religions share. Specifically, religions that are fully developed offer adherents systems of belief about the meaning of ordinary life and what transcends it. Such religions also symbolize these beliefs in highly condensed fashion in ritual settings where adherents act them out and provide guidance for everyday action in society that is consistent with religious belief. Finally—for all the presence of "Sheilaisms" at the end of the century—religions work to bond adherents in communities and to strengthen already-existing ties in groups.

From this perspective, it can be said that New Age beliefs about the nature of the world and human life, both proximate and transcendent, teach a version of the age-old cosmological theory of correspondence. This is perhaps most clearly expressed in New Age language about the "universe." In such language, the universe is the source of life's many manifestations, and it also possesses an intelligence that New Agers believe guides and guards them. But the relation of the universe to individuals is not the same

for New Age religion as the traditional relationship between God and creatures in Judaism, Christianity, and Islam. Rather, the New Age universe contains all of life and is also manifested within it. As understood by New Age adherents, the universe exhibits a design and order reflected on a small scale in individual existing things, and it embraces all of these things as part of an integrated whole.

Thus, New Agers hold to their own version of the dictum, "As above, so below." But they not only believe that the microcosm of human society reflects the macrocosm of the universe; they especially emphasize their conviction that the notion of separateness, of discrete existence, is finally illusory. In New Age belief, human beings are all expressions of one another and of the universe. With its mystical translation of the language of quantum physics, New Age theology posits a cosmology and anthropology in which matter and energy are different manifestations of one encompassing reality.

Still, if transformation between matter and energy states is relatively simple in this theology, the presence of a hierarchy is suggested. Vibrating energy is viewed as a "higher" manifestation of the universe than is matter. Provided the energy is ordered, cohesive, and integrated, New Agers believe, the greater the energy quotient, the greater the good for human life. On the other hand, another language implicitly counters that estimate by providing a different conceptual model. New Agers balance their references to the "universe" with others to the "planet." Here the macrocosm that was the universe has been transposed to an earthly setting to become the natural environment. In its teaching concerning the planet, the New Age reintroduces the theory of correspondence in its vision of an earthly macrocosm to which human society ideally conforms. For many, the earth is Gaia, the Earth Goddess or Earth Mother. For all, the earth is a living being, capable of being violated by the rapacious instincts of humans but capable, also, of being regenerated by human efforts at planetary healing.

Such views lead easily to the ethic of transformation that provides the moral ballast to the New Age. In fact, concern for transformation links the New Age movement in some respects to traditional American Christianity. For transformation among New Agers is, as already suggested, especially understood as a work of healing. Thus, New Agers construe the human situation as in some ways deficient, and they conceive present-day humans as existing in states that are metaphysical equivalents of sin. Sometimes, in New Age understanding, that deficiency finds material, physical expression; at other times, its expression is largely mental or "spiritual." In both cases, the description of the human situation—in need of healing—echoes, in another key, inherited notions of original sin. Hence, New Age beliefs in perfection and perfectibility exist side by side with an ethic predicated on ideas about imperfection and millennial expectations for healing/reconciliation that suggest the influence of Christianity.

All of this achieves practical form in New Age language about "harmony." Such harmony means, first, the healing and regeneration of the self, so that a person re-"members" forgotten aspects of body, psyche, and spirit, integrating and reconciling self to self. Transformation, thus, is personal and involves the harmonization of the individual who resolves inner conflicts. But more than the experience of peace, such resolution of conflict leads to continuing landscapes of self-discovery and self-reform. Much as nineteenth-century spiritualist theology viewed the progress of spirits in the afterlife as unending, New Age people view change as continual in a kind of pilgrim's progress. Indeed, one of the preferred New Age ways of reflecting on life is to see it as a series of lessons to be learned. In this conception, the pilgrim is understood more as a student, and the world has become a New Age schoolhouse.

This general ethic is specified by New Age people in numerous ways. It is here that a particular New Age teacher, favored text, and/or community lineage become especially significant. The specific action pathways available for applying the general ethic are options in a vast spiritual emporium of choices. Moreover, New Agers, with their strong predilections for synthesis, often follow multiple disciplines at the same time. Beyond the code for the individual, however, there exists the social ethic of the New Age. From the early days of their movement, New Agers have—in keeping with the theory of correspondence—linked the well-being of their lives to the well-being of the world.

The language of the "planet," already noted, underscores this connection. And the environmental ethic flows from it. New Agers have been for the most part concerned about allegations of human abuse of nature, and they have been willing to work to undo the damage they believe society has done. This ethic is connected to New Age theories of earth changes and purifications appropriated, typically, from American Indian teachers and, sometimes, other sources.

The ethic relates environmental healing to reforming action that ranges from ritual means to political organization, as in American versions of the po-

litical parties called the Greens. New Agers have defended animal rights, fought food irradiation, and demonstrated against nuclear power plants. They have lobbied against pesticides and airplane spraying of crops, promoted organic farming, and joined in grass-roots businesses to supply what are seen as "environmentally friendly" paper products. They have helped to promote Earth Days and supported environmental organizations ranging from the established Sierra Club to the newer and more controversial EarthSave, Greenpeace, and Earth First! Ecofeminism has become a strong suit among some New Agers as values of cooperation are preferred over competition and abuse of nature is linked to abuse of women. Peace activism absorbs others, from "visualizing world peace" to avoiding investments in mutual funds that support military weapons development.

Such visible expressions of a New Age ethic are linked to the cosmology of correspondence. They are also linked to condensed symbolic action in ritual that repeats the New Age vision, and in the fluid and informally structured world of the New Age the connection is especially noticeable. Without the strong presence of organized churches in which ritual religious action conventionally takes place, New Agers blur the line between moral injunction and ritual action by performing everyday acts in deliberate and self-consciously symbolic ways. Or, conversely, they stage ritual events as ways to affect public and political opinion.

As an example of this last, the large-scale event known as the Harmonic Convergence—on 16–17 August 1987—highlighted not only a series of planetary convergences said to be happening in the sky but also patterns of environmental harm New Agers said that humans had brought to earth. Conceived as a ritual celebration of heavenly events, the widely publicized gatherings and ceremonies also amounted to a New Age exhortation for planetary reform. Similarly, an organized series of annual visualizations for world peace, held simultaneously on 31 January at the same hour throughout the world, have provided collective ritual focus that is also an attempt at public persuasion.

One way to approach the issue of New Age ritual is to return to the symbol of the quantum and to the matter-energy equation so prevalent in New Age language. In this context, it is clear that some New Age rituals stress the material world and a felt need to bring it into harmony. Here, for example, ritual work seeks to "harmonize" body energies with larger natural forces and laws. On the other hand, a series of New Age rituals seek to facilitate mental journeying into nonmaterial worlds. In these rituals, the goal is to stimulate forces of mind and imagination so that they assume control over matter.

As an instance of the first, harmonial, type of ritual, we might consider the Japanese method of palm healing known as Reiki, which has been popular among New Age Americans. Gaining attention in the late 1970s and 1980s, Reiki posited the existence of "universal life-force energy" and its use through special "attunements" received from a Reiki master. These attunements were thought to enable an individual to receive and transmit life-force energy in a clearer, purer, and more powerful state. Receiving the attunements involved a series of initiatory rituals, as the individual passed through different "degrees" of Reiki attunement. Just as important, when the initiated Reiki practitioner began the actual practice of palm healing, that work also possessed ritual elements. Hand positions were stylized and serialized, and for higher degrees there were other secret instructions. During the healing exercise, the client and/or practitioner might report sensations of heat and cold or body tingling. Reiki would heal, they believed, because Reiki energy would transform bodily organs and functions. In that respect, the ritual acquired practicality and, for believers, provided material proof of the metaphysical system on which it was based.

As an example of the second type of ritual work that has featured the controlled use of imagination, perhaps the leading instance has been New Age shamanism. As has been noted, shamans take mental journeys to attempt both to acquire power and to use it. In traditional societies such as those of American Indian peoples, shamanic work was social in its intent and goal, with curing illness a significant focus. Although far less steeped in symbolic lore and, mostly, far less disciplined, New Age shamans have sought similar goals. They have sometimes been encouraged by specific organizations, such as anthropologist Michael Harner's Foundation for Shamanic Studies or adopted Huichol Indian Brant Secunda's Dance of the Deer Foundation. And they sometimes have learned shamanic techniques less formally, through audiotapes or shared experience.

Whatever their introduction to shamanic ritual, practitioners have aimed, typically, to "visit" several worlds. Mentally journeying through these various regions with the aid of drum and rattle and/or hallucinogenic plants, the shamanic practitioner has sought to live through a story that symbolically expressed the concerns with which he or she began.

That story might, for practitioners, illuminate a problem situation in everyday life, offer directions for healing, aim to effect the healing, or give advice for personal growth. Mind, in short, became the ritual focus, and it did so in ways that were not only symbolic but also practical.

Of course, Reiki palm healing and shamanic journeying are only two illustrations of the pervasive ritual activity that can be found among New Agers. In fact, seemingly nonritualistic activity has often acquired quasi-ritual status. The wearing of crystals and other forms of New Age jewelry is one example, with crystals and gemstones thought to possess certain powers to aid individuals, to protect them, or to develop aspects of their character. Whatever the particular ritual employed—and whether performed alone or in company—New Age ritual practice is based on beliefs and lifeways that are shared. Hence, questions about New Age ritual open, finally, into questions about New Age community.

What can be said about the body of people who, in late-twentieth-century America, follow the New Age? Little is known in the strict demographic or sociological sense, but there are clues that suggest the general nature of the New Age community. Different observers have spoken of New Agers as white, young, and urban, as middle-class and upwardly mobile, as better educated than average, and as not particularly alienated from society. High-priced and fashionable weekend workshops and conferences point to the appropriateness of these characterizations, although they do lead to questions, especially, about "youthfulness" and they hint of the predominance of the middle-aged, or soon-to-be-middle-aged, who have the necessary wealth to support conference fees. Beyond the conference circuit, there is a strong working-class component within the New Age movement, although its presence is quieter and less noticeable. There are also ethnic variants that link the folk traditions from, for example, rural black and Native American cultural enclaves to the New Age synthesis. Still further, impressionistic evidence indicates that more women than men are New Agers.

In terms of the organized religious traditions from which New Agers come, evidence suggests representative participation by mainstream Protestants, Catholics, and Jews. Geographically, New Agers appear to be well represented on both coasts, with California and the Northeast as bellwether regions. While New Agers are also strong in parts of the Midwest, they are probably weakest in the South.

Even more difficult to determine than the sociological characteristics of those who form the New Age community are their numbers. First, in a movement so fluid and individualistic, the criteria for "membership" are disputable. Second, even when criteria are arbitrarily established, information based on the selected criteria is hard to find.

At the broadest, it might be decided that nearly everyone who held, for example, reincarnational beliefs should be considered in some sense New Age. Surveys suggest that reincarnationists comprise some 20 percent of the American population, and—even excepting the presence among them of Asians who hold to their own traditions in accepting ideas of reincarnation—this number seems too large. At the narrowest, we could limit membership to those who subscribe to key periodicals, list themselves in New Age directories, or participate in New Age events, such as the Whole Life Expo (an annual New Age gathering and emporium). Or we might accept the results of a *New York Times* survey in 1991, which claimed 28,000 for the New Age. As another strategy, we might guess that many who are unaffiliated with an organized religious tradition are sympathetic to the New Age (roughly 7 percent of the population in the mid-1980s and, among baby-boomers and those younger, significantly more). And we might add to this number a further percentage to account for those church or synagogue members who also consider themselves New Age.

None of these strategies for estimating seems wholly satisfactory, however, and the best estimate probably lies somewhere between the extremes and closest to the last strategy. In fact, like the New Thought movement upon which, in part, it rests, the New Age movement has fostered a community so fluid that it merges finally with the rest of America. And in keeping with caveats against reification of what has, at best, only movement status, it is better to speak, perhaps, not of the "New Age" at all but of a "new spirituality" instead. To say this opens the way to identifying a way of configuring reality and of acting that has moved from being countercultural to being cultural.

## PROGNOSIS FOR AN AMERICAN FUTURE

In the beginning was diversity, it could be said of America, and in the end (of the twentieth century) thus, too, it is so. In the last decade of the century, it is clear that the Protestant establishment—that historic center that provided a species of religious unity to the nation—is crumbling, and, indeed, is no longer established, by most statistical measures. The ecumenical movement that aimed to bring churches together has not lived up to its promise. The media are dominated by the religious right. Schools and universities with mainstream religious ties have grown less and less attached to their heritage. Ministry has lost stature in denominational family squabbles and public moral scandals. Church periodicals have declined in outreach, while reform efforts have appeared in fits and starts and with ambiguous results.

Nor can Jewish sources report that institutional life is much better. Rates of intermarriage have continued to grow at what seems shocking proportions. Meanwhile, ethnic identity—Jewishness—is still intertwined with religion—Judaism—in the popular Jewish mind. For their part, Catholics hold their share of the church-going population precariously, with the church rocked by a series of scandals concerning sexual activity by priests and with a ministry declining numerically as well. A conservative pope seems less and less in touch with American Catholic mores of the late twentieth century, as polls have told of Catholics who practice birth control and countenance abortion in numbers not too different from those of the general population.

On the other hand, the fundamentalist-evangelical movement—that sizable portion of the Protestant community that has made a nontraditional and conservative Protestantism a new quasi-mainstream—can boast of considerable vitality. Although the religious right lost in 1992 with the defeat of George Bush, it has hardly come apart. Indeed, the most astute observers predicted that the defeat might fuel right-wing evangelical resolve and new and effective action among conservatives in what sociologist James Davison Hunter has called the "culture wars."

At the other end of the religious spectrum, new religious movements have shown themselves to be a growth industry. A good number are simply "new" in significant adherence in an American context. Others were "new" to nineteenth-century America, home-grown religious creations that endured into the twentieth century and, in a surprising number of cases, continue to flourish. Still others are "new" to twentieth-century America in that they have emerged in this time and place as viable religious realities. Perhaps most significantly of all, as statistical data from the baby-boom generation show, a new religious style has penetrated the former bastions of religious establishment. New Age is dissolving into a "new spirituality," and the new spiritual style promises to continue strong in the years ahead. If so, nontraditional religions may be poised to become the new tradition.

SEE ALSO Protestantism; Catholicism; Judaism and Jewish Culture (all in this volume); Ethnicity and Immigration (volume I).

## BIBLIOGRAPHY

Drew Kampion and Phil Catalfo, "All in the Family," *New Age Journal* 11 (July–August 1992): 54–55, report on a survey regarding the religious and spiritual profile of readers of the periodical. In *Religion and Personal Autonomy: The Third Disestablishment in America* (1992), Phillip E. Hammond gives compelling statistical evidence from four states for the declining role of organized religion and for the new and autonomous religious style of many of those who participate in church life. His colleague Wade Clark Roof, in *A Generation of Seekers: The Spiritual Journeys of the Baby Boom Generation* (1993), gives startling but persuasive evidence, based on extensive surveys and in-depth interviews, for the widespread appeal of a new spirituality existing outside the churches. For an ample demonstration of an early American world of occultism and popular religion, see Jon Butler, *Awash in a Sea of Faith: Christianizing the American People* (1990). And for an account of the Americanness of the religious vision of six New England transcendentalists, including Ralph Waldo Emerson, see Catherine L. Albanese, *Corresponding Motion: Transcendental Religion and the New America.*

In a study of a contrasting movement, D. Michael Quinn, *Early Mormonism and the Magic World View* (1987), impressively documents not only early Mormon immersion in folk occultism but also the widespread presence of occultism in rural and small-town New York in the antebellum period. The best introduction to nineteenth-century spiritualism may be found in a collection of essays by R. Laurence Moore, *In Search of White Crows: Spiritualism, Parapsychology, and American Culture* (1977). In a related volume, Ann Braude, *Radical Spirits: Spiritualism and Women's Rights in Nineteenth-Century America* (1989), offers an impressive study of the relationship between the public-speaking careers of entranced spiritualist mediums and their later public speech in nontrance states on behalf of women's rights. Bruce F. Campbell, *Ancient Wisdom Revived: A History of the Theosophical Movement* (1980), provides a sympathetic account of theosophy that is the most accessible and timely introduction to the subject. And for a suggestive survey of Anglo-American Buddhist converts and sympathizers, see Thomas A. Tweed, *The American Encounter with Buddhism, 1844–1912: Victorian Culture and the Limits of Dissent* (1992), which argues that these Americans understood their Buddhist leanings as a consent to basic American values.

The definitive work on the rise of early fundamentalism and its departures from the Protestant mainstream is George M. Marsden, *Fundamentalism and American Culture: The Shaping of Twentieth-Century Evangelicalism, 1870–1925* (1980). Mormonism's twentieth- as well as nineteenth-century saga is discussed in Jan Shipps, *Mormonism: The Story of a New Religious Tradition* (1985), an accessible account with a comparative religions methodology. For Christian Science, Stephen Gottschalk, *The Emergence of Christian Science in American Religious Life* (1973), offers a theological exposition, by an academic who is also an insider, of the denomination's teaching in the context of its development in American culture. For the best introduction to the New Thought movement—although problematic in many respects—see Charles S. Braden, *Spirits in Rebellion: The Rise and Development of New Thought* (1963). And for an introduction to Eastern Orthodoxy in America, although dated, see Anastasia Bespuda, *Guide to Orthodox America* (1965).

In a series of essays edited by Yvonne Yazbeck Haddad, *The Muslims of America* (1991) details Muslim growth and activity in the United States along with themes regarding Muslim women and identity, Islamic thought, and the perception of Muslims by other Americans. The best available work on South Asian traditions in contemporary America is Raymond Brady Williams, *Religions of Immigrants from India and Pakistan: New Threads in the American Tapestry* (1988). In *How the Swans Came to the Lake: A Narrative History of Buddhism in America* (1981), Rick Fields gives a sympathetic overview of the growth of Buddhism. Meanwhile, Robert S. Ellwood and Harry B. Partin, *Religious and Spiritual Groups in Mod ern America,* 2d ed. (1988), supplies basic information and interpretation for a series of new religious movements.

New religious movements are treated from a theological perspective in Mary Farrell Bednarowski, *New Religions and the Theological Imagination in America* (1989), which examines the answers to a series of theological questions provided by three nineteenth-century and three twentieth-century movements. For neopaganism, Margot Adler, *Drawing Down the Moon: Witches, Druids, Goddess-Worshippers, and Other Pagans in America Today,* rev. ed. (1986), by a participant-observer and journalist, is a detailed and helpful account. For a scientific-technological movement, Roy Wallis, *The Road to Total Freedom: A Sociological Analysis of Scientology* (1977)—based on documentary material, interviews, and a short period of participant observation—studies Scientology in transatlantic perspective.

Much more general in its purview, Robert N. Bellah et al., *Habits of the Heart: Individualism and Commitment in American Life* (1985), which introduces the memorable and individualistic religion of "Sheilaism," argues that Americans lack a language to express their deepest commitments because they no longer invoke either a Biblical or an Enlightenment communal vision. For the New Age vision that inspires many instead, J. Gordon Melton with Jerome Clark and Aidan A. Kelly, *New Age Encyclopedia* (1990), provides short entries on a series of persons and topics usually associated with the movement. In James R. Lewis and J. Gordon Melton, eds., *Perspectives on the New Age* (1992), a collection of essays that seek to provide information and interpretation for the New Age movement is offered. More historical in orientation, Catherine L. Albanese, *Nature Religion in America: From the Algonkian Indians to the New Age* (1990), studies nontraditional religious expression in American culture, including the New Age movement, under the rubric of "nature religion." Also historical in scope, William G. McLoughlin, *Revivals, Awakenings, and Reform: An Essay on Religion and Social Change in America, 1607–1977* (1978), explores—perhaps presciently—the period from 1960 to, roughly, 1990 as an age of emergence for what observers now call a "new spirituality."

A group of essays written with a common agenda and documenting the decline of mainline Protestantism come together in William R. Hutchison, ed., *Between the Times: The Travail of the Protestant Establishment in America, 1900–1960* (1989). A sociological account of religion in contemporary America may be found in James Davison Hunter, *Culture Wars: The Struggle to Define America* (1991), which interprets religious conflict along a fault line that divides conservatives from progressives. Finally, for a comprehensive reference volume, see J. Gordon Melton, *Encyclopedia of American Religions,* 4th ed. (1993), a one-volume work that divides American religions into some twenty-two "families" and offers the fullest treatment of nontraditional religions currently available.

Much of the material in this article has been adapted from Catherine L. Albanese, *America: Religions and Religion,* 2d ed. (Belmont, Calif.: Wadsworth Publishing, 1992). The material is used by permission of the publisher.

# JUDAISM AND JEWISH CULTURE

## Deborah Dash Moore

Jewish immigrants to the United States brought a blend of Judaism and Jewish culture to America. Judaism, the religion of the Jews, embraced faith and ethics, rituals and traditions, as well as a historical consciousness that stemmed from the study of sacred scriptures. Jews considered themselves members of a separate, chosen, consecrated people, possessing a fateful identity that was manifest in an exacting religious culture. Their separateness derived from God's covenant with the people, Israel, revealed in Torah, the Five Books of Moses, or literally "teaching," and elaborated in post-Biblical sacred texts. The dispersion of Jews, or Diaspora, represented exile—pervasive anti-Semitism emphasized the bitterness of exile—that would end when the Messiah, God's messenger, led Jews back to their homeland, the land of Israel. Since the people of Israel were God's instrument to bring salvation to the world, Jews understood their survival as a sacred obligation. But modernizing and secularizing trends influenced Jewish religious beliefs, as did economic hardship and political persecution. Many Jewish immigrants rejected Judaism, especially its fusion of universal faith with belief in national restoration and its posture of awaiting the Messiah while suffering misfortune. They seized control of their destiny, prepared to reinvent their Jewish identity and culture. Determined to shape a new future for themselves, their children, and perhaps the world, they perceived a congruence between their secular Jewishness and the American sense of exceptionalism as a democratic nation in a new world.

Jewish cultural norms included an acute collective self-consciousness and sense of responsibility for their fellow Jews, respect for educated individuals and the sacredness of learning, the goal of living a purposeful life, and a concept of an ideal, full human person—a *mensch*. Although Judaism synthesized nationality and religion, Jews also adopted ethnic traditions and languages developed in their countries of origin. Thus Russian Jews differed from German Jews despite their common religion. The former possessed a rich folk culture that blended mystical spirituality with earthy pragmatism; the latter embraced the values of universal education and enlightened cosmopolitanism. As immigrants, each group sought to craft an American Jewish culture that embodied their distinctive ethnic values.

Successive waves of migration—from the German states in the 1840s and 1850s and from Russia, Romania, the Austro-Hungarian and Turkish empires in the 1880s through 1924—fostered enormous cultural and religious creativity as well as conflict. Established native-born American Jews, situated in cities throughout the United States within a recently created but extensive Jewish communal network and middle-class cultural milieu, encountered increasing numbers of poor Jewish immigrants from eastern Europe at the turn of the century. Seeking new homes and new lives, immigrants faced not only a rapidly changing urban industrial society but also a second generation that claimed a dual American and Jewish heritage. These descendants of nineteenth-century German Jewish immigrants assumed the leadership of American Jews; their efforts to define the character of American Judaism sparked contention. Jewish secular and religious culture in the United States acquired its form and substance from this initial generational encounter prior to World War I, and from subsequent second generations as the twentieth century unfolded. The pivotal second generation mediated the process of acculturation for newcomers even as it modified its own heritage bestowed by immigrant parents.

This generational interaction occurred across and within ethnic divisions distinguishing Jews. During the twentieth century five distinct native-born generations came of age, products of the immigration of German Jews in the nineteenth century, the mass migration of 2.3 million east European Jews from 1881 to 1929 and a small minority of Sephardic Jews from the Turkish empire, and the arrival preceding and following World War II of 340,000 refugees from Nazism and survivors of the Holocaust. These second generations included the German-Jewish generation at the turn of the century, a first east European Jewish generation prior to World War I, a second east European generation of the interwar years, a third east European generation of the postwar era, and, since 1967, a generation descended from survivors and refugees of World War II of both German and East European Jews. Since 1965 and the liberalization of immigration laws, Jewish immigrants from Iran, South America, Cuba, South Africa, the Soviet Union, and Israel have settled in the United States with the potential to contribute a dynamic second generation. Among these new immigrants are many Sephardic Jews, augmenting the small numbers who arrived prior to World War I. Each second generation replicated many of its predecessor's innovative struggles, albeit under changed conditions, and produced varieties of Judaism and Jewish culture. At the century's close, despite the 500,000 new immigrants, bringing the total U.S. Jewish population to 5.5 million, this dynamic appears to have run its course as American Jews look inward for sources of renewal and revitalization.

The first native-born generation of the twentieth century to lead American Jews received its education in cities throughout the United States. In Philadelphia and Baltimore on the Atlantic seaboard, Cincinnati and Chicago in the Midwest, Atlanta and Charleston in the South, and San Francisco on the Pacific Coast, Jews established stable, middle-class communities that supported synagogues and charities, fraternal societies and women's clubs, Young Men's Hebrew Associations and Sunday schools.

Reform Judaism, a flexible rationalist American variation of Judaism, made its headquarters in Cincinnati. The association of Reform congregations (the Union of American Hebrew Congregations), founded the Hebrew Union College, the Reform rabbinical seminary, there in 1865. In 1889 Reform rabbis organized the Central Conference of American Rabbis and also settled in Cincinnati. Earlier (1885), Reform leaders had met in Pittsburgh to craft a consensus reflecting their belief that Judaism was a progressive religious faith analogous to liberal Protestantism in its rationalism, ethical imperatives, ceremonial simplicity, family orientation, and bourgeois aesthetic. The Pittsburgh Platform interpreted Judaism as an optimistic American religion adaptable to the democratic spirit of the age; it denied Jewish nationhood and the binding character of Jewish law,

radically reduced Jewish ritual requirements, and rejected a personal Messiah but anticipated the dawn of a messianic age when Jews would serve as a light to the nations of the world. Reform emphasized the universal and Biblical character of Judaism, especially the prophetic books with their calls for social justice, and eliminated the particularist, nationalist elements that set Jews apart. Thus Reform rabbis and laymen adapted Judaism to the American religious scene with its individualist, personalist, and biblically centered faiths. In Reform synagogues, called temples, men and women sat together, organ music played and a choir of mixed voices—male and female—sang, the prayers were read in English (not Hebrew), and the sermon dominated the formal worship service. Some Reform congregations even changed the Sabbath from Saturday to Sunday to conform to the rhythm of American life.

German Jews also established secular national associations to provide fellowship, sociability and unity while avoiding religious controversy. B'nai B'rith, the first Jewish fraternal order (established in 1885), and the National Council of Jewish Women (NCJW), the first organization of Jewish women's clubs (established in 1893), offered venues for gendered leadership. The NCJW originated in Chicago, where B'nai B'rith moved its headquarters when Adolph Kraus became president in 1904. Philadelphia served a conservative Jewish elite, the heritage of Isaac Leeser's rabbinical leadership of the city's premier congregation. This elite supported Dropsie College for Hebrew and Cognate Learning (1905), Gratz College (1897)—a nondenominational school devoted to Jewish studies—and the Jewish Publication Society (JPS)—an organization dedicated to publishing in English accessible and classic works of Jewish literature, history, and religion. Established in 1886, the JPS complemented an array of English-language Jewish weeklies addressed to a middle-class, Americanized community. The leading papers included the *American Israelite,* the nation's oldest Jewish journal (begun in 1854), edited, until his death in 1900, by Isaac Mayer Wise, the *American Hebrew* (1879) in New York, and the *Jewish Exponent* (1887) in Philadelphia. The weeklies combined personal, partisan journalism on religious questions with political analysis, literary and historical essays, and communal news. This bourgeois Jewish culture nourished a second generation, comfortable in its identity as American Jews and ready to confront the challenges of mass immigration of poverty-stricken east European Jews.

## NEW YORK CITY AND
## JEWISH CULTURE

The dispersed and diversified urban character of American Jewish culture and religion changed dramatically as a small but significant cadre of sons and daughters of German Jewish immigrants left their hometowns for New York City, the nation's emerging financial, commercial, and cultural center. The presence of such figures as Louis Marshall, Henrietta Szold, Judah Magnes, Lillian Wald, Stephen Wise, and Leo Levi helped to transform New York into the premiere city of American Jewry. In the two decades before Congress decisively restricted immigration in 1924, these leaders worked with such prominent figures among the recently arrived east European Jewish immigrants as Solomon Schechter, Israel Friedlaender, Samson Benderly, Hayim Zhitlowsky, David Pinski, and Joseph Barondess, and with the first American-educated descendants of East European Jews—including Mordecai Kaplan, Louis Lipsky, and Bernard Richards—to create many of the century's American Jewish religious, cultural, and political institutions. Wealthy German Jews, especially Jacob Schiff and Felix Warburg, and such enterprising east European immigrants as Israel Unterberg, Bernard Semel, and Harry Fischel, provided financial support for religious and cultural creativity.

To immigrant and native alike, New York was the city of opportunity, the place to realize one's personal and communal dreams. The lure of New York rapidly made it the largest Jewish city in the world, with approximately 580,000 Jews in 1900 and 1,100,000 by 1910. New York's overwhelming preeminence centralized American Judaism and Jewish culture; the city became the religious and cultural capital of American Jews, comparable to Paris for French Jews, London for English Jews, Berlin for German Jews, and Vienna for Austrian Jews. By 1930 almost 2 million Jews lived in New York. They were close to 30 percent of the total population–the city's largest single ethnic group. New Yorkers accounted for over 40 percent of the approximately 4,771,000 American Jews in 1940. Not until after World War II did American Jewry return to residing in cities and suburbs throughout the United States, a dispersed social and demographic pattern that resembled the structure of the native-born generation in 1900.

The impulse to centralize, synthesize, and lead; to blend nationalism with religious idealism; to create an indigenous, respected, and elite culture imbued with the best of both American and Jewish worlds inspired many native-born second-generation leaders. They embraced America, defining themselves as Americans. This common theme emerges from their parallel intellectual, organizational, artistic, and religious activities. Many interpreted the meaning of America to accommodate Jewish differences and imagined an America open to Jews, welcoming Jewish creativity. In the name of democratic ideals, the lawyer Louis Marshall helped to organize the American Jewish Committee in 1906 to protect Jewish rights abroad and at home, while the lawyer Arthur Spingarn tried to advance democracy by participating in the establishment of the National Association for the Advancement of Colored People in 1909. Similarly, social feminism motivated both Lillian Wald and Henrietta Szold. In 1895 Wald initiated a visiting-nurse service at the Henry Street Settlement on New York's Jewish Lower East Side, while in 1912 Szold transformed a women's Zionist discussion group into Hadassah, an organization to provide medical aid and health care for the residents of Palestine along American nonsectarian principles. A vision blending Jewish and American dreams of a better world animated such second-generation leaders.

Some second-generation Jews jettisoned the Jewish component of their identity while affirming their Americanness. Felix Adler, son of Samuel Adler, rabbi of New York's prestigious Reform Temple Emanuel, created the Society for Ethical Culture (1876) after his faith in Judaism collapsed under the assault of biblical criticism. Adler extracted Reform Judaism's concept of ethics from its interpretation of monotheism and Jewish chosenness, disengaging Jewish universalist faith from its particularist traditions. The anthropologist Franz Boas avoided Jewish associations but consistently used his scholarship to repudiate racism and anti-Semitism. One of the first New York Jewish intellectuals, Walter Lippmann, influenced American liberal politics through his writing but avoided discussing Jewish issues. A pioneer photographer, Alfred Stieglitz established his 291 "Little Gallery" in New York to promote a synthesis of artistic modernism and American culture. Stieglitz proclaimed himself an American with a passion for photography and ignored Jewish culture. The music critic Paul Rosenfeld, a friend of Stieglitz and contemporary of such other Jewish intellectuals as the writers Waldo Frank and James Oppenheim, similarly dismissed his Jewishness but championed an America, "the native soil of anyone who *feels* it to be his," that made room for Jews like himself. Rosenfeld edited the magazine *Seven Arts* with Frank and Oppenheim; as outsiders they viewed the Lower East Side as a model "community where race, nationality and culture were integrally related."

Between a committed Jew like Marshall, head of the American Jewish Committee and acknowledged communal leader, and a dedicated assimilationist like Lippmann existed numerous second-generation alternatives. Some Jews, like the economist Walter Weyl, who worked with Lippmann on the magazine the *New Republic*, or the novelist Fannie Hurst, found inspiration in the Jewish world of immigrant workers on the Lower East Side. Others, like Boston's "people's attorney," Louis Brandeis, moved from a posture resembling Lippmann's to a position comparable to Marshall's. The Kentucky-born Brandeis, the first Jew appointed to the Supreme Court and head of the American Zionist movement, discovered in Zionism an intellectual and emotional path back to his people that allowed him to claim his dual American Jewish identity. Irma Lindheim, elected the second president of Hadassah when Szold settled in Palestine in 1926, made a similar discovery. Zionism returned her to Judaism and the Jewish people, propelled her into a position of leadership, and ultimately led her to make *aliyah,* that is, to immigrate to Palestine.

Jewish immigrants produced their own leaders and intellectuals. Although often scornful of established second-generation Jews as capitalist exploiters or assimilationist traitors, immigrants championed equally diverse programs to transform Jews and America. Some espoused universalist secular ideologies that rejected national boundaries and ethnic sentiments. Socialism gained many adherents since it addressed Jewish exploitation and suffering, provided a sense of collective solidarity in a common struggle for a better world, and imagined an egalitarian future without injustice. Some immigrants subscribed to an ethnic version of socialism, rooted in Yiddish culture with solutions to specific problems confronting Jews as a persecuted minority. Others preferred a universalist version that emphasized their identity as members of a worldwide working class, an increasingly powerful proletariat. Socialist Meyer London, three-term congressman from the Lower East Side of New York City, represented the ethnic alternative while Morris Hillquit, long-time leader of the Socialist party in New York, represented the universalist one. In 1917 Hillquit defied the virulent nationalism of World War I and ran for mayor of New York on a peace platform, winning a fifth of the votes.

An articulate group of Jewish immigrants supported anarchism, a radical program that condemned capitalist society's constraints and considered all forms of government oppressive. Emma Goldman, the fore-

most anarchist leader, in her paper *Mother Earth* (1906–1918) also urged women to liberate themselves from the bonds of socially restrictive gender roles and claim a truly free sexuality that would transform the world. After the Bolshevik Revolution in 1917, some Jews rallied to the communist banner, advocating the abolition of capitalism and the establishment of a dictatorship of the proletariat.

A few immigrant leaders combined radicalism with nationalism. When the socialist ideologue and diaspora nationalist Hayim Zhitlovsky visited America in 1904, he imagined the United States as an international republic, model for a world government of nationalities. After immigrating in 1908, he wrote extensively on how to use Yiddish language and culture to develop a multinational socialist society. For Zhitlowsky, Yiddish national culture was Jewish and socialist, its literature inextricably bound up with an oppressed people's struggles. His many philosophical essays encouraged Jews to start supplementary schools to transmit radical Yiddish culture to their children. Debating Zhitlowsky, the socialist Zionist immigrant intellectual Nachman Syrkin explained where they differed in blending radicalism with nationalism: "Zhitlowsky takes everything that exists; I take everything that still does not exist. He has chosen the Yiddish which we have; I, the Hebrew which we do not have. He has chosen the diaspora which we have; I, the homeland which we still do not have."

Zhitlowsky's vision of a multicultural America proved less popular, due to its socialism, than Israel Zangwill's 1909 play, *The Melting Pot,* first performed in Washington in October 1908. The visiting English Zionist and territorialist, Zangwill, saw a new American being forged out of the intermarriage of immigrant peoples. "America is God's Crucible, the great Melting Pot where all the races of Europe are melting and re-forming," proclaims the hero David Quixano, a young immigrant Jewish musician. Since American nationality was unformed and "the real American has not yet arrived," Jews could help to shape a future American culture. Confronting the play's decadent, blue-blooded Yankee, David explains that even as a "Jew-immigrant" he "knows that your Pilgrim fathers came straight out of his Old Testament, and that our Jew-immigrants are a greater factor in the glory of this great commonwealth than some of you sons of the soil." Although praised by such prominent Progressives as Theodore Roosevelt and Jane Addams, the play's embrace of intermarriage angered some Jews, especially those, like the young, San Francisco-born Reform rabbi of New York's Temple

Emanuel, Judah Magnes, who thought that America did not demand such assimilation.

A Zionist immigrant intellectual, Israel Friedlaender contested both radical and secularist ideologies. Friedlaender considered America the new diaspora Jewish center; like Zhitlowsky, he grasped the mass migration's significance. Friedlaender also recognized America's seductiveness. "Jewry is dangerously ill" he wrote in an essay on the east European Jewish historian Simon Dubnov, in 1905, "assimilation proposes suicide; Zionism recommends transportation to a healthy climate. But the patient has still too much vitality to commit suicide and too little energy to bear transportation." American Jews could flourish only if they embraced Zionism by helping to establish a spiritual center in the land of Israel, their homeland, he argued. Opposing the secularists, Friedlaender emphasized the centrality of Judaism, the religion of the Jewish nation. No creative Jewish culture or viable Jewish community in the United States could survive without Judaism and Zionism.

Immigrant intellectuals brought more than their ideologies to the New World; they also transplanted Yiddish literary culture into uncensored American soil. They started Yiddish daily newspapers, ranging from the Orthodox *Morgen Zhurnal* (1901–1953) and *Tageblat* (1885–1953)—the latter started by Kasriel Sarasohn, the first successful Yiddish publisher, merged with its Orthodox competitor in 1928—to the Zionist *Tog* (1914–1971), to the socialist *Forverts* (1897) and communist *Freiheit* (1922). At the peak of its influence in 1917, the Yiddish press reached almost 600,000 daily readers. Besides New York, there were Yiddish dailies in Chicago, Cleveland, and Philadelphia. The press monitored events on the Lower East Side and throughout the United States and it reported on the Jewish situation in Europe. Yiddish papers also devoted attention to women in pages that included discussion of political issues as well as domestic matters. Perhaps most importantly, the press tried to guide immigrants in their adjustment to America, commenting on everything from elections to baseball.

An innovative editor like Abraham Cahan of the *Forverts* experimented with new features to attract readers. Cahan introduced the famous *bintel brief* column of letters, forerunner of "Dear Abby" advice columns. Immigrants wrote to the editor seeking help on how to cope with mundane problems. The *bintel brief* allowed immigrant Jews to see their troubles and perplexities reflected back at them. In addition, between 1910 and 1914 ads for national prod-

ucts flooded the Yiddish press: everything from Ivory soap, Pabst Blue Ribbon beer, Coca-Cola, and Gold Medal flour, to Ex-Lax, Colgate's talcum powder, Vaseline, and H. J. Heinz's beans and soups, sold an America to immigrants eager to adopt the mores of their new home. When the *Forverts* started a rotogravure section in the 1920s, it also began to purvey images of the Old World for the consumption of the new. Yiddish and English subtitles accompanying the photos encouraged immigrants to learn English.

The Yiddish press regularly serialized novels of both excellent writers and hacks as papers competed for readers. The relatively high literacy of immigrant women—higher than those remaining in Europe—made them a prime audience for serials. Sholem Asch, author of *Three Cities* (1929–1931) and a Christology trilogy beginning with *The Nazarene* (1939), published many of his dozen romantic novels in the press, as did I. J. Singer, whose family saga *The Brothers Ashkenazi* (1936) appeared in *Forverts*. The tradition of serialization continued even after World War II, with Chaim Grade in the *Morgen Zhurnal* and I. B. Singer, the Nobel prize-winning author, who published his many novels in *Forverts* despite its rapidly declining readership. The Yiddish literary world extended beyond dailies to weeklies and monthlies. Journals of opinion and letters, like *Tsukunft* (Future) (1892), and humor magazines (the most successful was *Grosse Kundes* [The big stick]), and political journals, like the *Freie Arbeiter Stimme* (The free voice of labor) (1899), an anarchist weekly, provided rich and varied fare for the Yiddish-reading public. The arrival in New York by 1914 of such leading literary figures as the poet Abraham Reisen, the playwright Peretz Hirschbein, and even the famed Sholom Aleichem, a founding father of modern Yiddish literature, formed a Yiddish literati that spawned scores of publishing houses.

Although transported from abroad, Yiddish poetry absorbed American literary influences: realism, expressionism, imagism, free verse, proletarian writing, and traditionalism. Such earlier "sweatshop" poets as Morris Rosenfeld were followed by Abraham Liessin and Yehoash (Solomon Bloomgarden), poets of *yidishkeyt,* literally "Jewishness," referring to values associated with the Yiddish culture. Together with Abraham Reisen they melded socialist and Jewish nationalist themes. Reisen wrote poetry that often entered the immigrants' cultural world as folklore, especially when set to music. Others, like I. J. Schwartz, whose epic narrative poem "Song of Kentucky" (1925) remained idiosyncratic, embraced America.

Soon talented circles of poets enriched the world of New York Jewish intellectuals. In 1907 *Di Yunge* (The young)—a movement loosely organized around several journals—emerged, rejecting political commitment in favor of aesthetic autonomy. The group included such poets as David Ignatov, Reuben Iceland, Mani Leyb, and H. Leivick, as well as several women, most notably Anna Margolin and Celia Dropkin. Moshe Leyb Halpern's volume of poems, *In New York* (1919), captured the texture and text of the city as an American and Jewish milieu, resembling in its language and imagery the poetry of his contemporaries writing in English. In 1919 *Di Inzikhistn* (The introspectivists) appeared, writing free verse poetry that explored personal feeling, an internalized social world. Poets such as Yankev Glatshteyn, Aaron Glanz-Leyeles, and N. B. Minkoff transplanted European Yiddish culture to America, maintained ties with the literary worlds of Warsaw and Odessa, Berlin and Vienna, and linked Yiddish readers to contemporary modernist trends by translating this new poetry into Yiddish. Kadia Molodovsky joined these literary circles when she arrived in New York in 1935. Alone among Yiddish women poets, Molodovsky edited a literary journal, *Svive* (Surroundings), during the early 1940s. Malka Heifetz Tussman knew English well but chose, like Glatshteyn, to write in Yiddish, though as a California resident she lived far from the centers of American Yiddish letters.

This elite literary culture spoke less directly to the immigrant masses than did the theater. Dramatists Jacob Gordin and David Pinski, and actors Jacob Adler and Boris Thomashevsky, helped bring Yiddish theater to the Lower East Side to escape Russian censorship. They quickly found an audience among immigrant workers and Yiddish playhouses proliferated on the Bowery and Grand Street. By 1918, four major theaters presented over a thousand performances annually for an estimated 2 million patrons. The plays engaged their audience's emotions, often presenting the trials of immigrant life, including the loss of old-country values in a commercialized America, conflict of immigrants with their second-generation children, decline of faith, and the temptations of sex brought by the ever-present boarder. Actors and actresses rapidly acquired loyal followings; debates raged in the press over the quality of plays and productions. Some critics tried to use their positions to influence popular taste by disparaging the simplistic, formulaic plays, many of which resembled ethnic versions of later television serials, especially those known as soap operas. Popular plays like Gordin's *Jewish King Lear* (1892) and its successor *Mirele*

*Efros* (1898) or the *Jewish Queen Lear* were known as "onion plays" or "three-handkerchief plays," suggesting the quantity of tears elicited from the audience.

The theater's popularity led to the formation of amateur dramatic groups and these, in turn, prompted the semiprofessional troupe. In 1918 the Fraye Yidishe Folksbiene (the Free Yiddish People's Stage) produced *Grine Felder* (Green fields) by Peretz Hirschbein. The production's unanticipated success encouraged the creation of the Yiddish Art Theater. Guided by Maurice Schwartz, the Yiddish Art Theater introduced sophisticated translations of European plays and provided a stage for serious Yiddish drama, including S. Ansky's *The Dybbuk,* and plays by Hirschbein and Asch. Schwartz also attracted a cadre of talented actors and actresses, including Jacob Ben Ami, Celia Adler, Bertha Gersten, and Ludwig Satz, who abandoned traditional Yiddish acting techniques for Stanislawski's psychological realism. Schwartz experimented as well with new theatrical forms, producing in 1926 a constructivist version of Abraham Goldfaden's *The Tenth Commandment* designed by Boris Aronson. Aronson's innovative production transplanted European avant-garde theater design to the United States. The popularity of serious Yiddish drama registered in 1933, when *Yoshe Kalb,* based on I. J. Singer's powerful novel, became one of the most successful plays on the Yiddish stage. Many artists initially associated with the Yiddish theater, most notably Paul Muni, later moved to Hollywood and Broadway. Located on Second Avenue, the "Yiddish Broadway," the Yiddish Art Theater nurtured talent, encouraged experimentation, and provided an alternative to popular musicals featuring such stars as Molly Picon, Aaron Lebedoff, and Menashe Skulnik throughout the interwar years.

A small Yiddish movie industry developed alongside the Yiddish theater. A technological innovation, movies extended Yiddish culture into a new medium. Yiddish movies relied upon the theater for stories and actors; movie themes echoed those of popular plays. A newcomer to the world of entertainment, Yiddish film competed not only with the theater but with American motion pictures that catered to the working classes. Yiddish movies never acquired the same following as the theater, nor did such popular innovations as theater parties extend to the movies to guarantee them an audience. Another new technology, radio, also offered listeners ethnic Jewish fare, from sermons to soap operas, songs, advice and advertising, even ideological messages. Ever attuned to media possibilities, Cahan encouraged the *Forverts*

Association to purchase a radio station in the late 1920s; WEVD, named in honor of socialist leader Eugene V. Debs, promoted itself as "the station that speaks your language."

Immigrants transplanted a diverse musical heritage that included the traditions of *hazzanut*, cantorial singing in the synagogue, an appreciation of classical instrumental music, and popular songs. Jewish immigrants enjoyed listening to classical music concerts and many dreamed that their offspring would one day achieve renown on the musical stage, like the child prodigies, violinists Jascha Heifetz and Mischa Elman, or pianist Artur Rubenstein. Immigrants considered the world of music respectable, unlike the theater. They encouraged their children to learn how to play an instrument; violin and piano lessons were particularly popular. For many these lessons represented the acquisition of culture and class; a piano in the parlor signified a tangible measure of upward mobility. Jewish appreciation of music extended to religious singing; the celebrated "King of Cantors," Yosele Rosenblatt, attracted as dedicated a following as any stage star. Immigrants bought seats, especially for the high holidays, to attend worship services to listen to a *hazzan;* they also went to concerts featuring their favorite cantors. When radio and phonograph extended music's reach, Jewish immigrants provided a large enough audience to support recordings—often on ethnic labels, subsidiaries of the large record companies—of famous cantors singing religious and Yiddish art songs.

Accompanying immigrant reverence for classical music came enthusiasm for popular musical entertainment, including Yiddish songs and klezmer music. Klezmer musicians in America not only transplanted an eclectic musical band style from eastern Europe but they also incorporated into their performances elements of American popular music, especially dance forms, jazz syncopation, and improvisation. Crossover musicians, like clarinetist and saxophonist Sammy Musiker who played in the orchestras of Gene Krupa and Dave Tarras, or clarinetist and comedian Mickey Katz, encouraged the mixture. Klezmer bands included instrumentalists on fiddle, flute, bass, clarinet, and drums. They played at weddings and other festive occasions; some worked as dance bands and vaudeville orchestras. The most popular *klezmorim,* such as Dave Tarras, Naftule Brandwein, and Abe Schwartz, recorded their hits. Yiddish popular songs were purveyed by pluggers for sheet music companies. Like the theater or *bintel brief,* the songs reflected the daily culture of immigrant life. They spoke of love and sorrow, suffering

and exhilaration, earning a living and yearning for home, the Old World and New. Most passed quickly from the scene, but a few endured.

After World War I, New York City commercial culture became national as Tin Pan Alley songwriters reworked melodies from the Lower East Side, Little Italy, and Harlem into sentimental ballads deracinated from any particular ethnicity. A song like "Bei Mir Bist Du Sheyn" (To Me You're Beautiful) traveled from the Yiddish cultural milieu of the Lower East Side up to Harlem's Savoy Ballroom for a jazz interpretation, acquired English lyrics written by two American Jews, and then became a big hit when sung by the Andrews Sisters. Such an odyssey suggested some transformations paradigmatic of American popular culture. New York's ethnic mixture proved fertile ground for cultural creativity. Its large Jewish population encouraged the transplantation of a Yiddish culture sufficiently vigorous and varied to sustain diverse forms incorporating popular American styles of entertainment. Such crossover experimentation produced new cultural styles that energetic and ambitious second-generation figures could exploit, transform, and sell to a larger American society.

Communal institutions sustained Yiddish culture as Jews left the Lower East Side for new homes in other neighborhoods. Opportunities for free association in the United States encouraged Jewish immigrants to organize. Politics provided a fulcrum for organization, but so did gender, religion, one's hometown in the Old World, one's job in the New World. The organizational diversity of immigrant society offered varied venues for cultural creativity. A lecture-and-concert circuit rapidly developed throughout the United States as immigrant organizations booked artists and intellectuals to provide education and entertainment for their many meetings. As immigrants elaborated networks of supplementary schools, they established a formal context to transmit Jewish culture to their children. Each organization chose to preserve and pass on selected elements of Jewish religion and culture transplanted by immigrants.

## IMMIGRANT ORGANIZATIONS: RELIGIOUS AND SECULAR

Many activities sponsored by secular American Jewish organizations derived from traditional Jewish religious culture. The synagogue in eastern Europe, a place for daily, Sabbath, and holiday prayer services, served as a study hall where men came to learn sacred texts—usually the Talmud, a compendium of Jewish law and lore—and as a meeting room for communal gatherings and discussion. The Jewish community also encouraged the formation of voluntary societies, segregated by sex, to care for social needs. The most important group, the *khevre kadisha* (holy society), oversaw all burials, from preparing the body to the funeral to interment in the cemetery. Other groups raised funds for dowries to enable poor women to marry or for the upkeep and education of orphans; still others visited the sick, provided travelers with accommodations, and assisted wandering beggars to keep moving.

Jewish religious culture embodied gendered norms of public and private behavior. Men participated in public religious activities in the synagogue; women's religious rituals centered in the home. Both men and women worked since they shared responsibility for earning a living. Adults were expected to marry and raise families. As the household head, fathers were responsible for their children's education. Although Jews prized study for its own sake as an ideal, only a privileged few pursued such learning. Most boys left school at the age of thirteen or fourteen to acquire a trade. Girls received domestic training from their mothers, whose duties included managing the household economy; many girls also went to school to learn to read, write, and cipher. As industrialization reached eastern Europe, promoting a migration of young people to the growing cities, girls increasingly learned trades to help support the household.

Jewish immigrants transplanted the popular, folk elements of this traditional culture to the United States before World War I, but the environment of the large cities—even within the immigrant enclaves—did not facilitate re-creating the elite Judaism of eastern Europe in America, especially its yeshivas, institutes of advanced learning. Voluntarism, congregationalism, the enormous pressures to earn a living, and the esteem accorded individualism and the self-made man of wealth undermined rabbinic religious authority and communal norms. East European rabbinic leaders considered the United States a spiritual wasteland, *trefe* (unkosher) and impure. Some even urged their followers not to emigrate. Nonetheless, observant Jews came, among them hundreds of rabbis, many of them young. A significant percentage graduated from the most eminent yeshivas of eastern Europe, including followers of Rabbi Israel Salanter, the founder of the *musar* (moral) movement that emphasized ethics and personal piety.

Contemporaries thought that immigrant orthodoxy replicated Old World patterns, but immigrants themselves recognized the adaptations necessary to survive in America. Synagogues narrowed their scope, serving largely as places of worship and occasionally as study halls. Lay leaders—often men of some wealth and standing, but not necessarily knowledge or *yichus* (pedigree)—assumed control of congregational affairs, deciding whether to hire a rabbi or cantor. Voluntary societies became independent organizations, since Jewish immigrants failed to transplant any form of organized communal self-government that might coordinate and supervise their associational life. Immigrant rabbis found their authority largely restricted to their congregations, and even then they were at the mercy of lay leaders. Only a few, like Bernard Levinthal of Philadelphia, established themselves as communal figures by virtue of their personalities and learning. Most rabbis no longer served as legal scholars and religious judges; many failed in the new role of preacher and pastor.

Public expressions of religious norms also weakened. Immigrants built relatively few *mikve*, ritual baths required by married women to observe the laws of family purity. Most immigrants worked on the Sabbath, inconceivable in eastern Europe. Even those who went to sabbath services often spent the remainder of the day at the shop or in the store. Death gradually ceased to be under the control of the *khevre kadisha*. Enterprising teamsters carrying the caskets to the cemetery, often located a considerable distance outside of the city where Jews lived, offered first to prepare the body for burial, and then to provide complete funeral services. Thus emerged a new field of Jewish entrepreneurship: the funeral home. Rabbis competed with each other and with religious slaughterers over the proper supervision of *kashrut,* the kosher laws. Women perhaps paid more attention to the cost of kosher meat than they did to its *kashrut*. When the price soared from twelve to eighteen cents per pound in 1902, militant New York Jewish housewives declared a boycott of all kosher butchers and forced their neighbors to eat meatless meals until prices declined.

Perhaps most significantly, Jewish immigrants transplanted only fragments of their educational system. They sent their sons and daughters to American public schools and relegated Jewish learning to supplementary education at best. Many neglected even the few years of *kheyder* or tutoring for their sons in preparation for bar mitzvah, the public religious ceremony at age thirteen that signified a boy's mastery of prayer texts and Torah. If daughters received a Jewish education, most learned superficially in Sunday schools, in settlement houses, or YWHAs. Only a few immigrants sent their daughters to innovative Hebrew schools. Ironically, in America experiments in Jewish education usually began with girls since there was no educational tradition to overcome.

If immigrants neglected the religious education of their children, they did not fail to organize their own social and cultural life. The most numerous Jewish immigrant organizations were the *landsmanshaftn,* societies of Jews from the same European town. A survey done prior to World War II under the auspices of the New Deal Works Progress Administration estimated that 25 percent of New York Jews belonged to a *landsmanshaft.* These groups maintained ties with relatives and fellow *landslayt* who remained in Europe by retaining such cultural practices associated with the old home as Yiddish dialects or traditions of chanting the sabbath prayers, and by sending aid to rebuild or strengthen local institutions. *Landsmanshaftn* also facilitated integration into American society through their use of credit unions and American protocols to conduct meetings and run elections, and by the material and spiritual assistance given to members. They often provided modest sums during unemployment, medical care when sick, burial in their own section of a cemetery, and death benefits for survivors and to cover funeral costs. Many met regularly as a congregation to observe the sabbath and festivals. Their religious practices followed orthodox custom, often incorporating local variations.

Organizational impulses behind the *landsmanshaftn* led to several innovations. Since most societies restricted membership to men, women occasionally formed auxiliaries. Age and year of arrival also spurred their establishment; younger immigrants preferred to associate with their peers rather than join older men in an existing group. Jewish ideological organizations, including Socialists and Zionists, encouraged the formation of *landsmanshaft* branches. The crisis of World War I brought several wealthy immigrant leaders like Bernard Semel, the head of the Federation of Galician Jews, to prominence. Federations of *landsmanshaftn* coordinated fundraising efforts to help Jews overseas; they also bestowed honor and recognition upon Jewish immigrants. The Hebrew Sheltering and Immigrant Aid Society (HIAS), the preeminent social welfare organization assisting immigrants upon arrival, partly originated among members of a *landsmanshaft* in 1902, and remained closely tied to that world until the interwar years.

Secular Jews who rejected Judaism turned to politics or work for a communal context for immigrant culture beyond the neighborhood. Zionism, Socialism, and labor unions offered immigrants a framework to shape and transmit their culture.

Zionists, in principle committed to Hebrew education, supported the efforts of a handful of dedicated Hebraists to revive the language. These stalwarts established the Histadruth Ivrith (Hebrew Language and Culture Association) in 1916 to disseminate Hebrew culture in the United States. Innovative educators introduced the modern *ivri b'ivri* method of teaching Hebrew, with its emphasis upon a spoken, living language. They developed a graduated system of supplementary schools that culminated in Hebrew teachers colleges. Established in such cities as Boston, Baltimore, Chicago, Philadelphia, Cleveland, and New York, these colleges produced an American-born generation of Hebrew speakers and scholars. Immigrant and second-generation Zionists also pioneered in establishing modern Jewish day schools and Hebrew-speaking camps to nurture a Zionist elite. They encouraged cultural creativity in music and dance. Dvora Lapson built an enthusiasm for Palestinian folk dances—later, Israeli dances—among American Jews. In addition to Zionist weeklies and monthlies published in Yiddish and English, *HaDoar* (The Post) appeared regularly each week in Hebrew starting in 1923. Hebrew journals helped sustain a modest Hebrew culture in America that included such immigrant poets as Hillel Bavli, Israel Efros, and Simon Halkin.

Zionists split into many parties. The ideological parties, European imports, ranged from the socialist Zionist Left, including Poalei Zion (1903), to religious Zionists in Mizrahi (1911) to Zionist Revisionists (1925). Following the first Zionist Congress in Basel, American Zionists organized the Federation of American Zionists in 1898, later the Zionist Organization of America, and most recently the American Zionist Movement, an indigenous American creation, like Hadassah, of the second generation. Most parties established a youth movement; many were authentically American, like Young Judaea (1909), later affiliated with Hadassah, and the Labor Zionist Habonim (the Builders, 1935). American influences also appeared in many parties' support of fraternal associations to provide social welfare benefits like the *landsmanshaftn* and in the creation of separate women's organizations, although Zionist ideology proclaimed the equality of men and women. Hadassah, the largest Zionist organization, usually avoided ideology, even as it developed an educational program keyed to the American scene. Despite the multiplicity of parties, fraternal and women's organizations, and youth groups, Zionists enrolled smaller numbers of immigrants than did socialist organizations and labor unions.

Committed to developing a workers' culture, Jewish members of the International Ladies Garment Workers Union (ILGWU) and Amalgamated Clothing Workers Union encouraged their unions to build housing cooperatives and vacation homes; supported labor lyceums with programs in education, music, and drama; and sought health and welfare benefits similar to those offered by *landsmanshaftn*. Like *landsmanshaftn*, unions blended Jewish customs with American ones. The Protocol of Peace ending the 1910 New York City cloakmakers strike that secured the ILGWU drew upon east European Jewish traditions of arbitration. Negotiated with Brandeis's help, the protocol used arbitration to govern the relations of Jewish workers and employers in a novel American situation of labor organization. Women workers brought their own cultural expectations to unionization. Although only a handful rose to leadership positions, like Rose Schneiderman in the Women's Trade Union League and Rose Pesotta in the ILGWU, women's radicalism prompted unions to develop opportunities for the pursuit of leisure extending beyond both socialist politics and bread and butter concerns.

As *landsmanshaftn* helped their overseas cousins, garment unions allocated funds to reflect their sense of socialist solidarity with workers throughout the United States and the world. Their publications, such as *Justice,* the ILGWU weekly, kept members informed about events involving workers. After the rise of Hitler in Germany, Jewish garment trades unions united with the Jewish socialist fraternal Workmen's Circle to create an explicitly Jewish Labor Committee (1934) to fight fascism.

Socialists, Communists, and Yiddishists blended the workers' culture of the immigrant garment trades unions with ideology in their fraternal organizations: the Socialist Workmen's Circle (1900), Communist International Worker's Order (IWO, 1929, later Jewish People's Fraternal Order), and Yiddishist Sholem Aleichem Folk Institute (1918). These fraternal groups enrolled ideologically committed men and women who supported their supplementary children's schools, camps and vacation homes, and music and drama groups. The semiprofessional Yiddish theater of both the Workmen's Circle, the Folksbiene, and the Jewish branch of the IWO, the Artef, nurtured considerable talents as well as providing members with entertainment. The Workmen's Circle Labor Lyceums sponsored lectures and concerts; impresario Sol Hurok began his career as Lyceum educational director. The organization offered unemployment insurance, health insurance and medical benefits, and burial rights in its cemetery. In the interwar years, the Workmen's Circle even established several old-age homes and sanitariums for tuberculosis victims.

The immigrants' antireligious radicalism agitated established second-generation Jews committed to Judaism. Such men as Louis Marshall and Cyrus Adler saw in the disarray of immigrant Orthodoxy the problem of how to transmit Jewish religious culture to the immigrants' children. They sought a solution in modernizing and Americanizing Judaism. There already existed an American Judaism, Reform Judaism, but even its supporters recognized that its American upper-middle-class mores repelled most east European Jews. So a group of leaders proposed a new American Judaism embracing American democracy, pluralism, congregationalism, and public schooling. These ideals would be linked with a Judaism that emphasized the binding character of Jewish peoplehood, the developmental nature of Jewish law, the importance of Jewish women as transmitters of tradition within the family, and the relevance of the new Hebraic culture created by Zionists in the Jewish spiritual center in Palestine.

When leading Reform laymen and some Orthodox rabbis brought the scholar Solomon Schechter from England in 1902 to head a reorganized Jewish Theological Seminary (JTS), they intended to create a modern American rabbinate prepared to lead congregations toward a new American Judaism. Schechter recruited a distinguished faculty from abroad, including rabbinic scholar Louis Ginzburg, Jewish historian Alexander Marx, and Jewish medievalist Israel Friedlaender. He also welcomed a young American-trained scholar, graduate of the seminary, Mordecai Kaplan. In 1909 Kaplan agreed to head the seminary's Teachers Institute, a school for men and women devoted to Hebrew culture. The Institute gradually developed close ties with Columbia University's Teachers College, absorbing the ideals of progressive education associated with John Dewey's theories. The rabbinical school required its students to be college graduates, thus assuring mastery of American elite culture. By 1913 enough rabbis had graduated from JTS to support the creation of a congregational union, the United Synagogue. The United Synagogue and the Rabbinical Assembly (1901), the organization of Conservative rabbis, gradually defined the pragmatic boundaries of Conservative Judaism, which included recognizing women's public presence within the synagogue through the practice of mixed seating.

Although Conservative Judaism expanded during the interwar years, its greatest growth came after World War II when it became the most popular form of American Judaism. Conservative Judaism appealed particularly to second-generation east European Jews. They liked its emphasis on Jewish peoplehood, its commitment to Zionist idealism, its democratic values—especially the equality offered women through family pews—and its affirmation of tradition. Unlike Reform, Conservatism stressed Jewish ethnic values and retained time-hallowed rituals, including a worship service conducted almost exclusively in Hebrew, while affirming American ideals and pragmatically accommodating the secular demands of American life. The decision of its Law Committee to permit Jews to drive to synagogue services on the Sabbath—riding is normally a forbidden activity on the Sabbath—represents a typical pragmatic accommodation to the suburban character of Jewish residential settlement after World War II.

Wealthy immigrant laymen like Israel Unterberg and Harry Fischel agreed that modernization was needed. They not only supported JTS, but they also contributed to the Rabbi Isaac Elchanan Theological Seminary (RIETS, 1897). RIETS combined rabbinical training with yeshiva study and, after student agitation in 1908, included traditional text study with secular subjects required by the New York State Regents for secondary schools. In 1915 its lay leaders invited a noted immigrant Talmud scholar and innovator, Bernard Revel, to head the institution. Revel created first a Yeshiva high school and then in 1928 a Yeshiva College. He intended this blend of the best of Western knowledge with advanced talmudic learning to produce the educated Jewish laymen needed to secure traditional Judaism in America, lead it out of the immigrant enclaves, and lift it above the folk religion of Jewish immigrants. Revel convinced supporters of RIETS to cooperate with the Zionist-oriented Orthodox teacher's institute established by Mizrahi and he moved all three out of the Lower East Side to a new campus in Washington Heights, an emerging middle-class New York neighborhood. Like Schechter, Revel recruited several brilliant European Jewish Talmudists, most importantly Joseph Soloveitchik, whose erudition in Talmud and Western philosophy strengthened the elite tradition of Jewish learning in America and laid the intellectual foundation for modern Orthodoxy.

Other religious innovators began with congregational life itself. Friedlaender and Kaplan, professors at JTS, encouraged a religious revitalization movement among immigrants on the Lower East Side. In 1912 they spurred the creation of the Young Israel movement of modern Orthodox congregations that encouraged participation and education, as well as socializing within the framework of synagogue life. Young Israel congregations demonstrated the attractiveness of orthodoxy, its ability to adapt to modern American life, its compatibility with middle-class mores and taste. By 1924 there were enough congregations to warrant a National Council of Young Israel. Herbert Goldstein developed the Institutional Synagogue in Harlem, its diverse activities for youth modeled on the urban institutional church. Still other Orthodox Jews gradually modernized congregations, as the history of Congregation Kehillath Jeshurun in New York demonstrated under the rabbinical guidance of Moses Margolies and his son-in-law, Joseph Lookstein. Lookstein initiated a new type of coeducational orthodox religious school, Ramaz Day School (1936), that blended American upper-middle-class private education with a modern form of traditional Jewish learning.

Not all Orthodox rabbis valued modernization. Resisters to American influences organized to repel accommodators. In 1902 resisters established the Agudath HaRabbonim, the Union of Orthodox Rabbis of the United States and Canada, a Yiddish-speaking rabbinical association led by Eliezer Silver, Bernard Levinthal, and Moses Margolies. During the Depression, some of its leaders shifted their allegiance away from RIETS to Brooklyn yeshiva Mesifta Torah V'daath, which included only the minimum secular studies required by law. Under the leadership of Shraga Feivel Mendelowitz, the school developed a rabbinical program. Growing conflict with resisters led younger English-speaking, RIETS-educated modern orthodox rabbis to reorganize the Rabbinical Council of America in 1935. The previously established congregational union, the Union of Orthodox Jewish Congregations of America (1889), tackled the challenge of *kashrut* and developed guidelines, national supervision, and the OU logo that allowed increasing numbers of products to be certified as kosher. By 1940, American orthodox rabbis had created two competing rabbinical associations, and a congregational union increasingly allied to RIETS and the Yeshiva College.

Thus the cooperation of immigrant leaders with the first American-educated generation of east European Jews produced the institutions that subsequently shaped American Jewish denominationalism. The Jewish Theological Seminary and its allied congregations and rabbis became the center of the Conservative movement while Yeshiva College—after World

War II Yeshiva University—and its seminary, allied congregations, and rabbis became the center of modern Orthodoxy. Together with the previously established Reform movement, they created the Synagogue Council of America in 1926 as a coordinating body to address Jewish religious issues. These three movements encompassed the major religious patterns of American Jews prior to World War II.

Similar coalitions led to innovations in American Jewish communal life. Jews had established many philanthropic institutions: hospitals, orphanages, immigrant aid societies—the largest was HIAS located in New York—charitable groups to help the poor, settlement houses, trade schools, and Young Men and Young Women's Hebrew Associations (YMYWHA). Now, younger leaders wanted to bring order and efficiency into the welter of competing organizations. Starting in Boston in 1895, wealthy Jewish men established federations of Jewish charities to coordinate fundraising and distribution. Through centralization, the federation system generated more money for worthy institutions. It also promised to promote communal cooperation rather than competition, to secure the prominence of an elite even as it recruited new wealth among the immigrants, to suggest the possibility of a communal vision rather than a narrow institutional one. The federation movement accompanied and supported the professionalization of Jewish social work and adopted the language of communalism, even suggesting that federations represented a modern American form of the traditional *kehilla,* the self-governing Jewish community.

Reform rabbi and Zionist leader Judah Magnes contested such a notion. He argued that American Jewish communal life had to be democratic. Magnes convinced the wealthy elite in the newly created American Jewish Committee to support an experiment in Jewish communal democracy: the New York Kehillah. Despite its brief existence (1908-1922), the Kehillah helped to shape a new type of communal educational system. Ambitious Jewish educators, men and women raised in America—including Alexander Dushkin, Isaac and Libbie Berkson, Emanuel Gamoran, Judah and Dvora Lapson, and Albert Schoolman—flocked to the Kehillah's Bureau of Education. There they designed a modern Jewish supplementary school system under the guidance of Samson Benderly, one of several Jewish educators to leave Palestine for work in the American diaspora. The Bureau championed a community-based transformative education to restore self-esteem to immigrant children, raise their ethnic and religious con-

sciousness, and encourage them to participate actively in both American and Jewish culture. To demonstrate that Judaism was a living culture, several educators established Jewish summer camps that provided an opportunity for learning by doing. Among the first was Camp Cejwin, founded in 1919 by Schoolman. When the Kehillah collapsed, many of the bureau's young recruits left New York and established similar educational bureaus in cities throughout the United States.

The Kehillah experiment fragmented in World War I factionalism and struggles over a larger democratic Jewish communal institution, an American Jewish Congress to unite Jews throughout the United States. Supported by Zionists led first by Brandeis and then by Reform rabbi Stephen Wise, agitation for a congress produced the unexpected cooperation of its opponents, anti-Zionist Socialists and non-Zionist capitalists in the American Jewish Committee. After democratic elections gave the Zionists victory, American Jews achieved a brief moment of unity focused upon obtaining a political solution to secure the rights of European Jews after the war. Through the congress, American Jews endorsed both the 1917 Balfour Declaration favoring the establishment of a Jewish homeland in Palestine and minority rights for Jews in Poland and the other states created upon the dissolution of the Russian and Austro-Hungarian empires. American Jews even sent Louis Marshall—the head of the American Jewish Committee and diligent opponent of the congress's democratic and Zionist character—to Versailles.

Although participants in the congress agreed that it would meet only once, Rabbi Stephen Wise decided to resurrect the American Jewish Congress in 1922. The new congress entered the Jewish communal world as a militant, mass-membership organization, a counterweight to the elite American Jewish Committee. Wise hoped that the congress would foster democracy in Jewish life and become the voice of American Jewry. Although he fell short of his goal, the congress soon acquired a reputation as an organization dedicated to fighting anti-Semitism through democratic political means. In the 1930s *Congress Weekly* kept constituents informed and generated lively political debate. Wise espoused mass rallies and aggressive interest group politics, tactics diverging sharply from those of the American Jewish Committee. Under Marshall's leadership, the committee preferred to negotiate behind the scenes, relying upon its members' prestige and wealth. In 1913, Marshall secured civil rights legislation in New York that prohibited discrimination at resorts. The congress's increasing support of Zionism also distinguished it from the non-Zionist committee. Unlike the committee, which remained the preserve of the first American-born generation of German Jews, the congress appealed to the new second generation of east European Jews.

As a mass membership organization trying to unify American Jews, the congress competed with B'nai B'rith. In 1913 the Jewish fraternal organization established the Anti-Defamation League of B'nai B'rith (ADL) in response to increasingly frequent stereotyping of Jews on stage and screen. The ADL immediately offered to help in the 1913 trial of Leo Frank, the young Jewish manager accused of murdering a teenaged woman worker in his Atlanta pencil factory. When a mob lynched Frank, many Jews expressed outrage. During the interwar years, ADL focused on defamation, working to remove anti-Semitic stereotypes from the media and fight libels against Jews. Though it preferred the American Jewish Committee's quiet tactics and found its supporters among descendants of German Jews, ADL championed group libel legislation as did the congress. B'nai B'rith also entered the academy by adopting the Hillel foundation program in 1925. Unlike Jewish fraternities and sororities or ideological youth movements, Hillel sought to unite all Jewish groups on campus by offering religious, cultural, and social activities. Under Abram Sachar's dynamic leadership, the number of Hillel groups expanded rapidly, making it the dominant Jewish campus organization by the end of World War II.

The struggle over the American Jewish Congress underscored the dissension within American Jewry and signaled the failure of immigrant ideologies or second-generation movements to propagate a sufficiently persuasive theory or practice of Jewish communal solidarity. The three major religious movements did not enroll a majority of American Jews; the secularist radical movements enlisted the support of a vocal minority; neither Zionism nor the federations, despite their limited success in uniting immigrant and second generation, provided a comprehensive vision of Jewish communalism. Even in the area of Jewish defense, the committee, the congress, and ADL competed more often than they cooperated.

Some theorists of Jewish community survival argued that the solution lay in relatively small, local community centers. Rabbi Mordecai Kaplan proposed that the synagogue assume the burden of centralizing Jewish life. Each congregation should create a synagogue center offering worship services, education for children and adults, recreation (including swimming pools and basketball courts), and social-welfare activities that reflected a Jewish understanding of social justice. Kaplan imagined that all neighborhood groups would meet at the synagogue center, from boy scouts to Hadassah chapters; families would celebrate important moments in the life cycle there, from bar mitzvahs to weddings. Within its walls the synagogue center would become a modern, American version of the traditional *kehilla*. In 1916 Kaplan oversaw construction of a model, the Jewish Center, on Manhattan's West Side. In the 1920s a burst of synagogue construction produced many elaborate synagogue centers, jokingly dubbed the *shul* (synagogue) with the pool and the school. But relatively stiff membership fees prevented all but the middle and upper classes from enjoying the facilities. Most synagogue centers affiliated with the Conservative movement. Congregational schools for children, however, competed successfully with communal schools; as parents increasingly enrolled their children in local synagogue schools, their choice gradually spelled the demise of the new communal education system Kaplan had helped to build.

## THE PLACE OF JEWS
## IN AMERICAN CULTURE

As a theorist of Jewish accommodation and persistence in America, Kaplan faced formidable opponents. His contemporary, Horace Kallen, a professor of philosophy and founder of the New School for Social Research, argued for a secular, Hebraist interpretation of American Jewish life. Rejecting the melting-pot idea of assimilation, Kallen proposed the concept of cultural pluralism and suggested the metaphor of America as a symphony orchestra. Each ethnic group provided its own timbre and played its own melody line in the American cultural symphony. For Kallen, Judaism was a component of the larger Hebraism. Yet he offered no proposals to preserve the distinctive Hebraist voice. Nor did he suggest, as Louis Brandeis did, that "to be good Americans, we must be better Jews, and to be better Jews, we must become Zionists." Brandeis linked Jewish and American identity, arguing that "Jews were by reason of their traditions and their character peculiarly fitted for the attainment of American ideals." Yet Brandeis and his supporters suffered a stinging defeat in a battle over leadership of American Zionists in 1921. Educators like Julius Drachsler, Emanuel Gamoran, Israel Chipkin, and Isaac Berkson theorized that America protected Jewish group culture. Education played a crucial role; "education has probably never meant as much to the preservation of Jewish group life, as Jewish education means at this moment to the continued life of our people," announced the inaugural issue of the *Jewish Teacher* in 1916. The Jewish school and summer camp became the institutional vehicles of Jewish cultural transmission and survival.

The seductive power of assimilation feared by the educators found expression in the writings of immigrants who published autobiographies or autobiographical novels in English. These books interpreted the immigrant experience to other Americans as well as to Jews. Many attracted a wide readership. Mary Antin's *The Promised Land* (1912) and Marcus Ravage's *An American in the Making* (1917) describe the transformation of immigrant Jew into American as a form of rebirth. The autobiographies graphically depict their author's willingness to discard their ethnic otherness for a new identity as American. "I must not fail to testify that in America a child of the slums owns the land and all that is good in it," Antin proclaimed in her paean to the new world. The fiction of Anoia Yezierska, especially *Bread Givers* (1925) and *Hungry Hearts* (1920), and Abe Cahan's *The Rise of David Levinsky* (1917) reveal some of the social and cultural costs of such self-transformations. Levinsky acquires wealth and influence but loses his soul and a chance for love; Yezierska's heroines similarly gain knowledge and culture but sacrifice any hope for a family and love. Both suggest that the price of Jewish assimilation to America is loneliness and alienation.

These writings anticipated themes that became increasingly popular as another cohort of second-generation Jews, the children of the earlier arrivals among the east European immigrants, came of age. These men and women struggled again with the issues faced by the first American-born German Jewish generation of 1900. Many of the earlier cultural battles—of religious against secular, socialist against Zionist, elitist against populist, bourgeois against proletarian—reappeared. Most of these replays occurred in English, the second generation's language.

These struggles of Jew against Jew occurred during a period of worldwide depression and war, a time of rising fascism abroad and increasing anti-Semitism at home. The apparently endless horizons that greeted Jews maturing at the turn of the century amid Progressivism's heady optimism changed into a sobering vision of limits. American Jews growing up in the years before World War I confronted as adults a less generous America, one that imposed an increasing number of restrictions on Jews. These

included quotas on Jewish immigration; quotas on admission of Jewish students to colleges, universities, and medical schools; restricted neighborhoods and apartment buildings; restricted hotels and resorts, fraternities and social clubs; even discrimination in employment. Newspapers regularly featured want ads specifying "Christians only need apply."

The publication of the anti-Semitic forgery, "The Protocols of the Elders of Zion," by the folk hero industrialist, Henry Ford, in his *Dearborn Independent,* epitomized for American Jews the appalling American embrace of anti-Semitism. Ford's public apology in 1927 hardly signaled a reversal in anti-Semitic discrimination. Hatred of Jews continued to increase, spurred on by the Ku Klux Klan in the 1920s, the preaching of Father Charles Coughlin and Gerald L. K. Smith, the rallies and propaganda of the German-American Bund in the 1930s. Anti-Semitism reached a peak during World War II and declined precipitously thereafter.

Social barriers constricted Jewish creativity. Seeking to come to terms with and shape their own America, Jews left immigrant enclaves and constructed ethnic neighborhoods and built Jewish resorts outside of the large cities in such places as the Catskills and Poconos. Thus Jews secured a piece of America where they felt at home. This ethnic milieu nourished local talent and proved a staging ground from which the ambitious few might try to conquer the other America. Their strategies ranged from assimilation to ethnic assertion, from the embrace of radical universalism to the championing of Zionist particularism, from seduction as the exotic other to entertainment as the girl next door. Each strategy embodied a vision of America and of the Jews' place within American society and culture.

Second-generation Jews played a singular role in shaping American urban culture, often using their ethnic world as a springboard. Broadway director Moss Hart, opera singer Richard Tucker, and abstract expressionist painter Mark Rothko all found employment as young men and a chance to hone their talents at the Brooklyn Jewish Center, a synagogue center built in 1922 on Kaplan's model. Tamiment Lodge, an adult summer camp sponsored by the socialist Rand School, acquired a playhouse supervised by Max Liebman that developed the intimate revue—a blend of "political satire, theatrical parody, Jewish camp, Yiddish sketches, romance, sex and spoofs on everyday life." The Tamiment playhouse encouraged such comics as Danny Kaye, Imogene Coca, and Carol Burnett, and such writers as Neil Simon and Woody Allen. The Catskills hotels nourished so many comedians, performers, playwrights, and producers that "the borscht circuit" acquired renown as a testing ground for talent.

The Educational Alliance, an early settlement house on the Lower East Side, started an art school in 1895 that fostered diverse talents: modernist painters Louis Lozowick and Abraham Walkowitz, abstract expressionists Adolf Gottlieb and Barnett Newman; sculptors Jacob Epstein and Louise Nevelson, the brothers Soyer, and the iconoclastic printmakers Ben Shahn and Leonard Baskin. Under Abba Ostrovsky's direction from 1917 when it reopened after a twelve-year hiatus, the "Jewish art school" nourished a Jewish artist's identity through participation in the social and cultural life of the people. A similar transformation occurred when William Kolodney became educational director at the 92d Street Young Men's Hebrew Association in 1934. He initiated programs that transformed the Y into a center of modernist culture. Through its concerts in contemporary classical music, modern dance classes and performances, and poetry readings in English, the Y discovered new voices. Young Jewish dancers like Anna Sokolow, Benjamin Zemach, and Pearl Lang created expressive forms of movement that helped shape a distinctive American modern dance. They also choreographed works with Jewish themes. In the 1950s Fred Berk established a Jewish Dance division at the Y that focused on Israeli folk dance. For many years the Budapest Quartet played there and the Y's Poetry Center encouraged such talents as Stanley Kunitz. Though the doors of the academy were largely closed, Jews found alternative forums for expression, encouraged by a bourgeois Jewish community that a younger generation would later condemn as philistine.

In 1922, Rabbi Stephen Wise established the Jewish Institute of Religion, a liberal seminary that offered rabbinical training outside of any denomination. Wise hoped that the institute would produce a generation of Jewish leaders dedicated to helping all Jews. He recruited eminent scholars—among them the philosopher Harry Wolfson and the historians Salo Baron and Ralph Marcus—but most left after brief tenures. Wolfson went to Harvard, Baron and Marcus to Columbia, Shalom Spiegel to JTS, and Julian Obermann to Yale.

Baron's presence at Columbia in the first chair in Jewish history at an American university, like Wolfson's position at Harvard, signified a new trend in higher Jewish studies. Initially, Jewish learning had found a home in Semitics departments in American universities, but Jewish Semitics scholars failed to nurture enough students to maintain the field's primacy as the model for Jewish university studies. By contrast, Baron used his position to articulate a Jewish academic agenda by establishing an interdisciplinary scholarly organization. In 1933, Baron and the philosopher Morris Raphael Cohen created the Conference on Jewish Relations (later Social Studies). The conference held annual meetings and began publishing a quarterly, *Jewish Social Studies* in 1939; both served to spotlight the legitimacy of scholarship on Jewish subjects and to foster a sense of community among often isolated Jewish scholars. The conference also assisted European Jewish scholars, located positions for them in the United States, and rescued them from Nazi persecution.

Jews also entered the American world of popular culture. From the streets of the Lower East Side Jews discovered pathways to fame and fortune through burlesque and vaudeville. Sophie Tucker and Fanny Brice popularized new female images, bringing visions of the Jew as "Red Hot Mama" and seductive singer to America. Other Jews embraced American sports, entering the boxing ring to win championships as Benny Leonard did from 1917 to 1925, or the baseball diamond, as Hank Greenberg did from 1933 to 1947. Leonard told apocryphal stories about how he defended Jewish neighborhoods and synagogues from anti-Semitic vandals. Greenberg's refusal in 1934 to play a game on Yom Kippur, the Day of Atonement, symbolized and legitimized a Jewish presence in the mythic center of American culture. Greenberg became the first Jewish athlete to cross over from ethnic to national favorite. With thousands of Jews moving to the Bronx—during the Depression Jews made up almost half of the Bronx's population—and to Brooklyn, the Yankees and Dodgers acquired a new generation of fans. Basketball, however, became the Jewish urban game of choice, so much so that sports writers associated it with stereotypical Jewish characteristics. One writer claimed that it placed "a premium on an alert, scheming mind" as well as "flashy trickiness, artful dodging and general smart aleckness." From the street courts of Brownsville, Brooklyn, to the synagogue-center courts, Jews of the middle and working classes played the game.

Others took illegitimate pathways out of poverty, climbing the criminal ladder of success. Jewish gangsters got their start in petty crime, then expanded during Prohibition into illegal liquor businesses, gambling, and labor racketeering. Men like Meyer Lansky and Bugsy Siegel helped to turn crime into a big business; organized crime became the American way.

Elements of continuity linked the new American-born generation with its second-generation and immigrant predecessors. Organizations did not disappear; the growth of synagogue centers did not eliminate the immigrant *shtiebl* (prayer room) or *landsmanshaft* congregations; Anglo-Jewish weeklies provided only meager competition to the Yiddish press; English language journals did not yet spell the demise of Yiddish literary culture; the popularity of Tin Pan Alley, swing bands, and the Broadway musical stage coexisted with Yiddish songs, klezmer music, and the Yiddish theater, despite the appeal of American culture. But without the renewal provided by mass immigration, the future pointed to the decline of Yiddish culture. Yet during the interwar decades, only the movies threatened immediately to entice all Americans—Jews and Gentiles—away from their favored entertainments.

Immigrant Jews entered the new field of movies as exhibitors selling moments of pleasure to the urban working masses for a nickel. Ambitious entrepreneurs like Marcus Loew and Adolph Zukor quickly realized that they could not depend on others to produce the product they displayed if they wanted to retain control over their theaters. Producing movies followed, first in New York City and then in Los Angeles, enticed by the mild weather and favorable political climate. In Hollywood, Louis B. Mayer, Carl Laemmle, William Fox, Samuel Goldwyn, and Harry Cohn created not just a form of mass entertainment but a version of the American dream that appealed to the middle and working classes. This ideal America knew no ethnic distinctions and offered all immigrants the possibility of rebirth. Jewish producers taught several generations of Americans how to dress and speak, to walk and flirt; movies manufactured dreams and spread myths of American heroes, most notably through the western. Due to threats of censorship, movies also propagated a stern morality in which sin was punished. In the 1930s, as anti-Semitism pervaded American society, Jewish characters and the general immigrant experience disappeared from the screen—because producers deemed them unprofitable—although Jews continued to work in most parts of the industry.

The first sound movie, *The Jazz Singer,* produced by the Warner brothers in 1927, expressed the melting-pot vision of assimilation embraced by most Jewish producers. Based on a story, "The Day of Atonement," by Samson Raphaelson that was inspired by the life story of Al Jolson, a successful vaudeville singer and blackface entertainer, the movie version had Jolson playing a fictional version of himself. The movie portrays the conflict of an aging immigrant cantor with his American-born son: the father wants the son to sing the songs of the synagogue but the son spurns these for jazz songs, the songs of African Americans which he sings with the peculiar pathos of Jewish suffering. Forced to choose between opening night on Broadway or chanting the opening prayers of Yom Kippur in place of his dying father, the son decides to return, briefly, to the synagogue. Having atoned for abandoning Jewish tradition, the jazz singer then reverts to the stage to perform in blackface before his adoring mother. This vision of capturing America after obtaining father's blessing—sustained throughout by mother's love—spoke to many Jews and echoed the ambitions of the new east European second generation.

These Jews now looked back on their childhood growing up in immigrant households and wrote about that world from their own perspective. Their version of the immigrant experience differed from that of the assimilationist autobiographies of the immigrants themselves with their hymn to America. The critically acclaimed novel of immigrant Jewish life, *Call It Sleep* (1934) by Henry Roth, imagines an America both seductive and threatening, both a veritable Tower of Babel and a new Israel. The novel chronicles a son's childhood experiences, the difficulties of securing father's blessing and the pain of separating from mother's love. Ironically, Roth's book failed to attract a wide readership. Michael Gold's proletarian novel appealed more broadly to Americans during the Depression; *Jews without Money* (1930) portrayed an immigrant Jewish world filled with exploitation, suffering, prostitution, and poverty that only a socialist messiah could redeem. A similarly dark vision of Jewish lowlife animated Daniel Fuchs's 1930s trilogy of the Brooklyn Jewish neighborhood of Williamsburg, a striking contrast to Charles Reznikoff's lyrical novel, *By the Waters of Manhattan* (1930). Chicago also served as a setting for second-generation writers reflecting on their immigrant upbringing. Albert Halper's *On the Shore* (1934) and Meyer Levin's *The Old Bunch* (1937) chronicled the rise of a young generation eager to discard its Jewish heritage for America. Boston's Charles Angoff in his 1940s trilogy portrayed a similar experience.

Alongside the second-generation Jewish novelists came the poets—Louis Zukofsky, Charles Reznikoff, George Oppen, and Stanley Kunitz—writing in English rather than Yiddish or Hebrew. Reznikoff, an imagist associated with the Objectivists, sought the beautiful in mean objects, often in an urban setting. The Objectivists, Zukovsky and Oppen, emphasized exactness, simplicity, and sincerity. Their younger contemporaries—Delmore Schwartz, Muriel Rukeyser, Karl Shapiro, David Ignatow, and Paul Goodman—avoided the experimental. Several of these poets received early recognition; Rukeyser won the Yale Younger Poets Prize at twenty-two and Schwartz, an editor of *Partisan Review,* was deemed a melancholic genius. "You can't fool me, the world is a funeral," remarks a character in Schwartz's "The World is a Wedding" (1948). A few, like Reznikoff and Shapiro, also wrote history and criticism; Goodman's book on adolescence, *Growing Up Absurd* (1960), influenced an entire generation coming of age in the 1960s.

Many successful Jewish artistic figures of the interwar years embraced American themes, despite America's reluctance to admit them. In music, literature, theater, and movies, Jews purveyed a vision of America that included them and all those who were outsiders. Sometimes this involved taking the language and style of popular culture and translating it into elite cultural forms. George Gershwin's "Rhapsody in Blue" (1924)—originally titled "American Rhapsody"—transposed jazz into classical music; his willingness to adapt African American culture outraged critics but brought him widespread popular acclaim. Aaron Copland in his dance suites, "Appalachian Spring" (1944) and "Billy the Kid" (1938) drew upon a western and rural heritage remote from his native Brooklyn. Copland originally had proposed a dance suite that took up the theme of immigration, but it was rejected in favor of the more "American" topic of the West. Ironically, the postmodern performance artist Meredith Monk returned to this theme in "Ellis Island" fifty years later. In a case reminiscent of Zangwill's hero, Ernest Bloch composed a symphony, "America" (1926), that critics considered an impudent act for one who also wrote "Schelomo, a Hebrew Rhapsody" (1916) or a "Sacred Service" (1930–1933). Irving Berlin's songs, especially the enormously popular "God Bless America" and "White Christmas," gently removed Christ by lyrically imagining a peaceful, nonethnic America. The musical-theater collaboration of Oscar Hammerstein II and Richard Rodgers produced a classic American western romance, *Oklahoma* (1943), that promised the reconciliation of sworn enemies: cowboys and farmers.

Similar visions animated some of the novelists of this generation. Edna Ferber did not ignore the Jewish saga—her novel *Fanny Herself* (1917) depicts a young Jewish woman's coming of age—but she devoted most of her energies to writing large American novels focused on the West and its vitality. By contrast, Ludwig Lewisohn's novels explored the sexual encounter of Jew and Gentile, a theme that the next generation would make central. After Lewisohn converted to Zionism, he wrote autobiographically in *The Island Within* (1928) about the inescapability of ethnic identity and the pain of anti-Semitism. Nathaniel West's bitter portrayal of the movie colony in *The Day of the Locust* (1939) shows the underside of Hollywood's American Jewish dream.

As second-generation Jews began to write for the Broadway stage and experimental theater, an audience of New York Jews developed for the biting humor of George S. Kaufman and Ben Hecht, as well as the serious drama of Lillian Hellman, Arthur Miller, and Elmer Rice. A circle of "Broadway intellectuals" appeared that included Moss Hart, Dorothy Parker, S. N. Behrman, and George Jean Nathan. The social-conscience dramas of Clifford Odets and John Howard Lawson also attracted Jews. In Odets's play *Awake and Sing* (originally titled *I Got the Blues,* 1933), the Jewish Bronx provides the cadence of the characters' speech, the inner rhythm of their lives, and the substance of their dreams of a better society. The critic Robert Warshow called Odets "the poet of the Jewish middle class" because he captured the "master pattern" of American Jews, the Jewish culture of New York City, with "its smallest forms of behavior, its accepted attitudes, its language."

Occasionally the transition from one generation to another occurred within an institution. The *Menorah Journal* began its forty-seven year literary career in 1915 as the "expression of all that is best in Judaism." Brandeis published his formulation of American Zionism, Kallen his views on cultural pluralism, and Kaplan his program for a reconstruction of Judaism in the journal's pages in its early years. Under the editorship of Elliot Cohen from 1925 to 1931, a new cohort of second-generation Jews published prose, poetry, and fiction. A number of these men, such as Lionel Trilling and Herbert Solow, espoused Marxism. Rather than seeing an open, egalitarian, democratic society in America as had Lippmann, Weyl, and Rosenfeld, they perceived a capitalist, biased, and philistine culture. Like their New York Jewish intellectual predecessors, they rejected notions of ethnic distinctiveness and cultural pluralism as forms of tribalism and bourgeois divisiveness. Later Trilling wrote that "to speak of the *Menorah Journal* as a response to 'isolation' isn't nearly enough—you must make the reader aware of the shame that young middle-class Jews felt."

The *Menorah Journal* acquired competitors in the

1930s when new Jewish intellectual journals appeared in English, testimony to the maturation of several east European second-generation cohorts. In 1935 Rabbis Mordecai Kaplan, Ira Eisenstein, and Eugene Kohn started a biweekly, *Reconstructionist,* to promote discussion of Jewish life in the spirit of Kaplan's pathbreaking book. A blend of philosophy, history, theology, and sociology, *Judaism as a Civilization* (1934) contended that American Jews were a people living in two civilizations, American and Jewish. Kaplan rejected Reform's view that Judaism was only a religion and challenged Orthodoxy by arguing that Judaism was an evolving religious culture. He avoided the Zionist term "nation" but recognized the spiritual importance of Zionism, especially the upbuilding of Palestine and the creation there of a new Jewish society and culture to nourish the diaspora. He also remained optimistic that Jews could cultivate their own religious civilization in the democratic United States even though that would involve discarding the Jewish concept of a chosen people because of its implicit chauvinism.

Labor Zionists, eager to reach an English-speaking public, launched a new monthly, the *Jewish Frontier,* in 1934. In its pages, socialist Zionists polemicized with members of the Jewish cosmopolitan Left such as Daniel Bell and debated Jewish religious thinkers, especially those like Kaplan who claimed to be Zionists yet denied that America was *galut* (exile). The *Jewish Frontier* united immigrant Zionist intellectuals like Hayim Greenberg and Maurice Samuel with the second generation, Ben Halpern and Marie Syrkin. Modern Orthodox Jewish intellectuals found a forum in Trude Weiss-Rosmarin's independent monthly; the *Jewish Spectator* (1935) began as a women's Zionist magazine, but after a decade of publishing it appealed to a broad, intellectual audience. This vibrant Jewish intellectual world coexisted with a similarly lively literary and political milieu made up of young Jewish and Gentile intellectuals clustered around competing journals and espousing different brands of Marxian socialism.

Most American Jews remained outside of this intellectual world, although they affiliated with ideological movements, including the radical Jewish Peoples Fraternal Order. Growing numbers also enrolled in Zionist groups. Zionism appealed to American Jews concerned about the rise of Hitler in Germany and the increasing anti-Semitism in Europe that forced thousands of Jews from their homes. Palestine offered a haven for Jewish refugees at a time when American immigrant quotas remained unfilled and immigration to the United States reached a nadir.

Zionist youth groups particularly expanded during these years, as did the young communist and socialist leagues.

Most Conservative congregations, as well as many Reform and modern Orthodox ones, came to support Zionist ideals. Responding to the escalating European crisis, a conference of Reform rabbis in Columbus, Ohio, in 1937 adopted resolutions recognizing Jewish peoplehood and the Zionist goal of rebuilding a Jewish homeland in Palestine. This Columbus Platform reflected the maturation of another generation of Reform rabbis, many of whom had grown up in east European immigrant homes. The new platform replaced the Pittsburgh Platform of 1885 that rejected Jewish nationality and denied the notion of a Jewish return to the land of Israel. Five years later, a small minority of Reform rabbis, angered by the movement's pro-Zionist endorsement, established the explicitly anti-Zionist American Council for Judaism. By then, many Reform rabbis were sanctioning the Zionist political goal of creating a Jewish commonwealth in Palestine. Several, including Abba Hillel Silver of Cleveland and James Heller of New Orleans, were Zionist leaders.

Zionists were not alone in their efforts to transform American Jewry into a national constituency. In 1917, settlement houses and Y's united in a coordinating organization, the National Jewish Welfare Board, to help provide religious and recreational services to Jewish soldiers. Subsequently, the board expanded its mandate to include Jewish community centers that were replacing many of the older settlement houses. Unlike settlements and Y's, community centers encouraged participatory leadership, men and women who used the facilities often serving on the board. Centers saw themselves as democratic organizations not as wards of wealthy philanthropists. Affluent Jewish leaders also looked beyond their local federations to the national scene. In 1932 they created the Council of Jewish Federations and Welfare Funds as a consultative body. Although jealous still of local prerogatives regarding the distribution of funds, federation leaders welcomed the council's assistance in fund-raising. Even the national organizations engaged in fighting anti-Semitism, or defense activities, agreed to establish a coordinating agency in 1944. The National Community Relations Advisory Council brought together the professionals, and occasionally the leaders of the defense organizations, to consult on policy and tactics. Given the diverse constituents and policies of each organization, not to mention the local community relations committees that sprouted during the Depression, Jews found it difficult to achieve agreement on how to fight American anti-Semites.

Despite all the national coordinating bodies created by American Jews, consensus continued to elude them. Even the unification of overseas fundraising in the United Jewish Appeal (UJA) in 1939 failed to produce a common perspective. The UJA brought the non-Zionist American Jewish Joint Distribution Committee that had been founded in response to the crisis of World War I together with the United Palestine Appeal that unified various Zionist parties into an uneasy alliance. As the Jewish situation worsened in Nazi Germany, as Hitler took Austria and Polish Jews faced increased anti-Semitism, American Jews struggled unsuccessfully to develop a viable program to resettle refugees and aid victims of Nazi anti-Semitism. The American Jewish Congress championed and led the anti-Nazi boycott movement over the protests of the other defense organizations and Wise frequently visited the White House of Franklin D. Roosevelt to solicit his aid. Zionists pressed for Palestine as the only viable place to absorb refugees, but they were stymied by a reversal in British policy. In 1939, the British issued a white paper severely limiting Jewish immigration to Palestine to 75,000 over five years. Jews were trapped in Europe, forced to flee their native lands, unable to enter the United States, Palestine, or most other countries in sufficient numbers. Before World War II began, 150,000 Jewish refugees, mostly from Germany and Austria, entered the United States.

## THE IMPACT OF WORLD WAR II

World War II marks a watershed in the history of American Jews. The war's horrors delegitimated anti-Semitism by revealing the consequences of such hatred. World War II also empowered American Jews; it inspired many to affirm and defend their identity. The war touched them directly and changed their lives. Half of American Jews aged eighteen to forty-four served in the armed forces; scarcely a Jewish family existed that did not have a son, father, brother, or uncle in uniform. Military service introduced American Jews to a distinctly foreign American world outside of the urban centers. They discovered how insular and provincial their lives had been, but they also learned that Judaism had a respected place alongside other faiths. America's wartime ideals rejected racism and anti-Semitism as inimical to democracy. During the war Judaism was incorporated into a biblically based Judeo-Christian ideology opposed to the idolatry of Nazism and fascism. Louis Finkelstein,

the new head of the Jewish Theological Seminary, brought leading religious and intellectual liberals, Jewish and Christian, into a Conference on Science, Philosophy and Religion in their Relation to the Democratic Way of Life in 1940. Finkelstein's initiative aimed to shape a new concept of American culture as grounded in a Judeo-Christian tradition in which Jews were a vital and integral component.

The destruction of European Jewry by the Nazis transformed American Jews. Stunned by the atrocities, many turned to militant politics to avenge relatives murdered in the death camps. The revelations of Hitler's extermination program filled American Jewish leaders with despair. They tried desperately to bury their differences to produce a rescue plan. In 1943, delegates to the American Jewish Conference that was organized by Henry Monsky, the first east European leader of B'nai B'rith, overwhelmingly supported the Zionist program of rescue. Galvanized by the powerful oratory of Reform rabbi Abba Hillel Silver, the delegates agreed that the establishment of a politically independent Jewish commonwealth in Palestine was the only answer to Hitler. Despite the majority vote to support the Zionist program, the non-Zionist American Jewish Committee and Jewish Labor Committee refused to accept their minority status and walked out of the conference.

Each Jewish group had its own rescue program. The Jewish Labor Committee worked to save Socialists, Jewish and Gentile, believing that the postwar world needed socialist leadership to survive. Orthodox rabbis created the Va'ad Hatzolah, a rescue committee, to save fellow rabbis and their students. Revisionist Zionists agitated for governmental action for immediate mass rescue. Only when Henry Morgenthau, Jr., the secretary of the Treasury, convinced Roosevelt to establish a War Refugee Board in 1944 was some meager progress toward rescue accomplished. But it was too little, too late.

When the war ended, American Jews found the joy of victory tinged with the bitter taste of defeat. The horrors of the death camps were more than they could possibly have imagined. The extent of Nazi atrocities stunned many American Jews, especially those who served in the armed forces. Stories soldiers brought home and newsreels of the camps overwhelmed Americans, especially American Jews. A new militancy took hold among them, a recognition of the deadly character of anti-Semitism and a renewed determination to rescue survivors and regain independent Jewish political power for the first time in almost two millennia. Americans appreciated this militancy. The Jewish defense organizations adopted more radical and vigorous programs. The ADL expanded its scope to include fighting all types of prejudice and discrimination. Under the leadership of its new executive director, John Slawson, the American Jewish Committee sought a mass membership base to sustain a broad antidiscrimination program that included sponsoring social science research on prejudice and cooperating with African Americans in the fight for civil rights. The American Jewish Congress endorsed an innovative proposal by Alexander Pekelis to establish a Commission on Law and Social Action to spearhead a drive to use the courts and legislatures to make discrimination in housing, employment, and education illegal. Led by Leo Pfeffer, the commission also became the leading advocate of separation of church and state; its successful court cases eliminated much of the Christian piety pervading the nation's public schools.

The loss of six million Jews in the war meant the end of European Jewish culture, the rich reserves of elite Judaism and intellectual life that periodically renewed American Jews through immigration. American Jews became by default the largest, most secure, and wealthiest diaspora Jewish community. As the United States became a world power, American Jews discovered new responsibilities of leadership in the international Jewish world. They exercised this leadership by cooperating with David Ben Gurion to establish a legally recognized Jewish state in Palestine. American Zionists like Silver, Wise, Louis Lipsky, and Emmanuel Neumann worked with such non-Zionists as Joseph Proskauer, head of the American Jewish Committee, to support partition of Palestine in the United Nations. After Israel declared its independence on 15 May 1948, most Jewish opposition to statehood declined dramatically as American Jews rallied to help the beleaguered and besieged nation. Only the American Council for Judaism, led by Lessing Rosenwald, continued its explicitly anti-Zionist program. In 1955 Israel served as a rallying point to unite American Jews in the Conference of Presidents of Major American Jewish Organizations.

As the United States became a more culturally cosmopolitan nation, American Jews recognized the intellectual and religious resources brought by refugees from Nazism. Although a few, like composer Kurt Weill or scientists Leo Szilard and Edward Teller, adapted quickly to America—only the physicist Albert Einstein immediately became a culture hero—most did not find a place for themselves until the war. Then the government tapped their considerable talents, recruiting many to work on the atom bomb.

After the war, the Jewish community drew upon the refugees' resources. The American Jewish Committee commissioned the social psychologists Max Horkheimer and Stanley Flowerman to edit a five-volume series, Studies in Prejudice. Theodore Adorno's jointly authored study, *The Authoritarian Personality* (1950), influenced Americans' understanding of the social bases of fascism and even reached the Broadway stage in the lyrics of the Rodgers and Hammerstein musical, *South Pacific:* "You have to be taught to hate . . . before you are six or seven or eight." The child psychologist Bruno Bettelheim coauthored with Morris Janowitz *Dynamics of Prejudice* (1950), another volume of the series, and suggested a model of human behavior under stress based partly upon his own experiences in Nazi concentration camps. Bettelheim thought that most Jews came to identify with their oppressors, thus losing their ability to withstand suffering, revolt, and preserve their own humanity. His interpretation influenced American historians writing on the enslavement of African Americans. The political philosopher Hannah Arendt researched her first major book while working for Jewish Cultural Reconstruction, locating and cataloging European cultural objects stolen during the war. *The Origins of Totalitarianism* (1951) posited the centrality of anti-Semitism to European politics and the essential similarity of fascism and communism. Her analysis affected the interpretation of communism by a new second-generation cohort of New York Jewish intellectuals. These studies generated considerable controversy among Jews, who questioned their disturbing conclusions.

Not only did individual refugees escape to the United States, entire institutions also fled their European homes. In 1940 the YIVO Institute for Jewish Research transferred its headquarters from Vilna to New York. Max Weinreich, caught abroad at a scholarly conference when the war began, made his way with his family to New York and immediately tried to reestablish YIVO's extensive program researching and documenting Jewish life and promoting the scholarly study of east European Jews, their Yiddish language and culture. As soon as the war ended, YIVO began to document the destruction of European Jews, and Jewish resistance. Among the early studies were those of Philip Friedman and Isaiah Trunk. YIVO recovered roughly half of its archives and a substantial portion of its library that had been plundered by the Nazis and brought these to New York.

Several Hasidic dynasties that escaped the Nazis similarly transplanted their institutions in America. Joel Teitelbaum, the Satmar rebbe, brought many of his followers with him when he settled in Brooklyn in 1947. Vehemently anti-Zionist, he opposed the State of Israel; he also refused to make any accommodations to American life but sanctified all east European manners and customs. Satmar became the largest Hasidic community in the United States and claimed to be the yardstick by which to measure the orthodoxy of other groups. Menachem Mendel Schneerson, the Lubavitcher rebbe, took positions diametrically opposed to Satmar. A supporter of Israel, Schneerson built an extensive network of outreach centers, Habad houses, to recruit non-Orthodox Jews. Lubavitch also embraced American media technology to spread the message of religious return. In the 1980s, Schneerson's addresses carried messianic overtones and many of his followers burned with messianic zeal. Other Hasidic sects also located themselves in Brooklyn, the borough with the most vigorous Orthodox congregations during the interwar years. They gradually reversed the acculturation process in several Jewish neighborhoods, creating insular communities.

The arrival of Rabbi Aaron Kotler in 1941 invigorated the recently transplanted Agudath Israel of America. Kotler encouraged the establishment of institutions for exclusively Orthodox interests, including the *kolel* (advanced talmudical institute), and transplanted his own yeshiva to Lakewood, New Jersey in 1943. The reestablishment of prestigious European yeshivas, like the Telshe Yeshiva in Cleveland, also strengthened several American yeshivas, including Yeshiva Metivta Tiffereth Jerusalem in New York under Moses Feinstein in 1938 and Ner Israel Yeshiva in Baltimore under Jacob Ruderman in 1933. Together, they produced the Yeshiva world, a group of American Orthodoxy. The separatist German Breuer community settled in Washington Heights, a Manhattan neighborhood that attracted many German Jewish refugees in the 1930s, and reestablished its entire parochial educational system, including the advanced yeshiva. Soon a network of Jewish parochial schools developed, including the Beis Yaakov schools for girls.

## POSTWAR ORGANIZATIONS AND CULTURE

American Jews similarly established new educational institutions. In 1948, Israel Goldstein, a New York Conservative rabbi and Zionist leader, and a group of wealthy Boston businessmen founded Brandeis University, the first nonsectarian liberal arts school sponsored by American Jews. Brandeis maintained an ethnic Jewish identity under the leadership of its first president, Abram Sachar. Sachar used his experience as head of Hillel to create a national constituency for the new university. Brandeis hired many Jewish intellectuals, including Philip Rahv, Milton Hindus, Herbert Marcuse, Ludwig Lewisohn, Irving Howe, and Marie Syrkin, who would not have found academic employment in the anti-Semitic environment of American higher education. Brandeis also made modern Jewish scholarship in philosophy, history, and biblical studies an integral part of its liberal arts curriculum through a program created by such refugee scholars as Nahum Glatzer, Alexander Altmann, and Simon Rawidowicz. Unlike Yeshiva College, Brandeis did not privilege Jewish learning.

During the postwar decades, the established schools of the Reform, Conservative, and Orthodox movements expanded. Yeshiva College became a university under Samuel Belkin's leadership, adding the Albert Einstein College of Medicine, Stern College for Women, and the Wurzweiler School of Social Work in the 1950s. In 1976 it started a law school, named in honor of Benjamin Cardozo, the second Jewish justice on the Supreme Court after Brandeis. Jewish involvement in law and legal education extended beyond the five justices—Felix Frankfurter, Arthur Goldberg, and Abraham Fortas, in addition to Cardozo and Brandeis—named to the Supreme Court. Jewish attorneys helped to shape legal theory on the bench and, starting in the 1950s, in the classroom. Despite such extensive participation in American law, Cardozo remained the only law school under Jewish auspices.

The Jewish Theological Seminary expanded by setting up a satellite school, the University of Judaism, in Los Angeles in 1947. In the 1960s, the university achieved a substantial measure of independence. The seminary explored alternative venues of learning, sponsoring a radio and later television series, "The Eternal Light" and "Frontiers of Faith" on NBC. Then JTS established another branch in Jerusalem. The Hebrew Union College acquired a New York campus when it merged with the Jewish Institute of Religion under the leadership of Nelson Glueck. Reflecting a move toward traditionalism in Reform, the combined Hebrew Union College–Jewish Institute of Religion (HUC–JIR) sponsored a School of Sacred Music to train cantors. In the 1950s HUC–JIR established a branch school in Los Angeles; in the 1970s it built a beautiful campus in Jerusalem to house another branch. Both HUC–JIR and JTS mandated the first year of rabbinical study in Israel for their students, an expression of the centrality Israel rapidly acquired among American Jews. Yeshiva University also set up a branch in Los Angeles in the 1960s. The decisions to establish branch institutions on the West Coast represented responses to the Los Angeles Jewish community's rapid growth due to internal migration. By the 1950s, Los Angeles overtook Chicago as American Jews' second city; in many of its social, religious, and cultural patterns, Los Angeles anticipated future trends among American Jews.

The growth of Jewish educational institutions accompanied the maturation of a third native-born generation, children of east European Jews who grew up during the Depression. These Jews fought once again the old battles, only they did so in a radically changed Jewish and American world. The advent of the Cold War hastened the dissolution of the Jewish Left. Revelations of Stalin's murderous policies disillusioned Jewish communists while many socialists embraced New Deal liberalism and anticommunism. A few, like Irving Kristol, Will Herberg, and Daniel Bell, eventually championed New Conservatism. The New Left avoided much of the Marxist polemics of the interwar decades, embracing a figure like Herbert Marcuse, a refugee intellectual who merged Marxism with Freudianism. Zionism also ceased to be a contested ideology as Israel became a living reality, defending itself against Arab armies, absorbing survivors from the displaced-persons camps, and helping hundreds of thousands of Jews to flee persecution in North Africa, Romania, and the Middle East and settle in the Jewish homeland. America itself gradually opened up to Jews: they found new homes in suburban subdivisions, new jobs in universities, elite law firms, and large industries, and opportunities to study in private colleges and to intern in prestigious hospitals.

The release of constraints encouraged an explosion of creativity. As New York became the world's cultural capital, Jews found themselves living in a cosmopolitan crossroads. New York artists became American artists, as New York intellectuals became American intellectuals, and the same transformation occurred among New York playwrights, writers, and composers. For those who remembered growing up within the old constraints, the transformation was startling, prompting a spate of autobiographies chronicling "the longest journey in the world," the odyssey from the fringes of the city in the Jewish neighborhoods of Brooklyn or the Bronx to the very heart of Manhattan, the American center of world culture. Starting with Alfred Kazin's bittersweet por-

trait of Brownsville, *A Walker in the City* (1951), through the music critic Samuel Chotzinoff's *A Lost Paradise* (1957), to the radical labor organizer Paul Jacobs's *Is Curly Jewish?*(1965), to the editor Norman Podhoretz's brash *Making It* (1967), through the travel writer Kate Simon's revelatory *Bronx Primitive* (1982), and on to the socialist Irving Howe's *A Margin of Hope* (1982), and the radical feminist Vivian Gornick's *Fierce Attachments* (1987), New York Jews never ceased to wonder at how rapidly the world had changed, how far they had come, and whether there still lingered an essential Jewishness within that shaped their identity. Several autobiographies also appeared that charted a return path to Judaism by those who had grown up within a privileged, affluent milieu, most notably the journalist Paul Cowan's *Orphan in History* (1982) and the writer Anne Roiphe's *Generation without Memory* (1981).

Others merely welcomed the chance to celebrate New York's culture as essentially American. Leonard Bernstein's musical scores, for such plays as *On the Town* and *West Side Story,* presented urban music as quintessentially American. Whether guest conducting Israel's Philharmonic during Israel's war of independence or leading the New York Philharmonic in an innovative televised series of youth concerts, Bernstein personified a harmonious identity as New Yorker, Jew, and American. The writer Grace Paley similarly found in her voice as New Yorker, Jew, and American a source of wit and insight that illuminated the world, as did Cynthia Ozick, Tillie Olsen, and Bernard Malamud. These writers also gave expression to the views of elderly Jews; looking back upon the immigrant past they wrote not about growing up but about growing old, about coming to terms with a heritage that was about to disappear forever.

In 1945 the American Jewish Committee sponsored *Commentary* magazine, initially edited by Elliot Cohen and then for most of its history by Norman Podhoretz. *Commentary*'s ability to attract Jewish and Gentile readers suggested that the problems facing an intellectual Jewish magazine in America had declined substantially since the *Menorah* Journal's heyday. *Commentary*'s success encouraged the appearance of other new magazines. In 1952 the American Jewish Congress sponsored *Judaism,* a quarterly devoted to Jewish life and thought edited by Rabbi Robert Gordis. Three years later another quarterly, *Midstream,* appeared; under Shlomo Katz's editorship it focused on Israel, Zionism, and Jewishness. A radical monthly, *Jewish Currents* (1946), edited for most of its history by Morris Schappes, signaled the transition of Jewish communists into English publication. The religious movements also entered publishing; these included *Conservative Judaism* (1945), and *Tradition* (1958), a modern Orthodox journal. In the 1970s, another round of publications burst upon the Jewish scene, including *Present Tense,* a Jewish alternative to *Commentary* edited by Murray Polner and sponsored by the American Jewish Committee; *Moment,* a liberal secular monthly edited by Leonard Fein; *Lilith,* a Jewish feminist magazine edited by Susan Weidman Schneider; and *Sh'ma,* a small biweekly of opinion edited by the theologian Eugene Borowitz. *Tikkun,* a left-wing journal of opinion, made its debut in 1986 under Michael Lerner's editorship.

Jewish poets coming of age after the war also discovered and explored the enormous range of opportunities available. Their diversity suggests an explosion of possibilities to find a poetic voice. Adrienne Rich and Allen Ginsberg, Kenneth Koch and Maxine Kumin, John Hollander and Ruth Whitman, Harvey Shapiro and Philip Levine were followed by such equally diverse voices as Allen Grossman, Marge Piercy, Alicia Ostriker, Paul Zweig, Grace Schulman, and Jerome Rothenberg. For some, like Rich and Ginsberg, Jewish concerns resonated through their personal politics. Ginsberg's "Kaddish" and Rich's "Yom Kippur 1984" speak directly out of Jewish suffering and knowledge. Others, like Grossman and Rothenberg, find Jewish vision in the mystic and mythological. A few, like Whitman, Piercy, and Marcia Falk, unexpectedly discovered that their feminist poetry spoke powerfully to Jewish women seeking alternative forms of spirituality. Several, like Hollander, Whitman, Falk, and Irena Klepfisz translated poems from Yiddish or Hebrew, thus enriching the world of American poetry with other Jewish voices.

Jewish involvement in Abstract Expressionism, dubbed "the triumph of American painting" and the major international art movement of the 1950s, reflected a similar movement to the cultural center. Painters like Adolph Gottlieb, Mark Rothko, Philip Guston, and Barnett Newman, and critics Harold Rosenberg and Clement Greenberg, influenced American aesthetics. Later Helen Frankenthaler and Morris Louis, and such Pop artists as Larry Rivers, Jim Dine, and the sculptor George Segal, found Jewish and Gentile audiences for their work, in the process blurring boundaries that once had set American Jewish artists apart. The subsequent movements of Neo-Expressionism introduced by Julian Schnabel and David Salle and the political art of Barbara Kruger and Sherrie Levine confirmed the vitality of Jewish artists as well as a continuing tension between artistic and Jewish cultural expression.

Nor did the literary voice of second-generation Jews stop at the Hudson. The most acclaimed of the postwar group of Jewish novelists, Nobel laureate Saul Bellow, grew up in Chicago. "I am an American, Chicago-born," begins Bellow's *The Adventures of Augie March* (1953). Philip Roth, too, used the experiences of his native Newark to write short stories and novels that captivated his fellow Americans even as they outraged an increasingly middle-class Jewish community that preferred the Jewish portraits of such writers as Meyer Levin, Irwin Shaw, Herman Wouk, and Leon Uris. In his best-selling novel *Exodus* (1958), Uris proudly wrote about Israelis, a new breed of Jewish hero that shattered old Jewish stereotypes. *Exodus* captured the imagination of Americans, Jews and Gentiles, decisively changing their image of a Jew. Otto Preminger's movie version similarly grabbed Americans through its portrayal of the phoenix-like rise of the Jewish state from the ashes of the Holocaust.

Israeli heroes, from the Milwaukee-bred Golda Meir to the young fighter pilot Ezer Weizman, rapidly acquired followers ready to translate their devotion to the young Jewish state into dollars. Each year Israelis came to the United States to raise funds for UJA and, beginning in 1951, for Israel Bonds. The annual rallies and fundraising drives kept Israel's needs before American Jews and encouraged them to identify with the Jewish state. Israel gradually acquired a hallowed place within American Judaism. Israeli Independence Day entered the Jewish calendar, celebrated with parades and services. Israeli art decorated new suburban synagogue sanctuaries, Israeli dances enlivened programs at community centers and camps, Israeli food entered Jewish kitchens through hundreds of cookbooks, even Israeli fashion and jewelry adorned women. Many of these items could be purchased at synagogue gift shops run by the "sisterhood"—a type of women's auxiliary first introduced during the interwar years—to raise funds for the congregation.

Jewish women, almost all of them married and with children, sought substitutes for paid employment outside of the home and found them in women's organizations. Not only Hadassah and the National Council of Jewish Women, but Women's American ORT (a transplanted east European service organization) the various Zionist organizations, the Women's Committee of the American Jewish Congress, B'nai B'rith Women, and the nationally federated Reform, Conservative, and Orthodox synagogue sisterhoods all experienced an enormous increase in membership, participation, and activity.

Synagogues, community centers, Zionist and women's organizations offered a rich fare of lectures, classes, and workshops on Judaism, Zionism, and the Jewish world, as well as politics, literature, and psychology. Men also turned to adult education to study what they had never learned as children; B'nai B'rith sponsored first a series of retreats with noted scholars and rabbis and then, like Hadassah, a great books series designed to introduce American Jews to basic Jewish texts and concepts.

## CULTURAL TRANSLATIONS AND RELIGIOUS TRANSFORMATIONS

As American Jews moved further away from their immigrant heritage they began to recast Judaism and Jewish culture in ever more distinctly American terms. Translation now became a crucial tool for a largely monolingual community. The 1953 translation of I. B. Singer's short story, "Gimpel the Fool," by Saul Bellow for publication in *Partisan Review*, in addition to launching Singer's English literary career, symbolized the new significance of English for Jewish culture. Many second-generation Jews still understood some Yiddish—enough to laugh at Yiddish jokes but not enough to support a Yiddish press and theater, or Yiddish poets and writers. The new second generation faced an American Jewish world in which English replaced Yiddish, synagogue centers dominated the communal landscape, American Jewish organizations shaped the contours of Jewish collective life. The philosopher Harold Weisberg considered American Jews to possess merely a "culture of organizations." Yet many of the innovative organizations transplanted to the United States or created by immigrants struggled to pass on their heritage to another generation. The new Jewish culture in English that flourished did so without facing the formidable competitors of an earlier era.

In 1945, the rabbis associated with *Reconstructionist* magazine published a sabbath prayerbook that included new English prayers. Although the Orthodox excommunicated Kaplan and banned the prayerbook because of changes in the Hebrew wording of several prayers, the Reconstructionists anticipated a trend. Soon the Conservative movement published a new translation of its prayerbook, an action soon followed by the Reform movement. Translations of modern Hebrew literature by contemporary Israeli writers increasingly found a broad audience in the United States and turned such novelists as Amos Oz, A. B. Yehoshua, and David Grossman into American Jewish cultural figures. Recognizing the significance of translation in making texts accessible to American Jews, the Jewish Publication Society decided to underwrite a major effort to translate the entire Hebrew Scriptures. Its earlier translation, published in 1917, relied upon previous versions by Christian scholars that were adapted for Jewish use. Although the ambitious undertaking took several decades, when the *Tanakh* appeared in 1978, American Jews had their first scriptures that spoke in a distinctly American accent.

American Judaism itself increasingly appeared American. Will Herberg described it as one of America's three great faiths in his influential book, *Protestant, Catholic, Jew* (1955). Herberg demonstrated the commonality of America's religions and argued that a triple melting pot was transforming American ethnic groups into religious denominations. Herberg's vision of the Jews' position of equality within American denominationalism won widespread acceptance, overshadowing Kallen's theories of cultural pluralism and enduring despite later interpretations of ethnicity in America put forth by Nathan Glazer. The pluralism of American Judaism also distinguished it, as did its willingness to accept women as religious equals to men. In 1954, a fourth, indigenous American Jewish movement appeared on the Jewish scene: Reconstructionism. Long a source of theological ferment and religious innovation within Conservatism, Reconstructionism became institutionalized in a school in 1968, the Reconstructionist Rabbinical College in Philadelphia under Rabbi Ira Eisenstein's leadership. Like its seminary predecessors, the College trained rabbis for a growing network of congregations and *havurot,* intimate fellowships of like-minded Jews who enjoyed praying, studying, and socializing together. An organization of Reconstructionist rabbis followed in 1974 to complement a previously established congregational union, Federation of Reconstructionist Congregations and Havurot. Although rapidly growing, Reconstructionism remains the smallest movement in American Judaism.

As Reconstructionists established a college for men and women, the Reform movement agreed to admit women to their rabbinical school and ordain them as rabbis. In 1972, Rabbi Sally Preisand became the first woman ordained by the Reform movement. Reconstructionists had been the first to introduce a ceremony for girls, bat mitzvah, that paralleled the bar mitzvah ceremony for thirteen-year-old boys. The new synagogue ritual became increasingly popular among Conservative Jews in the postwar decades. By the time Gerson Cohen became chancellor of the Jewish Theological Seminary in 1972, pressure for women's equality within Conservatism was mounting. Cohen encouraged the Law Committee to decide the *halacha* (law), on counting women in a *minyan,* the quorum of ten required for certain prayers. In 1973, the Law Committee ruled in favor of women's equal participation in the synagogue and, in 1983, women were admitted to the seminary to study for rabbinical ordination. Two years later, Amy Eilberg was the first woman ordained a Conservative rabbi. The decision to accept women rabbis and cantors precipitated a schism within the Conservative movement as several leading rabbis and scholars withdrew to form the Union for Traditional Conservative Judaism.

Typically for American Judaism, such radical changes grew more from the behavior of "Catholic Israel," as Schechter called the Jewish people, than from an intellectual or religious elite. Jewish theology in the postwar period generally ignored women's issues, though Judaism became more than a folk religion as theologians appeared to interpret its meanings. Joseph Soloveichik's *Halachic Man* (1945) posits the typical Jew as male as he confronts the commandments in their singularity. Abraham Joshua Heschel presented a more lyrical vision of faith, drawn from his Hasidic background, but he, too, understood theology as dealing with man and God. Even such American-born thinkers as Will Herberg or Arthur A. Cohen assumed men's centrality in Judaism. Only with the rise of feminism was this perspective challenged, most notably in *Standing Again at Sinai* (1990) by Judith Plaskow.

The impact of the Holocaust on American Jews registered only gradually in their religion and culture. Although Jews set aside a day of commemoration and many remembered the Warsaw ghetto revolt, discussion of the meaning of the Holocaust occurred fitfully. Holocaust survivors first drew attention to the destruction of European Jewry through memoirs and writing. Nobel laureate Elie Wiesel's powerful memoir of Auschwitz, *Night,* was translated into English in 1960, at the time that the trial of Adolf Eichmann in Israel captured worldwide attention. As American Jewish rabbis and philosophers searched for meaning in the Holocaust, a body of Holocaust theology developed. Richard Rubenstein's essays, *After Auschwitz* (1966), were among the first attempts to grapple with the theological issues. His death of God theology was challenged by Emil Fackenheim. In *God's Presence in History* (1970), Fackenheim uses midrashic method to argue for God's continuing presence in history. He also posits a 614th commandment that all Jews must obey: not to hand Hitler

any posthumous victories; Jewish survival is a sacred obligation. Irving Greenberg, a modern Orthodox rabbi, argues that the covenant, central to Judaism, has now become voluntary. His willingness to entertain a pluralism of covenants runs counter to much thinking among the Orthodox.

The Holocaust increasingly became a subject of discussion and debate among American Jews after the trauma of Israel's Six Day War in 1967. No longer could young Jews consider the Holocaust an isolated historical event; the Arab threat of annihilating Israel changed the views of many American Jews including those who felt estranged from Judaism or did not consider themselves supporters of Israel. In 1975 Lucy Dawidowicz's history, *The War against the Jews,* became a best-seller, unlike Raul Hilberg's earlier pathbreaking history, *The Destruction of European Jews* (1961). The debate among historians, reflected in the books' titles, echoed in the writing of American Jewish novelists. Edward Wallant in *The Pawnbroker* (1961) questioned the religious significance of survival through his painful portrayal of Sol Nazerman. Norma Rosen saw the universalism of the Holocaust in *Touching Evil* (1969) as poisoning everyone. By contrast, Arthur A. Cohen's *In the Days of Simon Stern* (1973) responded religiously and imagined a continuing post-Holocaust struggle between good and evil. More recent novels, like Lore Segal's *Her First American* (1985), Cynthia Ozick's *The Messiah of Stockholm* (1987), and Jerome Badanes's *The Final Opus of Leon Solomon* (1989), have probed the meaning of evil and guilt in their imaginative explorations of survival.

Movies and television also served as vehicles to portray the Holocaust and raise the consciousness of Americans against its evil anti-Semitism. Although there were many predecessors, none of the films and television dramas had the extraordinary impact of the television miniseries "Holocaust" (1978), produced by Herb Brodkin and written by Gerald Green. The series' popular appeal helped to transform the Holocaust into contested territory. Elie Wiesel damned "Holocaust" as an "untrue, cheap, offensive, soap opera." The struggle to define the meaning of the Holocaust continues with efforts to build museums and memorials. The Simon Wiesenthal Center in Los Angeles, established by Rabbi Marvin Hier in 1977, founded a successful Holocaust museum in 1979. The Center links its remembrance with an activist stand interpreting the lessons of the Holocaust for contemporary political, social, and moral issues. In 1993 the U.S. Holocaust Memorial Museum opened in the nation's capital. Located just off the Mall near other American monuments, it portrays the Holocaust from a distinctly American perspective.

The museum movement among American Jews itself suggests a new approach to Jewish culture, ritual, and history. The Jewish Museum in New York, established in 1904 as a gift from Felix Warburg to the Jewish Theological Seminary, only acquired a measure of independence in 1940. In the 1950s and 1960s, it generated a vitriolic debate over Jewish art and its place within a Jewish museum by sponsoring many shows of the latest contemporary art. The controversy spurred a redefinition of the museum's role in which Jewish elements, especially as expressed in historical and ritual culture, acquired prominence. The other major Jewish museum, the Skirball Museum of the Hebrew Union College in Cincinnati (1913), never strayed into modern art. During the postwar decades a number of historical Jewish museums were established, including the B'nai B'rith Klutznick Museum in Washington, D.C. (1957), the Judah L. Magnes Museum in Berkeley, and the Spertus Museum of Judaica in Chicago.

The experience of Jewish artists, writers, and musicians was duplicated in the fields of popular culture, where there had been little isolation or discrimination, and in the realms of academe and politics, where Jews had faced restrictions. The resulting diversity of American Jews and of their religion and culture prompted a search for a common denominator uniting American Jews. Some posited Israel as that common commitment. Indeed, the growth of the American Israel Public Affairs Committee (AIPAC) from 9,000 contributing households in 1959 to 55,000 in 1987 indicated Israel's importance for American Jews. Especially under Thomas Dine, executive director since 1980, AIPAC reached Jews throughout the United States, sensitizing them to their political responsibilities to Israel. Yet rabbi, historian, and Zionist Arthur Hertzberg contends that American Jews secured no future for themselves or for Israel by such narrow-minded pursuit of single-issue politics. Others proposed a common civil Judaism unifying American Jews. Devotion to Israel's security was one component of this civil Judaism, but so was dedication to liberal politics, a commitment to pluralism and social justice, and a sense of responsibility for Jews throughout the world. Still others suggested that a minimum of ritual behavior, including observance of Hanukka and Passover, some associational ties with other Jews, a sentimental liberalism and feeling of sympathy for Israel sufficed to unite American Jews.

The search for common denominators distinguishing Jews from other Americans reflected recognition of the rising rate of intermarriage between Jews and Christians. As barriers restricting Jewish access to suburbs, schools, jobs, clubs, and resorts crumbled under the assaults of the civil rights movement, Jews mixed ever more freely with their fellow middle-class, urban Americans, sharing their tastes, values, family life, and even their pathologies. Intermarriage rates, for many decades in the single digits, climbed slowly; in the mid-1960s, with the coming of age of the postwar generation, they jumped to double digits, and by 1990 a third of all Jewish marriages were intermarriages. In only a small fraction of these intermarriages did the Gentile spouse convert to Judaism. Current trends point to exogamy as the dominant pattern, reversing centuries of endogamy among Jews. Since 1985, over half the Jews who married chose a Gentile spouse.

Given the sacredness associated with Jewish survival as a separate people, American Jews have grown increasingly alarmed over what some fear is, as a *Look* magazine article in 1964 put it, "the vanishing American Jew." Others worry less about demography than the political and cultural significance of the declining numbers. They point to the importance of Jewish political efforts in behalf of Israel to secure its future in an Arab-dominated world. Fewer Jews poses a threat to continued support of Jewish organizations, despite remarkable Jewish achievements in electoral politics during the 1980s when many Jews won elections largely with the votes of Gentile Americans. Rabbis and Jewish lay leaders focus upon the shrinking core group of Jews and question whether they will be able to sustain the extraordinarily diverse religious and cultural life that Jews created in the United States. Some affirm optimism, citing creative programs of Jewish renewal; others express deep pessimism, often arguing that Orthodoxy offers the only hope and that Conservatism, Reform, and Reconstructionism are merely way stations on the path out of the Jewish people.

With permeable Jewish group boundaries and little sense of where Jews differ from their fellow Americans, most American Jews ignore the collective implications of their personal choices. For them, Jewishness has ceased to shape their identity and Judaism remains a matter of individual choice. If current trends continue, future American Jews will increasingly be "Jews by choice," that is, they will have consciously decided to live as Jews because Jewish identity, culture, and religion offer them meaning and community, personal fulfillment and collective continuity.

Clearly the transformative struggles of the second generation no longer shape American Jewish identity. American Jews have ceased to wonder whether they are American and what it means to be an American. Instead they have begun to ponder whether they are Jews and what it means to be a Jew on the threshold of the twenty-first century.

SEE ALSO Protestantism; Catholicism; Nontraditional Religions (all in this volume); Ethnicity and Immigration (volume I).

## BIBLIOGRAPHY

Naomi Cohen, *Encounter with Emancipation: The German Jews in the United States, 1830–1914* (1984), provides a comprehensive synthetic account of the religion, politics, and communal institutions of two generations of German Jews in America. Jonathan Sarna, *JPS: The Americanization of Jewish Culture, 1888–1988* (1989), deftly uses the history of the Jewish Publication Society of America as a vehicle to examine changing trends in English-language Jewish culture. Michael A. Meyer, *Response to Modernity: A History of the Reform Movement in Judaism* (1988), devotes the second half of his insightful account to the American scene. Deborah Dash Moore, *B'nai B'rith and the Challenge of Ethnic Leadership* (1981), surveys the organizational innovations of the leading Jewish fraternal order in response to American social developments. Faith Rogow, *Gone to Another Meeting: The National Council of Jewish Women, 1893–1993* (1993), focuses on the early years of this influential Jewish women's organization.

Moses Rischin, *The Promised City: New York's Jews, 1870–1914* (1962), is the classic account of the immigrant Lower East Side. Arthur A. Goren, *New York's Jews and the Quest for Community: The Kehillah Experiment, 1908–1922* (1970), incisively examines Jewish communal responses to the social, religious, educational, and political problems of Jewish immigrants, as well as the challenge of Jewish criminals. Irving Howe with Kenneth Libo, *World of Our Fathers* (1976), evokes the collective aspirations and spirit of the Lower East Side and probes the first forays of the children of Jewish immigrants into a wider American society and culture. Louis Wirth, *The Ghetto* (1928), articulates the classic sociological paradigm of urban immigrant settlement and the progressive stages of dispersion and assimilation. Susan A. Glenn, *Daughters of the Shtetl: Life and Labor in the Immigrant Generation* (1990), explores how working in the garment industry stimulated young Jewish women in Chicago to fashion a new understanding of female rights and responsibilities. Andrew R. Heinze, *Adapting to Abundance: Jewish Immigrants, Mass Consumption, and the Search for an American Identity* (1990), persuasively argues that Jewish immigrants on the Lower East Side successfully used consumption patterns to shape their acculturation strategies. Stephan F. Brumberg, *Going to America, Going to School: The Jewish Immigrant Public School Encounter in Turn-of-the-Century New York City* (1986), thoughtfully analyzes the mutual interaction of immigrants and the public schools.

Jack Wertheimer, ed., *The American Synagogue: A Sanctuary Transformed* (1987), is a fine collection of essays on American Jewish religious development. Jenna Weissman Joselit, *New York's Jewish Jews: The Orthodox Community in the Interwar Years* (1990), focuses on the creative adaption of economically prosperous, modern orthodox second-generation Jews. Mark Slobin, *Chosen Voices: The Story of the American Cantorate* (1989), is a major study of American Jewish religious music. Jeffrey S. Gurock, *The Men and Women of Yeshiva: Higher Education, Orthodoxy, and American Judaism* (1988), provides an insider's analysis of the changing dimensions of Orthodox scholarship and religious education by examining the leading modern Orthodox school of higher education. Marshall Sklare, *Conservative Judaism: An American Religious Movement* (1955), is a classic sociological study of the largest branch of American Judaism. Arnold Eisen, *The Chosen People in America: A Study in Religious Ideology* (1983), skillfully dissects the religious self-consciousness of American rabbis. Robert G. Goldy, *The Emergence of Jewish Theology in America* (1990), briefly surveys major Jewish thinkers and their thought. Samuel C. Heilman and Steven M. Cohen, *Cosmopolitans and Parochials: Modern Orthodox Jews in America* (1989), provide a sociological portrait of American Orthodoxy.

Three volumes of a comprehensive history of

American Jews, *The Jewish People in America,* ed. Henry L. Feingold, deal gracefully with the twentieth century: Gerald Sorin, *A Time for Building: The Third Migration, 1880–1920* (1992); Henry L. Feingold, *A Time for Searching: Entering the Mainstream, 1920–1945* (1992); and Edward S. Shapiro, *A Time for Healing: American Jewry since World War II* (1992). Deborah Dash Moore, *At Home in America: Second Generation New York Jews* (1981), argues that the children of East European immigrants created an enduring middle-class, urban, ethnic identity for American Jews. Charles Liebman, *The Ambivalent American Jew* (1973), provides an incisive portrait of the religious, ethnic, and political behavior of American Jews in the postwar era. William Helmreich, *Against All Odds* (1992), presents a broad view of the acculturation of Holocaust survivors in America. Leonard Dinnerstein, *America and the Survivors of the Holocaust* (1988), focuses on political strategies during the immediate postwar years.

Jonathan Shapiro, *The Leadership of the American Zionist Organization: 1897–1930* (1971), is a pioneering analysis of this influential Jewish movement. Melvin Urofsky, *We Are One! American Jews and Israel* (1978), covers the story of the transformation of American Zionism after the establishment of the Jewish state. Arthur Liebman, *Jews and the Left* (1978), explores Jewish involvement in labor and social movements, as well as in politics.

Neil Gabler, *An Empire of Their Own: How the Jews Invented Hollywood* (1988), argues that the immigrant Jewish producers, eager to assimilate, shaped the movies to reflect their vision of an ideal America. Susanne Klingenstein, *Jews in the American Academy, 1900–1940: The Dynamics of Intellectual Assimilation* (1991), discusses the complex interaction of a first generation of immigrant scholars with the values of American higher education. Alexander Bloom, *Prodigal Sons: The New York Intellectuals and Their World* (1986), presents detailed and nuanced portraits of the Jewish intellectuals of the 1930s, 1940s, and the 1950s. Norman L. Kleeblatt and Susan Chevlowe, eds., *Painting a Place in America: Jewish Artists in New York, 1900–1945* (1991), includes several useful essays on the art and politics of Jewish painters and sculptors. J. Hoberman, *Bridge of Light: Yiddish Film between Two Worlds* (1991), offers the best introduction to Yiddish movies in Europe and America.

Daniel J. Elazar, *Community and Polity: The Organizational Dynamics of American Jewry* (1976), clearly presents the complex structure of Jewish voluntary organizations and argues that these represent the polity of American Jews. Jacob Neusner, *Stranger at Home: "The Holocaust," Zionism, and American Judaism* (1981), consists of provocative essays on the relationship of American Jews to Israel and the Holocaust. Riv-Ellen Prell, *Prayer and Community: The Havurah in American Judaism* (1989), focuses on the *havurah* and its implications for American Judaism. Jonathan Woocher, *Sacred Survival: The Civil Religion of American Jews* (1986), argues that Jews share a common faith beyond Judaism.

# AFRICAN AMERICAN CULTURAL MOVEMENTS

## Kenneth W. Warren

In a 1926 address titled "The Criteria of Negro Art," W. E. B. Du Bois charged that "the white public today demands from its artists, literary and pictorial, racial prejudgment which deliberately distorts Truth and Justice, as far as colored races are concerned." Like many others before and since, Du Bois found himself remarking the fact that white supremacy proceeded along cultural as well as political fronts; white novelists, critics, painters, and filmmakers had aided and abetted the legal, social, and economic subordination of black Americans. One of the most dramatic examples of such collusion had been the popularity of Thomas Dixon's 1905 pro–Ku Klux Klan novel, *The Clansman,* which D. W. Griffith adapted for his film *The Birth of a Nation.* Without muting any of the racism of its novelistic predecessor, Griffith's film went on to become a landmark of American cinema. Along the way, it also enjoyed the honor of being the first movie shown at the White House, where its historical veracity was attested to by none other than President Woodrow Wilson— Dixon's and Griffith's paeans to white supremacy thus finding sanction at the highest levels of the American political system.

And while perhaps remarkable in its romanticization of the Klan and its striking visibility on the American scene, *The Birth of a Nation* was quite typical in bringing together aesthetic success and white racism. From popular entertainment through highbrow fiction, demeaning representations of African Americans had long littered the American cultural landscape. Even white authors who had championed black causes and black culture from abolition through the Harlem Renaissance, including Harriet Beecher Stowe, George Washington Cable, and Carl Van Vechten, could be charged with purveying stereotypical images of black Americans. In response, Du Bois called for a "Negro Art" and criticism that would counter white cultural propaganda by telling the truth about black people in the United States. Whatever else they claimed to be doing, black artists and critics could not remain indifferent to the racial climate within which they sought to create and evaluate African American aesthetic artifacts.

Although Du Bois's opinions on art and propaganda have had their detractors, the expectation that African American literature, art, and music have been and ought to be central to the struggle for black liberation has been broadly shared. Both abolitionist writers and turn-of-the-century proponents of black uplift argued for the political import of aesthetic production by pointing to the capacity of literature and art to change opinions and feelings. Other writers and scholars, following one strand of Du Bois's appropriation of German romantic historicism (which, in the words of Erich Auerbach, held "that each nation had its characteristic genius"), have stressed the importance of art and literature in establishing black group unity. Still others have attributed the survival of African Americans under slavery and Jim Crow to the development and maintenance of a resistant and oppositional black culture. And many others have embraced various aspects of all the above positions.

While there is merit in each of these arguments, it nonetheless remains difficult to assess with accuracy the role that literature, music, and art have played in the process of black liberation. Almost as tricky is deciding whether or not black aesthetic innovations and trends can be traced directly or indirectly to specific political changes. Writers, artists, and musicians often do attempt to represent or foment political and social change in or through their works. And political programs have included among their various demands calls for critical and institutional recognition of black aesthetic products and practices. Thus, with these issues and difficulties in mind, a central goal of the following discussion will be to chart significant attempts to employ aesthetic forms and practices in the larger political task of defining African American liberation. Another task, however, will be coming to terms with the persistence of the belief that substantive political change is best facilitated by interventions that define themselves as cultural. While changes at the level of aesthetics or style may indeed contribute to political or economic change, might it be possible that paying too much attention to questions of culture deflects attention away from more mundane but potentially more effective means of effecting social and political change? What, then, at the end of the twentieth century, are the benefits and liabilities in assuming that culture and cultural identity ought to remain central to political practice?

## AFRICAN AMERICAN CULTURE AT THE TURN OF THE CENTURY

The general visibility of African Americans in turn-of-the-century popular culture through such forms as minstrelsy, ragtime music (and the closely related "coon song"), and the cakewalk (a popular dance) at once belied and underscored the political fortunes of African Americans during these decades. While the spread of Jim Crow segregation, the dramatic outbreak of lynchings in the 1890s, the sweeping disfranchisement of African Americans in the South, and the removal of black officeholders throughout the southern states indicated that, for many white Americans, banishing blacks from the public mind, from public space, and if possible from the nation as a whole appeared to be the best way to deal with the "race problem," the popularity of cultural forms derived from black Americans made it clear that the black presence remained intensely on the mind of the nation as a whole. These popular images, which traded heavily in stereotypes of lazy and contented plantation darkies, lascivious black "wenches," and thieving, violent, and lustful black men seemed to sanction the disfranchisement and violence visited upon the black population during these decades.

Consequently, efforts to condemn racism necessarily took aim at the distortions and the falsehoods conveyed through these images. Through the founding of magazines and journals directed toward black audiences, a black elite sought to showcase African American writers and artists whose work provided uplifting images and stories for its audience. Part of a broader program aimed at redressing the wrongs of slavery, racism, and poverty, these magazines, perhaps best exemplified by the *Colored American* magazine,

which from 1902 to 1904 was edited by Pauline Hopkins, published fiction and essays that both celebrated the race and challenged racism. Racial uplift, as it shaped the novels of this era, foregrounded characters of mixed race whose morals, intelligence, and commitment to racial progress were exemplary. Fiction by such writers as Frances E. W. Harper, Paul Laurence Dunbar, Charles Chesnutt, Sutton Griggs, and Pauline Hopkins also attempted, not without ambivalence, to swathe the project of social uplift in robes of prestige and heroism. Denied access to the kind of social success to which their talents and education would have ordinarily entitled them, these authors' fictional characters, and to varying extents, the authors themselves, presented the commitment to the general welfare of the race as a higher calling than dedicating oneself to amassing riches. Although these attempts sometimes amounted to making a virtue of necessity, they did embody an awareness that the declining political fortunes of black Americans were correlated with large-scale changes in the prevailing economic order.

For Du Bois in his 1903 *The Souls of Black Folk,* the desire to husband black cultural resources centered in a respect for black sacred culture, such as "Negro Spirituals," which Du Bois termed the Sorrow Songs. In Du Bois's turn-of-the-century writings these songs and the vitality of the culture they represented served two purposes. In the first instance they constituted a more than ample down payment on the cultural contribution which the black race was making to the world. Endorsing a not uncommon view of race that saw the humanity of peoples as a function of the various achievements that could be attributed to members of that group, Du Bois argued that the future success of black Americans was pegged to their ability to make distinctive contributions to the society and culture of the world. In the second instance, and somewhat paradoxically, Du Bois presented the idealism infusing black folk culture as a repository of distinctly American values, proclaiming that "there are to-day no truer exponents of the pure human spirit of the Declaration of Independence than the American Negroes; there is no true American music but the wild sweet melodies of the Negro slave."

Although the cultural uplift program and the fictions it engendered neither entirely eschewed the pursuit of material prosperity nor dismissed the value of its less educated and less well-spoken characters, its emphasis on sobriety, moral uprightness, and behavior and tastes associated with middle-class status signaled the intensification of tensions between political and cultural elites and the largely southern masses whom they sought to represent and aid. Such tensions had emerged in the postemancipation era and, to some degree, had shaped the political choices of northern leaders. No less an eminence than Frederick Douglass claimed that he had decided not to seek office in the South during Reconstruction because the freedmen were accustomed to an oratorical style much different from his own, which had been developed before northern audiences. In fact, though Douglass had provided some astute commentary on slave music in his first autobiography, *The Narrative of the Life of Frederick Douglass* (1845), the popularity of southern black pulpit oratory disturbed him—black southern preachers seemed to him to be adopting outmoded white southern practices. And by the final installment of his autobiography, *The Life and Times of Frederick Douglass* (1892), he was lamenting that progress among the freedmen would be impeded so long as they insisted on "strutting about in the old clothes of the masters" by persisting in an emotional religious worship.

Thus whatever its intent, uplift necessarily presumed some degree of depravity, incapacity, backwardness, and general unfitness as being prevalent among the black population. Even when, like Du Bois, writers sought to praise black folk culture, racial advancement depended on an elite (in Du Bois's lexicon, the Talented Tenth) that could teach, lead, and guide. Its sympathies for the black masses notwithstanding, this elite viewed the folk with some alarm. Again to quote Du Bois, this time from his 1897 address to the American Negro Academy entitled "The Conservation of Races": "We are diseased, we are developing criminal tendencies, and an alarmingly large percentage of our men and women are sexually impure." Although the point of such statements was to rally the race to cleanse itself and to act on its own behalf, these sentiments not only tended to confirm prevailing stereotypes of African Americans but also dovetailed with the more accommodationist political program represented by Booker T. Washington, founder of Tuskegee Institute, which downplayed the need for radical political action and stressed the slow and steady progress of the race, primarily through the development of an economically viable yeomanry. Uplift could forestall demands for immediate equality between blacks and whites by focusing on the need to prepare black people for full participation in American society. Not surprisingly, when Washington acquired the *Colored American* magazine in 1904, forcing out Pauline Hopkins as editor, the magazine soft-pedaled direct condemnations of racism in favor of a line more compatible with Washington's overall philosophy.

The bourgeois elite's concern with the vice and sexual impurities presumably prevalent among the masses brought into view a major faultline between the cultural project of the Talented Tenth and a constantly changing black folk culture. The increasing secularization of black music, which resulted in part from the movement of black populations from the countryside to southern cities and ultimately to northern urban centers, and in part from the rise of a mass music industry, was an indication that many black Americans were defining their relation to culture and economics differently from the elites who spoke on their behalf. Booker T. Washington's vision for black progress presumed a largely agrarian future for the black masses. Thus when faced with the reality that more and more blacks were viewing cities as offering the best opportunities to escape the poverty and the open racism of the South, Washington was led in his autobiography, *Up from Slavery,* to wish "that by some power of magic I might remove the great bulk of these people into the country districts and plant them upon the soil." Not surprisingly, when blacks began to leave the South in large numbers in what became known as the Great Migration, Washington and his minions sought to choke off the northward flow of humanity through exhortation and propaganda.

Washington's vision was not the only one compromised by changes sweeping through the black populace. The desire on the part of elites like Du Bois and Harper to center black culture on its sacred aspects and to stress the black folk's inherent resistance to the materialism of the Gilded Age was complicated by the interpenetration of sacred and secular in black culture and by the popular demand, both black and white, for African American entertainment (or facsimiles thereof). The black spiritual, for example, could fade almost imperceptibly into secular forms. As Lawrence Levine observed in *Black Culture and Black Consciousness* (1977), "the structure, form, and tone of religious songs could be used to speak of secular events." And though attitudes varied from community to community, significant numbers of African Americans saw little need to maintain rigid distinctions between the sacred and the secular world. Moreover, as indicated by the persistence of minstrelsy and the rise of ragtime and blues, black folk forms, whether delivered straight or repackaged, were one means of achieving success in the material world.

By the turn of the century, black-face minstrelsy,

coon songs, and dialect literature, all of which had provided white entertainers and writers with a way of purveying their versions of black culture for fame and profit, were being reappropriated by blacks, who saw these forms not only as a way of making money but as a way to reinvest truth and authenticity into what had been warped and distorted by racist opportunists. In literature, Charles Chesnutt and Paul Laurence Dunbar gained national reputations largely on the strength of writing stories and verse in dialect, many of which would have appeared to their white audiences as little different from the literature being written by white writers. (In fact, early readers of Chesnutt's short stories were unaware of the race of the author.) On the stage, the comedians Bert Williams and George Walker applied burnt cork to their faces and gave performances that seemed at once to exemplify and to ridicule racist views of blacks, telling jokes that combined stereotypes, self-mockery, and veiled attacks on white racism. The two even produced musical comedies, *Dahomey* (1902) and *Abyssinia* (1906), set in Africa—shows which they envisioned as breaking stereotypes. As the name implies, coon songs, which circulated widely as sheet music, traded in stereotyped images and figures. Despite their obvious racism some, like Ernest Hogan's "All Coons Look Alike to Me," were written by black composers. But although ragtime (a complex, often syncopated music usually played on the piano), also employed racist lyrics, the artistic demands of the form gave black composers opportunities to display and develop their talents.

The aesthetic sophistication of turn-of-the-century popular forms allowed those elites who were not so wedded to sacred folk culture to find in an evolving black culture reason for celebration. James Weldon Johnson's picaresque novel *The Autobiography of an Ex-Colored Man* (1912) saw no contradiction in proclaiming the Uncle Remus stories, the Jubilee songs, ragtime music, and the cakewalk as equally significant African American contributions to world culture. In the words of Johnson's nameless narrator even the "lower forms of art . . . give evidence of a power that will some day be applied to the higher forms." But as the careers of many early-twentieth-century figures indicate, the attempt to harness popular forms to personal, aesthetic, and political ends was often a double-edged sword. Scott Joplin, the composer of "The Maple Leaf Rag" and the acknowledged master of ragtime, encountered disappointment and rejection when he attempted to get his audience to accept his opera *Treemonisha,* an allegory about black leadership and uplift, as the capstone

on the ragtime tradition. The difficulties in writing and producing the opera, which was published in 1911 and performed for the only time in 1915, taxed Joplin's health and contributed to his suffering a nervous breakdown. By 1917 Joplin was dead. Williams and Walker, too, wrestled with the ambivalence of having to caricature blackness in order to express it. And Paul Laurence Dunbar lamented in letters and in verse that the public and critical demand for his dialect poetry drew attention away from his writings in standard English. In fact, for some time Dunbar's short lyric, "We Wear the Mask," which includes such lines as, "We wear the mask that grins and lies, / It hides our cheeks and shades our eyes,— / This debt we pay to human guile," has been taken as the most poignant expression of the psychic costs incurred by blacks who sought to inhabit and give ironic twists to racist traditions.

Dunbar's pathos has been condemned as a bourgeois angst generated by a naive and misguided belief that genuine acceptance from whites was possible in a nation so invested in racism. Most blacks, in the argument of scholars like Houston A. Baker, Jr., recognized the game for what it was—a means of negotiating a racist society—and played it with a shrewdness that did not risk their personal integrity. Unconcerned with eliciting from whites any acknowledgment of equality, which they knew was impossible, the majority of black Americans, according to this argument, figuratively donned the minstrel mask whenever it was in their interest to do so and did not internalize the visions of themselves that they were compelled to project. What this position does not adequately account for, however, is not so much the psychological cost of dissimulation, which is after all, subject to various forms of dispute, but the extent to which African American activity, both political and economic, was predicated on the belief that the promise of equality in the nation's founding documents was a promise that should be honored immediately. The Great Migration was in its own way an expression by many thousands of blacks of their desire to escape from the conditions that made minstrel posturing necessary and a wish to seek equality on their own terms.

## THE HARLEM RENAISSANCE AND THE BLUES, 1919–1929

It was the perception, both real and imagined, of a new attitude prevalent among the masses that led many black writers and artists to begin to speak of a "New Negro"—the phrase that provided the title for a 1925 volume edited by Alain Locke. Locke surveyed the large number of migrants streaming into New York and proclaimed in his introduction that "the Negro is becoming transformed." More real than imagined was Locke's sense that he was witnessing a signal moment in American history: the urbanization of black America would change this nation drastically because race, which had erroneously been treated as merely a southern problem, would now have to begin to be addressed in national terms. More imagined than real, however, was Locke's belief that these changes heralded a consensus among African Americans that their political and economic destinies were intimately intertwined with the project of building a viable community of black artists and writers.

Black writers and artists did enjoy considerable critical success during this period. Jean (Nathan Eugene) Toomer's *Cane* (1923), a literary collage of poetry, sketches, short stories, and a play, was seen as the herald of a new literary age—a move from a literature of overt political protest to a literature that moved aesthetics to the foreground. In *Cane,* Toomer sought to evoke and preserve a black folk culture that he believed was dying out as a result of urbanization and the acculturation of blacks to a white bourgeois norm. The literary world's embrace of *Cane,* however, indicated that in the eyes of many writers and readers the spirit of black folk was not dying out but continued to define a black ethos distinct from a dominant white order.

While many African Americans could and did take pride in the achievements of well-regarded black writers, the sense that the destiny of the race required the ongoing financial support of a black literati characterized the beliefs of a small section of the middle class more so than the masses. To be sure, the Harlem Renaissance and the period immediately preceding it saw an unprecedented rise in the numbers of individuals supporting black periodicals. The *Crisis,* founded in 1910 as the voice of the National Association for the Advancement of Colored People, and edited by W. E. B. Du Bois, had achieved a circulation of 95,000 by 1919 (although these numbers declined steadily during the 1920s); the National Urban League's *Opportunity: Journal of Negro Life,* which commenced publication in 1923 under the editorial stewardship of Charles S. Johnson, had a peak circulation of 11,000; and A. Philip Randolph and Chandler Owen's *Messenger* topped out with a monthly publication of 5,000 copies. But to the degree that these magazines served partisan political purposes and were read for the news that they provided their readership

about black communities it is difficult to gauge the extent to which subscribers viewed literary aesthetics as a significant issue in the battle against racism.

The poet and writer Langston Hughes was among the earliest commentators to cast doubt on the political assumptions of the Harlem Renaissance, observing in his autobiography *The Big Sea* (1940) that "the ordinary Negroes hadn't heard of the Negro Renaissance." In Hughes's view the writings of black intellectuals existed in a world apart from the everyday cultural experience of blues clubs where the music of Bessie Smith, Mamie Smith, and Ma Rainey represented the vitality of a black culture that did not take its cues from an elite leadership, and harbored within itself a critique of the American dream. Variously defined, the blues is generally recognized by a "blueing" or flattening of the third and seventh notes of the scale, and a twelve-bar, three-line stanza with an AAB pattern. The sometimes bawdy wordplay and double entendre of blues lyrics seemed at odds with middle-class propriety. With this in mind, Hughes, writing for the *Nation* in an essay entitled "The Negro Artist and the Racial Mountain," skewered the black bourgeoisie for adopting mediocre white tastes over a much more vibrant black culture. The essay urged African American artists to cultivate an indifference to the expectations of white society and to ground themselves not in middle-class respectability but in the spirit of the blues.

That the blues vocalists singled out by Hughes were women points to another aspect of this historical moment. Hazel Carby has argued that female blues singers played a dynamic social role precisely by facilitating working-class women in resisting the moral policing of the black bourgeoisie and by bringing "to the black, urban, working class an awareness of its social existence." Dance halls, nightclubs, and recordings formed a network that validated desires and life-styles that the black bourgeoisie and the dominant white culture viewed as deviant. Given that racism severely constricted black female access to "respectable" work, the task of reconfiguring as respectable those occupational options that were open to black women, such as vaudeville, appeared to be crucial.

In deeming the blues paradigmatic of a black worldview that was antithetical to white and black bourgeois values, Carby and Hughes dissent in many respects from Lawrence Levine's argument that the blues "was the most typically American music Afro-Americans had yet created and represented a major degree of acculturation to the individualized ethos of the larger society." Blues represents less an antithesis to dominant styles than a synthesis of "black" collective and "white" individualistic norms. In contrast to the more communal content and performance structure of spirituals and work songs, blues featured the individual voice and tended to focus on personal loss, betrayal, and transcendence.

Although Levine's remarks evince a potentially troubling nostalgia for a lost black communal solidarity, his emphasis on the intersection of blues and individualism is instructive. For if the novels from the turn of the century through the Harlem Renaissance serve as somewhat useful guides, the project of racial uplift was, among other things, a way of consolidating a rather tenuous black bourgeoisie as a class which could experience itself as such, even as it sought to make racial identity a defining category. On their part, female migrant blues performers, like their middle-class "uplift" counterparts were equally, though differently, engaged in the process of constructing a consolatory, if potentially contestatory alternative to dominant norms and mores.

Uplift, then, constituted one side of a coin of which a working-class blues culture was the other. Both were complementary features of postemancipation migrancy and urbanization, a historical moment during which middle-class demonization of black working-class habits was always incomplete and ambivalent, as was working-class rejection of middle-class mores. Further complicating the picture was the fact that both groups often shared strategies for political betterment—even the greenest migrant was not unaware that the franchise might play some role in enhancing black urban life. Despite widespread disfranchisement in the South, there was still some experience with relatively effective uses of the franchise in such cities as Baltimore, where Republican party success depended on black voting.

Further, it appears that against the backdrop of the desires of African American individuals to have their interests acknowledged and material needs met, blues and uplift may have been the means through which lesser and better educated black Americans, respectively, came to realize or believe that their prospects for achieving individual success depended largely upon certain individual black voices being taken as representative of blacks in general. The individual stature of the blues singer, the politician, or the novelist was largely a function of the perception that each somehow adequately represented "the Race." But while this realization may have fostered a vision of the necessity and desirability of collective action and life, it also contributed to a politics of the spokesperson in which the collective was silenced

even as it was evoked. The ghettoization of the black population in urban centers like Chicago and New York, the need for black bloc voting, the intermittent effectiveness of the franchise, and the fact that representative black voices from Booker T. Washington to various musicians and singers could lead lives and exercise social clout well beyond the capacities of the vast majority of black Americans often appeared to make it clear that black Americans could only exercise power by delegating it to others. It was largely this set of factors, coupled with assumptions about economic well-being, that made possible the phenomenal success of Marcus Garvey, which we will look at below.

Whether one was from the working or the middle class, undergirding much of the optimism of the Harlem Renaissance was the relative economic prosperity enjoyed by a significant number of black urban dwellers in the 1920s. What James Weldon Johnson believed to be the irreversible character of the movement was, he argued in Locke's *New Negro,* guaranteed by the economic success of blacks in Harlem. "Black" capital accumulation would decrease the dependency of black artists and writers on white patrons and readers.

The presumption of eventual black economic autonomy was crucial and, in large measure, illusory. In the late 1800s, black colleges, perhaps the most visible black institutions on the national scene, had openly solicited white financial and philanthropic support. Beginning in the 1870s, the Fisk Jubilee Singers of Fisk University toured the United States and Europe securing critical acclaim for their presentation of black spirituals and monetary support for their university. Later in the century Booker T. Washington stumped the country on behalf of his Tuskegee Institute, emphasizing industrial education and articulating a vision of black progress that did not openly challenge racist norms, thereby eliciting needed dollars from wealthy northern whites. The artistry and accomplishment of the Fisk Singers was undeniable, but the image of educated blacks singing the old "slave songs" nonetheless fit rather comfortably into overarching assumptions about the nature of the black race. Likewise, while Washington's oratorical prowess made him much in demand as a speaker, he willingly moderated his expressions of black demands in order not to antagonize hostile whites. Whatever the success of Washington and the Fisk Jubilee Singers, it was clear that black culture and institutions presumed the support and endorsement of progressive whites.

From one angle, the Harlem Renaissance was to have changed all of that. Langston Hughes, as we have seen, assumed that black folk art in the form of the blues represented a dissent from white norms. Should the black writer dare to do so, the aesthetic and economic viability of blues artists attested to the possibility of successfully flouting bourgeois expectations. By the 1930s, Zora Neale Hurston's work in folklore and in the novel exemplified the aesthetic and intellectual avenues opening up for black writers who attended to folk culture. *Mules and Men,* her collection of black folklore, was published in 1934, and her most acclaimed novel, *Their Eyes Were Watching God,* appeared in 1937. Although her work enjoyed some success during her lifetime, it was not until the 1970s, more than ten years after her death, that the full impact of Hurston's contribution was felt. As a generation of black women writers sought literary models, *Their Eyes Were Watching God,* which drew upon the poetry of black vernacular speech as it chronicled the personal and sexual liberation of its heroine, became a touchstone.

To turn back to the twenties, however, is to confront the paradoxes facing those black writers who successfully mined folk materials for their own aesthetic purposes. Not only were Hughes and Hurston supported for a time by the same white patron, but the hostility to the white bourgeoisie championed in their work was also characteristic of a significant number of white writers who saw themselves as part of the avant garde and who readily, though often paternalistically, supported black writers and appropriated African and African American cultural forms. In addition, changes in the social sciences, particularly anthropology as shaped by the presence of Franz Boas (who influenced Hurston) helped lend legitimacy to the study and preservation of non-European cultures, while white American doubts about the viability of Western societies suggested that African art and black folk culture might be an antidote to the overcivilization of the West. As a result, the turn to Africa, the blues, or jazz by black artists was often a turn toward rather than away from white economic support.

## GARVEYISM

It was to be left to Marcus Garvey, a Jamaican-born activist who admired Booker T. Washington, to expound a vision of Africa that elicited rank-and-file black support. Founder of the Universal Negro Improvement Association (UNIA) in 1914 and its Black Star Shipping Line in 1919, Garvey preached a pan-Africanist vision that, for a time, caught the imagination of large numbers of blacks beyond the circle of

urban elites, claiming supporters numbering in the millions worldwide (although the exact figures are disputed). The UNIA was supported by dues-paying members and published a widely circulated weekly newspaper, the *Negro World,* which was published in French, English, and Spanish, and was banned by a variety of colonial governments. Garvey's Black Star Line was capitalized by selling shares at five dollars each to black Americans. The shipping line was to create commercial and interpersonal ties among black peoples the world over in order to achieve the UNIA's stated goals of fostering black nationhood, redeeming Africa, promoting black self-help, and inspiring self-love and respect. Although widely perceived as a back-to-Africa movement, Garvey's beliefs were a form of black imperialism, as signified by the phrase, "Africa, at home and abroad."

"Africa" and black cultural nationalism as they emerged in Garvey's speeches and writings did not so much specify black differences at the level of artistic form as stress a black content within recognized aesthetic forms and moral norms. Like his economic plans, which did not challenge imperial capitalism but insisted on black control of existing capitalist structures, Garvey's cultural ideals were not fundamental cultural challenges to the West. In fact, though he emphasized an African revivalism and advocated the teaching of black history to all descendants of Africa, Garvey's pronouncements on moral and artistic behavior sounded decidedly Victorian and Christian; African-derived beliefs, such as the practice of obeah in Garvey's home country of Jamaica, were frowned upon. Nonetheless, Garveyism, though controversial among other black elites, enjoyed a widespread appeal that other political movements of the 1920s were unable to approach. To a black population angered by the race riots of 1919, eager to realize the economic promise that had goaded their migration from the South, and deeply aware that the moment called for a collective response, Garvey's ability to combine inspirational and confrontational oratory, a highly visible business enterprise, and a vision of black nationhood made his UNIA and Black Star Line appear to be directly responsive to black Americans' desires for immediate redress of social and economic needs.

Poor financial decisions, political infighting, federal opposition, and Garvey's ill-considered meeting in Atlanta with the Ku Klux Klan in June 1922 led to the unraveling of the UNIA and the Black Star Line. Garvey was convicted of mail fraud in 1923, imprisoned in 1924, and deported to Jamaica in 1927. The success that he and his organizations enjoyed through the early 1920s, however, attested to the attractiveness of black cultural nationalism in the face of intransigent white racism.

## PULPIT ORATORY, MUSIC, AND BLACK CHURCHES

In 1934 the presses and editor of Garvey's *Negro World* gave themselves over to a new venture, the publication of the *World Echo,* which spoke on behalf of another spellbinding orator, George Baker, better known as Father Divine. Styling himself as "God at 20 West 115th Street," Divine headed a religious organization known as the Peace Mission, which drew into its ranks a significant number of former Garveyites on its way to establishing a following that was national (some would say, international) in scope. Divine's was one of the most flamboyant and successful of the ministries to come out of the phenomenon of the urban storefront churches common through the 1920s, but which gathered strength during the Great Depression when economic success became less than a dream for many African Americans. Preaching a gospel that mingled worldly and otherworldly success, Divine and other church evangelists struck a chord with many black urban dwellers whose various needs were not being met either by mainstream political and social institutions or by established black churches. Emotional services coupled with occasional outreach pulled in congregants far and wide. Divine's Peace Mission went beyond many of the other storefront churches in attempting, with some success, to reach beyond race, and in becoming actively involved in political movements.

Scholars have long differed over the question of whether the major impact of ministries like Divine's and black churches in general was more escapist than activist. There were often major disagreements both within and among denominations as to how, if at all, religious institutions should become involved in politics, making it somewhat erroneous to speak of the "black church" in any monolithic way. But it is clear that a variety of black church denominations cultivated styles of pulpit oratory and musical traditions, from spiritual to gospel, that sometimes became features of overt political movements as indicated by the prominence of Martin Luther King, Jr.'s oratory during the modern civil rights era. While King's effectiveness was arguably as much a function of his active participation in civil rights protests as of his speaking voice, his career provides evidence that when harnessed to progressive political movements, the tradition of the black sermon and of black sacred

music did lend an air of moral sanction and authority to acts of civil disobedience taken on behalf of changing the racial order of American society. Echoing Du Bois's efforts at the beginning of the century to locate in the black spiritual an alternative ethos to the Gilded Age, the attempt to center black cultural production and political protest in black church organizations was geared to present civil rights as a movement that went beyond the need to redress the grievances of a particular group and extended into the task of returning the nation to what were deemed to be its spiritual ideals.

## AFRICAN AMERICAN WRITERS AND THE LEFT

The apparent irrepressibility of cultural nationalism and its persistence in evangelical forms both inspired and bedeviled black writers on the left throughout the 1920s and into the thirties. African American life in the United States presented writers, artists, and performers with the dual tasks of representing and speaking to the largely segregated lives that the vast majority of blacks had lived in this nation in the rural South and in northern ghettoes. In a 1938 manifesto, "Blueprint for Negro Writing," the novelist and writer Richard Wright crystallized this paradox by proclaiming that "Negro writers must accept the nationalist implications of their lives, not in order to encourage them, but in order to change and transcend them." Yet creating a broadly based African American political movement through the articulation of "national" black cultural forms proved a difficult undertaking. The visibility of African American folk, jazz, and blues styles, along with the presence of black institutions made it easy to attribute the oftentimes disappointed longing for immediate political and social change to a failure among the black intelligentsia to establish effective cultural links between themselves and their erstwhile constituency. Correspondingly, these same black styles and institutions made it possible for elites to attribute any failure to rouse the masses to the narrowness, provinciality, or general unreadiness of blacks as a whole.

As the hopes of the Harlem Renaissance foundered on the shoals of the Great Depression, both rationales were given to account for the apparent failure of that movement. And for many black writers the waning of the Renaissance intensified their involvement with the Left. Jamaican-born writer Claude McKay, who had penned such novels as *Home to Harlem* (1927) and *Banjo,* (1929) and the militantly strident poem "If We Must Die," had joined the

Communist party in the 1920s, traveling to the Soviet Union to speak on black issues at the 1922 Fourth Congress of the Communist International. Langston Hughes, too, who had begun writing more explicitly political poetry in the late 1920s, thereby damaging relations with his white patron Charlotte Mason, also visited the Soviet Union in the 1930s, though he never joined the Communist party. Richard Wright, after moving North from Mississippi by way of Memphis, served his literary apprenticeship in Chicago's John Reed Club, joining the party in 1933. The actor Paul Robeson became a party member as well.

The notorious Scottsboro case of 1931, when nine black teenagers were convicted on dubious charges of raping two white women, galvanized Communist party efforts along the racial front. Moving with alacrity where some mainline black organizations had moved slowly, the American Communist party gained credibility and converts. Black writers like Hughes who had spoken out on and written about the Scottsboro case found support from the Left, and when mainline publications began to lose interest in publishing literature by black writers during the thirties, *Partisan Review,* the *New Masses,* and the *Daily Worker* continued to welcome submissions by African Americans. Richard Wright's early writings, including the 1938 collection of short stories *Uncle Tom's Children,* were suffused with his Marxist collectivist beliefs, but Wright's breakthrough 1941 novel, *Native Son,* which portrayed the violent shattering of black hopes in Chicago and the pathological character of white racism, also revealed his uneasiness with Party aesthetics. By 1942 Wright had left the Party. Hughes, attempting to regain his popularity as a writer in 1941 with the publication of his autobiography *The Big Sea,* repudiated some of his more strident left-wing poetry. McKay converted to Catholicism in 1944.

While some of the black difficulties with communism were the same as those of the American Left with the Soviet Union in general, stemming from reactions to Stalin's brutal suppression of dissidence and his signing of the Nazi-Soviet nonaggression pact in 1939, the ever-present problem of white racism within and without the party exacerbated the situation. Other objections were apparently aesthetic. Ralph Ellison, who had nursed left-wing affiliations while honing his craft as a writer, included in his National Book Award–winning novel *Invisible Man* (1952), an unflattering portrait of an organization modeled on the American Communist party, called the Brotherhood. Ellison's picaresque tale, which also vividly portrayed the seductiveness and the weak-

nesses of Booker T. Washington accommodationism and Garveyesque West Indian nationalism, was an imaginative brief against attempts to apply fixed formulas to representations of human experience, and for this reason was seen as an implicit critique of Richard Wright's naturalistic *Native Son.* When James Baldwin, whose *Go Tell It on the Mountain* (1953) established him as a major novelist, explicitly attacked Wright in an essay titled "Everybody's Protest Novel" for privileging politics over art, both Ellison and Baldwin were subjected to criticism from the black and white Left. The most visible of these critiques came in the early 1960s when Irving Howe's "Black Boys and Native Sons" took the younger novelists to task for not writing as directly out of their pain as had Wright—a critique which prompted a heated exchange between Ellison and Howe.

Notwithstanding the complicated involvement of black writers and artists with specific political movements and organizations, African American cultural figures retained a symbolic presence in American society through the 1940s and 1950s—a presence that helped keep visible the cause of racial justice and helped maintain pressure on the federal government to attack segregation. In 1939, for example, when the Daughters of the American Revolution (DAR) refused to grant a permit for black contralto Marian Anderson to sing in Constitution Hall in Washington, D.C., First Lady Eleanor Roosevelt resigned her membership in that organization. It was then arranged that Anderson would sing from the steps of the Lincoln Memorial on Easter Sunday when over 75,000 people watched her perform. Anderson's voice ringing out over the throngs in the nation's capital seemingly emblematized the capacity of African American artistic excellence to embarrass and eventually defeat white racism.

## JAZZ

Jazz, which had exploded onto the cultural scene during the Harlem Renaissance and had given the alternative moniker the "Jazz Age" to that decade, also contributed to a symbolic cultural politics of the 1930s and 1940s. The ensemble requirements of jazz performance—from combo to big band—and the fact that the music's sensual and improvisational style attracted white players as well as black meant that the performance stage at times became a visually integrated space. And as bands toured the country they often found themselves at odds with local Jim Crow ordinances, entailing resort to subterfuge or outright defiance in order to perform. With the major black political organization, the NAACP, pushing an integrationist line, the baseline demands of jazz performance (clubs, accommodations, and eating establishments that would accept blacks and whites, freedom from white racist violence on the nation's roadways) appeared to be in step with that of the civil rights mainstream.

The bandleader and composer Duke Ellington used some of his compositions explicitly to explore and celebrate African American history and liberation. *Creole Rhapsody* (1931), *Symphony in Black* (1934), *Jump for Joy* (1941), and most prominently *Black, Brown, and Beige* (1943), which premiered in Carnegie Hall, were testaments to the inevitable connection that Ellington saw between his music and the political fortunes of black Americans. As with blues, however, fixing a specific politics at the level of form has been a difficult if not impossible task. Responses to jazz by African Americans have been as varied as the musicians and styles that coexisted under the rubric of jazz; at the same time the willingness of whites to appropriate jazz styles or purchase jazz recordings was no real indicator of a willingness to endorse any particular variety of black political or economic demands. Clearly, however, within jazz the development of "bebop" or "bop" was a response to what was seen as the aesthetic limitations of big-band jazz and the crass commercialization of the form by white band leaders and white promoters. Associated with such figures as Charlie Parker, Dizzy Gillespie, and Max Roach and defined by a rhythmic complexity and an emphasis on virtuoso performances, bop moved jazz away from its dance-music dimensions. Socially, the intersection of bop, cool jazz, and the Beat generation helped foster a climate of aesthetic dissent from mainstream literary norms, particularly in the arena of poetry, creating the milieu that in Greenwich Village spawned LeRoi Jones/Amiri Baraka, who was to play a pivotal role in establishing and defining the Black Arts Movement.

## BLACK ARTS MOVEMENT

The assault on federally and state-sanctioned segregation in the late 1940s through the early 1960s once again pushed to the forefront the question of the artist's, writer's, or performer's relationship to a larger African American constituency. In the eyes of many, aesthetic achievement carried with it the responsibility of voicing the grievances and aspirations of the black masses, and the work of many black writers in the fifties—including Lorraine Hansberry, who authored the play *A Raisin in the Sun,* the novelist and

poet Gwendolyn Brooks, Ellison, and Baldwin—was looked upon as speaking on behalf of the less articulate. Baldwin, who had censured Richard Wright for remaining within the protest tradition, heightened his public profile in volumes of searing essays chastising the nation for its moral failure toward its black citizens. And novelist Paule Marshall, whose *Brown Girl, Brownstones* (1959) chronicled the coming of age of a Barbadian immigrant girl, expressed her fears during the U.S. Congress's discussion of the 1964 Civil Rights Act that the act would be watered down. In response Marshall called for the formation of an independent black political organization.

For underneath the overlay of elite eloquence, the civil rights decades—highlighted by A. Philip Randolph's proposed March on Washington in 1941 that prompted President Roosevelt's issuing of Executive Order 8802 establishing the Fair Employment Practice Committee; the series of NAACP court challenges that culminated in the U.S. Supreme Court's 1954 ruling in *Brown* v. *Board of Education* that separate but equal was inherently unequal; the 1955–1956 Montgomery bus boycott in Montgomery, Alabama; the establishment of the Southern Christian Leadership Conference (SCLC) in 1957; student sit-ins and the founding of the Student Nonviolent Coordinating Committee (SNCC) in 1960; the urban unrest of 1964 and 1965; and the passage of the 1964 Civil Rights Act and the 1965 Voting Rights Act—dramatically unveiled the creative power of mass action, or the threat of mass action, in its potential to reshape society.

In part for this reason, Willie Ricks and Stokely Carmichael's call in 1966 for Black Power in the political and economic arenas helped galvanize the voicing of an overtly political, presumably populist demand on the black artist or writer. If the arts somehow spoke for the black masses at a moment when revolutionary social change seemed possible, then it seemed pertinent to question the writer's or the artist's aesthetic protocols, social position, and audience. Such questioning, however, typically came not from the masses (leaving aside how such a question might be voiced) but from within the sphere of elite cultural production itself as writers and artists came to terms with the problematic status of the arts in late capitalist societies. What, other than mass consumption by African Americans, could define an art form as black?

The Black Aesthetic and Black Arts movement sought to answer this question along three related fronts, each of which presumed the ultimate possibility of creating and sustaining an organic role for the arts in black daily life. The first and most visible of these fronts was that of establishing a distinctive black literary and artistic style by discerning and refining black style as it was presumed to be contained and expressed in the voices and activities of African Americans generally. Jazz, and to a somewhat lesser extent, blues was paradigmatic here. Significantly, when Addison Gayle edited a collection of essays, *The Black Aesthetic* in 1971, included among the manifestos was a reprinting of Langston Hughes's "The Negro Artist and the Racial Mountain," which had called upon poets and writers to learn from blues and jazz performers. In a self-conscious attempt to rewrite the Harlem Renaissance, Baraka and Larry Neal published an anthology called *Black Fire* (1968), echoing the famous Renaissance *Fire*.

Articulated through the writings of Baraka, Neal, Stephen Henderson, Hoyt Fuller, and Maulana (Ron) Karenga, as well as Gayle and others, the black aesthetic expressed a great deal of skepticism about the applicability of mainstream cultural norms to African American cultural production, arguing that African American literature and art would evolve their own aesthetic protocols—the ultimate judges of artistic and literary value would be the people themselves, not an academic elite.

At a national level one of the most visible manifestations of the black aesthetic's dissent from the literary standards of the white literary establishment was the response to William Styron's 1967 novel, *The Confessions of Nat Turner*. A white southerner, Styron made his novel an ordeal of consciousness told from the point of view of the leader of the 1831 slave rebellion in Southampton County, Virginia. The novel was initially received with critical acclaim by reviewers, most of whom were white. But the publication in 1968 of *William Styron's Nat Turner: Ten Black Writers Respond* immediately changed the climate of reception for Styron's novel, as the responding authors, who included scholars and creative writers, faulted Styron on everything from his use of historical sources to his representation of black manhood. Perhaps more significant than the specifics of any of the criticisms of Styron was the context of the debate. Unlike in the past, in which black cultural elites had reacted to what were largely intentionally racist and demeaning representations of African Americans (as in the NAACP's campaign against D. W. Griffith's film *The Birth of a Nation*), the ten black writers had taken to task what Styron and a significant number of white critics had believed to be a sympathetic portrayal of black anger and revolutionary desire. The rancor of the disagreement made

it clear that the aesthetic standards prevailing in the black community were at odds with those held by most whites. Thus when Gayle published *The Black Aesthetic* in 1971 the question of black literary standards was so prominent that the book received significant critical attention.

Overlapping with the presumption of a distinctive black aesthetic at the level of style was also a presumption of revolutionary content and form within black arts, and the idea that this revolutionary aesthetic could be expressed only along nationalist lines. The ideological warrants for this aspect of the black aesthetic were drawn from a loose amalgam of theories that included Frantz Fanon's *The Wretched of the Earth* (1968) and *Black Skin, White Masks* (1967), strands of Marxist-Leninist thought, pan-Africanism, Negritude, Maoism, and various expressions of cultural nationalism including some of the tenets of the Nation of Islam. The various faultlines within this amalgam were often papered over by assertions that the celebration of black identity in a society that had deemed blacks ugly and inferior constituted in and of itself a revolutionary act. For black aesthetes, this assertion of identity was transmitted through a variety of means. At the most mundane and most long-lived level, the means of transmission were style of dress and habits of consumption—the wearing of African-inspired dress and the cultivation of African-inspired hairstyles. For writers, identity was asserted through the polemical essay and through a poetry of imperative that self-consciously crafted a diction intended to strike its readers as a street vernacular. Poets called for direct action from their readers and for a more immediate relationship between audience and artists. Poetry by such figures as Sonia Sanchez, Nikki Giovanni, and Haki Madhubuti (Don L. Lee) became a vehicle through which a younger generation of writers took on their already established predecessors, some of whom, like Gwendolyn Brooks in Chicago, responded by joining ranks with them in seeking out alternative venues for giving readings and publishing work.

As important as poetry in this process was the drama, which often took the form of street or guerilla theater, and which, when whites were among its audience, sought to confront them directly with the consequences of white racism. In the early sixties, Amiri Baraka, who played a defining role in the Black Arts movement, dramatically reoriented his Beat aesthetic (a process that included changing his name from LeRoi Jones) toward what he deemed to be a black revolutionary aesthetic. Establishing himself as a dramatist of significant power in such plays as *Dutchman* (1964) and *The Slave* (1964), he also founded the short-lived Black Arts Repertory Theater and School in 1965, which endorsed a chiefly pedagogical role for the theater.

Baraka's efforts at establishing a theater characterized the third front along which writers sought to bring into being a truly black art articulated with some version of black power politics. This period witnessed a variety of attempts to found and maintain black cultural institutions, including schools, theaters, magazines, literary presses, and even rituals and holidays. Maulana Karenga, for example, invented Kwanza in 1966, a family-centered African heritage festival celebrated from December 26 to January 1. In Chicago, Hoyt Fuller edited *Negro Digest,* and worked along with Gwendolyn Brooks, George Kent, and Haki Madhubuti in the Organization for Black American Culture (OBAC). Madhubuti, perhaps the most widely read of the black aesthetic poets, went on to become editor of the Third World Press.

The movement's larger goal, however, was to define a dynamic relationship between the cultural and political realms, as Harold Cruse dyspeptically reminded Black Power advocates in 1967 with the publication of his *Crisis of the Negro Intellectual.* Censuring black leadership for what he deemed its failure to establish a black "cultural identity," Cruse noted the absence of a "code of cultural ethics, an artistic standard, a critical yardstick or any kind of cogent and meaningful critique on society that might enable [the intellectual, artist, or critic] to fashion viable and lasting institutions in the cultural spheres that motivate progressive movements." Baraka, whose Black Arts Theater had received particular notice in Cruse's critique, expanded his sphere of activities, participating with Karenga in Newark city politics through the formation of a group called Black Community Development. At the national level Baraka became a prime player in the 1972 Black Political Convention in Gary, Indiana, which brought together cultural spokespersons and black elected officials for the purpose of working out a national black agenda. The 1972 convention was followed by another in 1974 (attended by fewer black elected officials), although, taken together, the two meetings did little to further the Black Aesthetic movement's stated goals of institutionalizing a revolutionary cultural nationalism.

## BLACK STUDIES

The privileging of cultural politics by black aestheticians did limn a trajectory for this movement that ran, both figuratively and literally, from the street into the classroom. Although some veins of this ideology issued forth in the establishment of alternate educational institutions, particularly at the preschool and primary grade levels, another vein poured its contents into white educational establishments as a part of, and as a result of the student activism of the late 1960s. Not only did some black aestheticians find employment within universities (Larry Neal, for example, after moving substantively away from the movement's tenets, taught at CCNY, Yale, and Howard universities before his death in 1981), but, largely in response to student demands, universities and colleges began to establish courses and sometimes departments in black studies that adhered in varying degrees to the larger outlines of the Black Aesthetic. As they began to crop up on campuses, departments of Black or African American Studies threw into relief one of the central contradictions of the Black Aesthetic movement, which had made cultural conservatorship a prerequisite to revolutionary action. On the one hand, the institutionalization of black studies at white universities entailed pursuing the legitimation of the discipline through a reform of existing institutional structures. To be perceived as a legitimate academic field, black studies had to look like other academic disciplines. On the other hand, the sometimes populist, sometimes revolutionary rhetoric that fueled black aesthetic pronouncements dictated that Black Studies ought to look different from traditional academic departments by maintaining an active political presence in black communities outside the academy.

For black aesthetic ideologies, gaining a modicum of legitimacy in the Academy proved in practice easier than the project of maintaining black studies as a progressive mobilizing force in black communities, although even here success was imperfect and often came with great compromise. Particularly within the humanistic disciplines, where in the late sixties and early seventies many fields underwent internal crises (not unrelated to, but not simply a result of, the challenge of black studies), the ideological weapons and cultural resources for making a case for the value of black writers were relatively close to hand. The outpouring of widely respected imaginative literature by African American women writers in the 1970s and 1980s such as Ntozake Shange, Alice Walker, Gloria Naylor, and most notably Toni Morrison, contributed to the burgeoning evidence of value in African American cultural production.

This outpouring was fostered by and in turn helped to foster a growing awareness of a history of African American women's writing that had not received much critical attention and commentary. As black women authors testified to the enabling result of this discovery, scholars and writers attempted to elaborate political analogues, positing cooperativeness rather than competitiveness as the central feature of black women's aesthetic choices and social interactions. These various elaborations helped point up the gendered assumptions that had undergirded much of the writing about African American literature and culture. At the same time they revealed the racism and racial exclusionism that had often gone unchallenged within a predominantly white feminist movement, which had too often cast its demands in a light responsive primarily to the needs of white middle-class women.

But during this period the role that the humanities in general were to play in larger society was being severely limited as a result of the increasing specialization demanded by a postindustrial capitalism. And while black aestheticians and their black studies heirs presumed that a turn to cultural history and practice could provide a perspicuous guide to social action, the prosecution of the Cold War and adjustments within the welfare state in response to the social and political demands of the late sixties placed the social sciences and the natural sciences in better positions to validate and substantiate their critical potentials relative to affecting policy development and implementation. And while the rise of theoretical discourses within humanistic disciplines, particularly the rise of structuralism and poststructuralism in literature departments, was responsive to these changes, the expanded purview of literary criticism was purchased by undermining long-held notions that literature and the arts were privileged sites for questioning, correcting, and evaluating society as a whole. Culture, in its traditional form, seemed able to claim little more than a hortatory, admonitory, or pedagogical role—its most cited office being that of teaching individuals their history, instilling in these individuals respect for that history, and producing subjects having the capacities and the wills to sustain communal mores and social institutions.

## AFROCENTRISM IN THE 1980s

Somewhat paradoxically, though, the rather restricted realm granted to traditional conceptions of culture accounts for the resiliency of the concept in discussions of African American political life in the 1970s through the 1990s. Focusing on the removal of state-sanctioned segregation and the enactment of policies intended to redress racial inequities, cultural critics have argued that something other than simple racism must explain the persistence of inequalities along racial lines in the United States. The economic devastation of the inner cities, intensified social segregation along racial and class lines within these cities, the impoverishment of largely black and Latino public schools, and the continued discrepancy between black and white academic success have provided dramatic evidence that large numbers of black Americans still exist on the margins of American society. To the degree that this marginalization has been discussed in terms of its psychic causes or effects, questions of culture are once again being given diagnostic centrality.

Conservative critics, both black and white, have often harkened back to Daniel Patrick Moynihan's 1965 report, *The Negro Family: The Case for National Action,* which argued that the legacy of slavery for the black family had been to create significant cultural differences between blacks and whites which stemmed from a preponderance of female-headed households in a society defined by a patriarchal family structure. These cultural differences, the report went on, tended to disadvantage blacks in the competition for economic success. Citing the interventions of the welfare state as exacerbating the problem, contemporary critics then have gone on to advocate policies targeted at those cultural habits presumed to cause disadvantageous behaviors. The aim of these interventions is to produce a culture and a set of behaviors more in keeping with dominant mores.

Popular Afrocentric beliefs often employ the same diagnosis of social breakdown in order, however, to argue that black psychic and moral unease derives largely from attempts to educate African Americans within Eurocentric traditions. Noting correctly the extent to which the teaching of literature and history in primary, secondary, and college education has neglected non-Western societies as a whole, and African societies in particular, Afrocentric scholars argue for a reorienting of education for black Americans toward a tradition centering on African-derived beliefs and cultures. This reorienting is offered as a corrective to falsifications of the historical record stemming from the attempt to valorize European cultures. And while in some cases the proposed good is limited to the production of a more accurate historical record, in other cases the benefits cash out at a psychic or spiritual level. Learning about African histories, societies, and values presumably recenters African Americans who have, according to this belief, been alienated from or taught to undervalue their culture and history.

Afrocentric scholars and pedagogues have gained a significant purchase in contemporary educational policy as a result of the crisis in public education at the elementary and secondary levels where blacks as a group do not achieve at the same level as whites and drop out in higher numbers. As school districts attempt to cope with these problems in the face of shrinking budgets and public support, low-cost curricular remedies that have the endorsement of local communities become very attractive, and Afrocentric scholars have been invited into a variety of districts to assist in the task of changing curricula. In 1989, however, attempts to implement Afrocentric-inspired curricular reforms in the New York City public schools touched off a firestorm of controversy about Afrocentrism with critics charging that the new curriculum sacrificed historical truth for ethnic and racial advocacy.

## AFRICAN AMERICAN POPULAR CULTURE

The emphasis on style and consumption habits that accompanied the Black Aesthetic movement also pointed to the growing degree to which popular black identity was being worked out through a mass-culture industry. Because profits were there for the making, the culture industry could be more responsive to black demands and desires than local, state, and federal governments where responses to black social needs required a commitment to redistributing economic resources in a political climate hostile to such ideas. As the progressive mobilization of black populations became more of a historical event than a present threat, and a black middle class found itself stymied by a less visible but still effective institutional racism, a form of "black power" could be most visibly exercised by

getting corporations to acknowledge the black difference through marketing techniques and the creation of products targeted toward that population. The troubling fact that mass consumption of a commodified black identity has not on the whole contributed to capital accumulation among black populations, and has facilitated the economic exploitation of those populations is, in the view of some scholars, mitigated greatly by the rise of a hip-hop or rap culture presumably made up of inner city youth. In this view rap culture has not only enriched individual black performers but has enabled a population that has been demonized by the larger society and denied access to most of that society's goods to create an alternative means of articulating its conception of the good life, while leveling a critique against racism. The playing of intentionally offensive, oftentimes angry rap music at high-decibel levels by black youth becomes a way of retaking a public space where the mere presence of these youth often evokes police scrutiny.

It is in many ways too early to tell whether the alacrity with which some academic cultural critics have seized upon rap as a potentially radical form of cultural politics is justified, or whether what is being replayed in this appropriation is merely another form of trying to work out at the level of culture a process that can only be effected through more overtly political mechanisms. The hope that African American cultural practices can create revolutionary consciousnesses is a longstanding one, and a notion not entirely without merit. Yet given the persistence of this belief and the various disappointments that have attended it, the presumption that a successful restructuring of society will precede primarily along cultural lines deserves continued scrutiny.

SEE ALSO Race (volume I); Literary Culture; Mass Media and Popular Culture (both in this volume).

## BIBLIOGRAPHY

The origins and early transformations within African American culture are ably discussed in the two following works: Sidney W. Mintz and Richard Price, *The Birth of African-American Culture: An Anthropological Perspective* (1976), addresses the formation of African American communities during the early slave era; and Lawrence W. Levine, *Black Culture and Black Consciousness: Afro-American Folk Thought from Slavery to Freedom* (1977), charts major changes in black folk culture from slavery through the late twentieth century.

Henry Louis Gates, Jr., *Figures in Black: Words, Signs, and the "Racial" Self* (1987), and Paul Gilroy, *The Black Atlantic: Modernity and Double Consciousness* (1993), help place African American cultural production within the context of Western intellectual thought. The former briefly sketches the relationship between race and aesthetic achievement in Western thought since the Enlightenment, while the latter argues for the political and philosophical roles that black vernacular cultures played in the historical development of modernity. Also indirectly useful in locating assumptions about race and culture in a broader historical context is the introduction to Erich Auerbach, *Literary Language and Its Public: In Late Latin Antiquity and in the Middle Ages* (1965), which, in outlining the assumptions of German romantic historicism, highlight the beliefs about culture and civilization that informed Du Bois's thinking in his early career. Du Bois's early intellectual and political development is treated in David Levering Lewis, *W. E. B. Du Bois: Biography of a Race, 1868–1919* (1993).

Aside from the aforementioned volume by Levine, insightful analysis of the cultural transformations accompanying the first significant migration of African Americans to northern cities include Hazel V. Carby, "Policing the Black Woman's Body in an Urban Context," *Critical Inquiry* (Summer 1992); Carle Marks, *Farewell—We're Good and Gone: The Great Black Migration* (1989); and James Grossman, *Land of Hope: Chicago, Black Southerners, and the Great Migration* (1989). The role of black magazines before, during, and after the period of the Great Migration is taken up by Abby Arthur Johnson and Ronald Maberry Johnson, *Propaganda and Aesthetics: The Literary Politics of African-American Magazines in the Twentieth Century* (1979).

A number of volumes are indispensable in coming to terms with the Harlem Renaissance. Nathan Irving Huggins, *Harlem Renaissance* (1971), is a now-standard, still eminently useful account of the Harlem Renaissance. David Levering Lewis, *When Harlem Was in Vogue* (1981), offers a critical, lively, and learned study of the Harlem Renaissance, the political assumptions that guided it and the historical restraints that seemed to end it. In a more revisionist vein are Carby, *Reconstructing Womanhood: The Emergence of the Afro-American Woman Novelist* (1986), which argues the need to rethink issues of cultural representation surrounding the Harlem Renaissance, and Houston A. Baker, Jr., *Modernism and the Harlem Renaissance* (1987), which takes issue with arguments that the renaissance was a failure.

The tradition of black nationalism through the rise of Marcus Garvey is illuminated in Wilson Jeremiah Moses, *The Golden Age of Black Nationalism, 1850–1925* (1978). Robert A. Hill and Barbara Bair, eds., *Marcus Garvey: Life and Lessons, A Centennial Companion to the Marcus Garvey and Universal Negro Improvement Association Papers* (1987), provides a useful collection of some of Garvey's significant writings along with a helpful introductory essay and chronology. Judith Stein, *The World of Marcus Garvey: Race and Class in Modern Society* (1986), astutely critiques

the political goals of Garveyism. Jill Watts, *God, Harlem U.S.A.: The Father Divine Story* (1992), provides a comprehensive discussion of the rise and impact of Father Divine in the wake of Garvey's decline.

Although obviously focused on individual writers, Michel Fabre's *The Unfinished Quest of Richard Wright* (1973) and Arnold Rampersad's two-volume biography of Langston Hughes, *The Life of Langston Hughes* vol. l, *1902–1941, I, Too, Sing America* (1986), and vol. 2, *1941–1967, I Dream a World* (1988), effectively portray black cultural and political life in the post–Harlem Renaissance era. Also from and on this period, see E. Franklin Frazier, *Black Bourgeoisie* (1957), a now-classic study of the political, social, and cultural shortcomings of the black bourgeoisie.

On the black arts movement one should see Harold Cruse's idiosyncratic yet powerful *The Crisis of the Negro Intellectual* (1967), which offers not only a prime example of the assumption that culture must predominate in black political practice, but also presents a useful history of black cultural movements and an unsparing critique of African American political and cultural elites since the Harlem Renaissance. Jennifer Jordan, "Cultural Nationalism in the 1960s: Politics and Poetry," in *Race, Politics, and Culture: Critical Essays on the Radicalism of the 1960s*, ed., Adolph Reed, Jr. (1986), scrutinizes successes and failures of 1960s cultural nationalism. Frank Kofsky's *Black Nationalism and the Revolution in Music* (1970) is a deeply flawed but provocative attempt to chart the relations between innovations in black popular music and the nationalist struggle for black liberation. Larry Neal's vexed relationship with the Black Aesthetic movement is evident in his essays collected in *Visions of a Liberated Future: Black Arts Movement Writings* (1989). Adolph Reed, Jr., "The 'Black Revolution' and the Reconstitution of Domination," in his edited volume, *Race, Politics, and Culture* (1986), offers concise critical examination of the political fortunes of black activism.

The effort to reclaim a black feminist cultural legacy is revealed in Alice Walker's somewhat belletristic collection of essays, *In Search of Our Mothers' Gardens* (1983). In a more straightforwardly scholarly vein is Patricia Hill Collins, *Black Feminist Thought: Knowledge, Consciousness, and the Politics of Empowerment* (1990).

Finally, Pierre Bourdieu, *Language and Symbolic Power* (1991), is extraordinarily helpful in thinking about questions of representations and minority group status.

# MUSIC

## Richard Crawford

Musically speaking, the United States must be considered both an independent democracy and a colony—an extension of European musical life. The "colonial" impulse in the United States, combining artistic idealism with patronage, has inspired a New World appropriation and adaptation of an Old World art form. Within a colonial perspective, performers in America have carried on a musical life devoted to the works of European masters, and composers here have followed similar models. At the same time, the "democratic" impulse, stemming from the public's appetite for functional music—music for worship, instruction, participatory recreation, and entertainment—and from musicians' pragmatic need to make a living, has given rise to a booming, varied marketplace. Popular songs, hymns, and dance music that were written for the moment have sometimes outlived the circumstances of their origin to become "classics." In addition, a third sphere, in which music circulates more through aural than written means, reflects the foreign provenance of the colonial sphere and the functional emphasis of the democratic—indigenous ("traditional" or "folk") music-making, embedded in social custom.

The notion of separate spheres, each reflecting different views of music's nature but open to other influences from within and outside the United States, offers an image modifying the familiar binary distinction of classical versus popular music (or the cultivated tradition versus the vernacular tradition, highbrow/lowbrow). The binary image suggests a spectrum, and the high/low metaphor tends to identify artistry with the "high" end. But musical activity, especially since electronic technology revolutionized its dissemination, more closely resembles a three-dimensional field than a spectrum. And few today would maintain that the colonial sphere holds a monopoly on artistic accomplishment.

As the century began, however, a hierarchical view of American musical life prevailed, with the colonial sphere on top, the democratic at the bottom,

and the traditional in between. Historians writing around 1900 treated the United States comparatively, as a nation whose relative youth had precluded the musical accomplishment other Western nations had enjoyed. Until recently, they believed, Americans had possessed neither the resources nor the will to build a proper foundation: a European-style concert life with such masters as Beethoven and Wagner at its center. But now a foundation was taking shape, and American composers seemed ready to add new works to the repertory. When that happened, the United States would deserve membership in the family of Western musical nations. In the meantime, however, promise outweighed fulfillment.

The lack of a traditional base in "folk music" especially hampered American composers. Except for the music of American Indians and Negro slaves, neither representing the entire nation, the United States could claim no folk tradition like those that had nourished European composers. From this point of view, the musical life of Old World nations, and especially Germany, seemed an organic whole: rooted in common people's song and reaching fruition in works for the concert hall and opera house. American musical life seemed fragmented by comparison. True, the country was rife with musical activity in the democratic sphere. But early historians found little to value in music-making driven by the profit motive.

These commentators' verdict follows the ideals of their day. In the colonial sphere, the prevailing ideal can be called *transcendence*: the belief that certain musical works, like certain poems, novels, plays, and paintings, possess an artistic greatness that assures their permanence; that such works form the basis of a healthy musical life; and that performers must sing and play them in a way that reveals their superior qualities. As a corollary, American composers in the colonial sphere were encouraged, while finding their own style, to emulate the artistic seriousness of European predecessors. The traditional sphere, in contrast, emphasized ways of life over music itself. Here the making of music called for the preservation of linguistic, cultural, and musical practices, and even, if the situation required, adopting an ideal of *continuity*. As for the democratic sphere, its key premise can be described as *accessibility*: an investment of authority in the audience, expressed in a determination to find and please them and to increase their size. Historical commentators believed music in both the colonial and traditional spheres to be based on aspiration that reached beyond practical concerns. In contrast, the economic motive fueling the democratic sphere's accessibility manifests a truth behind the words of composer Roger Sessions, who wrote with thinly disguised regret in an essay of 1948 that no fact about music in America was "more obvious, more pertinent, or more all-embracing in its implications than the fact that music here is in all its public aspects a business."

Around 1900, then, linking importance with idealistic aspiration, historians judged the democratic sphere historically insignificant despite the vast amount of music-making it inspired. Today things look different. With more than two centuries chronicled, it now seems clear that over the long haul the colonial and the traditional spheres have existed on the periphery of the democratic, commercially driven sphere. The latter, commanding opportunity, financial capital, and cultural power, has played a key role in shaping musical life in the United States. Even before 1800, in the marketplace that crystallized within the democratic sphere, musicians and customers with varying needs and interests began to come together to shape the professions of music—performer, teacher, composer, distributor, manufacturer, and writer—and to create what is recognized as "American music."

The first historian to reject the hierarchical view that prevailed around 1900 was Gilbert Chase, who, in *America's Music: From the Pilgrims to the Present* (1955), offered a fresh image. Perceiving that American music had flourished more fully in the democratic and traditional spheres than the colonial, Chase took that judgment not as a weakness but a strength growing from the heart of American democratic life. Rather than a late-blooming outpost of Western musical activity, as earlier historians had insisted, Chase saw the United States as a country realizing its musical destiny through, not in spite of, the variety of informal music its citizens made. Such music, Chase contended, carried its own vigor, aesthetic beauty, and artistic importance. And the composers in the colonial sphere who understood the United States best,

Charles Ives chief among them, celebrated music-making of that kind in their works for the concert hall.

Historiographically speaking, this shift in perspective has brought Americans closer to an unvarnished view of their musical selves. Most later writers on American music have taken Chase's interpretation as the starting point for theirs. Some, however, have written as if an appreciation of American accomplishments in the democratic and traditional spheres requires a devaluation of the colonial. Chase himself made no such statement. But he did leave it to his successors to reassess the colonial sphere's place and function, given that the musical facts of life in America undermine the hierarchy that earlier historians had confidently proposed.

Chase's central insight, while illuminating American music of all periods, should also be seen as a statement growing out of a particular time and historical situation. When earlier writers treated musical endeavor in the colonial sphere as part of a struggle to win for the United States a place of respect among Western musical nations, they wrote, in effect, against the democratic sphere, which seemed to them to oppose true artistic effort. By the same token, Chase's paean to the democratic and traditional spheres was written against the views of those who measured achievement by colonial values. In fact, however, Chase's stance signals that by the 1950s the colonial sphere had won its earlier struggle. Only its firm establishment and broad public acceptance could have evoked Chase's fervent denial that the colonial sphere provided an apt gauge of America's musical accomplishments.

Chase's perspective has served his successors well for almost four decades. Under its influence, historians have rewritten the history of American music, emphasizing events in the democratic sphere that earlier historians had missed or disdained. At this writing, the democratic sphere's fundamental place in American musical life is widely recognized. Relatively little discussion, however, has focused on how this change in the hierarchy reflects changing musical relationships among the colonial, democratic, and traditional spheres.

When one considers connections rather than divisions, what emerges most vividly is the democratic sphere's long-time reliance upon the colonial. That reliance, extending from the eighteenth into the twentieth century, testifies to the colonial sphere's artistic and intellectual hegemony, despite its art being actively practiced and cultivated by relatively few Americans. By the same token, nothing reveals that hegemony's decline more sharply than the way the democratic sphere has disengaged from the colonial sphere's influence since the 1960s. The musical split between democratic and colonial spheres constitutes a major event in American cultural history. Once considered a spin-off, a popular watering-down of forms and styles borrowed from the prestigious colonial sphere, the democratic sphere today finds inspiration and materials chiefly in the traditional sphere—especially in music making with African roots. And the public idea of music in this country today hardly reaches beyond what happens in the democratic sphere. Recent events in America have recast the colonial sphere as more an elite specialty than a legacy for society as a whole. At the end of the century, the colonial, democratic, and traditional spheres remained intact, but their changed relationship brought a shift in ideals. Transcendence, formerly the unquestioned province of the colonial sphere, has been redefined, connected with accessibility and continuity, and appropriated by the democratic sphere.

## MUSIC IN AN AGE OF HIERARCHICAL TASTE, 1900–1920

Writing in the 1840s, Alexis de Tocqueville warned against the canard that democratic Americans were "naturally indifferent to science, literature, and the arts." Americans did care about these things, he wrote, but they cultivated them "after their own fashion and [they brought] to the task their own peculiar qualifications and deficiencies." This country's treatment of music as an art imported from the Old World provides a case in point.

Even a glimpse at music in America around 1900 shows the need for an inclusive approach to its history. Because performances are ephemeral, while compositions form the enduring basis of musical life, historical accounts privilege composition over performance. In the United States, however, the colonial sphere was built around Handel, Beethoven, Mendelssohn, and other European masters. These composers' expressive power set the tone for the whole enterprise. Their music dominated the repertory, and it was by their standards that American music was judged. To consider the colonial sphere without the music of European composers would be to distort the experience that underlay its acceptance on American shores. Therefore, American music history challenges historiographical custom. An account limited to music created by citizens or residents of the United States would illuminate only the edges of the subject.

In American music history, both performance and composition must be considered.

By 1900, the colonial sphere had worked its way into a promising position. The labors of the conductor Theodore Thomas and others had helped to convince patrons that, as the nineteenth-century Boston critic John Sullivan Dwight had preached, Beethoven and Bach were indeed the musical equivalents of Dante, Newton, and Shakespeare. So important to humankind was the experience their music offered that Americans should not be denied the chance to hear that music performed, even if performances could not pay for themselves.

The support of colonial musical culture in the United States has historically been a local affair. In 1900, as before and since, local citizens worked to gain fellow community members access to the artistic greatness of Beethoven and company. With financial subsidies secured through appeals to the ideal of transcendence, symphony orchestras sprang up in major American cities as symbols of civic pride. Halls began to be designed and built for their performances: Carnegie Hall (New York City, 1891), Symphony Hall (Boston, 1900), and Orchestra Hall (Chicago, 1904). Concert life proliferated. In New York, resident companies performed whole seasons of grand opera, and the Metropolitan Opera Company toured other cities. Traveling virtuosi—singers, pianists, and violinists—brought their art to communities large and small. Performers who specialized in European art music were among the day's leading celebrities. (The tenor Enrico Caruso, widely known through his recordings, could earn a handsome sum for appearing in a *silent* film.) Metropolitan daily newspapers employed well-informed critics like Henry E. Krehbiel, W. J. Henderson, and Philip Hale, providing a forum where serious musical issues could be discussed: the merits of a new symphony by Mahler or an opera by Puccini; the significance of Wagner's works for American listeners; the place of American composers and performers in American musical life; the advent of musical modernists (for example, Debussy, Richard Strauss) and the meaning of their work for the future of the art. Whatever it suggests about the size and makeup of the audience, the sophisticated level of musical discussion in newspapers conveys the respect in which turn-of-the-century Americans held music in the colonial sphere.

Behind performances in concert hall and opera house lie years of apprenticeship, a fact reflecting the key role of teaching. The difficulty of many European masterworks adds to the spectacle of their performance. Only musicians who have mastered their me-

Elite music at the beginning of the century. American soprano Geraldine Farrar and Italian tenor Enrico Caruso in Bizet's *Carmen* at the Metropolitan Opera, New York, 1914. Photograph by Mishkin. Culver Pictures, Inc. PRINTS AND PHOTO-GRAPHS DIVISION, LIBRARY OF CONGRESS

dium's technique—tone quality, range, intonation, and agility—can present such music convincingly in public. Moreover, performers must also convey a work's spiritual essence: the truth behind the notes. Audiences understand that only by meeting both technical and spiritual demands can a performer bring a work to an audience as the composer has intended. Thus, artful performance of music in the colonial sphere is no simple matter, and only singers and players who can negotiate its perils and challenges with grace and panache have thrilled their audiences.

Through most of the nineteenth century, Americans had reason to believe that the tools needed for such performances could be gained only in Europe. Those who possessed them, after all, were either Europeans (the soprano Jenny Lind, the violinist Ole Bull, the pianists Sigismond Thalberg and Anton Rubinstein, all of whom toured the United States successfully) or Americans who had studied there (the pianist-composer Louis Moreau Gottschalk). But toward the century's end, a new development

undermined that belief: the performance of music in the colonial sphere began to be taught seriously in the United States. Conservatories of music, founded chiefly to teach beginners, added more Europeans or European-trained musicians to their staffs. Other skilled teachers set up private studios. The pedagogy of music in the colonial sphere began to be democratized, a development whose implications confirm Tocqueville's dictum that democracies find new ways of cultivating aristocratic legacies. For teaching—the bread-and-butter profession for which Americans have most willingly paid musicians—has provided the arena in which composers, performers, and writers in the colonial sphere have found ways to pursue their chosen musical calling.

An important step toward laying that arena's foundation occurred in the 1870s, when Harvard College made John Knowles Paine a professor of music. Other colleges followed suit (Horatio Parker at Yale, 1894; Edward MacDowell at Columbia, 1896), and the New England Conservatory named George Whitefield Chadwick its director in 1897. Paine, Parker, MacDowell, and Chadwick were composers who planned to continue writing music. Achievement as creative artists doubtless won them their appointments in the first place. And they continued to compose, with such works as Parker's *Mona* (1910; premiered at the Metropolitan Opera, 1912), MacDowell's *New England Idylls* for piano (1902), and Chadwick's lyric drama *Judith* (premiered 1901) among the results. Yet in these institutional posts, it was not composing that earned them a livelihood but rather their work as music educators who organized curricula, taught composition, orchestration, the history and theory of music, and perhaps even gave lessons in performance. In joining the teaching profession these men struck a bargain, trading freedom for economic security and taking on pedagogical tasks they may or may not have relished. Thus, they and their generation set a precedent that later American musicians have followed. The United States can boast neither a long tradition of aristocratic patronage nor many citizens with an appetite for European art music. But because Americans have believed in education and its edifying power, it was more in education's name than in the name of art that the colonial sphere established its beachhead in the academy, which has served as an unofficial but potent patron ever since.

Charles Ives is now widely considered the era's outstanding American composer, a judgment that would have astounded critics and musicians in turn-of-the-century America's colonial sphere. What makes Ives's achievement unique is that, after receiving a thorough musical education from his father and from Horatio Parker at Yale, he launched a career disconnected from other musicians. Neither a public performer nor a teacher by temperament (though he worked for a time as a church organist), Ives recognized early that no possibility of a satisfying musical livelihood lay open to him. Thus, he went into business in New York, succeeded at it, and composed in off-hours. Ives wrote in colonial genres: art songs, sonatas, symphonies. But, fired by the sincere, openhearted spirit with which musically untutored Americans sang and played, he staked out territory where the colonial, democratic, and traditional spheres seemed to merge. Ives's impatience with hierarchical boundaries could lead in his music to jarring juxtapositions—quotations from Beethoven symphonies, for example, next to fiddle tunes and gospel hymns—and opaque overlappings, such as two tonally unrelated events occurring simultaneously. In "Putnam's Camp," the second movement of *Three Places in New England* for orchestra, Ives creates the illusion of two bands, each playing a different piece, marching toward each other. In *The Unanswered Question*, a single trumpet intones repeatedly the same angular figure over a string ensemble's consonant, organlike chords while four flutes respond with growing stridency to the trumpet's calls. Harmonic dissonance in the former comes to a head in a cacophonous roar; in the latter, dissonance comes and goes, each time giving way to the serene string background. In both, Ives's use of sounds that stretch the ear allows him, following the lead of Emerson and Thoreau, to probe hidden unities and mysteries of human existence. Ives paid dearly for his isolation and originality; his music enjoyed few public performances during his lifetime. In retrospect, it stands as a remarkable accomplishment and resource: a quintessentially American contribution to the colonial repertory, a challenge to the boundaries separating that sphere from the democratic and traditional ones, and, for some, a critique of music itself, questioning where sound and nature stop and music begins.

At a time when Ives, for effect, was sometimes forcing colonial, democratic, and traditional elements together in deliberate disarray, the colonial and democratic spheres were engaged in a more regular intercourse. The latter openly took the former as its point of departure. In the Broadway musical theater, turn-of-the-century repertory was dominated by operetta: light opera, with elaborate musical numbers sung by operatically trained singers, interspersed with spoken dialogue. Among the American composers who

competed successfully with Gilbert and Sullivan (English) and Franz Lehar (Viennese) for the American stage were Rudolf Friml, a native of Prague, and especially the Dublin-born Victor Herbert, whose *Naughty Marietta* (1910) fits Friml's description of operetta's ingredients: "old things" (Herbert's work was set in 1780s New Orleans), "a full-blooded libretto" (Marietta, a disguised noblewoman, finds her destined lover through music), "luscious melody" ("I'm Falling in Love with Someone," "Ah! Sweet Mystery of Life"), "rousing choruses" ("Tramp, Tramp, Tramp," "The Italian Street Song"), and "romantic passions" (a jilted mulatto beauty's plight exposes Louisiana's caste system). Wind bands dominated the democratic sphere's concert world. John Philip Sousa, who formed and led the most successful one, included in the Sousa band's repertory his own marches and arrangements of popular tunes. But Sousa also toured with a concert violinist and an operatic soprano, as well as such virtuosi as cornetist Herbert L. Clarke and trombonist Arthur Pryor, whose solo performances followed operatic models. And Sousa featured in his concerts arrangements of

Charles Ives, American composer. NEW YORK PUBLIC LIBRARY FOR THE PERFORMING ARTS

shorter works from the symphonic or operatic repertory, Wagner being a special favorite. When in 1903 Broadway song and dance man George M. Cohan wrote the patriotic number, "I Want to Hear a Yankee Doodle Tune," he included the following lines:

Oh, Sousa, won't you play another march?
Yours is just the melody divine.
Now you can take your *William Tell*,
Your *Faust* and *Lohengrin* as well,
But I'll take a Yankee Doodle tune for mine.

Here is an apt symbol of opera's place in the turn-of-the-century United States: not, perhaps, an event for all to attend, but a reference point from which Americans could measure the prestige of the music they enjoyed.

As the twentieth century began, entrepreneurs had found two main ways to profit from music: organizing public performances, and selling published music to performers, mostly amateurs who played and sang at home. In the democratic sphere theatrical performance was the norm, with Tin Pan Alley—a nickname for New York City's music publishing district—and Broadway—New York City's theater district—serving the general population. Tin Pan Alley embodied unashamed commercialism, with publishers fighting to enlist performers to sing their songs, especially in vaudeville—the variety entertainment played on theatrical circuits throughout the country. Vaudevillians came to New York and Tin Pan Alley seeking new material. The more famous the performer, the harder the sell he or she received from publishers, who, when a headliner chose their numbers, could count upon "plugs" (i.e., performances) before audiences whose members would then presumably rush to music stores to buy copies. Profit in this arm of the music business depended upon sales of sheet music, with a typical song sheet containing several pages and selling for between twenty and thirty-five cents.

Broadway provided a more prestigious and demanding venue for composers than Tin Pan Alley, where the unit of production was the single song. On Broadway the show was the unit. Musical entertainments comprised a healthy proportion of Broadway's menu, from the operettas (chiefly imported) that dominated the century's first two decades, to "book shows" whose narrative plot was interspersed with songs, to revues (variety entertainment, usually with a unifying theme). Broadway shows proved highly effective in plugging songs, and successful shows spawned road companies and post-Broadway tours. Like Tin Pan Alley, Broadway also reflected

changes in popular styles. By all accounts, for instance, the most important new style to hit American popular music at the start of the century was ragtime, a syncopated dance music that originated among African Americans and brought into American popular music a new way of articulating musical time. By 1900, ragtime songs like "At a Georgia Camp Meeting" (1897) by Kerry Mills were circulating widely; Mills himself was white, but black influence stood behind this and other songs of the type.

The mention of black influence in American music brings up a fundamental issue. Given the social history of African Americans—brought to the New World as slaves and after Emancipation blocked by racial prejudice from the full rights of citizenship—most black musicians in this country have grown up in black communities, surrounded by traditional African American music. Thus, they have absorbed approaches and habits that leave the firm stamp of that tradition on the music they create. More than musical repertories, black folk tradition offers a unique approach to music-making—one based on what recent commentators have called "signifying"—where each performance becomes an occasion for spontaneous commentary. Syncopation played off against a strict dance-beat, the free bending of pitches (especially a major scale's third and seventh degrees), the exploring of varied instrumental and vocal sound qualities and techniques, and a freedom from fixed repetitions remake a piece of music in the performer's own image. As earmarks of a distinctive approach, they form black American musicians' common heritage, clearly advertising their provenance. As a set of traits that can easily be borrowed, they have also proved, in the democratic marketplace, to be an exploitable commercial resource (as in Mills's "At a Georgia Camp Meeting").

Against this background, the career of Scott Joplin shows a black musician in the democratic sphere, steeped in the traditional but aspiring to have his work accepted in the colonial. The traditional elements in Joplin's music—especially syncopated figures set against a strict beat—must have been absorbed as he grew up, the son of ex-slaves, on the Texas-Arkansas border. By the 1890s Joplin lived in the Midwest, where he studied, taught, and performed as a pianist. But unlike most other black keyboard players of his time, Joplin had a gift for composition. "Maple Leaf Rag," which he published as a piano piece in 1899, achieved popular success, selling over one million sheet-music copies. Joplin's piece shows the general traits of other piano rags: written in the form of a military march, with four

Scott Joplin. PHOTOGRAPHS AND PRINTS DIVISION, SCHOM-
BURG CENTER FOR RESEARCH IN BLACK CULTURE, NEW YORK
PUBLIC LIBRARY, ASTOR, LENNOX, AND TILDEN FOUNDATIONS

strains, each sixteen bars long, each repeated, and with the left hand providing a foursquare foil for the right hand's rhythmic trickiness. But within those conventions Joplin's inventiveness shines through. The first strain's opening twelve bars contain no fewer than four different patterns of accent and texture; yet for all that contrast—and the top register's sudden disappearance partway through the strain—the music coheres, its melodic integrity grounded not in vocal lyricism but in fresh ways of accenting measured musical time. Secure in his command of a novel idiom, Joplin moved to New York City in 1907, where he continued composing and marketing piano pieces as "classic ragtime." Within a few years, he was declaring ragtime not merely a popular fad, as some had charged, but a stately, stylized music that could inspire composition at high artistic levels. Accordingly, Joplin wrote two operas, the first now lost and the second, *Treemonisha* (1911), receiving full theatrical performance only in the 1970s, more than a half-century after his death. Joplin never managed to benefit from the New York entertainment world's acceptance of new black music styles. Working in a society where segregation was more the rule than the exception, he lacked the cultural and economic clout to parlay democratic success into a niche for ragtime and himself in the colonial sphere.

Instead of Joplin, Irving Berlin won the reputation of being America's chief purveyor of ragtime. A Russian Jewish immigrant who arrived in New York at age five, Berlin seems to have acquired his skill with words and music on his own. He took up songwriting while still a teenager, quickly grasping the trade's ground rules while seeking to perfect his creative flair. In 1911, Berlin wrote "Alexander's Ragtime Band," a major hit and a song whose muscular, declamatory urging—"Come on and hear/Come on and hear/Alexander's Ragtime Band!"—conveys so well the buzzing excitement of black-influenced vernacular music that Americans, and Europeans too, found it irresistible. (And this despite the song's avoidance of the rhythmic dislocations that are the essence of ragtime.) Through means closed to Scott Joplin, Berlin had positioned himself to benefit from the rewards in money and publicity that a hit song could bring. His success with "Alexander" led to a partnership in a Tin Pan Alley publishing firm. Thus, having shown, before the age of twenty-five, a pronounced knack for accessibility—for writing songs that a vast audience could embrace—while also cutting himself into the process by which such songs reached that public, Berlin seized leadership in American music's democratic sphere. A tough-minded, industrious craftsman who learned English on the streets of New York, he seemed better tuned to American public sentiment than his native-born rivals.

## THE JAZZ AGE AND AFTER, 1920–1945

In the years after World War I, a new musical style came to the forefront of American life that captured the spirit of the time so well that the 1920s are still sometimes called the Jazz Age. Most who wrote about it then described jazz as a peppy, syncopated dance music whose air of abandon carried messages of social liberation. Historical hindsight confirms that such African Americans as Louis Armstrong, Bessie Smith, and Ferd "Jelly Roll" Morton played and sang the most artistically satisfying jazz of the 1920s. These musicians' energy and inventiveness carried their music far beyond the expressive range of dance orchestras, such as those led by Paul Whiteman and Ted Lewis, that white audiences favored. Nevertheless, like the chief "ragtime" hit of prewar years, the most famous "jazz" composition of the jazz age was the work of a white songwriter with Russian Jewish parents.

On 12 February 1924, at a concert presented in New York's Aeolian Hall by Paul Whiteman's orchestra, George Gershwin played the featured piano part in the premiere of his *Rhapsody in Blue*, a "jazz concerto" commissioned for the occasion. Gershwin's piece lived up to the ballyhoo of precon-

George Gershwin. Photograph by Carl Van Vechten. PRINTS AND PHOTOGRAPHS DIVISION, LIBRARY OF CONGRESS

cert publicity. Touted as a work of historic significance, it has since come to be reckoned both as an American classic and a piece emblematic of its time.

The notion of American music's separate spheres lends itself well to an analysis of *Rhapsody in Blue*, which Gershwin wrote to challenge boundaries. One set of boundaries has to do with reputation and *Rhapsody's* introduction to the public. Billing his concert as "An Experiment in Modern Music," Whiteman caught the attention of New York's leading music critics, who went to hear an event—a concert promoting "symphonic jazz," the Whiteman orchestra's brand of dance music—that they normally would have ignored. Moreover, Gershwin was known as a writer of Tin Pan Alley and Broadway songs, not a composer in the classical sense. As Whiteman hoped, observers found the concert historic because of the gap it sought to bridge: a gap between the high cultural reputation of the colonial sphere—symbolized by the prestigious venue, the presence at the concert of famous classical musicians and critics, and the eye-catching classification of *Rhapsody* as a "jazz concerto"—and the lower standing of the democratic. Despite Gershwin's and Whiteman's

fame and earning power, neither they nor their audience doubted that their stature as artists ranked well below that of the musicians who usually graced the Aeolian Hall stage.

As for its music, to criticize Gershwin's *Rhapsody* for being a pastiche of styles is to misunderstand its strategy as a composition, which is to play upon the widely accepted boundaries that separate the colonial, democratic, and traditional spheres. Formally speaking, the work is a parade of references. It gathers elements from all three spheres, and it makes its impact through strong, memorable melodies of each kind. From the opening clarinet glissando through the blues-tinged themes to the syncopation animating many of its sections, *Rhapsody in Blue* claims traditional African American folk music, appropriated and transformed by Gershwin, as part of its pedigree. Gershwin's experience as a Broadway tunesmith also leaves its mark on the work's harmonic idiom and thematic structure, with phrases and periods cast in the four-, eight-, and sixteen-bar groupings of democratic popular song. Finally, *Rhapsody's* title and its length (approximately fourteen minutes), as well as its cadenzalike passages, sections of thematic development, and the soaring character of the final theme, all show the influence of the piano concerto as written by Grieg, Tchaikovsky, and other European composers. Unlike Ives's, Gershwin's references are not borrowed tune quotations but evocations of different musical styles. And it is precisely in the way they are juxtaposed that *Rhapsody's* eclectic essence shines through: the work of a composer who believed sincerely in the artistic worth of all three spheres of American music.

For all its fame, however, *Rhapsody in Blue* ranked at best as a diverting novelty in the colonial sphere's mainstream. The great names in American music between the world wars were star performers, including conductors (Arturo Toscanini, Leopold Stokowski, Serge Koussevitzky), instrumentalists (Fritz Kreisler, Jascha Heifetz, Artur Rubinstein, Vladimir Horowitz), and singers (Amelita Galli-Curci, Rosa Ponselle, Ezio Pinza, and Kirsten Flagstad). Most were foreign-born; all made their reputations presenting European masterworks to audiences in Europe and the United States. Live performance remained the chief avenue by which this music and these performers reached the public. But in the mid-1920s, electrical recording replaced the earlier acoustic process, and from that time on, record-buying listeners could experience, outside the concert hall, music in the colonial sphere in close approximation to the way it really sounded. In the 1920s, too, radio transmission began. By the 1930s, network broadcasts by the Metropolitan Opera Company and various symphony orchestras—most notably one formed by the National Broadcasting Company for Toscanini—brought this music into American homes throughout the country. The colonial sphere's performing branch, supported by civic pride and patronage, school music programs, private teachers and conservatories, and a knowledgeable if relatively small audience, confirmed its place in American life; by the 1920s virtually every major American city boasted its own symphony orchestra.

Events in Europe, however, helped to relegate the colonial sphere's creative branch in the United States to the periphery. By 1910, younger European composers were exploring beyond the major-minor tonal system that had served Western music for more than two centuries. Arnold Schoenberg in Austria and Igor Stravinsky in Russia and France, among others, began to compose music in which the arching melodies and goal-directed harmonies of earlier days were replaced by shorter thematic gestures, dissonant harmonies, and discontinuous rhythms. And when, after World War I, a new generation of American composers came of age, they took Stravinsky and Schoenberg, not older European masters, as models. Most performers in the United States gave such modern music a chilly reception. Hence, the Americans Aaron Copland and Roger Sessions had difficulty finding performances for their music. In America, amply supplied with the best work of older European composers, performers and their entrepreneurs had always carried more influence in the colonial sphere than composers; and by the 1920s, that influence seemed stronger than ever. It was as if the performance establishment, in league with critics and teachers, had decreed (1) that an age of musical greatness had ended but, nevertheless, (2) that preserving such greatness remained the highest musical calling. American composers who practiced a changing or experimental modern art found themselves largely unsupported by the colonial sphere's chief institutions.

They responded by forming institutions of their own, at first chiefly in New York City. With help from patrons, Edgard Varèse founded the International Composers' Guild in 1921, and two years later the League of Composers was established, the former devoted to performing modern works, the latter to the promotion and performance of new American music. Henry Cowell set up a publishing venture, *New Music* (1927), centered on "noncommercial works of artistic value" by such composers as Ives, Carl Ruggles, Ruth Crawford, and even Schoenberg.

Aaron Copland, American composer. NEW YORK PUBLIC LIBRARY FOR THE PERFORMING ARTS

*Modern Music*, the League of Composers' quarterly journal (1924–1946), surveyed the current scene from a contemporary composer's point of view. And of course, composers also tried, sometimes successfully, to secure commissions and performances in established venues.

The career of Aaron Copland symbolizes American achievement in the colonial sphere during the years between the wars. Born in Brooklyn and musically schooled in New York City and Paris, Copland returned from France in 1924 determined to write modern music reflecting the character of his native land. He turned first to the democratic sphere—to jazz, with which he had had no contact as a performer. In *Music for the Theater* (1925) and his *Piano Concerto* (1927), Copland borrowed jazz-inspired rhythms and melodic gestures and produced works whose verve and vernacular strut sought to reconcile American mannerisms with European neoclassicism, especially that of Stravinsky. In the 1930s, however, he set modernist aspirations aside, seeking to serve more directly the needs of a society in economic hard times. Aware that, with the help of radio, recordings, and film, a vast audience awaited musicians who could find a way to address it, Copland sought to broaden the appeal of his music beyond the concert-going public. Using tools he had already perfected, he looked to the traditional sphere for subjects and tunes. And he simplified his style, presenting borrowed "folk" melodies in uncomplicated harmonic dress while maintaining the rhythmic jolts and transparent texture of his earlier music. Working under commissions, Copland celebrated rural America in three ballets—*Billy the Kid* (1938), *Rodeo* (1942), and *Appalachian Spring* (1944)—and *Lincoln Portrait* (1942), in which a speaker delivered words of Abraham Lincoln over an evocative orchestral background. In these and other works of the period, Copland achieved a deft balance. Blending elements of musical modernism with more old-fashioned ones, he appealed to national pride and won a sizable audience without forfeiting his standing as a serious creative artist. Copland's avuncular public persona, coupled with his position as a spokesman for living composers, led some to see these works not simply as one composer's response to a particular historical moment but a recipe for American composers in the colonial sphere. Even for Copland, however, the folkloric approach proved confining; in the 1950s he returned to writing modernist works. As for other American composers, there were many, Sessions prominent among them, who had little interest in "sounding American" or courting a larger audience but instead accepted their peripheral niche, wrote music exploring modernist idioms, and hoped that performers and listeners would ultimately recognize their quality.

Copland's borrowings from the traditional sphere raise a question about professionally motivated music itself. To reach public forums such as the concert hall, theater, or even the mass media, music must show considerable technical polish. Its performers are presumably expert at what they do, its consumers conditioned to accept nothing less. In the traditional sphere, however, music exists for participation, not consumption. The polishing process, in fact, is foreign to the notion that music of value grows directly out of community life. From this perspective, which gained currency in the 1930s, professional sophistication, tied to the notion of art for art's sake (or perhaps for money's sake), might miss the simple yet profound human truth caught and preserved in folk music. Thus Copland, in borrowing from the traditional sphere, could be seen as seeking not only to widen his music's appeal, but to ground it even more deeply in the human condition.

By the 1930s, partly through the efforts of community members and partly through outsiders (whether working from scholarly or commercial motives), traditional music-making in the United States gained public attention. Because virtually every ethnic group in this nation of immigrants had maintained its own musical traditions in the New World, the range of practices that survived reflected enormous diversity.

The experience of the continent's first inhabitants shows the difficulty of preserving a separate musical heritage from a position of declining cultural power.

By 1890, scholars had begun to collect, both in hand-notated versions and on sound cylinders, music of various American Indian nations, recognizing that government policies and modernization threatened them with extinction. Scholarly study, though able to preserve parts of these traditions, could not stop the destruction of the ways of life from which they had sprung. While Indian nations struggled before and since to maintain their customs and rituals and music's place in them, most Americans have encountered American Indian traditions chiefly as folkloric bases for concert works in the colonial sphere or as formulas—for example, pounding tom-tom rhythms or melodies intended to sound "primitive"—quoted in songs and dances designed for the democratic sphere.

Among ethnic groups immigrating to America, the traditional musics of people of British stock and of African background have been the most influential, though in different ways. The prevalence of the English language in America has promoted the circulation of Anglo-American folklore. Ballads originating in the British Isles were already under study here before 1900. In the 1910s, the English collector Cecil Sharp discovered in the southern Appalachians English songs in versions older than those surviving in Great Britain, undermining an earlier view of the United States as a land without folk music. Sharp's investigations showed the South especially as a repository for a venerable British heritage and a place where indigenous folk music, both vocal and instrumental, had also blossomed. When in the 1920s the commercial music business began to expand into regional and ethnic markets, records made by musicians from southern Anglo-American communities proved economically potent as "hillbilly" music.

As for African Americans, within their own communities music had been a powerful expression of identity through both slavery and Emancipation. Unlike that of the American Indians, however, African music blended readily with European-based styles. Even in the nineteenth century, when they stood at the bottom of America's social ladder, the cultural power of African Americans was already evident in their music, which could not be confined to black communities. The "Negro spiritual"—an Africanized makeover of the Protestant Christian hymn—shows black music's syncretic force in that era; ragtime, blues, jazz, gospel, soul, and to some extent rock 'n' roll are twentieth-century results of a similar process. As already noted, the broad appeal of African American music has often worked against the economic interests of its black creators, who have found it impossible to maintain ownership of an approach to music-making so lively, accessible to audiences, and amenable to commercial exploitation. (The success of Kerry Mills, Irving Berlin, Paul Whiteman, and George Gershwin all testify to this fact.) Traditional African American music shows a volatility, a refusal to stay put—whether in its own culture or in the traditional sphere itself—that makes it seem perpetually poised to cross over into the democratic, or even the colonial sphere, which it has often managed to do without forfeiting its original character.

It was no accident that music in the traditional sphere came prominently to public notice in the 1930s. Several factors contributed: a wave of populist sentiment that appeared when rich and middle-class, as well as poor people, suffered the Depression's effects; government programs like the WPA's Federal Music Project (1935–1941), undertaken as relief measures, but suggesting that all Americans shared a common destiny; a growing acknowledgment of folklore's value as a repository of human experience; a corresponding increase in the collecting of folk music (the Library of Congress's Archive of Folksong was founded in 1928); the commercial music business's production, beginning with "race" and "hillbilly" recordings in the 1920s, of records by musicians from particular social or ethnic groups for members of those groups; and the start of a movement to press folk music into the service of social and political protest. Taken together, such events sparked a recognition of folk music as a valuable, perishable national resource. Its rootedness in the lives of plain people made it, when sung by the likes of Woody Guthrie, a convincing carrier of "truthful" messages that reached beyond the communities of its origin. Music in the traditional sphere gained prestige as it proved not only that it could enrich the colonial sphere but entertain and inspire in the democratic. Perhaps it was partly in that adaptability, and its obvious distance from the elite, that the roots of its later challenge to the colonial sphere's dominance lie.

In the democratic sphere, the years between the wars have been called a "golden age" in which songwriters—Berlin, the Gershwin brothers (Ira Gershwin wrote George's lyrics), Jerome Kern, Richard Rodgers, and Lorenz Hart (later Oscar Hammerstein II), and Cole Porter—created for the Broadway stage a unique body of popular song. Conventional subject-matter and forms prevailed; one practitioner described the trade's chief demand as "learning how to say 'I love you' in thirty-two bars." Nevertheless, a respect for and consciousness of the colonial sphere—its techniques, resources, and cultural position—pervades this repertory, whose musical vocabulary

Jerome Kern. PRINTS AND PHOTOGRAPHS DIVISION, LIBRARY OF CONGRESS

is essentially that of nineteenth-century European romanticism, spiced up harmonically and set in square-cut phrases. Its practitioners honed a special talent for transforming colloquial turns of word and tune into unpretentious art. That art required walking a fine line, avoiding both the high-flown sentiment of operetta and the Tin Pan Alley song's banality. Lorenz Hart staked out the songwriters' turf when he wrote a fellow lyricist: "It is a great pleasure to live at a time when light amusement in this country is at last losing its brutally cretin aspect."

Songs by Rodgers and Hart show the sensibility at work. Hart, a consummate versifier, could turn out hackneyed rhymes when required to do so, as in:

Blue moon,
you saw me standing alone,
without a dream in my heart,
without a love of my own.

But such sentiments, sung to music of comfortable triteness, were not Rodgers and Hart's metier. More often, as Philip Furia has shown, Rodgers set Hart's lyrics to emphasize their internal rhymes, sometimes showing romantic unguardedness, sometimes mocking romance, and sometimes simply reveling in wordplay. In "Little Girl Blue," wedded to Rodgers's tune, Hart's words unfold and drop into place with the precision of a well-made watch, as the aging character sings to herself:

Cole Porter. PRINTS AND PHOTOGRAPHS DIVISION, LIBRARY OF CONGRESS

you may as well surrender,
your hope is getting slender.
Why won't somebody send a
tender
blue boy
to cheer a
little girl blue?

Rodgers claimed that the secret of the team's best songs lay in a clash between "sentimental melody and unsentimental lyrics." But in "I Wish I Were in Love Again," an excessively repeated melodic fragment underscores a sarcastic portrait of love gone sour:

when love congeals
it soon reveals
the faint aroma of performing seals,
the double-crossing of a pair of heels,
I wish I were in love again!

Clearly, Rodgers and Hart were writing popular songs that took literacy, sophistication, and elegance of statement seriously.

By the same token, the career of Edward Kennedy "Duke" Ellington shows changes in jazz that kept traditional African American idioms at the forefront of the democratic sphere while still affirming the prestige of the colonial. Born in Washington, D.C., Ellington began to realize his destiny when, with the help of a white manager, the dance orchestra he led was hired as house band at the Cotton Club in Harlem in December 1927. Here Ellington blossomed as a composer. Required to provide music for floor shows as well as social dancing, he drew on the talents of his sidemen to create a distinctive jazz orchestra sound with a repertory chiefly its own. The Ellington orchestra was heard widely on recordings and radio broadcasts. It won engagements unusual for a black ensemble of the time: serving as pit orchestra for a Broadway show by Gershwin (1929); sharing a New York vaudeville billing with the entertainer Maurice Chevalier (1930); appearing in a Hollywood film with the comedians Amos 'n' Andy (1930); and touring Europe (1933). Projecting a persona of polished dignity, Ellington took well to the public spotlight. By the early 1940s, a remarkable and varied series of recordings had proved him master of the three-minute form available on one side of a ten-inch 78 rpm record, the democratic sphere's standard package. (Some of these pieces, such as *Mood Indigo* and *Sophisticated Lady*, with words added, were made into popular songs.) But such works as *Reminiscing in Tempo* (1935), which filled four record sides, and *Black, Brown, and Beige* (1943), a forty-five-minute epic of African American history premiered by the Ellington orchestra in Carnegie Hall, show Ellington seeking to expand jazz form to symphonic proportions.

As well as a leader with a fertile creative imagination, Ellington's orchestra boasted several outstanding solo improvisers—a mix that enabled Ellington to preserve the spontaneity of jazz in the context of composition. The trajectory of his career to the mid-1940s, for all his success in the democratic sphere, tended toward the colonial: toward longer pieces, references to the techniques and forms of art music, à la Gershwin (for example, in *Concerto for Cootie*, *Symphony in Black*, and *Fugue-a-ditty*, the latter written with collaborator Billy Strayhorn), and concert appearances. This is not to say, however, that all jazz musicians showed similar tendencies. From the mid-1930s until the early years of the World War II, a jazz-based style called swing, played chiefly by such "big bands" as the ones led by white clarinetist Benny

Goodman and white trombonists Tommy Dorsey and Glenn Miller, dominated the democratic sphere, proving the most popular music of "the swing era." Goodman himself felt somewhat constrained by the limits popular success imposed, commissioning clarinet works from such classical composers as Béla Bartók (1938) and Copland (1950) and featuring his jazz orchestra in a historic Carnegie Hall concert as early as 1938. But dance numbers with a solid beat, performed live for dancing or in theaters, and recorded for home and jukebox play, remained his and other big bands' stock-in-trade, continuing the democratic sphere's reliance on African American music for artistic vitality and commercial clout.

## MUSICAL DIVERSITY RECOGNIZED, 1946–1965

America's financial and cultural investment in the colonial sphere continued unflaggingly in the years after World War II. Many of the West's leading musicians, including Schoenberg, Stravinsky, Bartók, and Paul Hindemith, had settled in the United States as a result of the war's dislocations. American-born performers joined the ranks of opera troupes and concertizing artists—for example, the soprano Eleanor Steber, the baritone Leonard Warren, the conductor-composer Leonard Bernstein, the pianist William Kappell—not to mention symphony players. Evidence of serious participation in the colonial sphere can be seen both in this country's active concert life and the network of schools serving it. From conservatories such as the Juilliard School in New York and the Curtis Institute in Philadelphia to the colleges and universities that expanded their music programs as military veterans ready for further schooling returned to civilian life, Americans who sought more knowledge of this European-based art, or the skills they needed to make it, could find places to acquire them. This development took place in the spirit of democratic access; and the same spirit pervaded the music programs of one of the most self-consciously democratic of American institutions: the public school.

In the belief that music instruction enriched children's lives, American schools, as part of their curriculum, offered classes featuring group singing and listening to classical music recordings. In many parts of the country, from the 1920s on, they also provided free instrumental lessons (using instruments bought by the school and loaned out to students) and experience playing in bands and orchestras. This activity was carried on in the name of, and justified by faith in, the edifying power of education. Even if few students pursued musical careers, the philosophy held, those receiving school instruction would gain the discipline of learning new skills, the pleasure of aesthetically rewarding group endeavor, and respect for music as an art. Public school music programs were idealistic, practical, and hierarchical. Advocating the precepts of the colonial sphere, their leaders believed in musical transcendence and worked to increase opportunities for Americans to share in its fruits. They trusted that such musical experience, whether as performer, listener, or both, would have a broadening, civilizing effect upon participants.

But students were not the only beneficiaries of Americans' willingness to support school music instruction. Teachers benefited too. In a nation whose government offered no direct patronage for music, teaching remained an effective means of subsidizing unremunerative musical activity. That pattern became especially apparent in colleges and universities after World War II.

Music programs at tax-supported public institutions such as Indiana University, the Universities of Michigan and Illinois, and North Texas State University reflect Tocqueville's dictum that democracies cultivate the arts "after their own fashion." Founded and funded in the name of education, professional schools like these offered—together with instruction in the liberal arts—specialized courses for aspiring performers, composers, teachers, and writers on music. Their colonial pedigree was attested by their curricula; students studied the history and theory of Western art music and received intensive performance instruction, chiefly in its repertory. The schools met public accountability by granting degrees, placing graduates in professional posts, and mounting public performances: concerts for orchestras and choirs, chamber music, recitals by faculty and students alike, even operas. They also sponsored music-making of a more democratic cast, with school bands playing at athletic contests and glee clubs performing nostalgic college songs—an American college tradition begun in the nineteenth century. Behind this activity, many faculty members—like scientists and scholars in other university departments—maintained careers as performers, writers, and composers: subsidized by taxpayers, in effect, to expand, replenish, renew, and preserve music and musical knowledge in the colonial sphere.

Many composers took teaching positions in American colleges and universities after World War II. In an academic environment, it seemed natural to treat music both as a performing art and an endeavor inviting research. This research could be conducted not only by scholars but creative artists: by composers free to explore the nature of sound and to seek new ways of organizing, presenting, even inventing it—through electronic means, for example. Such activity reflected a notion that some composers in the colonial sphere had come to accept: that the reluctance of many performers and audience members to take seriously music composed in new idioms revealed their superficiality, and that therefore, the recent rupture between living composer and general audience had become a permanent condition.

During the 1950s, then, with such composers as Sessions at Princeton and Berkeley, Walter Piston at Harvard, William Schuman at Juilliard, Howard Hanson at Eastman-Rochester, Ross Lee Finney at Michigan, and Milton Babbitt at Princeton, schools took on the education of young American composers, most of them seemingly ready to write in dissonant chromatic idioms. In a time of growth for higher education, and with transcendence and research as ideological supports, composers won for themselves a high degree of autonomy: the freedom to pursue composition as research, the right to judge each other's work and to participate in the awarding of grants, prizes, and positions, independent of the views of other musicians or audience approval. A gap widened between living composers' role and their place in American musical life: as the heirs of Beethoven, they filled an indispensable role; but the place their compositions occupied in the country's, and even the university's musical life remained small. Writing in an idiom that demanded attentive, experienced listeners—to grasp Babbitt's musical discourse, he admitted, one should know the music of Schoenberg and Anton Webern—these composers and their students lived in an environment that encouraged the composition of music but paid little heed to its reception. Despite the predictions of Schoenberg (a teacher by trade), who saw his work as the logical next step in an evolutionary "emancipation of the dissonance" spanning several centuries of Western music, the idioms he inspired remain on the fringe of concert culture. Even at century's end—while it had earned respect as one suitable response, grounded in the history of the colonial sphere, to the realities of twentieth-century life—little of this music had been integrated into its performing branches, except for groups specializing in new music.

Recognition began to dawn after World War II that more than one American composer had explored the colonial sphere in ways not dependent on borrowing from the democratic or the traditional—ways,

John Cage, American composer. NEW YORK PUBLIC LIBRARY FOR THE PERFORMING ARTS

in fact, that questioned the colonial sphere's very existence, not to mention the idea of a hierarchy. By 1960, the critic Peter Yates was writing about an "American experimental tradition" of composers operating from independent, refracted views of the European orbit, who had rejected or perhaps failed to receive certain messages and techniques that had fueled the colonial sphere. Ives stood as the spiritual godfather and pioneering leader of this tradition. The arch-eclecticist Henry Cowell, whose piano recitals even before 1920 had featured fists, elbows, and string-strumming, was an active protagonist. Harry Partch—a hobo during parts of the 1930s and 1940s and a self-taught composer—invented, to accompany his own vocal chanting, instruments dividing the octave into as many as forty-three pitches instead of the usual twelve. But the New World composer who mounted the most radical challenge of all was John Cage.

The California-born Cage traced his approach to composition partly to an incapacity: he discovered as a student—Cage took counterpoint lessons with Schoenberg in the mid-1930s—that he had no feeling for standard harmony. Consequently, from early in Cage's life as a composer, he emphasized rhythm ("duration"). In the 1930s, he became involved with a dance troupe, and from that time on composed extensively for dance and theatrical settings. He also showed an early fondness for percussion instruments; a prewar innovation was the "prepared piano," in essence a new member of the percussion family with sounds determined by the insertion of screws, nails, pencils, erasers, and other objects between a conventional piano's strings. After the war, Cage also explored the use of prerecorded sounds, microphones to distort and alter natural sounds, and electronically synthesized sounds. A key moment in Cage's composing career occurred when he entered a supposedly soundproof anechoic chamber and heard two sounds. The high one, he learned, was his nervous system in operation, the lower his circulatory system. The experience taught Cage that there was no such thing as silence; there were only intentional and nonintentional sounds.

Cage began in the early 1950s to apply to his compositions what he had learned by studying Eastern philosophies and Japanese Zen Buddhism. He wrote his last "intentionally expressive" works in 1951. As he explained later (1966): "I had been taught in the schools that art was a question of communication. I observed that all of the composers were writing differently. If art was communication, we were using different languages. We were, therefore, in a Tower of Babel situation where no one understood anyone else." Against that background, Cage discovered in early texts from both East and West a reason to compose music he found better than either expressiveness or communication: "to quiet the mind thus making it susceptible to divine influences." In that spirit, Cage exercised his craft as a composer from the early 1950s on to reduce drastically the role of intended sounds in his music—to "let sounds be themselves," as he put it, and to encourage listeners to treat their environment, whatever it might be, as "music." Cage composed, in other words, to address a listener with "a sober and quiet mind" in which "the ego does not obstruct the fluency of the things that come into our senses and up through our dreams." Accordingly, he once named as favorite among his many compositions, *4′33″* (1952), a three-movement work that, because the performer remains silent, depends entirely upon sounds present in the hall during its performance. (In a public lecture of 1992, Cage explained to a group of music students that he continued to compose only because other people asked him to. He had no need of more new compositions himself, being content simply to listen to the sounds he could hear inside and outside the building where he lived on New York City's Sixth Avenue.)

Few performers of the postwar years paid Cage or the American experimental tradition much attention. But its presence broadened the range of stylistic options open to the new generation of American composers that came of age in the 1960s.

African American tradition stands behind the democratic sphere's most artistically demanding developments of the period. At mid-century, several jazz styles coexisted, all being performed and refined by some of their original creators. Older New Orleans–based jazz, rooted in the 1910s and 1920s, could be heard from Louis Armstrong, once an innovative trumpet player and now a famous American entertainer, or from "Dixieland" revival combos, mostly white. Larger orchestras, led by Ellington, the pianist William "Count" Basie, the white clarinetist Woodrow "Woody" Herman, and many others, continued to record and tour, playing both dances and concerts, and updating swing era styles. And in the mid-1940s, a new, consciously avant-garde style dubbed bebop came to the fore in New York, pioneered especially by the alto saxophonist Charlie "Bird" Parker, the trumpeter John Birks "Dizzy" Gillespie, and the drummer Kenny Clarke.

Bebop was chiefly an improvising solo instrumentalist's art, though singers like Sarah Vaughan and Betty Carter possessed the ear and technique to master its formidable demands. Rooted in a rhythmic conception in which players felt not quarter-note but eighth-note divisions of the beat, freely accenting any one (or more) of these divisions, bebop also encouraged players to invent asymmetrical phrases that cut across the foursquare structure of the tunes they performed. Heard in jazz clubs and increasingly in concerts, bebop was dance-based music aimed more at listeners than dancers. Its repertory mixed blues, songs from Broadway and Tin Pan Alley, and numbers composed by the performers themselves, some exploring harmonic twists new to jazz. Bebop carried with it an iconoclastic aesthetic that proclaimed jazz musicians as artists, not entertainers, possessing a "hip" view of society that rejected conventional values and cultivated its own language, manner of dress, and habits of living—including alcohol and drug use by many musicians who claimed such stimuli fed the imagination. Parker, the mythic figure of bebop, possessed a prodigiously inventive, orderly musical mind. His playing, firmly rooted in traditional African American blues, maintained a powerful, swinging impetus that seemed to sum up earlier jazz styles while also "signifying on" and extending them. And in Parker's work, and that of other jazz modernists of his generation, one could hear reverberations of a historical sense akin to that of twentieth-century music in the colonial sphere.

Jazz was the first music in the democratic sphere

Dizzy Gillespie. Photograph by Carl Van Vechten, 2 December 1955. PRINTS AND PHOTOGRAPHS DIVISION, LIBRARY OF CONGRESS

regardless of public response. (For jazz musicians of the time, however, performing remained the sole source of musical income.)

In churches and dance halls, other African American musicians proved more willing than jazz performers to privilege functional demands over aesthetic independence. It had long been the custom in black Pentecostal churches to cultivate, through preaching, praying, singing, and congregational response, an atmosphere of collective ecstasy. In the postwar era, this facet of the African American traditional sphere began to make its way into the democratic through broadcasts, recordings, and concert appearances of "gospel" musicians. When such singers as Mahalia Jackson or Marion Williams performed outside the church, what Stanley Crouch has called

Sarah Vaughan. PRINTS AND PHOTOGRAPHS DIVISION, LIBRARY OF CONGRESS

to become the subject of regular critical discourse. In journals devoted entirely to jazz—*Down Beat* (1934– ) was the most prominent, *The Jazz Review* (1958–1961) the most intellectually ambitious—as well as a few newspapers and journals of cultural commentary or literary criticism, one could read about recordings, concerts, and possible trends in jazz, while keeping up with recent books and discographies. One result was that jazz innovations—Miles Davis and "the birth of the cool," Art Blakey and the coming of "hard bop," and Ornette Coleman and the discovery of "free jazz"—now took place in an arena of public discussion and debate, unlike earlier landmark events, such as the beginnings of bebop itself. Hence, new jazz of the postwar era, while black in its cultural roots, shared with the colonial sphere a reliance upon dedicated, open-eared listeners, keen historical awareness, and a determination to pursue whatever artistic course its musicians chose, "the molten nobility of Negro religious emotion" was made manifest even to secular ears. As for the dance hall, perhaps saxophonist and bandleader Louis Jordan was the last black jazz musician whose musical appeal encompassed both aesthetically and functionally inspired members of the African American audience. In the 1930s and early 1940s, Jordan led groups specializing in blues-based performances that Basie's, or even Parker's fans might have appreciated. But by the late 1940s, Jordan and others were emphasizing simpler elements of his earlier style in a repetitive, beat-based, mesmerizing approach that music business functionaries dubbed "rhythm and blues" (formerly "race" records, that is, recordings aimed at black audiences). It was from that development that rock 'n' roll, the dominant democratic style of the century's second half, was born.

The story of rock 'n' roll's beginnings falls into the category of oft-told tales. From the perspective of its being a one-of-a-kind hymn to American populism, triumphant elements abound. The winning combination was produced by a fusion of southern white (country music) and northern black (rhythm and blues). Key figures include a white Mississippi-born truck driver who "sang black" (Elvis Presley) and a black Missouri-raised singer who sometimes sounded white (Chuck Berry). The corporate music business, which had long controlled the democratic sphere's production and distribution from New York and Hollywood, was caught unaware by rock 'n' roll's sudden popularity, and new producers and distributors sprang up elsewhere, especially in Memphis. Sexuality, long suppressed or veiled in commercial popular music, was thrust into prominence by the music's openly pelvic beat. White youngsters, never before the beneficiaries of a music addressed to the circumstances of their lives, now had one; and, rather than being a genteel brand of expression, rock 'n' roll (and its young consumers) seemed to glory in its lower-class origins. Finally, rock 'n' roll was quintessentially American, owing little to European antecedents or the colonial sphere—whose prestige, however, still stood high enough in 1956 for Chuck Berry to sing "Roll over, Beethoven, and tell Tchaikovsky the news." Rock 'n' roll, aggressively marketed through mass media, included the message that big money could be made in the "generation gap" between parents and their offspring.

The democratic sphere into which rock 'n' roll burst in the mid-1950s maintained in most of its popular styles a dependency upon the colonial sphere—not of the twentieth century but the nineteenth. Broadway shows put new emphasis on the

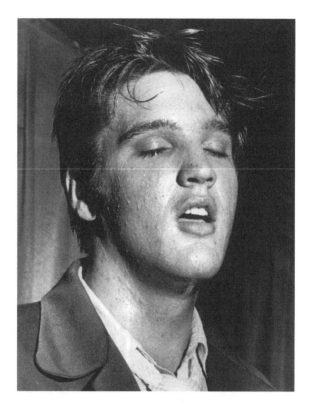

Elvis Presley. Photo by Bob Moreland, 1957. PRINTS AND PHOTOGRAPHS DIVISION, LIBRARY OF CONGRESS

operatic practice of having songs emerge from the story. Richard Rodgers, now working with Oscar Hammerstein II, helped to lead this trend with the highly successful *Oklahoma!* (1943). Critic Martin Williams has dramatized that show's impact by noting that on the night of its premiere, "a singer-actor, eventually revealed as dressed in a cowboy outfit, began [the show] by the offstage singing of a Neapolitan-style waltz . . . ['Oh! What a Beautiful Morning'] . . . and journalists were soon announcing that a 'real' American musical theater piece had finally arrived." This wry assessment confirms that, although the makers of Broadway musicals tinkered with earlier formulas, their composers broke no new musical or dramatic ground. Such hit shows as Berlin's *Annie, Get Your Gun* (1946), Rodgers and Hammerstein's *South Pacific* (1949) and *The Sound of Music* (1959), and Lerner and Loewe's *My Fair Lady* (1956), all maintained the musical habits of an earlier age; and even Leonard Bernstein and Stephen Sondheim's *West Side Story* (1957), with its jazz- and Latin-tinged score, owed much of its proclaimed innovativeness to standard opera dramaturgy.

Elsewhere in the democratic sphere, materials

Broadway musical. Scene from *Annie, Get Your Gun,* by Irving Berlin, 1946. ARCHIVE PHOTOS

and techniques from the colonial sphere were being recycled and recombined in search of tempered novelty. New popular songs maintained the styles of the previous generation. String sections were added to swing bands for richer accompaniment as new "high fidelity" recording techniques emphasized sound quality. Conductor-arranger Mantovani launched a long, commercially successful career playing popular songs in lush string-orchestra arrangements, and actress-singer Judy Garland won a devoted following singing these songs with near-operatic emotional intensity. In the meantime, a booming new branch of the democratic sphere—so-called country music—took shape in Nashville in the postwar years. Its roots lay chiefly in the traditional sphere: in the Appalachian string band, Anglo-American "hillbilly" music of an earlier age, and the blues-tinged songs of Jimmie Rodgers. Nashville radio station WSM helped to establish country music's identity, beginning in the mid-1920s, through weekly broadcasts of a show named after a more prestigious genre: "Grand Old Opry." The name caught both the musicians' consciousness of their humble place in the musical hierarchy and their commitment to old-fashioned styles and values. In the hands of an artist like Hank Williams, however, who sang in a strained voice songs touched by Tin Pan Alley sophistication, country music could pack an emotional wallop that enabled it to reach far beyond a local, or even a southern audience.

Country music shows music from the Anglo-American traditional sphere being tailored for commercial appeal in a regional market. Given a different tailoring, the same tradition, self-consciously preserved and presented with an anticommercial aura, proved successful elsewhere in the democratic sphere.

As noted above, in prewar years, guitar- and banjo-playing singers like Woody Guthrie and Pete Seeger had used traditional Anglo-American songs, or new songs composed in that style, to convey political messages as well as to entertain. After the war, such songs and styles, perceived as authentic because of their origins and modes of performance, won a large following, especially among northern college students, who preferred them to the popular songs of Tin Pan Alley and Broadway. ("Goodnight, Irene," a waltz recorded in 1950 by Seeger and the politically based folk group, the Weavers, sold two million copies.) Dressed in informal garb, playing unamplified instruments, and encouraging their audiences in coffee houses and at folk festivals to join in the singing, "urban folk" musicians cultivated an atmosphere of principled, if anachronistic collectivity. Younger ones, such as Joan Baez, who first featured Elizabethan ballads, and Bob Dylan, who, like Guthrie,

detailed social hypocrisy, expanded the democratic sphere's reach while taking an outsider's posture. From that viewpoint, rock 'n' roll seemed a commercial style calculated to separate teenagers from their money. And so, from the folk-music perspective, it remained, at least until the mid-1960s. When Bob Dylan in the summer of 1965 performed at the Newport Folk Festival with an electric guitar, backed by an amplified blues band, he not only angered folk fans but proclaimed that a new era of American music history had begun.

## A NEW HIERARCHY APPEARS, 1965–1993

In the cultural upheaval that during the 1960s saw rebellions by black Americans over race and by others, especially younger Americans, over the United States' involvement in an Asian war, rock 'n' roll, the music of teenage independence, came of age as

Woody Guthrie and Burl Ives rest in New York's Central Park before a radio appearance in 1940. PRINTS AND PHOTOGRAPHS DIVISION, LIBRARY OF CONGRESS

"rock," a music with a social conscience. As performed by Dylan, the Byrds, and the English groups the Beatles and the Rolling Stones, rock was a vocal music that defined itself through opposition to society's norms and values. Open distrust of authority—the government, the educational establishment, indeed "anyone over thirty," as a slogan of the day went—pervaded its messages. Rock songs, written by singers and players close in age to most of their listeners, offered a morally unambiguous perspective on the issues that divided society and that young Americans faced in their own lives. A convention of many early rock songs is that the musicians represent "the people," who carry a democratic vision of social change (they want peace, freedom, and racial justice), against their leaders, who preserve an elite position by opting for war, tyranny, and the status quo. Another rock convention, this one new to popular music, is that the performers' position carried a certain risk. The words they sang condemned authorities who presumably had the power to retaliate, and their public persona was provocative, rebellious, and topped off with clothing and hair styles calculated to offend common sensibilities. The music of their songs, novel in sound and often reaching toward the ecstatic, showed disrespect for the proprieties of music making in the democratic and colonial spheres, as had rock 'n' roll. And the music was easily understood.

Rock, which appealed chiefly to white Americans, claimed roots in rhythm and blues, relying on aggressively accented beats, usually in four-four time, played by guitars, keyboard, and a drummer. Vocal styles varied. The Beatles, sparked by the inventive melodies of John Lennon and Paul McCartney, sang their songs as earlier pop stars like Bing Crosby and Frank Sinatra had done, though in a higher register and with a much lighter voice quality. But Dylan, rather than singing, declaimed his texts in a rough timbre, his voice falling away from notes as if from world-weariness or disaffection, and other performers sometimes shouted or even screamed their words. Electronics played a key role in dissemination and performance. Recordings, formerly a means of securing lucrative concert engagements for popular artists, became rock musicians' chief money-making device and definitive performance format. (In live appearances some groups mimed their hit records.) Rock's embrace by the mass media made it immensely profitable, which in turn gave musicians access to the best recording studio technology. Standards of production were high. Consumers could buy recordings in handy packages: long-playing disc,

cassette tape, and, by the 1980s, compact disc. Radio stations, many specializing in one or more of rock's subgenres, gave repeated "airplay" to favorite selections, thus promoting record sales. In performance, instruments and voice were hugely amplified. Bass lines were "cranked up" so that their reverberations could be felt as well as heard. Rock fans took pride in the quality and voltage of their playback sound systems, whether at home or installed in their cars. High volume enhanced listeners' excitement.

Rock's adversarial stance—its power to catch, dramatize, and reflect upon moods of defiance and skepticism—won it wide attention in print. The periodical *Rolling Stone* (1967– ) was one of many journals celebrating the countercultural spirit. A new breed, the rock critic, though seldom writing from a knowledge of music, helped to form historical consciousness in musicians and fans through reviews, articles, and books. Rock's eclecticism provided one important historical narrative. Subgenres abounded: hard rock, soft rock, folk rock, art rock, rockabilly, heavy metal, jazz rock, acid rock, and others. All maintained common elements of rhythm and sound while expanding the style and the audience; and most, as writers explained, involved borrowings from the traditional or the democratic spheres. Stars' battles against complacency provided another historical narrative. Success had proved both goal and enemy for rock musicians. The example of such stars as Jim Morrison of the Doors, Janis Joplin of Big Brother and the Holding Company, and guitarist Jimi Hendrix, all of whom lived hard, behaved outrageously onstage, and died young, epitomized rock's demonic side. But those who succeeded and survived, like Elvis Presley, who harked back to rock 'n' roll days, grew so rich and reclusive that they risked losing the critical edge that had energized them in the first place. Thus, a development like punk rock—a mid-1970s genre in which inexpert but passionate performers gave a radically nihilistic view of society—was understood as an attempt to purge rock of greed and excessive professionalism and return it to the cutting edge, the only place for a true rock musician to be.

What made rock different from its mass-market predecessors was that it won intellectual respectability, doing so by rejecting, even flaunting the colonial sphere's customs and styles. Rock found little to use in the colonial sphere, except perhaps its critical posture. (Modern music, after all, had offered a sharp critique of both romanticism and modern society.) But whether or not rock musicians owed anything to modernism's critique, they presented theirs in a way that made the latter seem arcane, substituting repetitiousness for antiredundancy, "natural" declamation for classical singing, vernacular for cultivated diction, attention-grabbing costume for formal dress, electric for acoustic instruments, simple for complex harmonies, pulsating for irregular rhythms, and mass media distribution for a "new-music" concert ambience. (In fact, the "minimalist" music of a composer with a colonial pedigree like Philip Glass shares certain traits of rock—repetitiousness, electronic emphasis, simple harmonies, and pulsating rhythms— which helps to explain why it has won a substantial audience.) This is not to say that rock and classical musicians carried the same messages. But from the standpoint of some members of their audience, rock musicians had moved into "serious" territory formerly occupied by musicians in the colonial sphere. By the 1980s, sporting a history that featured its own pantheon of "classic" artists and works (the latter preserved on record), rock advocates were claiming the colonial ideal of transcendence for their own. Divorced from elite connotations and linked through its sources to both the traditional sphere's preservation of "natural," unpolished music-making and the democratic sphere's accessibility, rock's brand of transcendence proved convincing to many who a generation earlier might have sought such experience in the colonial sphere, or possibly in jazz.

It is a mark of Western art music's secure place in the nation's culture that when, with the founding of the National Endowment for the Arts (1965), the federal government began to dispense patronage, institutions devoted to that music's performance— like the Metropolitan Opera Company and leading symphony orchestras—were among its chief recipients. By the 1970s, due in part to economic inflation, the proportion of income that even well established performing organizations could realize from ticket revenues was declining. Deficits came to be expected; money from the government, corporations, and private donors had to be raised to meet them. But the values of transcendence, of the timelessness and power of great music, remained intact in the colonial sphere's concert life, justifying patronage as they have for more than a century. The motto *ars longa; vita brevis* (art is long; life is short) still sanctions the authority of star performers such as Jessye Norman, Yo-Yo Ma, and the Boston Symphony Orchestra (founded 1881): modern carriers of a time-honored tradition. Except that the audience seems older, colonial concert life has changed little in recent years. The repertory, while admitting more twentieth-century works, remains centered on music from the European past.

The most spirited challenge to concert hall customs has come not from living composers but performers with a new approach to older music. Beginning in Europe and taking root in the United States by the 1970s, the "early music revival" denounced as complacent the notion of the standard repertory's timelessness. Its advocates held that musicians should strive to locate the music they perform in time— specifically the time of its composition. The use of period musical instruments has provided one way to test received performance traditions, historical research another. Through these means, performers and scholars have been able to apply historically grounded performance conventions to music from the fifteenth to the nineteenth centuries. Early music advocates grant that no complete code of performing practices can be resurrected for earlier ages. Yet they believe that the orderliness of their approach has the effect not of constraining but of freeing performers' imagination, helping them capture some of the excitement and surprise that greeted older music when it was new. One outcome of their work has been a shrinking of the standard repertory's chronological span, fostered by a growing if not universal sense that music before 1750 is best left to specialist performers.

By some criteria, the place of the American composer in the colonial sphere's chief performing institutions seems secure as the century's end approaches. Employment for composers as teachers in higher education is available; private foundations, other granting agencies, and the government provide financial support for composers; ensembles specializing in new music offer the chance for performances and recordings. To be sure, there are more competent composers than there are jobs, grants, and performance opportunities, so competition among colleagues is keen. But while Americans generally believe that competition can measure quality, meaningful competition can take place only among comparable entities; and the styles of American composers today are so diverse that it is hard to find a basis for comparing them. At one end of the gamut stand Babbitt's systematic serial permutations, at the other Cage's exploration of unintended sounds. To summarize what lies between would take a very long list; to judge the value of individual styles and works would require a weighing of their premises— whether to explore, experiment, express, communicate, or quiet the mind.

Who is qualified to make such judgments? One critic or historian might describe such diversity as a musical consumer's paradise, the reward of hard-won freedom; another might deem it the decadent outcome of relativism. ("If they can't decide what's good themselves, what does 'quality' mean?") Performers' judgments, based perhaps on their friendships with composers, subsidies available to them, or their strengths and weaknesses of technique, are hardly more reliable. As for audiences, they seem already to have made their judgments. The consensus of the larger public is that, for all its prestigious legacy and financially protected status, the colonial sphere lacks the clear sense of purpose that would qualify it to speak to and for most present-day Americans. And the smaller audience for "new music" reflects the fissiparousness found elsewhere in the colonial sphere. Ultimately, therefore, composers will decide. Pieces of music define the historical moment more precisely than words can; and it is musical works themselves, by the use they make or do not make of earlier works, that render the most telling judgments.

The diffuseness of the colonial sphere's creative branch has surely helped undermine its place at the top of the American musical hierarchy. As recently as the postwar years, music still seemed an art whose essence was periodically reassessed and redefined by great composers. Schoenberg and Stravinsky were seen as filling that role for the century's first half, providing fresh direction for composers to follow. The experience of listening to music by them reveals their connections (or deliberate avoidance of connections) to Wagner, Beethoven, and earlier composers. Since the 1960s, however, no such consummate musical syntheses have seemed possible. How, in ways accessible to listeners, do Elliott Carter, George Crumb, Steve Reich, William Bolcom, Charles Dodge, and Christopher Rouse—living American composers in the colonial sphere—connect with their predecessors Schoenberg and Stravinsky, and with each other? The answer proves elusive. Connections and disjunctions abound with all of these composers, of course, but in ways revealing each as a free agent cutting a separate deal with tradition, rather than a contributor bound to a common enterprise. And that revelation proves in turn a reminder that common enterprises confer prestige on their participants as well as claiming it for themselves.

To say there are no Schoenbergs today confirms the point. Although comparatively few listeners have relished the music he wrote after abandoning the major-minor system, those works nevertheless project a vision of their creator as a pioneer carrying the art of music into new territory. They sustain the image of the composer as hero: an uncompromising artist who, through inspiration, knowledge, and strength of will, strives to embrace as a whole the

things about music that matter most. As long as composers believed in the integrity and scope of such syntheses, they had good reason to follow Schoenberg's example. But in the 1960s, as elite culture's superior position eroded, confidence in syntheses like Schoenberg's waned, as did faith in the colonial sphere as a locus for transcendence. For by modernism's values, transcendence has seemed more within reach for an artist seeking a grand synthesis than one working from a postmodern menu of diverse styles.

Something roughly parallel took place in jazz. By the 1960s, having splintered into many styles, jazz had won artistic respectability but lost much of its audience. As rock 'n' roll, rhythm and blues, and later rock—all based on a rhythmic impulse akin to jazz—took over the democratic sphere, work for jazz musicians in clubs and other entertainment venues dried up. Masters like Armstrong, Ellington, Basie, and Goodman performed into old age, revered figures keeping earlier styles alive into the 1970s and 1980s. Meanwhile, in the 1960s three jazz musicians, all black and all accomplished players of bebop, were recognized as having made their own transcendent reassessments: Thelonious Monk, John Coltrane, and Miles Davis. Monk, a pianist and composer, forged an astringent, elliptical style contradicting the notion that bop depended upon florid virtuosity. Relying on silences, novel note-choices, and a touch that rang, not rippled, Monk produced a sound unmistakably his own and explored jazz as an art of concentration, compression, and irony. Saxophonist Coltrane, a technician of near-demonic command and stamina, went in the opposite direction. Extending jazz virtuosity and improvising at greater length than anyone before him, Coltrane took a spiritual turn in his later years that invested his playing with an aura of hortatory gravity. Davis, trumpeter and preeminent jazz combo leader, sparked several heralded spin-offs from a bebop base—not only "cool" but "modal" (1959) and "fusion" (1969), the latter marked by albums made with rock musicians—without losing the distinctive approach and sound that made him instantly recognizable as "Miles." He sustained a reputation as a strong individualist, willing to reach even into the mass market as a way to avoid repeating himself.

By the 1980s, jazz had won a position in American musical life parallel in some ways to that of the colonial sphere: respected as an important art form; taught in school, college, and university programs; heard chiefly in concert settings; and supported by patronage and grants. Like those in the colonial sphere, jazz musicians now discuss weighty issues in public: whether, for example, any one musician or style can encompass the whole of the music today, or which styles show the most promise for future development. Trumpeter Wynton Marsalis has criticized the eclecticism that has resulted from borrowings outside the African American traditional sphere, especially in the cases of avant-garde jazz, "free jazz," and "fusion." In his own playing Marsalis has sought to summarize and extend a clearly defined jazz tradition rooted in the work of earlier greats, from Morton and Armstrong on. Whether a music with such an unschooled history will bend to the influence of an approach like his remains to be seen.

Recent developments in other genres of American music in the democratic sphere might have surprised postwar observers. Broadway is no longer a factor in the mass marketplace. The musicals of Stephen Sondheim—*Sunday in the Park with George* (1984) won the Pulitzer Prize for drama in 1985—show a professional sophistication and polish worthy of Cole Porter (who also wrote both words and music), but their audiences are relatively small. Indeed, the high cost of producing a show on Broadway has drastically reduced the number of new ones. Country music, still based in Nashville and still wedded to musical simplicity and themes of family, hard work, and disappointed love, enjoys a huge audience. (As country songwriter Bob McDill has put it: "You have to learn to do big things with little words.") Performers like Willie Nelson and Dolly Parton are national entertainment personalities who began as country singers. Within the black democratic styles upon which mainstream pop has drawn throughout the century, Ray Charles, James Brown and Aretha Franklin are seminal figures whose ecstatic approach derives from their early experiences singing gospel music in church. Rock, whose death has often been proclaimed, survives in the music of Bruce Springsteen, among others. And pop music, founded on a rock base, is widely understood as a major culture industry of the United States, with top stars like Michael Jackson and Madonna, each the apex of a huge marketing and publicity enterprise, among the most famous people in the world.

At this writing, a democratic style much in the public spotlight is rap—not surprisingly another borrowing from the African American traditional sphere. Rap depends on verbal and rhythmic "signifying": improvising rhyming words over a rhythmic accompaniment. Because rap, being declaimed and not sung, is without melody, some observers have questioned whether it deserves to be called music. But the virtuosity of rappers, who perform their incantatory

Michael Jackson. ARCHIVE PHOTOS/EXPRESS NEWSPAPER

truth-telling in rhythm and rhyme, is beyond doubt; and their commercialization has brought into the democratic arena authentic messages drawn from the lives of inner-city blacks, one of the most oppressed groups among all American citizens.

Elsewhere in the traditional sphere, most ethnic musics from Europe have by this time been assimilated or commercialized. Native American traditions still struggle to maintain themselves. Asian Americans and other groups of non-English speakers continue to bring their music-making to the United States. In regions where Hispanic Americans have settled in large numbers—New York City, Texas, Southern California, South Florida—they have preserved older traditions and formed new ones, including some of wide commercial appeal. In the midst of all these ethnic and community practices, the democratic world of pop stands poised, ready to promote any synthesis to which these "new" sounds might contribute, especially if it shows signs of turning a profit.

Madonna. ARCHIVE PHOTOS/FOTOS INTERNATIONAL

One such synthesis is a brand of dance music, developed in New York City in the 1950s and 1960s by musicians of Hispanic background, that in the 1970s began to be called "salsa." The word, which literally means "sauce," implies rhythmic vitality in something of the way that "swing" did in earlier jazz. Salsa boasts a diverse pedigree. Its origins are Cuban, but its musicians have borrowed elements from Puerto Rico and South America as well; it relies upon Latin rhythms played by conga and bongo drums plus other percussion instruments, overlaid with voices, trumpets (or trombones), and piano; and its harmonic language, styles of improvisation, and sound quality show the influence of jazz. In fact, salsa's syncretic character invites a consideration of its public. Created within Spanish-speaking communities, where it has provided the traditional sphere's expected cultural continuity, salsa has also managed to enjoy a certain amount of musical innovation without alienating its original audience. The unsuccessful efforts of some earlier salsa musicians to broaden that audience seemed ample testimony to the Latin community's position as an ethnic ghetto.

In 1984, however, singer/songwriter Rubén Blades won a recording contract with a major American company—the first salsa artist to do so. Since that time, he and others have claimed for salsa a place in the English-speaking democratic sphere, while also giving members of the Hispanic audience who are tuned into mainstream Anglo values and styles a popular music still rooted in their own culture.

As the century nears its end, music in American schools reflects a rearranged hierarchy. When the colonial sphere began losing prestige, school music programs forestalled charges of elitism and exclusiveness by incorporating more democratic variety, including jazz bands and gospel and show choirs; and general music classes broadened their listening exercises beyond the classics. As a result, many youngsters receive little or no exposure to music outside the democratic sphere. At the college and university level, some schools now offer, together with customary programs in the colonial sphere, preprofessional training in such genres as jazz and Broadway musical theater performance. It would seem that an academic environment in which so many different kinds of music are taught would be ideal for sorting out the positions of each, weighing their claims to artistic merit, and reflecting upon the conventions and values that unite and divide them. Perhaps, with the help of scholars, such winnowing is now taking place, though few musicians are inclined to view dispassionately the value of what they do.

A final thought, attesting the impact of music on American life, is that rock music's popularization of the metaphor of the principled opposer has proved the most successful cultural convention of the age. After rock's early days, musicians, promoters, and eventually even people outside music with a message to sell (advertisers and politicians) discovered that one did not need to hold radical political beliefs to borrow the anti-elite stance rock musicians had constructed. The rock sound, beat, and vocal style evoke the existence of an "other," a champion of outworn values, dividing listeners into friends and opponents. Where such opponents are perceived to lurk, advocates can unite around a cause more urgent than even friendship or consumption. To take just one example, "contemporary Christian" musicians, by setting sacred messages in a rock-influenced style, won from young listeners an allegiance all the more fervent for knowledge that some who shared the doctrine would bridle at the mode of its delivery. In other words, by performing in such a style, hence appearing to take a stand against elitism and outworn social values, a musician can claim both principle and wealth. In an environment where such claims are honored, it is not surprising that earning power, fame, and a high place in the hierarchy are widely believed to go together.

SEE ALSO Patronage of the Arts; The Mass Media and Popular Culture; African American Cultural Movements (all in this volume).

## BIBLIOGRAPHY

Gilbert Chase, *America's Music: From the Pilgrims to the Present* (1955; rev. ed. 1987) is the seminal history of American music as a whole. A noted black scholar presents an overall perspective with a different focus in Eileen Southern, *The Music of Black Americans: A History* (1971; rev. ed. 1983); and for a history featuring valuable comments on twentieth-century American composers in the colonial sphere, H. Wiley Hitchcock, *Music in the United States: A Historical Introduction* (1988), is recommended. Glenn Watkins, *Soundings: Music in the Twentieth Century* (1988), which deals with art music in Europe and the United States, offers musically schooled readers one view of how American composers have contributed. H. Wiley Hitchcock and Stanley Sadie, eds., *The New Grove Dictionary of American Music*, 4 vols. (1986), forms a starting point for research and reference on most subjects in the field, including the present essay. The historiography and economics of American music are discussed in Richard Crawford, *The American Musical Landscape* (1993), which also traces the history of musical professions in the United States.

The interdependence of artistry and economics, from the late nineteenth century into the 1960s, provides the story told in Philip Hart, *Orpheus in the New World: The Symphony Orchestra as an American Cultural Institution* (1973), written by an orchestra manager. Charles Ives, *Memos*, ed. John Kirkpatrick (1972), an autobiographical text with copious annotations, vividly captures the flavor of Ives's musical thought and character. For data on the musical stage, see Gerald Bordman, *American Musical Theater: A Chronicle* (1978, 1992), where every Broadway musical show from 1866 through 1991 is listed and given summary prose treatment. A symposium, Jon Newsom, ed., *Perspectives on John Philip Sousa* (1983) sets the composer/band leader in the context of his time. Russell Sanjek, *American Popular Music and Its Business: The First Four Hundred Years*, vol. 2: *From 1790 to 1909*, and vol. 3: *From 1900 to 1984* (1988), a former music business executive's encyclopedic account of his trade, documents in detail the evolution of popular music as an economically exploitable product. Charles Hamm, *Yesterdays: Popular Song in America* (1979), which posits a single, two-centuries-old tradition of American popular song, is full of historical and musical insights. The musical context within which Scott Joplin worked is the focus of Edward A. Berlin, *Ragtime: A Musical and Cultural History* (1980). And Laurence Bergreen, *As Thousands Cheer: The Life of Irving Berlin* (1990), illuminates the life and times of a secretive, successful songwriter.

While not a scholarly work, Edward Jablonski, *Gershwin* (1987), allows readers to glimpse the aura of fame within which George Gershwin led his musical life. The colonial sphere's mystique is the larger subject of Joseph Horowitz, *Understanding Toscanini: How He Became an American Culture-God and Helped Create a New Audience for Old Music* (1987). Aaron Copland and Vivian Perlis, *Copland: 1900 through 1942* (1984), and *Copland since 1943* (1989), locate the author's self-portrait within the activities of the colonial sphere in which he worked. A collection of articles published by the government-sponsored American Folklife Center, *Ethnic Recordings in America: A Neglected Heritage* (1982), documents one record-business response to music in the traditional sphere. Philip Furia, *The Poets of Tin Pan Alley: A History of America's Great Lyricists* (1990), deftly reveals the art behind "Golden Age" song lyrics; and Stanley Dance, *The World of Duke Ellington* (1970), uses oral history to capture the feel of jazz musicians' vocation.

Edward T. Cone, ed., *Roger Sessions on Music: Collected Essays* (1979), brings together writings from throughout the career of a respected composer in the colonial sphere, while composer Virgil Thomson's *The State of Music* (1939; rev. ed. 1961) offers a breezily worded but serious-minded analysis of practices and attitudes that endure to the present day. Peter Yates, *Twentieth Century Music: Its Evolution from the End of the Harmonic Era into the Present Era of Sound* (1967), is useful for its placement of American composers within Western art music. John Cage himself was an active lecturer and prolific writer, as documented in *Silence* (1961), *A Year from Monday* (1967), *Empty Words* (1979), and *First: Sixth* (1990); Richard Kostelanetz, *Conversing with Cage* (1987), a topically arranged anthology, draws together the composer's statements from published and unpublished interviews. In Albert Murray, *Stomping the Blues* (1976), a black writer interprets the artistry fostered by the blues, one of American music's most fecund forms. The comment about gospel music appears in Stanley Crouch, *Notes of a Hanging Judge: Essays and Reviews 1979–1989* (1990), chapter 1. A pair of related works by composer/conductor Gunther Schuller, *Early Jazz: Its Roots and Musical Development* (1968), and *The Swing Era: The Development of Jazz, 1930–1945* (1989), present a monumental, detailed study of the music's flowering, based on aural analysis of all available recordings. Martin Williams, *The Jazz Tradition* (1970, rev. 1993), offers an influential jazz critic's historically arranged essays on leading figures, and the same author's *Hidden in Plain Sight: An Examination of the American Arts* (1992) contains the wry comment about *Oklahoma!*.

Charles Hamm, *Music in the New World* (1983), is the first general history to give rock music a prominent place. Two books on rock 'n' roll's impact that can be recommended are Charlie Gillett, *The Sound of the City: The Rise of Rock and Roll* (1970, rev. ed.

1972), an early but still estimable appreciation; and Simon Frith, *Sound Effects: Youth, Leisure, and the Politics of Rock 'n' Roll* (1981), by an English sociologist and critic who loves the music and is good at explaining why. John Rockwell, *All American Music: Composition in the Late Twentieth Century* (1983), a series of twenty essays, covers a broad range of musicians, from serialist Milton Babbitt to salsa artist Eddie Palmieri. For a discussion of "early" Western art music performance, see Harry Haskell, *The Early Music Revival: A History* (1988). Chapter 6, "Nashville," of V. S. Naipaul, *A Turn in the South* (1989), describes country music as a regional institution; and Bill C. Malone, *Country Music U.S.A.: A Fifty-Year History* (1968, 1985), offers the first scholarly account of the subject. Don Michael Randel, "Crossing Over with Rubén Blades," *Journal of the American Musicological Society* (1991), offers provocative comments on popular music in general and Latin American pop in particular. Finally, Frederic Dannen's *Hit Men: Power Brokers and Fast Money Inside the Music Business* (1990) chronicles bruising battles for economic advantage within the world of contemporary pop music; and Jerry Wexler and David Ritz, *Rhythm and the Blues: A Life in American Music* (1993), presents autobiographical reflections of an important record producer.

# PHILOSOPHY

*David J. Depew*

The philosophical doctrine known as idealism was at the height of its influence in America at the turn of the twentieth century. From the fact that we refer to the world through a set of meaningful concepts, idealists infer that the world itself must be a unified field of meanings spread out before an experiencing mind. "Critical idealists" followed the great eighteenth-century philosopher Immanuel Kant in thinking that this inference is valid only for the world as we experience it. The "thing-in-itself" lies beyond the reach of our thoughts. The idealism that dominated American philosophy at the end of the nineteenth century, however, was "absolute" rather than "critical." The world as it is in itself must be a meaningful and knowable totality. Therefore, absolute idealists argued, it must be the coherent experience of a mind that does not suffer from our finitude. Accordingly, George Holmes Howison, who presided over the philosophy department at the University of California at Berkeley, could assert in 1895 without fear of contradiction that America's philosophers "were all agreed . . . that the only absolutely real thing is mind; that all material and all temporal existences take their being from a Consciousness that thinks and experiences; that out of consciousness they all issue, to consciousness they are presented, and that presence to consciousness constitutes their entire reality."

## IDEALISM: THE ROOTS OF CONFLICT

Why, we may ask, would absolute idealism, a philosophy formulated by Friedrich Schelling and Georg Wilhelm Friedrich Hegel in the neomedievalizing ambiance of early-nineteenth-century German Romanticism, take hold in forward-looking and newly industrialized America? Admittedly, American philosophers in the late nineteenth century were more influenced by German than by British philosophy. In any case, British philosophy itself had recently taken an unexpected idealist turn. In both places, it

seems, modernity was causing enough discomfort to draw many people back toward the numinous. In America, the religiously oriented philosophers of a largely religious nation were explicitly responding to a wave of materialism that had been stimulated by industrialization and the diffusion of Darwinism by inflating, rather than trimming back, claims that the world must be essentially spiritual if it is to be meaningful at all. If evolution takes place, idealists assured genteel Americans, surely it must be the unfolding of a grand plan rather than the meaningless slaughter of natural selection.

Josiah Royce was the most creative turn-of-the-century American idealist. Royce was as poignantly aware that our experience is fragmented as was his friend and Harvard colleague William James. As he pondered this condition, however, Royce became more rather than less absolute in his idealism. Even our sense of fragility and finitude, he argued, presupposes that coherent meaning lies at the horizon of our world, ingressing into it far enough to animate our lives with value and purpose. "All of our knowledge of natural truth depends," Royce wrote in *The Conception of God* (1895), "on contrasting our actually fragmentary and stubbornly chaotic individual and momentary experience with a conceived world of organized experience inclusive of all our fragments."

To keep this wholeness in view, Royce judged that it would be insufficient merely to oppose materialism. The respectable philosophical dualism of Descartes and Kant must be rejected as well. For Royce feared that dualism, according to which knowing, valuing, and choosing subjects must withdraw into a private inner world in order to protect the integrity of their experience in the face of a mechanistic and atomistic external world, would combine with the tendencies of the capitalist order and a rapidly secularizing civil society to undermine the sense of community through which, as Hegel had already argued, a meaningful and coherent human life is alone possible. Royce's idealism was aimed at protecting his communitarianism. "My deepest motives and problems have centered around the idea of the community," he remarked at a dinner given in his honor as America was about to plunge into World War I. "We are saved through community."

The threat that the meaningful and value-laden world hitherto protected by religion would disappear as society became more secular, and as natural science expanded its influence, was felt not only by philosophers who, like Royce and James, were reaching the height of their powers as the century turned, but also by those who were just then coming of age. They too came almost entirely from what George Santayana called "the genteel tradition," and felt keenly that vast social and intellectual changes were taking place to which they had to make a concerted and creative response. All but one of the thirty-four philosophers deemed by their colleagues in the American Philosophical Association to be worthy of contributing to a collection of intellectual autobiographies entitled *Contemporary American Philosophy* (1930) were white Protestant males, most of whom had matured around the fractious turn of the century. (The lone woman was Mary Calkins, who taught at Wellesley.) Many of these philosophers were the sons of clergymen whose adolescent spiritual crises had been defining events in their lives. Their confessions express studious ways, earnest demeanors, and genteel manners inherited from pious fathers or mothers. "Boyhood is religious," wrote Edward Singer in *Contemporary American Philosophy,* "while manhood forgets. But not all men forget. Those that cannot forget become . . . philosophers who seek—for philosophy either is, or else involves, the search for a religion."

At the same time, the coming generation was feeling pressures their elders had never experienced. In 1901, philosophers on the East Coast formed what was to become throughout the century the dominant professional organization of the field, the American Philosophical Association (APA). It soon incorporated the Western [Midwestern] Philosophical Association, and eventually budded off a Pacific Division in 1924. These efforts toward professionalization reflected the determination of progressive America to modernize a no longer agrarian or culturally homogeneous nation. In the case of philosophy, modernization meant recasting what had hitherto been a semi-clerical calling into a quasi-scientific profession. It was integral to the new professionalism that philosophers, like scientists, should generate what are now called "research programs," within which problems falling inside the field's proper sphere were to be cooperatively formulated and attacked. From the turn of the century, accordingly, we find proposals for and instances of cooperative work.

Royce embraced professionalism with verve. By using the broader German conception of science *(Wissenschaft)* as methodical inquiry of any sort, he was able to convince himself that philosophical work was indeed scientific, even if it was far from empirical or experimental. Indeed, he thought it was *more* scientific than empirical disciplines, since, according to idealists, philosophy is a foundational metascience at whose core is the a priori science of logic, out of which the conceptual structure of the world can be spun, leaving the empirical sciences to squabble over the contingent husks. Royce was acquainted with and enthusiastic about the new research programs in logic that were to have a profound effect on philosophy in the new century. Philosophers more attuned to natural sciences and to the emerging social sciences than Royce, however, still felt uncomfortable with this posture. The challenge was posed by empirical science, and by logic treated empirically. One result of this discomfort was that in the debates about the professional status of philosophy that racked the young APA, the idealist consensus that Howison proudly took for granted was shattered. With that consensus went any sense that religion and philosophy are comfortably continuous with and supportive of each other, and confidently dominant over other dimensions of discourse in society.

Soon two large camps of postidealist philosophers arose, each of which remained faithful to a different aspect of the idealist legacy. First came the pragmatists. They were prepared to surrender logic to the empirical science of psychology, but clung tenaciously to idealism's conception of philosophy as offering a comprehensive vision of life, an attempt to see "how things on the whole hang together as a whole," as James put it. Pragmatists were soon opposed by realists. They retained the idealists' insistence that the nonempirical or a priori, and hence certain and necessary, science of logic allows philosophy to set forth general criteria for knowledge, and so to retain its privileged status at the top of the disciplinary heap. Realists denied, on the other hand, what they took to be idealism's most basic claim, the distorting mind-dependence of the real, to which they thought pragmatists still clung. They also took a pluralistic rather than a "monistic" or holistic view of how the world is put together. (The term "realism" in philosophy resonates badly with its uses in politics, art, and literary history. Deriving from medieval quarrels about the reality of universals, realism contrasts with nominalism, which takes universals to be arbitrary human constructs. Since the notion that universals capture the genuine essences of natural kinds depends on the idea that we can portray reality without human distortions, realism has come to mean metaphysical or scientific objectivism.)

Conflicts between pragmatism and realism frame the history of American philosophy since 1900. The successive movements described in this essay—Anglo-American analytic philosophy, in both its logical empiricist and ordinary language versions, and so-called Continental philosophy, in its phenomenological, hermeneutical, and deconstructionist phases—have all been asked to testify on behalf of one or the other party to old quarrels between pragmatists and realists. We will see that, as the century ends, debates between pragmatists and realists remain as vivid as they were at its outset.

## PRAGMATISM

As a medium for articulating the policies of progressivism and New Deal liberalism, pragmatism has enjoyed much influence in America. It has impacted directly on the theory and practice of law, education, politics, social policy, and even art and religion. Of the movements we are recounting, it is the only one to have acquired a reputation for being distinctively American. Just because it means so many things to so many people and fields, however, and has been subjected to painful vulgarizations, it is necessary to be clear about what pragmatism meant in the context of professional philosophy, where it arose.

Pragmatists claim that ideas derive their meaning, and even get their truth, wholly from their utility in guiding behavior. If an idea fails to tell you how your conduct would be affected in case it were true, it tells you precisely nothing. If, on the other hand, an idea does successfully guide conduct, it is a true idea—or so, at least, William James believed.

The quirky genius Charles Sanders Peirce first explored the pragmatist conception of *meaning* in meetings of the Metaphysical Club at Harvard in the 1870s, which James also attended. Pierce's use of the term "pragmatic" was inspired by Kant's. Kant held that in fields like biology, history, and politics we cannot help but orient our thought and behavior by acting "as if" certain functional or purposive notions ("x is there in order to do y") are true, even though they seem to clash with the deterministic laws of mechanistic physics. For Kant, the validity of such "regulative" ideas is predicated on how they orient our conduct, especially in making further inquiries, rather than on whether they give us true representa-

tions. Hence such ideas are pragmatic (from the Greek verb *prattein,* to act). The sphere to which Kant assigns pragmatic ideas largely coincides with what was left of the old purposive or "teleological" Aristotelian worldview, from which Kant could not bear entirely to part after modern science had mechanized nature. Peirce realized, however, that since James Clerk Maxwell, Ludwig Boltzmann, Josiah Willard Gibbs, and Charles Darwin, science itself had been changing. A second scientific revolution was revealing a much less deterministic and mechanistic world than the one portrayed by Newton, Laplace, and Kant. It was a processive and unfinished world shot through with chance, contingency, and seat-of-the-pants adaptations, yielding its contours, therefore, to statistical and probabilistic rather than to deterministic models of reasoning. Peirce concluded that in such a world all our ideas must be pragmatic in something like Kant's sense. In an inherently changing world, ideas guide us from one point in inquiry to another, and are to be judged entirely by how well they do this.

This conviction undergirded Peirce's problem-centered model of thinking, according to which belief is the temporary cessation of genuine puzzlement and doubt through successful inquiry, "a demi-cadence," as he put it, "in the symphony of our intellectual life." Peirce went on to argue that in an inherently changing world, the only reliable (because corrigible) way of "fixing belief" and of guiding behavior so that it correctly anticipates the changing flow of events is the experimental method of modern science. This method allows knowledge to change in ways that can be distinguished from dogmatic belief. In this spirit, Peirce applied the pragmatic criterion of meaning to the concept of "truth" itself by defining it as a Kantian regulative ideal. We sort out what is known from what we merely opine, and move more surely toward an objectively correct account of things, by (tacitly) regarding truth as a property of a hypothetical state of affairs in the indefinite future when unconstrained inquiry would have produced universal agreement on the basis of total information.

Although James was attracted to Peirce's processive view of reality and to the pragmatic criterion of meaning, Peirce's restriction of the effects of our ideas on our conduct to what might eventually emerge from "laboratory habits of mind" seemed to James to ratify the longstanding prejudices of metaphysicians and natural scientists against the lived world of cultural experience, and so to draw the wrong lessons from the discovery of an inherently processive world, of knowledge that is revisable, and of the pragmatic criterion of meaning itself. James thought we live within the bounds of a profoundly useful, but variously interpretable, cultural inheritance, which comes up against the data of sensation only at the edges. Because there are so many good ways of describing one's experience and acting reasonably in the face of it, Peirce's conception of inquiry settling around a single world-version seemed to James wrong-headedly to retain relics of the changeless classical world-picture that Peirce himself had done so much to overthrow. The gap Peirce posits between pragmatic meaning and ultimate truth was thus radically narrowed by James. For James, a true idea is any idea that is "good in the way of belief," and not one that captures hypothetical agreement in eschatological time. (Peirce, it should be noted, was so appalled by this idea that he ceased calling his own philosophy pragmatism. Ceding the term to James, he dubbed his view "pragmaticism," a word, he remarked, "so ugly it will be safe from kidnappers.")

James's arguments for his pragmatism were informed by the "radical empiricist" psychology he had worked out in the *Principles of Psychology* (1890). There he boldly replaced the atomistic sensationalism of traditional British empiricism, which reached back to Locke, Berkeley, and Hume, with the notion that we are inescapably confronted with a perceptual manifold whose parts are not fully analyzable into constituent elements, but whose phases and flows provide multiple pathways through a "blooming, buzzing confusion." Experience, in this view, is too multiform, and our projects too various, to allow philosophers or psychologists to place prior constraints on ways of describing of it. "Truth," James wrote in *Pragmatism* (1907), "lives on the credit system." All that can be said with certainty is that since we are creatures living under a stern Darwinian imperative to adapt within a cultural even more than a natural environment, the function of thinking is to enable us to revise our beliefs in ways that do the least damage to their received coherence, so that we can muster enough physical, emotional, and moral energy to respond to threatening contingencies. "New truth," James wrote, "is always a go-between, a smoother-over of transitions. It marries old opinion to new fact as ever to show a minimum of jolt, a maximum of continuity." From this gradualist, adaptationist point of view, truth cannot be analyzed in terms of theory-oriented correspondence, but only in terms of action-oriented coherence.

James's place in the philosophical tradition now becomes somewhat clearer. It is a truth sometimes obscured by the division of labor among professional philosophers that philosophy is an effort to connect (or disconnect) the most general categories into which things and processes fall (ontology) with what is to be done (ethics) by enlarging or contracting our usual assumptions about what can be known (epistemology, from Greek for "study of knowing"). For example, Hume's famous contention that you cannot rationally get an "ought" from an "is," a value from a fact, uses a niggardly view of knowing in order to sever facts from values, and thereby to protect the latter from the withering skepticism of reason. James, by contrast, inherited idealism's effort to be generous about criteria for knowledge in order to be upbeat about the cognitive status of values. The general object of James's thinking, writing, and lecturing was to stiffen the resolve of genteel post-Puritans like himself to preserve their high-mindedness in the face of the collapse of the transcendent world view to which idealists (mostly in the person of his friend Royce) were still clinging. On these terms, James judged that "humanism," and even religious experience, could be pragmatically verified, and the deterministic biases of Enlightenment scientism, discouraging as they must be to free will and human self-assertion, deflated.

James famously distinguished between "tough" and "tender-minded" thinkers. As an empirical psychologist, he thought of himself as tough-minded by contrast to idealists like Royce. In the heady turn-of-the-century atmosphere of professionalization and progressive politics, however, where objectively valid results were increasingly expected from expert cooperation, James's Emersonian permissiveness about personal belief systems made him appear not just tender-minded, but even a bit old-fashioned. Proclaiming that "the philosopher is a lone beast dwelling in his individual burrow," James initially refused to join the APA. He reacted to his colleague Hugo Munsterberg's proposal that philosophers should contribute to a "Congress of Arts and Sciences" at the Saint Louis Exposition of 1904 by noting to himself:

> It seems to me . . . a kind of religious service in honor of the professional-philosophy shop, with its faculty, it departments and sections, its mutual etiquette, its appointments, its great mill of authorities and exclusions and suppressions, which the waters of truth are expected to feed to the great class-glory of all who are concerned. To me, truth, if there be any truth, would seem to exist for the express confusion of all this kind of thing.

Given his view of philosophizing as an edifying,

rather than a scientific, enterprise, James's dim view of the professionalization of his discipline could hardly have been otherwise. On this point, the young John Dewey begged to differ. Dewey first emerged into prominence in the early debates about the orientation of the APA. Upon graduating from the new German-model Johns Hopkins University in 1892, Dewey hoped to give philosophy a professional home in the newly founded American Psychological Association by turning philosophy's received problems into issues in experimental psychology. He wanted, that is to say, to "psychologize" logic and epistemology, and to professionalize them by so scientizing them, leaving grand metaphysics, the old metascience to which these disciplines were supposed to be propaedeutic, to molder in its grave. Where James rested pragmatism's claim to holistic wisdom on personal reflection and imaginative insight, accordingly, Dewey committed himself to the claim that only intersubjectively validated agreements, reached through a process he was pleased to call "experimental," could be said to constitute knowledge. On these terms alone could professional philosophers meet the cooperative conditions imposed on genuinely scientific work. When professional psychologists, who had been trained in Germany in the experimentalism of Wilhelm Wundt and Hermann von Helmholtz, proved indifferent even to such a severely chastened philosophy, Dewey tried to implant the same vision in the APA.

The fact that, like Peirce, Dewey identified the scope of knowing with the range of scientific method did not mean that he was much less generous than James about the scope of knowing, or that he disagreed with James about philosophy's role of offering, or helping people formulate, comprehensive visions of life. Admittedly, Dewey thought that philosophy's preachments about life's problems must be guided by the empirical sciences, including the new social sciences. At the same time, though, Dewey judged that the experimental method itself was only in the early stages of development. "The development of scientific inquiry is immature," Dewey wrote in *Reconstruction in Philosophy* (1920). "It has not yet got beyond the physical and physiological aspects of human concerns." As experimentalism was extended to the social sciences it would bring forth ways in which humans could deal effectively with their problems that would move well beyond the mechanistic and reductionist tendencies of early modern materialism, the first philosophical tradition to make the experimental method its own property. Accordingly, whereas James used pragmatism to extend the notion of knowing to dimensions of experience lying well beyond the reach of scientific method under any reasonable description of it, Dewey used it to extend the rhetoric of scientific method to dimensions of inquiry hitherto regarded as unscientific.

If Dewey saw a continuing role for philosophy in monitoring the changing culture of experimentalism, he also knew that this would require significant changes in the self-understanding of philosophers. Accordingly, Dewey worked hard to persuade his colleagues that in a world being rapidly transformed by the interaction between technologically applied science and industrial capitalism, philosophy could no longer present itself either as a foundational master science or as edification in the wispy spirit of Emerson or James. He tried to show up philosophy's traditional contemplative stance, in which the thinker stands in an essentially passive and private relation to the objects of experience, as an ideological instrument for sustaining the power of elites. Like Marx, he thought that by elevating the revisable, experimental, technical, and practical knowing of ordinary men and women over aristocratic and monastic contemplation of the changeless, he could provide support for democracy and working people. Simply deconstructing philosophy's illusory past would not, however, be enough. If philosophy was to preserve its claim to comprehensive wisdom, it must reconstruct itself as an agent of the public interest by offering to broker the relation between science and modernizing societies.

The transformation of the American economy into a cooperative and well-regulated kind of capitalism, for example, would require a social and not merely a political democracy. In turn, this would require reconstructing the idea of individualism. Dewey took it as a postulate that "it is through association that man has acquired his individuality and it is through association that he exercises it." In Dewey's ideal social democracy, people would interact with one another in most dimensions of their lives, an engagement for which they were prepared by habits acquired through the highly interactive style of childhood education Dewey championed. In such a world, citizens would not lose their individuality and autonomy, but gain it.

These convictions express themes that Dewey had absorbed in his Hegelian youth. Hegel was not only the philosopher of the overblown Absolute, but modernity's best critic of atomistic individualism. Reflecting on the glory and the tragedy of the French Revolution, Hegel had argued that it was the destiny of the modern age to secularize the Judaeo-Christian conviction of the infinite worth of the person. The mutual recognition of persons, however, and so their individuation itself, could occur only in and through the bonds of a strong social ethos. Concrete institutional conditions, legal, economic, and political, would have to be constructed, accordingly, in which mutually recognizing persons might develop and flourish. Throughout the nineteenth century, Hegel's best disciples tried with more or less success to disengage this vision from their master's short-sighted belief that the required bonds are those of an inherited monarchy rationalized and stabilized by a well-educated and well-oiled bureaucracy or "clerisy." Early and late, the point of Dewey's practice-centered reconstruction in philosophy was to preserve and deepen the Hegelian theory of individuation through socialization by identifying participatory (if also representative) democracy, already planted in the rich soil of American culture, as the medium in and through which the idealists' organicist vision was to be achieved. "The ordinary American expression of the sovereignty of every elector," he wrote in an early essay (1888), "is not a mere exaggerated burst of individualistic feeling, fostered through crude Fourth of July patriotism, but is the logical outcome of the organic theory of society."

Royce would have agreed with most of this. Dewey realized, however, that as long as abstract contemplation maintained primacy over practice, and spirit over nature, this vision could get no further than the timid and moralistic liberal communitarianism preached by idealists like T. H. Green in Britain and Royce in America. By about 1893, Dewey concluded that no version of idealism could avoid that fate. He thereupon took a decisive naturalistic turn, reconceiving Hegelian socialization as a form of adaptive learning in a naturalized social context interwoven throughout by technical and practical forms of intelligence, in which in an open and unfinished world humans appear as problem-solving animals, and the linguistically-mediated social environment appears as natural to them as water to fish.

This Hegelian background formed no part of James's inheritance. By Dewey's own testimony, however, it was James who gave him the arguments for his naturalized version of it. James had built his psychology on the stunning Darwinian idea that mind is an adaptation, and, like any other adaptation, a product of natural selection. The mind's ideas are, therefore, tools or instruments (hence Dewey's preferred name, "instrumentalism," for his brand of pragmatism) for negotiating experience rather than inert pictures of external reality. Any adaptation that

yields a capacity for reacting creatively to environmental contingencies is, ceteris paribus, more valuable than one that dictates only fixed reactions to relatively stereotyped occasions. On this score, the mind is a highly valuable set of adaptations, the spontaneity of which allows creative responses to the contingencies and indeterminacies of experience by way of revisable and creative versions of the world, which guide and shape further experience by trial, error, learning, and transmission. From this perspective, mind is not a passive recorder of the environment, as it is for classical empiricists like Hume, but an active determiner of a person's possibilities in an open world, "a fighter for ends," in James's fine phrase.

Dewey packed this adaptationist perspective into his use of terms like "experimental" and "scientific method." In the insightful autobiographical sketch he contributed to *Contemporary American Philosophy,* he remarked, "I doubt if we have as yet begun to realize all that is due to William James for . . . the return to a . . . biological conception of the *psyche,*" a return given "new force and value due to the immense progress made by biology since the time of Aristotle." But he also says that James himself "did not fully and consistently realize the implications" of his achievement, because "even when the special tenets of the prior [associationist] psychological tradition are radically criticized, an underlying subjectivism is retained, at least in vocabulary." In short, Dewey proposed to objectify and socialize James's adaptationist psychology by naturalizing Hegel's theory of the person.

Dewey began to formulate these ideas in the context of the progressivism that flourished in the Midwest at the end of the nineteenth century. In 1894, Dewey left the University of Michigan to serve as chairman of the Philosophy Department at the new University of Chicago, to whose founding president, William Rainey Harper, he had been recommended by James Hayden Tufts. Tufts had already worked with Dewey at Michigan. In turn, Dewey brought George Herbert Mead from Michigan as a third member of their emerging research group. The reunion of the Michigan philosophers coincided with the biter Pullman strike, during which the city, still fresh with the memory of the Haymarket Massacre, was under martial law. The philosophers and other Chicago academics entered into alliance with the progressive Chicago Civic Federation, a group of businessmen who were shaken by the specter of class warfare and sought to mediate the strike. "Stimulating and absorbing as it was to take part in the making of a new university," Tufts wrote in *Contemporary American Philosophy,* "I can now see that this was, perhaps, less crucial for my development in the long run than the contact with the city of Chicago." Soon the Chicago philosophers found themselves working with Jane Addams, with whom Dewey was linked through his reform-minded wife. Dewey's laboratory school at the University of Chicago, in which Alice Dewey played a leading role, was leavened with Addams's ideas about social work. Addams, meanwhile, learned to talk about her work in a Deweyesque idiom. Simultaneously, Dewey tried to keep Harper, who was dependent on the University's patron, John D. Rockefeller, mollified.

By 1903, the Chicago philosophers had turned out an important piece of cooperative philosophical work. *Studies in Logical Theory* was the product of a painfully self-conscious research program and thus an object of professional display. The idea was to portray logic as a tool of discovery, mediating between problematic situation and problem-solving response. Dewey claimed that if philosophers resisted this idea they must necessarily regard logical form as externally imposed on alien, sensuous matter, a point on which Hegel had long before criticized Kant, and Dewey had recently criticized Green. Dewey asserted that a practical logic of discovery, in which matter and form are fused and refused through problem-solving innovation, would better account for the quality of necessity that had traditionally been ascribed to logic than any theory in which contingency enters through a theoretical gap between empirical content and logical framework. After expressing a bit of supercilious surprise that an uncouth city like Chicago could give rise to a philosophical school, James gave his blessing in a 1904 review of *Studies in Logical Theory.* "The Chicago School," he wrote, "has formed a view of the world, both theoretical and practical, which is so simple, massive, and positive that in spite of the fact that many parts of it yet need to be worked out, it deserves the title of a new system of philosophy." Classical pragmatism, considered as a tradition that retrospectively embraced Peirce, James, Mead, and Dewey, was born at this point.

In the same year, Dewey, angered by Harper's failure to support the laboratory school, moved to Columbia University, where he continued to defend "instrumentalism" until his death in 1952. At Columbia, however, Dewey's primary philosophical opponents were no longer idealists of this or that stripe, but the "new," and later the so-called "critical," realists, who had their own, distinctly unpragmatic, ways of criticizing idealism. That made a good deal of

difference to the spirit of Dewey's later philosophizing.

## NEW AND CRITICAL REALISM

In 1910, working in a research program every bit as self-consciously cooperative as that of the Chicago School, six well-placed philosophy professors published a "realist," hence anti-idealist and by extension antipragmatist, manifesto in the *Journal of Philosophy,* which since its birth in 1904 had emerged as the official organ of the APA. Their "Program and First Platform of Six Realists" was followed by a fat book, *The New Realism* (1912). The new realists were dedicated to conserving, or if necessary restoring, philosophy's traditional foundational role over the sciences and culture. They worried that pragmatists, whose holism about meaning they considered a sign of imperfectly cured idealism, would destroy professional philosophy itself by undermining foundationalism.

Two of the six original new realists were Dewey's colleagues at Columbia, William Pepperell Montague and Walter Pitkin. Another was Ralph Barton Perry of Harvard. New realists denied the idealist assumption that reality is mind-dependent, and therefore that each of us is potentially trapped within the circle of his or her own consciousness, or what Perry called "the egocentric predicament." The new realists thought it a fallacy to infer from the premise that when we perceive an external thing we have an idea of that thing to the conclusion that the seemingly external thing is dependent for its existence or features on our idea. The root of the error is the representational theory of consciousness, or the "idea idea," in terms of which associationist psychology had been encoded since Locke's "new way of ideas," according to which the mind is in immediate cognitive contact only with its own representations and must infer whatever realities lie outside it, either as causes of its ideas or as their referents. Idealists moved from plain nonsense to what Bertrand Russell, then engaged in his own revolt against idealism in England, called "nonsense on stilts" when they assumed that the circle of consciousness is unbroken and then tried to make the consequences of this admission palatable by treating the real as an ever-expanding spiral, in which meanings are continuously relativized to larger and larger contexts. The new realists judged that pragmatists remained under the spell of this "coherence theory of truth," since using one's ideas to transform one's practical experience into a new holistic mélange was still to assume that one might be caught within an egocentric predicament, even if a commodious one.

The fallacies of the "idea idea" were based, new realists argued, on taking epistemology to be prior to logic. Logic teaches us that in valid inferences we refer to items whose meaning must remain fixed throughout the inference or sequence of inferences. It therefore presupposes a world that must contain many distinct things rather than one big monistic meaning. Indeed, if our ideas are as context-sensitive as idealists and pragmatists asserted, and our meanings as fluid, we would never be able to think valid thoughts at all, let alone grand ones. Since the notion that the things and processes that form the furniture of the world are necessarily plural, and are unaffected by our thinking about them, is difficult to sustain on a representational and psychologistic accounts of consciousness, the new realists replaced the "idea idea" with direct "presentational" realism, according to which the mind's objects, both particular and universal, have prima facie reality and do not have to travel through a thick veil of awareness to secure reference to things. On pain of opening the door to subjectivism and skepticism, new realists held that every object of consciousness must be accorded some sort of reality. If the parallel rails that I see in the distance converge to a point, let it really be so. Reality itself is replete with multiple, often intersecting, relationships, from which at any given point in time and space we select.

The new realism harked back to the "common-sense philosophy" of Thomas Reid, who attempted to block the skeptical conclusions of his fellow Scot, Hume, by insisting that our ideas grab onto things directly. Scottish common-sense philosophy is the "old" realism from which the new realists distinguished their own brand. It had deep roots in American intellectual life. "College philosophy" in the eighteenth and nineteenth centuries was based on it. Its realism about sensible intuition was intended to make us trust the reality of our moral intuitions, and by way of moral intuitionism to shore up the reasonableness of religious belief. The problem with the old realists, according to the new, was that they were still fixated on epistemology and psychology. In asserting the primacy of logic, the new realists were trying to protect realism from the tendency of any epistemology-centered philosophy to decline into the egocentric predicament. New realists could have added sophisticated support for their position from contemporary philosophers in Austria and in Britain, for at the turn of the century the realistic revolt against idealism was an international affair. In England, G. E. Moore was reviving Scottish common-sense philosophy by analyzing the logic implied by our language. Alternatively, they could have argued, with Austrian and German disciples of Franz Brentano, such as Alexius Meinong, Gottlob Frege, and Edmund Husserl, that it is of the very mark of the mental to be about something other than mind, the so-called "principle of intentionality." These resources were eventually exploited. At first, however, American new realism was largely a home-grown affair.

Dewey responded swiftly to the new realists' manifesto in hard-hitting articles in the *Journal of Philosophy* in 1910–1911. New realists, he noted, liked to portray themselves as on the side of common sense and the plain man. To this profession of innocence, Dewey retorted that they were not nearly naive enough. They assumed wrongly that the plain man's primary relationship to sensory objects is a contemplative gaze. The genuine article, however, refers to things by connecting them up as objects of his or her practical and productive interests. Ordinary persons, in scrutinizing their perceptions, do not regard them as objects of knowledge, but as sources of evidence. "While perceptions are the sole ultimate data," Dewey wrote in the introduction to his *Essays on Experimental Logic* (1916), "the sole media of inference to all natural objects and processes . . . we do not, in any intelligible or verifiable sense, *know* them. Rather, we know . . . things . . . *with* or *by* them. . . . Their nature as evidence, as signs, entirely overshadows their natural status, that of being simply natural events."

In saying this, Dewey was not calling into question the reality of the outside world, or our ability to know it. His thoroughgoing naturalism meant that he was "frankly realistic in acknowledging that certain brute existences . . . set every problem for reflection and hence serve as tests of its otherwise merely speculative results," as he put it in "The Shortcut to Realism Examined" (1910). However, Dewey did mean to reaffirm the protean theory of meaning associated with his idealist legacy. "The meaning of a term—mammal, species, metal, orchid, circle—is quite different at the end and at the beginning of scientific reflection." The realist, Dewey concluded, seems to "win an easy victory" only because he fails to "distinguish between the static ideal of possessed knowledge, in which meanings do not undergo change, and the active process of getting knowledge, where meanings are continuously modified by the new relations into which they enter." For Dewey, the experimental logic of discovery *is* the logic of justification, just as the genesis of things *is* their nature.

New realists were not above thinking about the causal conditions that produce our knowledge of common-sense objects. Since, however, the most plausible causal mechanisms suggest that our awareness of things comes heavily processed by perceptual machinery, they were forced to acknowledge that there are perceptual and cognitive errors, and that at least sometimes the theoretical entities, processes, and properties we uncover through scientific inquiry may replace the ordinary things that stimulated our inquiry in the first place, both as objects of knowledge and as its causal basis. If scientific learning displaces common sense, however, the realist's insistence that we are driven to understand the world as it is apart from our minds' contribution to it can end up undermining the direct or presentational realism that new realists sponsored. This problem became steadily more pressing as the new physics began to discount the objects of common sense, shifting the ontological weight downwards into the atomic and subatomic sphere, breaking up the substantialism of sensory objects through a more processive view of reality, and calling into question the status of the Newtonian space-time framework.

Reflections along these disturbing lines helped prompt the publication in 1921 of yet another manifesto by six American realists, who this time called themselves "critical realists." Critical realists were more tolerant of errors than their new realist brethren, but still insisted that error necessarily arises against a background of truth, so that we are presumptively, even if not infallibly, in a "veridical" or truth-capturing relationship to the world. Inadequate ideas or false representations admittedly fall back within the circle of consciousness. True ideas, on the other hand, which we acquire by inquiry, advance beyond the circle to make direct contact with the nature of things, revising or displacing common sense in the process. On the matter of how this trick is performed, however, critical realists grew puzzled. So many versions of critical realism proliferated that wags soon had it that while new realists could not explain error, critical realists could not explain truth.

Eventually, critical realists parsed themselves into two large categories. Some had naturalistic views about the nature of mind. Others, who formed the so-called "essence wing" of the movement, took a dualistic view of the relation between mind and matter. Roy Wood Sellars of the University of Michigan, who had introduced the phrase "critical realism" in a book of that name in 1916, was as thoroughgoing

a naturalist as Dewey. "Achieve the idea of mind as intrinsic to the living organism, and naturalism is full-fledged," he wrote in *Contemporary American Philosophy*. "Physical realism, plus the rejection of dualism, spells naturalism." In *Critical Realism* (1916) and *Evolutionary Naturalism* (1921), Sellars tried to turn the adaptationist theory of mind, hitherto monopolized by pragmatists, to the advantage of a realist theory of knowledge. Whereas Dewey took the adaptationist theory of mind to rule out contemplative picturing of the world as it is "in itself" as a meaningless irrelevancy to an organism's necessarily perspectival dealings with its environment, Sellars maintained that the reflective mind is an "emergent property" of the evolutionary process, whose payoff is not only the survival of the species, but an increasingly objective understanding of the nature of things. From this "emergentist" perspective, Sellars took a realistic, rather than an instrumental, view of scientific and philosophical theories. In ratifying the questions of traditional philosophy, Sellars also affirmed the role of the individual reflective ego in deciding what is and is not rational. Accordingly, although he was a convinced social democrat, and a self-proclaimed humanist, Sellars confessed that he "could never accept the tendency of the Chicago School to a social consciousness."

George Santayana, another of the six original critical realists, also sounded a note of naturalistic realism, but was more closely aligned with the "essence wing" of the movement. Santayana studied and taught at Harvard, where his Jamesian inheritance led him to recognize that we cannot viridically mirror the world in our thoughts. Our illusions will be all the greater, however, if we think with pragmatists that our ideas can do much to affect or reconstruct the world. The fact is that we live in a material realm that is largely indifferent to our thoughts about it. The only form of naturalism that can consistently avoid illusions, therefore, is one in which the ground of realism is "animal faith," the "natural attitude" from which some of the harsher truths about the human condition increasingly revealed by science, and by acute philosophical poets like the Epicurean Lucretius, arise. Certainly our mind is as free as James says it is to construct an indefinite number of world versions. But Santayana grants this on condition that we take a purely private, contemplative, aesthetic, indeed quasi-solipsistic, view of the mind's work of rationally harmonizing things. From this perspective Santayana proclaimed, "There is no opposition in my mind between materialism and a Platonic or even Indian description of the spirit." When we contemplate, it is aestheticized essences we contact, even though they are unembodied in a world of Democritean facts that leaves no room for values, the finest of which seem to us to transcend our subjective preferences and to thrust us into a world of ideal values. In this limited sense Santayana was a dualist. His remark that "The human mind is a faculty of dreaming awake" echoes Lope de Vega's assertion that "All life is a dream," and betrays Santayana's Iberian Catholic sensibility. Indeed, Santayana decried America's Protestant culture for elevating crass materialism and oppressive moralism over the imaginatively rich aestheticized contemplative life that is the home of intrinsic values that can never be apprehended or realized from an action-oriented point of view. In spite of recurring efforts to link him to the pragmatists, Santayana rightly took himself to be a realist.

Other members of the "essence wing" of the critical realist movement were more confident than Santayana that essences are more than dreams. Arthur O. Lovejoy, for example, who taught at Johns Hopkins, wrote with regret about the idealists' "revolt from dualism," the holism of which had started all the trouble in the first place by calling into question the solid distinction we must make between the mental world, and its proper objects of knowledge, and the physical world that is analyzed by science. "The distinction between the mental . . . and the physical," Lovejoy wrote in *Contemporary American Philosophy*, "is the beginning of wisdom in metaphysics." For Lovejoy, philosophy's questions are formulable and answerable when a dualistic philosophy of mind is taken as a starting point, and as an autonomous field full of questions that can never be held hostage to the passing whims of scientific fashion or experimental psychology. In these terms, Lovejoy defended the professional autonomy of philosophy and its competence in solving conceptual, rather than empirical, questions in debates about this issue in the APA. (Lovejoy and Dewey, it is worth noting, buried their considerable differences when they teamed up to defend academic freedom by founding the American Association of University Professors.)

Some critical realists in the twenties and thirties even found their way back to realism's oldest tradition, Aristotelianism. Aristotle had defined truth as "adequation of mind to thing." By this he did not mean, like Descartes or Kant, that the ego draws things into its own narrow circle. On the contrary, what Aristotle meant by the mind's power of abstraction was its capacity to transcend the egocentric predicament by assimilating itself to the inner structure of things. Aristotelian realism was most prominently on display in the Columbia Philosophy Department in the person of Frederick J. E. Woodbridge, founding editor of the *Journal of Philosophy* and Dewey's sympathetic but critical colleague. Woodbridge confessed in *Contemporary American Philosophy* that "Aristotle has said everything which I have ever said or shall ever say." Conscious of the fact that Dewey, America's most influential philosopher, held views which threatened to undermine the discipline's legitimacy, Woodbridge made strenuous efforts to push his colleague toward a more theory-centered and objectivistic position by asking him to recognize that he shared with Aristotle, Aquinas, and Woodbridge himself "the same" philosophy of mind, differing only about the biological machinery that supported it.

Dewey resisted these efforts. For him, the whole point of the Darwinian revolution was that there could be no difference between the essential "nature" of a thing and its mode of generation or coming-to-be, and no such thing, therefore, as unrevisable or purely conceptual knowledge. Nonetheless, as his career at Columbia went on, Dewey began to don the robes of an Aristotelian metaphysician himself, especially in *Experience and Nature* (1925). Just as Dewey's original psychologism was increasingly grounded in his biologism, so his biologism now became rooted in a naturalistic metaphysics in which the "generic traits of existence" presupposed by his adaptationist anthropology were to be related to the claims of the various empirical disciplines as Aristotle's "being *qua* being" was related to the subjects of the special sciences. It is difficult not to see in these developments Dewey's own adaptation to the environment in which he found himself at Columbia, where graduate students and junior professors such as Sidney Hook, Richard McKeon, John Hermann Randall, and Ernest Nagel vied to narrow the gap between Dewey's instrumentalism and Woodbridge's realism. Dewey's students even started calling themselves "empirical naturalists," thereby nesting in one of the pigeon holes of the "epistemology industry" that Dewey decried.

The steady tug toward realism during the twenties is evident in the fact that many social critics who had been nurtured by pragmatist teachers, such as Walter Lippmann, W. E. B. Du Bois, and Reinhold Niebuhr, now distanced themselves from pragmatism. It is also at work in Morris R. Cohen's attempt to usurp Dewey's place by presenting his own "public philosophy" as a criticism of pragmatism and an application of philosophical realism to social issues. Cohen, born in Russia, had been drawn into philosophy by Thomas Davidson, an intriguing character who haunted the margins of late-nineteenth-century American philosophy. Davidson plucked Cohen from the streets of Brooklyn and took him to the summer philosophy camp he ran in the Adirondacks, where the young man met the likes of Dewey, James, and Royce. Cohen then studied at Harvard under Perry. After a period of difficulty attaining a position because he was Jewish, he introduced to City College of New York a distinctive philosophical voice, much more committed to Enlightenment cosmopolitanism than either idealists or pragmatists had been, which he put to the service of the intensely discursive brand of liberalism that arose among the so-called New York intellectuals, many of whom were Cohen's students. He also sent Columbia some of its best philosophy students, notably Hook and Nagel, who, even when they declared themselves Dewey's disciples, betrayed more than a little of the rationalist influence of their first mentor.

Cohen took traditional philosophy, with its presumptively skeptical view of social discourse, seriously enough to empower it to hold political, social, and legal practice to intensely high standards of logical, evidential, and normative rigor. In his efforts to make philosophy relevant to social practice, Cohen pioneered the idea of designing courses in the "philosophy of" various fields, such as science and law. In 1934, for example, Cohen and Nagel published a textbook that became the prototype of books still used in now ubiquitous courses in logic and the philosophy of scientific method. The point of such courses was to sustain the claims of logic, reason, method, and scientific realism. Cohen argued that to treat scientific theories as instruments, conventions, or constructs, as Dewey did, was to undermine the power of science to distinguish truths from illusions and facts, and hence to deprive reason of its potential as a sharp instrument of social critique and amelioration. Cohen also regarded the law as a more effective instrument of democracy than the educational reforms Dewey favored. Like his friend Justice Oliver Wendell Holmes, whom he helped install as a liberal icon, Cohen seems to have had a more highly developed sense of evil than Dewey. He had the instinctive sense of Enlightened Jews since the eighteenth century that minorities could achieve real standing in an overwhelmingly Christian society only by defending the rationalistic, formal, even legalistic standards of a cosmopolitan society. Although Dewey and Cohen frequently spoke on behalf of the same causes and candidates, Cohen was, in this respect, a procedural liberal rather than a melting-pot progressive. At least implicitly, he saw Dewey's participatory pragmatism as sanctioning provincial, largely Protestant, cultural biases that would prove incapable of producing a fully secular and ideologically neutral democracy.

These facts suggest that, although there was little agreement about what a realist was, most philosophers in the twenties and thirties saw themselves as realists of one stripe or another. It is tempting to see the shift toward realism as a reflection of the political and cultural conservatism of the twenties. This point is inseparable, however, from the fact that realism, rather than Deweyan instrumentalism, represented the outcome of American philosophy's protracted effort to professionalize itself. Under this dispensation, professionalized philosophy would retain ownership of its old foundational problems. It would allow equal proprietary rights to experts in other fields, and it would intervene in social discussions only long enough to insist that the rational should be preferred to irrational. It would not, however, encourage philosophers to portray their discipline as devoted to Emersonian musings, or to dissipate their professional energy, which should be reserved for technical issues, in what Sellars called the Chicago school's "social consciousness."

## ANALYTIC PHILOSOPHY AND THE POSITIVIST ASCENDANCY

The turn from psychology to logic endured, but the ascendancy of realism did not. By the early forties, American philosophy had undergone another sea-change, in the course of which appeals to logic, which realists had used to confute pragmatists, now undercut realism itself. Often referred to as the rise of "analytic philosophy," or linguistic analysis, this shift was provoked by the migration of intellectuals from Germany and Central Europe following the rise of Nazism. The intellectual diaspora brought to America many prominent members of the Vienna Circle of "logical positivist," or as some preferred to call themselves "logical empiricist," philosophers. The influence of Herbert Feigl, Hans Reichenbach, Rudolf Carnap, Gustav Bergmann, and Carl Hempel, among others, began immediately to be felt on American philosophy. Although logical positivism, the first movement to be given a boost by linguistic analysis, eventually lost steam, analytic philosophy itself remained, dividing twentieth-century American philosophy into pre-analytic and analytic eras.

Analytic philosophy begins with what Bergmann

called "the linguistic turn." This is a piece of methodological advice urging philosophers to formulate their problems as problems about language. The hope was that by doing so philosophy's traditional issues would be solved at long last, or else discarded as pseudo-problems arising as artifacts of unanalyzed language. As a procedural recommendation, the linguistic turn may be contrasted with the "epistemological turn" of the seventeenth century (that is, with the "new way of ideas" we associate with Locke and Descartes, which appeared at the turn of the twentieth century as the old, tired "idea idea"), and with the even older Aristotelian "way of things," which asks what kinds of entities there are rather than what kind of ideas we have or words we use.

Those who took the linguistic turn conceived of meaning as a property of sentences, rather than of individual words, a point first made by Gottlob Frege. Following the Polish logician Alfred Tarski, who eventually settled in Berkeley, they then took the meaning of a sentence to be equivalent to the set of conditions under which it would be correct to assert it. The sentence "Snow is white," for example, is true if and only if snow is in fact white, for these are its truth-conditions. The general bearing of Tarski's disarming insight is well expressed in Ludwig Wittgenstein's startling answer to a question about how one knows that some item is red. "Because he knows English," Wittgenstein replied. To have a concept, that is to say, is to know how to apply it to cases. The truth-conditional analysis of meaning carries even more implications for the concept of truth than for meaning. Truth, rather than being obscure and distant, turns out to be something so pervasive that we overlook it all the time. Truth is simply what happens to sentences when their truth-conditions are fulfilled.

Analytic philosophers now recognized that Russell had long before produced a paradigm of linguistic analysis of this sort. In a 1905 paper "On Denoting," Russell assumed that the meaning of a name is the actual entity, whether particular or universal, to which it refers. The problem is that the mere mention of an apparently meaningful referent seems, on this assumption, to confer some sort of existence on it, even if no such entity exists in reality. The apparently meaningful sentence "The present king of France is bald," for example, uttered in 1905, must affirm the existence of a current king of France if the point is to deny that he had hair. Even a round square must, on this view, really exist, or at least "subsist." Meinong's brave embrace of something like this conclusion struck Russell, in his hasty retreat from the absolute idealism of his youth, as offending against the robust sense of reality that philosophers must always try to preserve. Russell resolved the dilemma by attributing the difficulty to a misleading feature of surface grammar, namely the subject-predicate form that had long retarded the development of logic itself. As Alfred J. Ayer put the point in *Language, Truth, and Logic* (1936), an influential tract commending the linguistic turn and logical positivism in particular to English and American philosophers, "In general, the postulation of real non-existent entities results from the superstition . . . that to every word or phrase that can be the grammatical subject of a sentence there must exist somewhere a real entity corresponding." Russell proposed to rid the world of such ghostly substances by analyzing an offending sentence into inoffensive elements. The sentence about the king of France, for example, is a conjunction of three propositions: "there is a king of France"; "there is only one king of France"; and "whatever is that one is bald." The falsity of the first conjunct entails the falsity of the entire set. But the first sentence is a simple negative existential sentence ("It is not the case that there is an x"). It does not mention a subject, and therefore does not leave anything behind when it is denied. Generalizing this perspective, Russell concluded that the illusions of the common-sense world, brimming as it is with the insupportable flotsam and jetsam of religion, political ideology, and folk psychology, have their source in bad grammar.

Russell's recommended antidote was a strong dose of traditional British empiricism. Any substantive idea that cannot be tracked down to the sensory experiences from which it derives should, as Hume had long before declared, "be consigned to the flames." Language hooks onto the world, Russell said, by way of "logically proper names," which pick out, and thereby posit the existence of, indubitable units or atoms of perceived reality. Propositional logic then allows true pictures of the complex world to be compounded out of classes of "atomic sentences" naming sense data, in a way that Wittgenstein, Russell's student and collaborator, proposed in his *Tractatus Logico-Philosophicus* (1921). Russell's "logical atomism," as this doctrine was dubbed, revived the flagging fortunes of British empiricism. It gave empiricism a realistic twist (since, like James, Russell regarded sense data as aspects of the real world rather than merely mental phenomena), and washed it down with more deductive logic than Hume and the psychologistic John Stuart Mill had been able to muster.

One of the advantages of logical atomism, Russell

believed, was that its injunction to tear experience down and put it back together again under the control of logic (and mathematics, which Russell and Alfred North Whitehead had shown in *Principia Mathematica* (1910–1913), to be deducible from logic) could anchor the new physics of relativity and quantum mechanics on an empirical base, no matter how offensive its concepts were to common sense. Thus was dreamed again the Enlightenment dream of resolving complex entities, ideas, and propositions into simple elements, discarding whatever is left as illusory—a dream that ever since Descartes has been dreamed again each time a new computational algorithm (in this case the new logic) appears on the scene. This development had a devastating effect on James's and Dewey's holism, which denied that the field of consciousness can ever be decomposed into units or reassembled into one and only one true, justified aggregation. To Russell, the pragmatists seemed hopelessly sunk in the same psychologism that had rendered Mill a philosophical primitive. When he visited the United States in the early 1940s, Russell ridiculed Dewey's logic as insufficiently a priori to preserve the necessary character of logic and mathematics, or to account for the profound new physical theories which depended on these formal sciences.

Russell took logical atomism to be a metaphysical thesis, a lean conceptual framework within which science would forever prosper and never again collide with philosophy. By contrast, the members of a research community of "logical positivists" that had been assembled in Vienna by Moritz Schlick and Otto Neurath after World War I were more inclined to interpret the insights of analytic philosophy, including Russell's, as a rejection of metaphysics altogether. The Vienna Circle, as it was called, was at least as familiar with contemporary physics as Russell. Unlike Anglophone philosophers, however, these philosophers had been forced to confront a cultural and intellectual crisis qualitatively different from any that had ever afflicted England or America. German-language philosophy had inherited Kant's conviction that the categories under which we have any experience at all are uniquely consistent with syllogistic logic, Euclidean geometry, and Newtonian physics. Modern logic, non-Euclidean geometry, and relativity physics now discredited this presumption, leaving neo-Kantians more disoriented than Pierce had been at an earlier point in the disintegration of Kantian philosophy at the hands of post-Newtonian physics. The Vienna Circle was even more upset when a wave of philosophical irrationalism, running from Friedrich Nietzsche to Martin Heidegger, attempted to preserve the Kantian claim that experience has a priori structuring principles by locating these principles at primitive, intuitive, prescientific levels of symbolic and emotional processing. The result of this neo-Romantic turn was to dismiss logic and scientific method as manifestations of a technological will to power, to concentrate ideological influence in the hands of antirationalist metaphysicians, and in the process to reinforce the destructive forms of social and political irrationalism then spreading in Europe. (The inability of Wittgenstein's English admirers, including Russell, fully to appreciate the poignancy of his philosophy reflects their indifference to his roots in this Continental crisis, and his curious way of combining its rationalist and irrationalist sides.)

Appalled by this flirtation with the demonic, the Vienna Circle defended the guiding role of scientific method in culture by attacking the Kantian idea that there are substantive a priori propositions, propositions that do not arise from experience because they make ordered experience itself possible. To reject this claim was to reject metaphysics itself, for since Kant metaphysics has been thought of as a quest for synthetic a priori propositions. The philosophers of the Vienna Circle are rightly called positivists because they inherited (mostly through the physicist-philosopher Ernst Mach) August Comte's conviction that the amelioration of the world by modern science depends on eliminating metaphysics. Comte, the father of positivism, encoded this belief in his famous "law of three stages," according to which culture moves progressively from theological and metaphysical stages to an empirical or "positive" stage, in which fruitless quests for essential realities behind appearances are given up, and inquiry is restricted to finding predictively useful correlations between classes of phenomena. They are called *logical* positivists because of their stress on deductive logic in scientific method and in philosophical analysis.

The Vienna Circle's most salient contribution to the positivist tradition was the so-called "verification principle," according to which the meaning of a sentence is simply the list of empirical conditions that must hold if that sentence is to be true. On the verificationist principle, meaningful statements fall into only two classes: the in-principle verifiable claims of empirical science, and the analytically true or false, but empty, calculi of logic and mathematics, which are used to track and concatenate sensory information. No room is left for a priori categories. Metaphysics, accordingly, is not full of falsehoods, or even of intelligible but difficult to assess, propositions, as Kant had thought. It is composed instead of pseudo-propositions with no definable meaning at all. This reworking of "Hume's [two-pronged] fork" between "relations of ideas" and "matters of fact" was tantamount to defending scientific method as the only way of getting real knowledge. Once metaphysical constraints had been set aside, the road of inquiry could no longer be blocked by turning dubious notions, including Kant's Newtonian prejudices, into inviolable truths. In these terms, the Vienna Circle attempted to launch a second Enlightenment, whose relation to the new physics would recover the lost relationship between the first Enlightenment and Newton.

Having put metaphysics out of play, logical positivists developed a philosophy of science with a number of components that remain influential even today: (1) philosophy of science is what remains of philosophy after its metaphysical pretenses have been cut down by the verification principle; (2) the scientific method is the only method of acquiring knowledge ("scientism"); (3) scientific theories are instruments for predicting and controlling phenomena, rather than pictures of underlying reality ("phenomenalism," "antirealism"); (4) scientific theories may originate in all sorts of psychological processes—what matters is that they are empirically confirmable, at least in principle, by experimental testing of the predictive statements they deductively entail (verification as demarcating science); (5) scientific theories are composed of deductively arranged propositions that follow *more geometrico* from a set of axioms; (6) scientific explanations are deductive applications of well-confirmed laws to cases, with the result that prediction and explanation are distinguished only by the temporal position of the investigator; (7) science progresses through efforts to reduce the empirical generalizations and laws of less general sciences to those of more fundamental sciences, notably physics ("reductionism," "unity of science program"); (8) questions of value, being neither confirmable nor falsifiable, can and should be separated from questions of fact ("fact-value dichotomy"); and (9) ethical claims are strictly speaking meaningless emotional responses ("emotivism"). (Another Viennese émigré, Karl Popper, offered an alternative to these ideas, according to which what demarcates science from nonscience is our ability to falsify, rather than to verify, hypotheses. Popper's philosophy of science has waxed as logical positivism waned. Initially it was more influential in Britain, where Popper settled, than in America.)

The Vienna Circle influenced American philosophers most deeply in the person of Rudolf Carnap, whose ambition to analyze scientific theories into sense data reports by way of elaborate logical transformations had been sketched in *The Logical Structure [Aufbau] of the World* (1928). In 1934 Carnap emigrated to the United States through the good offices of W. V. O. Quine, a young American logician from Harvard who had studied with him in Europe, and of Charles Morris, who found a place for him at the University of Chicago. Carnap was a bit put off by the medieval shades that neo-Aristotelian realists like McKeon and Mortimer Adler had drawn around the study of philosophy at Chicago. "In some philosophical discussions," he wrote in a memoir, "I had the weird feeling I was sitting among a group of medieval learned men with long beards and solemn robes, a feeling . . . further strengthened when I looked out the window at the other university buildings with their Gothic style." Carnap felt more comfortable with Morris, who had maintained a pragmatist presence at Chicago by refocusing it around Peirce's theory of signs ("semiotic"), his reworking of logic for a pragmatized world. From Morris, Carnap claims to have gained some understanding of Dewey's and Mead's pragmatism, and at least some sympathy for its hapless ambition to be a "scientific philosophy." (In Europe, pragmatism was crudely understood as an expression of America's vulgar commercial mentality.) Carnap became comfortable working in terms of the semi-Peircean distinctions Morris drew between syntactics, semantics, and pragmatics. At first, however, most of the influence went the other way. As editor of the *Journal for Symbolic Logic,* Morris was eager to infuse pragmatism with the nonpsychologistic stress on deductive logic that the Vienna Circle had brought to America.

Since the early thirties, reports about the Vienna Circle had been appearing with some regularity in American philosophy journals and books—by Hook in 1930, Feigl and Blumberg (who together coined the name "logical positivism") in 1931, Nagel in 1934, Reichenbach in 1936, Ayer in 1936, Morris in 1937. Graduate students quickly gravitated to the places where logical positivism was being taught. By 1940, it was clear that American philosophy had been infused with an exciting new spirit. American philosophers became proud of the fact that, like the artists, filmmakers, and architects who were welcoming German expressionists and Bauhaus modernists to America, they were providing a haven for the preservation of scientific rationalism even as Europe fell into totalitarian darkness. The émigrés found most of their converts among younger pragmatists, who saw in logical positivism ways of distancing their tradition from questionable, and certainly unfashionable, psychologistic conceptions of logic that they inherited from Dewey and James. Realists generally steered clear of a philosophy that attacked metaphysics, even if it did defend logic.

Negotiations between pragmatists and positivists centered on the analysis of meaning. The positivists took the pragmatic criterion of meaning to be a crude first approximation to their own verification principle. Morris agreed. "In spite of apparent divergences and real differences of emphasis," he wrote in *Logical Positivism, Pragmatism, and Scientific Empiricism* (1937), "it is possible for pragmatism and logical positivism to converge on an analysis of meaning." At the same time, Morris argued that pragmatism could help positivism by broadening the bounds of empirical meaning to include biological, social, and even valuational aspects of experience which the physics-centered iconoclasm of the positivists' forbade, but which Dewey's stress on the activities of organisms in environments had placed within the scope of empirical inquiry. Nagel too took this view. He devoted much effort to finding out how to align teleological or purposive phenomena, which had been central to the biocentric naturalism he had inherited from Dewey and Woodbridge, with physical laws. One eventual result was that Nagel's 1961 textbook, *The Structure of Science*, was considerably more leavened with positivistic philosophy of science than the one he had authored with Cohen so many years before.

The resulting assimilation of logical positivism to a wider range of quasi-pragmatized forms of linguistic empiricism was also a matter of prudent retreat on the part of the positivists. Since the early thirties, even its firmest advocates had recognized that logical positivism of the strict observance contained insoluble difficulties. For one thing, the status of the verification principle itself had long been in doubt. It was neither a definitional nor a purely empirical claim. Thus it did not fall readily on one side or the other of Hume's sacred fork. Moreover, suspicions that a priori categories float free of empirical control were raised when even Carnap had to concede that different languages (whether they are natural languages like English or Swahili, or formal languages like propositional logic and various computer languages) project different truth-conditions for the same empirical data, and so might equally well (or badly) predict a given body of data. Indeed, each language seems to structure empirical data in terms of a unique ontology in such a way that bare empirical facts do not testify in favor of one interpretive framework rather than another. "Ontological relativity," replete with the epistemologically discouraging implications of its cousin, cultural relativism, thereupon raised its head, conflicting with the antirelativist agenda that had given birth to positivism in the first place.

In offering a solution to these difficulties, Carnap took a pragmatic turn that he might never have taken in his original European context. He acknowledged, in the spirit of Morris, that our choices between languages or ontological frameworks are "pragmatic." Such choices are to be judged solely by which framework is most consonant with and useful for the economical and predictively fecund pursuit of up-to-date science. Yet no metaphysical consequences, Carnap proclaimed, whether realist or relativist, attend such choices. For there are no facts of the matter about conceptual schemes. "Five is a prime number" has a truth value only if one opts to use a framework of numbers. But the bare statement "Numbers exist," or substances, or universals, is neither true nor false. "External questions" do not demand "ontological commitment." Only "internal questions" do.

Quine was soon arguing that Carnap's ontological relativity entails a greater dose of pragmatism than Carnap suspected. Since each language has its own way of identifying and individuating objects, linguistic relativity implies "referential opacity": two languages will cut the sensational field up differently, even where they appear to pick out nominally the same thing, say a "rabbit" in English. Accordingly, we cannot justify the choice of one ontological framework, or scientific theory, over another by deciding which better accounts for and aggregates isolated, theory-neutral pieces of data. Unit for unit comparison must be abandoned for more holistic and heuristic considerations. As Quine puts it in "Two Dogmas of Empiricism" (1951), "Our statements about the external world face the tribunal of sense experience not individually but only as a corporate body."

Quine's view favored Jamesian coherence over Russell's ideal of logical construction and a correspondence theory of truth. For it meant that the project of reducing molecular to atomic propositions, each of which names a single sensory datum, cannot conceivably form the philosophical basis of theory choice in science. More radically still, Quine argued that if pragmatic criteria for theory choice are all we have, even the revered distinction between analytic and synthetic statements, and hence between conceptual and empirical truths, must be abandoned. In making comparisons between rival ontologies or languages we can choose to hold this or that statement more or less closely to our breast, and can "redistribute" truth values accordingly. No statement, however, including the allegedly analytic definitions and synonymies that are built into our preferred languages ("All bachelors are unmarried men"), will be immune to rejection or revision. Hence the very notion of a distinction between necessary (analytic) truths and revisable empirical (synthetic) statements collapses: "In repudiating such a boundary I [Quine] espouse a more thorough pragmatism [than Carnap]. Each man is given a scientific heritage plus a continuing barrage of sensory stimulation; and the considerations which guide him in warping his scientific heritage to fit his continuing sensory promptings are, where rational, pragmatic."

This famous sentence from "Two Dogmas of Empiricism" (1951) implies a radical answer to the positivists' conundrum about the logical status of the verification principle and the disciplinary status of philosophical claims and inquiry. By turning issues about theory choice into semi-empirical questions whose answers are to be guided by what the best physicists currently say about what objects really exist, what psychologists experimentally tell us about behavior, and how field linguists and anthropologists manage to devise translation manuals between the languages of different cultures, Quine claimed to be returning to Dewey's "naturalized epistemology," and to his once-spurned merger between philosophy and psychology. "When with Dewey we turn . . . toward a naturalistic view of language and a behavioral view of meaning," Quine wrote in "Ontological Relativity" (1968), "we recognize . . . that 'meaning is primarily a property of behavior.'"

It seems that American pragmatism, in the person of W. V. O. Quine, had rescued itself from defeat at the hands of realists by coming to the aid of positivists. In spite of his invocation of the shade of Dewey, it is, in fact, very useful to think of Quine as working out of the pragmatic tradition that James left behind at Harvard. Quine's conviction that our ideas are confronted by sensory data only at the periphery, leaving plenty of room for adjustment elsewhere, echoes James's proclamation that "Truth lives for the most part on the credit system." Indeed, in *Realism with a Human Face* (1990), Quine's colleague Hilary Putnam has perceptively written that Quine, Nelson Goodman, and himself "have been shaped by a continuous tradition of American thought . . . that can be traced from its beginnings in the debates at Harvard between Royce and James, as well as in the work of Peirce and Dewey, through the writings of our teacher C. I. Lewis, up to and including some of the most recent developments in American professional philosophy."

Lewis was the key figure in this transition, and Quine's main target in "Two Dogmas." He called himself a "conceptual pragmatist" because he thought that coherence among our beliefs is achieved more through formal logic than James thought, but that logic, whose application to the world depends on categories, is more open to revision than Royce, for example, assumed. Although Lewis was the first to recognize that the analytic consists in those statements we refuse to abandon or amend "come what may," and that the definitional truths of languages are as many and as varied as languages themselves, he stoutly advocated the "two dogmas of empiricism" that his student Quine attacked: the clean distinction between analytic and synthetic truths, and the "reductionist" dogma that Lewis vividly described in *An Inquiry into Meaning and Truth* (1946) by saying that "Our empirical knowledge rises as a structure of enormous complexity . . . all parts of which rest, at bottom, on direct findings of sense. . . . [It is] an Empire State Building made out of toothpicks." Lewis was able to defend the analytic-synthetic distinction largely because he had a traditional view of logical truth. A logical truth, such as a definition or a synonym, has meaning insofar as it states a criterion for identifying and classifying entities by way of their "essential" properties. By contrast, Quine had learned from Russell, Wittgenstein, Tarski, and Carnap to interpret logic "extensionally." The meaning of a term is simply the list of entities picked out and pushed around by an arbitrary classterm. Quine's extensionalism, when combined with his holistic conception of theory-choice, broke down the wall Lewis had erected between the analytic and synthetic, letting loose his submerged insight that what looks like analytic truth is simply a revisable decision to hold a statement constant while changes among our beliefs are made elsewhere.

If it is true that pragmatism revitalized itself by making these shifts, it is no less true that in the process American pragmatism was positivized. Quine, for example, assumes that in making conceptual choices that introduce greater coherence, economy, and predictive reliability into our beliefs, we do better in proportion as we are able to compute our way through the sensory field, identifying units and operating on them in a rule-governed way in order to control the flow of future experience. Quine thinks of the ontology of natural languages as embodying a weak predictive theory, whose chaotic, "folk-psychological" ontology of beliefs, intentions, desires, and actions is in the process of being replaced by predictively superior theories of behavior. Accordingly, he is dismissive of the computationally weak, and in his view epistemically impoverished, humanities, which utilize this primitive folk ontology. He looks favorably instead on the behaviorism of his Harvard colleague B. F. Skinner. Quine thus inherits and transmits positivism's Enlightenment prejudice against the ordinary. In spite of his attacks on its dogmas, Putnam has plausibly called Quine "the greatest positivist."

The difference between Quine's positivized pragmatism and older versions can also be seen in Dewey's response to the positivist ascendancy. In spite of the fact that the logical positivists assiduously courted his support, Dewey was from the start skeptical about, and even hostile to, their enterprise. Their treatment of scientific theories as axiomatic-deductive systems seemed to him too mathematizing, and too oriented toward physics, to square with his biocentric logic of inquiry. More importantly, the positivists' refusal to see valuation as a meaningful dimension of intelligence, rather than as emotivist "epithets or mere ejaculations," was, Dewey thought, of a piece with their assumption that the improvement of society would best be carried out by experts wielding powerful predictive theories rather than through the wide diffusion of Dewey's cherished habits of democratic inquisitiveness. Dewey did not think of people and their desires as irrational objects of expert manipulation. He did not think that intelligent social action could be represented as an engineering problem. Dewey did not, accordingly, mean by "behavior" quite what Quine, or certainly Skinner, meant. In treating intelligence as a property of behavior, he had no intention of depriving behavior of many "folk psychological" or intentional attributes. He wanted instead to treat these as objective, social forms of symbolic interaction rather than as private mental events. Accordingly, when Dewey reluctantly agreed to contribute to the positivists' *Encyclopedia of Unified Science,* his "Theory of Valuation" (1939) took the form of an attack on the positivists' emotive theory of value. Dewey repeated his main point in the 1948 introduction to a new edition of his *Reconstruction in Philosophy* (1921):

> When sociological theory withdraws from consideration of the basic interests, concerns, and actively moving aims of a human culture on the ground that "values" are involved, and that inquiry as "scientific" has nothing to do with values, the inevitable consequence is that inquiry in the human area is confined

to what is superficial and comparatively trivial, no matter what its parade of technical skill.

This remark arises out of a troubled background. Dewey had supported "Wilson's War" on the ground that the scientific coordination of production that it called for would at last give reformers an edge over capitalists by helping to construct a rationalized regulatory state. This had enraged his former admirers Randolph Bourne and Lewis Mumford, who spoke of this technocratic impulse as "the pragmatic acquiescence." Dewey later repented of his decision to support America's entry into World War I. By the twenties, however, many social scientists were hoping that institutions like the National Research Council and the Social Science Research Council, which had been created during the war, would be continued and expanded in peacetime. Among social scientists eager to contribute to this effort were many who had become disillusioned by the failures of their youthful populism, or who wanted to professionalize disciplines hitherto associated with the insufficiently quantified, and vaguely feminized, sphere of "social work," or whose hostility to the narrowness of their religious upbringings had stimulated a crusading scientism. Many political scientists, for example, embraced Walter Lippmann's conclusion, a product of his own disillusioned retreat from participatory pragmatism, that democratic consent must be "manufactured" from above because the "masses" are incapable of intelligent political judgment. Such people often found their way to philosophies of science which ratified a cult of expertise, such as the prelinguistic positivism of the eugenicist Karl Pearson. Dewey feared that the positivists who had arrived in the United States in the thirties would restimulate this tendency.

In many ways he was right. The diffusion of pragmatized logical empiricism, broadly construed, amplified the scientistic *ethos* within which a managerial "culture of expertise" acquired prestige in postwar America at the expense of the more participatory forms of liberalism favored by Dewey. Attempts to socialize production, economists now argued, would be less effective than the creation of a consumer society, watched over by economists charged with keeping employment and consumption levels high. If a "managerial revolution" was required to achieve that end, behavioral psychologists were there to recast their theories in terms of how workers and managers would respond to economic stimuli unmediated by such unmeasurable, and seemingly metaphysical, concepts as mind, intention, or values. Logical positivism helped legitimate the guiding hand of theory-wielding experts by furnishing managers with a suitably scientific self-image, and by allowing social scientists to present their diagnoses and prescriptions as "value free." The positivists' emotivist view of values also made it possible to portray ethical and aesthetic views as so subjective that no good reasons could conceivably be given why moralistic communities or invasive governments should be allowed to constrain the private preferences of individuals (if they harm no one else). Logical positivism thus helped reorient American liberalism around the ideal of protecting and enhancing personal choices against the very economic, legal, and social regimentation that positivistic social science was itself strengthening.

The home of this new liberalism was the reconstructed postwar American university, where the positivist dichotomy between fact and values was embodied in the disciplinary structure of a vastly expanded system of higher education. The social sciences were encouraged to assimilate themselves to the quantitative methods of the natural sciences, which were assumed to accord well already with the canons of positivist philosophy of science. Whatever disciplines could not meet this challenge were unceremoniously dumped into a new bin denoted by an old word, "the humanities," a category which assembled a heterogeneous collection of fields whose objects and methods were deemed too subjective to meet verificationist criteria, but whose mission (to cultivate the sensibilities of students by curing them of the dogmatic values they had brought from their homes, churches, and provincial or ethnic communities) seemed too important to drop.

## ORDINARY LANGUAGE PHILOSOPHY

The early fifties form a watershed in American philosophy. If many philosophers were unhappy with the positivists' deconstruction of the intelligibility of metaphysics, they were appalled by the self-immolation of philosophy implied by Quine's attack on the analytic-synthetic distinction and his calls for "naturalized epistemology." To blur the line between philosophy's conceptual issues and contingent, empirical matters was to deprive philosophy of the very air it breathed. Sensitivities about the future of philosophy became prickly in an academic environment in which philosophy's questions, and methods of answering them, seemed equally doomed whether they were absorbed into the empirical sciences, as Quine proposed, or were left to languish among the impressionistic humanities. In so eagerly embracing positivism, and successfully exporting it, philosophers seemed in retrospect to have been braiding the rope that was to hang them.

In this atmosphere, whatever heirs to the idealist legacy were still around took their distance from the APA, fully engaged as it now was with the linguistic turn. Some defected to a new Metaphysical Society of America, prominent members of which, like Charles Hartshorne and Paul Weiss, had regrouped around Whitehead, who had settled at Harvard in the twenties, and whose "process philosophy" of "concrescing occasions" bore some affinities to Peirce's evolutionary and probabilistic worldview. Many older critical realists responded no less suspiciously to the linguistic turn. Cohen, for example, professed relief in his waning years that Carnap did not "in my presence at least use linguistics as a refutation or substitute for metaphysics or ontology." At the same time, younger professionals began to doubt whether linguistic analysis was as deeply wedded to positivism as its friends and enemies assumed. They suspected that the linguistic turn might offer new ways of defending, rather than undermining, the line between conceptual and empirical issues, and of making it clear that philosophy's proper business is exclusively with the former. A canonical method for performing conceptual analysis in this spirit soon emerged. Designed in part to show academic colleagues that philosophers wield a standardized method that affords them as much scope for cooperative problem solving as the experimental method affords scientists, and practiced with a hair-splitting rigor and conventionally masculine bravado, the idea was to analyze the concepts that play important roles in traditional philosophical problems, such as "knowledge," "truth," "mind," "good," "right," "beautiful," by testing proposed sets of truth-conditions for the use of these concepts against often bizarre counterexamples.

Not surprisingly, linguistic restatements of virtually every preanalytical American philosophical orientation except idealism began to reappear in this idiom. Defenders of philosophical empiricism who opposed Carnap's and Quine's destructive view of conceptual questions looked to Russell's example. Had not Russell managed to be an empiricist, a linguistic analyst, and a metaphysician too? Thus in a book bearing the ironical, but perfectly serious, title of *The Metaphysics of Logical Positivism,* Bergmann, a member of the Vienna Circle transplanted to the University of Iowa, defended logical atomism as the best way to protect positivism's philosophy of science from the conceptual relativism with which Carnap's and Quine's pragmatic turn was infecting the field.

Unlike his father, Roy Wood Sellars, Wilfrid Sellars was impressed by the resources of linguistic analysis. The younger Sellars was unconvinced, however, that philosophy could skirt Quine's challenge as long as it remained sympathetic to empiricism. He thereupon set out to pry linguistic analysis loose from its contingent association with empiricist sensationalism and phenomenalism, and in the process to defend the critical realism that he regarded as his "paternal inheritance," by destroying what he called the "Myth of the Given." Language certainly gives us our world, Sellars argued, but not, as Russell had claimed, by way of "logically proper names" that hook onto atomized sense data. Language mirrors the world by aiming at "complete and systematic correspondence" between our sentences and the causally concatenated processes we learn to track ever more accurately as the "manifest image" of common sense slowly gives way to scientific realism. Accordingly, "in characterizing an episode or state as that of knowing," Sellars wrote, "we are not giving an empirical description of that episode or state. We are placing it in the logical space of reasons."

The linguistic turn was also used to support theses associated with the "essence" wing of the critical realist movement. Linguistic analyses of "mind," "consciousness," and related concepts seemed to some to show the irreducibility of mental to physical terms, and hence to affirm some sort of dualism, without, happily enough, committing anyone to metaphysical dualism between body and soul (an artifact of the old "way of things") or epistemological dualism between ego and external world (an artifact of the "way of ideas"). The implication was that our talk about mental acts will never disappear into physiology, nor will epistemology and philosophy of mind devolve into empirical psychology.

By the late fifties, it seemed to many that the most effective defense of the program of linguistically analyzing the concepts that figure in traditional philosophical problems, and the analytic-synthetic distinction on which that program precariously rested, had been put forward by a British school of philosophers who favored the syntax and semantics of natural or ordinary language over ideal or formal languages as both the medium and object of philosophical analysis. "Ordinary language philosophy," as it came to be called, resonates so deeply with the tradition of common-sense realism that it can usefully be considered a linguistic restatement of new realism. It can be traced to the stimulus given to work done earlier by Moore at Cambridge, and by Gilbert Ryle and John Austin at Oxford, by the confessional testimonials of the later Wittgenstein against his former logical atomist self. Wittgenstein now recognized that the assertoric mode into which he and Russell had once shoehorned every relationship between word and world had failed to acknowledge that to use language is to engage in a social practice. On this count, the notion of "logically proper names" to which he and Russell had appealed seemed too solipsistically conceived to count as language use at all. Nor are our ideas resolvable into computable sums of sense data. After World War II, a new generation of American graduate students made their way to England to study with Wittgenstein and with Austin at Oxford. British philosophers trained in this kind of analysis, meanwhile, began accepting lucrative positions in American universities.

Peter Strawson's 1950 paper "On Referring" was a milestone of ordinary language analysis. Strawson showed that Russell's theory of denoting, commonly thought of as the very paradigm of conceptual analysis and a definitive account of referring terms ("the x," "an x"), was mistaken. Its mistakes, moreover, illustrated the perils of disregarding the social dimensions of language learning and use. Russell assumed that the mere mention of a subject in the subject-predicate grammar of English deludes us into positing the existence of a present king of France or a golden mountain. Strawson argued that no such implication obtains, and that there is nothing inherently misleading about subject-predicate grammar. In mentioning a present king of France when I ascribe baldness to him, I do not thereby *assert* that he exists, but use a sentence-type that *presupposes* it. A person to whom such a sentence is addressed would reply inappropriately by contradicting the speaker's statement, but appropriately by informing her that the assumption under which she made it was unwarranted at the time she uttered it.

In Strawson's view, to analyze a concept is not to tear it down to its sensory roots, but to make explicit the conditions for using it appropriately in public discourse. This in turn suggested that the narrow concept of truth-conditions should be replaced with a wider semantics of appropriateness- or use-conditions, some of which were worked out by Paul Grice under the rubric "conversational implicature." We appeal to truth-conditions only when we are engaged in *asserting* something. It is clear, however, that, as Austin put it, we "do things with words" other than asserting, such as questioning, doubting, hoping, commanding, praising, and blaming. There are even some "speech acts," which Austin called "performative utterances," the fulfillment of whose appropriateness conditions actually brings about the state to which they refer. Satisfying the appropriate conditions for uttering the sentence "I pronounce you man and wife," for example, actually creates the marriage to which it refers, and thus can hardly be reporting or asserting it.

Ordinary language philosophers, rather than regarding formal or ideal languages as rapier-like instruments that deliver us from the muddles and illusions of the ordinary world, think of them as blunt tools that run roughshod over the fine discriminations which speakers of natural languages learn to use with finesse. Because most of our concepts are "open-textured," correct application is often a matter of sensitivity to context and nuance, which can be acquired only through a sustained process of becoming socialized into the practices of the communities that use the language in question. Armed with this conviction, Strawson and Grice joined forces to take on Quine. In "In Defense of a Dogma" (1956) they argued that we wield the analytic-synthetic distinction in normal speech quite effectively. In doing so, we leave room for long-term shifts and borderline cases that, far from falsifying the distinction in question, enhance its viability by allowing for flexible and open application.

Ordinary language philosophy had sobering effects on empiricist philosophies of science. Its advocates simply would not grant Quine the premise he needed to dismiss the "folk psychology" encoded in natural language as a predictively weak theory. Natural language, for ordinary language philosophers, is not a theory at all. It has a pretheoretical, world-constituting, or as Heidegger might put it, "world-disclosing," status. Natural language gives us the world that science, both social and natural, investigates. On pain of referential failure, accordingly, scientific theories cannot go on to cancel or replace that world. Rather, theorizing, predicting, and explaining are constrained to explicate the shared world we actually live in. Nowhere is the continuity between Scottish realism and ordinary language philosophy more apparent than in their realism about the ordinary objects of natural language and their suspicion about scientific ontologies. Given these suspicions, these philosophers went on to argue that the facts with which social scientists, psychologists, and historians deal are inextricably bound up with agent-centered descriptions of those facts, and connections among them, which refer to beliefs, intentions, actions, choices, reasons, practices, and cultural tradi-

tions. It followed that positivistic attempts to reduce the human to the natural sciences, either substantively or methodologically, and thereby to explain human affairs in ways that prescind from the apparatus of "folk psychology," lose contact with their subject matter, and do not meet criteria for good explanation. Aid and comfort was thereby extended to "interpretive" social scientists and historians who were trying to hold back the positivistic cult of law-governed, prediction-oriented explanation from their fields.

Ordinary language philosophy also helped American philosophers defend the cognitive worth of humanistic thinking. Stanley Cavell's work is illustrative. Cavell belongs to a generation of American philosophers who brought Austin's and Wittgenstein's way of philosophizing back to native shores after World War II. Inspired by Wittgenstein's conviction that authenticity requires us to remain within the bounds of honest, natural speech, Cavell argued that formal languages are correlated with our tendency merely to theorize about our experience, rather than to live it with aesthetic and moral sensitivity, and so with our capacity to avoid responsibility and to deceive ourselves and others. Cavell takes these existential concerns to be the authentic root of philosophical puzzles like skepticism and dualism. With Wittgenstein, he thinks that philosophy's problems are recurrent and important for everyone. The resolution of philosophical problems comes, however, not from the crystalline purity of formal languages, which dulls our moral sensitivities, but when what Cavell calls the "uncanniness of the ordinary" bursts our pretenses. Literature, art, and criticism leavened by ordinary language analysis provide good materials for doing philosophy in this spirit. Accordingly, Cavell has tried to call American philosophers, sometimes to their puzzlement, back to Emerson and Thoreau, who he thinks practiced philosophy in this spirit, and who need to be rescued from the trivializations they have undergone at the hands of the tender- and the tough-minded alike.

Cavell's example shows that ordinary language philosophy was appealing partly because it offered an able defense of the rationality of morality against the devastating effects of the positivist fact-value dichotomy. Logical positivists regarded moral claims as expressions of emotion with no cognitive content or normative force. Moral philosophy was to be restricted to "metaethical" analysis of ethical talk. Ordinary language philosophers were able to show, however, that agents are expected to and in fact do give binding, if contextually sensitive, reasons for their actions. Morality may depend, as emotivists like Ayer and C. L. Stephenson said, on persuasion. It is wrong, however, to assume that persuasion is not a matter of reason-giving. Arguments to this effect by British philosophers like G. E. M. Anscombe, Philippa Foot, R. M. Hare, Alasdair MacIntyre, and Stephen Toulmin were eagerly taken up in America. Arthur Murphy was the first among several philosophers to use ordinary language philosophy to rescue Dewey's communitarian conception of practical reason from its positivistic and technocratic distortions. By the seventies, the recovery of roughly Aristotelian conceptions of context-sensitive practical reason by ordinary language philosophers had even spurred calls for a return to Aristotle's "virtue ethics," according to which cultivating character traits that provide a basis for the flexible use of practical reason is more important than the rationalistic rule-following characteristic of many other ethical traditions. Somewhat later, Martha Nussbaum commended the study of literature, in the spirit of Cavell, as a way of articulating and applying Aristotelian virtue ethics.

Even when they resisted ordinary language philosophy and virtue ethics, moreover, analytic philosophers of every orientation soon came to believe that moral philosophy should not be restricted to analyzing the semantics of moral statements, as logical positivists had urged. Moral philosophers should insist on the importance of the moral point of view, and contribute to the resolution of difficult moral questions by bringing moral reasoning to bear on them. Richard Brandt, Kurt Baier, Alan Donagan, Gerald Dworkin, Joel Feinberg, Philippa Foot, William Frankena, and Thomas Nagel are among those who have contributed to the new seriousness with which "normative ethics," or moral problem-solving, has been taken by analytic philosophers. Stirred by worries that merely technical educations were dulling the ethical sensitivities of students, a movement arose in the eighties resulting in the rapid and pervasive spread of "applied ethics" courses in undergraduate curricula.

Concern with normative ethics also spilled over into political and social philosophy. The most influential American social and political philosopher of the postwar era is John Rawls of Harvard, whose *A Theory of Justice* (1971) uses penetrating thought experiments to defend not only the personal freedoms dear to liberals, but social welfare policies as well. Rawls revived the old Lockean tradition of "social contract thinking" by asking his readers to imagine themselves behind a "veil of ignorance," where, without knowing what place they would oc-

cupy in it, they would be asked to decide what sorts of political, social, and legal institutions to build into a society in which they would have to live. Rawls argued that rational self-interest itself would commend a set of arrangements in which a maximum amount of personal liberty is combined with a principle of distribution according to which no one can command a higher proportion of total social goods if that means those least advantaged will get less than they already have. At first, Rawls presented this theory as a product of reasoning from an abstract, universal moral point of view. Eventually, however, he reconceived it as a concrete and situated "political conception" of "justice as fairness," a product of constructive reasoning that might be undertaken by citizens living in a pluralistic society like ours, where not everyone can be expected to subscribe to the same substantive moral principles.

Although ordinary language philosophers and logical empiricists both call themselves analytic philosophers, the differences between their respective worldviews are vast. By the mid-sixties, a sort of methodological truce obtained between these orientations. Theories of scientific explanation sponsored by empiricists like Nagel and Hempel were assumed to be valid for the natural sciences. The human sciences and the humanities, on the other hand, were to be governed by methods suitable for interpreting value-laden phenomena and intentional acts. Soon, however, this tacit treaty was undermined by arguments suggesting that not even natural science works the way logical empiricists assumed. The most provocative stimulus to this view was Thomas Kuhn's *The Structure of Scientific Revolutions* (1962). Kuhn argued that neither verificationist nor falsificationist models of scientific progress can account for the development even of physics, the hardest of the hard sciences. Treating scientists as members of discursive communities, Kuhn showed that the way they assess evidence and change theories differs less from the way people do these things in areas like politics, art, and religion than inheritors of Enlightenment scientism would like to think. To establish this, Kuhn used ordinary language ideas about the context-sensitivity of concepts to reinforce arguments pioneered by cultural anthropologists to the effect that people in different language communities experience the world differently. Accordingly, commitment to "scientific paradigms," while not irrational, must be more like persuasion and conversion than like being compelled by raw data, as empiricists assumed.

Kuhn's theory was rooted in his experience teaching science-in-society classes with James Conant at Harvard. It was subsequently nurtured by conversations with Cavell and Paul Feyerabend when all three were teaching at Berkeley. In the early sixties, when Cavell had moved back to his native Harvard and Kuhn had gone to Princeton, Berkeley became the site of the Free Speech Movement and soon of opposition to the Vietnam War. The students who were forming a distinctively antiscientistic counterculture in and around Berkeley, together with their peers at Michigan, Columbia, and soon virtually everywhere, attacked the culture of expertise as a cause of the war and a culprit in the decline of older, populist, and participatory conceptions of democracy in America. The positivistic spirit, they acknowledged, may have helped millions of working-class people ascend to middle-class status. But the consumer ethic that was both means and end of that ascent was not, they thought, a worthy goal. Stimulated by humanistic educations, they saw the new postwar American "multiversity" and the bureaucratized government as positivist products, and vigorously challenged them. Some saw ordinary language philosophy, with its retreat from scientism, its defense of situated practical reason, and its aestheticized conception of the life-world, as an ally. Ordinary language philosophy, which began as a defense of the professional autonomy of philosophy against threats posed by Quine's naturalized epistemology, thus came to serve improbably as a medium for neo-Romantic defenses of the life world against the "system world." It did not take long, however, for dissident intellectuals to find their way to European philosophical styles, including Marxist methods of ideological analysis, that were more trenchantly critical than ordinary language philosophy had ever been.

## THE AMERICANIZATION OF CONTINENTAL PHILOSOPHY

In spite of standing differences between Anglophone and Continental philosophy, phenomenology, Europe's most vital twentieth-century philosophical tradition, shares common roots with analytic philosophy. Frege had answered Meinong's puzzles about round squares and missing kings of France by postulating that between the mental act of naming and the object named lies an intentional schema, or sense (*Sinn*), through which names are directed to objects. The object-directedness or intentional nature of thought, on which Brentano had insisted, need go no further in positing entities, therefore, than what a "sense" searches out. The fact than an object is "sensed" as an imagined object, for example, means

precisely that it is not a real one. Russell rejected Frege's solution to Meinong's puzzles because it appealed to intentional meanings that were inconsistent with his extensional interpretation of logic. It was precisely these features, however, that appealed to Edmund Husserl, whose triadic model of noetic act, *noema,* and object was based on Frege's three-fold distinction between act, "sense," and referent (*Bedeutung*). Philosophers, Husserl argued, could reflectively inspect the field of consciousness without making inappropriate commitments to its objects. For phenomenological description "brackets" existential claims by the act of reflection itself, leaving the field of consciousness undisturbed. Husserl's phenomenological method revealed that to each mental act—such as asserting, hoping, willing, doubting, desiring, imagining—there corresponds an essential meaning-structure that governs how the formal objects of these acts ("the willed," "the desired," "the asserted") are constituted and evidenced. The task of philosophy is to describe these a priori meaning-structures. Here at last, thought Husserl, was Kant's realm of synthetic a priori propositions, structural features of consciousness that make coherent experience possible. Here too was a good way to save neo-Kantianism from "the crisis of European science" that Husserl saw in both positivist scientism and Romantic primitivism.

As early as the twenties, American realists had latched onto Meinong's use of Brentano's "principle of intentionality," according to which mental acts transcend themselves by pointing to intentional objects. They had also become interested in how the directedness of consciousness to objects affects moral philosophy. Under the title "value theory," Meinong and other European realists were offering new defenses of the moral intuitionism that generally accompanies metaphysical realism. On this view, we not only possess a "moral sense," but "intend" an objective world that is constituted by and laden with compelling moral and aesthetic values. The African American philosopher Alain Locke even defended cultural pluralism in these distinctly antirelativist terms. Locke, who was Perry's student at Harvard between 1904 and 1907, and again in 1916–1917, received a Rhodes Scholarship that was only grudgingly honored by racist Oxford. There he was shunned by other American Rhodes scholars, except for Horace Kallen, a Jewish American pragmatist who opposed Dewey's monoculturalism, and who worked with Locke to develop the notion of cultural pluralism. Before returning to America, eventually to take up a post at Howard University, Locke studied in Berlin, where he encountered Meinong's value theory. Thereafter, he argued that evaluative judgments open up an objective world of intrinsic values, and for this reason command imperatively rather than instrumentally. In suggesting that it would be inconsistent for persons whose sense of their own intrinsic value is based on the activity of valuing itself to constrain the valuations of others, Locke turned a view of ethical obligation usually associated with Kant's absolutism into a normative theory centered on respect for diversity.

Marvin Farber, a philosopher at the University of Buffalo (later SUNY Buffalo), was the first American to import Husserl's version of realism into America. While studying abroad, Farber had been accepted into the circle of Husserl's students. Upon his return to the United States, he founded *Philosophy and Phenomenological Research* to foster dialogue between American and European realists. Roderick Chisholm, who eventually succeeded Farber as editor of this journal, recognized the affinity between Husserl's phenomenological analyses of mental acts and his own attempts to defend the irreducibility of mental concepts to the physical. Chisholm's anthology, *Realism and the Background of Phenomenology* (1960), made the Austrian tradition that had sprung from Brentano, and its relation to American realism, better known.

The American reception of phenomenology was greatly affected by the intellectual migration of the thirties and forties from Germany and Central Europe, which brought phenomenologists as well as positivists to America. The New School for Social Research in New York, founded in the twenties by Dewey, Kallen, and Charles Beard as a haven for academics who, like Thorstein Veblen, were victims of dismissal because of their progressive views, was an important reception point for these philosophers. Among them were Hannah Arendt, Aaron Gurvitsch, and Hans Jonas. These émigrés came to America acquainted not only with Husserl's work but also with that of his student, Martin Heidegger, whose *Being and Time* (1927) is one of the century's most influential books. Heidegger described the structures of the life world in "existential" categories in order to avoid the contemplative biases that, in his view, had led Husserl into a "metaphysics of presence" and ultimately into a version of idealism. Heidegger called his phenomenological method "hermeneutical," after the humanistic method of interpreting texts and persons. "Hermeneutical phenomenology" interprets human reality *(Dasein)* as "always-already" "being in the world." We are beings whose experience is contingent to the point of nau-

sea, and whose lives are so taken up with "care" *(Sorge),* a term connoting both anxiety and taking care of things, that they cannot conceivably be given a speculative gloss. Yet Heidegger's opposition to the metaphysics of presence did not mean that he opposed metaphysics itself. On the contrary, Heidegger announced that his hermeneutic of *Dasein's* lived world was only a preliminary to asking the old "question of being." He soon adopted an oracular tone borrowed from the ancient Greek poets to announce that Being "uncovers itself" not by a direct assault of speculative reason, but by erupting unbidden into the world of making and doing when the tools and instrumental reasoning through which we constitute our "average everydayness" breaks down. It is artists, whose receptive openness to the "Being of beings" "lets Being be," who take advantage of the breakdown of the ordinary to make a "clearing" in which Being can give glimpses of itself, confirming *Dasein's* Destiny as "the shepherd of Being." Heidegger went on to tell a Nietzschean story of the decline of Western philosophy into the "metaphysics of presence," a story that begins with the Greeks and ends with technology as the "fate" of the modern world.

The anxiety-ridden side of Heidegger's "care," together with his insistence on the necessity of ungrounded commitment, was developed after World War II by the French phenomenologist Jean-Paul Sartre. Sartre's existentialism was served up to middle-brow Americans in the fifties and sixties as a mild incitement to revolt against the conformism of consumer society. The caring side of Heidegger, and its biological embodiment in a lived body, was stressed by another French phenomenologist, Maurice Merleau-Ponty. (It was the "caring" side of Heidegger that Dewey himself noticed when he remarked that *Being and Time* sounded as if a German peasant had been trying to translate his own *Experience and Nature* into the gnarled idiom of the Black Forest.) Studies by American philosophers such as Marjorie Grene made existentialism better known in America, and led to increasingly accurate knowledge of Heidegger's seminal thought, although his complicity with the Nazis remained obscured until the seventies.

In many ways, Heidegger's place in twentieth-century German philosophy parallels Hegel's in the nineteenth. Just as there were right, center, and left Hegelians then, so there are right, center, and left Heideggerians now. Post-Heideggerians of all of these orientations, from the culturally conservative Hans-Georg Gadamer to the leftist Herbert Marcuse, a trenchant critic of consumer capitalism, either settled in America or visited frequently. Since their roots ran back to Hegel, these philosophers also helped acquaint American intellectuals with a Hegel who seemed to have little to do with the turn-of-the-century absolute idealist against whom Dewey, Russell, and Moore had revolted, as well as with a Marx who seemed to have little to do with "dialectical materialism," and even less with Stalinism. Influenced by these revelations, American philosophers began giving ordinary-language glosses to Hegel's defense of the life-world, and Hegelian glosses to Marx. Richard Bernstein tuned these voices to the American tradition by showing their affinity to Deweyan pragmatism, and by using the resources of contemporary European philosophy to suggest that Dewey himself was a defender of the life-world rather than an advocate of technological expertise.

American philosophers oriented to the Continental tradition soon recognized suggestive parallels between Austin's analysis of speech acts and phenomenological descriptions of mental acts like knowing, imagining, and hoping. Similarities between Heidegger's idea that Being "happens" when tools break down, and Wittgenstein's notion that "essences" reveal themselves when grammar misfires, stimulated Hubert Dreyfus, a phenomenologist, and his Berkeley colleague John Searle, a student of Austin, to portray Heidegger as a philosopher who describes precisely the kind of world in which Austin's ordinary language, and the Wittgensteinean practices it sustains, would be at home. These and like-minded philosophers were looking for ways to deepen the defenses already being offered by ordinary language philosophers of what Husserl and Heidegger called the "life world" *(Lebenswelt)*. They recognized that these thinkers and their disciples had given new depth to the long-standing conviction of German-language philosophers that the subjects, concepts, and methods of the human sciences *(Geisteswissenschaften)* must differ fundamentally from those of the natural sciences *(Naturwissenschaften)*. The former are "interpretive" or "hermeneutical," requiring the ability to identify, understand *(verstehen),* and even "relive" *(nacherleben)* the thoughts of agents, whereas the latter explain *(erklaren)* by subsuming instances under general laws. Dreyfus and Searle were soon trying to deflect psychologists from their new enthusiasm for reducing mind to brain by construing the former as a computer program. Lacking intentionality, Dreyfus said, computers cannot Think and have no World.

By the early eighties, the growing influence of Continental philosophy encouraged representatives of dissident research communities to make a concerted assault on analytic philosophy's grip on the APA. Calling for "pluralism," a motley coalition of humanist Marxists, deconstructionists influenced by Jacques Derrida, post–Vatican II Catholics, Whiteheadian process philosophers, feminists gathered in the Society for Women in Philosophy, and scholars who had remained faithful to pre-analytic American pragmatism in a separate Society for Advancement of American Philosophy joined forces to oust the established leadership of the Eastern Division. The pluralist movement did not spread as intensely to the Central and Pacific Divisions. Still, the revolt reflected not only the strength of the insurgents, as well as extramural calls for increased diversity within American society as a whole, but also weaknesses within the old analytic consensus that had dominated the APA during the postwar era. If philosophers of science, for example, were less disturbed by these events than they otherwise might have been, that is because they had already become a relatively autonomous discipline, with its own journals and professional organization, the Philosophy of Science Association (PSA). The fate of the APA was not a matter of supreme consequence to many philosophers of science, who were generally preoccupied with heeding Quine's call for a naturalized account of scientific knowing by getting closer to what goes on in actual scientific communities, while at the same time trying not to give too much ground to post-Kuhnian historicists, who regard scientific theories as little more than ideologically grounded "social constructions."

## ANALYTIC PHILOSOPHY AFTER EMPIRICISM

The pluralist revolt did not mean, however, that analytic philosophy was about to roll over and play dead as the century entered its final quarter. On the contrary, having absorbed the lessons of ordinary language philosophy without endorsing its conclusions, analytic philosophers have quietly slipped the albatross of programmatic logical empiricism from around their necks. In this way, they have found their way back to many of the issues that divided realists and pragmatists early in the century, albeit in a way that continues to depend on the linguistic turn. The title of an important collection of recent essays, *Post-Analytic Philosophy* (1985), is, on this account, misleading. For the most part, what the book contains are postempiricist, not postanalytic, pieces.

New research programs within the tradition of analytic philosophy often begin with novel accounts of referring terms. Russell's "On Denoting" was a cornerstone of logical empiricism. Strawson's "On Referring" was seminal for ordinary language philosophers. In the 1970s this happened again. The "new," "historical," or "causal" theory of reference independently proposed by Saul Kripke of Princeton, Hilary Putnam of Harvard, and Keith Donnellan of UCLA denies something assumed by positivists, ordinary language philosophers, and phenomenologists alike, namely, that the reference of a term is fixed by an associated description. (Lemons, for example, are supposed to be picked out by a bundle of terms like "sour yellow fruit," a set of marks that may or may not be further reducible to sense data.) According to Kripke, we actually keep track of things not by applying such criteria, but in the same way we keep track of persons. An entity is dubbed or "baptized" with a name that is passed down in an historical chain that rides serenely over even vast changes in the ways the bearers of these names are described, and the properties they acquire or discard. Surprisingly, what holds for proper names also holds for terms that pick out natural kinds. In using a word like "water," Putnam argues, I intend to refer to stuff having a certain underlying composition that makes it what it is, even if I have no idea what that composition is. As science reveals more about the nature of things, the referential chain goes with the underlying structure, and not with associated descriptions or empirical appearances. The proof is that if something bearing all the usual marks of water on a hypothetical planet, Twin Earth, turns out not to be made of $H_2O$, the correct inference is that the stuff is not water.

This amounts to a retreat from empiricism and a return to realism. Retreat from philosophical empiricism is not, of course, retreat from methodological empiricism in science. Scientific theories are, after all, tested by how well they fit empirically gathered information. Analytical realists merely recognize, with Peirce, that we live in a world composed of things whose essential properties, dispositions, and propensities have real causal effects, rather than a world in which we are merely acquainted with phenomena that we can at most predict and control. The point of science is to discover the underlying structures to which our referring acts point. Indeed, in "Naming and Necessity" (1972), Kripke startled philosophers by arguing that the new theory of reference allows us to say that necessary truths, in the form of constitutive identities between things and their underlying structures, can be discovered by way of contingent inquiries. According to Kripke, if water is actually $H_2O$, that is, if the thing to which I am referring is identical with certain proportions of hy-

drogen and oxygen, then it is necessarily $H_2O$ in every possible world. This implies that, although there are no a priori concepts that make experience possible, as Kant had thought, there are indeed analytical a posteriori propositions, that is, essential truths about constitutive identities discovered by contingent, empirical methods. Logical empiricists were wrong, accordingly, to subscribe so confidently to Hume's belief that there are only verbal tautologies and revisable empirical claims.

Kripke's interests are metaphysical. They hark back to the dualism of the "essence wing" of critical realism. Nor does Kripke show any great urge to reconcile science and common sense. In calling his own philosophy "internal realism," Putnam means in part to resist anything as scholastic as Kripke's brand of realism. For Putnam, the real lesson of the new theory of reference is that, once philosophy has freed itself from empiricism's dogmas, naturalistic critical realism can be defended without countenancing an unbridgeable gap between the "manifest image" of common sense and the reality uncovered by science. In referring to water and other such things, Putnam argues, I "defer" to experts as they learn more about the things and processes I am talking about. This very "linguistic division of labor," however, as Putnam calls it, shows that common sense implicates itself in explaining, revising, and enriching its interpretation of reality.

Putnam's "functionalist" philosophy of mind is an example of the linguistic division of labor at work. Mind depends strongly on its physical conditions, since a brain state is required for every mental state, and the same brain state will always give rise to the same mental state. Still, mind remains irreducible to brain because the mental act vocabulary of our speech, which names the processes into which psychologists and physiologists inquire, makes it possible to say that the same mental act can arise from ("supervene upon") different physical bases. The same thought, for example, might be carried out by brain-cells or by silicon-based machines like computers. Science and common sense work together in this case to obviate the dualist's overreaction to what turns out to be the baseless threat of reductionistic materialism. For similar reasons, Putnam says that worries about "the place of values in a world of fact" should be set aside. These worries reflect empiricism's misplaced distrust of the ordinary (as Putnam's colleague Cavell had already suggested), as well as old theological doubts about whether we see things quite the same way God does. For Putnam, we are securely embedded in the world precisely by our valuing, intending, and representing acts, through which run the myriad of referential chains that let us cooperatively inquire into the nature of things.

Donald Davidson's work also illustrates the contemporary revolt against empiricism. Davidson is, as he himself puts it, "Quine's faithful student." Yet he thinks that Quine fails to reap the full harvest of his own philosophizing because he clings to the misplaced worries of a latter-day empiricist. Quine assumes, for example, that extensional formal logic and intentional conversational logic are at odds, and that intention-ridden "folk psychology" will eventually be replaced by a behaviorist vocabulary closer to "stimulus meanings" and "observational sentences." For Davidson, on the contrary, the truth-conditional analysis of meaning embodied in propositional logic also underlies natural language. Moreover, since Davidson, like Putnam, believes that mind supervenes on physical events without being reducible to natural laws (a position he calls "anomalous monism"), he holds that scientific theories explicate, instead of replacing, ordinary human experience.

Quine stumbles on these points, according to Davidson, because, having freed himself from two of logical empiricism's dogmas, he succumbs to a third, namely to Carnap's view that languages are interpretive schemes that can be fitted onto bare sensory contents. For Davidson, genuine language use is too piecemeal to be represented that way. In making sense of what each other say, we necessarily employ a "principle of charity," according to which a vast number of another person's sentences must be presumed true if we are to be in a position to judge that one or more of them is false. If someone says, for example, "There's a beautiful yawl," apparently referring to what we take to be a ketch, we do not conclude that she has a wholly alien interpretive scheme. Instead, we say to ourselves, "What I call a yawl she must be calling a ketch," redistributing other truth values in such a way that a maximum number of beliefs will come out like our own. In insisting that error arises against a background of truth, and that science does not cancel the experiential world we all share, Davidson harks back to the new realists, and beyond them to a strain of common sense philosophy that is deeply rooted in the American intellectual tradition. In this spirit, Davidson's theory of "radical interpretation" shows to his satisfaction that "The Very Idea of a Conceptual Scheme" (1973), including Kuhn's paradigms no less than Carnap's and Quine's "languages," is incoherent. We all live in the same world. The world sets the truth conditions for our sentences by causing them to be true or false. If there is any general bond between words and world, then, it is a causal bond, rather than the illusory evidential bond demanded by empiricists, which gives rise to little more than useless skeptical doubts.

Richard Rorty believes that Davidson's theory of interpretation is the happy resolution of the problems that analytic philosophy set for itself. When we translate, disagree, redescribe, or play any of a number of other "language games," as Wittgenstein dubbed them, we are fully "in the world." For language gives us the world through our participation in the "forms of life" that constitute it. Any world that calls this into question, Rorty says, is "A World Well Lost" (1972). Rorty suspects, however, that Davidson has made things too easy for himself by hovering around simple interpretive cases about ketches and yawls. Where significant cultural and scientific change is afoot, as it is in what Kuhn calls "paradigm shifts," Rorty does not think we can reasonably hope that the world will ever testify in favor of one interpretation rather than another. Nor should we think with realists that the world will slowly and subtly shape our inquiries to conform to its own contours. Instead, our beliefs are warranted solely by "what our peers will let us get away with." If we do not want to put arbitrary roadblocks in the path of inquiry, then, we have no alternative but to let the meandering, contingent course of our debates generate whatever persuasive stories happen to arise. In this spirit, Rorty turns Davidson's recognition that in a world devoid of the scheme-content distinction there can be no principled distinction between metaphorical and literal talk into a historicist picture of rapid and radical changes in how truth-values are assigned as discourse goes its merry way, driven hither and yon by the life-cycles of the metaphors in and through which we converse. If we ever cease worrying about the mind-body problem, for example, it will not, according to Rorty, be because we have "reduced" the one to the other, but because we have "eliminated" mind simply by switching from one set of metaphors to another.

In saying such things, Rorty takes himself to be a pragmatist. Analytic philosophy, he believes, and Davidson's semantics in particular, frees the pragmatic tradition from the empiricism that led it into its misplaced alliance with logical empiricism, and that distorted James's and Dewey's best work. In spite of the fact that he has championed Dewey, and sees himself as a latter-day Deweyan public intellectual, Rorty is, in fact, something of a reborn James, who insists that sensory experience impinges on our discursive practices only at the periphery, leaving us free to invent whatever world-versions help us meet the contingencies of experience with high spirits. Yet in saying this Rorty does not want to validate pragmatic philosophy. By signing on to the pragmatist tradition, Rorty intends to deconstruct, rather than answer, philosophy's old questions, and so to put an end to philosophy itself. Philosophy, he argues, is so inherently biased against historicity, contingency, and self-creative human freedom that it can only distort and constrain our conversations. In this spirit, Rorty suggests that Davidson's misplaced fidelity to philosophy's factitious agenda prevents him from becoming the pragmatist that his own semantics calls for.

The discourse of philosophy, according to Rorty, is an unstable half-way house between religion and art. Modern philosophy arose to settle the hash of the theocentric world view. It solves its problems when it recognizes its dependence on the same background picture as religion. When philosophy sees through its worries about how words hook onto world, and whether our minds can "mirror" nature as it is "in itself," or as God sees it, it should go out of business. Philosophy's demise carries with it cultural consequences as large as those that accompa-

nied the displacement of theology. Tracing out the implications of the death of philosophy as resolutely as Nietzsche traced out the consequences of the death of God, Rorty argues that the torch of edification once held aloft by theologians, and carried for a time by philosophers, must now be passed to artists, novelists, and freewheeling cultural critics. Turning the tables on the postwar consensus in American philosophy, Rorty concedes that it may be the business of science, technology and bureaucracy to predict and control, and of the arts and humanities to edify. But in a postempiricist, and therefore a postmodern, culture, it is the latter task that is important, not the first. Having fled from Princeton's Philosophy Department to become Professor of Humanities at the University of Virginia, Rorty argues that artistic activity and criticism far better embody the promise of liberal democracy that each person should be free to reinvent him or herself than the earnest appeals to human nature and natural rights cherished by our philosophically bewitched Founders, or the religious conceptions of the human condition that their philosophizing both displaced and preserved. We close the century, then, as we began it, with realists and pragmatists contending over the legacy of religion and the solemn promises of democracy.

SEE ALSO Elementary and Secondary Education; The University (both in this volume); Political Ideas and Movements (volume I).

## BIBLIOGRAPHY

The first half of the century in American philosophy has been well studied by historians. Standard works include Elizabeth Flower and Murray Murphey, *A History of Philosophy in America* (1977); Herbert Schneider, *A History of American Philosophy* (1946); and Paul Kurtz, "American Philosophy," in Paul Edwards, ed., *Encyclopedia of Philosophy,* vol. 1 (1967). The most vivid guide to American philosophers, if not philosophy, between 1900 and 1930 is George P. Adams and William Pepperell Montague, *Contemporary American Philosophy* (1930, 1962), the two volumes of intellectual autobiographies from which I have quoted. On professionalization and the founding of the APA, consult Daniel J. Wilson, *Science, Community, and the Transformation of American Philosophy* (1990). Bruce Kuklick, *The Rise of American Philosophy* (1977), studies the professionalization of the Harvard Department in the Golden Age of

Royce, James, Perry, and Santayana. On the connection Royce saw between communitarian idealism and his boyhood in a California gold rush town, see John J. McDermott, "Josiah Royce's Philosophy of Community," in Marcus G. Singer, ed., *American Philosophy* (1985).

The historiography of pragmatism undergoes considerable revision from time to time under the pressure of new philosophical movements. Dewey's "The Development of American Pragmatism" (1925) is a good place to begin. It can be found in *Later Works,* vol. 2, pp. 3–21, of the superb edition of Dewey's works published by Southern Illinois Press, ed. Jo Ann Boydston. Many works on pragmatism reflect an easily overdone preoccupation with pragmatism as a uniquely American cultural phenomenon. These include John Smith, *The Spirit of American Philosophy* (1963); Morton White, *Pragma-*

*tism and the American Mind* (1973); and John McDermott, *The Culture of Experience* (1976). In *Uncertain Victory: Social Democracy and Progressivism in European and American Thought 1870–1920* (1986), James T. Kloppenberg offers a corrective to American provincialism by recontextualizing classical American philosophy within a wide range of contemporary British and Continental movements. See also Bruce Kuklick, "Does American Philosophy Rest on a Mistake?" in Singer, *American Philosophy*. On the progressive context of pragmatism, read David A. Hollinger, *In the American Province* (1985); and Andrew Feffer, *The Chicago Pragmatists and American Progressivism* (1993). The best collection of pragmatist classics is H. S. Thayer, ed., *Pragmatism: The Classic Writings* (1970, 1982). Another good anthology, unfortunately out of print, is Amelie Rorty, ed, *Pragmatic Philosophy* (1966), which also chronicles pragmatism's encounter with logical positivism. H. A. Thayer, *Meaning and Action: A Critical History of Pragmatism* (1981) focuses on the pragmatic criterion of meaning and truth vis-à-vis positivist verificationism. Affinities between Dewey's pragmatism, ordinary language philosophy, and continental philosophers like Heidegger are explored in Richard Bernstein, *Praxis and Action* (1971). How pragmatism looks from Quine's, Davidson's, and Rorty's perspectives can be seen in John P. Murphy, *Pragmatism: From Peirce to Davidson* (1990). Cornel West's *The American Evasion of Philosophy* (1989) is a postmodern "genealogy" of pragmatism.

For Peirce, begin with Joseph Brent, *Charles Sanders Peirce: A Life* (1993). Classic treatments of James are Ralph Barton Perry, *The Thought and Character of William James* (1935, 1948); and Gay W. Allen, *William James* (1970). The indispensable work on Dewey's life is Robert Westbrook, *John Dewey and American Democracy* (1991). Randolph Bourne's and Lewis Mumford's accusation that Dewey caved in to technologism is examined by Casey N. Blake, *Beloved Community* (1990). Larry Hickman defends Dewey from the charge of technologism in *John Dewey's Pragmatic Technology* (1990). Singer, *American Philosophy*, contains informative sketches of Mead by James Campbell and of C. I. Lewis by Susan Haack. Feffer (1993) is good on Mead and Tufts.

On American realism, start with William Pepperell Montague, "The Story of Realism," in *The Ways of Things* (1940). On the relation between American new realism and Continental realism, see Roderick Chisholm, *Realism and the Background of Phenomenology* (1960), which also contains the original "Program and Platform of Six American Realists." On Alain Locke, a start has been made by Leonard Harris, ed., *The Phi-*

*losophy of Alain Locke* (1989). Sidney Morganbesser, ed., *Dewey and his Critics* (1977), collects the papers Dewey wrote in the *Journal of Philosophy* against the realists, together with the relevant realist contributions. On Santayana, consult T. L. S. Sprigg's sketch in Singer, *American Philosophy*. On Lovejoy, see Daniel J. Wilson, *Arthur F. Lovejoy and the Quest for Intelligibility* (1980). On Cohen, read David A. Hollinger, *Morris R. Cohen and the Scientific Ideal* (1975). For more on Cohen, together with an account of Arthur Murphy, read Marcus Singer, "Two American Philosophers," in Singer, *American Philosophy*. Solid historical work on Sellars, *père et fils*, is badly needed.

Historiographical work on American philosophy after mid-century falls off precipitously. That is not only because events are too recent, but because analytic philosophers seem to have lost interest in their own history, while intellectual historians, preoccupied with the Americanness of American philosophy, too often see the analytic and Continental movements as intrusive disruptions of a native tradition. Studies of what linguistic analysis meant to figures like Morris, Nagel, Hook, and others in the first generation to receive it would be useful. The best introductions to analysis are still A. J. Ayer, *Language, Truth, and Logic* (1936), for logical positivism; and J. O. Urmson, *Philosophical Analysis: Its Development between the Two World Wars* (1956), for ordinary language philosophy. The impact of analytic philosophy's various programs on American philosophers can be perspicuously viewed by studying a sequence of canonical anthologies. Herbert Feigl and Wilfrid Sellars, eds., *Readings in Philosophical Analysis* (1949), was a logical positivist showcase. Feigl's *New Essays in Philosophical Analysis* (1972) shows increasing diversity in the movement. Richard Rorty, ed., *The Linguistic Turn* (1967), explores tensions between its ordinary and ideal language versions. The founding essays of the "new" or "historical" theory of reference are contained in Stephen P. Schwartz, *Naming, Necessity and Natural Kinds* (1977).

For Carnap, Tarski, Popper, and Quine (and indeed Dewey, Hartshorne, Santayana, and Weiss), see the relevant volumes of the Library of Living Philosophers, edited by Paul A. Schilpp, and published by Open Court, La Salle, Illinois, at various dates. George A. Romanos, *Quine and Analytic Philosophy* (1983), is good not only on Quine, but on Carnap and Wittgenstein as well. Richard Creath, ed., *Dear Carnap, Dear Van: The Quine-Carnap Correspondence* (1990), is informative. American philosophy of science after Kuhn and Quine is chronicled in an engaging way in Werner Callebaut, *Taking the Naturalistic*

*Turn, or How Real Philosophy of Science is Done* (1993). Bjorn T. Ramberg, *Donald Davidson's Philosophy of Language* (1989), serviceably introduces his work. James Conant, ed., *Realism with a Human Face* (1990), is a diverse enough collection of Putnam's essays to give an accurate account of this intriguing, but often elusive, philosopher. Also read Putnam's *Reason, Truth, and History* (1981). Rorty's *Philosophy and the Mirror of Nature* (1979) is a controversial account of how analytic philosophy brings the whole philosophical tradition to a benign end. The essays in Alan Malachowski, ed., *Reading Rorty* (1990), are mostly about this stage of Rorty's work. Rorty speaks for his postphilosophical pragmatism in *Consequences of Pragmatism: Essays 1972–1980* (1982); and *Contingency, Irony, and Solidarity* (1989). David Hall, *Richard Rorty: Prophet and Poet of the New Pragmatism* (1994), summarizes some of these themes.

How post-Heideggerian Continental thought fuses with the concerns of American philosophers who resist positivist accounts of the human affairs, including Rorty, can be seen in Robert Hollinger, ed., *Hermeneutics and Praxis* (1985); and in David R. Hiley, James Bohman, and Richard Shusterman, eds., *The Interpretive Turn: Philosophy, Science, Culture* (1991). John Rajchman and Cornel West's *Post-Analytic Philosophy* (1985) contains a wide sampling of postempiricist philosophers. Some informative essays in this collection are Bernstein's "Dewey, Democracy: The Task Ahead of Us," Davidson's "On the Very Idea of a Conceptual Scheme," Putnam's "After Empiricism," Rawls's "A Kantian Conception of Equality," Rorty's "Solidarity or Objectivity," and West's "The Politics of American Neo-Pragmatism."

# ARCHITECTURE

*Robert Twombly*

At the close of the twentieth century U.S. architecture can be categorized as signature, generic, and vernacular. A handful of buildings are designed by highly visible architects, widely known even to the general public as an elite coterie producing glamorous "signature" buildings internationally for public and private institutions with immense financial resources: I. M. Pei and the National Gallery East Wing in Washington, D.C., and the Louvre Pyramid in Paris, for example, or Robert Venturi with the Staten Island Ferry Terminal and the addition to the National Gallery of Art in London. A considerably larger second group of buildings is designed by architects, unknown beyond their immediate vicinities, who put up private and what little multifamily housing there is in the United States as well as local facilities for government and business—endless variations on what might be called basic generic types. The vast majority of construction (95 percent)—by convention called vernacular—is not designed by architects at all, consisting of easily replicable buildings that developers assemble for shopping malls, tract housing, storage, franchise, chain, and discount stores, and the rest of that sea of minimalism that Venturi praised in *Learning From Las Vegas* (1972) but that Peter Blake had already labeled differently in *God's Own Junkyard* (1964).

## ARCHITECTURE AND SOCIAL PLACE

When the twentieth century opened the situation was somewhat different. There were, to be sure, both an elite coterie in the United States, just emerging as a self-conscious group but without international reputation (except for Henry Hobson Richardson and Richard Morris Hunt, both already dead; Louis Sullivan; the firm of McKim, Mead and White; and perhaps a few others), and of course an invisible majority, many still unknown one hundred years later. Vernacular in 1900 referred to the forms and construction methods of the amateur or single-occa-

sion builder capable of erecting a dwelling or a shop with or without assistance. But during the twentieth century vernacular came to mean commercially produced mass construction based on textbook formats. The rural southern "dog-trot" house and the "false-front" of the West gave way to the suburban "Cape Cod salt box" and the split-level "ranch" (a.k.a. "splanch"), the strip's Pizza Hut, and countless other universal building types. Neither earlier nor later vernacular were generated by architects, although the latter on occasion was remotely based on professional designs. The difference is that whereas every dog-trot house was an idiosyncratic example of a collective building type that had evolved over generations in response to local climates and materials, the splanch and the salt box conflated time and place. If there never were cattle ranches on what became suburban Long Island, neither is it necessary today on the Great Plains to huddle for warmth around a fireplace in a box-shaped dwelling with a long sloping roof originally conceived to cover an added-on, lean-to kitchen at the rear; nor does the Pizza Hut roof, call it mansard or shed, reveal much about the work of the seventeenth-century French architect François Mansard or about country storage places.

What vernacular building of the late twentieth century does reveal, aside from dissociation from historical time and specific place, is a kind of architectural Reaganomic trickle-down, wherein ideas originating with the visible elite are homogenized by invisible colleagues either in their own designs or for vastly wider dissemination by contractors and developers. (By no means do all states require a licensed architect to sign off a developer's plans.) Take as an example the free-standing roofless gable with a hole punched through its facade of 1980s "postmodernism." It is difficult to determine who originated this element, but it was surely a well-known architect, possibly Venturi at his Tucker House (1975) in Katonah, New York, or Stanley Tigerman at the "Daisy House" (1976) in Indiana. Whatever the

Roofless Gable. Saturn of West Nyack (New York) automobile agency, early 1990s. Photograph by Robert Twombly.

source, by the 1990s the holey roofless gable was found at suburban shopping malls, atop skyscrapers, as new crowns for rehabilitated nineteenth-century business blocks, indeed, on every imaginable kind of structure. Starting out as an ornamental fillip for clients of means, it became a device for upgrading down-scale buildings as it devolved into a cliché for mass consumption.

The transformation of vernacular from folk to standardized forms mirrored the rise of a hegemonic architectural elite. By century's end, although little-known architects and builders were still responsible for more than nine-tenths of the nation's constructed fabric, important architects controlled the profession. Only they could advertise themselves by collaborating with publishers and "critics" on coffee-table monographs about their own work. Only they were featured on network television, taken up by national magazines (including Sunday supplements) or asked to design shopping bags for Bloomingdale's. A small number of architects controlled the organizations that, among other things, determine licensing standards and their own criteria for membership. Visible architects launched new stylistic mannerisms, set the agenda for polemical debate, and doubled as directors of prestigious training schools. Without elite sponsorship—without attending one of a handful of premier schools and later working for a prominent firm—it was nearly impossible for initiates to break ranks with the invisible. Graduates of publicly funded schools of architecture like City College of New York or the University of Wisconsin–Milwaukee for example, may have spent more time studying statics, structures, and mechanical systems, that is, what makes a building work, and less time studying history, theory, and critical opinion, that is, what makes a building famous, than an Ivy League counterpart, but they would find it infinitely more difficult to hire on with a "star" architect and eventually open a visible "shop."

This rigid stratification is the consequence of a professionalizing process that by 1900 was well under way and accelerating. Its beginnings may conveniently be dated with the formation of the American Institute of Architects in 1857, and it was essentially completed by World War II. As professionalization gathered unprecedented momentum during the 1890s, it generated two desiderata not new to architects but which for the first time were collectively and consciously, as opposed to individually and unconsciously, pursued. One was the necessity, in public perception and in fact, to sever historic ties with what were now deemed the lesser endeavors of construction and engineering because an emerging elite within what had been a trade chose to define architects generally, but especially themselves, primarily as artists with a calling nobler than that of mere artisan-builders. The second involved social location: the desire of leading architects to elevate themselves from a comparatively powerless, loosely associated group of independent gentlemen into a tightly knit coterie appended to the upper class.

The two desiderata intersected because only as creative artists would architects be indispensable to an emerging upper class aware of its own lack of historical rootedness and cultural connoisseurship. By providing it with a visual aura emblematic of social prominence, legitimizing power with artistic imagery, both purchaser and provider could address their objectives. But it was not solely through service to individuals that architects found opportunities to advance their agenda. During the nineteenth century the demands of a new network of architectural patrons—corporations and the republican state as well as plutocrats—surpassed in volume those of an older network—church, monarchy, and aristocracy—to which American architects for obvious reasons never had much access. The new demands were symbolic as well as material, equally if not more oriented than those of the older network toward social and political valorization.

Just as the social objectives of individuals and their organizations overlapped those of architects, so did the political objectives of the republican state. Its internal enemies in the decades bracketing the turn of the century, principally organizing labor and radical political movements, were also architects' enemies for quite tangible reasons: all visible United States architects opposed unionization, especially in the building trades, where struggles for and implementation of higher wages, safety measures, and the eight-hour day slowed construction while raising its cost. No United States architect of note, including stylistic "progressives" like Louis Sullivan and Frank Lloyd Wright, was associated with the political left, as were prominent Europeans like H. P. Berlage in the Netherlands, Tony Garnier in France, and Ernst May in Germany. The republican state's external objectives and furthermore, the expansion of economic and territorial empire overseas, helped solidify a national self-image of exclusivity and superiority that architects were internalizing about themselves personally and as a group. By cloaking the state and private entities in artistic imagery intended to validate the social order, architects not only embraced that order but also found a way to enter it in privileged positions. The images were carefully chosen to suggest analogies—that is, to obliterate differences—between American social and political intentions and European social and political achievement, and were mostly culled from history. Because scholars have grouped those images under the socially neutral rubric of "eclecticism," it is easy to overlook the precision with which they were applied.

There were dissenters from this historicizing agenda, to be sure. Principally in the Midwest, a younger generation inspired by Henry Hobson Richardson and Louis Sullivan argued that developing contemporary expressions of time and place was more important than perpetuating ancient forms or adapting foreign ideas. Their position was encapsulated in the slogan "Progress before Precedent," adopted in 1900 by the year-old Architectural League of America, briefly a rebellious organization whose members had started working mostly in the 1880s and 1890s. Their argument, however, was not with the notion of American superiority or exceptionalism, and rarely with the practices of plutocracy and state; nor was it with the emerging social role of architects or the political meaning of design. Rather, it was with the choice of imagery, that is, it maintained that eclecticism should give way to an "American" style, or, put another way, that "traditional" architecture had outlived its usefulness. By framing the debate almost entirely in stylistic terms, turn-of-the-century practitioners removed their work from analyses in other than the formalist terms in which, sometimes in literary and other times in architectural language, it has by and large remained, except for a minority of observers. Unlike most other architectures, that of the United States has been praised and condemned, debated, discussed, and critiqued, more in terms of aesthetics than in terms of social relations.

## STYLE AND SOCIAL AGENDA, 1890–1910

It is exceedingly difficult to maintain, as many have, that an American style has ever existed. There have certainly been building types—the skyscraper springs first to mind—as well as ways of expressing them—Louis Sullivan's interpretations, of course—that were invented here. Frank Lloyd Wright and his "Prairie school" followers developed a type of residence that specifically rejected other times and places. Ludwig Mies van der Rohe realized with steel, concrete, and glass what neither he nor others had in other countries. But even in their day these modes of articulation were only temporarily à la mode, no matter their influence on both visible and invisible architects; nor do three discrete mannerisms, or even ten or twenty, add up to a national style. United States architects, in other words, have not developed anything like a Gothic or a Baroque to which it might be said there was culturewide or even elite commitment over a long duration. Such commitment has occurred in the realms of folk and commercial building, but not in the fine art of design.

There were brief periods before the mid-nineteenth century, to be sure, when particular conventions and mannerisms captured regional or national fancy. But were these "stylistic mannerisms?" Some historians claim the so-called Federal style as the first national architecture, but during its heyday at the turn of the nineteenth century it was in fact a late and localized (concentrated in the Northeast) version of English Georgian, which had gingerly entered the colonies early in the eighteenth century and then swept them after 1760. Geographically broader in appeal was the Greek Revival of the 1820s to 1840s (lingering longer in the Old Northwest), also claimed by some as the first national style, mostly on the basis of ubiquity, begging the question, as is also the case with the Federal style, of whether an adaptation of an import can be considered indigenous. It was followed by the chronologically overlapping Gothic Revival, which lost its momentum with the outbreak of the Civil War.

From roughly the late 1860s until World War I the nation's architecture was no longer characterized by a succession of adaptations (Georgian, Greek, and Gothic revivals) or by distinctive regional conventions coexisting in time but not necessarily in space (as in the colonial period). The last four decades of the nineteenth century were, rather, an era of extraordinary diversity on a continental scale; historic and recent styles from the world over flooded the nation but no one of them prevailed, even locally or regionally. All was not as chaotic as it might seem, however; there were certain organizing principles for this eclectic potpourri. One was the application of specific historic styles to particular building types: Gothic for universities and churches, even Protestant churches; neoclassical and neo-Renaissance (sometimes called Beaux-Arts after the École des Beaux-Arts in Paris) for financial institutions and government buildings; "round-arch," a kind of simplified Romanesque, for warehouses; Tudor, "Italianate," "Queen Anne," and others for suburban and country villas.

A second organizing principle addressed a middle-class desire: to differentiate individual dwellings from what were fundamentally similar structures next door and across the street; for houses that were essentially the same size and shape, set back the same distance from the sidewalk and from each other, and with the same room designations, clients could insist upon a classical pediment here or a Tudor window there to reclaim their individuality. Or eclecticism could be organized in more idiosyncratic ways, by administering myriad historical flourishes to a single

structure—Frank Furness's Pennsylvania Academy of the Fine Arts (1871–1876) in Philadelphia, for example, sporting touches of neo-Gothic, French Second Empire, neo-Grec, Egyptian Revival, the Romanesque, and neoclassical salted with elements from an artful cornucopia of his own invention. Furness's was truly an "international style" which usually went under the name of High Victorian Gothic, and his, combined with other eclectic applications, turned the typical late-nineteenth-century American street into an architectural melting pot. Despite increasing clamor for culturally indigenous expressions, the nation's architect-designed buildings were adaptations—but almost never direct imitations—of usually historic, sometimes contemporary, but virtually always non-American structures.

Rummaging the world for historical inspiration seems to have been especially pronounced in English-speaking countries, the United States perhaps most of all, possibly because it lacked longstanding, universally endorsed traditions of its own. But another factor was the extraordinary influence here of the Englishman John Ruskin and the Frenchman Eugène-Emmanuel Viollet-le-Duc, whose immense popularity might in part be explained by the United States having no comparable influential home-grown architectural theorists. Ruskin's insistence that proper architecture was a moral force for social improvement and Viollet-le-Duc's emphasis on structural rationalism struck chords that resonated with other aspects of American culture, but their wide acceptance was also based on a shared preference for the Gothic, albeit gothics of very different sorts. The genius of visible eclectic architects in the United States, however, was to stand Ruskin on his head and to trivialize the import of Viollet-le-Duc.

Ruskin's interests were with working people, but the visible eclectics' were with employers. For him, the acts of building and of using good architecture would uplift the masses; for them, good architecture would keep the masses in their place while uplifting their patrons. All agreed that architecture could be a moral force. The question was, in whose interests? Viollet-le-Duc argued that good architecture clearly and rationally revealed its structural systems, as best demonstrated by French Gothic. American architects, ignoring the essential message that structure should determine form, took away only the notion that Gothic was rational and could thus serve as the compositional basis of the skyscraper, for example, to signal the efficient, rationalized business activities housed inside. Both theorists were thus divested of progressive implication—in the one case social, in the other aesthetic—and made to serve social and aesthetic reaction.

In the hands of an eclectic elite, modern functions and building systems were ordinarily disguised with socially loaded ornamentation, composition, and form. It remained for stylistic progressives to embrace structural rationalism, perhaps in part to muster authority for their artistic waywardness, which almost totally denied them access to upper-class and state patronage. During the middle third of the twentieth century, ironically enough, structural rationalism would be taken up by second and third generations of the privileged, administering a temporary setback to latter-day eclectics. But in the late nineteenth and early twentieth centuries, specific classical, medieval, and Renaissance models were selected as vehicles for appropriating Ruskin's sense of social purpose for exclusive use by the powerful and well-placed. An examination of upper-class residences, government edifices, quasi-public structures, and corporate headquarters demonstrates that eclecticism was never socially neutral or randomly applied.

The very rich were drawn to several styles for the dwellings with which they announced themselves, but what the architectural historian Marcus Whiffen calls the "châteauesque," typified by Richard Morris Hunt's work for the Vanderbilt family, and the neo-Renaissance, popularized in the United States by McKim, Mead and White, were the most exclusive. What the two shared and perhaps exhibited better than other possibilities was their association with prior aristocracies.

The châteauesque is sometimes called the Francis I style and in its sixteenth-century inception was a synthesis of Italian Renaissance and native Gothic forms. During the second quarter of the nineteenth century it underwent a revival in France at just the moment that Hunt—the first American to do so— was studying at the École des Beaux-Arts. The first major realization of the style in this country was his 1882 mansion on Fifth Avenue, New York, for William K. Vanderbilt, a building understood by the leading American architecture critic, Montgomery Schuyler, to refer "to the romantic classicism of the great châteaux of the Loire." Numerous other designers promptly followed with lesser counterparts, but the most lavish ever constructed in the United States was Biltmore (1888–1895) designed by Hunt for George Washington Vanderbilt near Asheville, North Carolina, with its stables over 1,000 feet long at the center of 120,000 acres laid out by Frederick Law Olmsted. Soon the Michigan, Woodward, and Commonwealth avenues of the nation's cities and the Newport and North Shore vacation colonies were dotted with Loire and other châteaux, collectively the most lavish architectural manifestations of recently acquired personal wealth ever seen in this country.

Also important was the neo-Renaissance, introduced here by McKim, Mead and White for Henry Villard's 1882–1885 house group on New York's Madison Avenue. Neither Charles F. McKim nor Stanford White had studied abroad. Both had attended the newly established architecture department (the nation's first) at the Massachusetts Institute of Technology and apprenticed with Henry Hobson Richardson before opening an office with William Rutherford Mead. It is instructive to compare the social location of their clients with Richardson's.

Richardson, who never leaned on neo-Renaissance forms, sometimes worked with aggressive new entrepreneurs like Marshall Field and John Jacob Glessner in Chicago, the Cheney department store family in Hartford, and the Ames industrialists in Massachusetts. But the people with whom he preferred to associate, including many of his clients, represented an older, socially established, often Harvard-educated, Yankee elite involved with regional commerce and manufacturing, public service, and the arts, men like John Hay, Henry Adams, Phillips Brooks, Frederick Law Olmsted, and Francis Lee Higginson. McKim, Mead and White, on the other hand, opening their operation in 1879, fourteen years after Richardson, attached themselves to a newer, much wealthier, more powerful but socially less established oligarchy comprising nationally oriented industrial and financial barons: the railroad promoter Henry Villard, the street-railway magnate William C. Whitney, Oliver Payne of Standard Oil, Jay Gould's broker Charles Osborn, members of J. P. Morgan's family, Cyrus McCormick, and the like. To accommodate his clients Richardson experimented at first with several historic styles, finally settling on variations of the Romanesque, which he developed so far beyond the original inspiration that it earned the label "Richardsonian Romanesque," indicating that for all practical purposes he had invented his own architectural language. To accommodate their clients, McKim, Mead and White went in another direction, passing through Richardson's and other mannerisms to settle on the Renaissance *palazzo,* particularly the *palazzi* of Florence. The choice made perfect sense.

The fifteenth-century "boom in the construction of family *palazzi,*" Lauro Martines writes, was the result of "a growing concentration of wealth." Princes, oligarchs, and other rich men "sought to

"Richardson Romanesque." Trinity Church, Boston, by H. H. Richardson, 1872–1877. Photograph by Robert Twombly.

affirm themselves by means of imposing *palazzi,* more organized and splendid facades," more elaborate interiors, decoration, and objects. The "passion" with which they "displayed their high status or proved their virtue," Martines continues, extended beyond the *palazzi* to other architectural projects, "such as churches, chapels, . . . and new public buildings. . . . As the political and monied élites spread out and pre-empted more urban space, all others had to be content with less." Ultimately, "the rising awareness that élites could reapportion or remake the urban space if they so willed" led to an interest in ideal cities, which was "politically a deeply conservative conception, a response," he concludes, "to the rising demand by princes and urban élites for grandeur and show, order and ample space, finesse and finished surfaces."

And so too in the late-nineteenth-century United States. The new, industrially based owning caste, still first and second generation in the 1890s and harboring a nagging sense of social insecurity,

wanted to make its cultural mark, to distinguish itself from the rest of society, to express its impressive power, perhaps also to disguise from itself and others the grubby ways in which it had accumulated that power. "There is nothing about a château after the manner of Blois," Jeanne Chase has written, "to remind its occupant about the railroad on which that château is based."

So it is not surprising that the American counterpart to the quattrocento oligarchy should have forsworn the circumspect brick and brownstone town houses of eighteenth- and early-nineteenth-century elites for granite châteaux and marble *palazzi,* or that, like their Florentine predecessors, that they sponsored privately funded civic projects like libraries, museums, opera houses, universities, and even municipal plans, almost invariably in the neoclassical mannerisms upon which Renaissance forms were based. The quattrocento was far enough removed in time for its seamier means of wealth and power accumulation to be conveniently forgotten in the American process of identification with it, but it remained so architecturally potent, if not hallowed, as to be reified into an endorsement of the new social order, of the legitimacy of the new American elite.

No matter the style—Florentine, Loire Valley, or something else—it was European aristocracies to which American architects referred when they designed mansions for the rich. And if that historicism was intended to validate those rich and, in addition, to persuade an older elite to accept new members, it nevertheless filtered down through the social hierarchy to middle-class dwellings in wood rather than stone, with eight rooms rather than fifty, on Roxbury side streets near trolley lines rather than Drexler Boulevard with carriage lanes, and from there to decorative touches over doors and windows and along the cornices of working-class tenements in South Philadelphia and New York's Lower East Side. No matter that paying the rent was difficult. This architecture proclaimed every man a king, someday at least.

A similar message was directed toward working-class immigrants even before they reached those tenements, as they arrived at the Ellis Island reception center in New York harbor. Federal takeover of immigrant processing in 1891, together with the destruction by fire of the island's original facilities six years later, required a new building, designed in 1898 by the New York firm of Boring & Tilton. In his review that year of plans for "such quarters . . . as were never seen before on this side of the Atlantic," a *New York Times* reporter concluded that so grand was the architecture that even the poorest newcomer

Ellis Island, by Boring & Tilton, 1905. PRINTS AND PHOTOGRAPHS DIVISION, LIBRARY OF CONGRESS

could "indulge in the inexpensive pleasure of imagining that in his role [as] a future American monarch the Republic has placed at his disposal a palace far . . . handsomer than many of those . . . in the Old World."

Opened in 1900, Boring & Tilton's building held out hope of upward mobility but also laid down rules on how to achieve it, with imagery characteristic of most government architecture at the time. In what was then called French Renaissance but is now referred to as the Beaux-Arts classical style, the processing center exemplified the notion that Greek and Roman structural systems could be codified and synthesized. The style and its archeological impulse reached their zenith in the United States in the 1890s and 1900s, mostly with prominent public and quasi-public edifices like Hunt's Administration Building (1892) at the Chicago World's Fair and the Metropolitan Museum of Art (1895) in New York, and Carrère

and Hastings' New York Public Library (1895–1902). Used to commemorate patriotic heroism, as with Palmer and Hornbostel's Allegheny County Soldiers and Sailors Memorial (1905–1908) in Pittsburgh, or for imposing urban portals like Warren and Wetmore's Grand Central Terminal (1903–1910) in New York, Beaux-Arts classicism made its greatest impact at early-twentieth-century international expositions, Bernard Maybeck's 1915 Palace of the Fine Arts at San Francisco's Panama–Pacific Exposition being perhaps its finest expression. The purpose of this architectural style was to impress the public with majesty and grandeur.

Like monumental railroad terminals of the period, Ellis Island's reception center was also a portal—hinting at wonders beyond its doors—not for a city but for an entire nation, and as such directed attention toward the government whose edifice it was. This was done architecturally by the striking contrast in color and texture between its imposing red brick walls and its ebullient gray stone trim, and by the overscaled heraldry and pilasters separating three larger than necessary arches at the entry. It was done by the prominence of four corner towers—capped with brilliant copper domes—that thickened as they descended, and by the assertive entablature partially blocking but thus accentuating semicircular attic windows. And it was done with crisp, copper-faced gables playing against the sloping clerestory roof. This was an architecture of exaggeration and contrast, designed to make a strong visual impact on arrivals long before they docked.

But its various design elements were also intended to turn entry through its massive central pavilion into a solemn and memorable event, extended though time and space by procession up the grand staircase to the Registry Room, 200 feet long by 100 feet wide, under a 56-foot vaulted ceiling. Three elaborate electroliers supplemented eight arched windows rising from an inspection gallery ringing the room. The scale, noise, and brightness surely produced the desired effect upon those who had never seen artificial light or witnessed such a vast and busy interior except, perhaps, in church. Such a building could hardly fail to move the dazed immigrant, in an intimidating situation, to heed the wisdom and respect, the power of the government that had created such a magnificent architectural display.

Government architecture in general—on state and local as well as the federal level—embodied similar ideas, less often in Beaux-Arts style than in a more highly refined neoclassicism referring directly to ancient Greece and Rome without fifteenth-century mediation. By and large neoclassical buildings were bigger, simpler, and of cleaner line than those in the Beaux-Arts manner. They tended toward monochromes of gray or white, with less assertive sculptural and decorative flourishes, fewer projections and recesses along their facades, and less elaborate attics. Given considerable momentum by the 1893 World's Columbian Exposition in Chicago—which received over 21 million visitors, equivalent to one-third the national population—and by the civic center component of the city planning movement it spawned, neoclassicism dominated American public architecture into the 1930s.

As the United States assumed "the white man's burden" overseas and encountered increasingly determined opposition to its collaboration with organized wealth at home, Greek- and Roman-inspired police stations, city halls, courthouses, and state capi-

tols mushroomed across the nation, followed after World War I by war memorials in Europe and embassies elsewhere. Chicago's prominent neoclassicist, Daniel H. Burnham, who was also the nation's premier city planner, spoke for the elite of his profession when he wrote in 1906 that the ceremonial sector of his Manila scheme would "put to the test . . . notable examples from the days of Old Rome." Well-known among the many domestic expressions of ancient architecture is George B. Post's Wisconsin State Capitol (1904) in Madison, the Shelby County Courthouse (1907) by Hale and Rogers in Memphis and, of course, most of Washington, D.C. Elsewhere are Egerton Swartwout's St.-Mihiel Monument (c. 1923) in Montsec, France, J. E. Campbell's embassy (1925) in Mexico City, and Jay Morgan's consulate (1932) in Yokohama.

Greek and Roman architectures were immensely serviceable to American governments for ideological reasons. Other Western nations were drawn to neoclassicism around the turn of the century, but according to an authority on the history of American styles, the "revival in its entirety [had] no parallel on the other side of the Atlantic. . . . Nowhere outside the United States were the classical orders . . . drawn up in so many parade formations." The sheer quantity of production here was staggering. "More marble was used in building in the United States in the years 1900–1917," Marcus Whiffen writes, "than . . . in the Roman Empire during its entire history." But even more significant was the intensity of commitment to what Greek and Roman architectures were said to represent as well as to what they in fact represented in, perhaps, a more subliminal way.

By 1900 the United States had successfully constructed one kind of empire—territorial across the continent—and was building another—economic as well as territorial—overseas. Whether in the service of economic expansion or not, federal officials spoke endlessly about the national mission to spread democratic ideals, which Greek architecture was said to represent. At the same time, indigenous peoples overseas and in the American West, not to mention native- and foreign-born farmers and factory laborers all around the country, were refusing in various ways to live happily with new police- and military-backed impositions of power that aimed to order their lives. Populism, socialism, the Industrial Workers of the World, and other radical movements were at their strongest between 1900 and 1917, and shattering disruptions like the 1886 Haymarket massacre and the 1894 Pullman strike—only the tip of the iceberg of social unrest—remained vivid for everyone.

As far as republican governments were concerned, the social order was under assault, and for the same reasons that national guard armories—crenellated like medieval castles—popped up on strategic sites in many American cities, government at all levels seemed fatefully drawn to the architecture of Rome, seat of the most enduring Western empire, in fact and in memory. The implication was, though hardly ever publicly proclaimed, that physical assault against the state or the private entities it chose to protect, and political assault on republican principles and forms of governance, would not prevail. Thus in the face of social upheaval and to announce its imperial objectives, government architecture often referred to that of the "eternal city."

Privately endowed quasi-public edifices served another kind of imperialism: the desire of the owning caste to control the urban environment, physically and ideologically, which can be understood as a collective extension of personal aspirations into the public realm. The great railway terminals—Grand Central, the many Union stations, and others—were strategic in this regard because they stood as introductions, as literally the first things travelers saw when they arrived, becoming icons of their cities; prototypical edifices, in the same way the Empire State Building today stands for New York, the Water Tower for Chicago, and the Gateway Arch for Saint Louis. Indispensability, exceptional visibility, and key location gave railroad terminals the ability to make statements few other buildings could.

When McKim, Mead and White made the waiting room in their neoclassical Pennsylvania Station (1902–1910) 25 percent larger than the tepidarium after which it was modeled in the Roman baths of Caracalla, they did at least three things for their clients, led by Alexander Johnston Cassatt: they helped them colonize a huge parcel of prime New York real estate, confirming their control over a significant measure of public space, in that a station is public in function and its construction required eliminating a public thoroughfare; they made them urban benefactors and icons; and they associated them with an age-old monument of art. In one fell swoop the clients and their architects' private decisions irrevocably changed the city's physical configuration while elevating their own cultural and civic standing.

In 1901 it took congressional action to remove a railroad terminal from the Washington Mall, which makes the implications of Pennsylvania Station all the more clear: members of the owning caste would order public space for purposes of their own. Their program certainly included, but was hardly restricted to, commercial gain, which becomes especially obvious when considering what is now called "cultural philanthropy." Late-nineteenth- and early-twentieth-century proliferation of vast new buildings for museums, libraries, historical societies, opera companies, symphony orchestras, and universities, invariably in Beaux-Arts or neoclassical garb, occurred in every American city of real or pretended standing coast to coast, sometimes in planned "civic center" clusters, like Cleveland's and San Francisco's, facing formal gardens. All had specific programs that were not so much sinister as caste-determined: to decide which art and knowledge was legitimate and which not, to limit access and instruction to acceptable individuals, to determine who would define, protect, and extend the cultural heritage.

Architectural strategies for achieving these objectives reinforced nonarchitectural. On the one hand, Chicago symphony and opera companies might refuse to perform German music in a vain attempt to perpetuate cultural control by eastern-rooted old Yankee families and, along with sister institutions elsewhere close their buildings after working hours and on weekends to exclude undesirables; on the other hand, stairwells, lobbies, halls, and myriad architectural elements were made as monumental and impressive as possible, both to intimidate the undesirables that might slip in and to instill in everyone acceptance of what was deemed proper art, including the building itself. Imposing facades and palacelike interiors of establishments like the New York Public Library were additionally intended to demonstrate the expertise, connoisseurship, and refined taste, and thus validate the elevated status, of those responsible for erecting them, whether patrons (whose own holdings further confirmed their rarified position) or their architects.

The architects of culturally philanthropic edifices for the public realm were, of course, also the architects of châteaux and *palazzi* for private consumption (and in financial and social terms they benefited mightily). If elaborate mansions signaled an individual's arrival in the aristocracy of wealth, railroad terminals, cultural palaces, and the like spoke to that aristocracy's collective determination to remake the city, either as a whole—witness Burnham's 1909 Chicago Plan sponsored by the Commercial Club, and others like it—or piecemeal, project by civic project, mostly in the imperial style that Burnham did not need to identify when he told the Brooklyn Chamber of Commerce in 1912 to show its citizenry "that it pays in dollars and cents that their city should be beautiful." That the republican state by and large settled on that same imperial style indicates, perhaps, a certain agreement on its usefulness.

## THE SKYSCRAPER AS ICON, 1890–1910

Notwithstanding the importance of the buildings thus far discussed, they did not raise the architectural problems posed by the skyscraper. During the 1950s and 1960s historians wasted considerable time defining and categorizing skyscrapers and attempting to identify the first one. All the layperson—and the expert, for that matter—needs to know is that a skyscraper rises noticeably higher than the norm of its built surroundings, which meant at least ten stories in 1900, when the vast majority were devoted to office space. Skyscrapers were ordinarily designed in historic styles or as a pastiche, even though they were developed in the United States to address new activity in certain sectors of the labor force: an exponential increase of clerical workers and significant growth of industrially based managers (and owners) and their dependent professional and commercial purveyors. This meant that skyscrapers were of two types: those built wholly or in part for rental purposes by real estate developers or speculators, and those built wholly or in part as headquarters for large companies by entrepreneurial or corporate owners. This division was by and large the rule, but there were exceptions.

Skyscrapers were massive urban intrusions, getting taller all the time—in New York Ernest Flagg's Singer Building reached forty-seven stories by 1908, Cass Gilbert's Woolworth Building stood at fifty-five stories by 1913—and were beginning to absorb entire blocks. Realizing their threat to outstrip human capacity to comprehend, let alone see, them in their entirety, owners and architects inserted banks and shops at ground level, while elaborately ornamenting entrances, lobbies, facades, and rooflines to catch the eye (and to advertise self and product). Owners also gave considerable attention to names. For company headquarters the choice was easy: Singer, Woolworth, Wrigley, or McCormick if individually owned; Metropolitan, Guaranty, Tribune, or Equitable if erected by a corporation. In the first case, at least, anthropomorphism brought the impersonal to life.

Builders of rental facilities had to be more imaginative. In Chicago, to take one example, builders mythologized local history to create an iconography of progress: the Marquette Building referred to an early French explorer, a priest; the Manhattan and

Early Chicago skyscraper. Manhattan Building, by William Le Baron Jenney, 1898–1891. Photograph by Robert Twombly.

the Virginia to areas of the country early Chicagoans had forsaken; the Montauk, Tacoma, Monadnock, and Pontiac to Indian tribes (which were especially popular); the Rookery to pigeon roosts in temporary buildings formerly on the site. A brutal record was thus sanitized: God's brave emissary opened the way for courageous settlers to remove the noble but obstructive savage in order to build a better world by improving the real estate. With the locality now tamed by heroic effort, past and present became a harmonious continuity of inevitable improvement, and the skyscraper its domesticating agent. But to accept its civilizing importance—and at first many would not for fear of height, fire, congestion, mechanical failure, inadequate light, and loss of commercial identity—was also to accept the corporatization and centralization of its big business builders via an unprecedented rate of mergers in the 1890s at the very moment the word "skyscraper" entered popular parlance. Business consolidation, progress, and the skyscraper were thus conflated. By 1900 it was universally seen as a symbol of national advancement and as the prototypical American building—which is what made it a major problem for architects.

How to turn this new building type into architecture was not obvious. Everyone agreed that "this sterile pile, this crude, harsh, brutal agglomeration, this stark, staring exclamation of eternal strife," as Louis Sullivan put it, was potentially a work of art, for skyscrapers were, after all, the possessions and workplaces of cultural and residential palace builders. But few agreed on the form the art should take. The most conservative approach was to design the tall building as though not tall at all, and two ways to do this were either to wrap every two or three floors with a heavy cornice or entablature so that the result resembled a stack of small identical structures (as with George B. Post's 1898–1899 St. Paul Building in New York) or to divide the facade into four or five units of different architectural treatment so that the result resembled a stack of small dissimilar structures (Post's 1889–1890 Union Trust Building in New York). Architects of more literal bent rummaged around in history for adaptable building types: the campanile (Napoleon Le Brun's 1909 Metropolitan Life Tower in New York), the classical column (J. W. and M. J. Reid's 1897 Spreckles Building in San Francisco), and the Gothic cathedral (the Woolworth Building) were popular.

These approaches shared two characteristics: they associated the modern with the ancient by dressing the new genre in old clothing—a way of doing what most architects believed, that design should change only incrementally, and then always remain close to historical precedent, which also suited the aesthetic inclinations of the owning caste—and they ignored the design potential of the steel with which all skyscrapers were constructed by 1900. This was certainly true in New York, where high-rises were ordinarily treated in historical terms, but less the case in Chicago, the other center of skyscraper accumulation at the turn of the century, where a group of commercial architects now known as the Chicago school (c. 1885–1910) turned away from history, it has often been said, which is partly true.

In general, the New York model, which included the tallest buildings in the world, was a solid block-and-tower with a pyramid or cupola top, more facing material than glass, elaborate multicolored projecting ornament, and was more often articulated vertically than horizontally but only ambiguously revealing the location of the frame. The representative Chicago skyscraper was a flat-roofed open block (hollow or U-shaped) with more glass than facing material, dec-

orated more restrainedly with flush ornament in the facade's color, and articulated horizontally as emphatically as it was vertically, thus following and openly revealing the location of the frame. Louis Sullivan's inclinations occasionally to disguise the frame by emphasizing only vertical members, and always to ornament his facades lavishly, were closer to mannerisms of his New York contemporaries than to his Chicago school colleagues who, by and large, pursued their own course until the early 1920s, when the two cities' skyscraper styles more or less merged.

The so-called Chicago school never proclaimed a collective design philosophy based on shared principles, objectives, or *solidarité,* and in that sense was not a school at all. But it cannot be denied that the work of Holabird and Roche, Burnham and Root (later D. H. Burnham and Co.), William Le Baron Jenney, Adler and Sullivan, and several lesser firms bore a strong family resemblance. Their simplified facades were the outcome of localized factors. The 1871 fire encouraged speedy, economical reconstruction with flame-retardant materials; spongy subsoil demanded lighter weight structures. Steel resting on spread-footing or caisson foundations satisfied both needs, in addition permitting greater spans, thus more window space. Masonry gradually lost its load-bearing function to become a skinlike protection against the elements, but as early as 1895 even that function was minimized by the nearly all-glass facade of Solon S. Bemen's Studebaker Building. The "great office and commercial buildings now found here" fulfilled "the business principles of real estate owners," compilers of the four-volume *Industrial Chicago* commented in 1891, which were that "light, space, air and strength were demanded . . . as the first objects and exterior ornamentation as the second." Five years later, Montgomery Schuyler added that "in no other American city has commercial architecture become so exclusively utilitarian."

*Industrial Chicago* had nothing to say about interior ornamentation, but recent analysis suggests why it was as commonplace and lavish as elsewhere, a condition usually ignored by those who locate the roots of stripped-down "functional" modernism in turn-of-the-century Chicago. Some of the reasons for ornamental richness are obvious: to impress transients and clients, to lend stature to owners, to advertise wares, to improve real estate value. Others are not so obvious: to instill company loyalty among employees; to engage in a kind of aesthetic competition with business rivals, all the while differentiating one from another; less obvious still is to add to the urban luster to enhance civic pride. A perfect example of concealing interior lavishness behind restrained facades is Adler and Sullivan's Auditorium Building (1886–1890), where a massive granite exterior prepares one not at all for incredibly ornate rooms within. This inside-outside rupture recalls the seventeenth-century bourgeois Dutch inclination in building matters to minimize public expressions of wealth, while the notion that interior architectural activity was actually civic improvement further privatized a form of urban adornment carried over from the exteriors of quattrocento Florentine *palazzi*.

The rupture of without from within made Chicago school architecture unique. The historically referential skyscraper facade common in New York extended into the business world the image of owner as *l'homme d'art* established by residential and quasi-public structures. In Chicago, the extension was accomplished less by facades than by interiors. These became the quasi-public spaces most closely associated with the owning caste by virtue of name identification and the myriad daily activities—waiting, meeting and greeting, buying newspapers, escaping the rain, making phone calls, getting haircuts, even using toilets—that increasingly occurred therein, and because, by attaching the idea of civic amenity to skyscrapers, entrepreneurs expanded the meaning of "public space," bringing it under closer control through direct ownership.

In Chicago, but not in New York, "utilitarian" exteriors defined the owner as *homo economicus*. (Concern for employee health and safety implied by the importance accorded in *Industrial Chicago* to "light, space, air and strength" can thus be understood as primarily a matter of productivity.) Being rational and gridlike, and so fundamentally similar, utilitarian facades were as visually neutral as the local plat map they would have resembled if laid on the ground and made two-dimensional. The industrial and topographical iconography of each was thus the iconology of all, because architects and owners had ceded to each other access to a common design language. In one way, the Chicago facade was socially neutral as well, revealing nothing individually about entrepreneurs and little collectively, beyond identification with efficiency, utility, modern technology, and businesslike demeanor. Yet, when these very characteristics were put into architectural form with geometric and mechanical precision and blown up in scale—Chicago skyscrapers were generally wider than others in relation to height, giving the impression of great bulk—they were socially loaded in another way: as statements of massive strength and uncontested power. Compared to more conventionally detailed tall buildings, Chicago facades were abstractions de-tached from familiar historical association, paeans to the "timelessness" of modern, rationalized production, implying that the values of the present-day commercial elite always were and always would be.

From the point of view of social relations, however, the rupture between inside and out was not a rupture at all, but a change in entrepreneurial strategy. *Homo economicus* was for the city at large, *l'homme d'art* for private and controlled public spaces. The former signified a single social characteristic, the latter many others that were heading indoors, seeking shelter from general scrutiny. Here is the first architectural indication—it would be a fixture of post–World War II "modernism"—that the business elite would retreat behind anonymous walls, that its cultural and social intentions would be less obvious, that it would operate less conspicuously, that it would be more discreet. It is unlikely that Chicago's business oligarchy was more prescient, socially responsible, well-intentioned or, on the other hand, more defensive than others. On the contrary, in a far from conquered physical and economic environment, in a place widely known as "the land of dollars," with few social constraints on how they might act, local entrepreneurs were likely to be as short-sighted, socially irresponsible, ill-intentioned, and aggressive as others elsewhere. In such a climate, subtle suggestions of artistic refinement carried less visual weight than utilitarian proclamations of power and strength, which is what Chicago school facades were all about. The irony is that what was offered in the early 1900s as a kind of braggadocio was transformed by later generations into an emblem of cool detachment. Taken together, Chicago facades and interiors announced that a shift of social style was in the offing, and therein may lie their real modernity.

## ALTERING HABITAT: NEW AGENDAS FOR RESIDENTIAL DESIGN, 1900–1930

Frank Lloyd Wright was a Chicago school product in that while working for Adler and Sullivan from 1888 to 1893 he imbibed many of Sullivan's ideas, including one of particular moment that only he among his contemporaries made the operational basis of his work. Sullivan had argued that since the skyscraper had become the prototypical American building, its proper facade expression could be the basis of a national architectural style. In some twenty or more built and unbuilt projects from 1890 to 1904, Sullivan developed two high-rise models: what he called a "system of vertical construction" emphasizing tallness (a structural interpretation of a visual characteristic: see the 1894 Guaranty Building in

Buffalo) and what can be called a "system of skeletal construction" emphasizing the frame (a visual interpretation of a structural characteristic: see the 1898–1902 Carson Pirie Scott store in Chicago). But like other Chicago school work, his "system" had limited application since it addressed only commercial exteriors for large-scale operations. Except for Sullivan's work and possibly John Root's (which ended prematurely with his death at age forty-one in 1891), the Chicago facade was economically and socially but not aesthetically motivated. It was not the outcome of artistic impulses; nor was it the consequence of fundamental cultural upheaval or intellectual reorganization. Chicago commercial architecture was less a style—even less the first American style, as many have claimed—than a mannered appliqué, like the neoclassic, for a self-serving plutocracy.

If Sullivan did not launch a national style, he certainly made a lasting impact on Wright, who took up his challenge. Like Sullivan's, but unlike the Chicago school's, Wright's conscious objective was to create a specifically American aesthetic suitable for all architectural occasions, and to a remarkable extent he succeeded. Wright's first great achievement—called the "prairie house" because its long, low, horizontal configuration interpreted characteristics of regional terrain—was the underpinning of a comprehensive Prairie style in which he designed structures as diverse as churches, commercial buildings, schools, boathouses, mortuaries, garages, banks, real estate offices, art galleries and installations, hotels, dance academies, and horse fountains, indeed, anything for which he was commissioned. Aesthetically, stylistically, in every possible case, his exteriors, interiors, landscaping, and furnishings were of a piece, conceived as parts of an architectural whole. Rejecting the customary practice of using particular styles only in certain circumstances—like Gothic for churches, neoclassical for banks—and assembling patchwork quilts of interior spaces unrelated to exterior form, Wright's work was ahistorical and holistic. And because it arose from confronting a social issue of national importance—the predicament of the middle-class urban family—it was the closest the United States ever got to having a home-grown basis for a style of its own.

Virtually unlimited stylistic applicability distinguished him from other architects—except for a few dozen mostly midwestern imitators collectively called the Prairie school—but what distinguished him most was the kind of work on which he concentrated. Historically, most elite architects are solely or best known for nonresidential buildings, even when luxury dwellings are a substantial part of their corpus;

even today, especially today, if they design private houses at all it is early in their careers before they are able to land more lucrative commissions. Wright was the first visible American architect since the Civil War to make his reputation with private houses and the first ever to do it with dwellings not intended for the rich.

From 1901, when he announced the prairie house in the *Ladies' Home Journal*, to roughly 1915 when as the first American architect of profound international standing he changed design direction, he executed approximately 120 structures, of which only 30 percent were nonresidential, including only four that were and are well known: the Larkin Building (1904) in Buffalo; Unity Temple (1905–1906) in Oak Park, Illinois; Midway Gardens (1913–1914) in Chicago; and the Imperial Hotel (1913–1922) in Tokyo. Even in the late 1950s, when as possibly the most visible architect in the world he was designing the Guggenheim Museum, the "Mile High" skyscraper, the Marin County Civic Center, and whole districts of Baghdad, nonresidential work dropped to 20 percent of his built total. Wright became famous and remained famous throughout a seventy-two-year career primarily because of single-family suburban houses for the middle and upper middle classes.

It is no accident that one of his heroes was Thomas Jefferson, whose idealization of American yeomanry Wright took to heart. Wright believed that the sturdily independent, home owning and therefore landed, resourceful small businessman, professional, and manager—the backbone of the nation, he insisted—was the modern version of Jefferson's eighteenth-century paragon of virtue. The prairie house was a complete residential reconfiguration based on a considered examination of the contemporary "yeoman" family, which Wright transformed into a cultural icon, the repository of "Americanness" itself.

But this family was imperiled, many observers thought, and Wright set out to save it. The prairie house literally encouraged and symbolically represented closer association with the natural world lost to city dwellers, withdrawal from disturbing urban problems into a visibly protective, visually inaccessible sanctuary, family togetherness via an open plan, orderliness via highly structured spaces, and psychic serenity achieved by holistic design. This amalgam of memory and desire—personal peace deriving from family harmony in a safe retreat wedded to nature—was intended to reassure anxious middle-class urbanites by recalling the happier if mythical past of the small town and rural areas from which they, their parents, or grandparents had migrated. If prairie

Prairie house. Isabel Roberts residence, River Forest, Illinois, by Frank Lloyd Wright, 1908. Photograph by Robert Twombly.

house reality and representation called to mind idyllic country chapels like the one in Wisconsin Wright had helped construct as a boy, it is because Wright had turned the middle-class dwelling into a sacramental place, a kind of shrine of traditional family values. But if its social orientation faced the past, its aesthetics pointed uncompromisingly to the future, for its architecture was daringly new, considered "radical" and disturbing by even intelligent culture critics like Chicago's Hornet Monroe. Wright's genius was to resolve this contradiction and sell it to fundamentally conservative clients. In so doing, he bonded avant-garde art to the rise of the middle class.

Wright's achievement had profound implications for the social relations of his profession. He extended the acceptable range of visible architectural activity downward into the middle class. He opened new avenues to visibility for architects who might not attain it otherwise and helped solidify the social position of all visible architects by expanding their possibilities for social usefulness. He delivered to them a new client pool by elevating its architectural requirements to fine art. And since that art was on the cutting edge, making serious waves in Europe as early

as 1910, he forced the American "academy," so to speak, to reckon with dissent. None of this happened overnight, and Wright did not act alone, but he was the principal player, and after his performance there was no going back.

Throughout all this and more vehemently as he grew older, Wright remained a professional loner, thumbing his nose at elite colleagues who came so to hate him that their premier organization, the American Institute of Architects, withheld from him its gold medal for lifetime achievement until 1949 when he was eighty-two, long after it had honored many lesser lights and long after it already owed him a huge debt of gratitude.

Principally because of Wright, middle- to upper-middle-class housing acquired artistic visibility before World War I. But he was not the only stylistic dissenter. Some of his Prairie school followers produced striking if derivative designs, particularly the husband and wife team of Walter Burley Griffin and Marion Mahony (the first female graduate of MIT), Barry Byrne (later excelling with ecclesiastical work), and the firm of George Grant Elmslie and William Purcell. Especially in California, others removed from

Wright's direct influence were developing their own original vocabularies. In Pasadena, the brothers Charles S. and Henry M. Greene applied Japanese joinery techniques to Gustav Stickley, "Stick," and "Shingle" styles in a series of stunning houses resembling Wright's at a distance but in fact artistically unique. And in San Diego, Irving Gill combined the local Spanish heritage, experiments in concrete prefabrication and in stucco, and his own geometrical ornament into clean-lined, asymmetrical compositions for all classes of families that sometimes eerily anticipated the so-called International style of the 1920s.

With clients from the rising middle class increasingly available, aspiring and elite architects gave them greater attention, so that in the interwar years, middle-class housing became a major, if not the major, area of design activity. Artistic innovation flagged, however, as visible architects moved into the field. Even during the Prairie school's heyday (which coincided with Gill's and the Greenes'), traditional architecture had been the overwhelming choice: in terms of style, almost all middle-class dwellings had been modest versions of elite preferences. But during the 1910s and 1920s, stylistic progressivism was even less evident.

There are several reasons for this. Personal difficulties temporarily removed Wright from a leadership role, and most of his followers drifted away. As visible architects appropriated middle-class housing, furthermore, their inclination to stick with the familiar was, if anything, welcomed by clients and residents happy to take artistic cues from the very rich. (Never in their wildest dreams would the 1880s and 1890s sponsors and agents of elite cultural hegemony have imagined how easy their success would be.) Then, too, more United States architects were training at the École des Beaux-Arts and its American derivatives, all bastions of stylistic conservatism. In addition, decades of imperial adventures and internal unrest had created a kind of yearning in certain circles for a supposedly simple and untroubled past, stimulating withdrawal into nostalgic regionalism that had made an early mark with the literary "local color" movement as well as with architectural revivals, first of New England and southern "colonial," then of Spanish, that peaked in the 1920s. United States participation in World War I also played a role, bringing Allied architectural traditions to a wider American audience through eyewitnesses and photographs, especially English Tudor, which was immensely popular prior to the Depression. Finally, as middle-class planned communities, including the garden variety, sprang up around the nation between 1910 and 1930, corporate, trade union, charitable, and plain old speculative developers saw no reason to go out on artistic limbs.

Sponsors of residential developments had diverse motives. But neither housing reformers, labor organizations, speculators, nor municipal officials thought stylistic experimentation would have much appeal. The tried and true was better, more marketable, than what some thought were artistic "un-American" activities. Other kinds of experiments there most certainly were, however: in separating pedestrian from vehicular traffic and in garaging automobiles, in cooperative financing and ownership, in communal space provision (play areas, gardens, and meeting rooms), in internal circulation, the handling of town centers, the arrangement of both attached and detached housing on irregular and superblocks, and so on and on depending on the project. Because of these and many other appealing provisions, the 1920s was something of a "golden age" for multiple housing in the United States. Not before nor since were so many handsome, affordable, well constructed, and still desirable units erected for middle-class residents—and replete with design lessons that are still applicable today, regardless of income level.

But stylistically there was little new and little to be built upon. Some of the best known communities are Grosvenor Atterbury's Forest Hills Gardens (1909–1913) in Queens, sponsored by the Russell Sage Foundation in English Tudor; Howard Van Doren Shaw's Market Square (1913), with an Austrian village look for the Lake Forest (Illinois) Improvement Association; Bertram Grosvenor Goodhue's Spanish revival Tyrone, New Mexico (1914), for the Phelps-Dodge Company; Henry Wright and Clarence S. Stein's Sunnyside Gardens (1924–1929) in Queens, financed by Manhattan investors, and the town of Radburn, New Jersey (1928–1929), financed by its residents—the first in a kind of friendly mill style, the second vaguely New England colonial. Stein and Wright were political progressives, members of the Regional Planning Association, hoping to build a sense of collectivity in self-sufficient communities. Atterbury cultivated his reputation as a social progressive by working for the Russell Sage Foundation (founded in 1907 for "the improvement of social and living conditions") but he was also quite comfortable designing country estates. Goodhue was an eclectic attempting to update one or another historic style depending upon the commission. Shaw flirted briefly with the Prairie style but preferred medieval mannerisms. Regardless of the political or aesthetic inclinations of its architects, in other words, collective housing—almost all privately financed, it should be noted—was stylistically *rétardataire*. Along with contemporary individual dwellings, they indicate a period of water-treading during which the visible elite consolidated its hold on middle-class architectural production.

## THE SOCIAL TRANSFORMATION OF MODERNISM, 1922–1940

There were, however, tiny rivulets of avant-garde activity during the 1920s. One came from Wright, not from his work, since he was designing little at the time and that a rather exotic dead-end, but from his continued call for a new American architecture. Another stemmed from among the 259 entries from around the world to the 1922 competition for new Chicago Tribune headquarters. A third resulted from the arrival of young Europeans, especially Richard Neutra and Rudolph Schindler from Vienna and William Lescaze from Zurich. And the fourth, the source of the second and third, was the gradual but inexorable penetration of the United States by new European architecture which in quantity of production was mostly social housing. Centered in Germany, Austria, the Netherlands, and France, modernism, so-called, was tentatively taken up during the decade by even a few quite visible architects who had previously depended upon historic styles. In residential design it would make its great impact after World War II, but in commercial architecture it made a significant mark before the Depression shut down building activity. By then it had helped point in a new direction the stylistic unification of New York and Chicago that had already occurred in the early 1920s.

The Chicago Tribune competition had contradictory but profound consequences for American architecture. On the one hand its medieval-style winning design administered a coup de grâce to the Chicago school, but on the other hand it compelled American architects to pay attention to new work in Europe. The Tribune competition was a very big deal, like the 1990s J. Paul Getty Center in Santa Monica, California, "the commission of the century" of its day, offering the winner not only the most important local undertaking since the Auditorium Building of the 1880s but also international notoriety. The winners were John Mead Howells and Raymond Hood, who produced (and built, from 1923 to 1925) a New York tower in Gothic akin to Cass Gilbert's Woolworth Building of 1911 to 1913. It had familiar

Tribune Tower, Chicago, by Raymond Hood, 1925. PRINTS AND PHOTOGRAPHS DIVISION, LIBRARY OF CONGRESS

Chicago elements, to be sure: its base, shaft, and crown were clearly distinguished. But it was not a building to sit comfortably with others that had set the local tone, although it would have sat comfortably in lower Manhattan. Had the competition not been so highly touted, the entries so highly scrutinized, and the winner so highly acclaimed, Tribune Tower itself might have quietly taken its place in the downtown architectural jumble. But its symbolic and corporate visibility made that impossible, and it was important enough to be a national bellwether. Since it was inevitably and correctly compared to its parent structure, the Woolworth, still the world's tallest building and already legendary, it told the architecturally literate that the winds had changed, that the Chicago school had succumbed to the New York style.

But had anyone in Gotham thought to claim

some sort of hometown victory, he or she would have been ill-advised, for the winds were swirling very unpredictably. Other competition entries were much more to be reckoned with, in both the long and not-so-long runs. Not that Tribune Tower was immediately forgettable; on the contrary, it remains one of the most handsome, best executed buildings of its kind, a landmark of its city and of "traditionalist" high-rise design. But even before it was finished it was artistically out of date.

Both the Gothic tower and the New York style were abandoned by Raymond Hood in his next important building, in 1924 for the American Radiator Company in New York, closely modeled after the Chicago competition's second-place finisher, which had been designed by Finland's Eliel Saarinen. Saarinen combined new ideas with old. His vertically emphasized columns were Gothic-inspired, but his arches were Romanesque, his sculptures would soon be called Art Deco, and, most importantly, his setbacks were soaring extensions of contemporary and earlier European work (that of Henri Sauvage in Paris, for example), creating a gradual diminution of mass upward through five recessions to the top. This was neither the Chicago nor the New York solution. The architect Claude Bragdon called the effect a "frozen fountain," and before it became a staple in such books as architectural renderer Hugh Ferriss's *Metropolis of Tomorrow* (1929) it was appearing in built form as the towering ziggurat. Soon, with greater ornamental restraint, the more fully developed and closely related Art Deco and "American moderne" styles dominated high-rise construction in New York. By the late 1920s and early 1930s, the Daily News, Newsweek, Chanin, Chrysler, and Empire State buildings, 500 Fifth Avenue, and Rockefeller Center were variations on Saarinen's themes. But so too were Trost and Trost's 1928 Luhrs Tower in Phoenix, John R. and Donald Parkinson's Bullock's Wilshire Department Store in Los Angeles the same year, Holabird and Root's 1929–1930 Chicago Board of Trade, and very tall buildings everywhere else.

Art Deco and Moderne were the first, and rather tepid, American responses to European modernism, but their triumph was almost as short-lived as the Gothic victory at Tribune Tower, partly because the Depression ended almost all large-scale commercial construction, and partly because other competition entries, unlike Saarinen's, were radical rejections of the architectural past and proved to have more lasting import. In their book accompanying a 1932 retrospective exhibition at the new Museum of Modern Art in New York, the curators Henry-Russell Hitch-

cock, an art historian, and Philip Johnson, an aspiring architect, labeled those rejections the International style, a misnomer based on a misconception because it subsumed under one rubric quite different work from several nations and architects. But the name stuck, probably because of shared mannerisms regardless of locale and designer.

In general, the new architecture replaced applied ornament with what might be called self-decoration: the composition resulting from the organization for visual effect of structural members, wall openings, and other requisites like downspouts, railings, terraces, and overhanging roofs. Long runs of ribbon windows flush with smooth, taut, skinlike walls were conceived as parts of the surface, not as holes in it. Roofs were flat, color usually monochromatic (often white), major facade components were organized asymmetrically, and the construction was generally skeletal. Form and material emphasized volume rather than mass, that is, interior spaciousness linked to outdoors as opposed to stalwart exteriors keeping outdoors at bay. These aspects of European social and private housing, schools, factories, and shops were just making their presence felt internationally in 1922 and, except for rare instances (such as early proposals by Mies van der Rohe), were not applied to skyscrapers (which were even rarer in Europe at the time). But the artistic vocabularies were there, and the Tribune competition seems to have stimulated their application to tall buildings, which, in turn, influenced the only two International style high-rises in the United States before World War II.

Less dramatic but more visually consistent of the two was the 1929–1930 McGraw-Hill Building in New York, the result of Raymond Hood's latest transformation, which took as its starting point the Tribune competition entry by Walter Gropius, director of the Bauhaus design school in Weimar, Germany. Gropius dramatized the frame as no American ever had, using the configuration of its structural members, its glass in-fill, and cantilevered and recessed terraces as his compositional scheme. His roofs were flat, his facades asymmetrical, his windows frequent and almost flush. The overall image was of a pristine, hard-edged, machinelike edifice. Hood softened the image and organized it symmetrically (except for one conspicuously off-set corner) with a Moderne tower at the center. Although its cage-like frame was evident, its strong green brick banding separating floors of dark ribbon windows with black mullions created a horizontal effect overlaid by a top-to-bottom triple stripe at the middle of the building indicating vertical circulation. From a distance,

McGraw-Hill Building, New York, by Raymond Hood, 1930–1931. Photograph by Michael Ross.

arrow of color complementing that of the vertical rear spine. Some wall planes were horizontal, others vertical, still others both. From every viewing angle, PSFS made a different statement. Like McGraw-Hill, it was a startlingly new example of structure determining composition, and with its Chicago school antecedents extended the line of alternatives to facade-thin historicism toward the 1950s. Art Deco and Moderne became footnotes to skyscraper history as "modern" began to rewrite its pages.

Outside the skyscraper genre, Rudolph Schindler and Richard Neutra produced the best known early International style buildings in America. Both worked with Wright briefly between arriving from Vienna and settling permanently in Los Angeles. Schindler's oceanside Health House (1925–1926) for Dr. Philip Lovell at Newport Beach, California, combined elements of de Stijl, Soviet constructivism, and internationalism in two large concrete volumes—one for bedrooms, the other for living areas—raised above the sand on five poured-concrete frames. A year later for the same client, Neutra lifted a glassy, steel-framed, cantilever-terraced residence from its hilly Los Angeles site on the kind of slender *pilotis* so favored by Le Corbusier. Neutra's design quickly became a landmark of American modernism, while Schindler's was neglected for years, apparently because it was thought too massive to represent the new, airy look.

Lescaze's other work—private residences for wealthy clients, unbuilt social housing proposals, commercial and cultural buildings—remained firmly in the International style throughout the 1930s. Hood, too, dabbled in the style off and on until his death in 1934. Elsewhere Albert Frey and A. Lawrence Kochner on Long Island, Gregory Ain and Ralph S. Soriano in California, as well as Neutra and Schindler, and a few other architects across the nation embraced the new style. But it was the arrival of three Germans in 1937 that gave great momentum to modernism here. Walter Gropius became a professor of architecture at the Harvard School of Design, collaborating with his former Bauhaus colleague, Marcel Breuer, in private practice until Breuer opened his own office in 1941. Ludwig Mies van der Rohe became director of the architecture department at the recently reorganized Illinois Institute of Technology (IIT) in 1938 and immediately began designing its new campus. From these secure bastions, Gropius and Mies broadcast modernism for the next thirty years, training legions of students at their own institutions while influencing legions more at almost every other. By the end of the 1930s, while

where its black verticals receded from sight into the window strips, McGraw-Hill appeared to be entirely circled by ring upon ring of glass, a study in horizontality unlike anything else in New York. It was as different from William Van Alen's Art Deco Chrysler Building (1926–1930) rising simultaneously down the street as Gropius's proposal was from the Woolworth.

More dramatic but less visually consistent was William Lescaze's (and George Howe's) Philadelphia Savings Fund Society (PSFS) Building of 1929–1932, which referred to the Tribune entry by Danish architect Knud Lönberg-Holm, itself based on the Dutch de Stijl movement, with boldly contrasting color fields, sharp edges, minimalist detailing, powerful asymmetry, and oversized graphics. PSFS had all this, including the graphics. But in addition, its upper stories were slightly cantilevered, its two-story banking mezzanine sheathed in glass, and its penthouse dining room roofed with a projecting slab that in a de Stijlian gesture fired into the building's core an

Philip Lovell residence, near Los Angeles, by Richard Neutra, 1927–1929. Photograph by Robert Twombly.

modernism atrophied in Europe, partly because after almost twenty years it had run its course, and partly because it met official opposition in Germany and the Soviet Union, the style was securing a strong foothold in the United States.

There were two other important developments during the decade. With a series of stunning designs from 1935 to 1938 Wright reappeared as a force to be reckoned with. His Fallingwater country house (1935–1936) for Edgar J. Kaufmann near Pittsburgh—considered by many the finest private dwelling of the twentieth century—translated modernist vocabulary into his own language: myriad pieces of rough fieldstone and small glass panels wedded to daringly cantilevered concrete terraces were attached so seamlessly over a waterfall to the hillside that the house at once became a reconstruction, an extension, an interpretation of and a tribute to its site. Few other buildings in the history of architecture were so much a part of their surroundings, so "organic," Wright would have said. Fallingwater was undoubtedly a tour de force, and very likely an "in your face" gesture to those in the younger generation—Wright turned seventy in 1937—who had pronounced him professionally finished. Then in 1936 came the Johnson Wax Administration Building in Racine, Wisconsin, possibly the finest of all the Moderne work

of the period, and the Herbert Jacobs residence in Madison, Wisconsin, the first in a series of partially prefabricated, modestly priced "Usonian" houses for middle-class clients generally with smaller incomes than their prairie house predecessors. In 1937 there was Wingspread, a luxury residence for the president of Johnson Wax, and in 1938 Wright's own Taliesin West school and studio complex in Scottsdale, Arizona, and the first of several buildings for Florida Southern College in Lakeland. In its strict adherence to basic geometries, its rectilinearity in many cases, its horizontality, its further diminished ornamentation, its occasional use of steel and concrete, Wright's work resembled the Europeans' by which it was probably influenced (although none of this was new to him), giving it a more "contemporary" look. In its regular use of natural materials—Wright preferred unpainted wood, brick, and undressed stone—and therefore in its natural color, its greater openness to the outdoors, its unmatched site specificity, and its equally unmatched exploitation of environmental factors for cooling and heating, however, the new work was distinctly his own. He liked to say it was modern but not modernistic, and it was indeed rather idiosyncratic.

Even so, it was included in the 1932 Museum of Modern Art Modern Architecture–International Exhibition, which was—more than Wright's return, Gropius's and Mies's arrival, and more than the growing number of American sorties into internationalism—the most significant architectural event of the decade because it heralded upper-class appropriation of modernism as its own—not Wright's modernism, of course, but the modernism of the International style.

The exhibition, which has become legendary in the annals of architecture, was divided into three parts. "Modern Architects" featured four Europeans (Le Corbusier from France, J. J. P. Oud from the Netherlands, Gropius and Mies van der Rohe from Germany) and five American design firms (Wright, Howe and Lescaze, Hood, Neutra, and the Bowman Brothers). According to the exhibition's historian, this section was "heavily skewed toward single-family house's [sic] and school projects." Of the forty-two works on display, only two by Oud and one each by Gropius and Lescaze qualify as social or public housing. "The Extent of Modern Architecture" contained forty projects by thirty-seven architects (six American) from fifteen countries. Only four were multiple housing, including one for professional women and another for senior citizens; none could be defined as social housing—publicly or collectively financed for working people—in the European sense of the term.

"Housing" featured only four projects, including Stein and Wright's Sunnyside, Queens. The other three—Otto Haesler's Rothenberg Houses (1930–1932) in Kassel, Germany; Ernst May and Associates' Römerstadt development (1927–1928) in Frankfurt-am-Main, Germany; and Oud's Kiefhoek housing (1928–1930) in Rotterdam—were the only social housing examined at any length in the entire exhibition. The quite considerable European effort to remove nineteenth-century and even earlier substandard speculator-built dwellings and to replace war-damaged stock was thus marginalized. Facades, furthermore, were given a good deal more attention than apartment interiors or floor plans; housing as art, as opposed to its solutions for social problems, took priority. The 1932 exhibition made it appear that the new architecture and its aesthetics were primarily in the service of wealthy villa owners and those responsible for erecting public or entrepreneurial structures, and only secondarily concerned with social issues when, in fact, it was the other way around.

Aside from redefining the new architecture, the 1932 exhibition helped put New York's Museum of Modern Art (MoMA) on the cultural map. Indeed, by 1939 it was a national institution, *the* national center of modern art, pursuing its policies as aggres-

Museum of Modern Art, New York, by Philip L. Goodwin and Edward Durell Stone, 1938–1939. ARCHIVE PHOTOS/ POTTER COLLECTION

sively as any American museum ever had. By then, Lillie P. Bliss, one of the founders, had donated 235 works and its treasurer, Abby Aldrich Rockefeller, an additional 181. With the museum's rapidly growing inventory, larger quarters were needed and were provided on Rockefeller-owned land in 1939 by architects Philip L. Goodwin and Edward Durell Stone in what the American Institute of Architects *Guide to New York City* calls "a catechism of the International Style: . . . an austere street front of marble veneer, tile, both opaque and transparent glass" that the *WPA Guide to New York City* said was a "rich but simple setting for the display of art."

There were two noteworthy features to this design. One was only partially executed. The new building was originally conceived as part of a complex including the luxury Rockefeller Apartments directly across a sculpture garden intended to serve as the apartments' rear court. Both were constructed, the apartments in 1936 (before the museum) to designs by Wallace K. Harrison, then working for the Rockefeller Center planning team, and the French architect André Fouilhoux, which explains why they so closely resemble housing for the affluent in Paris.

The part of the complex not constructed was a mid-block plaza linking MoMA's main entrance on 53rd Street to the 51st Street end of Rockefeller Center on land originally assembled for it. MoMA was thus conceived as an integral part of what in 1939 the *WPA Guide* called the "largest [commercial construction] ever undertaken by private enterprise" and as the backyard for rich New Yorkers. All this represented one sort of social appropriation: of modern art and architecture for investment purposes and to enhance social standing. Since the new style was incomprehensible to the general public at the time, it also became the latest indication of elite connoisseurship.

The other noteworthy feature of MoMA's new building was the use of marble, a luxury material historically associated with splendor but not with the new architecture (Mies's 1929 Barcelona Exhibition Pavilion is one exception), and especially not with social housing. This represented a second sort of social appropriation: of an architecture for the masses by those who ruled the masses. More than any other building in the nation by 1940 (Mies had not yet built at IIT, nor Gropius at Harvard), MoMA typified the International style of which it was also the most culturally visible example, as well as being the first indication of the new upper-class public facade.

### HEGEMONIC MODERNISM, 1940–1970

Within a year or two Mies's initial building at IIT, Minerals and Metal Research, was underway, the first of twenty-one low-rise structures he designed for the campus before retiring in 1958, not all of which were built. The majority were clad in black painted welded steel frames and sheets of glass, spanning up to twenty-four feet without interruption in the case of the 1952–1953 Commons Building. The steel-and-glass system moved off campus to his twenty-six-story twin apartment towers (1949–1952), known as 860–880 North Lake Shore Drive, Chicago, as did his reinforced-concrete column-and-girder system, used sparingly at IIT, to the twenty-one-story Promontory Apartments (1948–1949) on the South Drive. These apartments and his other work soon received enormous publicity, notably from the New York–based *Architectural Forum,* which brought him to national attention in a 1952 feature story. Even before the great fanfare accompanying his 1954–1958 Seagram Building in New York (in association with Philip Johnson, an up-and-coming devotee) and his numerous but slight variations on the same structural themes nationwide—mostly towers, many in his adopted city—Mies was "sufficiently influential," ac-

Seagram Building, New York, by Ludwig Mies van der Rohe and Philip Johnson, 1954–1958. Photograph by Michael Ross.

cording to Carl Condit, a partisan of Chicago architecture, "to produce a steady stream of derivatives."

This was a huge understatement. Mies imitators were countless, beginning with Skidmore, Owings and Merrill (SOM) at Lever House (1952) in New York. Here the frame was pulled behind glass curtain walls so as to be invisible from the street, a device Mies adopted at Seagram and with ever greater assurance after that, for instance, at the Federal Center (1961ff.) in Chicago. Although he had proposed the idea himself as early as 1919, the skyscraper curtain wall first appeared, but only on two facades, at the 1947–1953 United Nations headquarters designed by an international team of architects including Le Corbusier, although Wallace K. Harrison did most of the actual work.

After 1952, the curtain wall was everywhere. As buildings in the 1960s and 1970s regularly reached sixty and seventy stories, spreading beyond the traditional limits of city blocks, they not only gobbled up perfectly serviceable tenements, workplaces, streets, even neighborhoods, but they also became the most visible constructions in the nation. It was difficult to ignore SOM's John Hancock Center (1965–1970) in Chicago when it reached 100 stories and 1,170 feet, only to be surpassed by SOM's own Sears Tower (1970–1974), also in Chicago, at 110 stories and 1,454 feet slightly higher than Minoru Yamasaki's World Trade Center (1962–1977) in New York. In its twin 110-story towers, however, the World Trade Center contained ten million square feet, seven times the area of the Empire State Building, and consumed more energy than the city of Poughkeepsie.

From the early 1950s through the 1970s Miesian derivatives, in high-rise and low, spread across the nation. Not since Richardson was seized upon by hoards of imitators in the 1880s and 1890s had an American architect been so influential. And the why of it is no mystery: Mies's buildings were deceptively simple and very easy to copy: measure the distances between horizontals and verticals, vary their proportions, get a good structural engineer, add a touch or two of one's own (change the color, curve the surface, slice a piece off the top, angle the corners, stick in diagonals) and the product was avant-garde. SOM was better at this than most. Its four-story Manufacturers Hanover Trust Building (1953–1954) in New York, for example, is a crisp jewel of steel, glass, and light. But in general, quality went down as quantity went up. Drab, characterless behemoths stood shoulder-to-shoulder in every American city, including some that never before had skylines. Mies was not responsible for the mediocrity of what was built in his name, but he *was* responsible for launching an architecture of aloof anonymity. And those ubiquitous glass boxes—rectilinear, flat-roofed, artistically banal, and repetitive, repetitive, repetitive—were the preferred symbol of corporate America for almost thirty years.

The point is not that everything was curtain-walled, although that was the dominant corporate mannerism, but that so much of it was featureless, regardless of material, following MoMA's 1939 lead. Featurelessness was not unintentional, however, and it took on increasingly ominous overtones as the years passed. Three examples: Harrison, Abramovitz and Harris's early 1960s extension to Rockefeller Center for the Celanese, Exxon, and McGraw-Hill corporations, called the XYZ buildings because they are almost identical and lined up in a row, each on its own block, shot uninterrupted narrow granite columns alternating with uninterrupted window tiers of the same width over sixty stories straight up

XYZ buildings in Rockefeller Center, New York. The new McGraw-Hill Building and the Exxon Building (1251 Avenue of the Americas Building), by Harrison, Abramovitz, and Harris, 1973. Photograph by Michael Ross.

from sunken plazas. At One United Nations Plaza (1969–1976) Roche, Dinkeloo and Associates covered upwards of seventy stories with an unvarying glass and aluminum grid that the *AIA Guide* said resembled "folded graph paper." And in Boston, I. M. Pei wrapped the 1969–1977 John Hancock Tower's sixty-five stories in mirrored glass (which kept falling out, much to the irritation of passersby).

These buildings and many others like them reveal corporate priorities at the end of the 1970s. First there is unreadability: these facades give little indication of where the floors are, where supports are located, if interior spaces differ from each other, in short, of anything going on inside, human or not. They are also antisocial: mirrored glass, said to conserve energy and to be "contextual" by reproducing surroundings, acts as a self-protective barrier: one can see out but not in. Such glass on the gigantic scale of both UN Plaza and the Hancock Tower is, furthermore, a deliberate snubbing of their older, low-rise, masonry neighbors, which in Boston include Richardson's Trinity Church and McKim, Mead and White's Public Library, both distinguished landmarks. And that huge scale, thirdly, is a statement of arrogance, established in the XYZ buildings by row after vertical row of hundreds of feet of granite, so overpowering, so cold, brutal, and intimidating, particularly when multiplied by three, that years after construction pedestrians cross Sixth Avenue to avoid them.

What began in the 1950s as aloof Miesian anonymity evolved by the 1970s into haughty post-Miesian arrogance. The reasons for this lie in the changing ways big business had been perceived since the 1930s and in the ways it perceived the social and political climate. Investigations into World War I profiteering coupled with the general belief that corporate and financial machinations had brought on the Depression changed the image of the big businessman from rugged individualist culture hero to rapacious culture villain. For the upper class a new public facade was in order and it was demonstrated, first of all, in changing personal styles. For the second and third generations of the industrial and commercial elite, entrepreneurial swashbuckling was out. As new wealth got older, Ivy League educations, association with the arts, and charitable donations indicated cultivation, refinement, and taste. A low but socially responsible profile was in. On the level of personal architecture this meant selling off gaudy ancestral mansions and hundred-room Newport "cottages" to purchase completely invisible triplex apartments and secluded country retreats like those designed in the late 1960s and 1970s by Robert A. M. Stern, Michael Graves, Peter Eisenman, and Richard Meier in cool, neo-Corbusian or neo-Miesian vocabularies. As individuals in the postwar world, the rich were seldom seen and even less heard, except as society's benefactors.

Corporate architecture of the 1950's reflected similar factors, plus one other: that big business had been diversifying and consolidating simultaneously, becoming less identified with making a single product than with its range of servicing, manufacturing, marketing, and investing divisions. Ownership had grown more anonymous, less connected to individual names. Against a background of the changing structure of large-scale private enterprise, the subdued public profile of wealthy individual owners, and the negativity with which big business had been perceived since its last opportunity to build widely at the end of the 1920s, postwar corporate ownership

appropriated what it understood to be salient characteristics of 1920s and 1930s European architecture: cool competence, understatement, restraint, rationality, minimal disclosure, an international outlook and, most important, technocratic efficiency spurning historical association. When applied to the skyscraper, the International style was made to be aloofly impersonal and almost blank, hardly revelatory, completely reversing the pre-Depression corporate image. The new facades were a tabula rasa on which to rewrite the past by composing a more congenial future.

But with all this, of course, the International style was so altered as to be unrecognizable. Facades of new corporate headquarters bore no relation to structure or function: they simply covered everything over. They were neither symmetrical nor asymmetrical. They were not so much strikingly composed—in the Chicago school manner (or that of Gropius, Lescaze, or Hood) of making something of the relationship between voids and solids—as they were minimally patterned, often without direction or depth, like Scotch plaid but not as varied or visually interesting. They threw off ribbon windows, overhanging roofs, and cantilevers—anything giving facades texture or movement—and by the 1970s emphasized mass as often as volume. But they were not designed for *human* masses. If European architects of the 1920s had given serious thought to housing thousands of residents in what they believed were lively, healthy, variegated buildings, postwar American architects gave minimal thought beyond considerations of productivity to housing hundreds of thousands of workers behind facades that, if they said anything on the subject, pronounced employees to be interchangeable drones doing exactly the same things in interchangeable cubicles. But, of course, the buildings were less about workers than about corporate image.

And that had changed considerably by the 1970s. The shift from cool detachment to aggressive arrogance suggests that public hostility was seen to have waned, that the political climate was again friendly, that corporate muscle-flexing would go unchallenged. Thus there were audacious departures from the glass box, exemplified first by William Pereria's 1972 Transamerica Building in San Francisco, an elongated pyramid, with two twenty-story projections near the top rising straight from the street to a needlelike point fifty stories up, and by Philip Johnson and John Burgee's American Telephone and Telegraph Building (1978) in New York with a three-quarter round cutout at the peak of a false gable looking like a Chippendale highboy chest. It was obvious by 1980 that corporations were feeling a

American Telephone and Telegraph Building (Sony Building), New York, by Johnson and Burgee, 1978. Photograph by Michael Ross.

certain loss of individual identity in their look-alike boxes and that visual differentiation was again desirable, itself an indication of heightened assertiveness. So the Transamerica Building became the company logo while AT&T is often said to have inaugurated in skyscraper design a movement later called "postmodernism."

### SOCIAL FRAGMENTATION: ARCHITECTURAL CHAOS, 1970–2000

Visually, postmodernism meant the return of polychrome, ornament, and updated traditional design elements (like gables, Palladian windows, pyramidal roofs, classical orders), as well as huge cantilevers, trapezoidal shapes, giant stripes, tilted towers (like Pisa's), variegated levels and complicated profiles, protrusions, recessions, extrusions, the mixing-and-unmatching of almost anything in a kind of frenzied ostentation. (See the high-rise work of Helmut Jahn, Kohn Pederson Fox, and Johnson and Burgee, espe-

cially.) In some ways this has been liberating for the profession, especially for young architects, in creating an anything-goes attitude that rejects rigid modernist formulae.

But socially, postmodernism meant nothing. On the one hand, it did not reevaluate the essential element in such buildings: worker space, which has not in any substantial way been improved. On the other hand, the social meaning of commercial postmodernism is quite clear: visually, in relation to urban amenity, and to society at large, corporations can do as they please. Since postmodern skyscrapers tend to be bigger and bulkier than their predecessors—although not taller; nothing has yet surpassed Sears Tower despite several proposals to do so—what it pleased corporations to do throughout the 1980s was to colonize ever greater amounts of land, air, sunshine, and energy, cause unprecedented congestion, and put unprecedented strains on urban infrastructures. For all their stylistic showmanship, owners of postmodern skyscrapers have been profoundly antisocial in their treatment of cities and employees, and profoundly conservative in their unwavering commitment to a social order now more inegalitarian than ever.

If modernism had captured United States architecture in the 1950s primarily through high-profile commercial skyscrapers, it quickly spread to a pervasive vernacular—flat-roofed minimalisms with lots of glass held together by metal or concrete—for every kind of structure as far down the scale of social hierarchy as invisible architects worked, that is, to the level at which developers took over. There, middle-class suburban housing represented a kind of compromise between traditional and "vernacular modern." In ranch houses, the new consisted of lower, longer, simpler profiles, plate-glass picture windows in front and glass doors opening on patios in back, perhaps split-levels with playrooms downstairs, dens above for Dads, and for Moms functionally convenient kitchens off dining areas of standard "open plans." The old included slightly pitched or gabled roofs vaguely recalling bungalows, salt boxes, or the Georgian, remnants of trim around doors and windows, wood construction, little-used walks leading to still formal front entries, and similarity with neighbors.

Vernacular modern rarely filtered down to working-class detached or multiple dwellings, but it did reach the latter during urban renewal campaigns from the 1950s to the early 1970s as lowest common denominator versions of Le Corbusier's "towers in the park," where the poor were warehoused in low-to-no-income "vertical ghettos." Periodic outbursts of social conscience coupled with occasional budgetary munificence did not necessarily improve design quality. Seen as a model of excellence and efficiency, Yamasaki's award-winning Pruitt-Igoe Houses (1952–1955) proved to be such a sinkhole of misery for those forced to live there, who were constantly attacking it, that the city of Saint Louis dynamited it in 1972, revealing an enormous gap between what poor people needed and what architects and officials insisted they should have. By and large the little public housing built since then has not been much better.

In the interstices of visible modernism the number of subcurrents increased over the years until by the 1990s there was so little stylistic agreement among upper echelon professionals that a new eclecticism prevailed. Among the more important developments, all of which left residues, was the "new formalism" of the 1960s—strictly symmetrical structures with columns and the revival of arches, overhanging flat roofs, ornament in the form of metal grilles and screens or patterned masonry, and smooth, shiny, usually expensive materials—mostly reserved for institutional edifices: embassies, libraries, museums, cultural centers, and the occasional corporate headquarters. Minuro Yamasaki, Philip Johnson, and Edward Durell Stone were the most prominent designers in this manner.

"Neoexpressionism"—nonrectilinear, curving, sculptural work, often with sweeping concrete shells—was best executed by Eero Saarinen, at Dulles International Terminal (1960) in Chantilly, Virginia, at Yale University's Ingalls Hockey Rink (1956–1958) in New Haven, and at the Trans World Airlines Terminal (1962) at John F. Kennedy International Airport, New York. "Organic architecture" continued from Wright's late work out of his Taliesin homes in rural Wisconsin and Arizona through Bruce Goff's and Herbert Greene's houses (both lived and worked in Norman, Oklahoma), Paolo Soleri's Arcosanti (begun c. 1956) near Scottsdale, Arizona, to Fay Jones's current chapels, houses, and other small buildings issuing from Fayetteville, Arkansas. Although this earth- and nature-oriented architecture has not been taken up by prestigious design schools or realized in large urban centers, Jones's receipt in 1990 of the AIA's gold medal indicates its importance.

"Neo-" or "late modernism" refers to metal, glass, and concrete architecture evolving directly out of 1950s and 1960s precedents. In the hands of Richard Meier—the High Museum of Art (1980–1983) in Atlanta and the Getty Center (1990s) in Santa Monica, for example—who excels in this regard, along with others like Cesar Pelli, Gwathmey Siegel, and Hardy Holzman Pfeiffer, it reaches a high standard of excellence. Postmodernism, which is less a specific mannerism than a flamboyant attitude, has also spread to all types of construction. Outside skyscraper work its best-known names are Michael Graves, Robert Venturi, Frank Gehry, and the late Charles Moore. Along with Peter Eisenman, the French émigré Bernard Tschumi, and others, Gehry has been moving into what is now called "deconstruction" or "deconstructivism," an angular, hard-edged, optically deceiving, rule-breaking architecture said to be based on the work of the French philosopher Jacques Derrida. By the early 1990s, postmodernism was thought to be declining in popularity while deconstruction was limited to a handful of practitioners, with Eisenman's work—especially his Columbus, Ohio, convention center—among the best.

Nineteen-sixties "brutalism" is the last important subcurrent of modernism, requiring a lengthier treatment than the others, partly because of its disquieting social implications and partly because of what Louis I. Kahn did with it. Brutalism derived from the work of Peter and Alison Smithson in England and from late Le Corbusier, particularly his Unité d'Habitation (1945–1952) at Marseilles and his Couvent de la Tourette (1954–1956) near Lyon. Characterized by heavy, massive concrete forms left rough, exposed utility conduits, boxy or slab protrusions and insets creating dark shadows and deep penetrations of the building mass, it was most often used for government, educational, and occasionally religious edifices. Paul Rudolph is closely associated with brutalism in the United States. His Art and Architecture Building (1958–1964) at Yale, designed during his tenure as chair of the Department of Architecture, illustrates the style's social meaning.

As realized in New Haven, brutalism is an architecture of impenetrability and rejection. Entries are tucked under downward-bearing cantilevers or at the rear of slots cut into the facade. Enter at your peril, it seems to say. There is plenty of glass but it is beyond reach or visible access from the street. Its chunky blocklike forms in rough concrete and its jagged profile turreted against the sky suggest a bunker. Inside, its staggered levels and complicated spaces flow into each other vertically and horizontally making visual surveillance easy but circulation confusing. Physical and aural privacy are in short supply, but not skin abrasions from too intimate contact with walls. The Art and Architecture Building proved its worthiness in 1969: when out of anger and frustration protesting students set it afire, they caused considerable damage but could not burn it down. The only casualty was Rudolph, who had already resigned. (On the other hand, when his 1965 Christian Science

D. S. Ingalls Hockey Rink, Yale University, by Ero Saarinen, 1956–1958. Photograph by Robert Twombly.

Student Center in Urbana, Illinois, outlived its usefulness in the late 1980s and the church, after exploring every alternative for its use, was unable to sell it, it was torn down.) Perhaps it was only coincidence that student upheavals of the 1960s touched off a wave of similar campus constructions raised up on berms, platforms, and stilts, encasing everything in concrete with tiny windows and few, easily sealed entries: among the many examples are the science centers at the City College of New York and the State University of New York, Stony Brook, and the Elvehjem Museum–Humanities Building complex at the University of Wisconsin–Madison.

At Boston City Hall (1963–1968), Kallmann, McKinnell and Knowles applied brutalism to government structures. Sitting at the foot of a vast, empty, windswept plaza, it is raised on concrete girders and pylons of varying heights up to the equivalent of about five stories. Entrance through and under them is belittling enough, but arrival in the huge atrium-lobby with little indication of where next to proceed is especially disorienting. Its exterior, however, is far from ambiguous. Prominent concrete projections in different shapes identify city council and school com-

mittee chambers, the mayor's office, and the like, high above the plaza. Higher still, as if in the mansarded servants' attic of a nineteenth-century town house, small protruding fins designate dozens of identical clerical cells. And why not cells at City Hall, based closely as it is on Le Corbusier's convent near Lyon? However, in Boston they suggest nothing about community, nothing about the public service aspects of a republican government. Rather, with its clearly stated hierarchy of power and its formidable presence, City Hall stands as a fortress against assault, offering a 1960s iconography of the state under siege.

Marcel Breuer's 1966 Whitney Museum of American Art in New York embellished this imagery with drawbridge and moat, and when the city itself replaced its 1901 Beaux-Arts police headquarters in 1973 with a Gruzen and Partners late-brutalist design, it sent out a similar message. Indeed, precinct houses for police and fire departments across the nation—not to mention urban high schools, courthouses, and national guard armories—were frequently made to appear crowd-repelling. The successors to turn-of-the-century government architecture asserted power even more blatantly sixty and seventy

Boston City Hall, by Kallman, McKinnell & Knowles, 1961–1968. Photograph by Robert Twombly.

years later by being equally monumental and even more self-defensive but not at all historically oriented. The Roman empire no longer offered a secure visual harbor for the ship of state. When the "new radicalism," the civil rights and anti–Vietnam War movements, and other protest activities finally dissipated in the early 1970s, American cities were left with numerous architectural testimonies to the most recent period of social unrest—which should stand them in good stead for the next one.

Brutalism had a certain influence on Louis I. Kahn, the last American architectural master of modernism. His First Unitarian Church and School (1959–1969) in Rochester, New York, and his India Institute of Management (1962–1974) in Ahmedabad show brutalism's traces. But they, along with the Phillips Exeter Academy Library (1965–1972) in Exeter, New Hampshire, his government structures in Dhaka, Bangladesh, and other of his buildings are also among this century's finest. The Jonas Salk Institute for Biological Sciences (1959–1969) in La Jolla, California, may be the very best of his works. Its three components—research laboratories, housing, and community center—form an approximate U-shape, the latter two sitting on bluffs overlooking the Pacific. Further back, two parallel blocks of laboratories terminate at a pool from which issues an extremely thin channel of water bisecting a plaza between the blocks. Visually, the channel extends to infinity, linking laboratories to the sea, whose murmurs roll on gentle breezes back along the plaza which is hushed, tranquil in the sun. Trees rustle in the wind, shading outdoor seating, and form a border for the entire complex except where completed by the ocean. Fire, earth, air, and water—the sun, the landscape, the breezes, and the sea—are here united in serenity. All this to encourage the collective labor of a human community for the common good. At its best, this is what design can represent and nurture. That it often fails to do so in the United States is not an inherent flaw of architecture but a final indication of the narrow interests it usually serves.

SEE ALSO Visual Arts; Patronage of the Arts; Mass Media and Popular Culture (all in this volume).

## BIBLIOGRAPHY

Of the many general histories of the subject, three together provide a more than adequate introduction: Leland M. Roth, *A Concise History of American Architecture* (1979); Marcus Whiffen, *American Architecture Since 1780: A Guide to the Styles,* 2d ed. (1992); and in an international context, Henry-Russell Hitchcock, *Architecture: Nineteenth and Twentieth Centuries* (1958). For the seventeenth, eighteenth, and early nineteenth centuries Hugh Morrison, *Early American Architecture: From the First Colonial Settlements to the National Period* (1952), remains the best overview. For the remainder of the nineteenth century, it is best to consult biographies and monographs on specific activities. Still the most fruitful treatment of more recent work is William H. Jordy, *American Architects and Their Buildings: The Impact of European Modernism in the Mid-Twentieth Century* (1972).

Important architects are well served: Jeffrey Karl Ochsner, *H. H. Richardson: The Collected Works* (1982); Paul R. Baker, *Richard Morris Hunt* (1980); Leland M. Roth, *McKim, Mead & White, Architects* (1983); Robert Twombly, *Louis Sullivan: His Life and Work* (1986); and Robert Twombly, *Frank Lloyd Wright: His Life and His Architecture* (1979). By far the best book on Louis Kahn is David B. Brownlee and David G. De Long, *Louis I. Kahn: In the Realm of Architecture* (1991).

On cities, see Daniel Bluestone's *Constructing Chicago* (1991), by far the most stimulating analysis; for New York, see Cervin Robinson and Rosemarie Haag Bletter, *Skyscraper Style: Art Deco New York* (1975). There is much to be learned about 1920s housing from C. S. Stein, *Toward New Towns in America* (1957), and from chapters 5 and 6 of Richard Plunz, *A History of Housing in New York City* (1990).

Two books are crucial for the new European architecture in America: Henry-Russell Hitchcock and Philip Johnson, *The International Style: Architecture since 1922* (1932), and Terence Riley, *The International Style: Exhibition 15 and The Museum of Modern Art* (1992). For the architects associated with that style see Thomas S. Hines, *Richard Neutra and the Search for Modern Architecture: Biography and History* (1982); Robert A. M. Stern with Thomas P. Catalano, *Raymond Hood* (1982); Christian Hubert and Lindsay Stamm Shapiro, *William Lescaze* (1982); Sigfried Giedion, *Walter Gropius: Work and Teamwork* (1954); and Franz Schulze, *Mies van der Rohe: A Critical Biography* (1985).

For American modernism in an international context, see Charles Jencks, *Modern Movements in Architecture* (1973); and Kenneth Frampton, *Modern Architecture: A Critical History* (1980). On skyscrapers in general: Paul Goldberger, *The Skyscraper* (1981); Thomas A. P. van Leeuwen, *The Skyward Trend of Thought: Five Essays on the Metaphysics of the American Skyscraper* (1986); and Ada Louise Huxtable, *The Tall Building Artistically Reconsidered: The Search for a Skyscraper Style* (1984).

# VISUAL ARTS

## George H. Roeder, Jr.

What has happened in the visual arts in the twentieth century is what has happened more generally: everything. Artists have explored an unprecedentedly wide range of possibilities as regards form, subject matter, sources, manner of presentation, political and religious stance, materials, and concept of the nature and function of art. The loosening of constraints has not insulated artists from cultural currents that have favored some choices over others. Individual artists, or entire groups, have encountered, and continue to encounter, restrictions. These have been imposed by economic duress, an intolerant or inaccessible public, a hostile government, social prejudices, the insistent trends of a particular year or decade, and artists' ignorance of or indifference to options. But taken as a whole the story of twentieth-century art in the United States has been one of growing inclusiveness. The result often has been an art of contrary extremes: intensely personal or intentionally depersonalized, celebratory or confrontational, austere or extravagant, aleatory or rigorously structured, fastidious or visceral. This essay discusses representative and influential painters, sculptors, and photographers in terms of their interaction with the opportunities and burdens of this evolving condition of choice.

### TRADITION AND INNOVATION, 1900–1913

As viewed by eyes accustomed to paintings of soup cans and to sculptures made from discarded automobile parts, the art of the year 1900 seems to have been created under severe restraints. At the time, however, most artists who wrote about the condition of American art emphasized its expansiveness, the richness of its possibilities. The sense of excitement shared by many was captured by the sculptor Augustus Saint-Gaudens when he declared after a planning session on the ambitious art projects associated with Chicago's 1893 Columbian Exposition that "this is the greatest meeting of artists since the fif-

teenth century." Such experiences seem to give substance to a Danish critic's prediction in 1900, that if "the rate of progress" achieved in the past decade continued during the next, by 1910 "American painting would lead the world."

One reason for such optimism was the growth of institutional support for the visual arts during the century's opening decades. The building boom that followed recovery from the economic depression of the mid-1890s employed many muralists and sculptors. Industrialization and urbanization allowed increasing numbers of artists to subsidize their art by finding employment designing advertisements, packaging, stage sets, and department store windows. Many others taught. A 1911 survey counted 102 art schools, half founded in the previous twenty years, with a combined enrollment of over thirty thousand students. Places to display art proliferated as well. The 1913 American Art Annual reported that dedication of four new museums during the previous year brought to 119 the total of "art museums and like institutions" in the country. Most, including New York's Metropolitan Museum of Art, the Art Institute of Chicago, and the Boston Museum of Fine Arts, had come into existence since the Civil War. Books by Sadakichi Hartmann, Lorado Taft, and Samuel Isham published between 1902 and 1905 provided histories of American painting and sculpture more comprehensive than any previous attempts.

Yet in certain ways American artists had had wider access to the public in the mid-nineteenth century, when they could sell their work through such organizations as the American Art-Union. A New York court closed the Art-Union early in the 1850s, ruling that it was an illegal lottery. Many of the museums and galleries of 1900 presented only European art. America's newly rich collectors revealed similar preferences. Ralph Blakelock, a painter of somber visionary landscapes, was, according to the art historian Milton W. Brown, literally "driven to insanity by poverty and the callousness of dealers"

Augustus Saint-Gaudens. Portrait by Kenyon Cox. PRINTS AND PHOTOGRAPHS DIVISION, LIBRARY OF CONGRESS

and was unable to appreciate renewed interest in his paintings near his life's end. Industrial growth gave new force to old questions about the social utility of artists. Much of the citizenry considered art making an effete activity of little relevance to a society focused on practicality and the release of productive energies.

Despite such anxieties, artists created work of growing quantity and variety. Among those who had developed a mature style earlier but were still working in 1900 were Winslow Homer, Thomas Eakins, Thomas Anshutz, and Albert Pinkham Ryder. The widely honored Homer, having removed himself to Maine, found drama in undecorative depictions of the power of the sea and of human encounters with the natural world. Eakins painted portraits of unusual honesty and psychological penetration. Anshutz succeeded Eakins as director of the Pennsylvania Academy of Fine Arts after the latter was dismissed over controversies involving his personal behavior and use of a nude male model in a class with female students. Anshutz had his greatest impact as a teacher but like Eakins did portraits, as well as scenes of everyday life. Ryder worked in cluttered solitude and in a world of his own imagining, leading to the legend of his total isolation, although he had helpful associations with other artists and a few collectors.

Many American artists received their training in Europe and some chose to live there, including the master portraitist John Singer Sargent, Mary Cassatt, who showed with the leading French Impressionists, and Henry Ossawa Tanner. In 1891, the year he settled in Paris, Tanner, whose work included landscapes, portraits, and allegorical biblical paintings, said that he left the country because as an African American he could "not fight prejudice and paint at the same time." At work in the United States were artists as diverse as Frank Duveneck, whose flashing brushstroke, brought back from studies in Munich, had been a fresh influence in the 1870s; John F. Peto, who painted in the popular trompe-l'oeil manner; William Merritt Chase, influential as a teacher and an exemplar of the immaculately attired artist; and painters of the legendary American West such as Frederick Remington and Charles Russell.

Although Remington also made sculptures with western themes, officially sanctioned sculpture displayed less variety than painting. Sculptors achieved professional viability mainly through commissions to do works, nearly always figurative and thought of by the public as "statues," that adorned public buildings or similar structures. Leading figures included Saint-Gaudens, creator of the Charles Gould Shaw Memorial in Boston and the memorial for Henry Adams's wife Marion in Washington, D.C., and Daniel Chester French, eventually best known for the seated marble figure he did for the Lincoln Memorial in 1922. Others, such as Chicago's Lorado Taft, developed regional reputations.

The painters most likely to receive prestigious commissions belonged to New York's National Academy of Design (NAD), or one of its lesser counterparts in Boston, Philadelphia, or Chicago. Founded in 1826, the NAD held tightly controlled, professionally important annual or semiannual exhibitions. The equivalent organization for sculptors was the National Sculpture Society. Howard Mumford Jones characterized the tradition within which these academic painters and sculptors worked as "the fusion of idealism with craftsmanship that dominated high culture in this country from 1865 to 1915." This tradition had room for a variety of styles. Included among the ranks of academic painters were, in Brown's description, "disciples of the Barbizon school of landscape painting, slick portraitists in the tradition of Sargent and Chase, remnants of the Düsseldorf genre school, the brush wizards of Munich, students of the bastard style of French academic painting, Impressionists, [and] the American proponents of the grand manner of classicism and renaissance painting."

Within this variety, most academicians painted well-composed, carefully drawn portrayals of dignified subject matter, and used Renaissance conventions of perspective and other techniques that created an illusionary representation of the "real" world into which viewers could peer. They avoided excess, whether in the form of flamboyant color or conspicuous display of the artist's emotions. Many believed these traditions to be grounded in natural laws as well as sanctified by centuries of artistic practices. They considered moderate innovation to be part of their tradition, and aspired to create an art responsive to the particular conditions of a country whose national seal proclaimed a new order of the ages. The leading academician Childe Hassam said in 1892 that "I believe the man who will go down to posterity is the man who paints his own time and the scenes of everyday life around him." Three years later one critic noted the stylistic implications of this commitment: "in this day, when even steam is growing old-fashioned, and electricity is taking its place, it is not surprising that much of the work of our younger artists should resemble the telegraph."

One consequence was a strong interest in Impressionism, a style that emerged in France in the 1870s and received its first large American exhibition in 1886. By 1900 academicians used their widespread acceptance of this once-daring style to prove that they were progressive in outlook, although a few still considered it a retreat from more rigorous standards, and others a fashion whose time had passed. The historian H. Wayne Morgan notes reasons for the appeal of Impressionism, which, as interpreted by American artists such as Hassam, J. Alden Weir, and John H. Twachtman, "centered on depicting a new level of color and light without dissolving form and design." Americans found this art congenial because its subject matter, drawn from everyday life, was accessible, its frank sense appeal was refreshing, and its emphasis on motion and change helped identify it "with progress and modernization." Impressionist painter Theodore Robinson believed that such styles indicated that eyesight had evolved culturally: "the modern eye is being educated to distinguish a complexity of shades and varieties of color before unknown."

The lives of leading academicians confirmed for them their progressive credentials. John Alexander, NAD president from 1909 to 1915, advanced from telegraph company messenger to commercial illustra-

Daniel Chester French with sculpture group donated to the Corcoran Gallery, Washington, D.C. PRINTS AND PHOTO-GRAPHS DIVISION, LIBRARY OF CONGRESS

tor to leading portrait painter, including among his subjects Walt Whitman, Grover Cleveland, and Andrew Carnegie. Alexander believed that the "progressive idea" that art provided a vision of harmonious order animated the NAD. Edwin Blashfield, who was to serve as NAD president from 1920 to 1926, received praise from the critic Homer Saint-Gaudens as a "pioneer in American art" because of works such as his pictorial paean, *The Evolution of Civilization,* in the Library of Congress, the "crowning glory" of the building. When Blashfield said in 1910 "we must be modern and we must be American," he described what he and other academic artists believed they were doing.

Even the painter Kenyon Cox, who vigorously argued in writings such as *The Classic Point of View* (1911) that disregard for time-honored conventions of artistic representation invited social as well as aesthetic chaos, proclaimed his belief in "progress." Cox, who commemorated scientific advance in a Library of Congress mural, took pride in his earlier membership in the Society of American Artists, whose challenge helped revitalize the NAD. After the two merged in 1906 Cox wrote that their combined exhibition had "an air of life and vigor and freshness about it rare anywhere in the world." This personal history reassured Cox that he disliked paintings by Matisse and "his unspeakable followers" because of their work's deficiencies, and not because "I am merely growing old and stiff and unable to take in new things." Only such avatars of European aristocratic values as Sir Caspar Purdon Clarke, who came from London in 1905 to head the Metropolitan Museum of Art, admitted to a general dislike of change. Clarke declared soon after his arrival that "There is a state of unrest all over world in art as in all other things . . . and I dislike unrest." American academicians defined themselves against, rather than identified with, Clarke's extreme position.

It was the threat to their image as progressives, and to their sense of propriety, that concerned academicians most when Robert Henri mounted a rebellion in 1908. After study with Anshutz, in the 1890s Henri divided his time between Philadelphia and Paris, then lived in New York after 1900. His forceful personality and inspiring manner of teaching attracted a devoted following. Henri, who believed art school should be a "boiling, seething place," urged students to value originality and investigation in painting, but also taught them to respect nature's simple regularities and to honor kindred spirits from the past such as the Dutch painter Frans Hals. John Sloan, George Luks, William Glackens, and Everett

John Sloan. PRINTS AND PHOTOGRAPHS DIVISION, LIBRARY OF CONGRESS

Shinn met Henri while working as newspaper illustrators in Philadelphia. Guided by Henri's insistence that they bring life into their art, they sought to retain sketchlike qualities in their finished paintings, better to convey the bustling urban scene. Some also depicted gritty realities of the city, leading later observers to refer to them and their followers as the "Ash Can School."

Their artistic choices had political implications. One critic, praised the traditionalist Blashfield's depictions of "the American who labors with his hands" yet described the worker as "the man who as a unit so often makes our lives miserable." In contrast, Henri, who sometimes taught at the anarchist Ferrer

School, and others in his group identified with that "unit" of workers. Sloan, a Socialist Party member, served informally as art editor for *The Masses* and helped organize the Paterson Strike Pageant that brought together cultural activists and industrial workers. The Henri group had in mind both style and attitude when they boasted that they stood for "the spirit of revolution and radical change." Luks, flaunting his working-class background, assaulted genteel sensibilities with declarations such as: "Guts! Guts! Life! Life! I can paint with a shoestring dipped in pitch and lard." When the NAD rejected Luks's works for its 1907 exhibition, Henri withdrew from the show. The five exhibited together at the National Arts Club in January 1908, and in April—dubbed "The Eight" because of the addition of Ernest Lawson, Maurice Prendergast, and Arthur B. Davies—held a widely publicized show at Macbeth Gallery.

At the same time Alfred Stieglitz began showing modernist art at his 291 gallery in New York, complicating attempts by both academic artists and the Henri group to appropriate the imprecise "progressive" label. Often, modernist works did not, in the commonly understood meaning of the term, "look like" their depicted subjects. Their makers radically altered form and color for expressive and formal purposes, and in other ways flaunted academic conventions. American artists' first encounters with this art often took place in Paris at 27 rue de Fleurus, the residence of siblings from a prosperous California family, Gertrude and Leo Stein (and, later, Alice B. Toklas). Max Weber, Alfred Maurer, Marsden Hartley, Arthur Dove, Charles Demuth, and many others came there for conversation, food, and the chance to look at works by Paul Cézanne, Pablo Picasso, and Henri Matisse, none widely known even among other French artists when the Steins arrived in 1903. When photographer and painter Edward Steichen took Stieglitz to a Cézanne show in 1907, Stieglitz complained that the artist offered only "empty paper with a few splashes of color." Four years later he exhibited Cézanne's work at 291.

Son of a New Jersey wool merchant, the young Stieglitz became interested in photography while studying in Germany. After returning to New York in 1890, he began taking strikingly direct and well-composed photographs that revealed a well-organized mind, penetrating eye, and consummate technical mastery. He also encouraged the serious study of photography, editing the *American Amateur Photographer* (1893–1896), *Camera Notes* (1897–1902), and *Camera Work* (1903–1917). From 1839, when the artist and inventor Samuel F. B. Morse, among others, brought explanations of this new process from Europe to the United States, photography had an impact on American artists. Eakins drew motifs for his paintings from some of the hundreds of photographs he took. But usually photographers who considered their work "art" replicated conventions of subject matter, composition, and tone borrowed from painting and sculpture. Contemporaries considered photographs such as Lewis Hine's compelling images of the experiences of immigrants and of children employed in coal mines and factories as sociological documents separated from "art" by impermeable definitional boundaries. Despite the persistence of such conceptual limitations, by 1900 faster emulsion speeds, dry plate processes that eliminated the need for bulky equipment and timely development of negatives, and editing and enlarging techniques that allowed transformation of the original image expanded the choices available to photographers. Stieglitz explored the distinct aesthetic and technical possibilities of the medium, argued for its acceptance as a major art form, and displayed outstanding examples at 291, which he established in 1905.

Alfred Stieglitz. Photograph by Carl Van Vechten, 1935. PRINTS AND PHOTOGRAPHS DIVISION, LIBRARY OF CONGRESS

Site of the Armory Show. The 69th Regiment Armory, New York. Photograph by Michael Ross.

Stieglitz soon shifted the emphasis of 291 to non-photographic art. Convinced that modern painting complemented photography, which had eliminated the need for traditional painting, he offered path-breaking shows of works by Matisse, Henri Rousseau, and Picasso. Informed of the latest developments in European art by such associates as Steichen and Mexican-born critic and caricaturist Marius de Zayas, Stieglitz was an intense proselytizer who held forth in his gallery all day. Increasingly committed to American artists, in the years before World War I he exhibited works by the majority of the country's small number of thoroughgoing modernists, including Maurer, Weber, Hartley, Dove, Abraham Walkowitz, and John Marin. The beneficiary of modest support from family wealth, Stieglitz customarily took no commission. Hundreds of artists, intellectuals, and activists visited his gallery, but his audience remained limited. Although modernist art appeared occasionally in a few other venues, most in New York, few Americans knew anything of the arts revolution visible on the walls of 291.

That changed on 17 February 1913, when the International Exhibition of Modern Art opened in New York's Sixty-Ninth Regiment Armory. The show's principal organizers, Davies, Walt Kuhn, and Walter Pach, with a great deal of assistance from Maurer, Dodge, and others, assembled more than four hundred European paintings, sculptures, drawings, and prints, and twice as many American works. Smaller versions of the show traveled to Chicago, then Boston. The show displayed, among many others, works by Vincent Van Gogh, Paul Gauguin, Cézanne, Matisse, and Picasso, and by about one-half of the dozen or so American artists who already had adopted modernist styles. The exhibition became

headline news, attracting in excess of 300,000 visitors in the three cities.

Among the thousands who had something to say about the show were Theodore Roosevelt, John Reed, Walter Lippmann, and, writing from Paris on the modernist spirit, Gertrude Stein. Although they differed widely in their opinions as to whether madness, charlatanry, or genius inspired the new art, all agreed that it sharply challenged prevailing conventions. Defenders noted the importance of increased exposure to the varied art of different cultures, the breakdown of traditional beliefs in many fields of thought, and technical discoveries of concern to artists, such as how colors interacted. These developments made painters increasingly dissatisfied with the practice of merely reproducing on canvas the form and color conventionally associated with objects they depicted. The show's organizers, hoping to create a "big bang," adopted "The New Spirit" as their motto and warned that "To be afraid of what is different or unfamiliar is to be afraid of life." Painter Guy Pène du Bois declared that for American artists the show was "a fact as great as the declaration of our political independence." Such rhetoric led the editor of the Independent to report that the armory had become "a battleground where every day from 10 A.M. to 10 P.M. rages the eternal warfare between neophiles and neophobia."

He overstated the case. It is true that while Davies, one of the organizers, "became more and more enchanted" on each visit, the academician Chase, "the sixth time, left the show angrier than he did the first." But even as the show's organizers deployed symbols of revolution, they arranged it in a way intended to prove that "change is the result of a certain logical development." New York spectators could prepare themselves for the "Cubist Room" by studying works by Francisco Goya, J.-A.-D. Ingres, Eugène Delacroix, Edgar Degas, and other nineteenth-century masters. Promoters of the new art demonstrated their respect for both tradition and innovation, as did NAD leaders who unfurled their traditional art as a banner of progress.

## MIXED RESPONSES TO MODERNITY, 1913–1929

The Armory Show gave notoriety to a few Europeans but did not make any American artist rich or famous. Squabbling over finances soon led to disintegration of the organization that sponsored it. In the decade and a half after the show modernism enjoyed increases in institutional support widespread enough to encourage modernist hopes of artistic preeminence, and slow enough to sustain their fears of perpetual marginality. Traditional painters and sculptors, and, increasingly, artists whose work borrowed some features of modernist work without straying too far from established conventions, continued to enjoy far more opportunities for exhibition and sale of their work.

Yet the show had an impact. It transformed the work of such artists as Stuart Davis and Charles Sheeler and influenced the taste of collectors John Quinn (a corporate lawyer described by Kuhn as the show's "biggest booster"), Lillie P. Bliss, Arthur Jerome Eddy, and Walter Arensberg, among others. The art historian Lloyd Goodrich remembers that when he visited the show as a young man who had not yet decided on a career in the arts, it provided "a revelation of a new world of art, alive with a vitality beyond anything I had ever seen." A similar sense of excitement prevailed in enclaves of cultural innovation such as Greenwich Village and the salons hosted by Walter and Louise Arensberg, the Stettheimer sisters, and Mabel Dodge. There were approximately 250 exhibitions of modernist art in the next five years, most taking place at New York dealers' galleries. Museums continued to proliferate, and many admitted a few modernist works. In 1913 the prescient John Cotton Dana had exhibited Weber's work at the Newark Museum. In 1921 the curator Bryson Burroughs organized a controversial show at the Metropolitan Museum of Art that included works by Van Gogh, Picasso, and Matisse. During the twenties, museums in Philadelphia, Dallas, Cleveland, and other cities also exhibited modernist works. Critics such as Henry McBride developed a well-informed and sympathetic understanding of modernism, as did such writers and collectors as Duncan Phillips. Modern work became well enough known that in his popular history of the 1920s, *Only Yesterday,* Frederick Lewis Allen could define an intellectual as, among other things, someone who had heard of Cézanne.

Allen's choice of a French artist was significant. Most modernist works exhibited during and after the Armory Show were European. American modernists, who like many of their compatriots struggled with competing inclinations to emulate and react against European models, lacked visibility and a sense of collective purpose. Some sought to generate both through events such as the ambitious Forum Exhibition of works by seventeen American modernists organized by the critic Willard Huntington Wright at New York's Anderson Galleries in 1916. Wright hoped the show would "turn public attention for the moment from European art and concentrate it on the excellent work being done in America," but the weak response indicated the difficulty of this task. Uncertainty among nonacademic artists as to what counted as "art" became apparent in 1917 with the first annual exhibition of the Society of Independent Artists, modeled on a similar French organization. For a small fee any artist could exhibit two works, resulting in a "bouillabaisse" of 2,500 paintings and sculptures. The French artist Marcel Duchamp, whose *Nude Descending the Staircase* had been one of the most controversial paintings in the Armory Show, submitted for the 1917 exhibition a commercially made urinal, which he entitled *Fountain.* When the show's organizers refused to give it proper exhibition space, Duchamp resigned, insisting that "the only works of art America has given are her plumbing and her bridges." Some modernists sided with Duchamp, but others feared that his action invited charges that modernism was a spoof at best and degenerate at worst.

Americans had only selective exposure to European avant-garde art. Most early exhibitions of mod-

Marcel Duchamp. Photograph by Petersburg Press, London. PRINTS AND PHOTOGRAPHS DIVISION, LIBRARY OF CONGRESS

ernism, including the Armory Show, showed mainly French work. Katherine Dreier, a painter from a well-to-do family, hoped to change this. Her first exposure to modernism came at the Steins' five years before the Armory Show, which included two of her paintings. Soon after she published the first book in English on Van Gogh. Dreier also worked for women's suffrage, the settlement house movement, and other social causes. Influenced by the writings of John Ruskin, William Morris, theosophists (an American religious movement that drew on elements of Buddhism and Brahmanism), and the painter Wassily Kandinsky, she emphasized the spiritual foundations of modernism. With Duchamp and others in 1920 she formed the Société Anonyme, which arranged for exhibits of modernist works at places as diverse as Vassar College and the Manhattan Trade School for Girls. Its greatest achievement was a 1926–1927 exhibition at the Brooklyn Museum of Art that gave attention to German Expressionist, Russian, Dutch and Hungarian work largely unknown in this country. According to the art historian Ruth L. Bohan, this exhibition "helped prepare the way for the arrival the following decade of the many European artists displaced by the closing of the Bauhaus and the subsequent outbreak of the Second World War." But the confused and ill-informed critical response showed that modernist work continued to lack legitimacy for most Americans.

Despite the persistence of such mixed responses to modernism, the Armory Show irrevocably established the concept that in the twentieth century a condition of choice prevailed in arts. As Sheeler wrote about a Matisse painting in the show: "We had never thought a picture could look like that—but there it was to prove it. Pictures like this offered . . . evidence that a picture could be arbitrarily conceived as an artist wished." Tentative institutional acceptance of modernism took more permanent form with establishment in 1929 of what soon became the most publicized art museum in the United States. The name of this institution helped shape public perceptions of the visual arts. Before the Armory Show most writers used the term "modern" to indicate not artistic radicalism, but merely works of recent origin. In contemporary reviews of that show, among the interchangeable terms writers applied, seldom with any precision, to the unfamiliar art were "futurist," "postimpressionist," "cubist" and, less frequently, "expressionist" and "modernist." In the show's aftermath the term "modern" increasingly became associated with art that challenged the conventions of academic art. By 1929 it made sense for founders of a

The Woolworth Building (1911–1913; Cass Gilbert, architect), 792 feet tall, dominated the skyline of lower Manhattan at the beginning of the century. New York City Hall is in the foreground; the main post office is between it and the Woolworth Building. For two other views of the Woolworth Building against the skyline of lower Manhattan, see the article "The East" in volume I. PRINTS AND PHOTOGRAPHS DIVISION, LIBRARY OF CONGRESS

new museum devoted to this unconventional art to name it the Museum of Modern Art (MoMA).

Artists lumped under the label "modern" held diverse attitudes toward other attributes of modernity. Typical of those who affirmed conspicuous aspects of contemporary American life were participants in the 1921 Chicago "Salon des Refusés," who declared that they were "radicals" who wished to create art that would "rival the scientific and commercial strides made by our country." In New York visitors to the Armory Show encountered dramatic visual manifestations of these "strides" on their way to and from the armory. The Woolworth Building, which opened the month after the show closed, became, at 792 feet, the tallest in the world. Nearly three times as high as the steeple of Trinity Church (1846), Manhattan's tallest structure until 1890, it was a hard-to-ignore reminder of the obsolescence of previous restrictions on visual experience. The emerging world of human design transformed every aspect of perceptual experience of importance to the artist: space, time, vantage point, distance, size, duration, color, and light. For instance, Edison's introduction of an effective incandescent bulb in 1879, combined with the availability of electric power in large cities soon after, multiplied options for artists interested in depicting the effects of different types of illumination.

Changes in the visual environment invited new forms of artistic expression. As sculptor Jacques Lipchitz later asserted, "one cannot live on a visual diet of skyscrapers and produce the same sort of art as one who fed visually on the Acropolis." Many of modernism's earliest American adherents were involved with architecture or engineering in ways that required intimate awareness of the new technical world. Stieglitz had studied mechanical engineering at the Technische Hochschule in Berlin, Marin worked as an architectural draftsman, and Manierre Dawson, one of the few Americans to do nonrepresentational paintings prior to 1913, had graduated from Chicago's Armour Institute of Technology. H. Lyman Säyen designed the first military X-ray laboratory in the country in 1898, a decade before he became one of the country's first modernist painters. Among other early modernists with technical experiences were Morgan Russell, Man Ray, and Morton Schamberg.

Although American artists had more exposure than any others to visual manifestations of new technologies, Europeans often alerted them to their aesthetic implications. The French painter Francis Picabia proclaimed during a 1915 visit that "almost immediately upon coming to America it flashed on me that the genius of the modern world is in machinery and that through machinery art ought to find a most vivid expression." Art movements encountered during return visits to their native countries gave new visions to Louis Lozowick and Joseph Stella, two European-born artists who moved to the United States. When the Ukrainian-born Lozowick first came to the United States in 1906 he had found New York's skyscrapers "forbidding." Exposure to Russian Constructivism, as well as the paintings of Fernan Léger, inspired him to attempt "a new esthetic approach to the civilization of today—a new plastic interpretation of the machine age." He portrayed in his prints and paintings the underlying order of the American city, which he found "in the verticals of its smoke stacks, in the parallels of its car tracks, the squares of its streets, the cubes of its factories, the arc of its bridges, the cylinders of its gas tanks."

Futurist art seen on a visit to his native Italy in 1912 helped Stella appreciate the awesome spectacle provided by the lights and rapid movement of Coney Island and the innovatively structured majesty of the Brooklyn Bridge. One of many poets and artists, including Hassam, Marin, Weber, and Georgia O'Keeffe, to celebrate this bridge, Stella considered it "the shrine containing all the efforts of the new civilization of AMERICA—the eloquent meeting point of all forces arising in a superb assertion of their powers." In its presence he felt "as if on the threshold of a new religion or in the presence of a new DIVINITY." American writers such as William Carlos Williams also called for artistic exploration of the new landscape: "to take the machine and make its contours acceptable to our eye by using it in our compositions is admirable in a modern artist."

Others emphasized the more ominous implications of these new sights. In his 1921 oil painting *New York, Lower Manhattan,* Stefan Hirsch recorded what he described as his "recoil from the monstrosity that industrial life had become in 'megapolitania.' " George Ault's *Construction Night* (1922) offered his view of New York as "the Inferno without fire," with its skyscrapers serving as the "tombstones of capitalism." In Chicago Carl Hoeckner created paintings that suggested that mechanization threatened to standardize and dehumanize all aspects of American life. The First World War's revelations of the destructive potential of modern technology made such images more likely in the 1920s than they had been before. However, the war had less impact on American art than it did on American literature or on European visual artists. No recognized American artist was killed in the war. Marsden Hartley was influenced by military displays he saw in Germany in 1914, his interest given poignancy by his grief for the death of a German officer who had been his lover. Among other American artists who participated in or observed part of that war were Edward Steichen, George Biddle, Rockwell Kent, and Horace Pippin. Pippin, who served as a corporal in the 369th Colored Infantry, was shot thorough the shoulder by a German sniper and lay in a shell hole for one day before being rescued. He later said of his war experience, "I can never forget suffering and I will never forget sunset . . . so I came home with all of it in my mind and I paint from it today." The Dada movement spawned in wartime Europe had a New York variant sparked by the European visitors Duchamp and Picabia and involving American artists such as Man Ray. The postwar depression in his home town of Salem, Ohio, seemed to influence Charles Burchfield, who with the help of Sherwood Anderson's novel *Winesburg, Ohio,* "began to feel the great epic poetry of midwest American life" and express it in his haunting paintings. He wrote in 1928 that he hated "and would go on hating to my last breath—modern industrialism, the deplorable conditions in certain industrial fields such as steelworks and mining sections."

Charles Sheeler had a more ambivalent response. He recorded both the industrial landscape's austere, geometric beauty and its threat to individual identity. In his paintings people often are absent or dwarfed by immense industrial structures. In 1927 Sheeler began his most ambitious project, a series of photographs, which in turn led to paintings, of Henry Ford's immense Rouge River plant. He considered the subject "incomparably the most thrilling I have had to work with," although he acknowledged a wide range of influences, including the simplicity of Shaker furniture. The art historian Karen Lucic has noted similarities between Sheeler's Ford shots and others he made two years later of Chartres cathedral. Yet along with this obvious fascination with his subject was a fear, expressed years later in an interview, that the industrial sites had a deplorable "absence of spiritual content." A similar concern seemed present in the photographs of Sheeler's sometime collaborator, the photographer Paul Strand, who in images such as *Wall Street* (1915) showed the physical city visually overwhelming its human inhabitants. Lewis Hine's 1930 photographs of the construction of the Empire State Building were unusual for their dual celebration of the emerging vertical landscape and of the workers who constructed it.

Among many other artists who found rich visual material in the built landscape were the painters Preston Dickinson, Nils Spencer, and Ralston Crawford. Art historians often refer to them, along with Sheeler and some more thoroughgoing technological skeptics such as Ault, as Precisionists, or Cubist-Realists. The Chicago-born sculptor John Storrs, during and after World War I, created abstract sculptures, some of stainless steel, suggestive of skyscrapers and sophisticated machine parts. Revealing other dimensions of the contemporary cityscape in their paintings of large New York buildings, Marin, who wrote that "the whole city is alive," and O'Keeffe, gave steel and concrete diffuse organic qualities. Demuth also explored many compositional forms inspired by and devised in response to the modern environment. Many of these artists participated in the 1927 Machine-Age Exposition, hoping to prove that modern art made sense as an expression of "a life in which machine production, highly organized industry and commerce, science and invention play the dominant roles."

Artists also responded to other sensory consequences of modernity. Demuth's 1928 "poster portrait" of William Carlos Williams, keyed to a Williams poem inspired by a speeding fire engine, evoked the kaleidoscopic visual and sound juxtapositions of urban life. During the 1920s Davis, Stella, and Gerald Murphy incorporated advertisements and other commercial designs into their paintings. Davis, for instance, created a stunning 1921 painting with the then green Lucky Strike package as its principal subject. Reciprocally, business seized on the publicity opportunities offered by modernism. At the time of the Armory Show Wanamaker's department store ran an advertisement proclaiming "Color Combinations of the Futurists—Cubist Influence in Fashions," promising "for the first time in America" the "modern spirit in the realm of woman's dress." Critic Sheldon Cheney observed that by the late 1920s "the big department store advertisements, instead of sticking to properly photographic illustrations of their wares, are featuring artists who have caught all the surface earmarks of modernist painting—looseness, aliveness, and chasing of some elusive, abstract quality."

Stieglitz had long been stimulated and repulsed by the vulgar energy of urban America. Commercial exploitation of modernism after World War I strengthened his inclination toward the negative response. He expressed his state of mind in 1923 by entitling a photograph of a gelded horse "Spiritual America." When he opened his Intimate Gallery in 1925, eight years after closing 291 due to war-related and other pressures, he wrote that the sparse attendance did not bother him because he had no wish to attract "the mob." In his old age he concluded "I'm an absolute failure. The American church is the department store."

Others became even more discouraged. Influenced especially by encounters with Fauvist works, several years before the Armory Show Alfred Maurer abandoned the representational style that had won him success and began making expressive use of form and color. Rarely able to sell these new paintings, he depended for support on his father, Louis Maurer, a popular Currier and Ives lithographer who reportedly wept with dismay when he first saw his son's modernist work at 291. The younger Maurer lamented in 1922 that "for fifteen years not a living soul has said a kind word about my pictures." He lived on in his father's house, depressed by professional and personal problems. He hanged himself from a door frame in that house shortly after his one-hundred-year-old father's death in 1932. His final painting was a fragmented image of an agonized George Washington, whose two hundredth birthday the nation observed that year. Patrick Henry Bruce, another early modernist, also became embittered when his bold and original geometric abstractions received little notice, and committed suicide five years after Maurer.

Some responded to the perceived crassness of American society by embracing alternative cultures. Many nineteenth-century American artists had adorned their studios with antiquated and exotic artifacts. This interest took on new meaning for modernists, who found in West African sculpture and Navajo rugs license to include in their own work features banished from academic art, including explicit sexuality and unsubordinated decorative patterns. In 1909, when Max Weber returned from four years in Paris, he brought along a love for African art aroused by his contact with European modernists, who frequented the Trocadero and other museums stocked with trophies of ongoing imperialist ventures. In 1914, in part due to Weber's influence, Robert Coady displayed African works as well as examples of European modernism in his newly opened Washington Square Gallery. Several months afterward, Stieglitz showed wooden African statuary at 291. Marsden Hartley was also influenced by African art, which he first encountered at the British Museum in 1912, where Egyptian and Assyrian art also moved him. Later in the decade, during visits to the American Southwest, he developed a serious interest in Native American art, which he praised in his 1921 *Adventures in Art* as the product of cultures that provided models for harmonious relations between humanity and nature and between artists and society. Modernists were not alone in their respect for such art. John Sloan labored successfully to have American Indian art included in the Independent Exhibition of 1917, and in 1931 he helped arrange the first large showing of this art for aesthetic purposes.

Critics persistently condemned modernism's affinity for "primitive" art. In 1913 the artist Charles Vezin called modern art "the new coon in town," a 1917 reviewer for *Art News* said modernism overvalued the work of "the dusky sons of the Ivory Coast," a 1924 reviewer for *Arts* accused modernists of worshiping the "nigger gods of Africa," the critic Thomas Craven in 1925 described Matisse and his followers as "Negromaniacs," and in 1926 the *American Maga-zine of Arts* criticized modernists for giving "the blue ribbon to African sculpture, Indian totem poles, and the like." These attacks converged with others that classified modernism as subversive and alien. Soon after Russia's 1917 revolutions one art critic called modernism "lurid art Bolshevism." During the Metropolitan Museum of Art's 1921 modernist exhibition a committee of outraged citizens linked the art with a general movement intent on "the Revolutionary destruction of our entire social system." Royal Cortissoz's essay, "Ellis Island Art," published one year before passage of the severely restrictive 1924 National Origins Act, warned, "the United States is invaded by aliens, thousands of whom constitute so many acute perils to the health of the body politic. Modernism is of precisely the same heterogeneous alien origin and is imperiling the republic of art in the same way."

Modernism did have some influence on cultural values, including the way Americans thought about racial issues. North Carolinians enrolled in the state university's 1927 extension course on "Modern French Art" received assignments that required discussion of the impact of "Negro art" on Cubism. Perhaps such activities awakened some to black achievements that undermined assumptions of white supremacy. However, modernists shared as well as questioned prevailing prejudices. Stieglitz sponsored one of the first serious exhibitions of African art in the Western world, but he explained that it was not "thoroughbred art." It served a useful purpose just as "the greyhound was improved by introduction of the blood of the bulldog." Few modernists or other artists made an issue of discriminatory policies followed by art institutions. Art journals praised Fort Worth's museum for remaining open "for two evenings for the negroes," yet it continued to exclude blacks during the day. African American artists, such as Archibald Motley and William H. Johnson, encountered limits on what subjects they could address and what professional opportunities were open to them.

By 1929 racial restrictions had eased slightly in comparison with the beginning of the century. Motley attended the School of the Art Institute with financial assistance from a Chicago benefactor, and in 1928 he received an exhibition at the New Gallery in New York and a Guggenheim Fellowship that allowed him to study in Paris. Johnson was able to study at the NAD and in France. Like Motley he received some assistance from the Harmon Foundation, which began giving awards to black artists in the 1920s. Women artists also found their opportunities

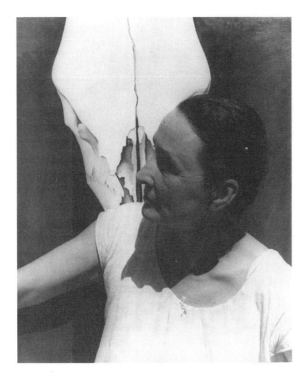

Georgia O'Keeffe. Photograph by Carl Van Vechten, 1936. PRINTS AND PHOTOGRAPHS DIVISION, LIBRARY OF CONGRESS

somewhat increased, although still severely limited. Early in the century the few women, such as the portrait painter Cecilia Beaux, who achieved recognition, worked in familiar and approved styles, although Mary Cassatt had pushed these categories to the limit through her early involvement with Impressionism. Less conventional artists, such as Florine Stettheimer and Marguerite Zorach, to an even greater extent than their male counterparts, were known mainly within their own circles.

Georgia O'Keeffe broke this pattern. After study in Chicago and New York and teaching in Texas, the Wisconsin-born O'Keeffe had her first New York show at 291 in 1916. She observed in 1930 that "I have had to go to men as sources in my painting because the past has left us so small an inheritance of women's painting that has widened life." Among her influences were teacher Arthur Wesley Dow, who transmitted his intense love of Asian art with its integration of pictorial and decorative art, and Stieglitz, whom she married in 1924. Her experience and feminist perspective convinced her that she must commit herself uncompromisingly to her art, which she did during a career that almost spanned the century. Impressed by two visits to Mabel Dodge Luhan

and the art colony at Taos, in 1930 she moved permanently to New Mexico. By that time her distinctive paintings had made her one of the best known and most financially successful of all American modernists.

The art of Motley, Johnson, and O'Keeffe took its place within a larger diversity that had unfolded in the fifteen years after the Armory Show. In 1914 Morgan Russell and Stanton Macdonald Wright exhibited their Synchromist paintings, nonrepresentational works that created form and structure through the interplay of colors. Abraham Walkowitz, one of several artists to make the dancer Isadora Duncan a favorite subject, anticipated many post–World War II artists by describing each of his works as "a record of an experience." Arthur Dove, also a member of the Stieglitz circle, used modernism's radical freedom to incorporate into his collage paintings of the 1920s such materials as fabric flowers, pipe cleaners, a ten-cent price card from Woolworth's, folding rulers, pieces of wood, and a scrap of music. In his *Fog Horns* he sought to create visual equivalents of sound. Man Ray created Dada objects, such as his 1921 *Cadeau,* a flatiron with nails attached at the bottom, and in *The Rope Dancer Accompanies Herself with Her Shadows* (1916) let chance play a major role in compositional decisions. In 1927 Gerald Murphy graphically represented in his painting *Wasp and Pear* the multiple levels of reality opened up by modern science by depicting both a wasp and a microscopic segment of the wasp's leg.

More conventional realist works also came in great variety. Henri's protégé George Bellows won great acclaim for his aggressive paintings of urban culture, including vividly depicted, bloody boxing matches, before his early death from appendicitis. Kenneth Hayes Miller, like Henri, painted scenes of New York life and had his greatest influence as a teacher, including among his students Bellows, Reginald Marsh, and Isabel Bishop. Also associated with what became known as the Fourteenth Street School of painting were the Russian-born Soyer brothers, Moses, Raphael, and Isaac. Artists who gave more political or satirical bite to their works included William Gropper and Peggy Bacon. Edward Hopper, another Henri student, created powerful, unsentimental images of human separateness. Other artists had begun the work that would bring them fame as "American Scene" painters in the following decade.

The opening of MoMA demonstrated the extent and limits of choice by 1929. Its founders came from the wealthy classes that had long dominated the arts through their bestowing or withholding of patronage, yet included among them were a number of women, who in contrast to their peripheral role in the governance of most traditional institutions had a shaping influence on this one. The inaugural show included works by Cézanne, Gauguin, and Van Gogh, art that caused great controversy at the time of the Armory Show, when a MoMA founding member, Lillie P. Bliss, bought some of the works on display in 1929, but that now seemed to many to represent a new establishment. Yet if this initial exhibition seemed merely to document options already won for artists, in the years ahead MoMA was to play a role in the ongoing enlargement of choice.

## ENVISIONING AMERICA, 1929–1945

Amidst their diversity, nearly all American artists celebrated the individual sensibility, and the related quality of originality. Deeply rooted in Western history, these celebrations became especially fervent in the Romantic era and reached new extremes with modernism. Not all would have gone as far as critic Benjamin De Casseres's definition of the artist's calling: "to have an individual vision and bugger the world with it!" But nearly all considered expression of individuality essential. In the decade and a half after the opening of MoMA, crises of depression and war called this emphasis into question.

Rampant individuality had not gone unchallenged. Early in the century Kenyon Cox, among others, had argued that esoteric personal expression deprived artists of the vital contact with society provided by shared traditions. But as of 1929 there was no one clearly defined tradition widely understood and accepted by both public and artists. During the 1930s many sought to establish, through an art grounded in a comprehensive ideology, or in observed realities of American life, a tradition that would offer direction to a society faced with threats to its existence. The felt need for strengthening communal ideals helped call forth the largest federal involvement in the visual arts in American history, which in turn provided a focus for struggles among competing viewpoints over how to define these ideals.

The federal government did not remain neutral. Under the prodding of his school classmate, George Biddle, a painter from Philadelphia's elite whose brother Francis later became solicitor general, President Franklin D. Roosevelt, as part of his response to record levels of unemployment and widespread

discouragement, initiated several art programs meant to help alleviate both. These included the Public Works of Art Project (PWAP, 1933–1934), the Section of Painting and Sculpture in the Treasury Department (1934–1943, with two name changes), the Treasury Relief Art Project (1935–1939), and the Federal Arts Projects of the Works Progress Administration (FAP, 1935–1943). Although the projects, which had different rules and goals, spawned a great variety of art, many officials encouraged painters to make pictorial records of American life. PWAP artists received explicit instructions to paint the "American scene" from the director, Edward Bruce. Assistant director Edward B. Rowan advised regional administrators that artists who wished only to draw foreign scenes "had better be dropped and an opportunity given to the man or woman with enough imagination and vision to use the beauty and possibility for aesthetic expression in the subject matter of his own country." A 1934 Treasury Department report concluded that PWAP successfully had led the American artist to "turn his mind away from theorizing for its own sake toward the life and people of his own country."

Some "American Scene" artists acknowledged their debt to Cubism and other modern movements, which others condemned as un-American and inaccessible. Diversity prevailed even among the most publicized of these artists, Thomas Hart Benton, Grant Wood, and John Steuart Curry. All became proponents of "regionalism," urging establishment of strong art communities committed to producing locally based art. In his autobiographical *An Artist in America* (1934) Benton told of early strutting in Parisian Bohemia, playing with some success at being a modern painter, and of equally disillusioning encounters with radical politics. He discovered in the 1920s the need to root his art in the rich soil of American life. In 1930–1931 he created *America Today* at New York's New School of Social Research, an ambitious mural documenting national life through cinematically stylized depictions of American types. A mural he executed for the Indiana pavilion at Chicago's 1933–1934 Century of Progress Exposition exemplified the range of subjects Benton incorporated into his works. The 250-foot-by-12-foot *A Social History of the State of Indiana* included depictions of Indiana's history and contemporary social customs, popular culture, agriculture and industry, and Native American crafts, and did not ignore such disturbing topics as war's devastation, violent labor conflicts, and the hooded presence of the Ku Klux Klan. In 1935 he returned permanently to his native Missouri,

Grant Wood. Self-portrait. PRINTS AND PHOTGRAPHS DIVI-SION, LIBRARY OF CONGRESS

accepting commissions such as a state capitol mural. By this time he had been featured, along with Wood and Curry, in a 1934 *Time* cover story.

Wood, born on an Iowa farm, spent most of his life in Cedar Rapids. After earlier training in the Midwest, in the 1920s he developed his mature style. A year spent mainly in Paris (1923–1924) strengthened his commitment to the artist's vocation and to high standards of traditional craftsmanship. Writers such as Sinclair Lewis, Ruth Suckow, and a local author, Jay Sigmund, stimulated Wood's interest in midwestern subjects. Ideas garnered from works by Hans Memling and other northern Renaissance artists during a 1928 trip to Germany combined with his long-time interest in local materials, such as county atlases, to help him find a way to portray regional subjects in whimsical yet solid and memorable paintings. Wood borrowed from modernism, but rejected, with less combativeness than Benton, nonrepresentational and explicitly theoretical art. Paintings such as the iconic *American Gothic* (1930) and *The Midnight Ride of Paul Revere* (1931) made clear his fascination, shared by Benton, with popular perceptions of American culture, as well as with contrasts between earlier and contemporary ways of life.

Curry left Kansas in his teens. A decade later he won recognition, as the art historian Sue M. Kendall noted, by "painting memories of Kansas from his studio in the fashionable art colony of Westport, Connecticut," beginning with *Baptism in Kansas* (1928). In 1936 he returned to the Midwest, becoming artist-in-residence at the University of Wisconsin. Between 1937 and 1942 he did a series of murals at the Kansas statehouse in Topeka featuring Coronado, John Brown, and a sturdy rural family. His final years were embittered by controversies over these murals. Although these three midwesterners received the most publicity, many artists in other parts of the country, such as Peter Hurd in the Southwest, painted the "American Scene" as they encountered it.

Government support for this emphasis received reinforcement from many other organizations, including the Whitney Museum of Art, opened in 1931 as successor to the Whitney Studio Club sponsored by sculptor and patron Gertrude Vanderbilt Whitney. MoMA also began showing American art, including folk art, although the nearly complete exclusion of American works from its 1936 "Cubism and Abstract Art" exhibition indicated the continuing difficulties of American modernists in finding an audience. Stieglitz called the gallery he opened in this decade "An American Place." Stieglitz and associates such as Hartley had long proclaimed their attachment to American traditions represented by Emerson, Whitman, Ryder, and other visionaries. Stuart Davis, like others who had studied with Henri, honored similar traditions; he considered Whitman the greatest American poet. Davis's jazz-inspired paintings made visible rhythmic links and oppositions that integrated, yet kept distinct, disparate elements in the seeming visual chaos of urban life. He titled a 1932 exhibition of these heterophonic works "The American Scene: Recent Paintings, New York and Gloucester." He explained he had been, "born in Philadelphia of American stock. I studied art in America. I paint what I see in America."

Davis also considered political radicalism a venerable American tradition. His commitment to left-wing causes began two decades earlier when he contributed illustrations to *The Masses,* as did the feisty independence that led him to resign from that publication to protest editorial interference with the prerogatives of artists. In the mid-1930s Davis became president of the American Artists' Union, editor of the union's magazine *Art Front,* and a leader of the American Artists' Congress. Although the numerous artists who joined these and other activist organizations ranged from loyal New Dealers to members of the Communist party, most believed that they should use their art to encourage working-class solidarity, racial equality, and resistance to international fascism, especially through support for the Loyalist side in the Spanish Civil War. Although social protest art remained more the exception than the rule, American artists produced it in greater abundance than they had in any earlier decade. Major influences included the Mexicans Diego Rivera, David Siqueiros, and José Clemente Orozco, who helped make murals a preeminent art form of the 1930s by demonstrating their galvanizing power, and artists such as Gropper who already had developed styles amenable to political expression.

Activists often defined themselves through contrast. Speakers at the first meeting of the American Artists' Congress chastised regionalists for depicting rural-urban differences at a time when artists should be helping poor farmers and factory workers recog-

nize their common interests. Others criticized modernists for overemphasizing personal expression; they insisted that artists must have a "social philosophy" in order to serve the needs of a society that "belongs to the masses." But Davis disputed formulations that ignored modernism's grounding in contemporary realities. Motion pictures and radio allowed artists "to experience hundreds of diverse scenes, sounds, and ideas in a juxtaposition that has never before been possible. . . . They force a new sense of reality and this must of course be reflected in art." He hoped that in the future "greater contact between artists and the broad masses of people" would make innovative art more accessible to the public. Davis's conciliatory approach became more acceptable to orthodox leftists in 1935 when the Communist International called for a "popular front," uniting without insistence on ideological purity all left-leaning antifascists. Thus the Artists' Congress welcomed all left/liberal

John Steuart Curry, *Baptism in Kansas,* 1928. COLLECTION OF WHITNEY MUSEUM OF AMERICAN ART, NEW YORK

Farm Security Administration as employer of artists during the Depression. Dorothea Lange's photo of a Texas family looking for work in the carrot harvest, California, March 1937. PRINTS AND PHOTOGRAPHS DIVISION, LIBRARY OF CONGRESS

artists of substantial achievement, whether they be "academician or modernist, abstractionist, realist, or surrealist." Perhaps the Congress's major achievement prior to its virtual collapse in 1940 (due to disenchantment with Soviet foreign policy) was helping to bring to New York in 1939, to raise funds for Spanish refugees, Picasso's *Guernica,* the century's most famous protest painting, created by its most famous modernist.

Scholars have documented numerous examples of censorship of politically or aesthetically radical work in the public projects. John S. Ankeny, PWAP's Texas-Oklahoma chair, said he would prohibit "the distorted forms of modernistic art" as well as anything "communistic." Local industrialists prevented Fletcher Martin from depicting a mining accident in an Idaho post office mural. Administrators discouraged works that called attention to conflicts among Americans, or challenged normal assumptions about class, racial, and gender roles. Barbara Melosh discovered that Rowan "advised Arthur Getz to fatten up the little boy in *Harvest,* his mural for Bronson, Michigan: 'His thin little arms are somewhat distressing in a scene of such

abundance.'" Administrators, often responding to local demands, sometimes warned against racial mixing in mural panels, precisely defined which jobs artists could depict blacks and whites performing, and discouraged scenes of violence.

Censorship affected other art as well. The Rockefellers destroyed a Rivera mural (1931) in Rockefeller Center because it included a portrait of Lenin. Washington's Corcoran Art Gallery rejected for its 1939 exhibition Peter Blume's 1937 painting *Eternal City,* allegedly because of its aggressive antifascist imagery. But much remained uncensored. In 1934 officials came under strong political pressure to force removal of radical imagery from murals done by several artists in San Francisco's Coit Tower. After extensive picketing by the city's Artists' and Writers' Union the murals, despite complaints that they overemphasized American shortcomings, went on display unaltered, except for one hammer and sickle removed under unclear circumstances.

Photographs taken for the Farm Security Administration (FSA) also made social problems visible. Photographers such as Dorothea Lange, Russell Lee,

Gordon Parks, and Ben Shahn recorded the ravages of flooding and soil erosion and the plight of migrant workers, the unemployed, and thousands of other Americans touched by the Depression. These photographs supported New Deal reforms, and as international crises began to seem more urgent than domestic problems FSA administrator Roy Stryker encouraged images emphasizing positive features of American life. Some extensively manipulated images posed as unmediated records. But overall the tens of thousands of FSA photographs provided a vivid, compassionate glimpse into the lives of many whose concerns would otherwise have been less noticed. Agencies such as the Soil Conservation Service also created photographic archives of lasting aesthetic and historical value, and federal funds supported other outstanding projects, such as the lucid documenta-

tion of New York's diverse physical and social landscape done for FAP by Berenice Abbott.

Photographers working on their own or only partially with government support created comparable images. Edward Weston carried out explorations of form as expressed in landscapes, organic objects, and the human body, as did Ansel Adams, Imogen Cunningham, and other members of the California-based F.64 group. Walker Evans, initially while on the government payroll, created for *Let Us Now Praise Famous Men,* a book he did with James Agee, his photographic vision of the life of southern tenant farmers. Helen Levitt sympathetically but unflinchingly photographed children's street life in her native New York City and other urban settings. Other work of the period ranged from the unapologetic sensationalism of Weegee's (Arthur Fellig) documentation

Farm Security Administration as employer of artists during the Depression. Bethune-Cookman College students, Daytona Beach, Florida, February 1943. Photograph by Gordon Parks. PRINTS AND PHOTOGRAPHS DIVISION, LIBRARY OF CONGRESS

Photography at war. Edward Steichen, head of the navy photography unit, aboard an aircraft carrier, World War II. PRINTS AND PHOTOGRAPHS DIVISION, LIBRARY OF CONGRESS

of urban horrors to Barbara Morgan's elegant depictions of the dancer Martha Graham.

Some of the best American photographers of World War II had gained experience on New Deal projects, including Carl Mydans, who worked for FSA. Mydans also had worked for *Life,* begun in 1936, as had W. Eugene Smith, whose sensitive photographs measured the war's costs for Japanese as well as Allied participants, and Margaret Bourke-White, who captured both the ironic visual beauty of aerial bombardment and the horrors of genocide. The war and the decade of conflict and persecution that preceded it brought many European artists to the United States. Among those who arrived between 1930 and 1945 were Josef Albers, Marc Chagall, Salvador Dali, Max Ernst, Hans Hofmann, Fernan Léger, André Masson, Lazlo Moholy-Nagy, and Yves Tanguy. Some of these émigrés founded in Chicago a "new Bauhaus" crucial in the history of American photography. Pearl Harbor and Adolf Hitler gave American artists a strong sense of common purpose during these years, intensified by the presence of refugee artists with personal knowledge of fascist brutality.

Artists as diverse as Benton, Davis, and the abstract gestural painter Lee Krasner made visual contributions to the war effort.

Underlying this apparent uniformity were circumstances that further enlarged the condition of choice. The war stimulated technological innovation, exposure to other cultures, and domestic social change. The diversity of American art in the postwar era was further assured by the vastly differing material and psychological circumstances the war thrust on concentration camp inmates, combat soldiers, and millions of other people whose wartime experiences would have some impact on that art. American Abstract Artists, an informal grouping formed in 1936 by George L. K. Morris, Balcomb Greene, Carl Holty, and others promoted nonrepresentational art of geometric purity. Diverse views of urban life were created by Romare Bearden, Marsh, Bishop, Shahn, Hopper (who painted one of the century's visual icons, *Nighthawks,* in 1942) and Alice Neel, whose refreshing city scenes had unsettling qualities as did many of the portraits for which she later became best known. Isamu Noguchi filtered ancient Japanese traditions through his contemporary sensibility in works such as a massive stainless steel sculpture in Rockefeller Center and in stage sets he fashioned for Martha Graham and George Balanchine. Motley and Johnson both developed distinct styles for depictions of African American life, and Jacob Lawrence began his brilliant career in the late 1930s with a series of narrative paintings dealing with figures such as Frederick Douglass and Harriet Tubman.

The best known American photograph of the war drew on decades of cultural and technical preparation. Joe Rosenthal's split-second picture of Marines raising the flag at Iwo Jima was made possible by a camera unavailable during World War I. American Scene and social activist art of the 1930s had laid groundwork for the attention to ordinary Americans represented by the picture's workerlike soldiers. As modernist art reified concepts of change and relativity of viewpoint, the photograph captured one passing, yet transcendent, moment of time. It was an authentic image of unified effort, falsely presented to detach that unity from its perishable wartime context. Contrary to rumors spread then and later, Rosenthal did not pose the photograph. But authorities obscured the fact that it documented the day's second and less hazardous flag raising. They shot holes in the flag to enhance its usefulness when returned to the United States, along with the three flag raisers not soon killed in battle, for war bond promotions.

Joe Rosenthal's photograph of U.S. Marines raising the American flag on Mount Suribachi, Iwo Jima, 6 March 1945. PRINTS AND PHOTOGRAPHS DIVISION, LIBRARY OF CONGRESS

Thus the unified purpose of American artists during the war years was real, but ephemeral and contingent.

## DOMINANCE AND DIVERSITY, 1945–1960

The energy generated by the collective effort of the war years did last beyond 1945. As the Chicago artist Leah Balsham recalled, art students, many of them veterans, "had an inner maturity, a certain strength of character. And they welcomed the fact that they were alive every day. It was a tremendous period, a tremendous sense of excitement." Yet, as expressed in works such as the photographer Minor White's portfolio entitled *Amputations* (1947), the war also left a legacy of tremendous sadness. And for many artists the Cold War did not generate the sense of common purpose with other citizens that the threat of fascism and Japanese militarism had. Amid the satisfactions provided by victory and postwar material prosperity, few Americans seemed seriously concerned with issues receiving urgent discussion in urban art communities, such as the implications of Hiroshima and the persistence within the United States of racism, cultural provincialism, and poverty. A few months after the war ended the Smith College art historian Oliver Larkin wrote a passage that repeated the concerns of 1929: "Our lack of a community concept of philosophy of life—beliefs and values which are shared by critic, artists and layman and whose existence can be assumed," made it "perhaps as difficult to be a whole critic today as to be a whole person."

This rupture of the tenuous wartime alliance between artists and society had an ironic result. Artists alienated from prevailing American cultural values gave rise to an art movement, Abstract Expressionism, that brought the United States unprecedented international influence in the visual arts. During the war several of these artists concluded that the prevalence of violence and injustice required an art saturated with a "tragic sense of life." In the postwar period they continued to act on this conviction, although they believed that it put them at odds with their society. Clyfford Still, the most abrasive of the group, later summarized his viewpoint: "Our age—it is of science—of mechanism—of power and death. I see no point in adding to its mammoth arrogance the compliment of graphic homage."

Personal circumstances contributed to the Abstract Expressionists' disaffection. In 1948 the critic Clement Greenberg described typical living conditions: "the shabby studio on the fifth floor of a cold-water, walk-up tenement on Hudson Street; the frantic scrambling for money; . . . the neurosis of alienation that makes you such a difficult person to get along with." Choices that required cash were of little benefit to them. Yet their art grew from, and contributed to, the emerging condition of choice that prevailed in the arts and in many other areas of life, although obscured and threatened by pressures for conformity during this era of political and cultural inquisitions. Most of the leading Abstract Expressionists had worked in New York, often on government art projects, during the 1930s, and in the early 1940s had become particularly interested in Surrealist explorations of the unconscious. During the next several years they had won small, enthusiastic followings after exhibiting at places such as Peggy Guggenheim's Art of This Century Gallery.

Among the major Abstract Expressionists were the Wyoming-born Jackson Pollock, a Benton student, who placed large canvases on the floor and covered them with elegantly and energetically intertwined trails of paint; Willem de Kooning, whose most characteristic paintings placed fragmented images of women in the midst of churning but carefully drawn and ordered seas of gestural color forms, sometimes applied with house painters' brushes; and Mark Rothko, whose overlapping fields of color seemed to shimmer and float. Barnett Newman sought monumental effect by plowing through his large fields of color with stark but nuanced verticals, and served as one theorist for the movement. Adolph Gottlieb hoped that by use in his paintings of elemental forms and symbols inspired by primitive art he could devise a universally valid imagery. Writers often referred to Pollock, de Kooning, and others, including Franz Kline, as "action painters" (a term applied to them by the critic Harold Rosenberg in 1952) or "gesture painters," while they later classified such artists as Still, Rothko, and Newman as "color-field painters." Sculptors included Theodore Roszak, Ibram Lassaw, and David Smith.

Arshile Gorky and Hans Hofmann taught Abstract Expressionists how to build upon the lessons of earlier modernism, as did the example provided by Piet Mondrian, in New York from 1940 until his death in 1944. The more numerous and noticeable émigré Surrealists kept Abstract Expressionists aware of alternatives to the formal emphasis of Cubism. John Graham, whose famously well informed if eccentric conversation had kept New York artists alert to developments in European painting during the 1930s, provided a link between various groups of modernists in New York in the 1940s. The recently opened Guggenheim Museum of Non-Objective

Art, where Pollock worked briefly as a custodian, exhibited works by Kandinsky and others who created an instructive tension between formalist and expressionist tendencies. Influences on different Abstract Expressionists included Carl Jung, Ruth Benedict, Martha Graham, the Hindu teacher Krishnamurti, and Martin Buber.

Some critics have argued that Abstract Expressionism "triumphed" partly because it could be interpreted in a way consistent with Cold War ideology. In a few instances government officials and others tried to use this art, with its apparent disengagement from collective efforts, to supplant more threatening social protest art, and to raise American prestige in the cultural phase of the Cold War, especially through brandishing the new movement as an advertisement for democratic freedoms. However, such objectives would have been as incomprehensible to most American leaders of this era as was the art itself. The immense postwar American global presence undoubtedly contributed to the growing influence of Abstract Expressionism, as did the originality and power of the art, the energetic efforts of some artists, dealers, and critics to promote it, and skepticism about explicitly ideological art prompted by recent memories of Hitler's Germany, Stalin's Soviet Union, and wartime propaganda in general. This movement also enjoyed publicity and persistence because of the growing importance of national media based in the same city as most of the artists, and multiplication of the art student population due to the postwar educational expansion encouraged by affluence and the GI bill. Although magazines such as *Time* played an essential role in winning attention for Abstract Expressionism, they were followers rather than leaders of trends established within the art community.

The federal government also eventually followed, but first resisted. In 1947 several politicians, journalists, and academic painters launched an attack on a collection of seventy-nine American paintings, including works by such established artists as Ralston Crawford and Stuart Davis, sent abroad by the State Department. The Republican National Committee distributed a sheet entitled "Art for Taxpayers." This document and congressional Republicans ridiculed the collection for including some paintings "so weird that one cannot tell . . . which side should be up" and others that presented an unfavorable view of American life. The State Department canceled the rest of the planned tour and sold the collection. Secretary of State George C. Marshall pledged there would be "no more taxpayers' money for modern art," and President Truman offered his opinion "that

Rockwell Kent. Photograph by Carl Van Vechten, 1933. PRINTS AND PHOTOGRAPHS DIVISION, LIBRARY OF CONGRESS

so-called modern art is merely the vaporings of half-baked, lazy people." Despite this Democratic refusal to defend works that challenged popular conceptions of what art should be, for the next few years Republicans such as George Dondero continued to try to make political hay from the issue. This representative from Michigan called modern art communistic because "it is distorted and ugly" and "does not glorify our beautiful country."

These politically powerful critics imposed significant limits on choice, restricting the international mobility of artists as well as of art. Cold War legislation and policies kept some foreign artists with alleged or actual Communist party affiliations out of the United States at the same time that they kept some Americans at home. Because of Rockwell Kent's decades of unconcealed left-wing activity, from 1950 until a divided Supreme Court ruled in his favor in 1958, the State Department withheld passport authorizations from this well-known American illustrator, painter, writer, and jack-of-all-trades. They also threatened him with prosecution for travel violations. The harassment endured by Kent and others, such as William Gropper, discouraged some artists from dealing with controversial subject matter. Philip Reisman's 1955 *The Trial,* with its depiction of rodentlike interrogators, was one of the few paintings from the era to directly attack the methods of Senator Joseph McCarthy and the House Committee on Un-American Activities. However, by the late 1950s the fame of Abstract Expressionism made it a diplomatic asset and the government gladly sent examples around the world. The English critic John Russell summarized the international reception of Abstract Expressionism with his observation that when asked what New York art meant to them most British artists would have replied "*nothing* in 1945, *everything* in 1958, and *something* in 1963."

Even at the peak of Abstract Expressionism's influence in 1958 Lloyd Goodrich remarked, "Representationalism, expressionism, abstraction, and all their innumerable variations—I doubt if there ever was a nation or a period whose art was more diverse than that of the United States today." Abstract Expressionism itself encompassed many distinct approaches, amplified by "second-generation" proponents such as Al Held, Grace Hartigan, and the Chicago-born artists Joan Mitchell and Richard Hunt. Hunt, a sculptor, was one of a growing number of African American artists who, although confronted by continuing inequities, had enlarged opportunities as a result of civil rights activism. For instance, the Container Corporation of America featured art by Jacob Lawrence in one of its 1946 advertisements. Lawrence was one of many artists who had benefited from government arts programs of the 1930s, the first use of federal funds to help establish and sustain the careers of a large number of nonwhite and women artists.

The diversity Goodrich noted also included such art as Hyman Bloom's disturbingly detailed and luminous paintings of cadavers and George Tooker's Orwellian *The Subway* (1950), which showed urban masses channeled into conformity by the bars and corridors of their constructed environment. In contrast to these works and to the Abstract Expressionists' heroic pieces, Richard Lippold's sculptures, intricate as cobwebs or snowflakes, reflected his interest in "the little delicate relationships of life." As he had since the 1930s, Alexander Calder put many of his colorful and carefully balanced sculptures into motion as "mobiles." Joseph Cornell remained at work on his poetic boxes. Ben Shahn, one of few artists who established close ties to organized labor, continued as he had at the time of the execution of Sacco and Vanzetti to use his work to call attention to

suffering caused by specific injustices. Increasingly he also created visual meditations on more general contradictions in the human condition. Jack Levine did social protest paintings in the Hogarthian style he had developed while working for FAP. Looking to different sources among the multitude available, Irene Rice Pereira sought in her abstract paintings "plastic equivalents for the revolutionary discoveries" in the sciences. Other painters, notably Helen Frankenthaler, who influenced Morris Louis and Kenneth Noland, developed brushless methods of applying painting to canvas with results that ranged from intense lyricism to intentional effacement of the artist's presence. Andrew Wyeth's finely drafted portraits and lonely landscapes made him probably the most popular painter in the United States.

Although no other city rivaled New York as an art center, part of the diversity came from the persistence of regional variations. Louis and Noland were living in Washington, D.C., at this time. Wyeth's work, done in Chad's Ford, Pennsylvania, and in Maine, carried on regionalist as well as genre traditions. Working in California, Richard Diebenkorn maintained a fruitful dialogue between his abstract and representational paintings, as did Philip Guston, who had worked earlier in Los Angeles then settled in New York. In the Pacific Northwest, Asian art and spirituality profoundly affected the work of Morris Graves and the widely traveled Mark Tobey. The Field Museum's collections of objects from Oceanic, West African, Native American, and ancient Mediterranean cultures, along with "outsider art" made by nonprofessional artists with little education, influenced artists who worked in Chicago, such as Ray Yoshida, June Leaf, and H. C. Westermann. Ivan Albright's unsurpassed ability to capture on canvas the inexorable process of human decay made him the logical choice when Hollywood needed an artist to paint the hidden portrait of Dorian Gray. Also working in Chicago at this time were the photographers Harry Callahan and Aaron Siskind, who in different ways probed the urban environment and the unique visual and physical possibilities of photography.

Other photography during the period stretched from the focus on human similarities in Steichen's immensely popular *Family of Man* exhibition at MoMA to Diane Arbus's disturbing images of the psychic distance separating people from one another, even within families. Ansel Adams and Eliot Porter produced images of the American landscape of such power that they made significant contributions to efforts to protect the country's natural environment.

W. Eugene Smith, one of the only photographers of stature to document the lives of industrial workers during this period, carried out a major project with this focus in Pittsburgh. He helped make possible the understanding of the United States achieved by Robert Frank. This Swiss-born photographer, who came to the United States in 1947, published twelve years later a challenging vision of his adopted country in *The Americans,* a project he had begun in 1955. Photographs such as one showing African Americans relegated to the back of a bus suggested contradictions central in the life of a nation that laid claim to leadership of the entire "free world." Such pictorial documentation of awkwardness and tension in Americans' relations with one another and a world of their making led Jack Kerouac to write in his introduction to the 1959 American edition that Frank had "sucked a sad poem right out of America onto film." Frank's photographs were immensely influential during the coming decades, as were the works of Robert Rauschenberg and Jasper Johns. Their impact began in the 1950s, but is most appropriately discussed in the context of the period after 1960, when the implications of their challenges to art's remaining boundaries became most apparent.

## ART WITHOUT BOUNDARIES, 1960–1990s

Until recent decades American painters usually presented their works in frames that fully contained them. In 1991 less than one in four of the artists, working in various media, in the prestigious Whitney Biennial exhibited paintings displayed this way. Boundaries that seemed essential at the century's beginning had lost their power to serve as constraints on artists' choices. By the late 1960s many of the country's artists were producing works that would have been unthinkable, physically impossible, or a criminal offense in the year 1900.

The boundary that came under most persistent assault separated works of art from everything else. In the avant garde of this assault had been Duchamp, who at the time of World War I presented as art such "readymades" as a store-bought bottle rack and the controversial urinal. Many others blurred distinctions between art and less "elevated" activities. In 1943 Stuart Davis declared that the most important influence on one of his recent paintings had been "the T-Formation as sprung by the Chicago Bears" in that year. Pollock and other action painters caused further blurring by creating works significant, according to critics such as Rosenberg, less for their

Whitney Museum of American Art, New York. Photograph by Michael Ross.

final appearance than for their documentation of the process that went into their making. Yet on the whole Abstract Expressionists left no doubt of their intention to create paintings and sculptures of exalted purpose that were distinct works of art. At the height of Abstract Expressionist influence, this concept of art as separable from other phenomena came under renewed probing by Rauschenberg and Johns, along with numerous other artists such as Larry Rivers, Claes Oldenburg, and, through the unique assemblages she created from wood fragments, Louise Nevelson. The Texas-born Rauschenberg, who described his social classification in his hometown of Port Arthur as "white trash," attended the experimental Black Mountain College in North Carolina, as did Noland and the sculptor John Chamberlain. The composer John Cage sometimes taught at this bastion of cultural ferment, whose visual arts component had been shaped by the émigré painter and color theorist Josef Albers, who came to the United States to teach at the college in the year of its found-

Andy Warhol with Nico, one of his superstars, 1966. ARCHIVE PHOTOS/TIM BOXER

ing, 1933. Visually omnivorous, Rauschenberg said that he considered the world "one gigantic painting." He included objects such as a stuffed goat, old bedding, tires, and cardboard boxes in his painted collages, later explaining that he worked in the "gap between art and life." Johns made a large impact with a 1955 painting, first exhibited in 1958, that in some senses was, but in others was not, an American flag.

These works helped set the stage for Pop artists such as Andy Warhol, Roy Lichtenstein, and James Rosenquist. Warhol's background in shoe design and advertising layout gave him the skills he applied in his multi-image paintings and prints of Campbell's soup cans, traffic accidents, movie stars, and other familiar subject matter. Lichtenstein's paintings at first glance appeared to be merely blown-up versions of comic strip panels; upon closer examination they presented the ironic spectacle of carefully hand-painted simulations of mechanically reproduced dots. Rosenquist, who had experience as a billboard painter, continued to work on a giant scale. He made paintings which juxtaposed realistic but fragmented portrayals of, to give examples from his eighty-six-foot-long painting *F-111,* a fighter plane, spaghetti with sauce, a garish beach umbrella with atomic blast residue, and a women under a hair dryer. Pop Art won national attention more rapidly than any earlier movement. Its major proponents developed in 1960 or 1961 the styles that won them recognition, received extensive publicity by 1963, and were at least

somewhat rich and famous within two or three years, although some were not yet thirty years old. This art emerged when memories of the Depression and war had faded, and when the accouterments of an ever more affluent society incessantly, blaringly, and seductively called attention to themselves. Whether particular Pop Artists meant to celebrate or ridicule the objects that they depicted, or simply explore their visual facticity, they opened their art up to the banality, immediacy, vulgarity, and vitality of popular culture.

The already long list of traditions, materials, and imagery absorbed by the gigantic sponge of contemporary art grew endless by the century's final decades. Artists such as Warhol and Ed Paschke, from their different vantage points in New York and Chicago, transformed images taken from the mediated visual environment of graphic design and television. Keith Haring was one of many artists who tapped into the energy of urban graffiti, as did works by Tim Rollins and KOS (Kids of Survival), a group whose changing membership Rollins formed from the talented, troubled teens he taught in the South Bronx, Brooklyn, and Harlem.

In addition to knocking some holes in the wall between art galleries and the streets, artists have questioned every distinctive feature traditionally associated with the fine arts. One of the criticisms of modernist art from the Armory Show onward had been that "a child could do it." Some took this as a compliment. Stieglitz had given a show of children's art at 291. Later, artists such as Red Grooms, often working in collaboration with his wife Mimi Gross, enlivened their works with childlike spontaneity, crudely delineated cut-out forms, and bright, clashing colors that defied learned rules of good taste. In the late 1970s Neil Jenney did a series of pieces that resembled finger painting, using garish and muddled colors. Warhol claimed that one of the purposes of his art was to demonstrate that "anybody could do anything." The complexities of works such as his disturbing electric chair series throw doubt on his claim, but his comments subverted the concept of art as a highly skilled activity.

The unskilled could not make sculptures such as Duane Hanson's life-size trompe-l'oeil re-creations of human figures, from tourists in Hawaiian shirts to uniformed museum guards. These works literally raised questions about distinctions between art and life, as in his *Janitor,* which uninitiated visitors to the Milwaukee Art Center assumed to be someone on the museum's custodial staff until close inspection revealed otherwise. Although their stark whiteness clearly marked the figures in sculptor George Segal's assemblages as objects rather than people, the fact that he had cast them directly from live models raised similar issues. Finely crafted Minimalist sculptures by Robert Morris, Donald Judd, and Sol Lewitt made visible complex concepts, but often intentionally excluded reassuring marks of the artist's physical participation in their making. Such marks were quite visible in the austere but transcendent grids drawn in pencil on bare canvas by Agnes Martin. Ad Reinhardt, who had been an abstract painter since the 1930s and a witty propagandist for this art, painted some canvases with nine squares of slightly different dark blues that at first glance appeared to be all-black paintings. Rauschenberg did do all-black, and all-white, paintings in the early 1950s; early works by Ellsworth Kelly and Frank Stella, influential in the subsequent development of minimalism, also had regular patterns and used only one or two colors. Supporting these works were theories defining a major thrust of modernism as the distillation of each medium to its pure essentials; often the results were beautiful, intellectually bracing, or meditative works. However, they raised the question of whether any meaningful boundary remained between art and nothingness.

Other artists challenged the notion of art as an exchangeable commodity. Determination to create works not confinable within a gallery was one of the reasons sculptors turned to massive outdoor earthworks in the 1960s and after. Robert Smithson's elegant *Spiral Jetty* (1970) in Great Salt Lake was fifteen-hundred feet long and fifteen feet wide. Constructing it required including a bulldozer among the sculptor's implements. Other ways to resist commercialization and to raise questions about art's nature were taken by conceptual artists who eliminated or minimized the material content of their work. In the late 1960s Jonathan Borofsky began counting, systematically writing numbers on paper, and for one period of almost two years did nothing else as an artist. After that, although he continued to spend some time counting, he also created a variety of other works, associating each with the point he had reached in his counting when they had their genesis, as in *Man with a Briefcase, 2,970,882.*

Borofsky's works included, in addition to a grow-

James Rosenquist. ARCHIVE PHOTOS/EXPRESS NEWSPAPERS

1717

*Gay Liberation* by George Segal, in Sheridan Square, Greenwich Village, New York City. Photograph by Michael Ross.

merger, not unique but uniquely widespread, and encompassing such new technologies as computerized manipulation of images, also included interactions between the visual arts and music, theater, and dance; between fine and commercial art; and between the arts and other disciplines. The mathematics prodigy Dorothea Rockburne, who studied at Black Mountain, visually articulated numerical systems in her mixed media works.

Contemporary artists also have made visible the structure, presumptions, and methods of art itself. In *According to What* (1964), Jasper Johns left intact one of the stencils used in making color circles on the painting, and in *Device* (1962) he screwed to the painting two rulers used to make the sweeping semicircles that are among its chief compositional features. In the late 1960s Morris, Richard Serra, and others, in part as an outgrowth of their own earlier minimalist work and of other' performance-type "happenings" of recent years, created "process art." Morris explained that such art revealed the "inherent tendencies and properties" of the materials they worked with. For example, Serra leaned heavy sheets of lead against one another in a stable but dramatically precarious manner that made clear to the viewer the counteracting forces maintaining the configuration. For another exhibition he splashed a large amount of silver paint along the meeting line between the gallery wall and floor, allowing the paint to assume the form determined by its own viscosity, gravity, and the particular space.

Many artists provided explicit visual commentary on earlier works. Particularly witty examples included paintings by Rauschenberg and Lichtenstein that meticulously reproduced the bold trails of surging paint, originally emblematic of spontaneity, of Abstract Expressionist action painting. Exploring connections between the making and perceiving of art, the painter Julia Fish wrote that she did not consider "that the appearance of the world has been established." Her multilayered works reflected her belief that the "analysis and reconstruction of appearances can be only a matter of imagination." James Turrell's poetic modifications of existing spaces sculpted and colored ambient light in ways that redefined visitors' perceptual experiences. Others pursued traditional artistic goals such as recording the results of careful observation. Wayne Thiebaud's sensually rich paintings reflected his understanding that "if you stare at an object, as you do when you paint, there is no point at which you can stop learning things about it."

Thiebaud's work also was an example of contin-

ing stack of counted-upon paper, mechanized and inanimate sculptures, drawings, many of which recorded his dreams, images traced directly in museum walls, found objects, and combinations of various forms. The works of many other contemporary artists also did not fit neatly into traditional categories. The Whitney Museum found it necessary to abandon its practice of holding separate annual shows of recent painting and sculpture, because the two so often overlapped. Photorealist painters of the 1970s and later, such as Chuck Close and Audrey Flack, used various methods to transfer photographic images onto their canvases, and often retained in these paintings visual features normally distinctive to photographs. Conditions approached that predicted by Man Ray in a 1951 interview: "a confusion or merging of all the arts, as things merge in real life." The

ued variations among and within regions. Existing regional traditions nurtured the carefully crafted, finely detailed, alternately whimsical and ominous paintings of erotically charged subjects, often from the cultural margins, done by Jim Nutt, Karl Wirsum, Christina Ramberg, and other Chicago Imagists. In Washington, D.C., Sam Gilliam displayed stained canvases as draped material rather than as framed paintings. California's growing population and economic power generated increased presence in the arts as well in major league sports. If one result was Thiebaud's use of creamy pigments to create paintings that seemed edible, whether they were of pastry displays or shoes, another was Ed Kienholz's construction of realistically scaled three-dimensional tableaux that intentionally repulsed viewers. For example, *The State Hospital* (1966), representing two mental patients strapped to their bunk beds, made grossly palpable the fetid, festering condition which the institution forced upon them. Many California artists were influenced by Simon Rodia, an Italian immigrant of modest means who created the majestic, mysterious Watts Towers out of industrial refuse, broken crockery, seashells and cement through decades (1921–1954) of solitary effort. Also in California, Ron Davis made glossy-surfaced, shaped illusionistic abstractions out of liquid fiberglass, Judy Chicago and Miriam Schapiro launched a Feminist Art Program in 1971 at the California Institute of the Arts that gave visual expression to their belief that "the personal is the political," and beginning about the same time a vigorous mural movement flourished, especially in Los Angeles's Latino communities.

The Los Angeles muralists were among the many artists who made the late twentieth century a time that surpassed every earlier period in the range of controversial topics addressed openly in art, including environmental and geopolitical matters and the status and identity of groups defined by concepts of race, class, religion, gender, and sexuality. The Vietnam War and the civil rights movement in the 1960s spurred the first widespread outburst of explicitly political art since the 1930s, an approach subsequently kept alive especially by participants in various rights and liberation movements, then by the AIDS crisis and social problems such as homelessness. Rosenquist's *F-111*, begun in 1964 and completed and exhibited in 1965, was an early example of art done partly as a critical response to American policy in Vietnam. Duane Hanson used his superrealist techniques to create a bloody *Vietnam Scene* (1969), and Kienholz assembled a sardonic *Portable War Memorial*. Leon Golub and Nancy Spero produced a substantial body of work related to Vietnam, such as Golub's wrenching *Napalmed Head* (1969). Subsequently he produced many large, raw paintings of torture and other indignities, often set in Central America.

Events of the sixties also invited a more general questioning of cultural values. This furthered an ongoing movement away from traditional art forms, such as painting and sculpture, toward those more amenable to direct political expression, such as performance and video. It also led to a sharp increase in the amount of ambitious art directed at audiences not likely to frequent museums. For instance, the United Electrical Workers, for their offices in Chicago, had José Guerrero and John Pitman Weber do a mural, *Solidarity* (1973), that showed workers struggling against oppressive workplace conditions. Other examples included Cythnia Weiss and Miriam Socoloff's New York mosaic mural *The Fabric of Our Lives* (1979), which "depicted the struggles of Jewish women for voting rights, equal wages, and the brutal reality of sweatshop work in a sewing factory," and the one-half mile long *The Great Wall of Los Angeles* mural. Done in the early 1980s under the direction of Judy Baca, its presentation of the history of the Americas began with an homage to pre-Columbian

Watts Tower, Los Angeles, by Simon Rodia, 1921–1954.
ARCHIVE PHOTOS/R. THOMPSON

1719

inhabitants and included such scenes as the zoot suit riots and internment of Americans of Japanese ancestry during World War II.

Responding to and helping to define other emerging public concerns, Neil Jenney was one of a number of artists who used their paintings to call attention to abuse of the natural environment. Deborah Butterfield's mud and stick horses and Martin Puryear's lyrical handcrafted sculptures were other works that implicitly expressed ecological concerns through their materials and manners of making. As these examples suggest, some artworks had political messages that were arresting but invited differing readings, such as Cady Noland's *Oozwald,* a more than life-size enlargement of a photograph of Lee Harvey Oswald at the moment Jack Ruby shot him, with holes cut in the Oswald image and parts of an American flag appended to his nose. Less ambiguous was painter May Stevens's *Big Daddy Paper Doll* (1971), which showed a bulky, phallic-headed white male figure with interchangeable uniforms as butcher, policeman, soldier, or klansman.

Some political art has made use of the new possibilities for sexual expression resulting from relaxation of legal restrictions in the 1960s and after. Artists such as Bruce Nauman and Vito Acconci used manipulations of their bodies as artistic and political metaphors. In his highly publicized work *Seedbed* (1973), for two weeks Acconci lay concealed under a ramp built over the floor of the Leo Castelli Gallery and, in his words, tried "to involve the viewers by fantasizing about them [through a loudspeaker] as I masturbated." The following year sculptor Lynda Benglis placed an advertisement in *Artforum* with a photograph of herself, naked except for a pair of sunglasses, holding a gigantic dildo to her crotch. She explained that she was "mocking" such things as the "hype" advertising of both art and sexuality. Although sexuality often was used in a depersonalized way, with equal frequency it contributed to an art of intense personal exploration, as seen in the photographic self-portraits of Lucas Samaras that often suggested metaphorical piercing and slicing of his body. Samaras also provocatively explored the contemporary artist's cultural legacy, as in his Polaroid pictures of himself assuming positions modeled after Michelangelo's Sistine Chapel ceiling frescoes. As all body functions came within art's expanding domain, in his 1982 sculpture *Doggie Bob* Robert Arneson placed his head on a dog's body, surrounded by ceramic turds. Also bringing the personal into the public realm were Sally Mann's photographs of the intimate private movements of her own children, which, in *Newsweek*'s words, mapped "the territory where innocence meets experience."

Alice Aycock made connections between art and the body as part of a more general exploration of relations between natural and fabricated forms, the latter an interest shared with other sculptors such as Nancy Graves. Some recent art, such as the paintings of David Salle and Eric Fischl coolly mimicked the form of earlier intensely felt expressionist paintings, thereby being more about the art of personal experience than the experiences themselves. Cindy Sherman exhibited hundreds of photographs of herself, but always in costumes and settings that provided different personae. Such extremely self-conscious work that took strength from appropriating usable parts of past styles often was called "postmodern," although the definition of this term usually depended on exaggeration of the previous dominance and uniformity of a formalist modernist aesthetic dedicated to reducing each art form to its essence.

The concept of postmodernism suggested also an emphasis on "deconstruction" of the assumptions and practices embodied in artworks and other cultural artifacts. Since the 1960s much art has probed racial- and gender-related stereotypes and celebrated previously suppressed or devalued aspects of female, African American, Hispanic/Latino, Asian American, Native American, and gay and lesbian experience. For example, David Hammons fashioned art from various manifestations of African American life, including his own body, hair clippings, and refuse found in the vicinity of his studio in Harlem. Hammons was one of a number of artists who, through such activities as on-site projects in impoverished areas, have continued the effort to make art in interaction with communities normally excluded from the art making process. Luis A. Jiménez, whose sculpture *Vaquero* adorns the entrance to the Smithsonian's National Museum of American Art, was one of many artists who made use of specific aspects of their cultural heritage in their works. Another was Fred Brown, who in *Geronimo with His Spirit* (1984) achieved a synthesis of his personal mix of African American, Native American, and Euro-American traditions. As artists paid more explicit attention to their ethnic identity, they became involved in struggles as to how their community should define that identity. Mario Torero's mural *We Are Not a Minority* (1978) at the Estrada Courts Housing Projects in East Los Angeles has been attacked frequently, sometimes physically, by those who resented the visual presence of Che Guevara in their neighborhood.

Women who have dealt with gender issues in

their art have shown a great diversity of viewpoints. However, most probably would agree with Miriam Schapiro's goal, stated in 1976, of using her work "to repair the sense of omission and to have each substance in the collage be a reminder of a woman's dreams." Artists such as Jenny Holzer and Barbara Kruger unveiled the social implications of language in their assertive works, adding another dimension to the earlier efforts of Eva Hesse and others whose sculptures and paintings established a nonverbal dialogue with male-defined types of art making. In her works painter Joan Semmel made a conscious effort to express "the eroticism of touch" from a female perspective, while Mary Miss challenged historical restrictions on women's mobility through installations such as *Screen* (1984) that mediated between the outside and inside of particular sites. Adrian Piper turned to video and performance to explore interactions between gender and race.

Public controversy was predictable, and often sought, the result of artists' increasing willingness to scrutinize prevailing values. The renewed government support for the arts indicated by the establishment of the National Endowment for the Arts (NEA) in 1965, combined with growing participation in and publicity for the arts, magnified these controversies. Politicians and religious groups able to tap into public anxieties about social change have led sometimes successful attempts to censor or deny government funds to controversial artists. In 1990 the director of Cincinnati's Contemporary Arts Center, Dennis Barrie, was charged with a felony for putting on display photographs by Robert Mapplethorpe, some of which depicted taboo subjects such as sadomasochistic homoeroticism; he was acquitted.

Such incidents demonstrated some of the many constraints that remained in the midst of the condition of choice. They indicated that one choice not readily available to artists was creation of works highly valued both by a wide popular audience and by particular constituencies such as other artists and different social groups struggling to achieve power and identity. In addition, many aspiring artists, and millions of others who would never have thought of having such an aspiration, did not have access to the financial, educational, social, or informational resources that opened up many options. Even established artists encountered frequent obstacles. Duane Hanson remarked on his inability to sell his sculpture of soldiers in Vietnam: "I almost sold them to a museum in Canada, but they had too much blood on them."

Limiting as these constraints could be, the most

striking difference between the circumstances in which artists operated in 1900 and in the 1990s was in the vastly greater array of possibilities available in the later period. Those American soldiers returning in 1900 from the nearly completed suppression of an insurgency in the Philippines would have found the visual arts almost completely bare of the means required had they wished to raise any questions about their country's policies there. In contrast, hundreds of Vietnam veterans found that the condition of choice achieved in the arts helped them fashion some expressive response to their experiences. C. David Thomas, in addition to arranging exhibitions such as *As Seen by Both Sides* (opened 1990) that brought together the works of Americans and Vietnamese veterans as well as others affected by the war, created drawings and paintings such as *Standing Figure* (1989), which showed a child with lines suggestive of barbed wire sketched on his face. In addition to addressing political issues beyond the reach of conventional American art of earlier eras, the work had compositional features that derived from post-1900 artistic innovations. The same was true of the artworks by most of the other American veterans in Thomas's exhibitions, such as Rick Droz, who lost most of his right leg as a result of his service in Vietnam. In 1988 he incorporated artificial limbs and weaponry into the powerful photographs in his childless "wounded children" series. Americans interested in expressing visually their innermost thoughts, political beliefs, erotic fantasies, or communal allegiances, or in exploring connections between traditional and electronic media, or in drawing on non-Western sources in their work, also had far more options than their counterparts of a century ago.

In the foreseeable future it seems certain that American artists will continue to operate within this condition of choice, unless their society suffers annihilation or massive repression. This condition will continue because it is rooted in the diversity of the experiences of Americans individually and among groups. One source of that diversity has been the constant influx of people from different cultures into the United States. Of the artists discussed in this essay whose native country has not yet been mentioned, are, from Canada, Ernest Lawson, Ralston Crawford, Philip Guston, Agnes Martin, Dorothea Rockburne, June Leaf, and Miriam Schapiro; from Russia, Max Weber, Abraham Walkowitz, the Soyer brothers, Peter Blume, Theodore Roszak, Mark Rothko, and Louise Nevelson; from Lithuania, Ben Shahn and Hyman Bloom; from Luxembourg, Edward Steichen; from Ireland, Augustus Saint-Gaudens;

from Armenia, Arshile Gorky; from Egypt, Ibram Lassaw; from Greece, Lucas Samaras; from Sweden, Claes Oldenburg; from Holland, Willem de Kooning; and from Germany, Louis Maurer and Eva Hesse.

To some the various group-based identities asserted in recent art was a sign of a fragmented society, where pluribus had crowded unum out of the national motto. But the seemingly greater unity of the visual arts at the end of the nineteenth century was like the limited harmony achieved by a chorus in which three-fourths of the voices remained silent. If the visual arts in the United States ever were truly to give equal place to the nation's many constituent cultural traditions, the seeming cacophony of the late twentieth century would have been a necessary prelude.

SEE ALSO Architecture; Patronage of the Arts; Mass Media and Popular Culture; African American Cultural Movements (all in this volume); Cultural Interactions (volume II).

## BIBLIOGRAPHY

A good place to begin studying twentieth-century painting, sculpture, and photography in the context of the overall history of American art is Milton W. Brown, Sam Hunter, John Jacobus, Naomi Rosenblum, and David M. Sokol, *American Art* (1979). Also useful for this purpose, although its coverage ends in mid-century, is Oliver Larkin, *Art and Life in America* (1964); and, for the transition into the new century, H. Wayne Morgan, *New Muses: Art in American Culture, 1865–1920* (1978). For an overview focused on this century, see Barbara Rose, *American Painting: The Twentieth Century* (1986). Sarah Greenough, Joel Snyder, David Travis, and Colin Westerbeck, *On the Art of Fixing a Shadow: One Hundred and Fifty Years of Photography* (1989), includes many Americans in its survey of major figures and developments in the history of photography. Wayne Craven, *Sculpture in America* (1984), covers in considerable detail the topic mentioned in its title.

On the century's early decades, see two books by William I. Homer, *Robert Henri and His Circle* (1969), and *Stieglitz and the American Avant-Garde* (1977). Milton W. Brown, *American Painting from the Armory Show to the Depression* (1955), remains essential for the period 1913–1929. Among the many other studies pertinent to understanding the century's first three decades are Marianne Doezema, *George Bellows and Urban America* (1992); and, on the conservative position, H. Wayne Morgan, *Keepers of Culture: The Art-Thought of Kenyon Cox, Royal Cortissoz, and Frank Jewett Mather, Jr.* (1989). Essays by Martin Green, Milton W. Brown, Edward Abrahams, and Rebecca Zurier in Adele Heller and Lois Rudnick, eds., *1915, The Cultural Moment: The New Politics, the New Woman, the New Psychology, the New Art and the New Theater in America* (1991), provide convenient summaries of their more extended works on changes taking place in the visual arts before and during World War I. On the postwar decades, see Karen Lucic, *Charles Sheeler and the Culture of the Machine* (1991); and Richard Wilson, Dianne Pilgrim, and Dickran Tashjian, *The Machine Age in America, 1918–1941* (1986).

Many scholars with an interest in interactions between artists and society have been attracted to the 1930s. Works that have resulted include Wanda Corn, *Grant Wood: The Regionalist Vision* (1983); M. Sue Kendall, *Rethinking Regionalism: John Steuart Curry and the Kansas Mural Controversy* (1986); Karal Ann Marling, *Wall-to-Wall America: A Cultural History of Post-Office Murals in the Great Depression* (1982); Barbara Melosh, *Engendering Culture: Manhood and Womanhood in New Deal Public Art and Theater* (1991); and David Peeler, *Hope Among Us Yet: Social Criticism and Social Solace in Depression America* (1987). The last book helps define key issues raised by the decade's rich photographic legacy, as do William Stott, *Documentary Expression and Thirties America* (1973); James Curtis, *Mind's Eye, Mind's Truth: FSA Photography Reconsidered* (1989); essays by Lawrence W. Levine and Alan Trachtenberg in Carl Fleischhauer and Beverly W. Brannan, eds. *Documenting American, 1935–1943* (1988); and those by Pete Daniel, Merry A. Foresta, Maren Stange, and Sally Stein in *Official Images: New Deal Photography* (1987).

Cécile Whiting, *Antifascism in American Art* (1989), describes some of the complexities of politically explicit art in the 1930s and early 1940s. Erika Doss, *Benton, Pollock, and the Politics of Modernism: From Regionalism to Abstract Expressionism* (1991), examines connections between major movements of the periods before and after World War II. Also extending the story into the postwar period is Frances K. Pohl, *Ben Shahn: New Deal Artist in a Cold War Climate, 1947–1954* (1989). Influential and sharply differing interpretations of Abstract Expressionism are given by Irving Sandler, *The Triumph of American Painting* (1970); and by authors represented in Serge Guilbaut, ed., *Reconstructing Modernism: Art in New York, Paris, and Montreal, 1945–1964* (1990). Also attentive to historical context in its analysis of art of the 1950s and 1960s is Sidra Stich, *Made in U.S.A.: An Americanization in Modern Art, the '50s and '60s* (1987).

Among the wealth of studies covering developments in the last few decades those especially pertinent include Diana Crane, *The Transformation of the Avant-Garde: The New York Art World, 1940–1985* (1987); Jonathan Green, *American Photography: A Critical History 1945 to the Present* (1984); Lucy Lippard, *Mixed Blessings: New Art in a Multicultural America* (1990); Peter Plagens, *Sunshine Muse: Contemporary Art on the West Coast* (1974); and, for a selection of artists' writings and statements, Ellen H. Johnson, ed., *American Artists on Art from 1940 to 1980* (1982).

Useful thematic studies that cover several time periods include Charles C. Alexander, *Here the Country Lies: Nationalism and the Arts in Twentieth-Century America* (1980); Ela H. Fine, *The Afro-American Artist: A Search for Identity* (1973); Susan Sontag, *On Photography* (1977); Alan Trachtenberg, *Reading American Photographs: Images as History, Mathew Brady to Walker Evans* (1989); and, to cite one of the historically richest of the many recent biographies of twentieth-century American artists, Richard J. Powell, *Homecoming: The Art and Life of William H. Johnson* (1991).

# PATRONAGE OF THE ARTS

## Kathleen D. McCarthy

The noted philanthropist John D. Rockefeller III proclaimed in 1963 that "the arts are not for the privileged few, but for the many. Their place is not on the periphery of daily life, but at its center." It was a prescient statement. At the outset of the twentieth century, cultural patronage was primarily the province of wealthy male elites, who cast their definitions of fine art in their own image, celebrating a largely European heritage. Although the arts were ostensibly open to the public as a whole, the audiences that passed through the urban museums, symphony halls, and opera houses that they created also tended to be white, middle or upper class, and of European descent.

By 1963, the country was poised on the brink of a cultural revolution. Within two years, the federal government would finally assume ongoing responsibility for cultural development with the creation of the National Endowment for the Arts; the first state arts council had been created by Rockefeller's brother, Nelson, two years earlier; and corporate and foundation funding was about to rise dramatically. As the funding base became more generous and more complex, definitions of the parameters of "fine art" expanded as well. By 1990, the cultural canon expanded to encompass works by an array of living American artists, from Hispanic choreographers to black playwrights and women painters, from leaders in the international avant-garde to community-based programs cast in the vernacular of the barrio and the street. Democratization, rather than art for the few, had become the prevailing theme.

The transition from localism to federal support, from elitism to cultural pluralism, has often been a rocky progression, surrounded by lively public debates. At least three periods can be traced in the history of twentieth-century American cultural patronage: the era from 1900 to 1925, when wealthy male patrons dominated the cultural scene; the years from 1925 to 1965, which witnessed the beginnings of national policy making by foundations and government; and the decades since 1965, which have been marked by increasing support from a variety of funders, increasing democratization, and increasingly vociferous debates about the scope, nature, and appropriateness of public funding.

## THE AGE OF ELITISM, 1900–1925

Turn-of-the-century high culture was steeped in an aura of elitism and exclusivity. Concentrated primarily in a few large cities on the eastern seaboard and the Midwest, America's major art museums and symphonies were still relatively new and novel institutions. Most owed their origins to the cultural reorganization that occurred in the wake of the Civil War, as commercial orchestras and galleries were superseded by the nonprofit museums and symphonies developed by wealthy male elites.

While America's first orchestras were profitmaking ventures that divided their receipts among players, conductors, and impresarios as they moved from town to town in search of audiences, nonprofit orchestras were permanently rooted in a single city. Musicians in these institutions had contracts and regular salaries, rather than a share of the gate receipts. And because most habitually ran deficits, the wealthy sponsors who created them made up the shortfalls through personal contributions and public subscriptions. In effect, the transition to nonprofit status changed these ventures from businesses to privately sponsored institutions for public edification.

In the process, their programs changed as well. Commercial cultural ventures often featured something for everyone, occasionally even mixing dramatic performances with music, jugglers, and animal acts. When these programs were removed from their dependence on market mechanisms and placed under the sponsorship of private patrons, their content became considerably more sedate. Moreover, by concentrating on the works of European composers of the past, symphony orchestras and their sponsors developed a new definition of fine art. And through the introduction of dress codes and higher admission prices, they effectively limited the consumption of fine art to those who could comply with these requirements.

Two models for development of cultural institutions emerged from the last quarter of the nineteenth century: plutocratic ventures sponsored by a single patron, and corporate initiatives backed by an array of donors. Perhaps the best example of plutocratic largesse was the reorganization of the Boston Symphony Orchestra by Henry Lee Higginson in 1881. Generally considered the first permanent orchestra in the United States, it was entirely Higginson's creation. He hired the musicians and the conductor, provided the necessary funds to cover the operating deficits out of his own pocket, and shaped the selection of the programs.

Although the corporate model was far more common, a number of important cultural institutions were developed around the turn of the century by individual patrons, including the Los Angeles Philharmonic Orchestra, founded by William Andrews Clark, Jr., the Isabella Stewart Gardner Museum in Boston, and the Morgan Library and the Frick Museum in New York.

Efforts such as these and their collective, corporate counterparts represented a uniquely American solution to the need for cultural support. Unlike Europe, America did not have hereditary monarchies to support the creation and display of paintings, music, and statuary. Nor did it have an aristocracy steeped in centuries of dynastic acquisition and traditions of cultural noblesse oblige. Religious institutions also played a relatively minor role in American cultural development, due to lingering Protestant antipathies to the ornate trappings of European Catholicism. Nor was there much in the way of state or federal support for the arts, aside from random commissions for paintings and public statuary for public buildings. In a country devoid of these traditional sources of patronage, cultural development logically fell to local elites.

Before the Civil War, these activities were limited by the fragile nature of American commerce and industry. But wartime profits laid the groundwork for a substantial number of individual fortunes, which were subsequently amplified with the completion of the transcontinental rail system and the opening of national and international markets. By the beginning of the twentieth century, northern industrial cities such as Chicago, Boston, and New York counted a growing number of millionaires among

their residents, who provided the necessary capital for the introduction of cultural initiatives on a new scale.

Most of these ventures were begun collectively, rather than as the gesture of a single individual. The Metropolitan Museum of Art in New York grew out of a group initiative sparked by the Union League Club in 1869; the Museum of Fine Arts in Boston emerged at the same time, under the sponsorship of a group of culturally active male elites; while the Pennsylvania Museum was created in 1876, with a core collection gathered from the exhibits at the Philadelphia Centennial Exposition. The Art Institute of Chicago was another of the great Gilded Age museums. Founded in 1879, it was created by a small group of postwar millionaires as part of a collective campaign to centralize their control over the city's charities and emerging cultural ventures, as well as its business affairs.

Most began with loaned collections and limited funds, occasionally backed by municipal assistance. American philanthropy, including cultural philanthropy, is steeped in a tradition of public-private partnerships that political scientists have termed third-party government. According to this theory, while European welfare states expanded through the growth of government bureaucracies, public programs in the United States often grew through public subsidies to nonprofit organizations, which received private donations as well. Thus, the lines between public and private charitable, educational, and social welfare services have historically been blurred, trends which became increasingly pronounced as the twentieth century progressed.

Although this type of public-private partnership became far more common at the state and federal level beginning in the 1930s, in some municipalities it dated from the nineteenth century. The pattern varied considerably from town to town: New York had a particularly strong tradition of public support for charities, but the tradition was less strong in Boston. Public subsidies of cash and land were often allocated for cultural institutions as well. Thus, the Metropolitan Museum was launched with $500,000 in land and construction costs from the city of New York, and Chicago's Art Institute secured land from the city and $200,000 for building costs from the promoters of the World's Columbian Exposition, matched by private donations. Boston and Cincinnati initiated their museums without the aid of private support; the Pennsylvania Museum received generous public funding from the outset. However uneven, this tradition of public-private support further distinguished the American system of cultural patronage from that of its European counterparts.

The level of private support for cultural ventures grew substantially after the turn of the century. Several factors contributed to the rising fortunes of institutions such as the Metropolitan Museum. By 1900, many of America's first generation of millionaires had begun to pass from the scene, bequeathing portions of their estates to the nonprofit institutions that they had helped to create and manage. Charitable deduction allowances for gifts to nonprofit institutions were written into law four years after the first permanent income tax legislation was introduced in 1913, providing additional incentives for individual largesse. By the 1920s, Jazz Age prosperity created a new generation of nouveaux riches, who also contributed some of their windfall to local cultural institutions.

The men who sat on the boards of these institutions generally represented the richest, most prominent families in their locales. For example, the legendary financier J. Pierpont Morgan served as president of the Metropolitan Museum of Art. The son of wealth, Morgan parlayed his inheritance into one of the country's great fortunes. He began to collect late in life, in his fifties, at which point he embarked on a virtual orgy of acquisition. Shakespeare's first folios, Leonardo da Vinci's notebooks, masterpieces of European painting and statuary, medieval vestments, and the trinkets of princes and kings all found their way into Morgan's holdings. In 1904 he assumed the presidency of the Metropolitan Museum, where he ruled with a firmly authoritarian hand. Through their acquisitions and their roles in institutional development, Morgan and his peers defined the parameters of fin-de-siècle fine art.

Morgan had an almost infallible eye for quality and a passion for collecting that was fed by his desire to make New York a cultural capital on a par with the major cities of the Old World. When he died in 1913, his collection was valued at $50 million (approximately half of his net worth), an enormous sum for that time. Although much of it was subsequently sold by Morgan's son to cover the inheritance taxes and other bequests, 40 percent of his holdings eventually made their way to the Metropolitan Museum. Collecting and cultural patronage at this level was a privilege that only the wealthiest could afford, a distinction that undoubtedly attracted men like J. P. Morgan to this field.

Morgan was also one of a small group of backers who contributed to the reorganization of the New York Philharmonic into a private, nonprofit institution under businessmen's control in 1909. By this time, several other major orchestras were operating in northern cities, including the Chicago Symphony Orchestra (1891) and the Philadelphia Orchestra (1900). There were several important opera companies as well, such as the Metropolitan in New York and the Chicago Opera Company. A few German Jewish bankers, such as Otto Kahn and Jacob Schiff, played a prominent role in the development of the Metropolitan Opera, backing it with million-dollar gifts, while Harold and Edith Rockefeller McCormick were the leading financial backers in Chicago, underwriting entire seasons with their gifts.

Nonprofit theaters and ballet companies took root more slowly and initially faced greater difficulties in raising funds. Many philanthropists were skeptical about the appropriateness of nonprofit theater, in part because the theater had traditionally seemed the most commercially viable of the performing arts. Even Andrew Carnegie, a strong advocate for cultural philanthropy, complained in 1902 that "the theater is not the proper field for private gifts." Nonetheless, a few fledgling repertory theaters did begin to appear in New York at the beginning of the century, including the short-lived New Theater, and a few more enduring ventures such as the Provincetown Players (begun by a group of actors and playwrights in Cape Cod in 1915) and the Civic Repertory Theater founded by Eva La Gallienne in the 1920s.

Several of the country's first major ballet companies took root during the depression years of the 1930s, struggling along with gifts from a few individual supporters until the advent of large-scale foundation and government funding began to place them on a firmer financial basis in the postwar years. The famed Russian choreographer George Balanchine came to the United States in 1933 with the aid of two young patrons, Lincoln Kirstein and Edward Warburg, forming the first of several ballet companies with their backing. The American Ballet Theater began six years later, aided by the family fortune of one of its leading ballerinas, Lucia Chase.

Until the 1920s, the development of such major cultural institutions as the Metropolitan Museum, the Metropolitan Opera and the Chicago Symphony Orchestra was carried out almost exclusively by men. Foundations, research universities, museums, orchestras, think tanks—all tended to be modeled on the modern corporation. Well-endowed, bureaucratically structured, and professionally staffed, these organizations played a pivotal role in setting professional standards in a variety of fields, recruiting, socializing, and certifying cadres of managerial elites, and providing local and national centers of policy making and authority.

There was a direct correlation between the degree of professionalization and the size of the organization's endowment. In museums, for example, professionalization developed in two stages. Many of the men who founded the nation's first museums were connoisseurs who wrote the catalogs, selected the art, and even occasionally conducted tours themselves. After the turn of the century, the larger museums were able to afford growing staffs of professional curators and administrators. In the process, responsibility for defining the scope and nature of fine art passed to technically trained decision makers who claimed their authority on the basis of "scientific" techniques and ostensibly "disinterested" expertise. As historian Neil Harris points out in *Cultural Excursions* (1990), "Museums were popularly expected to project cultural authority and therefore to represent the highest, most objective scholarship available."

Women played a far more limited role both as donors and managers within these institutions, in part because they often controlled more limited resources. Even when they did inherit substantial fortunes, these bequests were often hemmed in by restrictive trusts and the executors' whims that checked their access to liquid resources. Only one woman (Catherine Lorillard Wolfe) appeared on the list of the 105 charter subscribers of the Metropolitan Museum in 1870. Between 1900 and 1930, four women donated gifts of money or collections valued at $1 million or more, but none was invited to serve on the museum's board. Indeed, the first women to serve in that capacity were not appointed until the 1950s.

Women adopted a slightly more entrepreneurial role in orchestra development than in museums, but even here, management of the most prestigious organizations almost invariably passed to boards of prominent male trustees. There were stylistic differences as well. While men generally adopted the corporate form for their orchestras and museums, pooling local funds to ensure that their institutions were adequately endowed, the few female patrons who did create important arts organizations before the advent of the New Deal tended to do so on a smaller scale, with far less cash and more specialized goals.

Moreover, with the exception of Isabella Stewart Gardner, who built an elaborate museum to showcase her collection of Old Masters, female patrons made their greatest impact by sponsoring artistic forms that were inadequately recognized by the more established museums: nonacademic American painting, folk art, the avant-garde. The Whitney Museum, the Museum of Modern Art, the Abby Aldrich Rockefeller Folk Art Center, and the Shelburne Museum (of folk art) were all begun by women patrons.

The American expatriate writer Gertrude Stein established a strong female presence at the forefront of the avant-garde shortly after the turn of the century with her private gallery, her salons, and her early support of painters such as Pablo Picasso. A few women also played an important role in the Armory Show (1913), which introduced Americans to European modernism, including Gertrude Vanderbilt Whitney, who provided funding, and Mabel Dodge Luhan, who helped secure paintings. Sixteen years later, Abby Aldrich Rockefeller, Lizzie Bliss, and Mary Quinn Sullivan founded the Museum of Modern Art (MOMA) in New York, which quickly became the leading repository in this field. Afterward, other women took up the lead, including Peggy Guggenheim, whose gallery, Art of this Century, played a key role in promoting the careers of such leading American abstractionists as Robert Motherwell and Jackson Pollock.

Similarly, Elizabeth Sprague Coolidge became one of the country's most important patrons of contemporary chamber music with the creation of her foundation at the Library of Congress in 1925. An accomplished pianist and composer in her own right, Coolidge dedicated her fortune to promoting modernist fare. Some of the composers whose original works were commissioned by the Coolidge Foundation were Aaron Copland, Béla Bartók, Sergei Prokofiev, and Igor Stravinsky. Organizations such as the Coolidge Foundation and MOMA made their greatest contribution by testing the boundaries of fine art as defined by the nation's symphonies and museums, promoting the art of the new, the untested, the untried.

## THE BEGINNINGS OF NATIONAL POLICY MAKING, 1925–1965

America's first cultural institutions were rooted in local imperatives: boosterism, civic pride, and personal gestures of civic largesse. Beginning in the mid-1920s, nationally oriented initiatives began to appear as well. Most were fostered by private grant-making foundations, heralding the arrival of a new actor on the funding scene. However, this period also witnessed the creation of the first federal public cultural programs. Short-lived and often shrouded in controversy, these efforts nonetheless constituted a long-awaited first step toward national public patronage for the arts.

Like museums and symphonies, foundations were part of the emerging network of policy-making institutions fashioned by wealthy male philanthropists at the turn of the century. As historians Barry Karl and Stanley Katz point out, these institutions implemented social reforms on a national scale in an era of limited government and provided resources for the training and certification of managerial elites. Initially, the arts received short shrift in foundation agendas. Created to strike at the root causes of social ills, most turned their attention instead to medicine, scientific research, and the social sciences, fields that promised more immediate solutions to contemporary problems.

The first major foundation to initiate an arts program was the Carnegie Corporation, after Frederick Keppel assumed the presidency in 1923. The son of a prominent print dealer, Keppel was well acquainted with the world of art. Keppel tapped a group of such prominent critics and educators as Royal Cortissoz of the *New York Tribune*, art critic Frank Mather of the *Nation* (and director of Princeton University's art museum), and Paul Sachs, originator of the nation's first course in curatorial training at Harvard's Fogg Museum, for help in designing Carnegie's cultural initiative. Launched the following year, the program provided fellowships for curatorial, art, and music education, with courses at Harvard and Princeton netting the lion's share. Art-teaching sets were also distributed nationally, and funds provided for industrial art courses at Yale. Keppel's goal was twofold: to foster cultural outreach and art appreciation among the educated public and to speed the pace of professionalization. By 1930, Carnegie's arts budget topped the $400,000 mark, making it one of a trio of large cultural grantmakers, along with the Juilliard Musical Foundation and the Rockefeller-sponsored General Education Board. By the time Keppel's program was phased out thirteen years later, over $13.5 million had been invested in endowments for music departments in twenty colleges and universities, programs with the American Association of Museums and the American Federation of the Arts, and art and music appreciation campaigns.

The Rockefeller Foundation also began to make grants for cultural endeavors during these years, including a $500,000 gift to Harvard's Fogg Museum for curatorial training and art history courses under the guidance of Paul Sachs. During the 1930s, the foundation experimented with grants to regional theaters, part of a quest to extend access to good quality theatrical performances beyond major urban centers like New York and to establish viable theater programs on university campuses.

The drive to decentralize America's cultural resources reached unprecedented heights with the advent of the federal relief programs of the 1930s. Often considered a frill in the best of times, arts organizations experienced severe financial problems during the Great Depression, as did artists and performers. In 1933, Congress passed the first of several appropriations for relief work, part of which was earmarked to create jobs to help tide unemployed artists over the winter.

The resulting Public Works of Art Project (PWAP) was part of the Civil Works Administration (CWA) funded under the Federal Emergency Relief Administration. The CWA programs marked a major turning point in the history of American cultural patronage. Artists had been lobbying for increased governmental support since the early nineteenth century, particularly sculptors and painters who sought government commissions. The PWAP was the realization of an old dream, but with an ironic twist. Rather than wading into the quicksand of official connoisseurship, PWAP cast its support in charitable terms, emphasizing relief over aesthetic considerations.

Like the Carnegie program, it was national in scope, but the net was cast far more widely, with remarkable results. Building on older strains of third-party government, CWA administrator Harry Hopkins quickly conscripted a range of museum directors to make the selections. Juliana Force, the curator of the newly created Whitney Museum, was a natural choice to chair the regional committee in New York, since the Whitney specialized in American art.

The emphasis on personal poverty led to some embarrassing revelations. Respected painters such as John Sloan leapt at a chance to earn a steady weekly salary of $38.25 for their work. As Sloan reluctantly admitted, he had never supported himself on the basis of his painting alone, but relied instead on teaching and commercial work to sustain his career. The sculptor Alexander Calder was forced to confess that he had earned a scant $2,000 since 1931, and nearly exhausted his savings since the onset of the Depression, thus revealing the precarious financial position of some of the country's more distinguished artists. During its brief four-month run, almost four thousand artists, writers, and performers were given PWAP jobs, producing over fifteen thousand works of art for a total cost of $1.3 million.

Despite its brief existence, the PWAP was a harbinger of even more ambitious New Deal arts programs. The Resettlement Administration (RA) provided opportunities for photographers, who were hired to record the results of its work. Working under the Historical Section of the RA, and later the Farm Security Administration, photojournalists such as Dorothea Lange and Walker Evans preserved haunting images of the human costs of economic duress (for a photograph by Lange, see the article "The Visual Arts," in this volume; for a photograph by Evans, see the article "The South," in volume I). Painters were hired to create murals in post offices across the country under the Treasury Department's Section on Painting and Sculpture, which ran from 1934 to 1943. Unlike earlier cultural endeavors, the Treasury program was an exercise in grassroots democracy. Artists who were awarded commissions through regional competitions were required to design their projects in tandem with local citizens, who helped to select the subjects.

The most ambitious, and ultimately the most controversial project was Federal Project Number One: the national arts, music, writers, theater, and historical-records projects administered under the auspices of the Works Progress Administration (WPA) through a $5 million appropriation passed in 1935. The music program was one of the agency's most popular branches. An earlier music project had operated under the short-lived CWA initiative during the winter of 1933. Working through state and local governments under federal oversight, CWA orchestras provided free symphonic and chamber concerts, folk performances, and music festivals for audiences across the country.

Like painters and sculptors, many musicians lived a precarious existence during the Depression. Between 1929 and 1934, an estimated 70 percent of all American musicians were unemployed. Because unemployment rates among musicians were so high, and because most would have been self-employed (and therefore unable to document that they had been fired or laid off), participants in the music program had little trouble in meeting the WPA's qualification requirements. Under the direction of Cleveland Orchestra member Nikolai Sokoloff, the program produced impressive returns. Sixteen thousand musicians were employed at the program's peak, with five thousand performances attended by an estimated 3 million people per month. Twenty-eight symphony orchestras were formed, and over 1 million music classes provided for approximately 14 million students. Dance bands, folk music, opera units— all fell within the agency's purview, funded and disseminated to audiences on a national scale.

The Federal Arts Project, under the direction of the folk art specialist Holger Cahill, hired artists whose talents spanned the stylistic spectrum, from regionalist Stuart Davis to emerging abstractionists such as Willem de Kooning and Jackson Pollock. Assignments ranged from work in art-education centers to more individually creative fare. Approximately 100,000 easel paintings were finished under WPA grants, as well as 17,000 pieces of sculpture, 2,500 murals, and 9,500 prints. For a relatively meager investment of $5 million, WPA artists produced works that would be valued conservatively at $450 million three decades later.

The Theater and Writers Projects also produced substantial bodies of work. Under the direction of Hallie Flanagan, the Theater Project helped unemployed actors, stagehands, and directors. Over twelve thousand theater people participated, producing plays in six languages across thirty states for an audience of 30 million Americans. The Writers Project, headed by Henry Alsberg, also produced impressive dividends, resulting in over three hundred publications that included a respected series of state and city guides.

However, the significance of these programs far exceeded numerical gains. For less than the price of a single bequest, such as Frank Munsey's $10 million gift to the Metropolitan Museum in 1925, Federal One and the programs that preceded it brought art to Americans on a new scale. And they did so because public support was driven by different considerations than was private largesse. Men like J. Pierpont Morgan built their cultural ventures from a mixture of patriotic pride, princely personal riches, and a desire for personal gratification. The institutions they created greatly enriched America's store of artistic treasures, but they often did so in fairly narrow terms. Morgan wanted to collect, he wanted to define the contours of American taste and definitions of fine art, but he felt far less compelled to make these resources universally available. Because the WPA was backed by public monies, policymakers in Federal One adopted more democratic goals, bringing symphonies, original paintings, and live theater performances to some areas of the country for the first time. In the process, they broke the urban monopoly on high culture, and demonstrated the relevance of visual art, classical music, literature, and theater to the lives of the mass of Americans who formed the audiences for these works.

There were important gains for the artists as well. For example, the cultural canon developed by museums generally excluded the works of women artists.

Although unemployment was an important criterion in the WPA programs, race and gender were not. As a result, estimates place the percentage of women artists in the Arts Project at 25 to 41 percent of those employed, depending on the locale. Some of the most celebrated artists in postwar America, women like Louise Nevelson and Lee Krasner, were alumnae of Federal One.

African Americans benefited as well. Discrimination against blacks applying for WPA jobs was prohibited by an executive order issued by President Franklin D. Roosevelt. By the late 1930s, estimates held that 15 to 20 percent of the agency's employees were black, at a time when African Americans accounted for only 10 percent of the country's population. In the process, new types of artists and performers found audiences for their work, adding a more democratic strain to earlier interpretations of American culture.

Despite these gains, the notion of federal cultural patronage proved unpalatable to some policymakers, particularly in forms like the Writers and Theater Projects. By 1938, both were under congressional fire, led by House Un-American Activities Committee chairman Martin Dies. Dies launched a formal investigation into the agencies' activities, unearthing the names of several alleged Communists on their employment rolls. Branded as subversive, the Theater Project was disbanded in 1939, and the remaining programs passed to state control. Federal One formally terminated its operations in 1943.

Although Federal One and the Treasury arts program are the most familiar examples of Depression-era government patronage, the influence of the WPA extended to local cultural institutions as well, adding a new slant to the practice of third-party government. Despite often substantial endowments, many of the older urban cultural organizations saw their operations hobbled as the Depression deepened. They responded in a variety of ways. The Metropolitan Opera created an Opera Guild in 1934 to broaden its base of support through outreach activities. Designed to attract small donations, the guild presented lectures at such local institutions as New York University and branches of the public library, initiated low-cost concerts for schoolchildren, and arranged fundraising campaigns through local clubs and PTAs. By the decade's end, over $300,000 in additional income had been raised through these and other outreach activities.

Chicago's Art Institute was able to cover its deficits with its share of the residuary profits from the Century of Progress World's Fair. Other institutions that were more heavily dependent on public subsidies felt the pinch more strongly. Memberships at the Metropolitan Museum began to plummet in 1931, along with admission revenues and municipal allocations. Much of the problem was mitigated through creative bookkeeping, as endowment income was shifted from acquisitions to administrative costs. By 1933, the museum's investment income was diminishing as well, resulting in salary cuts. By 1936, however, staff costs were being offset by workers seconded from the WPA. Clerical staff, carpenters, painters, masons, lecturers, even guards were provided with support from the public till. The directors of the Cincinnati Museum also took advantage of the government's generosity, conscripting WPA workers to help in cleaning, restoring, and cataloguing the museum's holdings.

Statistics compiled by the Pennsylvania Museum (later renamed the Philadelphia Museum) provide some insights into the differing relationships that the major museums forged with the WPA. The Boston Museum of Fine Arts, which remained almost completely aloof from federally sponsored benefits, was also in the most stable position financially; despite constant laments about the need for building repairs, it was still able to derive 90 percent of its income from endowment funds, even at the height of the Depression in 1935. The Metropolitan, which culled 68 percent of its income from endowment funds, proved more amenable to federal assistance. And the Pennsylvania Museum, which gleaned a scant 22 percent of its annual operating revenues from endowment investments, amassed a brilliant record of securing federal grants and aid over the course of the Depression. Without this assistance, it would have been in deep financial trouble.

To a far greater extent than the other major museums, Philadelphia's repository was dependent on public monies. It also suffered some of the most stringent cuts in municipal support as the Depression deepened. Between 1931 and 1934, its local appropriations declined by 60 percent, as compared to a 29 percent reduction in New York and 14 percent at the Brooklyn Museum. Moreover, while the Metropolitan Museum had a hefty $31.5 million endowment in its coffers, Philadelphia had only $2.5 million in investment funds. Its sole advantage over its wealthier counterparts was that the bulk of its collections were "actually the property of the City, the Museum being merely in a position of custodianship," an unusual arrangement among the larger American art museums. Although shortfalls in its annual operating income necessitated layoffs and reduced exhibition hours, the Pennsylvania Museum was able to launch a major building campaign at the height of the Depression. As soon as the CWA was established, museum representatives submitted requests for assistance in everything from maintenance work to clerical help, all of which were granted. The advent of the WPA offered spectacular windfalls, providing money and manpower for architectural and engineering services, equipment, and construction costs. Between 1935 and 1942, over $2.5 million worth of improvements had been made, increasing the museum's gallery space fourfold. An "immense amount" of cataloging was also completed with the aid of WPA workers, and over thirty new galleries were opened.

Despite its brief duration, America's first brush with federal support proved an exhilarating experience. The fine arts, once the province of wealthy urban elites, arrived in the hinterland. Women and African American artists who seldom won the backing of the more established urban bastions of culture had been given more than an equal chance to test their talents before new audiences. Although the response varied from town to town, some cultural organizations began to test new types of public-private partnerships, using federal windfalls in creative ways. For a relatively modest investment, many of these projects produced enduring yields.

However, the largest cultural-funding program before the 1960s was based not in Washington, but New York. Begun as a local grant-making organization in Detroit in 1936, the Ford Foundation was reorganized as the nation's largest private grant maker in 1950. Backed by an endowment of just over $417 million, it boasted greater assets than those of the Rockefeller Foundation and Carnegie Corporation together; more than the combined endowments of the three largest American universities (Harvard, Yale, and Texas); and significantly more than the entire budget of the United Nations, including all its specialized agencies. By comparison, the $5 million allocation for Federal One was virtually a pittance. Even J. Pierpont Morgan's fabled outlays paled in comparison to the assets controlled by Ford.

Given the unprecedented size of these resources, the foundation was well positioned to make a considerable impact in whichever fields it chose. Although the arts were not initially flagged as an area of potential activity, by 1955 explorations were underway to test the climate for a national arts program. Headed by a former newspaperman, W. McNeil Lowry, the program was officially launched in 1957.

Lowry provided several reasons for Ford's entrance into this previously neglected field. As he explained, private funding was being diverted to other causes, from social work to medical research. Very few individuals and even fewer foundations focused solely on arts support. While governmental expansion was "crowding out" foundation donors in other fields, neither government nor industry had expressed a sustained interest in the arts. Despite the New Deal programs, the majority of the country's cultural institutions lay clustered in cities along the two coasts. Artists led financially precarious lives, as did the institutions that featured their works. Added to this were spiraling operating costs that threatened the continued operations of all but the most generously endowed organizations.

Backed by an elaborate rationale, Lowry had laid the groundwork for his program in 1955 with a two-year study of the contemporary arts scene that ultimately led him through over five hundred interviews in sixty-four communities in every region of the country. Two national conferences of arts leaders also were convened at the foundation's headquarters in New York, and other prominent arts representatives hired as consultants. Artistic directors, patrons, performers—all were polled for their ideas about current conditions and plausible programs and grantees.

The differences between this foray into national cultural policy making and earlier attempts by the Carnegie Corporation and the WPA are instructive. The country's earliest museums and symphonies were born of the ideas of small coteries of rich, occasionally well-traveled male businessmen, doctors, and lawyers who sought to realize their vision of high culture in American cities and towns. The Carnegie Corporation expanded this vision to national scale, but did little to alter its basic content. Admittedly, by the 1920s, professionals, rather than patrons, had assumed primary responsibility for defining and conserving the arts, trends Keppel had sought to hasten through his professionalization grants. But all were essentially elitist programs defined and devised by relatively small groups of administrators and trustees.

The New Deal programs considerably broadened the levels of participation, but they did so in a scatter-shot fashion and were hindered by time constraints and the necessity of quickly doling out relief checks. Within this milieu, charitable considerations often took precedence over more aesthetic aims. The Ford program was more carefully crafted, without completely abandoning the New Dealers' democratic intent. And, because of the resources at his command, Lowry was able to use the Ford Foundation as a sounding-board for emerging trends as defined not only by patrons, but by the artists themselves. As a result, Ford became the first central agency to study arts issues across the board as a necessary prelude to the creation of a national program.

Initially, the emphasis was on fostering individual creativity, taking up where the New Deal left off. In 1958, $800,000 worth of grants-in-aid were distributed among a motley array of writers, poets, painters, sculptors, playwrights, directors of arts organizations, and concert artists. The following year, $120,000 was awarded to enable ten performers to commission new works from the composer of their choice, which were then performed with three mid-sized symphony orchestras in different cities. Rather than selecting the candidates himself, Lowry solicited nominations from arts leaders across the country, entrusting the final selections to expert panels.

Institutions were added to the program in the 1960s. By 1962, Ford had become the largest arts donor in the United States and was contemplating a considerable expansion of its programs after the foundation's assets approached the $4 billion mark. Civic operas, repertory theaters, symphonies, and ballet companies—all increasingly fell within Ford's domain. The size of the grants grew as well, including $6 million to strengthen resident operas in 1962 and almost $8 million for seven ballet companies the following year. Seasons were lengthened, curators trained, and repertory theaters begun with Ford largesse. Audience-building was another important goal, beginning with a 1957 grant to New York impresario Joseph Papp to tide his New York Shakespeare Theater over a cash-flow crisis when promised municipal funds suddenly failed to materialize.

In 1963, the item at the top of Ford's agenda was dance, spurring a flurry of multimillion-dollar gifts to ballet companies in Philadelphia, Washington, San Francisco, Boston, and New York. Two of the largest recipients were the schools of the American Ballet Theater (ABT) and Balanchine's New York City Ballet (NYCB). To bolster his case for ballet support, Lowry noted the "surprising" interest in dance, especially ballet, that had developed since World War II. Yet only one professional company (NYCB) had what he termed "an important season." And even there, funds were desperately needed for new productions, new props, and day-to-day expenses. Many civic ballets in other cities managed to present only one production per year. Scholarships were provided for students and choreographers in these areas to study with Balanchine or ABT in New York as a means of developing a wider base of local talent.

The subsequent brouhaha served to underscore the lingering differences between public and private support. Ford was vociferously criticized in some quarters for favoring Balanchine's school at NYCB. A former member of Diaghilev's Ballet Russe, Balanchine was a Russian-trained master choreographer who was comfortable in both the idioms of Russian classicism and modern dance. Quality notwithstanding, complaints were made that Ford should have distributed its funds more widely, rather than concentrating so much money on New York.

In response, the foundation's president, Henry Heald, issued a formal statement in which he emphasized that "foundations are and ought to be free from the pressures often applied to government . . . of distributing their resources across the board by some formula." Heald's disclaimer was well taken; the strength of American patterns of cultural patronage lay in their diversity. Although they receive a form of public subsidy through tax deductions, individuals and private foundations are subject to limited public scrutiny and few constraints in rendering their gifts. Unlike government, foundations have the option of being elitist, populistic, or both, a fact vividly underscored by Lowry's grants and Heald's response. And, unlike government or corporations, they have no consumers, and no constituents to whom they are directly accountable. Until passage of the 1969 Tax Act, which required foundations to annually disburse at least 5 percent of their endowment earnings and prohibited abuses such as financial kickbacks for donors and trustees, foundations were subject to few federal controls. Then, as now, their primary accountability has been to their trustees, a fact that has given these institutions an extraordinary amount of leeway in determining the scope of their programs and gifts.

Ford took advantage of this freedom in 1966, when it donated $80.2 million to a group of sixty-one symphony orchestras in thirty-three states, the District of Columbia, and Puerto Rico. As Lowry explained, although symphonies were "the most universally established of cultural institutions," many still experienced endemic financial ills. Because salaries were habitually low, musicians often had to hold down two or more jobs to subsidize their performance careers. Unions were working to remedy this but had made little headway in institutions regularly hobbled by annual operating deficits. Ford's grants were designed to address these problems by building endowments, thus enabling orchestras to lengthen their seasons and improve the financial situation of their performers.

It was an unprecedented gesture. As Lowry un-blushingly pointed out: "The proposed program for orchestras far exceeds in size and scope anything which has ever been done for the arts, and only two agencies in the United States—the federal government and the Ford Foundation—could contemplate it." It was also a highly complex arrangement, with $25 million given outright to be used over the next decade, while the remainder was to be held in the form of Ford Motor stock in a "Symphony Orchestra Trust" until the mid-1970s. Unitary shares were to be assigned to most of the orchestras, which would receive a percentage of the annual income. When the stock was finally sold, each of the participants would receive an equal share for their endowments. The stock could be sold gradually, thereby solving the foundation's dilemma of how to divest itself of its holdings in the motor company without automatically depressing the market. The endowment grants also had matching requirements to generate local support and required recipients to do some outreach work, such as taking their concerts to parks and schools.

While Lowry was raising the level of foundation support to new heights, individuals such as John D. Rockefeller III had begun to experiment with public-private partnerships on a new scale. Precedents for these sorts of collaborative ventures dated from 1919, when the Detroit businessman Charles Lang Freer donated his outstanding collection of Asian art to the Smithsonian Institution in Washington, coupled with another $1 million for its upkeep. The financier Andrew W. Mellon gave his art collection to the federal government in 1936 as the nucleus for the National Gallery. In exchange for the collection and an endowment fund to cover staff salaries and future acquisitions, Mellon exacted a promise of congressional appropriations to cover the building and other operating costs.

Both were the gestures of single individuals. By the 1950s, however, cultural advocates had begun to build increasingly complex funding coalitions. For example, the promoters who developed the plans for Washington's cultural edifice, the Kennedy Center, put together a collaborative package that included public contributions of land and matching grants for the building costs, with the remainder to be supplied by private gifts.

The most ambitious of these projects developed in New York. In 1955, when plans for Kennedy Center were still on the drawing board, the Metropolitan Opera began to seek new quarters. New York's master planner and dealmaker Robert Moses

offered a three-acre site on the West Side that was slated for redevelopment under his Slum Clearance Project. Because it was already targeted for demolition, the site at the Lincoln Center Urban Renewal Project could be acquired quite reasonably. And, Moses reasoned, the presence of a major cultural institution would provide an important anchor for the revival of this previously rundown neighborhood. The creation of Lincoln Center would ultimately become the largest arts fundraising venture of its kind. John D. Rockefeller III was drawn to the challenge of heading this venture by his own desire to seek ways to broaden the base of arts support. The project that began with the Metropolitan Opera ended as a complex cluster of cultural institutions, including (among others) the New York Philharmonic, the New York City Ballet, the Juilliard School, and a branch of the New York Public Library. It was a tremendously complex undertaking that ultimately cost $185 million, the bulk of which was contributed by a handful of wealthy individuals, sixty-two corporations, foundations such as Rockefeller, Ford, and the Rockefeller Brothers Fund, the governments of West Germany and Austria, and Japan's premier business consortium, the Keidanren.

Gleaning public support was somewhat more challenging. Neither the state nor the city had permanent budget lines for arts support in the 1950s. The city's major arts project was City Center. Begun in 1943 as a means of continuing the low-cost concerts initiated by the WPA, it was housed in Mecca Temple, a rather exotic building that the city inherited when it was foreclosed upon for nonpayment of taxes. Although technically not empowered to conduct theatrical ventures, Mayor Fiorello La Guardia forged an ingenious compromise, leasing the property to a group of cultural entrepreneurs for the nominal sum of $1 a year. The city still owned the building, but the performances were paid for through private support from individuals, foundations, and corporations.

Rockefeller managed to garner the necessary public funds through a variety of means. The Public Library branch brought some funds, as did the construction of parking facilities. The biggest coup came when Moses became president of the 1964 New York World's Fair, a position that enabled him to secure state monies to build a dance theater for the fair. As in the case of City Center, the building would be state property, but it could be leased to the resident companies for a minimal sum. Construction of the New York State Theater brought in another $15 million in public support.

By 1965, a variety of new funding mechanisms had been set in place. Foundations had begun to leave their imprint on cultural patronage four decades earlier, with art appreciation and professional training courses that extended the tenets of the elite ideal nationally. While earlier efforts were rooted primarily in local gains, the foundation and federal programs of the Depression and the postwar years aimed at outreach, democratization, and the development of local and national cultural policy making on a new scale. Although short-lived, the federal arts programs of the 1930s revealed the potential for the development of genuinely national initiatives with strongly participatory aims.

The Ford program meshed these ideas with a respect for uniform excellence often missing from Federal One. In building his program, Lowry skillfully used Ford's resources and its name to build a national constituency for cultural policy making and reform. And collaborative ventures such as Lincoln Center underscored the extent of the era's gains, pulling together an array of public and private donors that presaged the funding partnerships that would fuel the cultural expansionism of the late twentieth century.

## PLURALISM AND DEMOCRATIZATION, 1965–1990s

If elitism was the catchword that best captured the nature of American cultural patronage before 1925, and nationalization described the tendencies of the intervening years, the leitmotif of the century's final decades was pluralism. And one of the driving forces behind this growing diversity was the National Endowment for the Arts (NEA).

The federal arts programs of the depression years were hastily implemented and hastily withdrawn. Although a few optimistic legislators such as Florida congressman Claude Pepper introduced plans for a permanent Bureau of Fine Arts in the late 1930s, their efforts were summarily dismissed. Nonetheless, the issue of federal support continued to surface during the coming decades. In 1951, President Truman asked Lloyd Goodrich of the Whitney Museum to study the question of the government's relationship to the arts; Goodrich's report, "Art and Government," was issued two years later.

The Eisenhower era witnessed the first full-scale hearings in the House of Representatives on the subject of federal arts support, in which New York congressman Jacob Javits began to emerge as an articulate champion of federal cultural patronage. At the same time, a new rationale was beginning to be forged from the competitive ethos of the Cold War. Cold warrior sentiments were particularly compelling during the 1950s, as Americans rhetorically embraced cultural endeavors along with nuclear saber-rattling as effective weapons in the battle for the hearts and minds of allies and foes outside the United States. In part, these sentiments were born of outright competition, as the Russians exported dancers and athletes as symbols of their cultural superiority. In part, they stemmed from a growing awareness that many foreigners condescendingly viewed Americans as intellectually vapid and mired in materialism. By nurturing the arts, it was reasoned, the country could burnish its image both at home and abroad.

By the 1960s, however, the discourse began to change, moving economic considerations to the top of the agenda. Two foundation reports were particularly important in developing this theme: The Rockefeller Brothers Fund Panel study *The Performing Arts: Problems and Prospects,* published in 1965, and *Performing Arts: The Economic Dilemma,* a Twentieth Century Fund volume by William J. Baumol and William G. Bowen, issued the following year. Taken together, these documents prophesied a gloomy scenario for the future of American artistic endeavors. Although the number of symphonies, operas, and dance troupes had increased in the years after the war, few enjoyed adequate support. Salaries were low, deficits common, and revenues rarely covered expenses. Ticket sales provided only a percentage of the necessary revenues. Rising labor costs were another problem, particularly when ticket prices had to be kept as low as possible in order to attract audiences. Seen from this perspective, the nation's postwar arts boom seemed to carry the seeds of its own destruction.

Backed by reports such as these, the movement to secure permanent state and federal backing for the arts steadily gathered momentum. By the beginning of the 1960s, influential public figures such as John D. Rockefeller III had begun to go on public record with pleas that the arts should be viewed as "a new community responsibility," akin to "already accepted responsibilities for health, welfare and education." The Kennedy administration provided additional backing, as the young president and his radiant wife highlighted the talents of major performers in their White House salons.

Twentieth Century Fund director August Heckscher joined the White House staff as a cultural consultant, where he drafted his report "The Arts and the National Government." Issued in 1963, the

Heckscher report strongly endorsed the need for government support. This in turn was followed by the report of the blue-ribbon Commission on the Humanities, which recommended the creation of a similar funding mechanism for scholarship in the humanities. President Johnson readily promised his support. As he explained, "History has shown that, if we are to achieve the great society for which we are all working, it is essential that the arts grow and flourish." Eight months later, in March 1965, Johnson bolstered his rhetoric with action, submitting a formal congressional proposal for the creation of a national foundation for the arts and humanities. By September, the National Endowment for the Arts (NEA) had been signed into law.

The initial appropriation, set at $2.5 million and backed by another $2 million in matching funds, was quite modest in comparison to the spiraling scale of Ford's grants during these years. Although the evidence suggests that Ford policymakers were not involved in working out the NEA's administrative logistics, in many respects the two programs were similar. In a move to sidestep some of the ideological problems surrounding the WPA projects, the government adopted an arm's-length approach: public monies were to be funneled through nonprofit organizations; advisory panels would determine the artistic merit of the projects; and recommendations were to be screened by a presidentially appointed national council and chairperson.

Moreover, in a move to use federal dollars to generate additional support, the proviso was added that grants to institutions would only cover up to 50 percent of the project costs, with the rest to be raised from other sources. Funds were also set aside from the development of state arts councils and for matching grants from individuals, foundations, and corporations. According to Senator Claiborne Pell, who helped to draft the enabling legislation, the notion of using the NEA "as a catalyst . . . [to] help spark nonfederal support . . . was the key to the entire proposal." With the creation of the NEA, the notion of public-private partnerships came to full bloom.

Of course, not everyone was enamored with the prospect of having to raise 50 percent of the necessary funds from other donors. Humorist Garrison Keillor's fictional character, Jack Schmidt, arts administrator, put it this way: "Matching funds! The perpetual curse of the arts administrator! . . . The girl says yes, but first I have to find a date for her ugly sister." Despite these misgivings, the program proved effective. By 1968, federal grants of $8.6 million had

garnered another $27 million in arts support from other sources.

Begun under the chairmanship of Roger L. Stevens (1965–1969), the NEA grew dramatically with the appointment of Nancy Hanks (1969–1977) during the Nixon years. Hanks had previously served as the executive secretary of the National Council for the Arts and as the staff director for the Rockefeller Panel Report. Between 1971 and 1976, the NEA budget grew exponentially, from $15 million to $82 million. Funding continued to rise under the chairmanship of Livingston J. Biddle, Jr., who served until 1981. By the time of his departure, NEA's annual appropriations reached almost $160 million. Frank Hodsoll's appointment during the Reagan era introduced the first declines, although by the time he handed the leadership of the NEA over to John Frohnmayer in 1989 the annual appropriation had grown by another $10 million (representing a gain in current dollars, but little progress if inflation rates were taken into account).

Other public monies grew as well. When the NEA was founded, only five states had arts councils; by 1978, every state in the Union had an arts council of its own. Nelson Rockefeller created the first American arts council during his tenure as governor of New York in 1961. Modeled on the British Arts Council, it was created (like the NEA) to fund existing arts organizations rather than to run programs of its own. From a modest $450,000 budget at its inception, appropriations for the New York State Council of the Arts (NYSCA) topped the $2 million mark by decade's end.

Funding also became available for arts organizations under the Comprehensive Employment and Training Act of 1972 (CETA), which provided job training and employment opportunities for the poor and those who had been unemployed for at least fifteen weeks. By 1979, an estimated 10,000 CETA employees were working in neighborhood-based arts groups and other cultural nonprofit organizations.

Private giving rose dramatically as well. According to figures compiled by the American Association of Fund-Raising Counsel, giving to arts and humanities programs from all private sources rose from $1 billion in 1971 to over $7 billion two decades later. Corporate giving increased particularly quickly, especially in the 1980s. In part, corporate interest was piqued by NEA challenge grants, in part by Americans' growing interest in cultural activities, and in part due to the efforts of intermediary agencies like the Business Committee for the Arts (BCA), founded in 1966. Organizations such as BCA provided a variety of services, from national research on corporate giving trends to technical assistance in shaping corporate contributions and matchmaking services to draw businessmen onto arts boards.

Corporate arts support dates at least from the 1920s, when Chevron made a $10,000 donation to the San Francisco Symphony. Texaco began its broadcasts of matinee performances from the Metropolitan Opera in 1939. Nine years later, Exxon began a similar radio project, broadcasting Sunday performances by the New York Philharmonic. Hallmark was an early participant in media support as well, launching its television series with an original opera, *Amahl and the Night Visitors,* commissioned from Gian Carlo Menotti. Companies such as IBM and DuPont began collecting art in the 1930s, and IBM opened the first corporate gallery to showcase its acquisitions in 1955. In 1959, corporations donated only 3 percent of their charitable contributions to the arts; by 1980, the ratio approached 11 percent. The dollar value of these donations rose as well, from $22 million in 1965 to over $500 million in the early 1980s. The pace began to accelerate in the 1970s, as Mobil undertook sponsorship of the Public Broadcasting System's popular series *Masterpiece Theater* and Exxon began to underwrite *Great Performances.* Similarly, the first "blockbuster exhibit" funded by a corporation, "The Great Age of Fresco," opened at the Metropolitan Museum under a grant from Olivetti in 1968. According to statistics gathered by BCA in 1989, corporate cultural patronage provided 58 percent more in funding than the NEA and all the state councils combined.

Unlike private support at the turn of the century, the driving force behind corporate arts support was the desire for public visibility. By sponsoring a major exhibit or a public television program of recognized quality, so the reasoning goes, the corporation will enhance its own reputation. And the more people who attend these events, the greater the amount of good publicity the corporation will receive. Some companies seek to achieve this through blockbuster exhibits like the King Tut show, which are likely to draw large audiences; other such as Mobil, focus on smaller communities. In the 1970s, for example, Mobil initiated a community-based arts program that provided funds for cultural organizations in over eighty cities and towns.

Foundation funding grew as well, as did the number of foundations. In the 1950s, when McNeil Lowry was fashioning his massive program, Ford was one of a few thousand American grant-making institutions. By 1990, that number had grown to over thirty thousand. Most were small; only about a quarter had assets of $1 million or more. And unlike the professionally staffed giants such as Ford, MacArthur, Mellon, and Pew, most undoubtedly constituted little more than extensions of their founders' personal giving, providing grants for local organizations. Yet by the 1980s, foundation support of cultural ventures had risen substantially, to approximately 15 percent of the total outlays.

Until recently, however, few grant-making institutions matched the generosity of Ford. Between 1957 and 1980, the foundation donated almost $60 million for theater development, over $40 million for dance groups, $22 million to the visual arts, and over $100 million for musical efforts, including the symphony grants. In 1984, Ford also created a National Arts Stabilization Fund to help strengthen the managerial and fiscal capacities of performing arts organizations.

When Carnegie and Ford began their arts programs, they were in the minority, pioneers in a neglected field. During the 1970s and 1980s, cultural patronage became a far more common foundation priority. Two of the largest foundations created in the 1980s—the J. Paul Getty Trust and the Lila Wallace–Reader's Digest Foundation—deal primarily with the arts, but in very different ways. One of the country's richest foundations, the Getty Trust pegged its endowment at $3.5 billion in 1991, bolstered by an additional $1 billion worth of original art. Getty's 1990 budget of $250 million exceeded the outlays of all fifty state arts councils combined. In addition to operating its own museum, the Trust is building the Getty Center for the History of Art and the Humanities near Los Angeles. Art education, museum management, conservation training—all will fall within the trust's ambit when the Center is completed. Like the Metropolitan Museum under Morgan, the Getty Trust is cast in the mold of earlier traditions of American cultural patronage, but on a more ambitious scale.

Conversely, the Wallace Foundation, the largest U.S. foundation donor to the performing and visual arts, actively commissions works by ethnic and minority artists, and aids organizations serving these groups. Created in 1987 through the merger of four smaller, independent trusts, it boasted an arts budget of $32 million by 1991, placing it well ahead of other major cultural donors such as the Mellon Foundation and the Pew Trusts. Together, the Getty and Wallace trusts combine the twin mandates of twentieth-century American cultural patronage, incorporating the connoisseurship and professionalism of the early-twentieth-century museum as well as the late-twentieth-century emphasis on outreach and cultural diversity.

Despite increasing levels of foundation giving, individual largesse remained the largest source of arts support in the 1990s, as it was at the century's beginning. Although precise data do not exist on the extent of individual cultural patronage, data from cultural umbrella organizations reveal that the 147 largest symphony orchestras received 38 percent of their donations from individual donors, as opposed to 26 percent from corporations, 9 percent from foundations, and 27 percent from other sources and benefits; while the largest opera companies and museums reported ratios of 44 percent from individual donors.

This increasingly diverse array of cultural donors was matched by a growing emphasis on cultural pluralism after 1965, as a small but growing stream of public and private funding was earmarked for black, Hispanic, and women artists, and other previously underrepresented groups. The response was not entirely altruistic. As riots erupted on urban streets across the country during the long, hot summers of the 1960s, city after city echoed with the angry cries of "Burn, baby, burn." In Watts, Chicago, Cleveland, Detroit, it was a decade seared in the idealism of the civil rights movement, a decade scarred by urban riots that erupted with staccato regularity. Televised reports brought the terrors of these urban upheavals into American households with the evening news. It was the beginning of a revolution, not just for political parity, but for social and economic justice as well.

This included demands for opportunities to participate in the arts as full partners. Foundations, corporations, and government funders all evinced a quickened interest in the works of ethnic, minority, and women artists by the end of the 1960s. NYSCA created its Ghetto Arts Program in 1967, providing training and resources to encourage the growth of cultural activities in minority enclaves. Ford's Social Development program was launched the same year. The Negro Ensemble Company, the Harlem School for the Arts, and Arthur Mitchell's Dance Theater of Harlem were among the earliest grant recipients. Ballet, art, and concert training suddenly became available for gifted ghetto residents, and the Negro Ensemble Company received over $2 million in Ford grants within a five-year period to train black actors, playwrights, directors, and theater technicians.

While Ford's munificence was probably somewhat atypical among private foundations, the drift toward cultural diversity was more strongly etched in the areas of public and corporate support. The riots heightened corporations' awareness of the need to cultivate better relations within minority neighborhoods, both as the site of potential customers and as a means of capping urban reprisals. Arts organizations were particularly appealing recipients for corporate largesse because they tended to be less controversial than some of the more radical advocacy groups. For example, Philip Morris broadened its longstanding program of arts support to include a twelve-city tour of works by contemporary black artists in 1970, the first of an array of exhibitions featuring black, Hispanic, American Indian, and female painters and sculptors.

Government programs also had a vested interest in broadening the parameters of fine art. Unlike private patrons and foundations, government funding agencies are highly sensitive to mass constituencies. The unvarnished elitism of a J. Pierpont Morgan would be out of place in the NEA. Geographical diversity has been an important part of the NEA's mandate since its inception, as it was in the earlier WPA programs. But by the 1970s, artistic pluralism had become an important priority as well. "No single voice or set of tastes predominates," noted one NEA report.

Not surprisingly, minority initiatives began to surface on the NEA's agenda at the same moment that they appeared at NYSCA, Philip Morris, and Ford. Beginning with a 1967 theater project in Watts, these projects quickly expanded to include a formal Community Arts Project to honor "the vibrant arts of the inner city," and a "Jazz/Folk/Ethnic" section by 1972. Begun with a million-dollar budget in 1971, within three years the appropriations for the Expansion Arts and Community Cultural Programs had grown fivefold. To quote Livingston Biddle, these programs were designed to "extend the boundaries of the arts world and to *assure* that no American will be denied the opportunity to reach his or her artistic potential because of geographic, economic, or other social or cultural constraints." Biddle also created an Office of Minority Concerns and a Hispanic Task Force during his administration, with funding for minority arts initiatives topping the $11 million mark within the first year of his tenure.

One way in which NEA grants helped to build audiences for nontraditional artists was through the support of nontraditional exhibition spaces. Although the works of women artists continued to be underrepresented in museum holdings, NEA-sponsored alternative spaces and galleries provided increased opportunities to show their work. Women artists had historically fared better under public rather than under private cultural support. Between 1900 and 1925, few women artists saw their works hung in the halls of institutions such as the Metropolitan and few performed with organizations such as the Chicago Symphony. Even if they were not consciously excluded from the cultural canon set by these citadels of elite culture, they were most decidedly overlooked.

Although a few female artists did find their works featured in such specialized artistic ventures as the Whitney Studio Club, they first began to achieve full parity under the federal relief programs of the 1930s. By the 1970s, an increasingly radical feminist push for recognition led to the growth of new federally sponsored projects that provided fresh alternatives for women's professional advancement and exhibitions. One reason why women artists have been more successful in wresting opportunities from public rather than private donors is because government programs are susceptible to public pressures in ways that a private museum, or an eminent collector such as Morgan were not. In effect, the politicization of patronage gave women a new weapon in their quest for professional parity.

The mid-1960s marked a crucial turning point in the history of American philanthropy as well. Steeped in the idiom of Progressive expertise, foundations and museums had devoted a major share of their resources to developing national cadres of technically trained managerial elites after 1900. By the 1960s, the underlying faith in the power of "disinterested expertise" that lay at the heart of these programs was beginning to lose some of its unquestioned authority in the arts, as in other fields. To quote the historian Neil Harris in *Cultural Excursions* (1990), there was suddenly a growing awareness of "the political and social implications of apparently neutral arrangements." And "when exclusions began to be noted, values challenged, and authority questioned, the apparent neutrality of the museums became less convincing."

Men like Morgan built their museums as neutral meeting grounds where citizens from different classes and backgrounds could meet in the pursuit of a common culture. The institutions they built would have been fairly representative of the populations of their cities at the time, which were predominantly European in origin. By the mid-1960s, many of the country's largest cities had become far more heterogeneous, with growing populations of Hispanics and African Americans, while the consciousness raising activities of the women's movement were beginning to encourage women to press harder for recognition as well.

The crisis of cultural authority that surfaced in the programs of NYSCA, the NEA, Philip Morris, and Ford marked a more fundamental shift from an abiding faith in the neutrality and fairness of "disinterested" professionals to a new emphasis on what might be termed "self-interested expertise": increasingly successful demands for inclusion in the canon on political and demographic, as well as aesthetic, grounds. Many felt that it was a leavening process that was long overdue. But it would not have succeeded as well as it did, nor have been accepted as readily, without the presence of new kinds of public and corporate funders who were more sensitive to the political pressures behind these demands.

Ironically, while definitions of the arts were being recast to include new idioms of gender, ethnicity, and race, funding began to contract. In the words of the noted historian, Arthur Schlesinger, Jr., the 1990s marked "a time of crisis in the state of the arts." The problems began a decade earlier, with the election of Ronald Reagan. President Reagan entered the White House in 1981 determined to trim government funding across a broad swath of educational, cultural, and social-welfare agencies, including the NEA. A Heritage Foundation report issued the same year suggested that the NEA was particularly ripe for cuts, evoking decades of earlier debates about the propriety of federal arts support. However, Reagan's efforts were quickly checkmated by the recommendations of his Presidential Task Force on the Arts and Humanities chaired by Charlton Heston, which produced an unequivocal endorsement for the continuation of the NEA.

The following year, the President recommended a 50 percent cut in the agency's budget; the final appropriation dropped its funding by a more modest ratio of 10 percent. When Reagan suggested that the appropriation be pared to $100 million two years later, the budget was upped to $162 million instead. In justifying the President's request, OMB Director David Stockman announced: "Reductions of this magnitude are premised on the notion that . . . for too long, the Endowments have spread federal financing into an ever-widening range of artistic and literary endeavor. . . . This policy has resulted in a reduction of private, individual and corporate support in these key areas." Nonsense, countered arts advocate Senator Claiborne Pell, noting that private support for the arts and humanities was pegged at $2.7 billion in 1983, a sum that dwarfed the annual appropriations of the NEA.

Although President Reagan was never able to trim the endowment's budget to the levels he sought, he did eliminate the CETA funds that had provided professional and staff support for many neighborhood and community arts organizations. Some observers reasoned that since arts groups received a far smaller share of government outlays than most other nonprofit organizations, they would be better positioned to survive cutbacks than similar institutions in other fields. Viewed in terms of current dollars, NEA appropriations continued to grow incrementally during the 1980s, despite the Reagan administration's repeated attempts to reduce the level of federal support. But in terms of constant dollars, with 1967 as a baseline year, there were significant declines over the course of the decade, constituting a 27 percent reduction in purchasing power.

Funding issues ceded stage center to ideological concerns after the Bush administration was voted into office in 1988. Questions of censorship, state control, and ideology surrounded the demise of the Federal Writers and Theater Projects in the 1930s, only to reemerge in more vitriolic form at century's end. Two grants, in particular, triggered the ire of conservative critics in Congress and on the fundamentalist Right: funding for an exhibition of homoerotic photographs by Robert Mapplethorpe, an artist who had recently died of AIDS, and another photographic exhibit by Andres Serrano, which featured a depiction of a cross in a jar of urine. Led by Senator Jesse Helms, conservatives balked at what they deemed the use of public monies to display works that they considered to be obscene.

The battle lines were drawn when the NEA came up for reauthorization in 1990. Helms presented a resolution barring government support for projects that disseminate or produce "obscene or indecent material," thus placing the government in the role of censor, at least in terms of federal support. The Helms proposal sparked heated protests throughout the art world. John Frohnmayer, the new chairman of the NEA, tried to defuse the issue by asking artists to sign a pledge not to produce artworks depicting sadomasochism, homoeroticism, sexual exploitation of children, or graphic depictions of individuals engaged in sex, a suggestion that was met with angry resistance.

Both Bush and Frohnmayer were caught in a political bind, trapped between the fundamentalist enthusiasms of the conservative Right and cries to preserve artistic freedom and freedom of speech from artists and arts advocates across the country. Pat Robertson's Christian Coalition mounted a $200,000 fundraising campaign to quash the agency's reauthorization, while Reverend Donald Wildman's American Family Association asserted the right of taxpayers to ensure that their funds were not expended on works they deemed blasphemous or obscene. President Bush's rejection of the Helms proposal sparked protests from these and other groups, while artists continued to campaign to have the antiobscenity pledge dropped from NEA acceptance forms. A compromise was finally reached in October 1990, granting the NEA a three-year reauthorization with the proviso that arts organizations would have to return their grants if the works completed or presented with federal funds were judged obscene by the courts. This at least removed responsibility for determining whether a work was obscene from the shoulders of government bureaucrats and private citizens and placed it in the more dispassionate setting of the juridical system. It was a damaging contest, prompting conservative commentators such as William Safire of the *New York Times* to call for end to the NEA in the name of free speech, arguing that the danger of government control is always implicit in government support.

For some, the prognosis for American cultural patronage seemed bleak on the threshold of the twenty-first century. A lingering recession was making inroads into the budgets of state arts councils, and corporate giving began to stabilize in 1986, after years of steady growth. Revenues were dwindling as well, as audiences cut back their attendance at cultural events due to the recession, and individual giving began to drop. Some of the largest corporate donors, such as Exxon, discontinued the bulk of their arts programs in the sluggish economy of the 1980s, severing longstanding ties such as Exxon's support for the *Great Performances* series on PBS. And conservative commentators and critics such as Representative Philip Crane continued to lobby for the abolition of the NEA.

John Frohnmayer stepped down from his position as the NEA's chairman in 1992, following public attacks by the archconservative presidential candidate Patrick J. Buchanan in the New Hampshire primaries. With his return to private employment, Frohnmayer finally had a chance to air his views, charging that the reauthorization bill was "patently unconstitutional, overbroad, vague, and without standards." The one consolation, in his opinion, was the fact that "no project funded by the endowment has ever been found legally obscene in any court anywhere." As he explained, " 'obscenity' has become a label freely attached to anything that some people do not like or understand, rather than being a legally defined term. . . . We must demand that our legislators decide on the basis of facts, not 'outrage.' "

Yet despite ongoing debates about the appropriateness of federal cultural patronage, the perspective from the 1990s was not as bleak as some artistic jeremiads might suggest. By 1990, a highly diversified array of public and private funders at the local, state, and national level was fully in place. As new donors entered the cultural arena, opportunities to create, to present, and to view increased as well. Between 1965 and the mid-1980s the number of major American symphonies increased twofold; resident professional theaters fourfold; and professional dance companies tenfold. Rather than the province of the urban few, culture had become the entitlement of the many. And those who could not get to see a major exhibition, dance company, or opera in their area could enjoy many of these art forms on radio and television, courtesy of coalitions of public, foundation, and corporate donors.

The nation's artistic canon had become more inclusive as well. Former NEA chairman John Frohnmayer eloquently underscored the importance of the new pluralism, noting that "Some claim that the only way the Endowment can be saved is to return to 'safe' grants—to dead white male Eurocentric art. . . . [We cannot] let our government retreat to such a fortress mentality. As a nation we must celebrate and accommodate our diversity." By the 1990s, John D. Rockefeller III's vision of a society in which access to art would become a democratic prerogative open to all had been realized, due in large measure to the changing contours of American cultural patronage.

See Also Foundations and Public Policy; Visual Arts; Architecture; Music (all in this volume).

## BIBLIOGRAPHY

Lawrence W. Levine, *Highbrow/Lowbrow: The Emergence of Cultural Hierarchy in America* (1988), provides a useful overview of nineteenth- and twentieth-century cultural trends; while Neil Harris, *Cultural Excursions: Marketing Appetites and Cultural Tastes in Modern America* (1990), includes essays on cultural philanthropy and some of the controversies surrounding the democratization of American culture. Helen L. Horowitz, *Culture and the City: Cultural Philanthropy in Chicago from the 1880s to 1917* (1976), and Kathleen D. McCarthy, *Noblesse Oblige: Charity and Cultural Philanthropy in Chicago, 1849–1929* (1982), examine the growth of cultural institutions in a single city. Art museums have been particularly well studied. One of the earliest institutional overviews was Daniel M. Fox's imaginative book, *Engines of Culture: Philanthropy and Art Museums* (1963). Nathaniel Burt, *Palaces for the People: A Social History of the American Art Museum* (1977), surveys the development of a variety of American museums; while Walter Muir Whitehill, *Museum of Fine Arts, Boston* (1970), and Winifred E. Howe, *A History of the Metropolitan Museum of Art* (1913, 1946), provide detailed studies of specific repositories. For an overview of orchestral developments, see John Henry Mueller, *The American Symphony Orchestra: A Social History of Musical Taste* (1951).

Kathleen D. McCarthy, *Women's Culture: American Philanthropy and Art, 1830–1930* (1991), examines the differing roles of male and female artists and patrons in museum development; while Aline B. Saarinen, *The Proud Possessors: The Lives, Times and Tastes of Some Adventurous American Art Collectors* (1958), provides a lively introduction to the activities of an array of prominent art patrons. The best biography of J. Pierpont Morgan is Ron Chernow, *The House of Morgan: An American Banking Dynasty and the Rise of Modern Finance* (1990), although Chernow deals with Morgan's cultural activities only in passing. Avis Berman, *Rebels on Eighth Street: Juliana Force and the Whitney Museum* (1990), examines the events surrounding the creation of the country's first major museum of American art. Nicholas Fox Weber, *Patron Saints: Five Rebels Who Opened America to a New Art, 1928–1943* (1992), surveys the careers of Lincoln Kirstein, Edward Warburg, Agnes Mongan, James Thrall Soby and A. Everitt Austin, Jr., providing a particularly useful discussion of the origins of the New York City Ballet. John Ensor Harr and Peter Johnson, *The Rockefeller Conscience: An American Family in Public and Private* (1991), is an excellent biography of the Rockefeller "brothers," including John D. Rockefeller III.

Barry D. Karl and Stanley N. Katz, "The American Philanthropic Foundation and the Public Sphere, 1890–1930," *Minerva* 19 (Summer 1981): 236–270, provides an incisive discussion of foundation activities in the early twentieth century; while Ellen Condliffe Lagemann, *The Politics of Knowledge: The Carnegie Corporation, Philanthropy, and Public Policy* (1989), has a good chapter on Frederick Keppel's arts programs. The notion of third-party government is discussed in Lester Salamon, "Partners in Public Service: The Scope and Theory of Government Nonprofit Relations" in Walter W. Powell, ed., *The Nonprofit Sector* (1987): 99–117.

Jane De Hart Matthews, *The Federal Theater, 1935–1939: Plays, Relief, and Politics* (1980), examines the history of one of the more controversial of the WPA arts projects; Jerre Mangione, *The Dream and the Deal: The Federal Writers' Project, 1935–1943* (1972), is a first-hand account by that project's National Coordinating Editor. The history of the Treasury Department's art programs are detailed in Karal Ann Marling, *Wall-to-Wall America: A Cultural History of Post-Office Murals in the Great Depression* (1982), and Marlene Park and Gerald E. Markowitz, *Democratic Vistas: Post Offices and Public Art in the New Deal* (1984).

Gary O. Larson, *The Reluctant Patron: The United States Government and the Arts, 1943–1965* (1983), affords the best discussion of the debates leading up to the creation of the National Endowment for the Arts. Serge Guilbaut, *How New York Stole the Idea of Modern Art: Abstract Expressionism, Freedom, and the Cold War* (1983), is a sophisticated analysis of the complex interaction among politics, ideology, and cultural patronage at mid-century.

Dick Netzer, *The Subsidized Muse: Public Support for the Arts in the United States* (1978), remains one of the most useful overviews of the development of federal cultural support, with an emphasis on economic as well as political issues. Patricia McFate, ed., "Paying for Culture," *Annals of the American Academy of Political and Social Sciences* 471 (January 1984), is an important collection of essays on the impact of federal cutbacks on arts organizations, including pieces by Claiborne Pell, Livingston Biddle, and Frank Hodsoll. Livingston Biddle also wrote his own account of the National Endowment for the Arts in *Our Government and the Arts: A Perspective from the Inside* (1988). Two other edited volumes, Paul J. Di-Maggio, *Nonprofit Enterprise in the Arts: Studies in Mission and Constraint* (1986), and Martin Feldstein, *The Economics of Art Museums* (1991), provide insights into the political, social, and economic issues surrounding public and private cultural patronage in the late twentieth century.

# LEISURE AND RECREATION

## Randy Roberts

Slowly they marched through the streets of Worcester, Massachusetts—hundreds of them, huddled close together in the December chill. They carried signs and banners and placards that announced their demands. Trade unionists all, they were attempting to gain control over some aspect of their lives. One long banner, carried by local carpenters, proclaimed, "Eight Hours for Work, Eight Hours for Rest, Eight Hours for What We Will." As they marched, they sang stanza after stanza of the most popular labor song of the period:

> We mean to make things over;
> We're tired of toil for naught;
> We may have enough to live on,
> But never an hour for thought.
>
> We want to feel the sunshine,
> We want to smell the flowers; We are sure that
> God has willed it,
> And we mean to have eight hours.

"Eight hours for what we will." A simple demand, but one loaded with political and social implications. What these Worcester workers were fighting for in their 1889 march was time for and control of leisure. Too often, historians have focused on labor's struggle to improve the workplace, win higher wages, and obtain job security. Of course, they have traced the battle over a shorter workday, but they have seldom discussed the meaning of an eight-hour day. Few historians have followed workers home and watched what they did with their leisure hours. For them work is serious, play frivolous. As sociologist David Riesman remarked, "Many people are uncomfortable when discussing leisure; as with sex, they want to make a joke of it." But in their struggle for leisure, twentieth-century American workers have enjoyed some of their greatest successes. Indeed, during the twentieth century, leisure has been profoundly and fundamentally altered. Unlike industry, leisure has been democratized.

## SEGREGATED LEISURE

Leisure has always occupied an important position in the lives of the wealthy. Games, sports, and travel were woven into the fabric of their social and economic interaction. By the late nineteenth century, the wealthiest Americans had begun to use leisure to insulate themselves from their economic and social inferiors. They had developed such summer colonies as Newport, Rhode Island, where they vacationed in roomy mansions and filled their leisure hours with sports and the activities of their athletic clubs. For them, leisure activity served a social function; it provided the arena where the wealthy could come together and mix socially in exclusive subcommunities.

The wealthy used leisure to insulate themselves in several ways. Often they engaged in activities that took great amounts of leisure time and wealth. Only the wealthiest Americans, for example, could afford to maintain a yacht or a stable of thoroughbred race horses. By the late nineteenth century, membership in the New York Yacht Club or the New York Jockey Club was a clear indication of social and economic standing. In a time of booming economic expansion, when fortunes were being made daily and the captains of commerce, politics, fashion, and culture often came from different backgrounds, membership in the most exclusive clubs announced who were indeed the "leaders" of America.

Memberships in athletic clubs and country clubs were also signs of distinction. Often modeled after the London Athletic Club, American athletic clubs mixed sports with purely social activities. By the beginning of the twentieth century, every major city had at least one athletic club that was normally tied by its membership to other clubs. Members of the New York Athletic Club, for instance, were often also members of either New York's Knickerbocker, Union, or Century clubs. And if athletic clubs sponsored amateur sports, they also filled their calendars with social activities. As historians of the New York

Athletic Club commented, "Wine, women, and song became more than a catch phrase—they were woven into the texture of NYAC activities."

Country clubs served a similar function, mixing cricket, golf, tennis, and swimming with nonathletic social occasions. Based on the ideal of the English country home, the American country club attempted to replicate the architecture and ambiance of an English manor. Tudor architecture, interiors of wood and leather, and British servants catered to Anglophile American tastes. But if the mood was affected, the purpose of the clubs was often practical. They were meant to bring together the business and social leaders of a community. Historians of the Country Club of Brookline, Massachusetts, founded in 1882 and America's oldest country club, noted its exclusive social nature: "Everyone [in Boston Society] was either in it or out of it; and those who were in it were proud of the fact and guarded its boundaries jealously. They played with each other, not with others; they competed with each other, not with others; above all, they married each other only, and so their children carried on the good (?) [sic] tradition."

In areas where the elite could possibly come into athletic contact with less wealthy Americans, the development of the code of amateurism curtailed the extent of the association. Once again, the inspiration was English. The object of the amateur code was the athletic separation of the classes. The constitution of the Amateur Rowing Association (1892), for example, defined an amateur oarsman, sculler, or coxswain as one who had never rowed for money, never knowingly rowed against a professional for any prize, never "taught, pursued, or assisted" in athletic exercises for money, never been "employed in or about boats, or in any manual labour, for money," and never been "by trade or employment for wages a mechanic, artisan or labourer, or engaged in any menial duty." Although amateur codes for other sports were not quite so severe, they all carried an underlying class bias. The message of such codes was that participation in certain leisure sports was a restricted privilege, not a universal right.

Sports and clubs did not consume all the leisure hours of the wealthy. Travel and cultural activities were also important. The grand tour of Europe had been essential to the education of young wealthy American men since the seventeenth century, and by the end of the nineteenth it had become a central feature of a young woman's education as well. Inspired by Jefferson's notion of a worldwide "republic of letters," Charles Sumner, Henry Adams, Henry James, Theodore Roosevelt, and thousands of other wealthy Americans traveled to Europe to round off their educations. They made lengthy stops in London, Paris, Berlin, and Rome and visited the important ruins and mountains of Europe. The success of the Adams men, Henry Adams commented, "was chiefly due to the field that Europe gave them." Although by the end of the nineteenth century group tours had brought European travel within the reach of the upper middle class, it remained a vital element of upper-class leisure.

Wealthy Americans paid homage to Europe in the United States as well as abroad. They supported high culture that was decidedly European. German and Italian opera, French painting, and English literature received the support and patronage of culture-conscious Americans, often to the detriment of American productions. In several areas, in fact, the elite appropriated for their own entertainments that had cut across class lines for most of the nineteenth century. Shakespeare's plays, for example, were once performed before audiences of all economic levels. The Bard was popular entertainment, and audiences were quite vocal in their appreciation and condemnation. A bad performance might provoke boos as well as a shower of eggs and rotten fruit from the pit. Describing an evening of Shakespeare, Washington Irving noted that a chorus of "coughing and sneezing . . . *whistling and thumping.* . . . The crackling of nuts and the crunching of apples saluted my ears on every side." Toward the end of the century Shakespeare moved out of popular culture and became a staple of "polite" culture and the "legitimate" stage. A new code of conduct—emphasizing proper dress and manners—became de rigueur, and the popular appeal of Shakespeare was sacrificed on the altar of clean clothes and soft hands. The same march toward orderliness and decorum changed audience behavior at concerts and museums as well as the theater. Increasingly toward the end of the nineteenth century, elite leisure culture had less and less in common with popular culture.

Middle-class Americans in the nineteenth century regarded leisure differently than the elite. For them, productivity and self-improvement were cherished ideals, and the entire notion of leisure was vaguely scandalous. In no other class was the tug of Protestant piety, Victorian respectability, republican ideology, and the industrial work ethic so strong. The Victorian emphasis on sobriety, delayed gratification, thrift, and domesticity often clashed with popular leisure activities. For many earnest middle-class Americans, Frederick Law Olmstead's Central Park was the ideal leisure space. He designed Central Park

Central Park, New York, 1906. PRINTS AND PHOTOGRAPHS DIVISION, LIBRARY OF CONGRESS

as a rural retreat in the midst of the busiest city in America. It was meant as a haven for New Yorkers, a place where they could quietly contemplate tranquil lakes and green meadows. Olmstead even claimed that the park exerted a "refining influence" on all who visited it, "an influence favorable to courtesy, self-control, and temperance."

By the end of the nineteenth century, however, middle-class Americans were beginning to engage in a wider range of activities. They, too, enjoyed sports, both as participants and as spectators. Baseball was a particular favorite. "Baseball," wrote Mark Twain, "is the very symbol, the outward and visible expression of the drive and push and struggle of the raging, tearing, booming nineteenth century." The ideology of baseball, which stressed teamwork, competition, and clean living, seemed to mirror corporate and industrial values and held a particular appeal to Americans anxious for social and economic advancement. Professional baseball courted middle-class fans.

Since the games were played on spring and summer afternoons and seldom on Sundays, most spectators came from the middle class. In addition, ladies' day and other such promotional schemes encouraged men to bring their wives and families to the games. To tie baseball to bourgeois respectability, team owners even gave clergymen free season passes. By 1903, the year of the first World Series, baseball had become the country's most popular sport.

The middle class participated in other sports as well. They attended college football games and played croquet. Some even followed boxing, perhaps the most antibourgeois sport. William Lyon Phelps, professor of English literature at Yale, recalled reading a newspaper to his father, an elderly Baptist minister, the day after James J. Corbett defeated John L. Sullivan for the heavyweight championship: "I had never heard him mention a prize fight and did not suppose he knew anything on the subject, or cared anything about it. So when I came to the headline CORBETT

DEFEATS SULLIVAN, I read that aloud and turned the page. My father leaned forward and said earnestly, 'Read it by rounds.' "

The middle class also contributed to the growth of the leisure travel and culture markets. Mark Twain's national reputation was made with *The Innocents Abroad* (1869), a book that recounted a trip of largely middle-class Americans to the Holy Land and the Mediterranean. Indeed, faster and less expensive ocean travel had brought European vacations into the price range of those at the top of the middle class. In addition, "travel experts" began to package tours to conform to middle-class tastes and expectations. As early as the 1840s, Thomas Cook was packaging tours in England to Ireland and Scotland. In 1856 his "grand circular tour of the Continent" included stops in Antwerp, Brussels, the field of Waterloo, Cologne, the Rhine and its borders, Mainz, Frankfurt, Heidelberg, Baden-Baden, Strasbourg, Paris, and Le Havre before returning to London. Many Americans traveled to London to become part of one of Cook's packaged tours to Switzerland or the Holy Land.

The art critic and traveler John Ruskin likened a Cook railroad tour to being sent to a foreign land much as a parcel is sent. This was not travel at all, he believed. Travel, as Ruskin and other traditional travelers defined it, implied effort and some trouble—the word *travel* comes from the same root as *travail,* meaning "trouble," "work," or "torment." But Cook's ideal, not Ruskin's, captured the imagination of middle-class America. In the United States, American Express moved into the field of middle-class tourism. In 1891 it copyrighted its first American Express Travelers Cheque, and in 1895 it opened its first European office. Like Cook, American Express developed its own packaged tours that guaranteed that the traveler would see all the "important" sights of the lands visited. And the travelers would see the sights in comfort without work or worry. American Express's first "all-water round-the-world" excursion was not so much a trip as a "pleasure cruise" aboard the *Laconia.* As historian Daniel J. Boorstin observed, "Foreign travel now had, of course, become a commodity. Like any other mass-produced commodity, it could be bought in bargain packages and on the installment plan."

Culture, too, became a commodity for the middle class. During the mid-nineteenth century such entrepreneurs as P. T. Barnum demonstrated that culture, like travel, could be packaged and sold. Although Barnum is more closely associated with Tom Thumb, the "Fejee Mermaid," the American Museum, and the circus, he appealed to the desire for information and culture as much as the curiosity to see freaks and fires. The Jenny Lind concert tour was one of Barnum's greatest successes. Barnum arranged for Lind, the coloratura soprano called "the Swedish Nightingale," to tour the United States in 1850. Her successful tour became a pseudoevent, which Daniel J. Boorstin defined as a "planned happening that occurs primarily for the purpose of being recorded." Barnum's skill at packaging and marketing Lind drew criticism from some observers. The London *Times* commented, "That which can be done by a private adventurer, may with more ease be accomplished by the leader of a faction." Politics, the editorialist feared, might also become a commodity, for in the United States Senate "the same reckless system of exaggeration, the same intense vulgarity of means and littleness of ends" as Barnum has brought to high culture already existed. The London *Times,* however, failed to diminish the success of Barnum's achievement.

Public tours, often based on the Lind model, attracted millions of middle-class spectators during the late nineteenth century. The tours mixed high culture with popular entertainment. Charles Dickens made several successful tours of the United States. He read from his novels and lectured on various social and literary subjects. Before Mark Twain was a successful writer, he was a popular public speaker who lectured on the exotic behaviors of Hawaii and the American West. Oscar Wilde also made a popular tour of the United States. His lectures on the English and Italian Renaissances and on home decoration entertained his American audience.

When Wilde spoke about "the home beautiful," he touched on a subject close to middle-class America's heart. For many Americans, and particularly for women, leisure activities were largely confined to the home. The home, noted one popular advice book, should be "a place of repose, a refuge from the excitement and distractions of outside . . . , provided with every attainable means of rest and recreation." The middle-class Victorian home revolved around the parlor, the area where private and public concerns merged. The emotional if not the physical center of the parlor was the parlor table. Here the family read the Bible and more secular books together and gathered during the evening to play board games. Close to the parlor table was often a piano. Religion, education, music, entertainment, sociable conversation— all could be obtained in the parlor. The parlor fulfilled the Victorian notion of leisure being uplifting and self-improving. And such late-nineteenth-century

Saloon interior, c. 1906. PRINTS AND PHOTOGRAPHS DIVISION, LIBRARY OF CONGRESS

institutions as the soda parlor attempted to extend the ideal of the parlor into a purely public space.

Lower-class leisure was more public than middle-class leisure, as dictated by work schedules, as well as the design of working-class homes and ethnic cultural patterns. During the late nineteenth century, most laborers worked six days a week, often ten or more hours a day. In 1890, for example, bakers averaged sixty-five hours a week, steelworkers over sixty-six, and canners nearly seventy-seven. Working in a steel-mill blast furnace was a twelve-hour-a-day, seven-day-a-week job, including one twenty-four-hour continuous shift and one free day every two weeks. Even as late as 1920, skilled laborers averaged 50.4 hours a week and the unskilled 53.7 hours. In addition, working-class women normally faced hours of household work after they returned from their other jobs. In 1900 the typical housewife labored six hours a day on just two tasks: meal preparation and cleaning.

If such schedules left little time for leisure and little energy for recreation, working-class homes provided poor shelter for leisure activities. The private space provided in the mansions of the wealthy and the parlors of the middle class was absent in the cramped, uncomfortable homes of the working class. Urban tenements were cold and drafty in the winter and hot and stuffy in the summer. They encouraged the people who lived in them to find their leisure elsewhere.

For many working-class males, that elsewhere was the saloon, the working-class equivalent of the social, athletic, and country clubs of wealthier Americans. Dubbed "the one democratic club in American life," the saloon became a basic institution for the urban working class, especially after industries barred drinking on the job and the technology of pasteurization and refrigeration improved. By 1884 there were more than 3,500 saloons in Chicago, and they were nearly ubiquitous in other industrial cities as well. Often located across the street from the main gates of factories or close to the entrances of mines, saloons provided comforts that many working-class men could not obtain in their homes. Beer was often healthier to drink than water or milk, and for a nickel or a dime the saloon keeper served a meal.

Saloon keepers offered inexpensive meals to attract customers, especially during the late nineteenth century when the saloon business was the most competitive. They also attempted to attract patrons by providing leisure and recreational outlets. Boxing, billiards, and bowling, the three sporting B's of saloon life, were all sponsored by saloon owners. In addition, saloons also functioned as banks and employment offices. In his local saloon, a worker could get his paycheck cashed, borrow a few dollars to meet an emergency, learn about a new job, or simply relax with a beer and read a newspaper. He could also discuss politics with his friends or gamble on the turn of a card or the pluck of a fighting cock. The saloon, in short, was the department store of clubs, offering entertainment, edification, nourishment, and fellowship.

Given the many functions of saloons, politicians and labor leaders often used them as unofficial headquarters. Like the saloon keepers, political and labor organizers were after recruits, men who would vote for them on election day and support their efforts to unionize. They used logic and patronage jobs as well as recreational opportunities to attract supporters. Politicians especially provided the money for the organization of saloon-based social and athletic clubs (SACs). As one authority on SACs commented, "The Boss pays the rent and is generous in his donations for all club enterprises. He is the patron saint of the gang and often leads the grand march or makes a speech at gang dances and in return his protégés work for him in innumerable ways and every gang boy in the hive is expected to gather honey on election day." Richard Daley, Chicago's powerful political boss, got his start in the Hamburg Athletic Club, and other politicians, police captains, labor leaders, and gamblers emerged from the ranks of the SACs.

Ethnic clubs similarly often operated out of saloons. German American Turner societies, Scottish American Caledonian clubs, and the Irish American Gaelic Athletic Association and Clan na Gael often had strong ties to neighborhood saloons. They attempted to preserve their native language and literature as well as their Old World sports and customs. The Irish Athletic Club of Boston, for example, was established in 1879 and promoted such traditionally Irish sports as goaling, trapball, and stone throwing. The Gaelic Park in Chicago was the heart of the South Side Irish community.

Saloon culture—and, for the most part, the activities of the SACs and the ethnic clubs—was male-oriented. Termed the bachelor subculture, the world of the saloon revolved around satisfying the social, emotional, sexual, and recreational needs of men. Most women in this world served those ends, either as prostitutes, servants, or distant observers. Although many married men belonged to this bachelor subculture, they accepted the ethos of a single man once they entered the world. Certainly until well into the twentieth century, saloons made no attempts to bridge the gender gulf.

Working-class women turned to other leisure and recreational outlets. Married working-class women faced the bleakest prospects. Outside and inside their homes, they labored long hours at physically demanding jobs. Whether they worked in sweat shops or as domestic servants, their labors did not end when they returned home. Then, as today, they had to prepare meals, keep their home clean, and care for their children. For many, religion provided an emotional outlet. Whenever possible, they tried to mix leisure with work. If they took their children to a park, for example, they could often discuss family and community affairs with other women. During hot summer nights they might escape to house or apartment stoop for an hour or so pleasant conversation or enjoy an after-dinner promenade. Seldom, however, did their leisure involve a commercial component.

Single working-class women had greater opportunities. By the turn of the century, beer gardens, dance halls, and the popular theater had begun to cater to single women. P. T. Barnum and Moses Kimball, two nineteenth-century entertainment entrepreneurs, attempted to attract women to their shows, and the legitimate theater banned prostitutes and drinking in an effort to encourage respectable women to support its product. Dance halls were particularly popular with young, single, working-class women. Commenting on the rise of dance halls, historian Kathy Peiss noted, "Although many working-class halls had their origins in the saloon trade, managers differentiated this mixed-sex arena of pleasure from the world of male culture by welcoming women attending alone or in groups, sponsoring fancy dress balls and masquerades, and mixing unusual cocktails to appeal to their female customers."

Although there were no homosocial, commercialized leisure opportunities for women—no female equivalent of the male-dominated saloon—by the early 1900s heterosocial opportunities for single, working-class women abounded. Such amusement parks as Coney Island actively sought male and female customers. They offered exotic, dreamland landscapes; wonderful, novel machines; and a free, loose heterosocial environment. In the nation's amusement parks, men could remove their coats and ties and both sexes could enjoy a rare personal freedom. As one immigrant claimed, for the young "privacy could only be had in public." Increasingly, vaudeville circuits and variety houses also aimed their shows at mixed-sex audiences. They advertised ladies invitation nights and provided matinees that conformed to women's schedules. If variety shows continued to be considered low, vulgar, male entertainment, vaudeville did attract female patrons. "At the big

Luna Park, Coney Island, New York. Stereograph, 1903. PRINTS AND PHOTOGRAPHS DIVISION, LIBRARY OF CONGRESS

time level," wrote one historian, "managers insisted on refined language and drawing-room manners, leading some to call it the Sunday School circuit."

## THE BATTLE FOR TIME AND INCOME

As the nineteenth century gave way to the twentieth, the leisure difficulty confronted by the working class was not so much a lack of choice as a lack of the opportunity to exercise that choice. Time—long, six or seven-day-a-week work schedules—was the problem. This gave a greater urgency to workers' demands for a ten or eight-hour day and a six-day or five-day work week. By 1900 most workers had Sunday off. But observation of religious customs and blue laws made Sunday a poor day for commercialized leisure. Blue laws—the term comes from the blue paper on which the Sunday restrictions were written in New Haven in 1781—curtailed leisure opportunities on Sunday. Many states prohibited Sunday baseball and closed stores and saloons on Sunday. As late as 1985, observed Witold Rybczynski about the blue laws, on Sunday "somewhere in the United States, it is illegal to barber; bowl; play billiards, bingo, polo, or cards; gamble; race horses; hunt; go to the movies; sell cars, fresh meat or alcohol; organize boxing or wrestling matches; hold public dances or sporting events; or dig oysters." Sunday,

the early Puritans and many politicians and religious leaders afterwards believed, should be a day of prayer, not a day of play.

During the first half of the twentieth century laborers won many of their demands for shorter workdays. The first battle centered on Saturday work. First employees sought a five-and-a-half-day week, ending their workweek at midday on Saturday. The Typographical Union won this concession for its workers early in the century and gradually the practice spread to other industries. By the 1920s, the five-and-a-half-day week was a reality for most workers. Other workers, however, clamored for a five-day week. The movement started among Jewish workers who demanded all day Saturday off to observe their Sabbath. A five-day week, they reasoned, allowed both Christians and Jews to faithfully observe their religious duties. In 1929, the Amalgamated Clothing Workers of America, a union with a large Jewish constituency, proposed the five-day week for the clothing industry.

Some industries made a smooth conversion to the five-day week. The Jewish-dominated clothing industry, the heavily unionized construction industry, and the printing and publishing industries all adopted the five-day week. In addition, a few industrialists advocated the shorter workweek. Henry Ford opposed unions but not the five-day week. In 1914 he had shortened the workday in his factories from nine to eight hours, and in 1926 he adopted the five-day week. His decision was based on economic self-interest. Just as higher wages allowed his employees to purchase automobiles, the shorter workweek gave them more leisure time to use automobiles. Greater leisure time, he believed, would be good for his business. In fact, he told other industrialists that leisure and business—play and profits—were two sides of the same coin.

Few business leaders listened to Ford until economic conditions dictated the adoption of the "weekend." During the Great Depression, when industrialists and manufacturers reduced the size of their labor forces, the weekend was seen as a way to save money without massive layoffs; laborers would work less and be paid less, but they would keep their jobs. The weekend received the official blessing of the government in the Fair Labor Standards Act of 1938. Although it exempted farm laborers, domestic servants, and professional workers, the act—and the 1940 extension of it—set the five-day, forty-hour week for all enterprise engaged in or affecting interstate commerce. Although many Americans returned to longer hours and a six-day week during World War II, the change was temporary. After the war, the five-day week became an American institution. The support for the five-day week became so strong that in 1990 the United States insisted that its trade agreement with Japan include the promise that the Japanese government institute a five-day week for all government employees and encourage private companies to do the same. Although one American editorialist labeled this provision a "vow of future sloth," it demonstrated the commitment of America to the ideal of the weekend.

If weekends and shorter workweeks gave laborers more leisure time, higher wages allowed them greater freedom in how they filled that time. During the late nineteenth and early twentieth centuries, real wages for blue-collar and lower-level white-collar workers remained fairly constant. Unions failed to improve the wages of most unskilled and semi-skilled workers. For their own economic interests, a handful of industrialists raised their employees' wages. In 1914, Henry Ford introduced a five-dollar minimum daily wage in his plants. But as with the weekend, few industrialists voluntarily followed Ford's example. If conditions seemed to improve in the 1920s, it was more the result of steady or declining prices than significant wage increases. Actually, the economic gap between upper- and lower-class Americans widened during the 1920s.

The Great Depression of the 1930s began the movement to narrow the economic disparity between classes. The National Labor Relations Act of 1935 (better known as the Wagner Act) put the government's stamp of approval on unionization, and during the next few years the country's leading industries—automobiles, steel, and coal—were unionized. Two other 1935 acts similarly affected individual incomes: the Social Security Act began the process of restructuring the economic lives of elderly Americans, and the Revenue Act increased the tax levels of wealthier Americans and expressed the government's intention to redistribute wealth. In 1938, the Fair Labor Standards Act established a national minimum hourly wage of forty cents. Although these measures did not immediately change the economic conditions of most Americans, after the Depression ended industrial workers' wages rose significantly.

The acceptance of the weekend and the real increase in wages were the most significant measures in the democratization of leisure in the United States. Along with paid vacations, they have allowed working-class Americans to enjoy leisure activities that were once beyond their reach. To be sure, no change in working conditions could fully democratize leisure. The five-day week did not mean that steel workers could take up yachting. Nor did it mean that black or Jewish or Catholic Americans could now join exclusive WASP country clubs. Economic, racial, ethnic, and religious divisions continued to limit and define leisure opportunities. The five-day work week and higher wages, however, were preconditions for significant change. They allowed blue-collar workers to regularly attend Saturday baseball games or visit museums that were closed on Sundays. They gave middle-class and working-class Americans more control over their time, and this in turn contributed to the twentieth-century leisure revolution, a revolution that has altered the economic, racial, ethnic, and religious nature of leisure activities.

## THE DEMOCRATIZATION OF TRAVEL

Technology has similarly altered and democratized leisure activities. The automobile, for example, has given Americans greater control over their movements. In the late nineteenth and early twentieth centuries, only wealthy and upper-middle-class Americans could afford to tour the country or travel abroad. The costs of train or steamer tickets and carriages, or the recently invented automobile, were prohibitive for most Americans. Although the horseless carriage was invented in the 1890s, early automobiles were considered rich men's toys, and automobile companies targeted wealthy individuals as consumers. In 1901, Ransom E. Olds began to produce a less expensive product, but the cost of his "merry Oldsmobile," as it was dubbed by Tin Pan Alley, was still high for most Americans. Henry Ford put America on wheels. In 1913, he began to mass produce automobiles, aiming his product at middle- and working-class Americans. An early Model T cost $950; by 1925 the cost had fallen to $290, or less than his lowest paid workers made in three months. He also mass marketed his product, building branch assembly plants and establishing dealerships in thousands of towns across the country. With installment buying, most American families could afford to purchase an automobile. In 1920, 10 million automobiles cruised the nation's roads; a decade later the number surpassed 26 million. After the Great Depression and World War II, family ownership of automobiles increased dramatically. In 1948, 54 percent of American families owned at least one automobile; by 1970, that figure had risen to 82 percent. An even more telling measure was the rise in families with two or more automobiles; that percentage rose from three in 1949 to twenty-eight in 1970.

Ford's product virtually mandated the construction of more and better roads. The dust and mud of unpaved roads belonged to the age of horse-drawn carriages, not the century of the combustion engine. Congress passed the Federal Aid Road Act in 1916 to improve rural post roads and distributed the money through state highway departments. In 1926, Connecticut began construction of the Merritt Parkway, the first high-speed, limited-access highway, and other expressways were built around other cities. Some states followed Pennsylvania's 1940 lead and constructed turnpikes that ran the length of their states.

Most American families could now take a Sunday drive in the country, and millions could afford to take an occasional vacation to tour some part of the country. Leisure travel increased significantly after World War II. The return of prosperity, coupled with the end of wartime travel restrictions and gasoline and rubber rationing, ushered in an era of unprecedented travel. Improvements in the country's basic transportation infrastructure contributed to this increased travel. The National System of Interstate and Defense Highways Act of 1956 earmarked $26 billion to build 41,000 (later expanded to 42,500) miles of highways. Although it took longer to complete and was more expensive than anticipated, the interstate highway system influenced the very nature of American cul-

ture and leisure activities. It accelerated the movement of Americans to the suburbs and spawned the development of drive-in theaters, suburban shopping malls, roadside motels, and mobile homes. Attempts to "beautify" highways by removing unsightly billboards and prohibiting littering recognized the central place highways occupied in American life.

Travel and automobiles became an important part of millions of Americans' leisure lives. Middle-class and working-class families drove to the mountains and oceans for vacations. Trips to Atlantic City and the Jersey Shore, the Pennsylvania Poconos, the New York Catskills, the Grand Canyon, Lake Tahoe, Yellowstone Park, or the Pacific Coast became commonplace. Only the poorest Americans could not afford a few such trips. In addition, automobiles occupied a central place in the youth culture that emerged after World War II. Drive-in theaters and restaurants, drag races and customized hot rods, speed and danger—millions of teenage Americans enjoyed some if not all aspects of a leisure culture that revolved around the automobile. Souped-up '57 Chevys and chopped '32 Fords—the classic "street rod"— became part of the teenage experience and were celebrated in the film *American Graffiti* (1973). As a teenage character in *High School Confidential* (1958) commented, "Don't tell me you never rode in a hot rod or had a late date in the balcony?" That film—and many similar ones—suggested that hot-rodding and making-out were part of the democratic youth experience. They were as American as listening to a rock 'n' roll radio station and singing along when "Teen Angel"—a song about a teenage girl killed in a car crash—was played.

The new leisure opportunities opened by the mass production of automobiles and a better highway system were increased by the development of inexpensive air travel. Not only did the airplane allow for faster travel within the United States, economically it unlocked the gates to Europe and Asia for millions of Americans. Although the cost of steamship travel dropped during the 1920s, it was still too expensive for most Americans. And initially, air travel was equally costly. In 1939, when Pan American Airlines began service to Europe, only wealthy Americans could afford the luxury of risking their lives on the four-engine Boeing aircraft. By 1955, however, over one million Americans traveled to Europe, and twice as many went by air as by sea. The number of Americans traveling abroad increased to 5 million in 1970 (only 3 percent of whom traveled by sea) and took another sharp rise during the 1980s. Daniel J. Boorstin observed, "The United States was the first nation in history so many of whose citizens could go so far simply in quest of fun and culture." If in the 1960s air travel was associated with jet setters—men and women who ate breakfast in New York, skied in Aspen in the afternoon, and consumed a late dinner in Los Angeles—by the 1970s air travel had been effectively democratized. Discount fares, group packages, and an aggressive advertising campaign aimed at middle- and lower-middle-class Americans made air travel a common experience. Spending on air travel became so significant that it affected world trade and the balance of payments. Leisure travel became a boom industry, and American and foreign agents competed for travel dollars.

Statistics suggest the democratization of leisure travel. In 1986 over 50 percent of all American adults took at least one trip, and one out of every three trips was for pleasure. Rich Americans traveled more frequently than poor Americans but not significantly more than the middle class. The same year, business receipts for travel exceeded $275 million and the travel industry employed 8.7 million people. In all, Americans took almost 600 million trips of two hundred miles or more. Two hundred million of those trips were for pleasure, and millions more combined business with pleasure. The result is a nation of people with shared experiences. A family vacation at Disneyland or Disney World, a camping trip in the mountains, an airplane flight across six time zones, a night in Paris or London or Rome—millions of Americans can discuss the pleasures and nightmares of such experiences.

### MOVIES: THE DEMOCRATIC ART

Other technologies have also increased these shared experiences and contributed to the democratization of American leisure. Film, radio, music recording, and television have all contributed to the breakdown of regional, religious, ethnic, racial, and class barriers. By providing the country with a shared popular culture—the content that fills leisure hours—they have blurred lines that were clearly drawn before the twentieth century.

The invention of motion pictures was the first important twentieth-century advance in popular culture. The film industry began as a result of a bet. In 1872, Leland Stanford, a California millionaire, bet a friend $25,000 that "at some point in its gallop a race-horse lifts all four of its hooves off the ground" simultaneously. To prove what no person could detect with the naked eye and what was denied by nineteenth-century graphic artists, Stanford hired pho-

tographer Eadweard Muybridge to get photodocumentary evidence. Five years later, Muybridge had the proof Stanford desired. In the process of obtaining that proof, he also refined the technique of series photography that led to the invention of motion pictures. Other inventors followed Muybridge's lead. Étienne-Jules Marley, Hannibal Goodwin, George Eastman, Auguste and Louis Lumière, Oskar Messter, Thomas Armat, William K. L. Dickson, and Thomas Edison all contributed to the development of motion pictures. By the end of the nineteenth century, Edison's Kinetoscope was ready for commercial application. Motion pictures made the transition from inventors' workshops to public "parlors" where they served the country's growing demand for leisure entertainment.

The first commercial movies were shown as part of vaudeville programs or in amusement arcades. They presented slices of reality—waves crashing against the shore, two men engaged in a boxing match, a woman dancing, a man sneezing, a building burning. The emphasis was on the novelty of the invention, not the subject of the entertainment. This soon changed. Movie producers began making films that told a story. Silent narrative films were particularly popular in immigrant neighborhoods. For a nickel a person could enter a nickelodeon and be entertained by a series of short movies. Movies served the entertainment needs of the working class: they were inexpensive, accommodated easily to a busy work schedule, and did not demand a verbal or written understanding of English. And, particularly attractive to the filmmakers, distributors, and exhibitors, the individual nickels added up to a fortune. By 1907, there were five thousand theaters in operation throughout the country.

During the early twentieth century, the film industry shifted from the East Coast to the West Coast and control of the industry switched from a handful of WASP businessmen led by Thomas Edison to a group of primarily Jewish entrepreneurs. The move to the West Coast made sound artistic and commercial sense. California had a better climate for outdoor filming and more varied landscapes, and it was three thousand miles from Edison's Motion Picture Patents Company, the trust that attempted to drive independent filmmakers out of business. The film industry matured and flourished in California. Jewish producers—led by Carl Laemmle, William Fox, Adolph Zukor, Louis B. Mayer, Harry Cohn, Joseph Schenck, Samuel Goldwyn, and the Warner brothers—sought to expand the industry beyond its immigrant, working-class base. They attempted and suc-

Ornate movie house. Crowds line up outside New York's Roxy Theatre, 1930. ARCHIVE PHOTOS

ceeded in making movies that attracted patrons of every class, race, and religion in the country. Under their guidance, film became a democratic entertainment form.

The new producers were motivated by two goals: the desire for quality and the need for respectability. In the pursuit of quality, they experimented and took chances. Instead of adhering to the standard Edison format of short, inexpensively made films, Laemmle and the other independents followed the European lead and made more expensive and longer, feature-length movies. These, they maintained, would appeal more readily to the large middle class. They also introduced the star system, giving actors and actresses on-screen credit and publicizing their careers. Florence Lawrence, previously only known as "the Biograph Girl," became the first named actress in a movie, but more followed as star identification became im-

portant to industry growth. Finally, the new producers brought respectability to their product by surrounding it with opulence and luxury. Movies moved out of storefront arcades and into "movie palaces." S. L. "Roxy" Rothapfel, pioneer of the movie palace, lived by the philosophy, "Don't 'give the people what they want'—give 'em something better." Ornate theaters, uniformed ushers, orchestral music, trappings of royalty for the price of admission—Rothapfel turned movie houses into pleasure domes fit for Kublai Khan. Patrons of all classes came to Roxy's theaters, saw the splendor that he brought to movies, and were conquered by the pure sensuality of the experience. Never was leisure more democratic than when Roxy greeted a packed theater with his standard opening line, "Hello, everybody." The greeting embraced all classes, religions, races, and ethnic groups.

By the 1920s, the movie industry dominated American popular culture and leisure. The industry itself matured into an integrated vertical monopoly. The leading studios—Paramount, Metro-Goldwyn-Mayer, Warner Brothers, RKO (Radio-Keith-Orpheum), and Twentieth Century Fox—controlled production, distribution, and exhibition. Studio leaders decided what shaped the dreams that Americans consumed. Each year during the studio era, the eight leading studios—the five vertically integrated studios and United Artists, Columbia, and Universal—made several hundred movies. Almost all of the pictures were pitched toward a broad general audience. Until the late 1940s and 1950s, none of the leading executives gave much thought to the idea of segmented audiences, and before the 1960s, there was no rating code to warn viewers about the content of movies. Movies constituted a democratic art. They reflected the goals, yearnings, fears, and frustrations of their audience. And that audience responded. In 1939, for example, the Big Eight studios produced 376 pictures, and movie box office receipts exceeded $673 million. Each week of the year between 52 million and 55 million people paid to watch at least one movie. In the United States, there were 15,115 movie theaters, one for every 8,777 Americans and more than the number of banks, department stores, or cigar and cigarette stands. Furthermore, film was one of the largest industries in the country and second only to the cement industry in executive remuneration as a percentage of total volume of sales. Nor was 1939 an unusual year. In terms of the number of Americans going to the movies each week and corporate profits, there were better years during the 1920s and World War II.

Americans paid millions of dollars and spent countless of their leisure hours sitting in darkened theaters to learn that all was right with the world. To be sure, many of Hollywood's movies had messages. Film historians have located strong messages in Progressive-era social films, comedies of the 1920s, early 1930s gangster films, and the problem films of the mid-1940s. But even in these message films, Hollywood never spoke with a single voice. During the early twentieth century, as many social films would oppose birth control, socialism, or woman suffrage as support those movements. The majority of films in the first half of the century, however, avoided any social message save faith in the triumph of truth, justice, and the gentle heart. The comedies of Charlie Chaplin and Frank Capra praised the American everyman, the man—or woman—who stood for democratic values and defended the de-fenseless. As Robert Sklar noted in his history of American movies, "Even satirical movies like the screwball comedies, or the socially aware films like *The Grapes of Wrath,* were carefully constructed to stay well within the bounds of essential American cultural and political myths. . . . Hollywood's contribution to American culture was essentially one of affirmation."

To ensure this affirmation and to fend off demands for censorship, studio executives agreed to follow the Motion Picture Production Code. The code set down what subjects could be treated and how. For example, no brutal killings could be presented in detail and no illegal drug trafficking could ever be shown; adultery could never be justified and any reference to sexual perversion, white slavery, miscegenation, or venereal diseases was forbidden; religions could not be ridiculed or the flag treated disrespectfully. The ultimate design of the code was to shield the industry from controversy and keep movies broadly democratic.

In the late 1940s, the movie industry began to veer from its democratic tradition. Several factors contributed to this change. Charges of communism and several well-publicized HUAC investigations shook the industry. At the same time, the Supreme Court in the *Paramount* decision (1948) decreed that the vertically integrated studios were monopolistic and had to divest themselves of their theater chains and stop all booking and pricing arrangements that discouraged free trade. Finally, television emerged as a rival for Hollywood's audience. The movie industry responded in a number of ways—some sound, some foolish—but in terms of its democratic form, the most significant was the decision to make films for special interest groups. This move toward segmented markets—preteen, teenage, adult, and special interests within each of those markets—ended the era of films designed for a broad audience. Although the film industry still provides leisure entertainment for millions of Americans, it is no longer the country's primary entertainment choice.

## EMPIRE OF THE AIR

While going to the movies emerged as the most popular public entertainment form in the 1920s and 1930s, a new technology began to dominate private and family entertainment. Radio originated in the desire to communicate with other people in far-off places. It began with the experiments of Guglielmo Marconi and the development of wireless telegraphy. Early radio operators—mostly middle-class, white, urban boys and men—communicated with each other, transmitting and receiving messages encoded in Morse code. These hams formed an unofficial fraternity of tinkers. They set up a national relay system and read magazines aimed at ham operators. To belong to the fraternity—this empire of the air—one had to master Morse code and the technology of the craft.

Commercial radio began in 1919, when Frank Conrad, a ham operator and Westinghouse engineer, used an Audion—a vacuum tube that allowed for the transmission of works and music—to broadcast music from a transmitter in his Pittsburgh garage. He broadcast piano and saxophone solos, and they proved so popular that Westinghouse decided to start the first commercial station, KDKA in Pittsburgh. The company hoped to profit not from the broadcasts themselves but from the demand for receivers created by the broadcasts. KDKA demonstrated the public potential of the new technology when it broadcast the election returns of the 1920 presidential race between Warren G. Harding and James M. Cox. Harding won, and so did radio.

Radio, like automobiles, boomed during the 1920s. By 1929 there were more than eight hundred independent radio stations, and the marketing of radios helped to fuel the economic growth of the 1920s. Soon, wired networks began to dominate the new industry. The National Broadcasting Company (NBC) began operation in 1926 and the Columbia Broadcasting System (CBS) commenced business the following year. They made profits not through the sale of radios (although NBC's parent company RCA did) but by the sale of commercial air time.

Commercial radio was the most democratic of mediums. Although the consumer had little control over programming, everyone could listen to the same programming. If a person lived in a house with electricity, for the price of a radio one could hear symphonies, operas, vaudeville routines, plays, and a wide range of other programming. Entertainment that had previously been only within the grasp of the affluent was now suddenly within the reach of almost every American. Critics complained about the commercials and the rigid structure of broadcasts, dubbing radio a vast wasteland. But their criticism usually revealed an underlying class bias. The important point was that radio did entertain millions of Americans, not just occasionally but nightly. The finest popular talent—Eddie Cantor, Burns and Allen, Jack Benny, George Jessel, Fred Allen, Ed Wynn, Orson Welles, Bing Crosby, and many more—performed on radio. Popular shows like *The Rise of the Goldbergs*

and *Fibber McGee and Molly* contained the same messages as the films made in Hollywood. They normally celebrated America and the human spirit, confirming, not challenging, basic institutions.

Any class, political, or economic criticism on radio was particularly muted. Even more than films, censors carefully regulated the content of radio shows. The goal of commercial broadcasting was first and foremost to sell products. Seldom was the message of the entertainment allowed to interfere with this primary purpose. Susan Smulyan commented in an essay about radio, "Comedians smoothly made the transition from gently spoofing the Great Depression to gently spoofing World War II, always mindful that the federal government regulated radio broadcasting and that major corporations paid the bills." And if network writers and producers ever forgot who regulated and who paid, network executives were always on hand to remind them.

During its most popular phase, from the early 1930s to the mid-1940s, radio's major accomplishments were providing entertainment for millions of Americans and rendering a generally uniform interpretation of world events. This second accomplishment was most clear in radio's coverage of the events leading to World War II. After H. V. Kaltenborn's radio coverage of the 1938 Munich crisis, where he made 102 broadcasts in eighteen days and dramatically presented the events that moved Europe to the edge of war, radio became most Americans' leading source of news. Kaltenborn and the other radio commentators were never neutral. As David Holbrook Culbert noted in his study of the commentators, "After August 1938 . . . none of the most popular commentators opposed the foreign policy objectives of Franklin D. Roosevelt. . . . If some newspapers continued to attack the President, the same was not true for the major medium that provided information about the rest of the world for the average person. . . . Radio commentators played a major role in creating a climate of opinion favorable to an interventionist foreign policy."

In the late 1940s and early 1950s, radio began to decline as the primary private and family form of leisure entertainment. Its popularity sank as television's rose. Like radio, television could present entertainment, news, and educational programs, and it had the added advantage of pictures. Radio could not compete with television, and it did not try. Instead, it shifted directions, phasing out dramatic programs and returning to the broadcasts of Conrad's garage: music. Taking advantage of transistor technology, prerecording, and new markets, radio transformed itself into a primarily music medium. And, like television, it adopted a segmented market strategy, pitching programs for special interest groups rather than a large general audience.

The most important of the new markets were blacks, white southerners, and teenagers. The invention of the transistor in 1947 allowed for the manufacture of small, portable, inexpensive radios that were affordable for virtually every American. The transistor took the radio out of the family parlor or living room and placed it into the hands of the individual listener. Radio stations, freed from having to cater to a mass audience, programmed music that appealed to more select groups. The growth in the popularity of country-and-western music as well as rhythm-and-blues and rock 'n' roll music originated in this change in radio programming policy. Programming on the FM spectrum increased the opportunities for special-interest stations. With its better fidelity and fewer commercial demands, FM stations were free to program more experimental music.

By the 1970s and 1980s, special interests dominated radio programming. Not only individual shows but entire stations revolved around market segments. Some stations played only classic rock or easy listening; others were devoted to sports or talk shows. In some respects, the call-in talk shows of the 1990s have fostered a revival of the original fascination of radio: communication over distance. For hosts Larry King and Rush Limbaugh the telephone acts as a mini-transmitter for their audience. The result—if not the technology—is similar to radio's ham years.

## THE TUBE

Although both radio and movies have altered American culture and filled millions of leisure hours, neither has had the impact of television. In the late twentieth century, the average American spends one-quarter of his or her life watching television. One study suggested that in most American homes television is the first electrical appliance turned on in the morning and the last one turned off at night. Television dominates the information most Americans receive and their interpretation of that information. Mr. Gardner, a character in Jerzy Kosinski's satirical novel *Being There* (1970), when asked what he did in life, spoke for many Americans: "I watch." For him, leisure meant watching and watching was being.

Television emerged from the NBC laboratories of the 1920s and 1930s. Several experimental telecasts were made in 1936, but the possibilities of television were first apparent to the general public in 1939,

when NBC telecast the opening ceremonies of the World's Fair as well as a college baseball game. After World War II, commercial television blossomed. Following the examples of film and radio, television attempted to satisfy the demands of a large mass audience that included all ages, classes, races, and religious groups.

Initially, however, television was largely an urban entertainment medium. Almost every television set was located in a city—particularly New York and several other eastern cities—and many of them were in bars. Programming was designed for this urban market. Sports shows—particularly boxing and wrestling—were popular in bars and such programs as the *Texaco Star Theater* with Milton Berle and *The Honeymooners* with Jackie Gleason appealed to urban, ethnic viewers. Berle, television's first star, never played well in middle America. After the FCC lifted its 1948–1952 freeze on licensing new stations and television expanded across the country, Berle's ratings dropped.

But television grew even without "Mr. Television." When the freeze ended, the nation had 108 operating stations located in 63 cities. By 1965, there were 572 stations in the United States. In 1950, only 9 percent of all American homes had a television set. The figure rose to 55.7 percent in 1955, 78.6 percent in 1957, 85.9 percent in 1959, and 92.8 percent in 1966. As a point of comparison, in 1966 only 80 percent of American households had a telephone. The emergence and expansion of television, commented Leo Rosten, was a "marvelous, exciting, depressing, promising, wonderful, deplorable miracle." And as the numbers indicate, it was a democratic experience.

Television has altered leisure patterns in America by privatizing leisure. Even more than radio, television kept people at home. Before television, Americans looked outside their homes for leisure recreation. They ate at restaurants and went on picnics, they drank in saloons and attended sports events, they went to concerts, movies, and plays. After television, TV dinners and Budweiser provided the food and drink and television took care of the rest. For millions of Americans moving to the suburbs, television provided the single most important leisure outlet. Television offered everything the inner city did without the traffic and crime. Television carried public events to private spaces.

The importance of television to Americans was underscored in a 1992 study. By that date, the average American devoted forty-one hours each week to leisure activity. Watching television consumed one-third of those leisure hours during workdays and one-fourth during weekends. No other leisure activity was even close to television. Socializing, a distant second, consumed less than 10 percent of Americans' leisure time; reading less than 6 percent; shopping less than less than 3 percent; and outdoor rest and recreation about 2.5 percent. Other studies indicate that the dominance of television is on the increase. In 1965, Americans on the average watched television eleven hours each week; in 1985, they spent fifteen hours in front on their sets.

But recent technology has begun to alter the democratic nature of television. Cable television and the rise of independent superstations has broken down the monopoly of the three major networks. The major networks' audience share had fallen from 90 percent in 1970 to 70 percent in 1990. The result is special-interest television. Similar to radio, television broadcasters have begun to specialize. ESPN programs only sports, MTV only music, and CNN only news. Some stations appeal to younger viewers, others to older viewers. A few stations program for the educated, more for the uneducated. Critics complain, as they did about radio and the movie industry, about the nature of television programming, but as David Karp commented in 1966, "TV is not an art form or a culture channel: it is an advertising medium." Its purpose is to push products and make money for manufacturers. "Obviously," Karp continued, "if their object is to make money—and they do make money—it seems a bit churlish and un-American of people who watch television to complain that their shows are lousy. They are not supposed to be any good. They are supposed to make money."

## THE TRIUMPH OF DEMOCRACY

More than any other factors, technology and mass production have democratized leisure. Coupled with more leisure time and greater disposable incomes, most Americans can now afford to do what only wealthy Americans could afford a hundred years ago. A century ago, most Americans could not afford to dine out regularly. In the 1990s, McDonald's—started in 1955 by Ray Kroc—and other fast food chains offered inexpensive, nourishing, and instantly available food. Critics charge that McDonald's hardly offers a luxurious dining experience of the sort that the wealthy can obtain at one of America's finest restaurants, and they are correct. But McDonald's is inexpensive, clean, and democratic—patrons carry their own food to their tables and clear their tables

when they are finished. The same is true with reading and owning books. The paperback revolution that began in 1939 with the publication of the first ten Pocket Books has changed the publishing business, an industry that once catered almost exclusively to the affluent. The typical reader in the second half of the twentieth century is more likely to purchase a book in an airport, department store, drugstore, or grocery store than a bookstore.

The hallmark of modern leisure is choice. Although income is still an important factor, racial, ethnic, and religious barriers have largely crumbled. The choice of leisure is also a defining process. In the nineteenth century, German Americans joined Turnverine, Czech Americans joined Sokols, Irish Americans joined Gaelic Leagues. They defined themselves by their leisure choices. Participating in body building, jogging, golf, or jazzercise similarly helps to define an individual, but that definition does not have an ethnic, religious, or racial component. Once leisure was tied to communities based on ethnic origins or class. Now leisure is anchored to subcommunities based on choice.

In addition, modern leisure is increasingly tied to consumption. This, of course, is a natural consequence of the importance of leisure in the lives of Americans. Surveys of leisure behavior indicated two telling developments in the 1990s. For the first time, Americans' leisure week was longer than their work week, and they commented that their leisure time was more important to them than their work time. Many reported that they worked to earn enough money to support their leisure habits. Some of those habits, such as watching television, are relatively inexpensive. Others, such as shopping, traveling for vacations, eating out regularly at expensive restaurants, and attending theater and concert performances could be more expensive. But around almost every leisure activity a thriving business has grown. The progressive movement of women into the work force has contributed to this development, creating families with more disposable income and greater willingness to dispose of that income on eating at restaurants, traveling to Europe, and buying the latest machines that promise slimmer waists, firmer stomachs, and better lives. Even children have become part of the consumer binge; television shows, toys, games, amusement parks, and camps cater to their tastes and interests.

One final trend has become clear. More than ever, leisure has become privatized. During the century, the heart of leisure life has moved from city to suburb, from suburb to home, from home to individual. The social critic Louise Bergheim has noted the "pluggy" phenomenon. Televisions, radio headsets, computers and modems, and video games have created individualized, privatized leisure worlds. Although the consumption of leisure has become more democratic during the twentieth century, the forms of that leisure have become more individualized.

It remains to be seen whether this burrowing tendency will continue or whether excessive individualism will eventually give way to group concerns. For most of the past, leisure and sociability have been inseparable. Shared pleasures have been the norm, rooted undoubtedly in a psychological need for fellowship. In recent years the growth of the cruise-ship industry, spas and resorts, and meditation centers suggest that total privatization of leisure is an unfulfilling pursuit.

SEE ALSO Consumption (volume III); Mass Media and Popular Culture (in this volume); Sports (in this volume).

## BIBLIOGRAPHY

A number of books provide a useful introduction to aspects of leisure and entertainment in America; they include James L. Baughman, *The Republic of Mass Culture: Journalism, Filmmaking, and Broadcasting in America since 1941* (1992); Daniel J. Boorstin, *The Americans: The Democratic Experience* (1973); and Mary Cayton, Elliott Gorn, and Peter Williams, *The Encyclopedia of American Social History* (1993). Two useful texts are Michael Chubb and Holly R. Chubb, *One Third of Our Time: An Introduction to Recreation Behavior and Resources* (1981); and John R. Kelly, *Leisure* (1990). Witold Rybczynski, *Waiting for the Weekend* (1991), looks at the subject across time and cultures and is wonderfully insightful.

Recently film history has begun to receive the attention that it deserves. Among the best studies are Tino Balio, ed., *The American Film Industry* (1976); Andrew Bergamn, *We're in the Money: Depression America and Its Films* (1971); Eileen Bowser, *The Transformation of Cinema: 1907–1915* (1990); Kevin Brownlow, *Behind the Mask of Innocence: Sex, Violence, Prejudice, Crime: Films and Social Conscience in the Silent Era* (1990); David A. Cook, *A History of Narrative Film* (1981); Neal Gabler, *An Empire of Their Own: How the Jews Invented Hollywood* (1988); Garth Jowett, *Film: The Democratic Art* (1976); Richard Koszarski, An Evening's Entertainment: The Age of the Silent Feature Picture, 1915–1928 (1990); Charles Musser, *The Emergence of the Cinema: The American Screen to 1907* (1991); Robert B. Ray, *A Certain Tendency of the Hollywood Cinema, 1930–1980* (1985); and Robert Sklar, *Movie-Made America: A Social History of American Film* (1975).

Radio and television have received less attention than film, but that too is beginning to change. Useful treatments of radio include Erik Barnouw's two volumes in *A History of Broadcasting in the United States*, volume I, *The Tower in Babel, to 1933* (1966), and volume 2, *The Golden Web, 1933–1952* (1968); David Holbrook Culbert, *News for Everyman: Radio and Foreign Affairs in Thirties America* (1976); Susan J. Douglas, *Inventing American Broadcasting, 1899–1922* (1987); Tom Lewis, *Empire of the Air: The Men Who Made Radio* (1991); J. Fred MacDonald, *Don't Touch That Dial! Radio Programming in American Life, 1920–1960* (1979); and Arthur Frank Wertheim, *Radio Comedy* (1979). Television's complex history is explored in Erik Barnouw's volume in *A History of Broadcasting in the United States,* volume 3, *The Image Empire,* (1970), and Barnouw, *Tube of Plenty: The Evolution of American Television* (1990); Leo Bogart, *The Age of Television: A Study of Viewing Habits and the Impact of Television on American Life* (1972); George Comstock, *The Evolution of American Television* (1989); Jeff Greenfield, *Television: The First Fifty Years* (1977); David Marc, *Demographic Vistas: Television in American Culture* (1984); J. Fred MacDonald, *One Nation under Television: The Rise and Decline of Network TV* (1990); and Benjamin G. Rader, *In Its Own Image: How Television Has Transformed Sports* (1984).

All aspects of popular culture and leisure activities have begun to interest historians, from sports and reading to eating and drinking. Some indication of the range of subjects under consideration is suggested in Max Boas and Steve Chain, *Big Mac: The Unauthorized Story of McDonald's* (1976); Richard Butsch, ed., *For Fun and Profit: The Transformation of Leisure into Consumption* (1990); John G. Cawelti, *Adventure, Mystery, and Romance: Formula Stories as Art and Popular Culture* (1976); Kenneth C. Davis, *Two-Bit Culture:*

*The Paperbacking of America* (1984); Foster Rae Dulles, *America Learns to Play: A History of Popular Recreation, 1607–1940* (1940); Allen Guttmann, *From Ritual to Record: The Nature of Modern Sports* (1978); Russell Nye, *The Unembarrassed Muse: The Popular Arts in America* (1970); Benjamin G. Rader, *American Sports: From the Age of Folk Games to the Age of Spectators* (1990); Steven A. Riess, *City Games: The Evolution of American Urban Society and the Rise of Sports* (1989); and Roy Rosenzweig, *Eight Hours for What We Will: Workers and Leisure in an Industrial City, 1870–1920* (1983).

# SPORTS

*Peter Levine*

Sport today is an ever-present part of daily life. Popular sports heroes not only adorn our morning cereal boxes, but appear on billboards, in newspapers and magazines, and on television selling everything from running shoes to automobiles. Cable networks provide 24-hour sports programming, supplementing the deluge of golf, tennis, basketball, baseball, football, and even the luge provided by the major television networks. Everything from Australian football to the America's Cup is available without ever having to leave the comfort of our own homes. For those with more exotic tastes, creative programmers even have manufactured the likes of *American Gladiators,* athletic contests of strength and endurance that pit well-developed men and women in quest of fame and fortune against "professional" warriors. And for Americans with discretionary income who live in large metropolitan areas deemed prosperous enough by marketing executives to financially support a professional sports franchise, or in towns with universities that field their own array of mens' and womens' sports teams, there are ample possibilities to take in the action live, either in outdoor stadiums or in state-of-the-art domed structures sophisticated enough to provide climate-controlled comfort and protection from the elements, as well as real grass.

Passive spectatorship parallels equally expansive opportunities for participation. Be it organized competition or informal activity, millions of Americans engage daily in one form of athletic endeavor or another. Aerobics, ultra marathons, three-on-three basketball tournaments, swimming, golf, tennis, and innumerable recreational sports—each with its own magazine, equipment, and instructional guide—provide opportunities for health and good fun.

What at times appears as a national preoccupation with sport—witness professional football's Super Bowl extravaganza, which annually attracts tens of millions of television watchers in the United States and abroad—is in fact a relatively recent phenomenon. Not until well into the 1870s did anything approaching mass spectator sport appear in the United States. And even these early attempts at mounting baseball as "America's national game" and first professional team sport pale in comparison to later versions. Simply put, sport today is a significant cultural, social, economic, and, at times, even political, institution in American life. How did this transformation come about and what does it reveal about American life and culture?

## TURN-OF-THE-CENTURY PRECEDENTS

Writing on the eve of the Civil War, Thomas Wentworth Higginson—minister, literary confidant of Emily Dickinson, abolitionist, and supporter of John Brown—declared in an essay, "Saints and Their Bodies," that "physical health . . . a necessary condition of all permanent success," was of "stupendous importance" to "the American people . . . because it is the only attribute of power in which they are losing ground":

> Guaranty us against physical degeneracy, and we can risk all other perils—financial crisis, Slavery, Romanism, Mormonism, Border Ruffians, and New York assassins. . . . Guaranty us health and Mrs. Stowe cannot frighten us with all the prophecies of Dred; but when her sister Catherine informs us that in all the vast female acquaintance of the Beecher family there are not a dozen healthy women, we confess ourselves a little tempted to despair of the republic.

National physical torpor was not the only reason Higginson might have despaired about his country's future in 1858. But his belief that the United States had the resources to become "a nation of athletes," balancing his assessment of American physical disability, appeared justified by 1900. Whether measured by the bicycling craze of the 1890s, the growth of organized, professional baseball, the rise of college football, the birth of the country club, renewed interest in boxing, the organized play movement or the emergence of the sporting-goods industry, the last quarter of the nineteenth century witnessed a popular explosion of sport.

This new enthusiasm resulted from a confluence of factors that included Higginson's belief that athleticism did more than simply provide personal pleasure. His advice to Emily Dickinson that lifting weights might improve her poetry was only one manifestation of a firm belief shared by many Americans that productive social gain would be served by being physically fit. Buttressed by the popularity of Social Darwinist thought that extolled the survival of the fittest and advocated racial purity while justifying the increasing division of wealth between social classes, it took on added importance for middle- and upper-class white Americans who began to wonder, by the turn of the century, whether the official close of the frontier as testing-ground for American character and virility threatened their preeminence. Even their own success, measured by material comfort, opulent homes, and a sedentary urban lifestyle, appeared as a potential sign of decay and "overcivilization." The arrival of millions of eastern and southern European immigrants, who brought their own customs and values to the large cities where they worked in factories, and increasingly displayed their displeasure with the harsh demands of industrial capitalism by participating in violent strikes and protests, only heightened concerns about social crisis and race dilution. Sport, both as a new frontier for preserving American character and as a way of "Americanizing" new immigrants, provided one avenue of regeneration and social control.

Intellectual justification for sport—be it Theodore Roosevelt's praise of the "strenuous life," calls for American "Muscular Christians," or more popular manifestations echoed in the adolescent fiction of Gilbert Patten's Frank Merriwell stories—involved the belief that individualism and the savage instinct inherent in all men could be channeled into socially productive activity that would assimilate unwashed immigrants, shape American character, and produce a new generation of leadership. While it is a critical component of the emergence of modern sport and an essential precursor of the place and role of sports heroes in American culture, sport's spiritual potential is not sufficient explanation for its growing popularity and peculiarly modern shape during the last quarter of the nineteenth century. Aware of new urban markets and the potential for profit in the promotion of sport, enterprising capitalists actively persuaded Americans to join in as spectators and participants in a wide range of sporting activities that they creatively organized and designed.

The rise of professional baseball and the promotion of the sport as "America's national game" best exemplifies the coming together of these concerns. Organized versions of baseball appeared in the United States as early as the 1830s, particularly among white, middle-class, urban men who played the game for fun, prestige, and to boost the image of their cities as attractive places to live and work. Lasting popular and professional versions of the game, however, awaited the formation of the National League in 1876. The National League established the game as a rational, business enterprise, centered in large urban markets and played under formal rules. It also created clear controls by management over who could play and under what terms, including the reserve rule that gave the team a player originally signed with exclusive rights to sign or trade him, salary caps, and even unwritten agreements about the exclusion of blacks. As baseball's first two-hundred-game winner and as captain, manager, and principal owner of the Chicago White Stockings, baseball's most successful team in the 1880s, A. G. Spalding, more than any other person, rationalized and organized the game into a mass spectator sport controlled by owners and promoted as both respectable entertainment and a shaper of American values. He did so by serving as the key architect and enforcer of league policy, establishing agreements with competing professional leagues in hopes of guaranteeing monopoly control of the game and by putting down a players' revolt against the reserve rule in 1890 known as the Brotherhood War. Through it all—be it by fabricating the myth that Abner Doubleday invented baseball as America's "immaculate conception" in Cooperstown, New York, in 1839, by taking American baseball players on a world tour in 1888–1889, or by running for the United States Senate on his credentials as a baseball man—Spalding extolled the virtues of the game in nurturing American character. Whether talking to boys who came from his own midwestern Protestant stock or addressing Jewish immigrant children on New York's Lower East Side at play days sponsored by the Playground Association of America, Spalding, as he put it in his *America's National Game*, alphabetically declaimed that baseball was "the exponent of American Courage, Confidence, Combativeness; American Dash, Discipline, Determination; American Energy, Eagerness, Enthusiasm; American Pluck, Persistency, Performance; American Spirit, Sagacity, Success; American Vim, Vigor, Virility."

Organized play activists and settlement house workers who consciously offered baseball and other sports to immigrants as a way of teaching them to be Americans provided another impetus to sport's acceptance as a significant part of American culture. Spalding, however, was not a social reformer. First and foremost he was an aggressive capitalist out to enhance his own fortune who recognized that it was good business to promote sport in terms of its social promise. He employed the same energy and purpose in founding A. G. Spalding and Brothers, a sporting-goods firm established in 1876 with the help of his brother and an $800 loan from their mother. Armed with a logo of a large baseball over the door and a motto on A. G.'s desk that declared "Everything is possible to him who dares," they transformed the company into a multimillion dollar business in less than two decades, dominating a new industry that they were instrumental in creating.

Spalding's contributions to organized, professional baseball, the emergence of a new consumer industry, and the acceptance of sport as a socially beneficial activity, underline important trends that were to mark the growing importance of sport in the twentieth century. But it is clear that these developments hardly depended on one man or even solely on capitalists or social reformers. Physical educators and skilled athletes, sensing new opportunities for careers as coaches, teachers, and performers, made their own contributions. Women physical educators, for instance, like Senda Berenson, who popularized basketball for women and served as the head of physical education at Smith College for many years, helped forge a whole new career for women out of this new interest in sport. And a particular historical context that demanded new ways of organizing human activity encouraged all these groups that, in promotion of their particular and at times overlapping interests, emphasized rational organization, control, and the importance of professional experts to solve the problems of an increasingly unfamiliar and complex world.

Also critical to sport's emergence as a significant part of American life was the way in which Americans, often living in cities and distinguished by class, race, and gender, embraced and shaped their participation in the new range of sporting activities offered to them at the turn of the century.

Wealthy white Anglo-Saxon Protestant Americans, always on the lookout for ways to distinguish themselves from the mass of people below them and spurred by intellectuals and reformers who bemoaned their lack of physical strength and their imminent decline, bought up land on the outskirts of large cities and built America's first country clubs.

The first club, Boston's Brookline, opened in 1882, with facilities for polo, racing, and the hunt. By 1900 every large American city boasted similar facilities for the urban elite, a boom that continued apace through the 1920s.

Typical was one New York club, built on 205 acres on Long Island Sound that boasted a forty-room stone mansion. Appointed with furnishings from the Italian Renaissance period and remodeled to serve as a clubhouse, it featured a thirty-foot hallway leading to a "distinctive dining hall," adjoining tea and breakfast rooms, a smoking room, a billiard room, and a library, "sumptuous bachelor suites on the upper floors," as well as seven sun-parlors overlooking 32 acres of flower gardens. Replete with opulent clubhouses, golf courses, tennis courts, and hunting and fishing grounds, these exclusive domains of the white, Gentile rich were off-limits to those of lesser means, as well as to blacks and other ethnic and religious minorities regardless of wealth.

Although lauded as a "safety-valve for an overworked Nation" and capable of fostering a new generation of virile American leaders, the country club primarily served to divide the rich from the masses of Americans by opulent displays of self-indulgence, including participation in sport and social activities that by time and price were off-limits to any but the elite. Eschewing sports like baseball and bicycling, which they identified as middle- and lower-class attractions, they sailed on their yachts, hunted fox from automobiles on private estates, or summered at Saratoga Springs or Newport. Engaging in purposeless leisure, the rich aptly provided evidence for Thorstein Veblen and other social critics who took such signs of conspicuous consumption as sure signs of social decay. Whether Veblen was correct or not, and even though the sports of the wealthy were clearly out of the reach of most Americans, their involvement provided another impetus for general acceptance and participation in sport, especially by suggesting the legitimacy of consumption without purpose beyond pure enjoyment.

There also were other positive, if unintended consequences. Golf, for example, the centerpiece of most country clubs, experienced a growing popularity in the United States. By 1917, 472 golf courses had been built in the United States, mostly in the Northeast. Although catering primarily to the wealthiest classes, there were increasing numbers of courses open to business and professional men, as well as some public courses open to all classes of society.

More important, the country club movement encouraged the participation of women in sport,

Del Monte, California, Country Club, early twentieth century. PRINTS AND PHOTOGRAPHS DIVISION, LIBRARY OF CONGRESS

even if limited by class, race, and by activity consistent with prevailing Victorian sexual attitudes. Participating among themselves as individuals or as part of ladies' auxiliaries, the wives and daughters of America's wealthiest men also played tennis and golf at country clubs. Although at first encumbered by floor-length skirts and bustles, women's interest in these sports complemented the introduction of physical education as part of the regular curriculum of colleges and universities that catered to educating the daughters of the elite.

Encouraged to see sport differently than men—not as activity that prepared them for the rigors of the public sphere of business and politics but as preparation for the private world of domesticity and femininity—some women nevertheless viewed their participation as nothing short of a revolution. Writing in *Munsey's Magazine* in 1901, Ann O'Hagan proclaimed that "the athletic girl" who played tennis, golfed, and even rowed, challenged notions of the frail, physically weak female while promoting women's health, less restrictive clothing, and even the psychological well-being of women. When O'Hagan spoke of a revolution, not unexpectedly she ignored

the fact that her optimism concerned only white, wealthy women like herself and did not attempt to break the boundaries of gender discrimination that limited women's opportunities, not only in sport but also in virtually every other area of American life.

Nor did her views go unchallenged. Women physical educators at elite women's colleges, while fully supportive of female athletic participation, argued against competitive athletics of any sort for fear that the aggression and physical violence associated with the will to win might destroy woman's feminine nature. In the early 1920s they lobbied to limit women's participation in Olympic competition on these grounds. Although working-class women participated in a wide variety of competitive sports sponsored by the Amateur Athletic Union in these years, eventually producing such outstanding athletes as 1932 Olympic track-and-field champion Mildred "Babe" Didrikson, the achievements of such athletes were often ridiculed as freakish aberrations accomplished by less than feminine women. Even sports enthusiasts less radical than O'Hagan, who suggested that participation in sport would improve the childbearing capabilities of women, were challenged

Women's sports in the early twentieth century. Vassar College field hockey team, c. 1915.
Photography by E. L. Wolven. PRINTS AND PHOTOGRAPHS DIVISION, LIBRARY OF CONGRESS

by others who conjured up more ominous consequences of such behavior. A 1921 *New York Times* editorial, "College Sport and Motherhood," for example, chastised women for frittering away energy on frivolous involvement in sport. "Every girl," the *Times* opined, "has a large store of vital and nervous energy upon which to draw in the great crisis of motherhood. If the foolish virgin uses up this deposit in daily expenditures on the hockey field or tennis court, then she is left bankrupt in her great crisis and her children have to pay the bill." Two years later, the House of Representatives pigeonholed in committee an equal rights amendment to the Constitution, where it remained for the next half-century—a motion defended by one congressman who argued against notions of equality between the sexes on the grounds that "there is more difference between a male and female than between a horse chestnut and a chestnut horse." It would remain for other generations of women, operating in far different social and political circumstances, to challenge such views effectively.

Also contributing to the popularity and expansion of sport were the way in which millions of new immigrants to the United States responded to increased opportunities for involvement. When John O'Sullivan, the "Boston strong boy," won the heavyweight championship of the world in 1882, he endeared himself not only to Irish working-class immigrants but also to other American newcomers. Abraham Cahan's fictional "Yekl," a Russian Jewish immigrant, proudly marked his identification as an American by his infatuation with Sullivan and "Gentleman" Jim Corbett, the man who took the title away from the great John L. in 1892. Indeed, the success and bravado of Sullivan, the country's first national sports hero, who liked to introduce himself by boasting that he could "lick any son of a bitch alive" and who came from beginnings no better than other immigrants, affirmed their own American possibilities. Where else were the values of competition and individual effort so transparently important? What other kind of activity more easily provided opportunities for immigrants to participate as American consumers by purchasing a ticket to a boxing match or a baseball game, to learn about something identified in their minds as distinctly American, to take pride in the American triumphs of their own kind, or to root for a local boxing champion or home team, an act that underlined the freedom of choice that made American life seem unique?

Certainly social reformers who encouraged the children of immigrants to participate in boxing, baseball, and other sports organized through such agencies as YMCAs, public school athletic leagues, settlement houses, or playgrounds sponsored by the Playground Association of America hoped for such results, albeit in a more controlled environment. Sporting activities supervised by trained social workers would Americanize their wards, teaching them to become competent, cooperative members of society. As one Chicago settlement house worker put it, "we consider baseball one of the best means of teaching our boys American ideas and ideals."

There is no question that immigrant children flocked to settlement houses, public parks, and YMCAs, taking advantage of the opportunities offered to participate in baseball and other games in numbers large enough to encourage the growth, popularity, and persistence of sport. The expansion of such urban facilities, only rarely in neighborhoods that contained large numbers of blacks, as well as statistical counts kept by proud social workers, testify to this fact. Clearly some children did become more American through their participation. Most impressive, however, was the initiative and control immigrants themselves took in shaping these sporting opportunities to their own purpose. Coupled with the informality of the streets, these experiences contributed to their passionate interest in American sport and their development as Americans precisely because they did so on their own terms. Remembering his childhood days on New York's Lower East Side, George Burns, the legendary comedian and entertainer, recalls in his autobiography, *The Third Time Around*, that his "playground was the middle of Rivington Street." Along with his friends, Burns

> only played games that needed very little equipment, games like kick-the-can, hopscotch, hide and go seek, and follow the leader. When we played baseball we used a broom handle and a rubber ball. A manhole cover was home plate, a fire hydrant was first base, second base was a lamppost and Mr. Gitletz, who used to bring a kitchen chair down to watch us play, was third base. One time I slid into Mr. Gitletz; he caught the ball and tagged me out.

Not every immigrant boy was fortunate to have a Mr. Gitletz on his block, but scattered throughout the reminiscences of immigrant childhoods is ample

testimony to the sense of freedom, opportunity and control that participation in sports provided. Be it in New York, Chicago, Detroit, or any city with large immigrant populations, the children of immigrants, in the streets and at playgrounds and YMCAs, organized their own baseball and basketball teams and competed as independent amateur teams against neighborhood teams as well as in organized leagues. At times they became so proficient in their sport that they cashed in their success, charging admission for their games and even traveling beyond the confines of their ethnic neighborhoods to take on all comers.

In their love of American sport and play, by dint of their own enthusiasm and inventiveness, the children of immigrants learned about American values, American capitalism, and even the possibilities of success that had often eluded their first-generation parents. Their interest not only encouraged sport's growing popularity but also established it as a part of everyday life that at times served as a battleground between parents and children about how to live in America. European parents struggling to make a living in an unfamiliar economic world with little time for or attachment to American games or ways often found it difficult to understand their children's infatuation with baseball or basketball. Time might be better spent, they argued, doing homework, earning money, learning the catechism, or preparing for bar mitzvah.

Even some of these parents, however, could understand how the public athletic triumphs of their own kind confirmed both ethnic identities and American status, a point not lost on sports entrepreneurs. Boxing promoters, for example, creatively pitched fights between boxers in terms of their racial and ethnic connections, hoping to attract paying customers who came out as much to see a good fight as to vigorously cheer their own kind to victory. Anxious to bolster the New York Giants' sagging baseball fortunes as they fought a losing war at the gate in the 1920s against Babe Ruth and the New York Yankees, John McGraw sought out good Jewish ballplayers who might attract Jewish fans to the Polo Grounds. His efforts were no different from the Yankees' attempt to sell "Poosh 'Em Up Tony" Lazzeri as an Italian hero to New York's large Italian population or attempts in Cincinnati or Saint Louis to attract German audiences to the ballpark by advertising their club in German-language newspapers. The success of these endeavors varied—the Giants' "Rabbi of Swat" Mose Solomon lasted only two games in 1923, while Andy Cohen became a hero to Jewish immigrants in the Bronx five years later—yet the very

College football in the 1920s. Stanford faces the University of California, 8 April 1928. Photograph by Waters and Hainlin. PRINTS AND PHOTOGRAPHS DIVISION, LIBRARY OF CONGRESS

effort to cash in on ethnic attachments suggests another way in which immigrant audiences contributed to making sport an integral part of American culture.

## THE 1920s: THE GOLDEN AGE OF SPORT

For most contemporary observers, by the 1920s, sport was an important part of American life both as participatory activity for millions of Americans and as part of a growing national entertainment culture. The sportswriters Grantland Rice, Paul Gallico, Damon Runyan, and Ring Lardner, who declared the decade "the golden age of American sports," could offer abundant evidence to justify their claims.

College football, which had begun in the nineteenth century as a sport for elite youth, organized and controlled by students and later defended as a strenuous sport that would produce "muscular Christians," became big-time business and popular spectator sport open to an increasing number of youth attending schools throughout the land. In 1914 alone,

450 colleges, 6,000 secondary schools and 15,000 other teams involving over 150,000 players participated in organized versions of the game. Led by full-time, well-paid coaches like Amos Alonzo Stagg, Walter Camp, and Fielding "Hurry-Up" Yost, the University of Chicago, Yale, Michigan, and other institutions built highly successful programs that attracted alumni financial support considered crucial to building large universities. Between 1921 and 1930 attendance at college games doubled and gate receipts tripled. Both private and public universities built new, immense concrete stadiums to accommodate their fans. In 1920 only one college stadium held 70,000 people. The number increased to seven by 1930.

Inherent in this expansion and growth was an important shift in attitudes about sport that also marked other aspects of American life. Begun as a sport that emphasized social purpose, by the 1920s football's character-building possibilities had been firmly supplanted by its commercial potential, fueled in large measure by the desire of a consumer-oriented public eager simply to enjoy the ways in which they spent their leisure time. For the game itself, the result in many instances, according to a 1929 Carnegie Commission report on intercollegiate athletics, was a corruption of amateurism. The emphasis on winning at all costs in order to attract alumni financial support as well as paying customers encouraged colleges to illegally pay athletes to compete, accept students to play football who otherwise could not have met admissions standards, and to engage in a whole range of activities that called into question the integrity of higher education.

For the nation at large, it was one of many signs that marked the culmination of a dramatic shift in American culture—from a time dominated by a belief in the virtues of a rural society, Victorian morality, and the Protestant work ethic to a new urban age that encouraged Americans to enjoy an orgy of self-indulgence—all made possible by the abundant material riches of a modern industrial world. Continued urban growth that produced new markets for consumer goods, a communications revolution that included the radio and increased coverage of sports in the nation's newspapers, and aggressive advertising that advised people on how to enjoy their time and money, encouraged new attitudes about leisure and consumption. Americans now were urged to enjoy themselves for their own sake—be it at the ball park, at the movies, at amusement parks like New York's Coney Island, or even by taking a car ride in a Model T Ford. This transformation from a producer to a consumer society gave less attention to moral or social purpose, placing emphasis instead on the simple enjoyment obtained in the consumption of goods and activities that provided pleasure.

College football's appeal as spectator sport was hardly the only indicator of the explosion of sport in the 1920s. According to U.S. Department of Commerce figures, in 1929 alone, Americans spent $3.4 million on tennis equipment and $17 million on golf. In 1927 104,000 people crowded into Chicago's Soldier Field and paid $2.6 million to watch Jack Dempsey fail to regain the heavyweight championship of the world from Jim Tunney. Over 50 million listeners tuned into the fight, carried by seventy-three radio stations on the NBC network, the same one that for the first time that same year began national broadcasts of major league baseball's World Series. Overcoming the infamous "Black Sox" scandal of 1919, in which several players on the Chicago White Sox, with the help of gamblers and gangsters, fixed the 1919 World Series and allowed the underdog Cincinnati Red Stockings to win, major-league baseball averaged over 10 million paying customers

George Herman "Babe" Ruth. PRINTS AND PHOTOGRAPHS DIVISION, LIBRARY OF CONGRESS

a year throughout the decade. Although the National Hockey League, the National Football League, and the American Basketball League came nowhere close to attracting such fan support, the very emergence of these professional leagues provides still another indication of sport's growing importance.

Babe Ruth's status as a different kind of sports hero symbolized the emergence of a new American consumer culture and sport's place in it. Unlike fictional and real sports heroes of the past whose athletic skill provided evidence of their moral fitness and Christian values, Ruth, the son of a tavern keeper and his wife, who spent much of his childhood in a Baltimore orphanage, delighted an American audience with his prodigious feats both on and off the ball field. The Babe's numerous and mighty home runs—60 in 1927, 40 or more in eleven seasons, and 714 over the course of his career—ushered in a new era of power baseball that made the New York Yankees the game's dominant team in the 1920s. Known as well for his other quantifiable achievements—a love of fast automobiles and an insatiable appetite for food, women, drink, and gambling—the "Sultan of Swat" personified a culture that encouraged Americans to believe that it was possible and permissible to partake of a new world of affluence and plenty. By 1927, Ruth earned a salary of $70,000, far more than any other major leaguer and even American presidents. Three years later, when told that his salary was higher than President Hoover's, he responded by reminding reporters that "I had a better year than he did." As one sportswriter put it, Ruth was the "uncrowned king of the diamond, the master figure of baseball, the big noise in the biggest game on earth." In a society fascinated with things that could be measured and counted, Ruth was a natural attraction. The fact that he succeeded even as he broke the rules and seemingly rose from rags to riches by dint of his own individual effort and talent also made him appealing to Americans who found the complexity and organization of a modern industrial world stifling. Not surprisingly, like another hero of the twenties, Charles Lindbergh, Ruth was often depicted as a throwback to a less complicated time when the exceptional individual mattered. As one sportswriter put it, Ruth was a "superman" who "throws science itself to the winds and hews out a rough path for himself by the sheer weight of his unequalled talents."

Ruth's success certainly had much to do with the regeneration of baseball as "America's national game" after the infamous Black Sox scandal. Also important, however, were the efforts of baseball capitalists who took steps to formalize control of markets and labor in the hopes of maximizing their profits. Often more successful than their counterparts in other sports and in other sectors of the economy, professional baseball's control over its own house established important precedents that were to govern the operation of professional sport over the next half-century.

Between 1913 and 1915, the new Federal League attempted to lure National and American League players to their clubs by promising long-term contracts and by doing away with the reserve rule. Major-league baseball went to court to protect its monopoly control over the game. The New York State supreme court ruled that baseball was not subject to antitrust laws because "as complete a monopoly . . . as any monopoly can be made . . . baseball is an amusement, a sport, a game . . . not a commodity or an article of merchandise." Judge Kenesaw Mountain Landis,

in U.S. District Court in 1915, offered similar sentiments and then helped work out an agreement that ended the Federal League's challenge in exchange for monetary compensation paid to its club owners by the major leagues. Six years later, in the aftermath of the Black Sox scandal, Landis became the first commissioner of baseball, with dictatorial powers to clean up the sport and protect its financial promise. His efforts to do so without interference were enhanced by a decision of the United States Supreme Court in 1922 that reaffirmed the owners' monopoly control of the game.

The successful efforts of baseball owners to establish monopoly control over their sport in many ways were no different than the efforts of capitalists in other industries to rationalize their business operations, seek stable markets, regulate competition, and control their labor force. Prior to World War II, capitalists in other professional sports such as basketball and football had less success and also less incentive to pursue such goals. The National Football League remained a small-scale operation compared to major-league baseball, which was really the only truly national team game in these years. Prior to the advent of the National Basketball Association in 1949, a variety of such regional professional leagues as the Eastern League, the National Basketball League, and the American Basketball League existed by hiring players on a game-by-game basis at a time when players often suited up in the same season for several different teams. Not until another marked expansion in the sports world's economy, this time made possible by the emergence of television, did other sports expand.

## THE BLACK EXPERIENCE, 1900–1950

Increased opportunities for both participation and spectatorship certainly marked sport's full emergence as a significant way in which Americans spent their leisure time during the first quarter of the twentieth century. Even though class and gender distinctions affected certain individual choices, an increasing number of Americans took advantage of those opportunities as they eagerly embraced a new ethic that encouraged them to enjoy the fruits of a modern industrial society. Black Americans, too, found sport attractive. Their experiences, critically limited by racism and discrimination, offer their own important perspective on the place of sport in American society during the first half of the twentieth century.

In 1875, to the delight of thousands of white residents of Louisville, Kentucky, a horse named Aris-

Jack Johnson (*right*) and Stanley Ketchel before their 16 October 1909 world heavyweight bout. Johnson won in twelve rounds. ARCHIVE PHOTOS/AMERICAN STOCK

tides raced to victory in the first Kentucky Derby, ridden by a black jockey named Oliver Lewis. Fourteen of the fifteen jockeys in the race were black. Over the next fifteen years another black jockey, Isaac Murphy, rode three mounts to victory in the Derby. In 1884, the same year Murphy won the Kentucky Derby, Moses Fleetwood Walker became the first black man to play in baseball's major leagues. In 1900, Marshall Taylor, a black cyclist, repeated his 1899 accomplishment as professional world champion. A decade later, in Reno, Nevada, on 4 July 1910, Jack Johnson, who in 1908 in Australia became the first black man to win the heavyweight boxing championship of the world, successfully defended it on home soil by annihilating "white hope" Jim Jeffries in fifteen rounds. By 1894, however, blacks were forced out of major league baseball, not to return until 1947. Soon after his victory over Jeffries, Jack Johnson fled the United States, harassed by government officials and a white America appalled that a black man was heavyweight champion of the

world. Indeed, despite some important exceptions, for the most part the twentieth-century black experience in sport prior to World War II paralleled the larger experience of blacks in American society. Patterns of racism deeply imbedded within the fabric of American society, reinforced in 1896 by the United Supreme Court's *Plessy* v. *Ferguson* decision legitimizing segregation, guaranteed limited opportunity for African Americans. Barred from full access to the white world of American sport, nevertheless they took an active interest in sport both as spectators and participants, creating opportunities for themselves that provided their own sense of enjoyment and pride.

Black involvement in professional baseball aptly illustrates these tendencies. Denied the chance to prove themselves in the major leagues, black ballplayers sought opportunities elsewhere. Some organized barnstorming teams and traveled throughout the country, playing each other and all comers. Especially prominent were the Cuban Giants, the first salaried

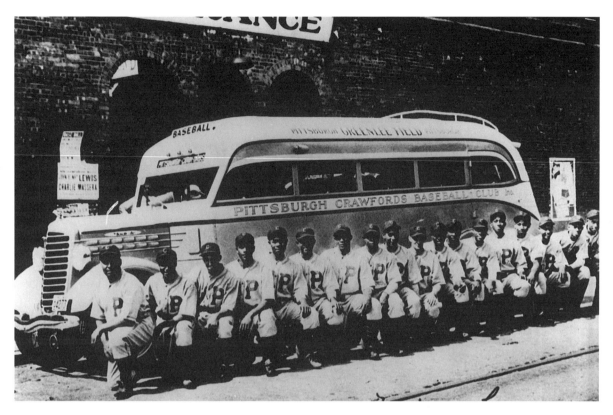

Pittsburgh Crawfords, 1935 National Negro League champions. The team included five Hall of Fame members: Oscar Charleston, Judy Johnson, James "Cool Papa" Bell, Josh Gibson, and Leroy "Satchel" Paige. PHOTOGRAPHS AND PRINTS DIVISION, SCHOMBURG CENTER FOR RESEARCH IN BLACK CULTURE, NEW YORK PUBLIC LIBRARY, ASTOR, LENNOX, AND TILDEN FOUNDATIONS

black professional team, who in 1887 played an exhibition game with the Detroit Tigers, the National League champions. Several times in the 1920s, there were even attempts to organize black professional leagues that failed because of weak financial support and poor organization. In 1933, however, thanks to the efforts of black entrepreneurs and gamblers such as Rube Foster and Gus Greenlee, as well as white entrepreneur Abe Saperstein, who also owned the well-known Harlem Globetrotters basketball team, the National Negro League (NNL) was formed. Franchised in cities with large black populations, the NNL brought quality baseball to tens of thousands of loyal black followers for almost two decades. The league's annual East-West game annually attracted 50,000 fans to Chicago's Comiskey Park. Dominated by stars like Cool Papa Bell, Buck Leonard, Josh Gibson, and the legendary Satchel Paige, NNL teams not only played each other but also continued their barnstorming efforts, including successful efforts

against white major-league ballplayers. Although never provided full equality in the world of professional baseball, nevertheless they recognized that their lives were generally better than that of most blacks living in the United States.

Black involvement in other organized team sport, for the most part, reflected similar patterns. All-black professional basketball teams like the Harlem Rens and the Harlem Globetrotters, denied admission into white leagues, barnstormed around the country, playing each other as well as white professional and college teams. Occasionally, exceptional black athletes, such as Rutgers's Paul Robeson and Columbia's George Gregory, played for integrated college teams. Robeson, who went on to greater fame as a singer, actor, and black activist, also was an All-American footballer at his alma mater between 1917 and 1919. And Jackie Robinson, who was to break baseball's color line in 1947, lettered in three sports at UCLA in the early 1940s. For the most part, however, both in the college and professional ranks, black athletes rarely were given the chance to compete on an equal footing with whites.

Important exceptions, especially in the area of individual sports, while demonstrating continued black interest in sport, only confirm the inherent racism within American society that denied full equality and opportunity to a whole race of people. Jack Johnson's ring dominance in the early 1900s, for example, evoked both black pride and vitriolic white response. At a time of increasing segregation and limited opportunity in an openly racist society, Johnson's triumphs gave blacks a measure of revenge, even as they realistically assessed their situation in the United States. One poem by an unknown North Carolina black writer, commenting on Johnson's victory over Jim Jeffries put it this way:

The Yankees hold the play,
The White man pulls the trigger;
But it makes no difference what the white man
    say,
The world champion's still a nigger.

Papa Jack's fistic power, his flamboyant lifestyle, and his publicized affairs with white women that flaunted white standards of black behavior and appeared as arrogant threats to white supremacy, were dealt with accordingly. Determined to destroy him as a symbol of black pride and resistance, government officials confronted Johnson with a variety of charges, including falsified sexual misconduct accusations under the Mann Act, which made it a crime to transport a woman other than one's wife across state lines for the purpose of having sexual intercourse. Convicted by an all-white jury in 1913 and sentenced to a jail term, Johnson fled the country. In 1915 he fought for the title once again, this time against Jess Willard in Cuba. Willard knocked Johnson out in the 26th round, part of a deal Johnson said he made with the FBI for the right to return to the United States. Whether or not his claim was true, Johnson lost his heavyweight crown, a victim of his bold attempt to live his life as he saw fit rather than as white society sought to determine.

A quarter-century later, Joe Louis's popular reign as the next black heavyweight champion of the world revealed similar circumstances. Louis's promoters understood that the Brown Bomber's talent was not enough to give him a shot at the title. Determined to make him acceptable to white America, they encouraged Louis to dress conservatively, comport himself with politeness, and to stay away from white women. Most importantly, at a time of increasing tensions between the Western democracies and fascist regimes in Italy and Germany, Louis appeared as an American hero, thanks to his smashing first-round knockout of German champion Max Schmeling before 70,000 fans at New York's Yankee Stadium on 22 June 1938. Louis's victory over a man who had defeated him a year earlier and who had been lauded by Adolf Hitler as proof of Aryan supremacy, made him democracy's champion. Ironically, however, America's hero was a black man whose own people were still subject to lynchings, discrimination, and oppression. One southern white newspaper unintentionally captured the paradox. While applauding Schmeling's defeat as proof that the Germans were "stupor Men" rather than "supermen," it reminded Louis that he was still a "colored boy." Black Americans who rallied around Louis as a hero that challenged racist stereotypes and provided hope and pride for their own future, recognized only too well the inequities and violence of a racist America. The poet Maya Angelou, in *I Know Why the Caged Bird Sings*, recalls the affection and pride that her small black community in Stampps, Arkansas, had in Joe Louis. She also remembers that on a night in 1938 when he successfully defended his title, something he did twenty-five times between 1937 and 1949, "it wouldn't do for a Black man and his family to be caught on a lonely country road on a night when Joe Louis had proved that we were the strongest people in the world."

Jesse Owens, another prominent black athlete, also became an American hero in the 1930s, as American nationalism transformed this Olympic gold medalist into an American hero at a time when the Olympic Games, for the first time in the twentieth century, became international extravaganza and political theater. American blacks had competed and succeeded in previous Olympics. In 1932 in Los Angeles, for example, Eddie Tolan won gold medals in the 100- and 200-meter dashes. But none achieved the fame accorded Owens in 1936; the Ohio State track star, son of Alabama sharecroppers, captured gold medals in the 100- and 200-meters, the long jump, and the 400-meter relay, setting world records along the way. Like Louis, Owens became a national symbol of the triumph of American democracy over Nazi fascism. In part, he owed his fame to Adolf Hitler, who spent millions to make the 1936 Berlin games a showcase for German rebirth. Determined to use German Olympic triumphs and a rebuilt Berlin to demonstrate Aryan supremacy, Hitler set precedents in politicizing international athletic competition that were to shape the Olympics and American participation in them down through the 1980s.

Owens, who returned home in triumph to a ticker-tape parade in New York, found his own Olympic moment short-lived. White newspaper reporters who billed him as democracy's answer to theories of Aryan supremacy nevertheless took care to explain to their readers that his speed came naturally or, as Grantland Rice put it, that Owens and other black Olympians who had also done well at the games had "easily, almost lazily, and minus any show of effort . . . turned sport's greatest spectacle into the 'black parade of 1936.' " Stripped of his amateur status because of a dispute with Avery Brundage, the czar of the American Olympic Committee, Owens lost his track-and-field scholarship and was unable to finish college. Unable to find a job in a society still wrought by depression and that always provided limited opportunity for blacks, he made his way by racing horses, trains, and motorcycles.

## AMERICAN SPORT SINCE WORLD WAR II

Owens's Olympic experience is a far cry from that of a more recent generation of American Olympians, the 1992 men's basketball "Dream Team," a predominantly black contingent of millionaire professional basketball players headed by two of the most famous athletes in the world, Michael Jordan and Earvin "Magic" Johnson. Effective corporate spokesmen for everything from basketball shoes to automobiles and even, in the case of Magic Johnson, able to mobilize international attention to the health catastrophe of AIDS, their visibility and success, prominently kept before an incalculably large international television audience, suggests, for some, dramatic improvement in the situation of all black Americans. While that proposition remains to be examined, less in doubt is that the last half-century has produced significant alterations in the American sporting landscape. Black, white, male or female, poor, rich, or middle-class—Americans at the end of the century find more opportunities to participate in sport either as players or spectators than A. G. Spalding would ever have imagined.

Elite athletes and everyday "wannabes," lured by economic rewards and popular commercial images of physical beauty, risk their health and even their lives by using steroids and other drugs to enhance their physical appearance and strength.

These changes are a product of a variety of forces.

Building on precedents established prior to World War II—especially the continued existence of consumerism fueled by aggressive sports capitalists and a corporate America intent on maximizing profit and acceptance of sport as an integral part of a national entertainment culture—the arrival of television and space-age communications technology, feminist and civil rights movements that have challenged traditional racial and gender limits, and even the Cold War, have all played a part in transforming American sport radically over the last half-century, providing a mixed legacy for the twenty-first century.

On 17 May 1939, Bill Stern, the well-known radio sports broadcaster, called the television play-by-play of a college baseball game between Columbia and Princeton played at Columbia's Baker Field in upper Manhattan. At stake was fourth place in the Ivy League. Only 400 television sets, many in the corporate offices of the National Broadcasting Company (NBC), were tuned in to this first televised sportscast. Commenting on its quality, one reporter noted that the players looked like "white flies" and that the "ball was seldom seen except on bunts and other infield plays." Although World War II demanded other priorities, communications executives and the advertising industry recognized the revolutionary possibilities for selling consumer goods to Americans through the cathode tube. Over the last half of the century, this new medium, taking advantage of a successful space program that launched the age of satellite communications and pay-for-play cable television, became a significant part of American culture, with a deep impact on the way in which Americans participate in sport and even on the economic and social landscape in which sport takes place.

Statistics provide an initial measure of television's importance. As late as 1950, most Americans had never seen a live professional baseball game. Only sixteen cities, located mostly in the Northeast and upper Midwest, fielded teams. There was no National Basketball Association (NBA). Altogether, only forty-two franchises in the major professional team sports existed. Although Hank Greenberg became the first baseball player to sign a $100,000 contract, the salaries of most professional athletes were hardly impressive. Many of the players in the American Basketball League, as late as 1948, earned no more than $75 a game.

By 1971 the number of professional baseball, football, basketball, and hockey teams had swollen to 87; by 1980 to 101. Baseball, alone, almost doubled the number of franchises in the space of forty years, the addition of the Colorado Rockies and the Florida Marlins swelling the total to 28 as the 1993 season opened. Five teams now play in California; two even play America's national game in Canada. An increased number of franchises, not surprisingly, encouraged increased attendance in baseball and in other sports as well. In 1989, 56 million people came out to major-league ballparks. Many more watched the game on national television networks and on cable television channels, out in the hinterland and also in cities coast to coast that had been awarded franchises because of the size of their television markets. Similar patterns exist for professional football, which became part of the national sports culture thanks to television. In 1959, the American Football League came into being only because the ABC television network agreed to broadcast its games for a five-year period at a cost of $2 million. The continued existence of the league in the early 1960s, before its eventual merger with the National Football League (NFL), depended on NBC's offer of $42 million over five years after the network had failed to outbid CBS for the rights to televise NFL games. In 1967, some 575,000 fans attended NFL games each week, while over 11 million households watched the games on television. By 1980, that number had increased to 20 million, in a year when an average of twenty-five hours of professional football broadcasting became available each week. In 1992, the Super Bowl attracted over 280 million viewers worldwide, while corporate America paid $835,000 for each thirty seconds of advertising on the telecast.

No less dramatic has been the increase in players' salaries, made possible, in part, by the increasingly lucrative television contracts secured by professional sports leagues. Again, consider baseball as an example. In 1989 the major leagues signed a four-year contract with CBS and ESPN, the twenty-four-hour all-sports television network, which guaranteed major league baseball total revenues of $1.75 billion. This agreement was made possible by the National Sports Broadcasting Act of 1961 that suspended antitrust restrictions so that such negotiations could take place. Leaving aside local broadcasting fees negotiated by individual clubs (beginning in 1991, for example, the New York Mets received $42 million per season from a local cable company), for the first time in the history of the game, major-league franchises earned more money from the broadcast rights to their games than from paid admissions to the ballpark. Not surprisingly, the value of baseball franchises increased as well. In 1962, when the New York Mets began play for the first time, the value of the franchise was put at $2 million. By 1980 its market value was $21 million.

Players' salaries, not without real struggle, have risen accordingly. In 1935, Detroit Tiger Hank Greenberg held out for $18,000. Five years earlier, the entire payroll increase for the New York Giants stood at $30,000. As late as 1975, the average salary for a major-league ballplayer was $46,000. Fifteen years later it stood at $578,930. In 1990, José Canseco of the Oakland Athletics signed a four-year contract worth over $25 million, a figure put to shame within two years when Bobby Bonds inked a $43 million, six-year deal with the San Francisco Giants.

Similar numbers could be generated for other professional team sports, especially the NBA. And there is no question that sports entrepreneurs every bit as creative as A. G. Spalding—people like Roone Arledge of ABC sports and David Stern, the commissioner of the NBA—have played critical roles. Arledge's creation of *Monday Night NFL Football,* his packaging of it as prime-time entertainment managed by the engaging if often exaggerated duo of Don Meredith and Howard Cosell, and his creation of *Wide World of Sports* are but two instances of his impact. Much as Pete Rozelle helped professional football become major entertainment spectacle, so too has David Stern transformed a somewhat unstable business venture into a worldwide success. Clearly, however, it was television that created the possibilities for such men to exploit.

And exploit it they did, affecting every aspect of the games we watch and play and the nature of the relationships between players and owners, fans and franchises—even who plays and where. Determined to maximize advertising dollars and increase exposure, television and sports executives have literally transformed the nature of competition and even the rules and organization of sport to suit television tastes. Professional baseball's decision to create two divisions within each league with intra-league playoffs, first three of five games and later best of seven, to decide pennant winners, for example, was dictated solely to increase the number of games on television in order to maximize commercial possibilities. So too has been the decision to play virtually all playoff games (and an ever-increasing number of regular season games) during prime-time evening television hours. The result has been to extend the season well into autumn, with the summer game often played in forty-degree weather by players with frost on their lips. More than once, major-league sports have rescheduled games to take optimum advantage of television time. Nor have they been remiss in introducing television timeouts, regularly scheduled intermissions to allow advertisers full exposure of their products, regardless of how these breaks might affect the flow and momentum of the game.

Team sports have not been the only ones affected by the power of television and corporate America. The popularity of golf and tennis, both as spectator and participant sports, certainly was influenced by new stars like Arnold Palmer, Jack Nicklaus, Billie Jean King, Jimmy Connors and Bjorn Borg, who attained worldwide acclaim because of their television appearances. Also critical were changes in the rules of both sports dictated by the medium. In 1958, for instance, the Professional Golfers Association changed the format of all its tournaments from match to medal play on the assumption that a television audience would be more apt to watch a format that pitted everyone vying for the top spot over four days rather than head-to-head competition. Similarly, tennis introduced the tie-breaker concept as a means to end long matches that might interfere with television scheduling and the supposed limited attention span of television viewers.

Not surprisingly, with so much at stake, both sports capitalists and professional athletes sought to capture their share of the pie, with dramatic effect on long-standing practices that had traditionally governed professional team sports. Professional sports leagues, ever since the early days of baseball's National League, had always sought to restrict competition, dictate markets, and control their workers. Every team sport, for example, had some version of the reserve rule that restricted an athlete's freedom of movement and bargaining power. Drafts of new players each year that arbitrarily dictated which club a player could negotiate with enhanced capitalists' control over their labor force. League executives also retained authority as to where to place new franchises or move existing ones, conditions, including monetary compensation to the league, under which expansion might take place, and even approval of new owners. Television, as a new source of immense revenue, intensified owners' interests in these concerns.

Population shifts that saw a new flow of people to the Southwest and West Coast encouraged demographic studies of television markets and control of local broadcasting rights that increasingly became critical factors in determining the location of new clubs, the movement of old ones, and even the types of stadium to build. The advent of domed stadiums, beginning with Houston's Astrodome, meant that advertisers could be assured that nature would not interfere with the scheduled broadcast of baseball or football games, and, most importantly, the commercial spots that came with them. Even more so than in the past, when sports entrepreneurs had worked closely, even illegally, with politicians to determine location of franchises, the potential economic benefits that a professional sports franchise might mean for a metropolitan area, in large measure due to the power of television, allowed sports entrepreneurs to parlay their power to obtain lucrative tax benefits and outright subsidies to move or maintain teams in particular locations. In 1977, for example, New York City, already in severe economic crisis, renovated Yankee Stadium to the tune of $100 million in order to satisfy the demands of the New York Yankees, who threatened to follow the NFL's New York Giants to the Jersey suburbs. All this at a time when the ball club paid a token $150,000 in annual rent for use of the stadium while grossing over $14 million through the turnstiles. Also attractive were federal tax laws that permitted creative accountants to depreciate players as the real assets of a ball club, a legal avenue that produced large tax write-offs for sports investors that made owning a professional sports franchise profitable even if the ball club was unsuccessful at the box office or on the field.

The economics of professional sport, dramatically transformed by television, brought a new type of owner to sport—very wealthy individuals and corporations who bought and sold professional sports teams for personal prestige and the bottom line, not because of their knowledge or love of the game. It also brought new challenges by athletes who demanded their fair share. Baseball players had challenged the reserve rule before. In 1885, they organized themselves into the National Brotherhood of Professional Baseball Players to lobby for the repeal of the reserve rule. Five years later, many of them bolted their American Association and National League clubs to join teams in what became known as the Player's League, one in which the reserve rule did not exist and players shared in team profits. This effort failed. In 1970, demanding that he no longer be treated as a slave, Curt Flood, an All-Star outfielder with the Saint Louis Cardinals for twelve years who had been notified by form letter that he had been traded to Philadelphia, went all the way to the Supreme Court to challenge the reserve rule. Although he lost, five years later two pitchers, Andy Messersmith and Dave McNally, with the help of the Major League Professional Baseball Players' Association led by labor negotiator Marvin Miller, who had worked hard to secure players the right of binding arbitration in disputes with management, successfully overturned the reserve rule, ushering in the era of free agency and immense player salaries that spilled into other professional team sports.

Professional sports owners did not give in easily. Throughout the 1970s and 1980s, baseball's establishment attempted to regulate free agency even as the more affluent clubs sought pennants by entering the bidding wars. As players' salaries skyrocketed, fans expressed exasperation and resentment at the millionaire status of even journeymen ballplayers, forgetting perhaps the long history of labor exploitation experienced by professional athletes whose own opportunities to cash in on their exceptional athletic talent was limited by age and injury. Lockouts, strikes, and negotiated settlements—patterns either real or threatened that marked other professional team sports—were all part of the picture, one that at times seemed to reorient sports pages into business columns, with more attention paid to salaries and strikes than to game-winning home runs or last-quarter touchdowns.

Amateur sports have not been immune to television's influence. Both the promise of amateur athletics and its potential for corruption existed long before its invention. We know, for instance, that the popularity of college football in the early part of the twentieth century promised to promote American character and virtue but often encouraged corruption and greed even as it helped build great universities. Some twenty years after the 1929 Carnegie Report noted such problems, a handful of New York city college boys from a free public university, the City College of New York, coached by the legendary Nat Holman, became the only college basketball team to win both the National Invitational Tournament and the National Collegiate Athletic Association (NCAA) men's basketball tournament. Their triumphs were lauded by the university and the press as proof of how young working-class boys who put education first could still triumph on the athletic field. Yet within months, this illusion was shattered on the heels of a point-shaving scandal that involved CCNY players as well as athletes from other schools, including the University of Kentucky. As in 1929, calls for reform resulted in little change, a fact made most evident by a repeat of the 1950–1951 scandal only ten years later, this time involving more players and more schools.

Over the last quarter century, as reported almost daily in our nation's newspapers and magazines, the corruption of intercollegiate athletics, measured by illegal financial inducements to recruit athletes, transcript tampering, bogus courses, academic programs maintained to keep athletes eligible while mocking the very purpose of the university, and the use of steroids and other supposed performance-enhancing drugs that cause permanent physical disability and even death, has escalated more intensely. The tragic death of Len Bias in June 1986, an All-American collegiate basketball player from the University of Maryland, felled by an overdose of cocaine while celebrating his good fortune to have been chosen by the NBA's Boston Celtics as their first-round draft pick, represents only one of many examples of these tendencies. An investigation of the school's basketball program following Bias's death revealed that he had either failed or withdrawn from five classes that spring and that the grade point average for the entire basketball team was barely above a D.

Television did not cause these events, but the huge amounts of money available through network contracts to broadcast men's football and basketball games and the lure of professional careers in a variety of sports made popular by television, encouraged alumni, coaches, and athletes to engage in illegal practices that call into question the compatibility of the purpose of the university and athletics and even threaten human life. In the mid-1980s, for example, the NCAA, signed a four-year contract with ABC and CBS, assigning the networks the right to televise Division I college football games for $280 million. In 1983, UCLA and the University of Michigan earned almost $3 million for participating in the Rose Bowl. And in 1991, Notre Dame became the first school to sign its own independent contract with a network, NBC, giving NBC the exclusive right to televise Notre Dame's home football games for five years in exchange for $32 million.

Aware of these high financial stakes and the opportunity for national attention afforded by television, coaches, who at major basketball and football schools regularly earn more than university presidents let alone professors, urge their young charges to cut corners, stay eligible, build bodies, and risk all for alma mater. As one investigation of the state of big-time college athletics concluded in 1980, "from the moment the student-athlete sets foot on campus, the name of the game is 'majoring in eligibility.' "

The NCAA, first organized in 1905 to reform the violent game of college football, continues as the agency responsible for monitoring intercollegiate athletics—setting and enforcing eligibility requirements and investigating charges of corruption. For the most part, however, its efforts to contain abuses have not been successful. Especially since the advent of television, many of its most visible functions focus on negotiating and managing the increasingly lucrative television contracts that ironically contribute to the problems of intercollegiate athletics today.

Although not all colleges and universities share equally in the abuses of a system that has transformed collegiate amateur sport into big business, the abuses have resulted in a variety of proposals that aim to address them. They range from formally professionalizing college athletes by paying them salaries and postponing their education until their playing days are over to abolishing big-time college sport altogether. The activities of the Knight Commission, a panel of university presidents, who in 1990 and 1991 offered a general blueprint for reform that (among other things) suggested more stringent entrance and exit requirements for college athletes, momentarily influenced the NCAA and individual athletic conferences to reconsider requirements and enforcement procedures. It remains to be seen, however, if this call for change will have any more impact than the cosmetic effects of previous reform efforts. Most likely, without a more fundamental reordering of the social and economic context within which intercollegiate athletics unfolds, it seems naive to hope for a dramatic reversal of behavior.

## RACE AND SPORT

As television raised the stakes and heightened the tensions in both professional and amateur sport, it both encouraged and made visible the increased presence of African Americans and other racial minorities. Although able to compete in integrated international competition in track and field, prior to World War II American blacks primarily participated in intercollegiate sport on a segregated basis and remained virtually excluded from organized professional team sport. Over the last half of the twentieth century, however, the situation changed dramatically. Annual college and professional all-star teams in football, basketball, and baseball are disproportionately dominated by highly paid black athletes. Although hardly as visible behind the scenes in coaching and administrative roles, there is definite movement at every level to increase the number of blacks in such positions. While more white athletes than black serve corporate America as spokespersons, increasingly accomplished black performers and multimillionaires sell Wheaties, Nikes, and Nissans with élan and style.

Television certainly facilitated this increased presence, through its impact on the expansion of sport that demanded new pools of athletic talent and its powerful presence as advertising medium. But black activists both in and out of sportsworld, fully aware of changing historical circumstances, were also critical players in the increased integration of American sport.

Anti-Semitism, racism, and segregation did not end in the 1940s but World War II softened its edges. Jews, Irish, Italians, all Americans—even blacks, albeit in segregated units—were urged to repel fascism and preserve democracy. No less a united effort seemed required to turn back the supposed new menace of communism as it appeared in the late 1940s. Encouraged by federal government policies such as the Fair Employment Practices Act, the desegregation of the armed forces in 1948, and the 1954 Supreme Court decision, *Brown* v. *Board of Education*, that made segregation illegal, civil rights activists, and black and white journalists like Wendell Smith, Heywood Broun, and Shirley Povich, pressed the case for full equality in sport, targeting professional baseball first.

Bombarded by demands to make America's national pastime a fully integrated game, and aware of population shifts that had brought large number of African Americans from the South to eastern and northern cities in search of new jobs, white professional baseball owners were reluctant pioneers in this battle for integration and civil rights. Despite the claims of baseball commissioner Albert "Happy" Chandler, who said of black ballplayers, "if they can fight and die on Okinawa, Guadalcanal [and] in the South Pacific, they can play ball in America," as late as 1946 baseball owners secretly voted by a margin of 15 to 1 to keep their sport segregated. Against the wishes of the baseball establishment, in October 1945, Branch Rickey, principal owner and general manager of the National League's Brooklyn Dodgers, signed Jackie Robinson to a contract with the Montreal Royals, the Dodgers chief farm club. Eighteen months later Robinson opened the 1947 season at first base for the Dodgers, becoming the first black ballplayer to play for a major league professional baseball team in the twentieth century. Counseled by Rickey to turn the other cheek when confronted by the racist tirades of players and fans, Robinson endured much publicized abuse during his rookie season yet managed to play well enough to earn rookie of the year honors and the hearts of many Brooklyn fans, both black and white.

Over the next few seasons, Robinson, along with Don Newcombe, Roy Campanella, Joe Black, Sandy Amoros, Charlie Neal, and Junior Gilliam, transformed the Dodgers into sport's only truly integrated team. Outspoken as ballplayer and activist, Robinson, some have even suggested, encouraged arguments and tactics in the service of integration that became essential parts of an expanding civil rights movement that took shape in the 1950s and blossomed fully in the 1960s. Although certainly Martin Luther King, Jr., Roy Wilkins, and a host of other black and white activists were the critical figures here, Robinson's role as a national symbol of racial pride and American possibility cannot be underestimated. As African American writer Robert Curvin put it, who first saw Robinson play when he was a young child, it was his "courage that thrilled us, inspired us and held us to him even after he had moved on. His spirit had entered the bloodstream of a generation."

Despite these efforts, the sportsworld did not respond with overwhelming enthusiasm to the prospect of integration. Although Bill Veeck brought Larry Doby and other black players to the Cleveland Indians in the late 1940s, as late as 1960 baseball's American League had only six black ballplayers. The Boston Red Sox signed their first black player, Pumpsie Green, in 1959, almost a decade after the Boston Celtics became the first team in the NBA to sign a black ballplayer. By 1973, however, 25 percent of all major league baseball players, 33 percent of NFL regulars, and 54 percent of the NBA's players were black—percentages that have increased as the years have gone by. Similarly, college sport, especially the revenue-producing tickets of football and basketball, underwent similar transformation. Consider the appearance of black-dominated teams by the 1980s at Deep South institutions such as the University of Alabama that no more than twenty years earlier considered using force to keep blacks from their classrooms, let alone their football fields or basketball courts.

Numbers tell only part of the story. Both in football, and most noticeably in basketball, a "black" style of play that emphasized speed, leaping ability, and flamboyant artistry changed the way in which games were played. Nor was a new black presence limited to popular team sports. Although blacks had always excelled in track, individual sports from figure skating to golf have seen the lifting of racial barriers. The courageous and dignified efforts of Althea Gibson and Arthur Ashe even broke down the lily-white establishment of amateur and professional tennis. Even boxing, a sport that always encouraged some degree of integrated participation so long as black participants remained visible in limited ways dictated by whites, experienced change, thanks to the efforts of a young black fighter from Louisville, Kentucky, named Cassius Clay, or as he became known to millions worldwide, Muhammad Ali.

Clay became a national hero in 1960 when he won a boxing gold medal at the Olympics and proudly paraded around the ring waving an American flag. Brashly predicting victory, four years later the young Kentucky boxer, backed by a group of white Louisville businessmen, astonished the boxing world by taking the heavyweight crown from Sonny Liston, another black boxer and a former prison inmate who was not a popular champion. Even more surprising, however, was Clay's announcement immediately after the fight that he had joined the Nation of Islam and changed his name to Cassius X. Several weeks later, it became Muhammad Ali.

Clay's conversion to a religious faith outside Christian tradition with a particular slant that emphasized black superiority and separatism troubled some Americans. His flamboyant lifestyle and penchant for self-assertion reminded many of a black champion of another era, Jack Johnson. Ali's friendship with Malcolm X, his decision in 1967 to refuse to be inducted into the military in the midst of increasing American involvement in Vietnam, and his subsequent status as a hero of the antiwar protest and black nationalist movements in response to losing his heavyweight crown because of his political stance only intensified his significance as a cultural symbol of a society torn apart by the assassinations of Martin Luther King, Malcolm X, John and Robert Kennedy, and Medgar Evers, and the deaths of black and white college students protesting the war and racial intolerance at Jackson State and Kent State.

By the early 1970s, however, growing protest within the United States against American participation in Vietnam encouraged a new appraisal of Ali. Championed throughout his exile by prominent sports journalists such as Howard Cosell and Robert Lipsyte, Ali was allowed to box again. And box he did. Regaining and losing his title several times over the next decade, he became an American hero—the underdog who had fought back and won his right to compete and who in 1980 was appointed by President Jimmy Carter as a special "ambassador of good will" to help convince African nations to boycott the 1980 Moscow Olympics. Honored in 1990 as the most prominent athlete of the last half-century, Ali, long retired from boxing and still suffering from the effects of too many punches and too many fights, celebrated his fiftieth birthday with a two-hour special on national television, showered with birthday wishes from a who's who of American politics and entertainment.

Ali's elevation to national icon, along with the visible success of other black athletes, clearly demonstrates that for the gifted few, segregated barriers to full competition and opportunity in competitive sports have been successfully challenged. But the sports activist and sociologist Harry Edwards, as well as other critics, suggest the prominence of black athletes as highly visible symbols of black success obscures the extent to which American society still denies real opportunity to the large majority of American blacks, especially lower-class residents of neglected, deteriorating, burned-out, drug-infested inner cities. Edwards even argues that a racist, white society consistently reluctant to allow blacks full economic and political freedom channels blacks into sports—an area where black accomplishment does not threaten a dominant white power structure. In 1971, a *Sports Illustrated* editorial offered explicit testimony to his view, asserting that "in recent years sports has opened some very special doors. Every male black child, however he might be discouraged from a career with a Wall Street brokerage firm or other occupational choices, knows he has a sporting chance in baseball, boxing, basketball or track. . . . The black youngster has something real to aspire to when he picks up a bat or dribbles a basketball."

Although not all contemporary critics of American sport would agree with Edwards's charges, most accept the fact that black college students especially, enticed with scholarships to play football and basketball for alma mater as a prelude to the starry life of the professional athlete, in overwhelming numbers are sold a false bill of goods. They find themselves either unprepared for the rigors of college or encouraged to take meaningless educational programs in order to stay eligible. They graduate at far lower rates than comparable groups of white athletes, and in the end are confronted with the sad fact—by one estimate, odds of over 20,000 to 1 for any college athlete dreaming of a career as a professional football or basketball player—of how elusive sport is as a path to a better life. And for those who do make the grade, their opportunities for managerial or administrative positions in sport after their playing days are over, relative to those available to their white counterparts, remain scarce, both implicitly and even explicitly, because of racism.

## WOMEN AND SPORT

This mixed picture reflects larger patterns in the ongoing struggle for racial justice in America. Influenced by similar forces, women's situation in sport also changed dramatically since World War II. Just as the war provided new opportunities for work and hope for African Americans, it also encouraged, indeed, demanded that women take on new roles in society. Between 1940 and 1945 the percentage of women who were part of the American work force increased from 20 to 35 percent. Formerly limited to jobs like teaching, nursing, clerical, and domestic labor defined as consistent with a traditional, gendered construction of women's capabilities and character, women, spurred by the demands of a wartime economy and a depleted male work force, took on a wide variety of jobs in the past defined as men's work. Although hardly a picture of full equality—women were still paid less than men, still asked to fulfill "feminine" responsibilities of raising children and caring for the home even as they built airplanes and battleships, and lost their jobs when the war ended and American men returned home from the battlefields of Europe and the Pacific—new opportunities even appeared briefly for women in the world of sport.

In 1943 Philip Wrigley, the chewing gum king who owned baseball's Chicago Cubs, launched the All-American Girls Professional Baseball League (AAGPBBL), a money-making venture designed as a novelty to keep up public interest in baseball even in the midst of war. Wrigley established franchises in a number of midwestern cities, drawing players from Amateur Athletic Union and industrial league teams. The league lasted for over a decade, peaking in attendance in 1948 at 1 million, all the while providing important opportunities for Sophie Kurys, the league's most valuable player in 1946, and other talented women athletes to earn good money while doing something they loved.

Although they gained entrance into the world of professional sport, just as their counterparts who took up riveters to build airplanes and battleships, women who played in the AAGPBBL found themselves caught in a double-bind. Both to attract fans and to maintain accepted societal distinctions between male and female roles, Wrigley required that all players maintain their feminine image even as they slid into home plate or dove for fly balls in the outfield. Players were required to wear short skirts and make-up when they took the field. Contracts insisted that all players go to charm school before they took up bat and ball, where they would learn how to apply make-up, move like a woman, and even "how to take a call third strike like a lady."

Like women workers in other industries, when

the war ended, so too did the professional baseball careers of these female athletes. For women, in general, however, even as they returned to their traditional roles as mothers and homemakers and limited "domestic" employment, both the new pride they took in their abilities and the resentment many felt about being deprived of continued opportunity to fulfill new expectations contributed to a revival of feminism in the late 1950s and early 1960s that was to have a revolutionary impact on women's involvement in sport.

Urged on by Betty Friedan and other feminists who demanded women insist on total equality and the choice to lead their lives as they saw fit, and encouraged by the activities and beliefs of civil rights activists and a growing movement protesting the American war in Vietnam, women employed a variety of tactics and arguments to change peoples' attitudes and behavior in their own battle for equal rights. The fact that organized sport had traditionally been seen as a visible bastion of male superiority and dichotomous sex roles for men and women made it an especially attractive arena for feminists who wanted to challenge traditional attitudes and practices.

Billie Jean King became a symbol of these developments by leading the demand for full equality in the world of professional women's tennis. A U.S. Open and Wimbledon champion several times over, she was a critical figure in demanding equal prize money for women. Her threats to lead a boycott of women professionals at these prestigious tournaments was responsible for producing the huge increases in prize money that brought women to full parity with male professionals. She also was instrumental in establishing the Virginia Slims as a separate professional circuit for women in 1971. Although spurred by her love of the game and her desire to maximize her personal talent, King understood and accepted her importance as a feminist. In one instance she combined both her political interests and opportunity for personal profit in a televised "Battle of Sexes" tennis match against a middle-aged former tennis great, Bobby Riggs, in 1973 before 30,000 spectators at the Houston Astrodome and a television audience of 40 million people. More staged entertainment than competitive tennis, this much publicized match that attracted large amounts of spectator interest and advertising dollars, provided symbolic importance of the gains women were making in sportsworld.

Between 1960 and 1990, a virtual revolution in women's sports took place. Be it in Olympic mara-

thons, ten-kilometer road races, gymnastics, golf, basketball, or aerobics, both in organized competition and recreational activity, women enjoyed far greater opportunity and participation in American sport than ever before. Sports pages listed with equal attention the huge earnings of professional golf and tennis players of both sexes. Mary Lou Retton's Olympic gold medals in gymnastics in 1984 received as much coverage as any other Olympic competition by American television. More significantly, between 1970 and 1977 alone, the number of girls involved in organized high school sports programs rose from 300,000 to 2 million. The NCAA regularly holds national championships in seventeen women's sports, encouraging competition and an emphasis on winning far different from the "play day" mentality and the intramural emphasis on women's colleges athletic programs that were dominant during the first half of the twentieth century. Although financial support for women's programs at American universities and colleges still lags behind male programs, in 1977 alone 460 colleges awarded over 10,000 athletic scholarships with a total value of $7 million to aspiring female athletes. At the 1992 Winter Olympics, of the eleven medals won by American athletes, women won nine, including all five of the golds, despite the fact that only 55 of the 161 athletes the United States sent to Albertville, France were female. According to a 1992 survey research report, in the space of a quarter-century, sports has become a respectable and legitimate activity for women rather than something unfeminine that should be avoided. Indeed, women posed in athletic garb of one kind or another—be they celebrity athletes like Chris Evert and Mary Lou Retton or models decked out for the occasion—selling everything from Wheaties to Tampax to fast automobiles, symbolize both the changing image of women and corporate capitalism's awareness of their potential as advertising tools.

A critical factor in these developments was the enactment by the United States Congress of the Educational Amendments Act of 1972. A specific provision of this bill, usually referred to as Title IX, said that "no person, on the basis of sex, should be excluded from participation in any educational program or activity receiving federal financial assistance." Vague in description and redefined by government agencies and the federal courts over the years, Title IX barred sex discrimination at institutions receiving federal aid and forced male-dominated athletic departments to take seriously the demands of women for full equality.

Although real progress has been made, gender

equity had not yet been reached by the early 1990s. At the intercollegiate level, according to NCAA statistics, as late as 1992 men received 70 percent of athletic scholarship money available; men's sports programs receive 77 percent of the operating funds and 83 percent of the recruiting dollars. Despite an initial surge in the hiring of women as coaches and administrators of women's athletic programs after the enactment of Title IX, progress thereafter diminished. In 1972 more than 90 percent of the people in these positions were women. By 1990, less than 50 percent of the coaches and less than 20 percent of the administrators were women. Although not clear from the evidence, it is reasonable to suggest that the renewed emphasis on winning, and a desire of male-dominated athletic departments to have their own kind in command of new programs for women that might threaten the dominance and financial superiority of male programs, encouraged this shift.

Nor have changes in the socialization of gender roles and in the kinds of opportunities open for girls and women in American society demanded by the feminist movement been fully achieved. An explosion in recreational sport since World War II that increasingly encourages women as equal participants also sells specialized shoes and clothing for everything from aerobics to basketball in ways that reinforce images of women as male sex objects and cater, almost exclusively, to the affluent, upwardly mobile, young, white, heterosexual woman. Yet it is clear that not even those women who succeed at the highest level of athletic competition are viable symbols of social change. Paul Wylie, who won a silver medal in figure skating at the 1992 Olympics, much in the spirit of Harry Edwards's critique of the black experience in sport, suggested to a *Sports Illustrated* reporter that the comparative success of American female athletes over their male counterparts at the 1992 Winter Olympics had to do with the fact that men are more ambivalent about pursuing their sport because it might mean delaying other opportunities for careers in the business world or elsewhere. Women athletes, he insists, "don't have that ambivalence. They see athletics as one of the few places they have a chance to be Number One, where they are judged purely on merit, and their sex matters not in the least."

Women physical educators like Donna Lopiano, the director of intercollegiate athletics for women at the University of Texas, appointed in 1992 as the executive director of the Women's Sports Foundation, continue the struggle for full equality, just as women in other walks of life fight the same battle.

Sport, both as a battleground itself and as symbol of a larger struggle, continues to hold a prominent place in one of the most important social developments of the twentieth century.

## POLITICS AND SPORT

The same visibility sport offered women intent on making their case for the creation of a more equitable society—testimony itself to sport's significant place in twentieth-century American culture—also made it increasingly important as a vehicle of political protest and celebration. Adolf Hitler's attempt to make the 1936 Olympic Games, held in Berlin, a showcase for Aryan supremacy and a new Germany, set precedents that both the United States and other countries have employed throughout the four decades following World War II in their efforts to win the ideological battles of the Cold War.

Building on the celebration of capitalism and democracy inherent in the way in which Americans applauded the victories of Joe Louis and Jesse Owens against German opponents in the 1930s, Americans have been encouraged to view the victories of their athletes in international competition, especially in the Summer Olympics, as evidence of the superiority of their system and values. The efforts of the Soviet Union and of East Germany consciously to promote and support its athletes in this spirit and the desire of television and advertising executives to cash in on American athletic successes by transforming individual athletic victories into national medal counts encouraged these tendencies.

In one way or another, virtually every Olympic Games since Berlin has been subject to this kind of political manipulation and confrontation. The 1952 Helsinki Olympics marked the first of successive Olympics where the ideological conflict between communism and capitalism spilled over into international athletic competition. The United States, to be sure, never undertook the development of state-sponsored athletic programs on the scale of East Germany or the Soviet Union. But after it finished third in the medal count at the 1976 Montreal Summer Games, behind the Soviet Union and East Germany, a Presidential Commission on Olympic Sports urged the United States government and corporate America to increase financial support for American athletes in order to combat the way in which other nations used sporting success as a tool of international politics. One year later the Amateur Sports Act allocated $16 million to help Americans prepare for the 1980 Games. Even the end of the Cold War did not mean the disappearance of sport's use as a vehicle of celebration. In the midst of the Persian Gulf War of 1992, when the United States led a multinational assault on Saddam Hussein and Iraq, it became de rigueur for American collegiate basketball teams to wear American flag patches on their uniform to show their support for the war effort.

International athletic competition has also served as a vehicle of protest. In 1936, for example, many Americans openly questioned whether American athletes should participate in the Berlin Olympics—games organized by a fascist country with professed racist policies that included open hatred and overt discrimination against Jews and other "non-Aryan" people. Although attempts to organize an American boycott of the games as a protest against these policies failed, other efforts to exploit the Olympics to similar purpose followed. In 1968 Harry Edwards tried to organize a boycott by American black athletes of the 1968 Mexico City games, both in sympathy with a threat by African nations not to participate unless South Africa was excluded because of its apartheid policies and in protest against the discrimination faced by blacks within American society. Although the boycott was not successful, two black Americans, John Carlos and Tommy Smith, gold and silver medalists in the 200-meter dash, used the occasion of their victory to protest the condition of black America by raising their fists in the black power salute on the victory stand. Their individual acts of defiance, punished by the American Olympic committee with immediate expulsion from the games, underscored the way in which both black and white American athletes, in the turbulence of the civil rights, feminist, and anti-Vietnam War activities of the 1960s, used sporting opportunities to publicly demonstrate their discontent with the state of American society and politics. Twelve years later, with a different target in mind, President Jimmy Carter demanded that American athletes boycott the 1980 Moscow Olympics in protest against the Soviet invasion of Afghanistan. More broadly, some social critics even blame the emphasis on winning and the kind of character developed by serious attention to athletic success as contributing to increased violence and drug abuse, not only in sportsworld but throughout American society.

Sports may exhibit these tendencies, just as it may reflect significant social developments such as civil rights or feminism. It is also clear, however, that to blame or praise sport for producing certain values or encouraging certain kinds of behavior puts a misplaced emphasis on its importance. While events in sports certainly have had both a symbolic and actual influence on larger issues, racism, sexism, and the development of a win-at-all-cost mentality have roots far deeper and in far more significant areas of American life than sports. While social attitudes and values are affected by who manages organized athletic programs in elementary schools and colleges, who coaches Little League teams, or the athletes young people choose as their heroes, too much attention to sport as a shaper of American character or as a focal point of social concerns detracts attention from more basic consideration of both the promise and problems of American life on the eve of the twenty-first century.

It also obscures something else—something that often is forgotten in the expansion of sport in the twentieth century and the attempt to keep track of the variety of forces that impelled it—the sheer joy of participation. In daily lives that provide little opportunity for freedom and excitement or for moments of physical excellence, the simple act of participation—now more available and acceptable for most Americans than at any other time in their history—should not be forgotten. Although not an American, Roger Bannister, the first person to run a mile in under four minutes, offers his own testimony and provides fitting closure to this brief examination of twentieth-century American sport. Standing on a beach in his native England, awed by the power of the waves and the stillness and beauty of the moment, the adolescent Englishman begins to run:

> I was startled, and frightened, by the tremendous excitement that so few steps could create. I glanced around uneasily to see if anyone was watching. A few more steps—self-consciously now and firmly gripping the original excitement. The earth seemed almost to move with me. I was running now, and a fresh, new rhythm entered my body. No longer conscious of my movement I discovered a new unity with nature. I had found a new source of power and beauty, a source I never dreamt existed. . . . However strenuous our work, sport brings more pleasure than some easier relaxation. It brings a joy, freedom and challenge which cannot be found elsewhere.

See Also Mass Media and Popular Culture; Leisure and Recreation (both in this volume).

# BIBLIOGRAPHY

Two useful general accounts of the history of American sport are Allen Guttmann, *A Whole New Ball Game: An Interpretation of American Sports* (1988); and Peter Levine, *American Sport, A Documentary History* (1989). Donald Mrozek, *Sport and American Mentality, 1880–1910* (1983), provides an important overview of the emergence of modern sport in the late nineteenth century.

Peter Levine, *A. G. Spalding and the Rise of Baseball: The Promise of American Sport* (1985), explains the development of early professional baseball and Spalding's role in the process. Solid multivolume general histories of the game are Harold Seymour, *Baseball* (1960, 1971); and David Q. Voigt, *American Baseball* (1966, 1970, 1986). Eliot Asinof, *Eight Men Out* (1979), nicely recounts the story of the 1919 Black Sox scandal, while the most insightful biography of Babe Ruth is Ken Sobol, *Babe Ruth and the American Dream* (1976). Andrew Zimbalist, *Baseball and Billions* (1992), makes clear the impact of big business on America's national game. For discussion of labor-management conflict in the game, see Lee Lowenfish and Tony Lupien, *The Imperfect Diamond* (1980).

Steven Riess, *City Games: The Evolution of American Urban Society and the Rise of Sports* (1989), offers a comprehensive analysis of the connections between urban settings and sport. Warren Susman, *Culture and History: The Transformation of American Society in the 20th Century* (1984), imaginatively imparts a sense of the new consumer culture.

On the connection between immigrants and sport, see Elliott Gorn, *The Manly Art: Bare Knuckle Prize Fighting in America* (1986); and Peter Levine, *Ellis Island to Ebbets Field: Sport and the American Jewish Experience* (1992).

William Baker, *Jesse Owens: An American Life* (1986), is a first-rate biography of Owens that puts his life in historical context. Harry Edwards, *The Revolt of the Black Athlete* (1968), offers an activist's account of black protest and proposals for change. Thomas Hauser, *Muhammad Ali: His Life and Times* (1991), based heavily on interviews with Ali and his contemporaries, best explains the importance of Ali. Randy Roberts, *Papa Jack: Jack Johnson and the Era of White Hopes* (1983), is a solid biography of Johnson that explains his importance as a symbol of race relations in the United States in the early 1900s. Robert Peterson, *Only the Ball Was White* (1973), offers a good history of the Negro leagues. Jules Tygiel, *Baseball's Great Experiment: Jackie Robinson and His Legacy* (1983), not only recounts the struggles of the first man to break baseball's color line in the twentieth century, but also his place in the civil rights movement.

Television's impact on sport is best discussed in Benjamin Rader, *In Its Own Image: How Television Transformed Sports* (1984); and William O. Johnson, Jr., *The Super Spectator and the Electric Lilliputians* (1971). The commercialization of college sport is captured in Murray Sperber, *College Sports Inc.* (1990).

Allen Guttmann, *Women's Sports: A History* (1991), is the best comprehensive survey of the history of women and sport. Also helpful are essay collections by Ellen W. Gerber et al., *The American Woman in Sport* (1974); and Carol Oglesby, ed., *Women and Sport: From Myth to Reality* (1978). Stephanie Twin, ed., *Out of the Bleachers: Writings on Women and Sport* (1979), is useful for the first-person accounts of twentieth-century women athletes.

Richard Mandell, *The Nazi Olympics* (1971), clearly shows Hitler's attempts to politicize the 1936 Olympics. For the larger connections between politics and sport, see also Richard Lapchick, *The Politics of Race and International Sport* (1972); and Robert Lipsyte, *Sportsworld: An American Dreamland* (1975).

# CLOTHING AND APPEARANCE

## Nancy Rexford

Clothing is one of the more sensitive instruments a society uses to express its values and concerns, and changes in American dress over the course of the twentieth century reflect the accelerated pace of both technological and cultural change. Our clothing is made from materials unknown in 1900, and we have fashion and ready-to-wear industries that barely existed when the century began. We have steadily become more informal in both dress and manners, and new fashions tend to originate on the street rather than in the upper class. Yet clothing still speaks eloquently of the wearer's class, gender, and status. Now that women wear pants nearly as often as men and work beside men in most businesses, we are no longer sure how men and women should be differentiated in their dress. This insecurity, intensified by an uncertain economy, has made the end of the twentieth century a period in which concern with appearance is stronger than ever before.

## CLOTHING AND CLASS ASPIRATIONS

When historians of dress try to explain why we dress the way we do, their comments can often be reduced to two themes: gender roles (including sex attraction) and class distinction. Clothing is particularly important as a class identifier because it is usually the first thing we perceive about a person and because twentieth-century American culture distinguishes a wide range of socially meaningful variations in clothing. Although classes theoretically are fluid in the United States, details of dress often provide the clue to the wearer's background. Anyone trying to rise on the social scale can disassociate himself from a shabby home or vulgar relatives, but speech, manners, and clothing cannot be divorced from the individual, and it is by these things that he is judged. Even people who are consciously trying to improve their speech and appearance may not recognize the critical attributes that identify the class to which they aspire and may inadvertently reveal the lower-class background they would like to escape. In *The Woman's Dress for Success Book* (1977), John T. Molloy explains that "we have twenty-twenty vision when we look down the social scale. Most of us speak better than 'Toity-toid Street.' . . . We immediately recognize the imperfection of such speech. But the people who say 'Toity-toid' . . . don't hear themselves speaking any differently from anyone else. We are myopic when we look up the social scale. The same is true of nonverbal communicants that have social significance, such as clothing." People who wear really fine clothes recognize equal elegance in others. Those who do not wear them may not perceive the difference between a made-to-order haute couture dress and the inexpensive knockoff they can afford to buy themselves.

Wealth and status traditionally have been expressed through clothing made of high-quality and often eye-catching materials, carefully fitted to the particular wearer and displaying careful workmanship. All too often ready-made clothing is badly finished, with ragged stitching and buttons that fall off at the first wearing. Couture clothing, by contrast, is characterized by hand-sewing and careful finishing, including overcast seam allowances and bound buttonholes. Made-to-order clothing also ensures the wearer a degree of fit harder for ready-made customers to achieve. According to Paul Fussell in his 1983 book *Class: A Guide through the American Status System,* the gap between the collars of the shirt and and the suitcoat is the stigma that betrays a working-class wearer. "The distinction . . . is not one between the tailored clothes of the fortunate and the store clothes of the others, for if you try you can get a perfectly fitting suit collar off the rack, or at least have it altered to fit snugly. The difference is in recognizing this as a class signal and not being aware of it as such."

Historically, the most important signal of wealth has been the wearing of rare and costly materials. In America at the time of the Revolution, the costliest materials were silk, cotton, and high-quality wool broadcloth. Working people wore linen and coarse wools. After the invention of the cotton gin and the growth of southern cotton production in the early nineteenth century, cotton became cheaper than linen and replaced it in the working-class wardrobe. The most highly prized fabrics, however, were still made of silk, and the first silk dress was a milestone in the lives of many middle-class women. Those who could not afford the real thing wore fabrics made of half silk and half cotton, or of cotton woven to maximize the sheen. Cheap silks were also available, but they were adulterated with metallic salts that made them self-destruct.

What the middle-class market wanted was an inexpensive and lustrous substitute for silk, and this was supplied by the introduction of artificial fibers in the twentieth century. The advent of manmade fibers entirely altered the structure of social meaning attached to the natural fibers, making the latter more valuable than they had been before. The first new fiber to appear was rayon (developed in the 1890s but not named until 1924), which was made of a cellulose solution extruded as a filament. Because it was so much shinier than silk, rayon was limited in its usefulness until 1926, when chemists learned how to control the degree of luster. Early rayon also creased very easily, but manufacturers learned to mix it with other fibers and to develop softly draping crepe and velvet weaves that minimized its defects. In such materials, rayon was widely used in dresses and coats from the 1930s on. Nevertheless, real silk was always preferred by those who could afford it since rayon carried the stigma of being an imitation rather than the real thing.

Rayon was successful enough, however, to encourage chemists to work on other artificial fibers. The most important of these were nylon (developed in 1934) and polyester (1941). Both are made from petroleum products and have the advantage of being thermoplastic, that is, they will permanently retain a shape set in with heat, making permanently embossed fabric patterns, permanent pleats in skirts, and permanent creases in trousers new features of twentieth-century clothing. Made into fabric, their qualities vary depending on the way they are processed and combined with natural fibers. Nylon was introduced in 1938 but was rarely available for domestic purposes until after World War II. Polyester was introduced in the United States under the name Dacron in 1951, and at first was generally combined with cotton to make "wash and wear" shirts and blouses. By the late 1960s, polyester was being used by itself, often in knit fabrics made up into women's

dresses and both men's and women's suits. Although all-polyester fabrics are easy to care for, they are nonabsorbent and tend to feel hot in summer and cold in winter. For these reasons, people who could afford the costs of laundry and drycleaning abandoned polyester for cotton and wool, and polyester became a distinctly lower-class textile until better weaves and blends were introduced in the 1980s.

Along with the prevalence of home washing-machines and dryers after World War II, the advent of cotton/polyester blends that needed no ironing threatened to reduce at least one long-established class distinction to insignificance: the clean white shirt. For over two hundred years, the spotlessly clean and pressed white shirt with clean, unfrayed cuffs had been the hallmark of the real gentleman. The white shirt had the class advantage of showing every smudge of dirt, making it a garment impractical for the laboring man to wear. It required frequent and careful laundering and ironing, implying that the wearer had the money to buy these services. Even if one's work was clean, a white shirt was nearly impossible to keep white if the laundry was done in a tenement with only one faucet for several families. Therefore, to hide the dirt, laboring men wore colored shirts, this being the origin of the distinction between "white-collar" and "blue-collar" workers. Middle-class men who worked and lived in cleaner environments might still have trouble meeting the standard of cleanliness for a gentleman. For these men, shirts were made until the 1920s with button-holes for attaching separate collars and cuffs (preferably linen), which were easier to launder than the whole shirt. A bit further down the scale, the man who could not afford to buy separate linen collars and cuffs could buy them made of cotton, or even of stiff paper embossed to suggest the texture of fabric and stitching and coated to shed dirt and imitate the gloss of starch. Collars and cuffs were also available in celluloid, an early plastic that could be washed, dried, and replaced in a few minutes. These makeshifts would have done well enough when it came to the overall impression, but they would never have passed close scrutiny.

When the permanent-press shirt came into wide use in the 1960s, shirts were no longer the significantly labor-intensive items they had been before. For this reason it eventually became a matter of class chic to wear only 100 percent cotton, in spite of, indeed because of, the fact that it wrinkled easily and had to be pressed carefully and changed frequently, sometimes more than once a day. All-cotton shirts imply that the wearer can afford either a live-in maid or to send his shirts out to the laundry. They can of course be worn by anyone willing to iron his own shirts or to marry his maid, but this demands a sacrifice not required of the rich. Once cotton became an upper class symbol, it naturally came into wide demand among all classes, even those who had no time for ironing. To overcome the ironing problem, manufacturers in the 1980s offered dress cottons with a crepe-like finish that produced all-over wrinkles, presenting the wrinkliness as a fashionable characteristic rather than a defect. This was possible because of the interest in all things "natural" in the 1970s and 1980s. Because wrinkles were natural to cotton (even though artificially produced), wrinkles were acceptable. By the 1990s, manufacturers had developed a finish that made cotton wrinkle-free without the addition of polyester fibers, permitting a neater, more formal look in no-iron cottons.

Underlying this concern with laundry and ironing is the idea that upper-class people are clean and lower-class people are dirty; literally, that they get dirty in the process of earning a living and do not have the means to wash their clothes or their bodies as often as rich people do. With the advent of essentially universal modern plumbing, cleanliness is less trenchant a class indicator, this being another case where technology has undermined old class indicators. At the same time, however, standards have also been raised. At the beginning of the century, a weekly bath and hair-washing was considered sufficient. At the end of it, the daily shower is the rule for most Americans, and hair must not look greasy. Americans do not generally tolerate any body odor, though there has been some acknowledgment since the 1980s that the particular kind of sweat produced by working out on expensive fitness machines has a certain attractiveness. Once out of the gym, however, the first stop is the shower, and most Americans past puberty would not think of skipping the deodorant.

Traditionally, affluence has always been reflected in the size of one's wardrobe—the rich can simply afford more clothes than the poor. In the late nineteenth and early twentieth centuries, however, sheer quantity was no longer perceived as being sufficiently impressive. Any Horatio Alger might have money, but that did not mean he had class (the revelation that Imelda Marcos had two thousand pairs of shoes did not make people view her as a classy lady, but only as a greedy and heartless one). The real test of class was manners, knowing precisely what clothing was appropriate for every kind of occasion (and then of course having it to wear). By the early twentieth century, the distinctions enjoined by etiquette be-

came very fine and at the same time a huge variety of styles were available. Many people were uncomfortable negotiating the shoals of good taste by themselves and looked to the women's magazines for advice. For example, if a woman could afford only one pair of dress shoes, what kind should she buy? According to the *Ladies' Home Journal* in 1925, "If she goes to more evening functions than afternoon, the satin pump is suggested. If, on the other hand, afternoon teas and bridges overtop the dances, patent leather or suede is better. The suede is a little more durable than the patent and harder service would definitely call for the suede." The wealthy woman, of course, need not make such decisions. She could buy the best kind of shoe for each dressy occasion, perhaps one to match every dress in her wardrobe.

Until the mid-twentieth century, it was also a sign of wealth when a woman felt free to discard clothing before it was worn out. This kind of conspicuous consumption was conveniently made obvious to the observer because of the constant seasonal changes in fashion. While a general silhouette might remain in style for several years, the fashion-conscious knew what materials or details were new each season, and therefore could tell how many seasons a garment had been in use. Those interested in flaunting wealth by this means bought new clothing and accessories every spring and fall. Last season's clothes they gave to their servants or to charity. It did not matter to them if a style was so extreme that it would soon look dated. Indeed, all the better. By the time it looked dated, they would be wearing something newer.

Less affluent women could not be so cavalier about their clothes. Women who cared about changing fashions remade their clothes every year or two, but makeshift styling, dated textile designs, and the tired look of much-worn fabric would make such alterations obvious to the discerning eye. The growing ready-to-wear industry changed this, making fashionable clothing so inexpensive that even middle-class women could throw out their old clothes in favor of something more up to date. Keeping up with Paris fashion became a good deal less satisfying as a way of setting oneself apart from the hoi polloi when you were all too likely to see on the other side of the shop counter a gum-chewing teenager in a cheap rayon copy of your silk couture dress.

## THE TREND TO INFORMALITY

When technology, inspired by lower-class aspirations, brings established upper-class indicators such as "silk" dresses and "ironed" shirts and "up-to-date" fashions within reach, the upper class needs to find new ways to differentiate itself. This accounts for the upper-class view that "the wearing of clothes either excessively new or excessively neat and clean . . . suggests that your social circumstances are not entirely secure." According to Paul Fussell, "The upper and upper-middle classes like to appear in old clothes, as if to advertise how much of conventional dignity they can afford to throw away." This is one force that has contributed to make American dress increasingly informal in the second half of this century.

Traditional class conventions in dress have been distorted not only by technological advances but also by the American democratic tradition that elevates the common man as the exemplar of common sense and homespun virtues. Existing side by side with the impulse of the lower class to better itself by imitating the clothes and manners of the upper class, is an impulse on the part of middle class people to experience "real" life and express solidarity with the working class by imitating their clothes and manners.

The most important characteristics of working class clothing are that it is cut to allow full movement of the body and that it is made of sturdy, easily-cleaned materials. It is neither too tight for ease, nor so loose that it gets in the way. In contrast, clothing that inhibits movement or is designed to be uncomfortable or inconvenient suggests that the wearer does not have to perform physical labor, and therefore belongs to the upper class. The more elaborate the occasion, the more restrictive the clothing tends to be.

The discomforts that the upper class accepts most of the time, the working class will shoulder as a sign of respect for a special occasion. Thus powerful men wear suits and ties whenever they appear in public, while men of less consequence put them on only for weddings and funerals. If a politician takes off his coat in public, it probably means that he wishes to look (1) as if he is working very hard, or (2) as if he is in touch with the people. The association of shirtsleeves with the common workingman goes back hundreds of years. Omitting the coat in public was still a lower-class phenomenon in 1900, and the guardians of etiquette fought to keep it from creeping upward as it was clearly threatening to do. Writers in ladies' magazines begged women to discourage "the shirtsleeve habit." In John P. Marquand's novel *The Late George Apley,* Apley's father tells him how his grandfather bought a house in the South End, being "under the impression that this district would be one of the most solid residential sections of Boston instead of becoming, as it is to-day, a region of room-

ing houses and worse. . . . One morning . . . he observed the brownstone steps of the house across the street. 'Thunderation!' Father said. 'There is a man in his shirt sleeves on those steps.' The next day he sold his house for what he had paid for it and we moved to Beacon Street. Your grandfather had sensed the approach of change; a man in his shirt sleeves had told him that the days of the South End were numbered." But the Boston Brahmins and the ladies' magazines were were fighting a rearguard action. Shirtsleeves were only the beginning. By the end of the twentieth century, even the undershirt would have become acceptable public dress.

The vanguard of informality was generally in sportswear. By the 1920s, men might wear sweaters instead of coats while playing golf, and colored shirts (borrowed from the working class) were permissible for informal occasions. In the 1930s, informal summer shirts had short sleeves and ties were no longer required. Sweatshirts and sweatpants made their appearance for active sports, and by 1938 the T-shirt was advertised as either outerwear or underwear. In the late 1930s, rib-knitted T-shirts were worn for golfing and other active sports, and buttoned shirts were occasionally shown hanging out over the trousers. The 1950s saw the advent of Bermuda shorts for men, the 1960s the acceptance of patterned shirts for men in the office and of jeans worn with a sport coat. By the 1970s, T-shirts had acquired color and decoration and were assumed to be outerwear, and by the 1980s, they too were seen with sport coats. In 1980, designer Norma Kamali presented a collection made of fleecewear inspired by athletes' sweatshirts and sweatpants, and fleecewear now takes a prominent place in many wardrobes. By 1995, informality in dress had become so pronounced and widespread that *Newsweek* ran a cover article under the headline "Have We Become a Nation of Slobs?"

## READY-TO-WEAR AND THE AMERICAN FASHION INDUSTRY

At the beginning of the twentieth century, although the very rich might still choose to have their suits made to order, the vast majority of American men bought all their clothes ready-made. The quality of men's ready-to-wear was good enough by 1900 to make all American men look at least superficially equal. Claudia B. Kidwell and Margaret Christman quote one foreign visitor, Giuseppe Giacosa, as saying that "no European would be able to pick out by eye who there represents the infinite variety of professions, trades, states, fortune, culture, education, that may be encountered among the whole people. . . . [T]he shape and texture of the clothing in all shows the same care, the same cut, and almost the same easy circumstances."

Although good-quality ready-made underwear, cloaks, and accessories were available and widely worn by women in 1900, most women still preferred to have their dresses made to order because fashion required a wrinkle-free bodice precisely molded to fit the individual corseted body, a look that no ready-made dress could achieve. The situation changed radically between 1900 and 1915. As early as the 1890s, American women had been gravitating toward garments the ready-to-wear industry could produce very well: the blouse (known as a shirtwaist) worn with a tailored skirt and jacket. This became the uniform of the active American girl (immortalized as the Gibson girl in countless illustrations of the period), and it was a breakthrough in women's ready-to-wear. The less fitted lines of the shirtwaist and jacket having been accepted, fashion proceeded to reduce and then remove stiff boned linings from dresses, to use easily draped fabrics, and to arrange them softly over the body. By 1915, loosely fitting fashions meant that extreme accuracy of fit was no longer any greater an issue for women's clothing than it was for men's, and it became as practical to mass-produce women's dresses as any other garment. At the same time, early twentieth century ready-to-wear manufacturers were also learning how to make clothes to fit various kinds of bodies, using newly available pattern drafting systems and measurements garnered from thousands of customers.

Not only did ready-made clothing fit better, it also became cheaper, thanks to the use of power machines and fast, accurate, underpaid workers. Sewing machines, introduced about 1850, had made production faster and quality more uniform. By 1900, electrically powered cutting knives and saws permitted the accurate cutting of many layers of cloth at once. Steam pressing machines replaced hand irons in the early twentieth century. Just as the ready-to-wear industry was growing between 1880 and 1920, a stream of immigrant laborers willing to work for next to nothing poured into New York, some, like many Russian and Polish Jews, bringing tailoring experience with them. Making clothing was divided into many small individual tasks, allowing every worker, though not paid very much, quickly to become expert in the one task for which he was responsible. Workers generally were paid by the piece rather than by the hour in order to encourage speed and efficiency.

By the 1920s, both the ready-to-wear and the shoe industries had developed enormous production capacities, but the American public did not have the buying capacity to match. Although the rich were spectacularly rich and gave to the decade a gloss of luxury and frivolity, they were far outnumbered by the poor who could barely afford the necessities of life. The stock market crash of 1929 spelled the beginning of a long decline for the American shoe industry, and dangerous times for the rest of ready-to-wear. By 1933, the number of clothing manufacture establishments had dropped to 70 percent of what it had been in 1914. Since World War II, the ready-to-wear business has continued to face serious competition from foreign manufacturers with far lower labor costs. At century's end, the design, marketing, and sales departments of major American ready-to-wear firms are centered in Manhattan as they have always been, but the clothing itself is likely to be manufactured wherever management can find lower rents and cheaper labor, whether that is Central America, Southeast Asia, or eastern Europe.

American women had always looked to Europe, especially Paris, for their fashions. This was natural in the eighteenth and early nineteenth centuries before the American textile industry matured and when all but the most utilitarian fabrics had to be imported, but by 1900, American mills were producing silk, wool, and cotton fabrics of every type, especially the mid-grade fabrics needed by the burgeoning ready-made clothing industry. In spite of their production skills, American manufacturers habitually looked to France for designs for both women's clothing and dress fabrics. Manufacturers, department stores, and dressmakers all bought models and sketches from French couture openings merely to copy them in quantity. Some of the better American copies were provided with false couturier labels and high price tags to make the deception complete. Many others were mass-produced in cheaper fabrics with less careful workmanship and sold for as little as one-twentieth of the original price.

Nevertheless, Americans in New York and Hollywood in the late 1920s and 1930s were learning the business of fashion design. They copied, then adapted, and eventually departed from French designs, gradually developing a style of dressing more suited to active American women. Some of these designers worked for the new ready-to-wear industry, while others worked in specialty dress shops like Bergdorf Goodman or Henri Bendel, or in the dressmaking departments still maintained by department stores such as Saks Fifth Avenue. Almost none of their names were known to the general public until

1932, when Lord and Taylor decided to showcase a number of American designers as part of an attempt to stimulate interest and sales during the Depression.

One of the earliest of these successful American designers was Hattie Carnegie, who had opened a hat shop in New York City in 1909. She began to import dresses from France in 1919 and her business expanded until, by the 1940s, it employed a thousand people and included millinery, ready-to-wear, and custom departments selling clothing designed under her name. Two others were Anne Lowe, an African American custom dressmaker best known for having designed the wedding clothes for Jacqueline Bouvier Kennedy, and Sophie Gimbel, the in-house designer for Saks Fifth Avenue during the 1930s. But the most influential of these early New York designers was Claire McCardell, who came to the public's attention in 1938. McCardell designed for ready-to-wear manufacturers, specializing in informal separates and sportswear for middle-class American women who led active lives. She is considered the founder of the sportswear tradition that is at the center of American style. At the same time that these New York designers were becoming better known, American designers on the West Coast were exerting their influence through the medium of film. Among them was Gilbert Adrian, who designed clothes for actresses such as Joan Crawford at MGM until he started his own fashion house in 1942.

During World War II, American designers gained greater prominence and publicity simply because the war put Paris out of reach, but they still did not have the authority of Paris couture. It was the federal government that in 1942 laid down the law concerning clothes by regulating such things as skirt length (short) and width (narrow), as well as the amount of fabric that could be used. Federal regulations were designed not only to conserve materials important to the war effort, including wool, silk, nylon, and leather, but also to prevent the styles current when the war began from becoming obsolete, to ensure that women would not buy new clothing until they really needed it. The result was that American designers strove for excellence in design rather than novelty, and they frequently produced elegant suits and dresses that used even less fabric than the regulations allowed.

When the war ended, however, and restrictions were lifted, everyone was ready for a change. The nature of that change was defined not by an American but by a French designer, Christian Dior, in his January 1947 collection. Dior's clothing used waist-cinchers, bodices with boned linings and padded busts, and long, full skirts with padded hips to impose an exaggeratedly feminine silhouette on women's bodies. Many American women objected to "The New Look" because it was not comfortable, not well-suited for the active lives they led, and could not be approximated by altering clothing women already owned. It did, however, match the postwar impulse to return to "normality" by putting women back in the home as decorative helpmates to male breadwinners. It was a ladylike style that suited rich married women with nothing better to do than look sophisticated and elegant. While dress fashions did change over the next fifteen years, this mood of ladylike dignity continued to dominate the couture until the mid 1960s.

In the twenty years following the war, the French fashion legend and the male couturier both seemed to be renewing their grip on American clothing. Most of the prominent Americans working in the postwar couture tradition were men (Charles James, Mainbocher, Oleg Cassini, James Galanos, and Norman Norell), but none of them were as famous as Paris designers like Dior and Balenciaga. American women designers included Bonnie Cashin, who designed sportswear in the McCardell tradition, Pauline Trigère, master of the princess cut, and Anne Fogarty, who in her 1959 book *Wife-Dressing* advised women to wear girdles with everything. Almost all American couturiers in this period also designed ready-to-wear.

From about 1964, both the American fashion industry and clothing began to change. The most influential ideas in style were no longer originating from Paris couture or major New York designers, but from young people on the streets, first in London and later in San Francisco and New York's Greenwich Village. New young designers like Betsey Johnson and Elisa Stone concocted brief, simply shaped dresses suitable for young women, employing cheap, throwaway materials like vinyl, polyester, and even paper, in bright, unsophisticated colors. The new styles were showcased in modish boutiques like New York's Paraphernalia rather than in established department stores. During these same years, hippie culture burst into the national media. Intent on celebrating life and love and on glorifying the senses, but having little money to do it with, the hippies (who included professional designers such as Linda Gravenites) combined their old jeans with a hodgepodge of secondhand and ethnic garments gleaned from antique and import shops and army-navy stores. Such counterculture dress encouraged a generation of younger women not to look to Paris or Seventh Avenue for their clothes. Indeed, the established designers were often accused of stealing ideas from the young fashion radicals.

After the upheavals of the 1960s, the couture was rather less successful in imposing new styles on the ordinary women who bought ready-to-wear, especially when they introduced sudden and drastic change. When designers tried to establish long skirts in the late 1960s, most women ignored them and continued to wear short skirts and, even more routinely, pants. Moderately longer skirts were eventually accepted in the 1970s and were even found advantageous for working women who wanted to be perceived as equal professional partners rather than sex objects. In 1986, when the industry decided to revive the miniskirt, women rejected that too. Since 1970, American women have insisted on having a variety of styles to choose from, some with longer skirts, some with shorter ones, some with pants, some severely man-tailored, others with softer lines, others with frills. Their choices depend on their age and class, their personal taste and the occasion, not merely on the dictates of the couture.

Caroline Milbank suggests that "1970s designers could not force elaborate styles on women, who wanted easy-to-wear clothes that were versatile enough so that they decided when and where to wear what. [Forced to compete at producing rather simple, repetitive styles], Seventh Avenue began to concentrate on image rather than on the actual designs. American designers saw to it that their faces (and antics) became well known by managing to be in the right place at the right time to be snapped by the paparazzi . . . and they resorted to placing logos, initials, and even their entire names on their clothes. In short, the label went from the inside to the outside of the clothes." Since 1970, the designer's name, personality, and public image have increased in importance until it has become in many cases the most valuable thing the designer has to sell. Among the American designers who made themselves household names in the 1970s were Liz Claiborne, Calvin Klein, and Ralph Lauren.

Making a name as a major New York designer toward the end of the twentieth century has entailed not merely the showing of two collections of clothing each year but the development of a conspicuous public image through expensive advertising linked to subsidiary businesses in cosmetics, perfumes, jewelry, shoes, handbags, and household furnishings. This kind of big business requires significant financial backing, and the designers who get such backing, being indebted to the investors, may have less independence than those who are forced to work more

quietly. Until recently, investors were more likely to back male designers, partly because of the mythos of the male couturier, partly because men are assumed to be more able at business, and partly because men have often been better at promoting themselves. However, since the death of Perry Ellis from AIDS in 1986, and that of many other young men in the fashion industry, discrimination now works the other way and financial backers have tended to consider female designers a safer long-term investment.

## COMMUNITY, COUNTERCULTURE, AND THE CLOTHING OF AFFILIATION

To follow mainstream fashion, even at a distance, implies a feeling of connection to mainstream culture. Therefore, many American subcultures that assume distinctive dress do so to clarify their repudiation of mainstream culture and to symbolize their solidarity with others of like mind. Some of these sartorial rebels have themselves been rejected, often by racist and homophobic elements in the dominant culture. When the dominant culture offers no real opportunities for advancement or reward, why not dress in a way that expresses dissatisfaction with the mainstream and identification with the fringe community? Counterculture styles of dress have become an important feature of postwar American life, and reflect the fragmentation of American society as the century draws to a close.

Ted Polhemus in his important book, *Streetstyle* (1994), defines two major modes of counterculture dressing: dressing up and dressing down. In general, people who start their lives in poverty enjoy the newly won opportunity to wear luxurious clothing without necessarily accepting upper-class conventions about how wealth should be displayed. Middle-class malcontents, on the other hand, tend to dress down, rejecting mainstream standards of dress and cleanliness in favor of working-class garments that symbolize their sympathy with the oppressed.

At the beginning of the century, newly arrived immigrants experienced a degree of poverty and want far beyond what was known in American cities ninety years later, but they did not feel utterly hopeless. Although often disliked and feared by people longer established in the new world, most immigrants seem to have believed that America really would reward hard work and sacrifice, and in order to expedite the process, they attempted to look as American as possible. Only a minority of elderly immigrants, as well as certain isolated religious communities such as the Hasidic Jews in New York City and the

Amish in Pennsylvania, persisted in wearing archaic clothing and hairstyles as a means of setting themselves apart from the mainstream and emphasizing the cohesiveness of the group. Certain occupations, such as nursing and the priesthood, required distinctive clothing, and fraternal orders often wore special costumes and symbolic garments during their meetings. Otherwise, American dress was surprisingly uniform for the first forty years of the century, and the uniformity did not entirely break down until the mid 1960s. Essentially, the lower middle class wore the same kind of clothes as the rich, and they willingly accepted the rich as sartorial role models.

This began to change in the late 1930s. Twenty years earlier, large numbers of African Americans had streamed into northern cities, creating densely populated and compact communities in which African American culture gained both focus and public acknowledgment (chiefly because of jazz). Like other early-twentieth-century immigrants to the cities, blacks tried to look as much like mainstream America—white America—as possible, but dark skin and distinctive hair made it impossible for most to blend in. In 1905, a black woman named Madame C. J. Walker invented a thermal straightening comb that removed the natural kinkiness of African American hair. Her invention made her a millionaire, but cosmetics claiming to help black people look white only reinforced the assumption that to be black was somehow inferior. The Great Depression hit the black community particularly hard. The unemployment rate, about 25 percent in the country at large in 1933, ran as high as 70 percent among African Americans in some cities. The welfare system instituted in the 1930s provided assistance to women having no male breadwinner in the home, thus encouraging black men to leave their families. Without jobs or families, they were denied the normal cultural structure in which most men created a sense of identity and self-esteem. By 1940, they had begun to create their own.

It was in this environment that the first true counterculture clothing developed: the zoot suit. The zoot suit consisted of a huge, slightly waisted, knee-length jacket worn over trousers that were enormously baggy at the knee and narrow at the cuff. It was made in bright colors (Malcolm X wore one in sky blue) and was frequently worn with a feathered hat, excessively long gold watch chain, two-toned shoes, and a narrow bow tie that stood out stiffly over the lapels. This reinvention of the suit intensified it as a status symbol (the wearer clearly "has it made"), while subverting it as a symbol of sobriety and respectability. Zoot suits did not buy into mainstream culture, but distorted it in order to create an alternative collective identity for the suit's wearers, who were primarily young black and Hispanic men ("pachucos"). In 1942, when the federal government regulated the amount of wool permitted in suits and dress, zoot suits fell outside the limits. Unwilling to give them up, black and Hispanic men continued to have zoot suits made in violation of the regulations. In 1943, white servicemen in southern California started beating up and stripping any zoot-suiters who crossed their path. In June, there were riots between police and pachucos in Los Angeles, and zoot suit riots spread to cities around the country. According to Polhemus, "what had begun as aspirational Dressing Up and as a marker of youthful subcultures suddenly became a focus of racial identity. . . . [T]he 'zoot suit riots' served to sow the seeds of that sense of black and Hispanic consciousness which would blossom to profound effect in the 1960s."

Just as the zoot suit is the first example of counterculture dressing up, jeans exemplify dressing down. Jeans had been worn by laborers well back into the nineteenth century. Levi Strauss, California's first clothing manufacturer, started making them in 1850 during the gold rush, and jeans had come to be associated with cowboys and the American West. Unpretentious western-style clothing became common everyday dress in many parts of the Southwest, the important elements being jeans, a leather belt with a fancy buckle, a shirt with a pointed rather than a straight yoke, leather boots with a moderately high heel, and a hat with a large brim and deep crown. Not all of these are necessarily worn together. Sometimes the belt buckle is the only detail that conveys the western look in an otherwise mainstream ensemble.

Country-and-western singers and the rural southerners who identified with them also adopted western-style clothing beginning in the 1940s, but they developed it as a way of dressing up, not dressing down. The dressed-up cowboy look characteristic of Gene Autry and Roy Rogers movies was never historically realistic, and over time it became more and more ostentatious and highly decorated. The western outfits made by "Nudie" Cohen, the designer most closely associated with the style, were covered with embroidery and rhinestones just like the outfits he had previously made for strippers. This glitzy western style was worn by singers such as Elvis Presley and Dolly Parton and its attributes appear in the 1990s in the couture collections of both American and European designers.

In *Streetstyle,* Polhemus carefully differentiates nearly forty counterculture styles of dress, both British and American, beginning with zoot suits and cowboy outfits around 1940 and continuing through cyberpunk in the 1990s. For the United States, the most important of these since World War II have been beat, characterized by all-black clothing, sandals, and goatees; hippie, characterized by brightly colored or ethnic clothing, jeans, and long hair; black pride, characterized by fabrics or garments of African origin and Afro or other distinctly African hairstyles; biker, characterized by jeans, boots, and black leather jackets; punk, characterized by fetishist garments such as corsets, stiletto heels, and garterbelts combined with black leather jackets and partially shaved heads with the remaining hair brightly dyed; and grunge, characterized by thrift-shop clothes, heavy work boots, unkempt hair, and body piercing and tattoos. The original complexity and significance of each of these life-styles was to some extent simplified and diffused by the media. In those simplified forms, they were then adopted by many young people who never understood exactly what the original beats or hippies or punks were trying to say, but for whom the style was just vaguely "cool," a way to show off to their friends and distance themselves from their parents.

Historically, counterculture clothing has often been associated with a particular set of opinions or beliefs, but it is even more often connected with youth and popular music: the beats with jazz, the hippies with folk music or acid rock, black power with soul music and rap, punk with groups like the Sex Pistols, and grunge with Nirvana and Pearl Jam. Music and clothing, rock concerts and clubs, have become the means young people use to create for themselves a community of affiliation. That youth became a separate subculture is due partly to the baby boom, which caused the number of teenagers to swell in the 1960s, and partly to late-twentieth-century economic realities. In a country that does not have enough jobs for the population, it is important to keep young people from entering the job market too early. In order to ensure this, society offers, indeed requires, more schooling, enforcing the requirement by making one or more degrees the passport to a job, whether or not the material studied is really essential for doing the work. The teen years are a time when human beings gradually need to become more independent by making a place for themselves in the larger society (as apprentices did in earlier periods). Yet in modern culture, young

people are cut off from the adult world of work and massed together in schools (or on the streets) with hundreds of other kids at the same stage of immaturity. Having no place else to turn for a sense of self-worth and membership in a community, they naturally turn to each other. Immature and insecure, they use clothing, language, and manners to determine who is "in" and who is "out."

If teenagers cannot be valuable as producers, they can certainly be valuable as consumers, and advertisers work hard to ensure that unformed and malleable young people learn to define themselves and their communities in terms of material goods. The trick is to get your product identified as the one that is really cool, the one worn by everyone who is "in." As a result of pressure from advertisers and peers, teenagers conflate their self-worth with the ownership of a particular style of jacket or shoes—especially shoes, in the last decades of the century. It is not unknown for young people to be beaten up or even killed for their clothes.

Just as streetstyles have been divorced from their original meanings and adopted generally in youth culture, they have also been the source of new ideas for the couture. Since the 1960s, fashion designers have repeatedly incorporated streetstyle elements into their new designs. But once taken up by the dominant culture, sartorial symbols lose their power clearly to signify an alternative affiliation. The response on the street, where clothing is still supposed to mean something, is to go to yet greater extremes, to invent something so outrageous that no one else would dare to wear it. But the fashion industry seems capable of absorbing it all, not seeming to care that in the 1980s and 1990s runway fashions have ceased to have any relationship to the clothing ordinary women wear. Given time and sufficient exposure, even shaved heads, red and green hair, corpselike faces with black mouths, tattoos, fetish garments, work boots worn with corsets, and pierced nipples, navels, and noses may lose their power to shock, and perhaps watered-down versions of these outrages will be looking back at us from our own mirrors before many more years have passed. Meanwhile, as long as high fashion plays with lower-class iconography, those well-to-do people who do not choose to look as if they are slumming take refuge in simple, timeless styles made in very high-quality materials and wear their clothing until it is quite worn out. This kind of dressing, long referred to as "preppy" (as in "college preparatory school"), also surfaced in the late 1970s as a popular style.

Like fringe groups and teenagers, the amorphous

middle class has also developed its own version of the clothing of affiliation, that is, the habit of wearing labels, logos, and slogans on one's clothing. The roots of this practice go back to the nineteenth century, when the college athletic "letter sweater" made its appearance. These were augmented in the 1920s and 1930s by T-shirts and sweatshirts bearing the college or team name or logo (and later by decals the student's parents could put on the family car). Souvenir shirts began to be produced in the 1930s, and after World War II, children wore printed shirts featuring television heroes like Roy Rogers and Davy Crockett. Thanks to refinements in printing technology, the first elaborate, multicolor printed T-shirts appeared in the mid 1960s. Protest and counterculture groups began using T-shirts to display their various messages (a clenched fist, a peace symbol), but at the same time promotional T-shirts came into wide use for advertising (Budweiser was one of the earliest). Baseball-style visored caps had long been worn by farmers, and by the 1970s, farm-supply companies were giving out caps with the product name on them as a promotional gimmick. By the later 1980s and 1990s, partly inspired by the fad for cap-wearing among black teenagers, boys throughout America began wearing visored caps, generally those bearing the names and logos of their favorite professional sports team.

Paul Fussell, writing in 1983, commented that "when proles assemble to enjoy leisure, they seldom appear in clothing without words on it. As you move up the classes and the understatement principle begins to operate, the words gradually disappear, to be replaced, in the middle and upper-middle classes, by mere emblems, like the Lacoste alligator. Once, ascending further, you've left all such trademarks behind, you may correctly infer that you are entering the purlieus of the upper class itself." Fussell further suggests that wearing labels and logos are generally signs of personal insecurity. "By donning legible clothing you fuse your private identity with external commercial success, redeeming your insignificance and becoming, for the moment, somebody."

Molloy also observed this trend in 1977, but his concern was whether this new habit of identifying oneself by means of merchandise trademarks was good for one's image in the workplace. "We tested the effect of women wearing or carrying designer items in the office. The reaction of other women was mixed. About one-third responded favorably, and the other two-thirds had either a neutral or a negative reaction. Of the men, 90 percent reacted negatively. They treated the women who wore or

carried the designer items as lightweights, and they assumed that these women were more interested in form than substance."

The increasing importance of clothing that communicates affiliation reflects an significant change in American culture. As the twentieth century has progressed, more and more Americans have moved great distances, often several times during their lives, making communities less tightly knit and homogeneous than they used to be. At the same time, chain stores and restaurants allow people to repeat familiar experiences in their new locations so that the consumer habits they learned in one town may not change radically in the next one. Television news, talk shows, and commercials also encourage people to identify themselves in terms of lifestyle and opinion rather than geographical community. Whereas at the beginning of the century, there was essentially one fashion that all Americans followed as well as their circumstances allowed, there is at the end of it, a multiplicity of fashions, each with adherents living similar lifestyles scattered across the country.

## CLOTHING AND GENDER

Perhaps the most basic task of clothing in western civilization is to indicate which people are male and which female. In our culture, even people who affirm the essential similarity and equality of the sexes become quite uncomfortable when they cannot tell whether they are talking to a man or a woman. To make this essential distinction, women in the West have, for the last six hundred years or so, covered their legs with skirts while men have covered them with some variety of bifurcated garment. Therefore it was a change of the first magnitude when women began to wear pants in this century.

In 1851, a few early women's rights advocates espoused the bloomer costume, essentially an ordinary dress cut off at knee level and worn over a matching set of ankle-length trousers. This costume never gained wide currency for the street, but women did begin to wear knee-length bloomers whenever they engaged in strenuous exercise, if the occasion was not too public. College girls, for example, wore them for playing basketball in the 1890s, but if a mixed audience was viewing the game, the girls had to put knee-length skirts over them. College gym suits continued to be made with bloomers (eventually much shortened) until about 1970.

Pajamas had been available for women since 1900, and working overalls with bloomerlike bottoms were introduced in 1917–1918, when some women needed a more practical outfit for their wartime work. Another breakthrough in the 1910s was the adoption of rompers as everyday playwear for all toddlers. The earliest rompers were not gender-differentiated, but they soon took the form of shorts and overshirts for boys, and bloomers with longer overdresses for girls. Slightly older girls continued to wear dresses with matching bloomers underneath through the 1920s and 1930s and occasionally later. As boys got older, they graduated from rompers to knickers and suits, and in the early 1920s, girls too began to wear knickers. These were intended only for rough outdoor sports, but they opened the way for grown women to wear them for hiking, golfing, and skiing by the mid 1920s.

A surprising addition to a woman's wardrobe was the beach or lounging pajama, which enjoyed great popularity in the late 1920s and early 1930s. These were generally made of silk, with long loose-fitting trousers and a simply cut front-fastening overblouse. In 1930, Sears advertised both athletic shorts (without bloomerlike gathered bottoms) and "new, practical, popular overalls for women." More elegant tailored pants were popularized in the 1930s and 1940s by actresses such as Katharine Hepburn and Marlene Dietrich. By the 1940s, pants and overalls were offered for little girls, and by the 1950s, pants seem to have been nearly universal outside of school, made long in flannel-lined corduroy for winter, short or calf length (pedal pushers) in cotton for summer. Teenagers in the 1950s, both boys and girls, wore dungarees (blue jeans). Adult women, too, were wearing pants and shorts more and more often in the 1950s and early 1960s, but pants were still not appropriate to wear on the street downtown. Students at Vassar were expected to wear skirts to dinner until 1968.

The next breakthrough came in the 1960s with the invention of the women's pantsuit, a suit jacket with matching pants instead of a skirt. The American designer Norman Norell offered pantsuits for daytime wear in 1963, and for evening in 1965, but even into the late 1960s, some prestigious New York restaurants refused to admit women wearing them. Meanwhile, on college campuses, jeans were almost the only thing anyone wore, and by 1970 most elementary and secondary schools began to allow girls to wear pants to class. Thus women born since 1960 have grown up in a period when it was possible to wear pants for almost all occasions at every stage of life.

However, this did not mean that there were no longer any gender distinctions in clothing. For example, black women who wore unisex Afro hairstyles in the late 1960s added large earrings to identify themselves clearly as women. After little girls began wearing pants to school, a system of color-coding was adopted in clothing for prepubescent children whose gender might otherwise be ambiguous. Dresses could be made in a range of colors because the form of the garment clarified gender, but when unisex garments like pants, shorts, T-shirts, jackets, and sneakers were marketed for girls, they incorporated the color pink almost as if it were law. Pink was combined with white, lavender, purple, and occasionally shades of aqua or yellow, but bright primary colors were reserved for boys. It is possible to argue that Americans are more concerned about the gender of their children now than they were in 1900, when all infants and toddlers wore identical white dresses. Even disposable diapers have been gender-differentiated since the mid 1980s.

For most of the last six hundred years, both men and women wore a rich variety of fabrics in bright and dull colors, and in plain and conspicuous patterns depending more on their income than their gender. But during the nineteenth century, men's clothing became gradually simpler and less colorful. Sober colors came to be associated with power and responsibility while conspicuous patterns or colors came to imply weakness of character. No longer permitted to display their prosperity in rich and elaborate clothing of their own, men displayed it through the clothing of their wives and daughters, a phenomenon pointed out in 1899 by Thorstein Veblen in *The Theory of the Leisure Class.*

Thus at the end of nineteenth century, men and women's clothing was more thoroughly differentiated than it had ever been before, a fact that reflected the period's need to distinguish the roles men and women were expected to play. Women's clothing, characterized by constant change and conspicuous color and decoration, was associated with weakness, dependence, frivolity, and extravagance. This meant that when women began to gain greater power in the world at large, becoming teachers, office workers, writers, editors, even doctors and lawyers, the associations carried by their clothing worked against them, and they began to look for a way of dressing that would better fit their lives. A prototype of the tailored suit appeared as early as the 1860s, and it was fully realized by 1890, in the tailored suit with shirtwaist blouse of the Gibson girl. There was a reaction toward ornamentation in women's suits in the early 1900s, but the tailored version returned in even greater force by 1910, and continued to be made through the rest of the century, echoing the lines of contemporary fashion.

When color returned to men's wardrobes after World War II, it was in sportswear and leisure clothing, not business suits. Young men enjoyed wearing brighter colors during the "peacock revolution" of the late 1960s, but this did not fundamentally change the meaning color in men's clothing has had in the twentieth century. If anything, it may have reinforced the association between bright colors and bold patterns, on one hand, and leisure, even idleness and irresponsibility, on the other. This cultural association caused women with professional ambitions to limit their use of color when they entered the workplace in the 1970s. John T. Molloy, in *The Woman's Dress for Success Book,* notes that women project authority better when dressed in colors associated with menswear, such as a gray or blue suit with a white blouse.

Molloy's research also indicated that although pants for women had apparently been accepted in American society, women who wore them to work did not project as much authority as women who wore skirts, especially skirted suits. He found that pantsuits in traditionally male fabrics such as pinstripes made women look like imitation men, not like powerful women. Even skirted suits in pinstripes tested poorly, but a gray pinstripe dress tested very well, suggesting that the dress projects enough femininity to balance the masculine associations of the fabric. Clothing that appears to be playing games with gender roles, Molloy found, looks sexy, not professional. Women's business clothing needs to acknowledge gender but without incorporating characteristics the society considers sexy or ultrafeminine. Working women also need to take class factors into account. Molloy found polyester knit pantsuits (very common working garb for women in the mid 1970s) to be "failure outfits" that destroyed a woman's effectiveness in dealing with men, especially when made in bright or pastel colors, as many were in that decade. Polyester knits sent such a loud "prole" message that women who wore them could not command respect, while the bright and light colors were associated with leisure and therefore looked unprofessional in an office.

Molloy felt that women would do well to adopt a business uniform that, like a man's suit, every businesswoman wore as a universally understood sign of professionalism. He understood that the successful uniform would have to take into account, like it or not, the subverbal, almost subconscious associations we all make with clothing. His research put into words what many women already recognized, that

women must choose between "the bedroom and the boardroom." They may choose to look powerful or to look sexy, but their clothes will not let them do both at the same time because our culture associates sexy clothing with dependence. That is because for at least two centuries, many men have been attracted to young, decorative women who, clinging to a man's arm, emphasize his virility and economic success by their dependence. Men's suits, by contrast, let a man look both powerful and sexy, because women are attracted to men who appear to be competent, powerful, and successful, qualities symbolized by the business suit.

The dress-for-success era of the 1970s developed in the 1980s into "power dressing," which according to Caroline Milbank, "managed to be both more masculine and more feminine than the 1970s dress-for-success style. Masculine aspects of the new business clothes included bold tailoring, larger shoulders, and men's fabrics used in interesting combinations." She identifies the padded shoulder as a masculine characteristic, but large shoulders are actually more ambiguous than at first appears. Because they tend to appear in clothing that also obscures the waist and narrows toward the knees, the effect is to reduce the apparent size of the hips and to make the woman's body appear triangular, like a man's. Some women believe this makes them look powerful, but it also implies that the kind of body most women have, narrow through the shoulders and wide through the hips, is undesirable. Asked why they like the broad-shouldered look (and many women do), women often say that it makes them seem more in proportion, and it does, if the male body is the norm. But exaggerated shoulders can also make women look as if they are playing at being men (like little girls dressing up in Daddy's jackets), or as if they feel the need to work very hard at being authoritative. Whenever women raise their arms (as political campaigners do when they wave to the crowds) the shoulder pads bunch up in an awkward way as if women are not supposed to make large gestures.

Like padded shoulders, women's high-heeled shoes also carry a mixed message. They imply that the wearer is not a manual laborer, and they even out the height difference between men and women, making it possible to look men in the eye without having to look up to them, a significant advantage in business. On the other hand, very high heels are associated with sexual fetishism, and shoes with rather high heels imply sexual availability since the woman who wears them puts it out of her power to flee an assault.

Historically, short skirts have been considered liberating, but only in comparison to the cumbersome long skirts worn by women for so many centuries. A very short skirt, like any extreme exposure of the body, carries sexual overtones. If a woman who wears one does not really wish to seem provocative, she must carefully control her posture and body language. Narrow skirts, unless very short, restrict the stride and imply deliberate hobbling.

Feminist writers such as Susan Faludi and Naomi Wolf perceive 1980s fashions as part of a backlash against women after the feminist advances of the early 1970s. They condemn the fashion industry for promoting demeaning images of women and for using the rhetoric of feminism to do it. Faludi quotes a fashion consultant as saying in 1988 that wearing suits "shows you aren't successful because you have no freedom of dress, and that means you don't have power." According to such thinking, dressing-for-success made women squelch their sexuality, but once women are economically successful, they can be afford to be sexually liberated as well. "Older women want to look sexy now on the job," the head of Componix, a Los Angeles apparel maker, insisted. "They want men to look at them like they're women. Notice my legs first, not my appraisals." Even the designer Donna Karan, who built her reputation on clothes for working women and who, as a working mother herself, felt a great deal of empathy for their needs, said in 1986, "there has been a shift in saying to a woman, 'It's okay to show your derriere. . . . I questioned it at first. But women's bodies are in better shape." But if Molloy was right about what women need to wear to work, they are making a serious mistake by combining imitation masculinity with a sexy exposure of the body. It seems unlikely that associations so long and firmly established with female clothing would change radically over a mere ten or fifteen years.

## BEYOND CLOTHING: BODY FASHIONS

The twentieth century has been characterized by a decrease in the amount of clothing worn and an increase in the amount of bare skin it is permissible to show. For public and formal occasions, men may still wear clothing that covers nearly the entire body, as they did in 1900, but vest, hat, and gloves are normally omitted, and even white-collar workers often leave off the coat, working in shirt and tie alone, the shirts having short sleeves in the summer. For informal wear, men now wear shorts and short-sleeved shirts or T-shirts, and may go bare-chested if they choose (although stores and restaurants still require shirts and shoes). Women's clothing has changed even more dramatically. In 1900, almost all women's day clothing had long sleeves and high necklines. Within the decade, elbow-length sleeves and lower necklines were common, and by the late 1920s, day dresses could be made sleeveless. Skirts shortened gradually through the 1910s and were at knee-level by the late 1920s, although they rose and fell intermittently thereafter.

Bathing suits have always offered the greatest opportunity for displaying the body. Even in 1900 women's bathing suits were revealing compared to ordinary dress. They consisted of a short-sleeved blouse attached to bloomers with a knee-length skirt worn over the top. Usually made of black or navy blue wool or heavy cotton, they were worn with black stockings. Men went naked when swimming only with other men, but mixed bathing required knee-length knit breeches worn with a high-necked, short-sleeved knit top. By 1930, both men and women wore simple, body-hugging knitted styles that left arms, legs, and neck entirely bare, but men's suits also exposed much of the back, while the lower edge of women's suits suggested a modest vestigial skirt. Men could swim without tops by the end of the 1930s, and two-piece suits were available to women in the 1940s. In the 1950s women's bathing suits were generally one-piece, but they were followed by bikinis ("Itsy Bitsy Teeny Weeny Yellow Polka Dot Bikini" was a hit song in 1960), cut low enough to expose the navel. Although more conservative suits are available, many now advertised for women expose the entire body except for three or four triangular patches covering genitals and breasts. Men's suits may be equally minimal.

The invention of better elastic yarns using man-made fibers (Lastex in the 1930s, Helanca in the late 1940s, and spandex in the 1960s) has made it possible to design clothing that molds itself exactly to the body, covering and revealing at the same time. With the growing concern about fitness in the 1970s and 1980s, spandex began to be used not just in bathing suits but in other kinds of athletic garments, notably bicycling wear. Betsey Johnson designed a spandex collection in 1978 for women who wanted to show off their bodies.

As more and more flesh is exposed, the body becomes as important to appearance as clothing, and there has been a tendency through the century (much accelerated after 1970) to alter and remake the body itself. In many historical periods, cosmetics were worn without apology, but for most of the nineteenth century, women were not supposed to look "painted." Women began wearing makeup more openly after 1900, and by the 1920s, it was permissible to apply powder and lipstick in public. The permanent wave and the thermal straightening comb, invented shortly after 1900, made possible relatively permanent changes to the hair. Hair bleaching and dyeing became gradually more common as dyes became safer and more natural looking. With the advent of sleeveless dresses and sheer stockings in the 1920s, underarm and leg hair began to be shaved off or removed with a depilatory. Such minimal body alteration, however, pales in comparison to what was coming in the second half of the century.

Realism was never the purpose of fashion illustration, and hand-sketched fashion figures have generally been taller and slimmer than real women. Thus when magazines began featuring photographs of clothing on live models in the early decades of this century, the real women looked dumpy compared to the drawings. The problem was solved by the 1930s by employing thinner models and using camera angles that emphasized their slenderness. In the 1950s, models were still extremely slim, but they were also wearing waist-cinchers to narrow the waist and padding to increase the bust and hips, and ordinary women understood that foundation garments were necessary to create the exaggerated fashion silhouette. In the late 1960s, the pressure to be very thin grew stronger with the advent of short little-girl A-line dresses that demanded sticklike thighs and no bust (the supermodel who epitomized that look was nicknamed "Twiggy"). The desire to look well in clothes designed for very tall, thin women explains, in large part, why dieting has become an obsession among American women. An entire industry has grown up around the determination to shed a few pounds before the swimsuit season arrives, or before the wedding, or after the baby. But it is an industry that exacerbates the weight problem rather than cures it, by implying that an unrealistically "ideal" figure can be achieved by sufficient effort.

Because the dynamics of weight loss and gain are not yet widely understood, gaining weight gives rise to feelings of guilt and self-hatred, while losing weight is thought to show strength of character and self-control. In their need for a sense of control, and in the struggle to look like the images held up for their admiration, many young girls take self-starvation to an extreme. Anorexia nervosa is recognized as a serious, even life-threatening illness, as is its companion illness, bulimia, characterized by a pattern of binge eating followed by self-induced vomiting. These illnesses are still very common, especially among teenagers and among women in the media, whose appearance is their livelihood and whose visibility makes them likely role models for the young.

In the 1970s and 1980s, exercise joined dieting as a method of losing weight, and it too became an obsession, one affecting both men and women. Running, or "jogging," the early exercise of choice, was prized as a way of strengthening the heart and for the "high" some runners experience, but it was hard on the legs and did not develop the upper body. Soon, serious fitness was felt to require a complete program of exercise for all parts of the body, and it became fashionable to have a body shaped by fitness training. *Jane Fonda's Workout Book* and companion video were published in 1982 and were followed by scores of others. To be thin and muscular was easiest for the rich, who could afford to buy not only VCRs and exercise tapes but also stylish bodysuits and costly shoes to wear while exercising, as well as weights, exercise bikes, ski machines, and memberships in fitness clubs where even more expensive and complicated machinery was available.

In the 1980s, muscles became fashionable for both men and women, although the results of women's weight-training paled beside that of media stars like Sylvester Stallone and Arnold Schwarzenegger. To see the change in the masculine ideal, one need only compare the pudgy figure of the 1950s television Superman with the bulky-shouldered Superman of the 1978 film. Exaggerated images of musclebound masculinity assaulted young men not only from the movies but also from cartoons, comic books, and the world of sports. Athletes who worked out regularly with weights to build strength and endurance inspired teenagers to imitate them. Young boys sometimes damaged their bones and stunted their growth by training too hard too early. Others resorted to dangerous steroid drugs to build their muscles artificially. This kind of self-destructive behavior was in the past associated primarily with women, and the fact that it is spreading to men suggests that Americans are far more obsessed with their bodies in the 1990s than they have ever been before.

Since the 1930s, the ideal female body has been thin, in spite of the fact that women carry by nature a higher proportion of fat on their bodies. Since the 1980s, women have also been encouraged to develop noticeable muscles, even though bulky muscles do not come easily to women. In the 1990s, women are also called upon to have large breasts, a trait very hard to combine with thinness. In fact, the only way to do it is through plastic surgery, a growing business in the 1990s. The pressure to have a perfect body has led, literally, to body sculpting. Having failed to achieve the desired shape through diet and exercise, women have excess fat removed from bellies and thighs through liposuction, enlarge breasts by means of silicone implants, and get plastic surgeons to make their noses straighter, their lips fuller, their cheekbones higher, whatever the world of fashion has seen fit to promote as the only beautiful look. There is no real model in nature for this beauty. Even screen actresses get it from their plastic surgeons. Men, too, have begun to have body-altering surgery in increasing numbers, only in their case, they remove fat, add pectoral muscles, remove wrinkles, and augment thinning hair. Given the increased acceptance of this kind of body alteration, the pierced noses and extensive tattoos affected by young people seem merely less expensive expressions of the zeitgeist.

Why this obsession about body appearance as the century ends? The reasons are not yet clear, but some of it appears to be rooted in economic insecurity. Certainly one of the major reasons both men and women have plastic surgery is to look youthful in a job market where older people are not valued for their wisdom or experience, but are considered out of touch in a world of fast technological change. Another economic threat, one that hits hardest at women, is divorce. While there are many reasons for divorce, it is the tendency for middle-aged men to try to increase their own self-esteem by taking up with younger women that encourages the middle-aged wife to get a facelift or go to a diet center. The insecurity that leads men to look at younger women may also be economic in origin, the fear that they have already stopped advancing in their profession.

Historically, Americans have always tended to measure personal value in terms of appearances and material acquisition, a practice that intensified in the 1980s. The body, not just the clothing, has become a way of indicating class. Thin looks rich, fat looks poor. In fact, thinness and wealth are now being seen as signs of virtue, being the visible results of self-discipline and strength of character. On the other hand, fatness and poverty are considered the visible signs of laziness, slovenliness, and weakness of character. But in spite of all the medical advice and cultural pressure to eat less and exercise more, Americans are getting steadily fatter. Perhaps the ideal body image presented everywhere we turn seems so unattainable that there is no point trying. Perhaps this is just another expression of the increasing disparity between rich and poor that developed in the 1980s. Certainly, many people eat to compensate for stress,

many have little time or opportunity for exercise, and many find inexpensive fast-food tempting when everyone comes home from multiple jobs too tired to cook.

Several industries have an interest in keeping those of us who have money convinced that there is only one right way to look and that it is not the way we look right now. As long as flat bellies, narrow hips, bulky muscles, full breasts, perfect noses, pouty lips, unwrinkled eyes, lots of hair, lovely complexions, and designer underwear are associated with the rich, the successful, and the famous, Americans will continue to buy products and services from diet centers, plastic surgeons, and the makers of exercise equipment and designer clothing. While people in our society must wear clothes, they do not actually need to wear makeup or perfume, or to change their bodies to fit the latest fashion. Those needs are artificial and must be cultivated by clever advertisements. Because the women's magazines depend on advertising from the manufacturers of makeup, perfume, and designer jeans, they are under pressure to promote a lifestyle in which makeup, perfume, and designer jeans are important.

The feminist theory that there has been a backlash against women's equality with men in the 1980s probably also has some truth to it. The kind of female body being promoted is one designed to give men sexual pleasure by means of its youth, large breasts, sexy mouth, and provocative posture without creating any unwanted consequences, since very thin, fitness-obsessed women often temporarily lose their ability to conceive children. The wide hips that are natural to most women are considered an affliction. Judging by this model, most real female bodies are not particularly desirable. Indeed many, perhaps most, women live out their lives in bodies they have been taught to consider unattractive, and self-hatred is an underlying current in their lives. When a woman goes to work, the female body is considered such a liability that the fashion industry offers her huge shoulder pads and high heels to help her look less inadequate.

But the obsession with appearance affects men as well as women. When old structures of gender begin to break down, when women begin to encroach on territories long held by men, when distinctions such as trousers and skirts no longer hold true, then perhaps we need to reassure ourselves that the sexes are finally not really alike. The fact that men's and women's lives have become more similar since 1970 may account for the desire to emphasize the difference between the sexes, symbolized by the exaggerated display of basic sex characteristics. Even the fashion for wearing stubble beards in the 1990s may be a way of calling attention to maleness, making more of a point of male facial hair than a conventional beard would. Bustiers and Wonderbras are provided to help women emphasize their breasts, while men are encouraged to develop their muscles until they present a caricature of masculinity. In the twentieth century, the woman may have learned to wear the pants in the American family, but it is still the man who wears the muscles.

SEE ALSO Class (volume I); Consumption (volume III); Mass Media and Popular Culture (in this volume).

## BIBLIOGRAPHY

American scholarship in the field of costume is still in its infancy and many of the titles generally available are little more than picture books. *Dress,* the journal of the Costume Society of America, is the only American periodical dedicated to costume history. For a guide to conducting research in the field, consult Valerie Burnham Oliver, *Costume/ Clothing/Fashion: Information Access Sources and Techniques* (1993).

There is no single work describing American clothing for men, women, and children through the entire twentieth century. Shirley Miles O'Donnol, *American Costume, 1915–1970: A Source Book for the Stage Costumer* (1989) is the best available overview. For men's clothing, see Richard Martin and Harold Koda, *Jocks and Nerds: Men's Style in the Twentieth Century* (1989). Martin and Koda suggest that menswear is best understood not as a chronological succession of styles but as a collection of choices, ways to reveal the wearer's identity or community of affiliation. For a series of articles focusing on African American dress, consult Starke, Holloman, and Nordquist, *African American Dress and Adornment: A Cultural Perspective* (1990).

Secondary works on American high fashion have drawn heavily on *Vogue* magazine. See Jane Mulvagh's *Vogue History of 20th Century Fashion* (1988), Nicholas Drake's *The Sixties: A Decade in Vogue* (1988), and Carolyn Hall's series, *The Twenties in Vogue* (1983), *The Thirties in Vogue* (1985), and *The Forties in Vogue* (1985). Joel Lobenthal, *Radical Rags: Fashions of the Sixties* includes information gleaned from personal interviews and is highly recommended for the 1960s.

The best description of how the fashion industry worked in both New York and Paris in the 1920s and 1930s is still to be found in Elizabeth Hawes' lively book, *Fashion is Spinach* (1938). Hawes learned the fashion business in Paris and was one of the earliest American designers to set up an independent business in New York. Carolyn R. Milbank provides a useful overview of the New York fashion industry and the work of its major designers through the 1980s in *New York Fashion: The Evolution of American Style* (1989). See also Sarah Tomerlin Lee, ed., *American Fashion: The Lives and Lines of Adrian, Mainbocher, McCardell, Norell, Trigère* (1975) and Beryl Williams, *Young Faces in Fashion* (1956). The role of women in the world of haute couture, including several Americans, is discussed in Valerie Steele, *Women of Fashion: Twentieth Century Designers* (1991). Claudia B. Kidwell and Margaret Christman provide a broader view of the development of ready-to-wear in *Suiting Everyone: The Democratization of Clothing in America* (1974).

Middle-class clothing is illustrated but not discussed in selected reprints from mail order catalogs edited by Stella Blum, *Everyday Fashions of the Twenties as Pictured in Sears and Other Catalogs* (1981) and *Everyday Fashions of the Thirties as Pictured in Sears Catalogs* (1986), and by JoAnne Olian, *Everyday Fashions of the Forties as Pictured in Sears Catalogs* (1992).

Thorstein Veblen's seminal work, *The Theory of the Leisure Class* (1899) is still required reading for his perspective on clothing and class at the end of the nineteenth century. While presented as self-help books, John T. Molloy's *Dress for Success* (1975) and *The Woman's Dress for Success Book* (1977) are noteworthy for their careful research. Molloy's perceptions and recommendations about clothing have been repeatedly attacked by the fashion industry but in many parts of the business world they have held true for twenty years. For a lighter look at the role clothing plays in revealing class, see Lisa Birnbach, *The Official Preppy Handbook* (1980), and Paul Fussell, *Class: A Guide Through the American Status System* (1983).

Gender issues in dress are discussed in Claudia Kidwell and Valerie Steele, *Men and Women: Dressing the Part* (1989), and in Anne Hollander, *Sex and Suits* (1994). More militantly feminist viewpoints are expressed by Rita Freedman, *Beauty Bound* (1986), Susan Faludi, *Backlash: The Undeclared War Against American Women* (1991), and Naomi Wolf, *The Beauty Myth* (1991). In *Wife Dressing* (1959), the American designer Anne Fogarty expresses postwar attitudes about femininity, clothing, and women's roles. The diet industry and the destructive role of dieting in women's lives are analyzed by Diane Epstein and Kathleen Thompson in *Feeding on Dreams: Why America's Diet Industry Doesn't Work and What Will Work for You* (1994).

For an exhaustive overview of counterculture clothing, see Ted Polhemus, *Streetstyle: From Sidewalk to Catwalk* (1994). Mick Farren, *The Black Leather Jacket* (1985) and John Gordon and Alice Hiller, *The T-Shirt Book* (1988) take a closer look at the history of the two garments most important in counterculture dressing.

# ELEMENTARY AND SECONDARY EDUCATION

## Carl F. Kaestle

The American concept of public schooling did not spring full-blown from the U.S. Constitution, nor did public schools as we know them begin in the early national period. The basic characteristics associated with public schooling were established in the North between 1840 and 1860. During these decades most state legislatures decided to require local school committees to provide tuition-free elementary schooling to all children. Public high schools became common after the Civil War, and by 1880 high schools had surpassed private academies as the predominant form of secondary education. The second half of the nineteenth century also witnessed further bureaucratization of public schooling, both at the state and local levels. Judged by late-twentieth-century standards, the level of organization was modest, but some centralization occurred. Many towns consolidated their small district schools under the supervision of a single committee. Larger towns hired professional superintendents and established graded schools with principal teachers and assistant teachers. At the state level, legislatures began to regulate teaching credentials, the length of the school year, and some matters of curriculum.

### AMERICAN PUBLIC SCHOOLS IN 1900

In the meantime, a number of nonpublic alternatives persisted, and some new ones developed. Many private academies survived, but most of them catered increasingly to the children of affluent families. Tensions between Protestants and Catholics continued, creating fierce controversies on educational issues; the Catholic hierarchy had decided by the late nineteenth century that the provision of separate schooling was a high priority, and so parochial schools had become more numerous by 1900. Racial minorities were widely denied access to the public schools that served white children, either through formal or informal means of segregation. Cheated out of equal public funding for their own segregated schools, they sometimes supplemented public funds with their own meager resources. By the late nineteenth century African Americans faced public education systems in the South that spent four to eight times as much on white students as on black students, and the ratios became even more steep in the early decades of the twentieth century. Southern blacks relied on self-help and on philanthropic aid from such sources as the Julius Rosenwald and Anna T. Jeanes funds to build and maintain local schools. Such resources were not enough to close the gap in the supply of schools, and many black children could not afford to be in school. As a result, in 1900, 36 percent of black children aged five to fourteen were enrolled in the South, compared to 55 percent of white children.

In the case of other racial minorities, as well, white Americans pursued a policy of segregation, neglect, and inferior education. In the Southwest, Mexican Americans experienced segregated, underfunded schools, with shorter school years. About half of Mexican American children did not attend school in the early decades of the century; very few reached high school. Very little public education was offered to Native Americans; most children were left with whatever informal, indigenous education their communities devised. The federal government, having placed most Native Americans on reservations, abrogated treaty obligations to provide schooling. The much-discussed boarding schools, which aimed to extinguish Native American culture in their students, touched only a small minority of Indian children. Asian American children were allowed to attend public schools in some cities, but in San Francisco, where the largest concentration of Chinese and Japanese immigrants lived, attempts to maintain segregated schools led to court challenges and nativist agitation.

For white European immigrants, however, the policy was one of inclusion, not exclusion, in the public schools. As in race relations, there was prejudice and ethnocentrism, but the goal was behavioral and political assimilation. Immigration had mushroomed in the late nineteenth century; in 1900 over 30 percent of the population was either foreign-born or had one or two foreign-born parents. Americanization of immigrants—adults as well as children—was a major policy issue.

As the states developed free public school systems, more children came to school for more years. Educators, parents, employers, and reformers of various types approved of more schooling for a variety of motives: moral education, work discipline, enlightened citizenship, cultural assimilation, and the custody of children during the working day in an increasingly nonagricultural society. Many children had to work to augment family income, but increasingly there was a shift from work to school among both rural and urban youth. Thus by the early twentieth century most white children, from all social groups, attended school for at least two or three years. The result was higher enrollment rates at any given point in time for whites than for nonwhites. For example, in 1900 about 53 percent of whites aged five to twenty were enrolled, compared to about 31 percent of nonwhites. The age at which students left school was heavily influenced by their parents' social class, and high schools were still fairly elite institutions. About 11 percent of youths aged fourteen to seventeen were in school. Among those enrolled in school in 1900, the average number of days attended was ninety-nine, up from eighty-one days in 1880. Schooling was becoming a bigger part of childhood. Not only were public school systems expanding, but their programs were becoming more diverse. As the students became more varied in ethnic background and family income, the schools began to develop practical courses such as commercial or industrial arts.

Public education in 1900 was both a big success and a big problem. Educators had created a workable school system and a new professional field. Although nonwhites were left outside, and some groups chose to forge private alternatives, public schools were otherwise increasingly inclusive. Teaching jobs were a major white-collar employment opportunity for women, but education also provided a variety of administrative and supervisory jobs for both men and women as principals and county supervisors. These administrators built infrastructures of influence, support, and leadership for local and state school systems.

Despite such signs of expansion and professional development, and widespread popular faith in education, many people thought the public schools were not doing a very good job. People looked to the schools to produce cultural unity, political stability,

and appropriate training for adult work life, and problems in these areas had mounted to alarming proportions. The deterioration of urban environments, the increasing proportion of children with foreign-born parents, alienation and political activism in rural areas, conflict between labor and management, and the specter that radical ideas would take hold in such an environment all exacerbated the sense of social crisis at the turn of the century and threatened the prospect of a cohesive, productive society that the public schools were supposed to ensure.

## EDUCATION REFORM IN THE PROGRESSIVE ERA, 1900–1930

Against this backdrop came the most vigorous school reform movement since the pre–Civil War days. Some people called it "progressive" education, but many educators did not use that label. School reforms in the early twentieth century expressed a multitude of impulses and problems. Some of the suggested solutions were contradictory; most of them were influenced by the development of America's highly specialized, industrial society and by the increasing diversity of its population. On the one hand, reforms partook of the impulses in industrial management to organize more centrally and to worry about efficiency and the measurement of outcomes. On the other hand, many reformers combined the nineteenth-century faith in education with new alarm about the fate of children in industrial society. These reformers linked progressive education with larger currents of social reform in the Progressive Era. The connection can be seen in the emphasis on children in Jane Addams's settlement-house work and in the muckraking book of John Spargo, *The Bitter Cry of the Children* (1906). Spargo wrote poignantly about the 2 million undernourished schoolchildren in the country, and about another 2 million laborers under sixteen, many in brutal industries like glassmaking and mining. He exposed bad sanitary conditions, infant mortality rates among the poor, and other abuses of childhood. Some of his recommended solutions were implemented in his day, like the creation of a Children's Bureau, health standards for food and milk, and child labor laws. Some anticipated later policies and debates, like his advocacy of day nurseries for working mothers, free meals in school, and medical assistance as a right.

Leading educators of this turn-of-the-century era looked at the public schools and saw rigid institutions too devoted to rote learning, isolated from real life, mechanical, and standardized. Reformers' solutions varied, but they all faced two major questions: How can schools deal with individual differences among students? What is the proper connection between schools and adult life? One set of answers to these questions came from John Dewey, who taught philosophy and education at the University of Chicago from 1894 to 1904. There Dewey and his wife, Harriet Alice Chapman, developed a laboratory school that demonstrated many of their ideas about education. Around the turn of the century John Dewey wrote two small treatises that launched his prominent career in educational philosophy: *The School and Society* (1899) and *The Child and the Curriculum* (1902).

In *The School and Society* Dewey argued that schools had lost touch with modern industrial society—children were not active enough, cooperative enough, or productive enough in school endeavors. Schools must become "embryonic" communities that model a good society, he argued, and they must build on children's natural impulses toward intellectual and social growth: their propensity to communicate, to construct things, to investigate, and to be creative. In *The Child and the Curriculum* Dewey described the teacher as an arbiter between traditional knowledge and the child's interests. The teacher's task was to connect the two in a dialectical fashion to motivate the child, to turn passive education into active inquiry, and yet to respect the historical and scientific traditions that the society valued. In these and later writings, Dewey linked school to society in an effort at reform, not the reproduction of the status quo, and he addressed individual differences by emphasizing individual inquiry and children's interests. Because Dewey wished to move schools away from the tradition of teacher-centered pedagogy and discipline-based content, he has often been associated with the "child-centered" school that became the stereotype of progressive education. But his own ideas were more complex and more difficult to achieve.

The notion that schools should help reform industrial society by producing inquisitive, active citizens, and that teachers should engage children in traditional, organized knowledge by continually consulting their interests and spurring active learning gained little ground in most schools. Even the simpler but nonetheless radical idea of child-centered pedagogy remained on the fringes, in private progressive schools and a handful of experimentally minded public schools. Still, progressive ideas about pedagogy and curriculum had some effects on mainstream public schools. Innocuous offshoots like field trips, homerooms, extracurricular activities, and the "project"

method spread widely. Public schools also implemented other ideas loosely described as "teaching the whole child." In the name of child development and social priorities, schools began offering lessons on personal relations, health, and etiquette. Such elements in the curriculum became widespread enough to upset traditionalists. Progressive challenges to traditional education actually changed some subject areas. Advocates of "social studies" challenged the discipline-based curriculum in history with a problem-centered approach, and the ensuing debate continues today.

Two major reports of the National Education Association (NEA) frame the changes in curriculum thinking that occurred over the twenty-five most active years of the debates about "progressive" education. In 1893 the Committee of Ten, chaired by Charles Eliot, president of Harvard, faced demands for modernizing the curriculum by de-emphasizing preparation in Latin, granting equal status to modern academic subjects like science and modern languages, and arranging them in four alternative academic curricula, each equally valid for college entrance or for life. In the 1890s, about 7 percent of the high school–age group was attending high school, but only about one-fourth of them went on to college. Faced with an elite institution, but not one attended mainly by college-bound students, the Committee of Ten moved in the direction of a broader academic curriculum, thus upsetting the classicists. Their actual impact was modest, and soon they were being criticized from the other side—by self-consciously twentieth-century educators who wanted schools to relate more directly and functionally to modern adult life.

In 1918, another NEA committee, the Committee on the Reorganization of Secondary Education, reflected these concerns for relevance and efficiency. Chaired by Clarence Kingsley, a high school mathematics teacher and inspector of high schools in Massachusetts, the committee announced that there were seven "cardinal principles" or objectives for high schools: education in health, home-making, vocational skills, civic participation, use of leisure, ethical character, and, as an academic afterthought, "command of fundamental processes." Even this document, the soul of social-efficiency thinking, was too "academic" for some who wanted separate high schools for different vocations. Like the Committee of Ten report twenty-five years earlier, the *Cardinal Principles* did not have dramatic effects. Few schools wholly reorganized their curriculums, and subject-matter disciplines remained the main organizing principle. But the report is a reflection of two things:

first, the gradual drift toward nonacademic functions as high schools in the twentieth century enrolled larger and larger percentages of teenagers (by 1920, about 32 percent of the fourteen- to seventeen-year-olds attended school); and second, some roads not taken—the dominance of Latin and Greek was rejected, but so were separate vocational high schools.

Whatever effects child-centered pedagogy and the demand for relevance had on American schoolrooms, the most consequential educational changes of this era concerned the control and organization of public schools. Educators such as David Snedden, Commissioner of Education in Massachusetts from 1909 to 1916, and Franklin Bobbitt, who became a professor of curriculum at Chicago in 1909, argued the case for highly centralized, highly "efficient" school systems. In 1913 Bobbitt wrote that "Education is a shaping process as much as the manufacture of steel rails . . . . Within the past decade we have come to see that it is possible to set up definite standards for the various educational products." In *The Curriculum* (1918) he summarized the dominant view of his day, that objectives and behaviors from adult life could be minutely specified and made into different curricula for different groups of children in schools. Snedden reinforced the view that schools must differentiate children's futures and train them accordingly. In "Education for a World of Team Players" (1924), Snedden wrote that only "a Utopian" would expect "the rank and file" to like opera or the fiction of Henry James. Most children were destined to be followers because "leadership, planning, management, protracted responsibility . . . present intolerable difficulties."

At this same time, psychologists were developing theories and tools that would help educators centralize systems and differentiate curriculum. Two products of this fertile period in psychology were very relevant to education: behaviorist theory and intelligence testing. In his *Educational Psychology* (1913) Edward L. Thorndike of Columbia detailed the implications of behaviorism for education. The major tenet of this theory is that learning is conditioning, the formation of a bond between a stimulus and a response. Undesired responses can be weakened by negative reinforcements, and desired responses can be reinforced by rewards. This psychological theory allowed minute specification of tasks and learning strategies. It fit well with Franklin Bobbitt's desire to achieve efficiency through constant measurement of results and David Snedden's plan to elaborate different curricula for various social roles. Thorndike also contributed to the testing movement, along with

Lewis Terman, who devised the hundred-point intelligence quotient, and Robert Yerkes, who was active in the testing of Army recruits during World War I. Like Snedden and other social efficiency theorists, Thorndike believed that children are destined for different roles depending upon ability and that testing could help identify different groups for different training. "It seems entirely safe to predict," he wrote, "that the world will get better treatment by trusting its fortunes to its 95–99 percentile intelligences than it would get by itself." Ideally the schools would provide different programs for students according to their talents, as measured with intelligence tests and other assessments. In practice, of course, children's fate in schools were also much influenced by teachers' subjective judgments, class and ethnic biases, and, within these constraints, children's own choices. As educators differentiated their programs and attracted more students to high schools, the school system became a more important arbiter between the family and the student's future workplace.

Armed with such concepts and tools, efficiency-minded educators (those that the historian David Tyack has called the "administrative progressives") set out to centralize control of education. Centralization had two aspects: political and professional. In terms of political control, centralization meant the consolidation of rural school districts and the abolition of large ward-based urban school boards. Rural school consolidation had begun in the mid-nineteenth century, and by 1900 featured an effort to make rural schools relevant to life (thus the "country life" movement) but also to professionalize control of the schools. As in urban school reform, there was an ethnic dimension to the reformers' discontents. They had always been hostile to small-scale district control because it seemed unprofessional, an excess of democracy. Then, in the Progressive Era, this tension took on an ethnic flavor as well. In his book on *Rural Life and Education* (1914) Ellwood Cubberley said that when "Jose Cardoza, Francesco Berolini, and Petar Petarovich are elected as school directors," it is "of course educative to these newcomers, though a little hard on local government." The consolidation of small districts and increasing professional supervision were the answers.

In cities, there was a widespread effort to reduce the size of school boards and to shift from ward-based elections to city-wide elections or mayoral appointments. The reform was aimed at wresting control of the system from ward representatives, who were often associated with machine politics and diverse ethnic groups, and placing it in the hands of a smaller group of people elected or appointed city-wide, who (it was argued) would act for the common good and not for partisan interests. New York City eliminated ward-level school committees in 1896 and consolidated all five boroughs under one seven-member board in 1917. Philadelphia's board was cut in half in 1905 and replaced by a smaller group appointed city-wide. Milwaukee moved from a large, ward-based board to a small board elected at large in 1907. Similar reforms took place in Saint Louis, San Francisco, and elsewhere. There were big battles over these reforms, but time was on the side of the centralizers. During the early twentieth century, large-scale organization, hierarchy, differentiated roles, and efficiency became leading ideals in school administration as in American industry, and they remained dominant until the 1960s.

In terms of professional organization, attention focused on the superintendent of schools, whose role was likened to that of the executive of a corporation. At the same time as reformers sought to centralize school board elections to ensure governance by upper-status, professionally oriented people, they also aimed to give more authority and prestige to the superintendent of schools. Professionalization, bureaucratization, and centralization went hand in hand, and the most profound legacy of early-twentieth-century school reform is the professionally trained superintendent at the top of a hierarchy of schools and rules.

But such control was not easily won or held unchallenged. Many arguments about education policy in the early twentieth century reflected the tension between democracy and efficiency, between education for open-ended growth and training for an identified end, between broad participation and hierarchical control, between an emphasis on environmental factors in learning and hereditary constraints. Looking at the leading advocates and their ideas, one can often see the sides clearly, almost as pure types. Edward Ward defended free speech and the use of schools as adult social centers in Rochester in 1910. Political boss George Aldridge, who wanted no socialist speeches being made in public school facilities, slashed Ward's budget. John Dewey joined hands with organized labor in 1913 to oppose the Cooley bill for separate vocational schools in Illinois, and he argued with David Snedden in the pages of the *New Republic* in 1914 about the undemocratic nature of vocational education. Walter Lippmann ripped into Lewis Terman and others for making hereditarian assumptions and abusing intelligence testing in a six-part series of articles in 1922.

But at the grassroots level, many educators blended contrasting ideas in pragmatic ways. Superintendent Frank Cooper in Seattle, Washington, Superintendent Richard B. Dudgeon in Madison, Wisconsin, and many of their counterparts elsewhere spoke with enthusiasm about both democracy and efficiency, about both academic work and socialization. In Gary, Indiana, Superintendent William Wirt devised a "platoon" system of schools which, he claimed, promoted efficiency and socialization on the one hand, plus an active, communal experience for students on the other. And the famous *Cardinal Principles* report of 1918, sometimes characterized as the triumph of social-efficiency thinking, was nonetheless a compromise among competing academic, vocational, and social values.

Despite such pragmatic compromises and the commitment of many individual teachers to democratic and pluralistic values, the drift in public school administration and curriculum was toward centralization, efficiency, conformity, and scientific measurement. In the follow-up to their classic sociological study, *Middletown Revisited* (1937), Robert and Helen Merrell Lynd wrote that by the 1930s social-efficiency ideas had permeated Muncie, Indiana. "In the struggle between quantitative administrative efficiency and qualitative educational goals," they wrote, the "big guns" were all on the side of efficiency. Schools are large organizations with limited resources and multiple tasks; the appeal of bureaucratic solutions and hierarchy is strong. And as the high school population moved from 32 percent of students aged fourteen to seventeen to 51 percent by 1930, the appeal of testing, guidance, and vocational training grew. Thus in Gary, for example, the 1920s saw more and more emphasis on patriotism, work socialization, and vocational training.

## PRIVATE SCHOOLS IN THE EARLY TWENTIETH CENTURY

Despite educators' attempts to reform public schools, to make them more relevant and lively, some groups did not feel well-served by the public schools. Roman Catholics had waged debates with public school officials throughout the nineteenth century. The traditions, the personnel, and the textbooks of the public schools tended to have a Protestant bias. Even if the public schools had not been biased, they would have been problematic for Catholics, many of whom believed that teaching in all subjects should be infused with religion, whereas most public schools had retreated either to a vague, generalized Protestantism or to a secular morality, in order to reduce religious controversy. The Roman Catholic Third Plenary Council, meeting at Baltimore in 1884, ordered priests to provide parochial schools in every parish within two years. While disputes between Catholics and Protestants continued, the Catholic school system expanded. In 1880, before the Third Plenary Council, there were about 400,000 children in Roman Catholic schools, or about 26 percent of the school-age Catholic population; by 1900 there were 850,000, or about 34 percent of Catholic children; and by 1920 the figures stood at 1,700,000, about 38 percent. Most of these schools had a distinct ethnic affiliation, so the appeal was both religious and cultural. In Chicago in 1900, for example, about 45 percent of the Catholic schoolchildren were in schools attended mostly by Irish; 25 percent were in schools affiliated with Polish churches, and another 23 percent affiliated with German churches. Even when residential patterns changed, Catholics clung tenaciously to the ethnic identity of their schools. For Poles, Germans, Italians, Lithuanians, French, and others, ethnic parishes were havens of national identity, and Catholic schools were an instrument of language preservation.

The most publicized nonreligious private schools of the early twentieth century were child-centered schools. Among the more prominent and long-lasting were Marietta Johnson's school at Fairhope, Alabama, featured in John and his daughter Evelyn Dewey's book, *Schools of Tomorrow* (1915), and Caroline Pratt's City and Country School in Greenwich Village, founded in 1914. Following Rousseau's ideas about education as natural growth, children in Johnson's school moved around, made handicrafts, told stories, and took field trips. In her book, *I Learn from Children* (1948), Pratt described a similar program, arguing that iron discipline and bolted-down desks would be appropriate training for dictatorship, but not for democracy. Despite the creative and democratic aspects of child-centered private education, they appealed mainly to an avant-garde middle-class clientele. In *The Child-Centered School* (1928) Harold Rugg and Ann Shumaker estimated that such schools "constitute but a corporal's guard as compared with the great regiments of formal schools."

Another distinctively twentieth-century form of private education was the "prep" school. As public high schools became more available, private academies became more expensive and selective. Some became elite feeder schools for private eastern colleges, among them old academies for boys like Andover, Episcopal schools like Groton and St. Mark's, and

newer boarding schools like Choate and Hotchkiss. Similar private elite schools for girls developed, such as Miss Porter's School in Connecticut and Chapin, one of New York City's prestigious day schools. Although they were most popular in the Northeast, similar schools in other regions provided a small sector of monied privilege to American schooling.

## EDUCATION IN THE 1930s

When the Depression of the 1930s hit America, some educators were inclined to doubt their longstanding admiration of business organization; some were even doubtful about the capitalist system. Several of the leaders of this "reconstructionist," group were faculty members at Columbia's Teachers College, to which Dewey had moved in 1904. They thought that they were applying Deweyan principles to the social crisis of the 1930s, though Dewey himself shied away from the socialist leanings of leaders like George Counts. Counts argued that if the schools did not take a stand for a new social system, they would just support the status quo, which was literally bankrupt. He made quite a splash with a speech to the Progressive Education Association in 1932, published that year as *Dare the School Build a New Social Order?*, but his radical ideas were uncongenial to most school administrators, who were more worried about fiscal retrenchment than a lack of social analysis within their classrooms. And for Counts to imagine that teachers would lead a move toward fundamental social reform, wrote Agnes de Lima in the *New Republic,* "is fantastic indeed," since teachers were "a class long trained to social docility."

As the Depression deepened after 1932, educators tried every technique they knew to shore up respect and support for education. At the federal level they argued for federal funds for purposes like salaries and construction, with no strings attached. This argument has never been popular with federal officials then or since, and in the Depression, when the Roosevelt administration was beset with emergency priorities, it got nowhere. Educators felt that the New Deal had left them in the cold. And it is true that President Roosevelt's people were unwilling to provide general aid for local schooling. Nonetheless, several New Deal programs affected the schools themselves, or educational goals outside the schools. The National Youth Administration provided work-study grants to allow poor youth to stay in school, and the Civilian Conservation Corps paid males aged eighteen to twenty-four to work on environmental projects accompanied by some education programs during nonwork hours. The Federal Emergency Relief Agency provided some emergency payments of teachers' salaries in poor districts, and the Works Progress Administration and other agencies put some money into school construction. The approach of the New Dealers, then, was to target federal aid to education toward particular disadvantaged groups and to do it temporarily.

The Depression did not constitute a turning point in federal involvement with elementary and secondary education, nor did it alter professional educators' attraction to business models and methods. American faith in education survived the crisis, and schooling continued to expand into the lives of more American youths. High school attendance increased from 51 percent of those aged fourteen to seventeen in 1930 to 73 percent in 1940.

## DIVERSITY AND AMERICAN SCHOOLING TO 1940

The public school system served some groups better than others, but patterns and levels of discrimination were continually changing. During the nineteenth century, barriers to the attendance of females had gradually given way, first at the elementary level and then, with the advent of public high schools, at the secondary level. In 1900, females actually predominated in high schools, constituting 58 percent of the students and 63 percent of the graduates. Girls took mathematics, physics, and chemistry almost as frequently as boys; and more girls (56 percent) than boys (47 percent) took Latin in 1900. By the turn of the century, then, differential treatment of girls in elementary and secondary education was not a matter of access to the classroom. It was more a matter of the messages that were conveyed, the roles and expectations that were portrayed. Reflecting the culture and the workplace of American society, schools reinforced the image of women as wives and mothers. At the very time when access to secondary education was becoming more equal, educators like G. Stanley Hall emphasized that a highly advanced society featured strong differentiation of roles. Arguing against coeducation in high schools, Hall said that schools should "push distinctions to their uttermost, to make boys more manly and girls more womanly." He lost his campaign against coeducation, but the sentiment about gender roles was widely shared. Although most male and female students studied similar subjects at the core of the curriculum, schools developed home economics and secretarial courses that reinforced certain expectations about adult roles for women, and

the gender composition of the education profession itself modeled images of appropriate female and male roles. As the century progressed, some women challenged such generalizations by seeking access to higher education and entry into such traditionally male occupations as laboratory science. But stereotyping receded only gradually and partially, and not all role models proved permanent. Female college faculty increased substantially in the early decades of the century, from 19 percent in 1910 to 33 percent in 1930, and then declined. The peak of 1930 was not reached again until the 1980s. Similarly, women held 62 percent of elementary school principalships in 1905, dropping to 38 percent in 1950 and 17 percent in 1985.

Classroom teaching, of course, was a popular occupation for women. In 1900, 70 percent of elementary and secondary teachers were female, which increased to about 84 percent in 1920 and then gradually decreased (except during World War II) to about 68 percent in 1960, a ratio that has persisted to the present, within a few percentage points. Women teachers have been more heavily concentrated at the elementary level. They held 90 percent of public school elementary teaching jobs in 1930, a ratio that has altered little in the years since (86 percent in 1986); secondary school teachers, in contrast, were 65 percent female in 1930 and 50 percent female in 1986. More men came into the profession after World War II, and most of them entered the secondary school ranks. Meanwhile, the number of women in top administrative positions in school systems has gone from near zero to a handful (1.6 percent in 1928, 3 percent in 1985).

While prejudice toward women is an important element in the history of twentieth-century American education, affecting the educational experiences, aspirations, and careers of half the population, discrimination against racial minorities was more severe and more open. Until the Supreme Court's decision in *Brown* v. *Board of Education* signaled the beginning of a federal commitment to begin rectifying the situation in 1954, equal educational opportunity did not exist for nonwhite children. Reactions to this discrimination varied, as minority leaders recommended different strategies for their groups. The most celebrated debate among African Americans involved the ideas of Booker T. Washington, head of the Tuskegee Institute, a famous college for blacks that was devoted to manual labor and occupational training in such practical trades as carpentry, even though most of its graduates became teachers. Washington, raised in slavery, advised social segregation and gradual economic progress for black Americans, and he developed a strong following through persuasion, personal networks, and control of the black press. Challenging Washington's dominant "accommodationist" stance was William E. B. Du Bois, a Harvard-trained sociologist and a founding member of the National Association for the Advancement of Colored People. Du Bois advocated more forthright demands for access to education, especially for the "talented tenth" of African Americans who would provide the leadership for the betterment of the race.

Important issues were at stake between Washington's supporters and those who favored Du Bois. But many black educators found ways to combine the ideas of the two camps. In this regard they were like the grassroots white educators who blended ideas about democracy and efficiency. One can thus find, in the history of black education before the *Brown* decision, much emphasis on rudimentary literacy and vocational education, and, on the other hand, much pride in the accomplishments of the minority of black students who attended high school and colleges, where most pursued the same classic liberal arts high school and college curriculum as white students.

In the North, black Americans lived mostly in large cities, and even there, they constituted a small percentage of the population in the early twentieth century. Sometimes their children attended school with white children. But the black population grew rapidly during the "great migration" of blacks northward, and whites acted to segregate school systems which had in some cases been somewhat integrated. In Chicago, for example, the black population in 1900 was under 2 percent; in Philadelphia it was 5 percent. In Chicago, black residents recalled, access to public schools was fairly open in 1900, and many black children went to mostly white schools. Tensions mounted as the black population grew, but Superintendent Ella Flagg Young resisted agitation for segregation in the first few decades. In Philadelphia a similar situation existed in 1900, with some separate black schools but most black children in mixed schools. Superintendent Martin Brumbaugh, unlike Young, favored more segregation. Yet he was resisted on both counts by activists within the black community. After 1920 the migration increased whites' anxiety to segregate schools, and the memory of violent race riots added to the alienation. Northern urban school systems became segregated not only through rigorous residential segregation ("de facto" segregation), but also directly, through education policies such as the creation of black-only schools or the drawing of district boundaries that deepened segre-

gation. While some blacks supported separate schools, pointing to the employment opportunity for black teachers and to the lessening of racism for their children, many others argued for equal access. Their fears—that segregated black public schools would receive unequal resources—became reality in both the North and the South.

Native American children received even less equal educational access in the early twentieth century. Very few local district public schools admitted American Indian students as of 1900. The federal government operated two kinds of schools for Indians, boarding schools and reservation day schools, and the number of these schools had increased in the last few decades of the nineteenth century, numbering 106 boarding schools and 147 reservation day schools by 1900. The Bureau of Indian Affairs (BIA) had rid such federal schools of cultural input from Native American educators. Federal officials condemned Cherokee, Chickasaw, and Choctaw schools as too broad in their aims and too tribal in their culture, and they replaced them with federally controlled boarding and day schools based on explicit theories of white racial superiority. Such schools enrolled about 20,000 Native American students, which, according to the government, equalled about half of the school-age children. But enrollment varied greatly in different areas and among different tribes, and daily attendance rates were much lower than enrollment rates. BIA officials reported strong resistance to government schooling, for example, among the Pueblo nation and the Navajo. In 1892, only 95 Navajo children, out of 16,000 of school age, were enrolled in government schools, said the BIA superintendent of education; only about 900 Indian children were enrolled in California at the turn of the century.

Native Americans mounted many challenges to this situation, often suing for access to public schools. Courts in the various states responded quite differently, but gradually the percentage of Native American schoolchildren who were in local public schools (sometimes segregated) increased, and the percentage in federal BIA schools decreased. The federal boarding schools were severely criticized in the Meriam Report of 1928, and under John Collier, head of the Bureau of Indian Affairs from 1932 until 1945, the boarding schools were urged to change to a policy more sympathetic to Native American culture. But these reforms did not change all the boarding schools and did not touch the great majority of Indian children. In 1934 Congress passed the Johnson-O'Malley Act, which authorized the BIA to contract with local public schools for Indian education, but its intent was subverted by many local districts, which simply incorporated the Johnson-O'Malley funds into their general budgets, diverting the money to white students.

Similar patterns of exclusion and discrimination characterized Hispanic Americans' experiences with public schooling, with similar responses of protest and legal action, largely unsuccessful before World War II. In the Southwest, Mexican Americans faced public school systems that either excluded them or segregated them in inferior facilities. Public schools in Texas, California, New Mexico, and elsewhere emphasized English training, rudimentary skills, and vocational education for Mexican Americans. This unequal treatment prompted the formation in Texas in 1929 of the League of United Latin American Citizens (LULAC), headed by middle-class Mexican American integrationists. However, challenges to the exclusion of Mexican American children from Anglo schools in Texas and elsewhere were not effective for many years. The California state attorney general declared in 1930 that local authorities could treat Mexican Americans as "Indians," who could be segregated under the separate-but-equal doctrine and state law. In a Texas case (*Salvatierra*) in 1930, the state supreme court treated Mexican Americans as white and forbade segregation in principle but denied that their segregation was based on their ethnic identity. In a case (*Mendez*) that was more legally satisfying to integrationists, a federal judge in California ruled in 1945 that it was unconstitutional that Mexican American children had been systematically segregated in four communities. Despite this long-sought admission, de facto segregation of Mexican American schoolchildren continued in the postwar period.

Asian Americans faced some similar conditions: in some communities, notably San Francisco, there was white resistance to their attendance in mixed schools, while in other communities they attended public schools with whites. Issues of the language barrier and cultural adjustments required of Asian American students were not addressed by the public schools in the immediate postwar decades.

## PENDULUM SWINGS IN EDUCATION REFORM, 1940–1990

Two important shifts in education policy were hastened by World War II, but the origins of each reached back before 1940. One moved in the direction of greater intellectual emphasis in the school curriculum, and the other in the direction of greater equality of opportunity. The first shift took the form of an attack on "Life Adjustment Education," a version of progressive education that was popular in public school circles in the 1940s and 1950s. Life Adjustment Education did not place a high priority on academic subject matter, or on socially critical thinking. Thus it fit neither the inclinations of the radical progressive educators of the 1930s, who wanted to use the schools for social reconstruction, nor the various academic critics of the schools, who wanted a return to subject matter emphasis in the traditional disciplines. It was the latter who surfaced in strength in the mid-1950s. In his *Educational Wastelands* (1953), the University of Illinois historian Arthur Bestor complained that in a Life Adjustment curriculum, "trivia are elaborated beyond all reason," teaching children how to improve their appearance and how to choose a family dentist. This critique received a tremendous boost when the Soviet Union launched its *Sputnik I* satellite into orbit in 1957. Leading American educators like James B. Conant had become accustomed to thinking of public education in terms of "manpower" development for international competition during World War II, but it now became a matter of public concern and of constant comment in the popular press. *Life* magazine complained that schools were "trying to be all things to all children," while "the geniuses of the next decade are even now being allowed to slip back into mediocrity."

President Eisenhower, like many commentators, blamed it on John Dewey. Teachers, he said, must "abandon the educational path that, rather blindly, they have been following as a result of John Dewey's teachings." Eisenhower informed his cabinet officers that domestic legislation would fare better in this immediate post-*Sputnik* period if it carried the phrase *national defense* with it. Thus arose the National Defense Education Act of 1958, the first sizable entry of the federal government into funding local elementary and secondary education since the Smith-Hughes Act of 1917 had begun funding vocational education programs. Like Smith-Hughes, NDEA provided funds on a voluntary basis to local districts that applied through their states. But NDEA money was targeted at math, science, and foreign language training. Despite a huge amount of publicity, and despite the Cold War anxieties associated with this educational crusade, subsequent studies showed only modest changes in elementary and secondary school curriculum. There was a slight rise in foreign language study, and NDEA funds built a lot of new language laboratories. Surprisingly, course registrations in ad-

Table 1.   TWENTIETH-CENTURY LEGISLATION AFFECTING ELEMENTARY
AND SECONDARY EDUCATION

| Title | Year Enacted | Description |
|---|---|---|
| Smith-Hughes Vocational Education Act | 1917 | Provided federal grants to vocational education in local elementary and secondary schools. |
| Johnson-O'Malley Act | 1934 | Authorized Bureau of Indian Affairs to contract with local school districts for education of Native American children. |
| National Defense Education Act | 1958 | Provided federal grants to local elementary and secondary schools for improved education in math, science, and foreign languages, and to universities for improved programs and graduate fellowships in these areas. |
| Vocational Education Act of 1963 | 1963 | Increased the level of federal funding for vocational education; broadened the definition of vocational education, making more programs eligible for funding. |
| Elementary and Secondary Education Act | 1965 | Provided aid to local elementary and secondary schools for compensatory education for children in low-income districts; also for improved libraries, pilot projects, and educational research. |
| Bilingual Education Act | 1968 | Funded local school district programs in bilingual education. |
| Indian Education Act | 1972 | Increased funding of Indian schools; established bilingual and multicultural programs; established Office of Indian Education. |
| Education Amendments | 1972 | Title IX forbade discrimination based on sex. |
| Rehabilitation Act | 1973 | Guaranteed civil rights of handicapped persons. |
| Education of All Handicapped Children Act | 1974 | Established right to education for handicapped persons. |
| Education Consolidation and Improvement Act | 1981 | Allowed more discretion to local districts through block grants. |
| Goals 2000: Educate America Act | 1994 | Title II created a board to certify voluntary national content, performance, and opportunity-to-learn standards and related assessment systems. Title III provided funds for states to develop such standards at the state level. |

SOURCE: Adapted from *Encyclopedia of the United States Congress* (New York: Simon & Schuster, 1995), p. 689.

vanced science and math did not increase, despite the emphasis on these subjects in James Conant's best-selling *American High School Today,* published in the year after the *Sputnik* launch. But there was, with additional monies provided by the National Science Foundation, much innovation in "new" mathematics and science curricula, following the psychological principles laid out in Jerome Bruner's influential 1959 book, *The Process of Education.* NDEA also became a precedent for later legislation providing federal aid to elementary, secondary, and higher education in the 1960s and beyond. (For a summary of federal legislation, see table 1.)

In the meantime, the 1950s witnessed the rise of the civil rights struggle into a visible and expanding movement. The famous Supreme Court case, *Brown* v. *Board of Education of Topeka* (1954) was both the culmination of a long legal campaign and, on the other hand, only the very beginning of a revolution in public education in the South. In *Brown,* the justices declared unanimously that school segregation arising from state statutes, such as existed in twenty southern and border states, was unconstitutional. This decision overturned the reigning court doctrine, promulgated in *Plessy* v. *Ferguson* (1896), which declared that separate public facilities for different races were permissible as long as they were equal. The pre–World War II precedents of the *Brown* decision include cases in the 1920s and 1930s in which the Supreme Court increasingly applied the Bill of Rights to state laws, as well as efforts by black plaintiffs to sue school districts in the South for unequal resources. Some of these cases resulted in concessions, but always on the basis of the separate-but-equal doctrine. World War II led to pressures to integrate the armed forces, raised issues of racism more generally because of the Nazi Holocaust, and, at home, led to the GI bill, which gave many minority students a chance to go to college, where they encountered and challenged segregation. By the late 1940s, the Legal Defense Fund of the National Association for the Advancement of Colored People, led by Thurgood Marshall, had decided to argue not just for equal resources but also to argue the inherent inequality of separate school systems. Black lawyers developed these arguments in the early 1950s, winning some influential federal court dissents in the cases that eventually came to the Supreme Court. In the meantime, the Supreme Court decided some higher education cases in favor of black applicants to white law schools, cases that undermined the separate-but-equal doctrine (especially *Sweatt* v. *Painter,* 1950). In *Brown,* the Court, led by Chief Justice Earl Warren, cited the great importance of education in providing equal opportunity, and argued that the stigma attached to legally separate public schools made them inherently unequal, and a violation of the Fourteenth Amendment guarantee of equal protection of the laws.

At first southern states interpreted *Brown* to mean only that they had to erase school segregation laws from their statute books. During the first ten years after *Brown,* very little integration of children occurred. Indeed, in 1964, only 1 to 2 percent of all black children went to school with any white children in the South. But in a series of cases between 1964 and 1973, the Court made it clear that the time for action had come, that integration and not just nominal desegregation would be required, that compulsory busing had to be used if other techniques were ineffective, and that integration would also be required in the North, wherever segregation had resulted from decisions made by local school boards, such as how they drew district boundaries, how they assigned students, and others. In the meantime, the Congress and the executive branch got more aggressive in support of integration. Title VI of the 1964 Civil Rights Act allowed the government to withhold federal funds from discriminatory programs; then, the next year, the Elementary and Secondary Education Act (ESEA) of 1965 began to provide unprecedented funds to local districts for the basic

skills training of children from poor neighborhoods. Thus the secretary of education had some leverage to encourage integration. All these developments moved in the same direction, but the tougher stance of the federal court system, in the wake of Supreme Court decisions clarifying and extending *Brown,* was crucial. By 1975 only 23 percent of black students in the South attended schools that were more than 90 percent black (compared to 58 percent in the Northeast and 63 percent in the Midwest). As the integration effort moved into the late 1970s and 1980s and the scene shifted more to the North, progress was impeded by urban demography (density of minorities in the inner city, white flight to the suburbs), flagging political will, a more conservative stance from courts and the White House, and increasing skepticism by African Americans about the benefits of integration. In 1988, almost half of black students in the Northeast and Midwest still attended schools that were 90 percent or more black. Three decades of research on the effects of integration are inconclusive but suggest modest positive effects on black academic achievement and opportunity with no negative effect for white students.

The administrations of John Kennedy and Lyndon Johnson (1961–1969) witnessed a shift in federal educational policy from the emphasis on Cold War technology to an emphasis on ameliorating the effects of racism and poverty. Title I of ESEA (1965) provided aid to districts with a high proportion of low-income families, to spend on compensatory instruction on basic skills; it became the largest federal education program and the most pervasive instrument of federal presence in local schools. Head Start, the preschool program aimed at disadvantaged children, also appealed across bipartisan lines and became a fixture in local communities. As with integration, research has shown modest positive effects of these programs, but they have found strong support in Congress and from Republican as well as Democratic administrations.

The 1970s also saw the successful assertion of education rights by a variety of groups. Building upon the civil rights achievements of African Americans as well as upon their own struggles over the many years, women, Hispanic Americans and other language groups, handicapped children and their advocates, and Native Americans, among others, received new legal guarantees of more equal access and more voice in determining education policy. The politics of the time were right for it; the momentum was there, albeit briefly. If race and poverty were the central education themes of the mid-1960s, their expansive cousins, diversity and pluralism, were pre-occupations by the mid-1970s. In 1968 Congress passed the Bilingual Education Act (Title VII of the reauthorized ESEA), which provided grants to districts on a voluntary basis to conduct bilingual education programs. This and subsequent legislation underscored the government's basic policy to support transitional bilingual education, with English fluency as the goal. In 1974 the Supreme Court (in *Lau* v. *Nichols*) declared that Chinese American students with limited English proficiency in San Francisco were discriminated against, in violation of Title VI of the Civil Rights Act; the Court did not specify the remedy but demanded that school systems respond to children's language needs. Subsequently, the Department of Education promulgated guidelines for "Lau remedies," which specified bilingual instruction as the remedy.

The movement for women's rights also had its education component. Title IX of the Education Amendments of 1972 provided for the withholding of federal funds from any program that discriminated on the basis of sex. The most visible and publicized area of Title IX enforcement became inequities in men's and women's athletic programs, but the law applied also to a much wider range of issues: recruitment, admission, and financial aid of students, for example, and the hiring and compensation of faculty and staff. Meanwhile, the rights of handicapped citizens were gaining advocates in Congress. The Rehabilitation Act of 1973 was called the Civil Rights Act for the Handicapped, and it was followed by the Education of All Handicapped Act in 1974. Three major policies resulted: first, improved physical access to public buildings, including schools; second, mainstreaming, the integration of children with special education needs into regular classrooms as often as possible; and third, collaboration with parents of handicapped children on an individual educational plan for each child.

In the case of Native Americans, the general ethos of protest and group assertion was exacerbated by the termination policy of the 1960s, which ended protected reservation status for many tribes that elected to do so; in some cases, like the Menominee of Wisconsin, the result was widespread destitution, with a great majority of Menominee on welfare by 1970. Among other reactions to the crisis, and to perennial problems of Native Americans in public schools, parents protested against prejudice and lack of Indian culture in the curriculum. Such agitation led to the Indian Education Act of 1972, making more funds available to Indian schools, requiring

parental input into public schools, encouraging bilingual and multicultural programs, and establishing an Office of Indian Education in the Department of Education. Various amendments in the 1970s encouraged local input and cultural diversity, but the problems were not easily solved. In the late 1980s an Indian Nations at Risk advisory committee was still urging the Department of Education to respect Native American cultures and build better partnerships with parents.

Related to these assertions of group rights were issues of pluralism and mainstream values in the public schools. After the pendulum swung away from "teaching the whole child" in the 1940s, to focusing on advanced subjects and academically talented kids in the late 1950s and early 1960s, the pendulum seemed to swing again to concerns about equality, pluralism, and the problems of those whom the public schools served least well. It had at least two major effects: one was that more school resources and policy analysis went toward compensatory education and less toward high-level academic achievement. A second was a heightened sensitivity to bias in curriculum materials, causing somewhat greater diversity of materials and discussion about bias in such matters as testing.

Critics argued that the drift of the 1960s and early 1970s not only de-emphasized academic achievement but promoted moral relativism in the schools and a failure of confidence and conviction about moral education, patriotism, and traditional roles. Furthermore, much of the school reform of the period was initiated at the federal level, entailing a great deal of bureaucratic regulation. Even before the election of Ronald Reagan in 1980, there was much backlash, and some retreat by officials of the Carter administration, on such issues as Title IX enforcement and integration. President Reagan promised reduced federal involvement, and although he could not make good on his pledge to abolish the Education Department, his education officials did reduce regulations, give much more discretion to states and localities, and change the themes of research and program initiatives. Public concern about declining college-entrance-test scores and poor functional literacy, linked in the public press to recession and poor productivity, found expression in the report of the President's Commission on Excellence, *A Nation at Risk* (1983). The pendulum had swung again. Once again the focus of the agenda moved to academic achievement and excellence in the service of international competition—this time more economic than technological. With the federal government more in the background, the states assumed a greater role. States had always been the main regulators of curriculum, teacher certification, and other matters; they now became the major players in school reform. The 1980s reform packages enacted by many states included tougher high school graduation requirements, improved teacher training, increased teacher salaries, teacher career "ladders" with new roles for experienced and master teachers, increased testing, and, toward the end of the decade, widespread experiments in decentralized governance, often called site-based management, in which councils of teachers, administrators, and parents made decisions about personnel, curriculum, and other matters that had previously been made by system-level administrators or building principals.

Some schoolchildren, of course, were not part of the public system. The Roman Catholic schools, after a financial crisis that caused many school closings in the 1970s, stabilized in the 1980s. Although the total percentage of American schoolchildren in private schools (about 12 percent) did not rise in the 1980s, the number of conservative Protestant Christian schools increased, and private schooling in general received more sympathetic treatment from journalists, researchers, and politicians. The Supreme Court had in the 1970s drawn a line around permissible aid to private religious schools, which, though vague, prohibited general payments like salaries, construction, or tuition reimbursement. But in 1983 the conservative majority, in the spirit of alternatives and parental choice, allowed a tax deduction for school tuition payments by low-income parents in Minnesota (*Mueller*). With the legal situation more fluid, "choice" in education became an important issue in the early 1990s.

The history of educational reform is one of pendulum swings in debates, proposals, and rhetoric. Americans have charged their schools with numerous responsibilities, some of them in tension. Among these tasks are to socialize children, teach them moral values, promote academic excellence, train people for life, provide equal opportunity, and be a melting pot of cultural and social understanding. When reformers perceive that some task they value is not being well served in schools, they tend to emphasize that theme, and denigrate the other goals the schools are pursuing. Thus, in 1900 reformers criticized the schools as too academic, too cut off from modern industrial life; in the 1950s critics bemoaned schools' attempt to "teach the whole child" at the expense of academic excellence, especially for the top students. By the late 1960s the most common criticism

of the schools was their cultural biases and failure to serve poor and minority children well. In the 1980s the values swung back to academic achievement and excellence.

But real schools do not change so fast; their history is more of continuity and accretion. Field trips, movable desks, and group projects are legacies of the progressive movement, the comprehensive high school the result of long discussions about democracy and tracking from the 1910s to the 1950s, and schools' constant testing inherited from the rise of assessment from the 1910s to the 1930s. Reform movements call for "revolutions" and "total restructuring," but they tend to nudge schools first in one direction then in another. Some reform demands are cyclical: teaching the whole child versus promoting academic excellence, or responding to episodes of international competition through education. Other trends are long-term developments, moving more or less in one direction, for example, the expanding access to schools and the corresponding increase in school attainment. These long-term trends have also been the result of reforms and struggles. They were not foregone conclusions, nor did they always move in straight lines. The long-run trend toward greater and more integrated access has been a major feature of public school history in the United States. Whether this trend is reversible is one of the interesting questions for the coming decades, since the 1980s witnessed some resegregation on racial lines.

A different sort of example is the process of centralization, long the ardent goal of reformers, from 1900 to the 1950s, resulting in more and more state and federal involvement, more professionalization of administration, and more centralization of local districts. There was resistance, to be sure, from some educators and some parents, but the professional orthodoxy, supported by the popular press, was that big, centralized systems provided better education. This faith eroded in the 1960s, when attacks on bureaucracy and demands for decentralization arose. Not only the inefficiency of bureaucracy and bigness was attacked, but the power relationship embedded in the bureaucracy, namely, that big school systems like New York City were managed largely by whites, when some schools had mostly black students and teachers. Attempts at decentralization aroused huge controversy in New York City in 1968 but resulted in undramatic and inconsequential compromise. The issue arose again in the 1980s, in the context of very different politics. The 1980s reform movements, driven more by local and state reformers, discovered that central control was keeping schools from responding to students' needs and from recruiting the best teachers. Restructuring was promised. At the same time, President Reagan bucked a historic trend by decreasing federal involvement in elementary and secondary education. Whether these two attempts to decentralize control will prevail in the face of such a long, sturdy historical trend will be another interesting question to assess in the next century.

Whatever happens concerning these two trends, the public schools will continue to struggle with an enduring agenda, one which has taken different forms in different eras, but has long included these daunting tasks: to create equal opportunity for all Americans through schooling, to be the main arena in which American diversity is faced and adjudicated, to be the main arbiter between families and the economy, and to be the main provider of literacy, essential to democracy as well as to the world of work. Reflecting the society in which they work, the schools have always come up short on these tasks, but that has not allowed them ever to escape the demands of the agenda for very long. Furthermore (and finally), the demands of advanced capitalism and democratic pluralism are complex and continually evolving; thus, Americans tend to notch up their expectations about what it means to be treated equally, to be tolerant, to be a competent worker, and to be literate. This guarantees future performance gaps for the schools and future school reform movements.

SEE ALSO The University (in this volume); Philosophy (in this volume); Political Ideas and Movements (volume I).

## BIBLIOGRAPHY

Among works that cover the whole sweep of twentieth-century educational history, one must begin with the third volume of Lawrence A. Cremin's magisterial synthesis, *American Education: The Metropolitan Experience* (1988). Focused more on the history of schools, David B. Tyack, *The One Best System* (1974), is the classic study of urban education in the twentieth century, essential to understanding the development of public educators' administrative mentality. Donald Warren has edited an anthology of the latest work on the recruitment, training, and professional activities of teachers in American history, entitled *American Teachers: Histories of a Profession at Work* (1989).

For the history of particular groups, see James D. Anderson, *The Education of Blacks in the South, 1860–1935* (1988), which covers an ambitious subject, emphasizing the "self-help" aspects of African Americans' educational ventures, and Guadeloupe San Miguel, Jr., *"Let All of Them Take Heed": Mexican Americans and the Campaign for Educational Equality in Texas, 1910–1981* (1987), which chronicles the goals and activities of the League of United Latin American Citizens. A now-dated but still indispensable overview of the education of racial minorities in American history is Meyer Weinberg, *A Chance to Learn: A History of Race and Education in the United States* (1977). More recently, Paula S. Fass has analyzed the cultural commitments of school reformers by looking at the experience of women, Catholics, blacks, and European immigrants in *Outside In: Minorities and the Transformation of American Education* (1989).

For works focused on the Progressive Era, we begin once again with Lawrence Cremin; his book, *The Transformation of the School* (1961), is still the best narrative account of progressive education, though it uses a light touch on social conflict and inequality. Edward A. Krug, *The Shaping of the American High School, 1880–1920* (1964), comprehensively analyzes debates and documents about curriculum in the Progressive Era; Krug's work should now be complemented by Herbert M. Kliebard, *The Struggle for the American Curriculum, 1893–1958* (1986), which dissects the major strands of curriculum thinking in the Progressive Era, clarifying tensions in school reform. Two other recent, influential works deal with the Progressive Era: in *Power and the Promise of School Reform* (1986), William J. Reese examines education at the grassroots level in four cities; and, in *Education and Women's Work* (1991), John L. Rury analyzes the relationship between the economy and female participation in secondary education from 1870 to 1930. The only broad historical study of education during the 1930s is excellent; it is David B. Tyack, Robert Lowe, and Elisabeth Hansot, *Public Schools in Hard Times* (1984). On the period since World War II, see Joel Spring, *The Sorting Machine* (1976), which chronicles and critiques government intervention from a perspective on the left, and Diane Ravitch, *The Troubled Crusade* (1983), which analyzes national and federal trends from 1945 to 1980 with an equally troubled but more conservative eye. Richard Kluger, *Simple Justice* (1976), chronicles in stirring fashion the landmark Supreme Court case, *Brown* v. *Board of Education*.

# THE UNIVERSITY

## *Hugh Hawkins*

A striking characteristic of American higher education in 1900 was its institutional variety. What some called healthy democratic multiplicity others saw as anarchic provincialism. It was not just the number of institutions claiming to be part of higher education that struck observers, but those institutions' widely differing missions and structures. This range of types had grown out of a history that combined efforts to imitate alternative European examples, tolerance for innovation, and local entrepreneurship. Charters, scarce before the American Revolution, had proliferated in a country that gloried in new beginnings, where state governments were eager to encourage residents' ambitions.

Harvard, modeled on the English residential colleges and created by a legislative act of the Massachusetts Bay General Court in 1636, sought to prepare clergymen, civic leaders, and learned gentlemen. It was the only college in the English colonies until a royal charter in 1693 established William and Mary in Virginia, but before it got around to holding classes, the school that was to become Yale had opened in Connecticut (1701).

By 1776 there were nine colonial colleges, headed by clergymen and sharing modestly in the new learning of the Enlightenment. Most colonies desired to prepare an elite without the need for training in England. New Jersey already had a college (later called Princeton) when in 1770 the founding of a second college (later called Rutgers) by the Dutch Reformed Church forecast an important new source of such institutions: a denomination's assertion of its special identity. By 1860 at least 180 colleges survived out of a good many more founding efforts.

In the wake of the Revolution came a movement for "state universities," notably in the South. Those that opened differed little from older colleges, carefully maintaining student discipline and religious nurturance and receiving very little support from state funds. An exception was the University of Virginia, which began instruction in 1825, with freedom of course election for students and a minimum of clerical influence. Hoping to serve the "learned professions," older colleges began to establish chairs, and later schools, of law, medicine, and theology. Independent professional schools, such as the law school of Tapping Reeve in Litchfield, Connecticut, also gained ground.

As the population spread into newly acquired territory and newly prosperous cities, state universities, denominational and local colleges, and independent professional schools all proliferated. So did misnamed secondary schools and utterly fraudulent "degree mills." Normal schools, founded as early as the 1820s, made no claim to be colleges until late in the century. Early women's "seminaries," such as Mount Holyoke (opened 1839) might offer college studies, but cautiously avoided the name. Vassar (1865) and Wellesley and Smith (both 1875), however, granted the bachelor's degree and declared that their students received an education virtually equivalent to that in "the best men's colleges." Largely excluded from existing institutions, African Americans joined sympathetic whites in founding Wilberforce University in Ohio in 1856. This pattern of separate colleges for blacks was followed elsewhere after the abolition of slavery. Oberlin (1833) was a notable exception in both its racial and gender inclusiveness.

All was not variation, of course. New colleges imitated older ones. Many looked for guidance to the Yale Report of 1828. This faculty statement, responding to accusations that the curriculum was impractical, made a careful case for liberal education as "the discipline and the furniture of the mind," with mental discipline and cultural grounding best provided by continued requirement of the traditional studies of Greek, Latin, and mathematics. Specialized education for professions or business, the report argued, should come later in separate schools or departments, or through apprenticeship. Two influences moderated this stark curricular regime, the president's

Table 1.   LANDMARK LEGISLATION AFFECTING HIGHER EDUCATION

| Title | Year Enacted | Description |
|---|---|---|
| Morrill Land-Grant College Act | 1862 | Provided grant of federal lands to states to establish and operate college programs in agricultural and scientific education. |
| Smith-Lever Act | 1914 | Provided matching grants to states for agricultural and home-economics extension programs. |
| Army Defense Act | 1916 | Established Reserve Officers Training Corps (ROTC). |
| Servicemen's Readjustment Act (GI Bill) | 1944 | Provided federal grants to individual veterans for further education. |
| Fulbright Act | 1946 | Arranged college student and faculty exchanges abroad. |
| National Defense Education Act | 1958 | Provided federal grants to local elementary and secondary schools for improved education in math, science, and foreign languages, and to universities for improved programs and graduate fellowships in these areas. |
| Higher Education Act | 1965 | Created a general system of federal loans and scholarships for undergraduates. |
| Education Amendments | 1972 | Title I expanded college scholarships and loans. Title IX forbade discrimination based on sex. |

SOURCE: Adapted from *Encyclopedia of the United States Congress* (New York: Simon & Schuster, 1995), p. 689.

course for seniors, usually called moral philosophy, which sought to lend coherence and ethical force to earlier studies, and the student literary and debating societies, where new books and new ideas promoted fresh thinking and argument.

With almost no exceptions colleges required attendance at daily chapel and Sunday church services. A revival could cancel all class sessions as prayer meetings multiplied. The college was a community, perhaps even a family, and the president, devout and fatherly, set the tone. The religious atmosphere at most of these colleges diminished with time, but if revivals became a rarity, the institution's obligation to students' spiritual development remained part of the collegiate idea as the nineteenth century ended.

For some time West Point (opened 1802) and Rensselaer Polytechnic Institute (1824) had the field of applied science and engineering virtually to themselves. By the 1840s, however, things were stirring with the creation of scientific schools attached to older colleges and "parallel courses" that avoided the classics in favor of science and modern languages. By the 1870s the RPI example had found several imitators in new independent technical institutes.

These practicalist tendencies, given a boost by agricultural societies, were strongly advanced by the Morrill Land-Grant Act of 1862, the favorite project of Sen. Justin S. Morrill of Vermont. Under this law, revenue from the sale of federal lands was used to support at least one institution in each state with the main purpose of teaching subjects "related to agriculture and the mechanic arts." States reacted in multifarious ways, but usually with either a new "agricultural and mechanical college" or new support for an existing state university. Admission requirements varied widely. (For a summary of federal legislation, see table 1.)

In the last third of the nineteenth century, complex universities dramatically altered the educational landscape. Based on the German model, but unlike it encompassing an undergraduate college, "true universities," as they were often called by their advocates, included a faculty oriented toward research, a graduate school that granted the Ph.D. degree, and professional schools requiring some collegiate preparation. Both older foundations, like Harvard and Yale, and new ones made possible by private fortunes, like Johns Hopkins (opened 1876) and the University of Chicago (1892), embraced these new ideals.

As the twentieth century dawned, such universities were dislodging many traditions of higher education. Independent technical and professional schools, coming under suspicion of inferior standards and mercenary motives, began to accept the shelter provided by university affiliation or by themselves began to expand into universities. Liberal arts colleges, still claiming a special function in mental training and character building, began to rely on teachers and textbooks developed in universities. Nevertheless, many institutions with local or regional reputations and clienteles (including some state universities) clung to older ways, such as offering subcollegiate preparatory programs.

No one could seriously assert that American higher education constituted a coherent system, but influential academic leaders urged clearer definitions and better coordination. Their considerable success came during a century that brought vast increases in the number of students and the number of institutions, budgets that grew but never seemed big enough, administrative exfoliation, rising faculty professionalism, a continued gain of prestige for research over teaching, easing of institutional controls over students, intensified government and business influence along with weakened religious involvement, and a public that generally respected academia but could also grow skeptical.

## COORDINATION AND OUTREACH, 1900–1918

Higher education resembled much of the rest of society in the years preceding World War I. Reform was in the air, but while some reformers sought more efficient and orderly institutional arrangements, others focused on improving the lives of groups that had suffered negative effects from the nation's pell-mell industrialization and urbanization. Then, like most of the nation, colleges and universities threw themselves uncritically into a war to "make the world safe for democracy." The sudden onset of peace in 1918 left them with a host of new problems, but also a new sense of their importance.

There were somewhat more than nine hundred colleges and universities at the turn of the century. A movement to limit proliferation in the name of standards appears to have been effective, as the number remained under one thousand through the end of World War I. The average institution was expanding to absorb more students. In 1910, the University of Chicago ranked as the largest, with 5,000 students; Columbia, Harvard, and the state universities of Michigan and Minnesota enrolled approximately 4,000 each. By 1920 the University of California surpassed them all with 13,000 students. Midwestern colleges also grew. Carleton, with just above 200 in 1900, had more than doubled its enrollment by 1915.

If number of students can serve as a guide, higher education was already prosperous in 1900. The 238,000 resident students that year constituted 2.3 percent of the nation's eighteen- to twenty-four-year-olds, double the percentage of thirty years ear-

lier. Accelerated by World War I army training programs, the percentage attending rose to 3.6 in 1918. (It must be borne in mind, of course, that the population of college-age youth was itself increasing.) The national student-faculty ratio was an impressive 10:1 in 1900 and 12:1 in 1920. Faculty salaries were improving, the average at Wisconsin rising 11 percent between 1904 and 1907. The highest salary for a professor at Yale in 1910 was $5,000.

The federal government had in 1890, with a promise of steady increases, begun annual subventions to institutions designated by states as beneficiaries of the Morrill land grants. Even more propitious, state funding rose after that year. In most states by 1900, tax revenues—sometimes by millage, a guaranteed fraction of all state tax revenue—regularly went to state universities, Morrill-grant colleges (where these were separate from state universities), and normal schools. Private benefactions, which had allowed institutions such as the University of Pennsylvania and Washington University in Saint Louis to become complex universities, continued in the prosperous opening years of the new century, with many earlier gifts continuing their effect as endowment income. But a crucial portion of financial receipts in private institutions remained student payments, and legislators were more likely to increase public institutions' appropriations when enrollments rose. Accordingly, administrators strove to increase student numbers.

The institutional untidiness of a system without central definitions or controls distressed some who shared in a general social movement toward order and coordination. Regional accrediting associations began in 1895 to set standards, first for secondary schools, then for colleges. The Carnegie Foundation for the Advancement of Teaching, led by Henry S. Pritchett (formerly head of Massachusetts Institute of Technology and earlier of the U.S. Bureau of Standards), set eligibility requirements for its professorial pension program that put upward pressure on admission, graduation, and other standards. National organizations, notably the Association of American Universities, joined in the accreditation venture. An effort by the U.S. Bureau of Education to appraise institutions, however, ran afoul of political opposition stimulated by the outcry from institutions given lower rankings.

Gradually, professional schools (whether parts of universities or independent) began raising their entrance and graduation requirements. The state normal school at Greeley, Colorado, pioneered in requiring high school graduation for admission (1897) and elevated its name to Teachers College in 1911. A series of research studies by the Carnegie Foundation promoted this tendency, most effectively Abraham Flexner's 1910 survey of medical schools, which led to closings and mergers that reduced the number of schools from 155 to 85 by 1920. Colleges, once competing with professional schools for students, were becoming a necessary preliminary and hence more likely to hold their students for four years. Engineering remained an exception, the professional training for which could be entered without prior higher education, and so did school-teaching.

Along with this ordering process of admissions and degree standards, went national organization by institutions, beginning with the Morrill-grant colleges in 1887. State universities followed in 1895, and the leading Ph.D.-granting universities in 1900. Fearing that universities were squeezing them out, and resisting secularization of higher education, liberal arts colleges (most of them Protestant) formed a national association in 1915. These and other groups sought coordination during World War I by forming an umbrella organization, the American Council on Education (1918).

As beneficiaries of corporate wealth and an enriched tax base, colleges and universities generally supported industrial capitalism. Still, they sought ways to humanize the new industrial system, offering a hearing to proponents of reform. New business administration programs and training for social workers both shared in university expansion. Most famously at Wisconsin under President Charles R. Van Hise, but at other state universities also, academics consulted with legislators and regulators to help create and carry out new social legislation. There was nothing new in the claim that liberal arts colleges trained worthy leaders for government, but for Woodrow Wilson, holder of a Ph.D., to reach the White House added luster to the advanced training which had more than anything else identified the "genuine universities."

Hoping to counteract stereotypes of pedantry, impracticality, and snobbishness, higher education developed a variety of programs to win public support, some of them minimally connected with older ideals of intellectual discipline, character building, and pursuit of truth for its own sake. Extension programs brought professors face to face with small-town audiences. Farmers' institutes invited rural folk to campus for short training programs. The Smith-Lever Act of 1914 provided matching grants to states to support Morrill-grant institutions in offering agricultural and home economics extension work. The

joyful acceptance of this program, which the land-grant college's own association had done much to design, signaled a moment of high assurance. There could be no question about the appropriateness of tax monies for universities, advocates reasoned, since such outreach by experts clearly served the public.

Presidential tours and addresses reassured the middle class that the educational ladder was available to all. Inventions such as the milk-fat test were touted as demonstrating the benefits of support for university scientists. In 1900 Harvard briefly hired a private "Publicity Bureau," and when during the 1910s the term "public relations" emerged, it was soon taken up by universities as well as businesses, for the press found good copy in higher education and institutions wanted positive coverage. Interviews with presidents abounded, and intercollegiate athletics made the front page. However, Edwin E. Slosson, in his muckraking *Great American Universities* (1910), found tedious lectures, inefficient faculty meetings, and student shallowness, although he also cited such positive developments as the linking of abstract thought with technical applications and well-designed new engineering programs.

Shortly before World War I, some private universities added military training, hoping to match public universities' reputation for rendering social service, and in 1916 academics helped shape federal legislation that set up the Reserve Officers' Training Corps program. American entry into the war brought unqualified statements of willingness to serve the purposes of the state. Faculty left campus to create new weapons, War Department training programs in the fall of 1918 turned colleges into virtual military camps, and humanists violated their obligations to truth by disseminating lurid and inaccurate accounts of enemy atrocities. As Carol Gruber observes, this was a corruption of the service ideal by scholars who failed to recognize "that they could serve society best as free and independent thinkers, who contributed to the expansion of human knowledge and . . . exercised the function of social analysis and criticism."

Largely from middle-class families, students aspired to ascend one of the American career ladders, no longer limiting themselves to traditional professions. By 1910 over 40 percent of Wesleyan University graduates were entering business, quadrupling the rate of the early 1880s. At Kansas State College, children of farmers learned about agriculturally relevant occupations in science, government, and teaching that could be followed without the backbreaking toil their parents knew. At Harris Teachers College in Missouri, a largely female student clientele prepared for school-teaching, though not necessarily thinking of it as a lifelong career.

Denominational student clubs, plus YMCAs and YWCAs adjacent to campus, may have countered rumors of godlessness, and were especially welcomed by state universities that had long been objects of suspicion from denominations sponsoring their own colleges. But even at church-related colleges, required instruction in religion gradually gave way to courses on "the Bible as literature." Ethics courses developed that explored nontheistic grounds for pursuing the good, and the burgeoning humanities, especially literature and philosophy, were justified as religious training had once been—as helping students toward timeless values and self-transcendence. Elaborate new chapels still rose on prosperous campuses, as at Stanford and Chicago, but they served more as personal memorials or exemplars of architectural magnificence than as centers for a shared religious life. Required Sunday church attendance grew easier to escape, or was abolished, and weekday chapel services grew less daily, less religious, and less strictly required.

Extracurricular activities began to proliferate as an extension of liberalizing the curriculum. "Well-rounded" students immersed themselves not only in proms, yearbooks, and pregame rallies, but in social and community service. A series of deaths from football injuries led in 1905 to a national association to regulate play and diminish violence, a development that helped preserve the sport that often came closest to determining morale on campus. The football star, the head of the "women's association," the editor of the student newspaper (as Franklin D. Roosevelt was in 1903–1904) won their peers' admiration as valedictorians did not. Seeking votes for women, chapters of the College Equal Suffrage League, launched in 1900, spread to many campuses by 1912. Students before and after graduation began to participate in the settlement house movement, going into cities and learning about the life of urban poverty by more direct experience than books could give. Student government, generally under close control from deans, allegedly provided practice in citizenship. At Earlham, links to Quakerism did not prevent the introduction of drama by 1910, though dancing and smoking remained forbidden.

While some faculty members were pushing to revive the humane tradition against a curricular regime that, as Irving Babbitt put it in 1902, measured learning "in foot-pounds" and welcomed everything from "boiler-making to Bulgarian," others worried more about getting their due respect as professionals.

J. McKeen Cattell's *University Government* appeared in 1910 with accounts of presidential highhandedness and trustees' obscurantism. Within institutions, faculty asked for a larger role in governance, but when they got it, they often complained about long agendas and onerous committee assignments. Faculty members who sought more than a local reputation attended conventions and published in scholarly journals. Departments, taking on sharper disciplinary identities, sought not only to attract majors, but also to win respect from fellow specialists at other institutions.

As they became more specialized, individual scholars felt a divided loyalty between their home institution and their discipline. A spate of organizing in the 1880s and 1890s left a few gaps, mostly filled with the founding of one disciplinary association per year between 1901 and 1905, ending with the American Sociological Society. The inadequacy of these bodies in meeting general professional needs of academics led in 1915 to the formation of the American Association of University Professors, which promptly investigated the abrupt firing of a professor at the University of Utah. In the sterner test of World War I loyalty hysteria, however, the AAUP failed to offer adequate protection to professors discharged for their real or suspected political beliefs.

The inner structure of governance was shifting in ways that made presidential autocracy, benign or otherwise, less and less likely. Deans increasingly served as intermediaries with both faculty and students. Departments began to have more say in faculty appointments. Senates, often made up of the institution's full professors, shared new responsibilities. But presidents' visibility and influence remained high. They, after all, represented the institution to the public and made the case for funding to donors and legislators. Trustees often preferred to back them, even in questionable decisions, rather than embroil themselves in the inner workings of the institution.

Although required concentration (the major) and distribution (breadth), as established at Princeton, Harvard, and elsewhere, provided a credible response to the alleged anarchy of electivism, students soon informed each other of the less constricting majors and of "snap" courses which filled breadth requirements. Still, highly demanding teachers found followers among students who hungered for learning or saw upward mobility in intellectual achievement. The term *grind,* applied to the student rather than the process, had emerged in the United States in the 1890s, and preceding the epithet with *greasy* heightened the implications of social unacceptability. But at Yale, students and faculty joined after 1900 in an effort to restore respect for intellectual achievement. Cheating lost its acceptability, and the Phi Beta Kappa chapter was revived. Elsewhere awards were created for the best scholar-athlete or the fraternity with the highest grade average.

Already established at ten institutions by 1900, the perquisite of sabbatical leave gradually spread. New "research professorships," at Cornell and elsewhere, relieved their incumbents of most teaching responsibilities. Carnegie support in 1903 for the new Research Laboratory of Physical Chemistry at MIT forecast future development of research institutes. Newly minted Ph.D.-holders, starting out in college teaching, wrote back to their mentors complaining of teaching demands that excluded time to continue productive scholarship. The increased pressure for active scholarship by faculty in professional schools diminished the reputation of mere teacher-practitioners. In medicine, a great battle for "full-time" teaching and research by all professors began in 1911, with philanthropic foundations pushing to separate professors from financial relationships with clients.

Despite their earlier participation in the reformist ferment of the Progressive Era, the universities came out of World War I elated by victory and loath to criticize American society. With Europe exhausted, American higher education launched programs to bring in foreign students, raised funds to rebuild shattered European libraries, and established the American Council of Learned Societies largely in order to help foreign scholars. The new assurance came not just from economic capacities. American academics could credibly claim that they had built institutions deserving to rank with the ancient European centers of learning and that they had shaped these into a coherent system.

## GROWTH IN FLUSH TIMES
## AND HARD TIMES, 1919–1941

The sharp growth in enrollments during the 1920s, close to double (from 600,000 to 1,101,000, with the percentage gain of eighteen- to twenty-four-year-olds as resident enrollees rising from 4.7 to 7.2), was brought on by more than recovery from wartime disruption. Male enrollment increased more rapidly than female, a trend which continued until World War II. More and more occupations required academic training, but economic motives explained only part of the mounting attendance. Prosperity allowed

children of the middle class to spend time on a liberal education, which in the rhetoric of the time prepared one for life rather than for earning a living, and such education helped protect social status. The offspring themselves might insist on being part of the college scene, popularized by the media and romanticized by older friends.

Distinctions between universities and colleges grew, the former seen as large, renowned, and working occasional scientific miracles, the latter as intimate, concerned for all-around student development, and staffed by dedicated pedagogues. The institutions in the Association of American Universities increasingly committed themselves to the ideal of research, appraising candidates for membership by the quality of Ph.D. dissertations and faculty scholarly achievements. With Beardsley Ruml, an officer for Rockefeller philanthropies, taking the initiative, and with Chicago sociologists and Yale psychologists conspicuous among the beneficiaries, some universities developed elaborate research institutes with staff members who did little or no teaching.

Teachers colleges and the then-labeled Negro colleges were both moving toward the standard liberal arts college model. At Fisk University, long steeped in white philanthropy and paternalism, student protests in 1925 forced out the president, eased rules such as one forbidding conversations between male and female students, and opened the way for fraternities and more ambitious intercollegiate athletics. Catholic colleges, seeking accreditation, began adopting the usual system of departments and credit hours. Newly self-conscious urban institutions, many Catholic, others growing out of YMCA evening business schools, hoped to serve cities as land-grant colleges served rural populations. Sometimes an ambitious urban elite took over a local church-related college, as when Buchtel became the Municipal University of Akron in 1914. Junior colleges, usually in smaller communities, varied from expensive private finishing schools to publicly supported extensions of high school that made starting college more economical.

The creation of new women's colleges slowed, but some among those that opened, like Bennington and Sarah Lawrence, proved notably innovative. In the South, separate women's colleges continued as a long-established tradition, existing even as separate parts of state universities (as in Virginia and North Carolina), although Tulane allowed its women's college, Sophie Newcomb, to move to the main campus in 1918. Eastern elite universities continued to resist coeducation, with Harvard, Brown, and Columbia claiming to meet the need with their coordinate women's colleges, developed in the l890s. In the case of Catholic women's colleges the rate of foundings did increase in the 1920s, providing for a group that had previously lagged in college attendance.

The sharp inflation of 1919–1920 helped focus attention on academic budgets. A new sort of fundraising began—the organized drive, targeting alumni, often with a matching grant from a foundation. On the whole, these drives succeeded amid a rising sense of prosperity. Between 1921 and 1930, Yale's endowment rose from $26 million to $94 million. State legislatures proved more willing to loosen the purse strings, as presidents, playing down student frivolity and faculty radicalism, stressed their institution's practical social benefits. The state's appropriation to the University of Wisconsin, at $3.2 million in 1921–1922, peaked at $5.2 million in 1930–1931.

Direct support from business corporations also mounted in the early 1920s. The University of Michigan successfully invited business contracts with its new department of engineering research but did not obtain the federal subventions for engineering research stations that Michigan, along with Purdue, Illinois, and others, claimed would appropriately parallel agricultural research stations, aided under the Hatch Act of l887. At the University of Colorado, an electrical engineering professor accepted a trade association subsidy for a report that depreciated municipal ownership. He told critics that he was fostering good relations and helping the university's graduates get jobs. By the 1930s many such programs were in abeyance, partly because they appeared to violate academic autonomy, partly because corporations were in financial trouble.

During the Great Depression, endowments shrank as stock values collapsed. Lower interest rates also cut endowment income. A declining tax base could not maintain the previous level of public support for higher education. Accordingly, the proportion of income from student fees rose in the early thirties, even when total enrollment dropped in 1933. (It began to rise again in 1934. Given the absence of jobs, some students felt they could scrape by better at college than at home.)

Although colleges never got the loans from the Reconstruction Finance Corporation that they wanted, federal aid did increase. Public works projects expanded academic plants, and aid reached students through the National Youth Administration and other agencies. Even though the proportion of funds from state governments fell sharply in the

1930s, it remained well above that from the federal government (in 1940, 23 percent state, 11 percent federal). Not until 1943 did federal revenue surpass state.

Ethnic barriers rigidified after World War I. Black students were not admitted to Princeton, and Harvard barred them from freshman dormitories in the early 1920s. But it was the announced limitation on Jewish admissions at Harvard that caused an uproar over exclusion. President A. Lawrence Lowell insisted that Harvard was being open about a policy other institutions practiced sub rosa. Protests by Jewish alumni and faculty brought a formal withdrawal of the policy, but by complicating the admission procedures and emphasizing "character," the barriers were kept up. Similar practices were adopted at other institutions.

Such issues were of little concern to the students who dominated the decade after World War I, those whom Helen Lefkowitz Horowitz identifies as pursuing "College Life." Women students seemed different, less worried about proving that females could be as serious in the pursuit of learning as males. Students of both genders paid more attention to learning by direct experience about life in general and sex in particular. Apart from fraternity parties and rides in jalopies, there were fascinating extracurricular activities that for many made up the real life of college. Courses and examinations, accepted as necessary evils, formed a background for more congenial pursuits with the campus newspaper, intramurals, drama clubs, and choruses. In *The Damned and the Beautiful* Paula Fass shows that students tended to be culturally liberal in the 1920s while remaining politically conservative, with the student press embracing the rights of self-expression as its favorite cause.

Secularization accelerated with wartime disruption and the larger, more diverse student bodies after 1918. Yale, the model for many colleges further west, reestablished required chapel following a wartime suspension, but had to give it up in 1926 under student, alumni, and faculty pressure. The official rationale, of course, was that religion would be more influential when freed from compulsion. The ideal of the college as a Christian community survived at conservative evangelical institutions like Wheaton in Illinois, but was ill-adapted to complex universities or the many colleges that shared an ideal of truth as an open-ended quest. Academics who feared institutionalized religious authority as a threat to free inquiry joined in making the Scopes trial of 1925 a symbol of religiously based repression. Most liberal arts colleges still made religious nurture part of their rationale, but presidents spoke ever more vaguely, referring to "religion in its largest terms" or to their "historically Protestant" college.

During the hard times of the 1930s, the studious and the radical gained new prominence among undergraduates. There were new and urgent reasons for students to engage public issues. They felt directly threatened by the inability of the nation to counteract persistent unemployment, but they also manifested an altruistic concern with social inequalities. Organized labor gained their support, and off-campus social projects expanded. The class inequities of higher education drew student protest, and extension courses for union workers and the more elaborate "labor colleges" sponsored by unions (one was a summer school at Bryn Mawr) let some students reach across class lines.

Departmental identity intensified, even at smaller colleges. Psychology broke off from philosophy, political science from history. Professors were busy trying to keep up with developments in their specialties. Those from different departments might meet at the Faculty Club, where complaints about the president or the students usually provided common ground, and representatives of different departments might work out the politics of a new curricular distribution requirement. Generally, however, colleagues were content to go their own ways.

Faculty salaries fell far short of matching the postwar inflation. The professoriate dropped in the professional income scale, even as clearer standards for tenure increased job security. AAUP investigations gained influence, but efforts to work out formal standards dragged on. When the national "Statement on Academic Freedom and Tenure" was finally issued in 1940 by the AAUP, only one of the several institutional associations—the liberal-arts-oriented Association of American Colleges—agreed to cosponsorship, though others later joined in.

More European scholars began to appear on American faculties in the late 1920s, their number increasing as fascism grew more menacing. Within the social sciences these newcomers (such as Theodor Adorno) introduced theoretical work to counteract the narrow empiricism of American scholarship. In language and literature, the presence of representatives of the culture being studied (such as Ramón Sender) gave new vividness and authenticity. Scientists who had once attracted American students to Europe (such as Enrico Fermi) were now available at American institutions. A notable beneficiary was the New School for Social Research in New York,

but even small provincial institutions began to include émigré faculty members.

At complex universities, "the administration" came to mean a large number of officers, and jokes about presidential absence from campus went the rounds. Alumni relations directors and public relations officers appeared, the latter often under euphemistic titles. New deanships sought to address the needs of students perceived as coming from a wider range of backgrounds, many "crude" and "lacking in culture." Also part of the "personnel movement," with expertise in psychology the chief avenue of entry, were admission officers and counselors, who promised to reduce cases of poor adjustment and to increase academic achievement.

Various foundation studies encouraged a drive for standard accounting procedures. The discovery of a college president who kept bills and receipts in his hat emblemized the problem of fiscal backwardness. Soon there were national handbooks, with procedures modeled on the best-run businesses, and treasurers and comptrollers with specialized training headed retinues of clerks. The drive for efficiency was not limited to financial matters. Registrars headed growing staffs dedicated to the accuracy of schedules and transcripts.

While freshman orientation programs sought to help all newcomers adjust to college, remedial freshman composition classes targeted those with special needs. Some state universities were required by law to accept any graduate from the state's public high schools. In that case, the university might create a separate track for the less able, as the University of Minnesota did by opening its two-year General College in 1932. The often imitated honors program at Swarthmore stimulated abler students with special seminars and concluding orals conducted by outside examiners. Major foundation backing for the program was won by Swarthmore's president, Frank Aydelotte, who had been inspired by Oxford methods as a Rhodes scholar.

Foundations also played a major role in encouraging faculty research. Rockefeller fellowships sent American physicists and biologists to Europe for study, and various postdoctoral fellowships allowed new Ph.D. recipients to advance beyond the dissertation stage before they embarked on full-time teaching. University laboratories now had to reckon with industrial research laboratories, some of which, like General Electric's, made important theoretical breakthroughs. Industry drew talent away from the academy, as did the federal government with such agencies as the National Bureau of Standards and the Food and Drug Administration. But these could also be viewed as new opportunities to place those with university training.

In the 1920s, the arts began to be taken more seriously as part of a liberal curriculum. A national study surveyed art appreciation courses and suggested ways to prevent trivialization. Yale founded a drama department and lured George Pierce Baker away from Harvard to develop advanced training through his workshop method. The University of Michigan made much of having Robert Frost as a writer in residence, and other institutions concluded that having artists and writers about was one way of preparing their graduates for "cultured" lives. The presence of Grant Wood at the University of Iowa fine arts school (founded in 1929) led to a bitter struggle between the historical-critical and the creative wings. Basking in reflected glory as Wood's works became national icons, the university gave him considerable autonomy. Paul Green's historical pageants, such as *The Lost Colony,* stimulated theater studies at the University of North Carolina and spread its fame. Sometimes the arts flourished at small maverick institutions, notably Black Mountain College, where the teaching of Josef and Annie Albers inspired a handful of students who went on to distinguished careers in the visual arts.

The academy's unhappiness with American culture tended during the 1920s to stress small-town provincialism (as did Sinclair Lewis's novels) and nationwide commercialism (as did Thorstein Veblen's treatises). Professors of English like Norman Foerster and Stuart Sherman reached more than a campus audience with their strictures on philistinism and shallowness. The onset of the Great Depression worked a startling change. It seemed inappropriate to dwell on the faults of the unemployed, especially as members of the middle class fell into that status, and criticism shifted to the American political and economic system. In Wisconsin, the best social insurance system in the nation owed much to scholars at the state university, and these experts went to Washington to help design the Social Security Act of 1935. Professors who became New Dealers or published exposés in the *Nation* and the *New Republic* became models for idealistic students and a thorn in the side for conservative trustees. Capitalism having failed, the more daring academics reasoned, socialism must be recognized as the hope of the future. If Marxists were never a majority of any faculty or student body, they were determined and articulate. Students could choose between the Young Socialist Alliance and the more radical Student League for Industrial Democracy. At City College of New York,

Stalinists, Trotskyites, and various splinter groups made the lunchroom a debating center, struggling to adapt to international turnabouts as Europe drifted toward war.

## THE EXPANDING FEDERAL PRESENCE, 1942–1973

During World War II, academic leaders were busy coping with the drain on civilian students, worrying about federal policies that brought service personnel to campus for training, and trying to give intellectual depth to the wartime slogans of freedom and democracy. Still, there were efforts at postwar planning, and some institutions regarded the hiatus of war as a chance to let certain traditions die and to set new goals. National and local committees continued to advance ideals of general education, still seeking to counter excessive or premature specialization. All in all, the universities' governmental negotiations showed greater sophistication than during World War I. Scientists often performed military research under contract at their home institutions, and university officials learned not to ignore overhead costs. Some results of this work were known during the war, such as radar, chiefly developed at MIT; whereas the world's first release of energy by a self-sustaining nuclear reaction, achieved at the University of Chicago, remained secret until the dropping of the bomb on Hiroshima in August 1945. The much less noted completion in 1946 of the computing machine ENIAC at the University of Pennsylvania presaged revolutionary developments in electronics.

Although the higher education establishment in Washington supported the 1944 GI Bill of Rights, which included aid to returning veterans for college attendance, virtually no one foresaw the wide utilization of this educational benefit. GI bill students peaked at over a million in 1947, and in all 2.2 million enrolled, 3 percent of them women. Overcrowding by student veterans encouraged the opening of branch campuses and new institutions, as did the democratic ideology of the war, which put new emphasis on accessible higher education.

Creation of community colleges proved one of the few promptly enacted suggestions of the President's Committee on Higher Education, appointed by Harry S. Truman in 1947. Often linked to high schools, but also created independently, the number of community colleges (as the junior colleges were rapidly renamed) rose from 461 in 1942 to 886 in 1970. By then close to three-fourths were public (up from half in 1942), and two-year colleges constituted about one-third of all institutions of higher education.

In a similar spirit of democratic expansiveness, Connecticut, Massachusetts, and Rhode Island transformed their agricultural colleges into state universities. Branches of older state universities opened in Baltimore, Chicago, and Milwaukee. Upgradings and coordination of various public institutions into the State University of New York sprang in part from evidence that private institutions limited admission of African Americans, Catholics, and Jews, and in part from the national political ambitions of Governor Thomas Dewey. California's "master plan," adopted in 1960, created separate functional definitions for three public higher education systems with different missions: the university (with sole authority in training for certain professions), the state colleges (with strong teacher-training components), and the junior colleges. The university promptly began developing new branches at Santa Cruz and San Diego.

Private urban institutions also responded to the increased postwar demand. The University of Southern California and others were able to create or upgrade professional schools, bringing themselves closer to the most inclusive university model. In 1949–1950, there were 1,851 institutions of higher education in the United States, 62 percent private; by 1971–1972, there were 2,606, with the private group still the majority. When enrollments are compared, however, the change is striking. Close to equal in 1949, the enrollment in public institutions more than tripled that in private by 1971. There seemed to be plenty of students to go around, since overall enrollment rose (1950 to 1970) from 2.3 million to 7.9 million. With instructional staff up from 190,000 to 551,000, the student-faculty ratio increased from 12:1 to 14:1. Complaints about oversubscribed classes and impersonal methods mounted accordingly.

Women's proportion of total degree enrollment, at 35 percent in 1952, scarcely budged during the rest of the decade. Women students still heard themselves urged to preserve culture, do volunteer work, and be intelligent wives and mothers. But a counterargument began to gain power even before the women's liberation movement, an argument that emphasized proving gender equality by having a career, even if motherhood delayed that career. The 1960 figures showed a rise in the proportion of women students.

The chances for African Americans to obtain higher education improved, although slowly. In 1950, the Supreme Court ordered admission of black students to state-supported professional schools and forbade any segregation of black students once admitted. *Brown* v. *Board of Education* (1954), though it dealt with lower schools, challenged the whole apparatus of educational segregation. The admission of a black veteran, James Meredith, to the University of Mississippi in 1962 brought violence and tested the resolve of the Kennedy administration, but Meredith stayed to graduate in 1963. Historically black institutions were torn by recognition of the righting of an old injustice and the wish to keep their own special traditions alive. Strategies varied: merger with a previously all-white neighbor, admission of whites and attaining full racial integration (successfully pursued in the case of West Virginia's black land-grant college), emphasizing remedial work for black students deprived of adequate secondary preparation, or (increasingly after the revival of black nationalism in the mid-sixties) stressing the specialness of a black community and a black heritage.

New modes of federal support went far beyond the GI bill and funds to construct student housing. Vannevar Bush's *Science: The Endless Frontier* (1945) had warned that for both military and economic reasons, the government must increase and regularize its support for basic research. Sponsorship of research, basic and applied, continued under various agencies, such as the Atomic Energy Commission, the National Institutes of Health, and the armed forces. MIT, the top recipient of militarily oriented funds, created a giant Division of Defense Laboratories, and President James R. Killian declared that MIT's long experience with sponsored research proved it to be educationally enriching. Summer conferences between national security officials and MIT faculty swelled the stream of contracts, and in 1957 Killian became the first White House science adviser. Other institutions followed MIT's example. At Stanford and elsewhere, government contracts became so important that administrators often based hiring decisions largely on candidates' ability to win federal financing. Even at smaller institutions scientists won federal grants and tapped funds from the National Science Foundation, established in 1950 after a long legislative struggle, with special responsibilities for science education. By 1960 the central government's contribution to total academic income stood at 18 percent, including land-grant moneys, research grants and contracts, and payment for services to the military. But that statistic only hinted at the effects on the academic ethos of Washington's involvement. The old service ideal took on a national, defense-oriented coloration, and professors with large government grants or contracts emerged as the new academic elite.

The Korean War of 1950–1953 proved less disruptive than World War II in part because the federal-academic alliance had continued in force. Then in 1957 the Soviet launching of Sputnik, presumably showing that the United States had fallen behind in science and technology, turned Cold War anxieties dramatically toward improving the quality of education. The favored fields in the National Defense Education Act of 1958 were natural science, engineering, and modern languages, with direct funding to private as well as public institutions. NDEA undergraduate loans and graduate fellowships introduced new ways of directing government dollars to individual students.

If such widely welcomed developments owed much to the Cold War, the ideological struggle clearly damaged higher education in other ways. Accusations of radicalism and suspicions of disloyalty distracted institutions. The few cases of institutional courage were overshadowed by the more numerous occasions when trustees, presidents, and colleagues participated in dismissing faculty members accused by the FBI or congressional committees of being or having been Communists, or of refusal to assist investigators by identifying other radicals. "Lack of candor" proved a convenient ground for dismissal.

Most academics had put this sordid record out of their mind by the mid-1960s, when they found themselves among the beneficiaries of Lyndon Johnson's Great Society. The Higher Education Act of 1965 brought the first federal scholarships for undergraduates—those with "exceptional financial need." It also provided insured loans for students and expanded existing work-study programs. The act was carefully drawn to benefit students from middle-class as well as poor families, and settled a long battle among the higher education lobbyists over whether the bulk of federal aid should go directly to institutions or to students.

The Education Amendments of 1972, enacted by a Democratic congress and a Republican president, unified virtually all federal programs aiding higher education. Its authorization of $19 billion over three years for what was now broadly labeled postsecondary education would have been unthinkably high only a few years before. The omnibus act provided for "basic educational opportunity grants" as an entitlement, linked only loosely to family income. During the next two decades the act was periodically renewed with relatively minor modifications. With massively increasing academic budgets, federal money came to seem an absolute requirement for institutional fiscal health. Federal dollars made a new world for administrators, faculty, and students.

As fears of renewed depression after World War II had faded, academics felt challenged to demonstrate their contributions to continuing economic expansion while seeking to attract an increasing share of national product to their institutions, whether from public or private sources. Economic analyses demonstrated the advantage of higher education to individual incomes and to gross national product. *Economics of Higher Education,* a 1962 government study, stressed human capital's role in economic growth and indicated that in 1949 college graduates had a mean lifetime income double that of the population at large. Shortages of faculty placed aspiring academics uncharacteristically in a seller's market. A study of thirty-six institutions found salaries had lagged behind price increases from 1939 to 1957, but that by 1968, real salaries showed an increase of nearly half over 1939. Nationally, the annual faculty salary increase averaged (unadjusted) 5.5 percent between 1957–1958 and 1967–1968, years of relatively low inflation. Since institutions persistently stressed their needs, it only gradually became clear that they were sharing in the remarkable prosperity of the 1950s and 1960s. From 1950 to 1970 state support for public higher education rose from $1.1 million to $12.9 million, and higher education endowment income from $113 million to $668 million.

In the new era of rising expectations, Clark Kerr, chancellor at Berkeley (1952–1958), then president of the statewide University of California, stood out among successful academic leaders—a manager, a negotiator, an entrepreneur, a Quaker idealist, and yet a pragmatist. Suggestions that a major party might select him as its presidential candidate indicated the rising status of universities. His classic volume *The Uses of the University* (1962) captured the ethos of the new giant universities, serving multiple constituencies, surrendering old ideas of academic community, and stressing research as the route to professorial and institutional success.

A longstanding concern about the lack of system in American higher education and alarm over the campus turmoil of the mid-1960s led the Carnegie philanthropies to set up a special commission in 1967. The commission and its successor, the Council on Policy Studies, both headed by Kerr, became potent influences in institutional and governmental decisions. If some of the nearly two hundred reports which had appeared by 1979 got lost in this welter of publications, their general case for ordered diversity effectively reasserted traditional American pluralism.

Rapid internal changes suggested the brevity of collegiate generations. A campus which in 1947 would have been packed with older student veterans, whose dwellings (surplus housing contributed by the federal government) dotted once open green spaces, had taken on a different look by 1957. Dubbed "the silent generation," students were busy sampling the good life, which their degree would presumably guarantee in the future. In 1965, more bachelor's degrees were awarded in business and commerce than in any other field. Marriage and parenthood while still in college grew more likely, and women left college for marriage with few apparent qualms.

In the mid-sixties things changed. Coffee houses featuring folk songs appeared near campuses. Haircuts for men and permanents for women went out of style. Dress became daringly casual, with army surplus clothing a favorite. Use of drugs, some stronger than marijuana, spread from campus to campus. Students began, as the slogan urged, to "question authority." Harbingers had appeared in 1960. That year in San Francisco students protested against House Un-American Activities Committee hearings, at Oberlin others created the left-oriented Student Progressive League, and in New York a group refused to take cover during a civil defense drill. But the major sources of the new student culture were the civil rights movement and the war in Vietnam.

When black college students in Greensboro, North Carolina, began a sit-in to protest segregation at a local lunch counter, they sparked a direct action program that soon ignited other southern campuses. Nashville became one center of black student activism, Atlanta another. As the objectives widened to include desegregation of interstate bus travel and voter registration, some white students joined in. The protesters suffered beatings, jailings, and lynchings, but their numbers grew.

Students who had spent a year or a summer in protest activities returned to campus in no mood to accept the shibboleths of the American way and gradualist reform. This new radicalism erupted at Berkeley when campus officials blocked recruiting and money-raising on campus for various causes, including the Student Nonviolent Coordinating Committee. The resulting Free Speech Movement attracted students from across the political spectrum and opened an era of direct action, including sit-ins, marches, and strikes. Mass media quickly spread the image of embattled students. A rhetoric of revolt developed, applying the themes of oppression di-

rectly to student life, as in the article "The Student as Nigger." A new model of student protest was now available for widespread imitation.

The escalating war in Vietnam deepened student anguish. For male college students of draft age the war became a highly personal issue, with minimal consolation in student deferments that were palpably inequitable and distinctly temporary. Although opinion polls showed most of the public supporting the war, it came to symbolize all the nation's imperfections. Students seeking ideological support often drew on the arguments of the Port Huron Statement issued by Students for a Democratic Society in 1962, and many could give a fair summary of C. Wright Mills's *The Power Elite*.

Richard M. Nixon's ending of the draft relieved one source of student anxiety, but his continuation of the war, even while deescalating, made him an object of academic wrath. Reactions against the American invasion of Cambodia in 1970 brought new student uprisings and the fatal shooting of students by police at Jackson State, a black college in Mississippi, and by the National Guard at Kent State in Ohio.

Students' mounting critique of the society turned to the institution closest at hand. They challenged virtually the whole range of academic values. The seizure in 1968 of four buildings at Columbia University, the violence of police called onto campus, and the ensuing breakdown of educational activity shocked the academic world more intensely than had the initial Berkeley uprising. Some who had sympathized with the original Free Speech Movement were appalled at the invasion of a university president's office and the burning of a faculty member's research notes. Protests at the University of Wisconsin reached a gruesome climax when a late-working student was killed in the nighttime bombing of the physics building, presumed to be the site of secret military research.

The more prestigious the institution the more likely an outbreak of student militancy. But it was a rare campus during the Vietnam era that did not experience some sort of demonstration against local academic practices. A look back in 1972 (the last year of numerous student protests) would have found changes large and small that had followed a period of questioning, first by students, then by nearly all participants in academic life. Authorities loosened curricular requirements, began active efforts to increase black enrollments, and gave students direct access to boards of trustees. New experimental colleges included the private Hampshire College in

Massachusetts and the public Evergreen State in Washington.

Faculty reformers won power in various national scholarly organizations, notably the Modern Language Association. Rank and file gained more influence in policy-formation, and radical papers began to spice formerly stodgy annual meetings. Meanwhile, the associations continued their traditional function of advancing professional values. At conventions members heard about new faculty benefits on other campuses, and more importantly, gave each other the prestige of visibility among peers. Specialized journals and university presses proliferated, providing new outlets for scholarly writing. The practice of peer review spread to nearly all matters of research support, publication, and promotion. Although the "locals" could still be admired and valued, the "cosmopolitans," with their ability to enhance institutional reputations, benefited most from higher salaries and more generous leave policies.

Presidential heads rolled in the late 1960s. One could rise toward the top of the AAU's seniority list with surprising rapidity. Only Theodore Hesburgh of Notre Dame (1952–1987) and William Friday of the University of North Carolina (1956–1986) had the staying capacity of earlier patriarchs. With increasing size and more complicated external relations, it grew ever harder for presidents to imagine themselves as scholars or mentors. Clark Kerr's emphasis on the president as mediator was accurately placed, but his own troubles with the various constituencies of the University of California dramatized how extremely difficult that function had become, and after Ronald Reagan exploited campus unrest to win the governorship, Kerr was dismissed.

General education gained strength in the aftermath of World War II. Amherst College's core curriculum, launched in 1947, introduced a set of new required courses that filled over half the freshman and sophomore years. The Harvard faculty report of 1945, familiarly known as the Red Book, made an impressive case for attending more closely to preparing the "responsible human being and citizen," not just the specialized pursuer of a vocation. Still, the report's limited results at Harvard—the requirement to choose one general education course each from three divisions—showed the power of a specialized faculty to resist large core courses. Columbia had developed such courses after World War I, but found it difficult to keep them staffed.

Inspired by the nation's new sense of its global responsibilities, older departments yielded ground to area studies. New programs in American Studies,

comparative literature, and neuroscience sometimes took on departmental status. The pattern set by these interdisciplinary programs was available when pressures mounted from groups of students who felt their identities demeaned by absence of curricular representation. The late sixties saw the emergence of black studies programs or departments, the seventies of women's studies.

Evidence of the mounting attractiveness of careers in academia came in the steady increase of new Ph.D.'s. The number of earned doctorates conferred (most of them Ph.D.'s) rose from 3,300 in 1939–1940, to 6,400 ten years later, to 9,800 in 1959–1960. Until the mid-sixties, the total of faculty positions was rising faster than the number of new Ph.D.'s, and when this situation reversed, there was little slack, since the rate of Ph.D.-hiring by government, business, and the nonprofit sector began a decided increase.

Amid mounting prosperity, more institutions could afford to engage visiting writers and artists, and formulas for promotion began to allow for "creative work." Women's colleges continued in the forefront of developing arts programs, including dance, but more institutions now followed their example. Grants from the new federal humanities and arts endowments, founded in 1965, though not restricted to academics, brought them new support for independent projects. In all departments, filling out grant applications became a chore, but often a remunerative one.

By the time the Korean War ended in 1954, an observer could clearly discern that Cold War liberalism had become the dominant force in the country. Daniel Bell's essay, "The End of Ideology in the West," caught the spirit of the times better perhaps than any other work. Although some, like Bell, became professors (he left *Fortune* for Columbia in 1958), the "New York intellectuals" made their hyperarticulate transition from thirties radicalism to fifties "liberalism as conservatism" in the role of independent social critics, not as academic scholars. The fifties did bring academic criticism of conformity and "mass culture" (*The Lonely Crowd* reached near best-seller status), but this censure rarely touched on the distribution of wealth and power. Some academics used independent journals like *Dissent* to object to the national direction, but it was far safer to find a nonideological field in which to perform scholarship, or to join the American celebration, or to become part of a government-subsidized research institute that treated carefully selected public problems.

Many intellectuals on the left found academic

1831

careers shut off. To the disputed question—should Communists be allowed to teach?—only the boldest answered yes, usually while taking pains to make their own anticommunism crystal clear. In 1950, the University of California regents dismissed thirty-one faculty members for refusing to sign a new oath denying they belonged to the Communist party. Across the country, however, thousands signed without objection various loyalty oaths required by state laws.

"Action intellectuals" like Harvard's James B. Conant and Henry Kissinger left academic life, accepting major roles as national policymakers. Paul Douglas, a University of Chicago economist, was one of several professors who became U.S. senators. While the elite New York and Washington law firms remained the richest source of top advisers and cabinet members, the professoriate offered ready recruits for national administrations of both parties. Indeed, in the seemingly endless pursuit of the Vietnam War, the prominence of those with Ivy League connections laced with irony the phrase "the best and the brightest."

## NEW CONSTRAINTS, NEW CRITICISMS SINCE 1973

Warnings of a numerical decline in potential students had begun when the birth rate took an unusually large drop in 1965. A slight dip in total enrollment did indeed come in 1984 and 1985, but then the figures rose again. Behind this surprising growth lay several new sources of students, including those past traditional college-going age, whom worried colleges now courted. In the 1980s, enrollment of persons twenty-five and over rose nearly five times as fast as that of younger students. By 1989, undergraduates over thirty-five had risen to 12 percent of the total.

The proportion of all enrolled students who were white, non-Hispanic males, still above half in 1976, thereafter began a steady decline. Women surpassed men among part-time students in 1980, and among full-time in 1987. Members of ethnic groups who had once felt unwelcome were now urged to apply for admission. The number of African Americans in college grew, hovered around 9 percent of enrollment from 1976 to 1988, then declined slightly, while Hispanics rose to 5 percent and Asian Americans to 4 percent.

Federal loans and scholarships made family income somewhat less a determinant of college attendance. The appropriations for basic and supplemental educational opportunity grants mounted steadily from 1973 to 1979, by which time 2.7 million students were receiving the former, 600,000 the latter, which were particularly directed to students from low-income families. In the first half of the 1970s, the median family income of entering freshmen was dropping, even though national median household income was rising or holding steady. Although from 1983 to 1987 the income status of freshmen's families was rising more steeply than the national figure, this trend appeared to reverse as the decade ended.

As competition for students intensified, some colleges were forced to close or enter face-saving mergers. Dwindling enrollments and the inflation of the 1970s proved fatal to Eisenhower College, founded with high hopes but little endowment in 1968. Between 1960 and 1990, 167 private four-year colleges disappeared. Despite the demise of smaller institutions, there were still 1,321 in 1989 with enrollments of under one thousand. Their students, however, made up only 4 percent of the national total; whereas slightly over half of college students attended institutions with enrollments of over ten thousand. Multiple branches became the usual arrangement for state universities, and some private institutions also established colonies.

The Catholic institutions, once viewed by outsiders as a strange mixture of religiosity, urban utilitarianism, and athleticism, increasingly adopted the dominant national patterns in higher education. Lay faculty and trustees came to outnumber clerics and religious. Catholic colleges for women suffered as single-sex institutions lost favor, and most all-male Catholic colleges began in the 1970s and 1980s to admit women, sometimes absorbing nearby Catholic women's colleges. By the 1980s, fundamentalist institutions like Jerry Falwell's Liberty University in Virginia appeared further from the mainstream than did Catholic universities, where non-Catholic students and faculty felt increasingly comfortable.

In 1973–1974, amid the welter of the Watergate scandal, an Arab-Israeli war, an unprecedented energy shortage, and stagflation, academic institutions reported unexpected deficits. The general sense of financial well-being which had somehow lasted through the student revolts rapidly dissipated. By the end of the 1970s, institutions shared with much of society a new sense of limits—financial, ecological, and world-political.

The terrors of stagflation contributed to the rise in business influence in higher education. Administrators in both public and private institutions looked to corporations for cooperative research and training programs as well as outright gifts. Careers in business so appealed to students that by 1980, 16 percent of undergraduate majors were in that field, far outstripping other choices.

In order to avoid losing federal aid, schools were forced to examine institutionalized prejudice. Rooted in Title IX of the Education Amendments of 1972, regulations mandating redress of gender or racial discrimination, widely known as affirmative action, gained influence from sympathetic bureaucrats and determined victims. Citing millions of dollars in federal contracts at risk, Rutgers University agreed in 1974 to $375,000 in back salary for underpaid women and minority group members, and Brown University settled a lawsuit by accepting a consent decree that placed it under court supervision in all promotion and tenure decisions. Such headline-making cases of the 1970s brought general consciousness-raising, and when officials in Washington grew less interested in the cause, aggrieved women or members of minority groups could still pursue redress through the courts. Alan Bakke, a white male, made landmark use of equal rights standards when he charged that guaranteed quotas for blacks had excluded him from the medical school of the University of California at Davis. The 1978 Supreme Court decision ordered him enrolled, but also declared ethnic diversity a legitimate goal of institutional admission policy.

The Reagan victory in 1980 with its promise of lessened federal activism had mixed results for academia. "Laissez faire" hardly described the approach of Secretary of Education William J. Bennett, whose allegations of academic shoddiness brought equally spirited rejoinders. Although the new administration repeatedly proposed reducing federal support for higher education, skillful lobbying kept most cuts moderate. White House directives to the Internal Revenue Service to grant tax-exempt status to Bob Jones University, which barred interracial dating and marriage by its students, proved a political embarrassment well before being ruled unconstitutional in 1983.

The Bush years brought a new set of federal initiatives aimed at influencing higher education. Exposures of overbilling for federally supported research projects embarrassed several distinguished universities and hastened the resignation of the president of Stanford. An antitrust investigation forced dissolution of the Overlap Group, through which certain elite institutions had regularly equalized their financial aid packages to accepted applicants. Perhaps most startling, though undoubtedly linked to the backlash against affirmative action, the Department of Educa-

tion threatened to cease recognizing regional accrediting agencies that made ethnic diversity a required goal for approved colleges and universities. Since most federal aid programs were restricted to accredited institutions, such loss of authority for a voluntary accrediting agency would be deadly, and the requirement was dropped. The chickens of federal aid were coming home to roost. Those who had scoffed at fears of federal interference began to have second thoughts. Brigham Young University's refusal of federal money because of strings attached no longer seemed so eccentric. Most institutions, however, were in no position to withdraw from the network of federal programs. In 1987–1988 these provided on average 13 percent of current-fund revenue, quite apart from the direct federal grants to over one-third of undergraduates, a major facilitator of tuition increases.

Sure that government funding could never be enough, administrators strove to keep private income sources flowing. Some institutions managed successful fund drives in the 1970s despite stagflation, though others postponed them or settled for less than their announced goals. Emory University benefited from a Coca Cola–based fortune when it received $105 million from Robert W. Woodruff in 1979. A decade later comedian Bill Cosby, spectacularly successful as a television performer, gave another Atlanta institution, Spelman College, $20 million, the largest benefaction ever to a historically black college. Stanford, in the midst of Silicon Valley, tapped new computer industry fortunes and reached its $1.1 billion campaign goal. For many institutions, annual giving by alumni became a staple of budget planning. Alumni influence rose accordingly, but in 1984–1985 corporate gifts surpassed those from alumni.

Borrowing from procedures developed in business, institutions enlarged student applicant pools by direct mail campaigns and hired professional managers to maximize return on endowment. Justifiable as rational stewardship, such methods still raised public doubts about higher education's nonprofit status. As both admission applications and direct student aid from government mounted, private institutions turned to higher tuition charges, an expedient also adopted by public institutions when they found income from state government dropping in the early nineties. Critics objected that this step further undercut public higher education's somewhat dubious claims to be accessible to all classes.

Scandals in the late eighties and early nineties caused nightmares for public affairs officers. In sports, repeated exposures of rule violations by recruiters and coaches led institutional presidents to seek reform through the National Collegiate Athletic Association. Although faculty members bringing charges of denial of tenure on racial or gender grounds lost their cases more often than they won, news stories about such disputes suggested institutions in disarray. Among several cases of scientific misconduct, the most notorious involved allegations of falsified data in an article coauthored and long defended by the Nobel laureate David Baltimore. Shortly after agreeing that the article should be withdrawn, he stepped down as president of Rockefeller University.

Humanists experienced at least a twinge of schadenfreude at the chagrin of their high-flying scientific colleagues. But humanists too faced embarrassments as cases of plagiarism surfaced with unexpected frequency and Paul de Man, a leading light of deconstruction, was shown to have published numerous profascist articles during World War II. By the time of this mortification, deconstruction had already suffered diminution, its self-reflexive irreverence interpreted as nihilism and its jargon as a way of rendering literature inaccessible.

"Political correctness" became the catch phrase of those accusing universities of blocking free expression of ideas by punishing speech that offended minorities or women. The American Civil Liberties Union joined conservative groups in challenging some new campus regulations, and the University of Michigan found its speech code ruled unconstitutional by a federal court in 1989. Another aspect of the political correctness debate, the allegation that curricular multiculturalism meant neglect of essential achievements of Western civilization, inspired two new organizations. The National Association of Scholars defended curricular tradition, countered by Teachers for a Democratic Culture.

Student demonstrators who demanded curricular recognition of non-European cultures also called for admission reforms to increase ethnic diversity. Campuses mounted new recruitment efforts, and Talent Search, soon renamed A Better Chance, sought to prepare minority students for college by supporting them at superior secondary schools. Administrators' heavy reliance on Scholastic Achievement Test scores made it more difficult to admit African Americans and Hispanics. Once viewed as objective, these tests now came under fire as ethnically biased. Some institutions stopped requiring them of applicants, and admission officers reverted to a more complex basis for admission, including something as old-fashioned as strength of character. They also exerted themselves to seek students in high schools where few had pre-

viously imagined college as a possibility. A few wealthier schools adopted a "need-blind" policy, with ability to pay playing no role in the admission decision and all needed financial aid guaranteed. Graduate and professional schools also bestirred themselves, and in 1990 the Johns Hopkins medical school ceased requiring the long-revered Medical College Admission Test. The revision of immigration laws and the many refugees from the Vietnam War swelled the number of college-aged Asian Americans. In the 1980s, admission staffs began including them in calculations of the proportion of "minorities" in entering classes. At Berkeley, however, Asian Americans argued that they were discriminated against because the university's efforts to attain ethnic balance led to undervaluing their higher average SAT scores. Meanwhile, foreign students came in gradually increasing numbers, roughly one-third of a million each year during the 1980s.

If diversity made for a better school, why not diversity by gender? Gradually such reasoning and equal rights legislation prevailed in all-male bastions (mostly in the East and South), and even in the U.S. Military, Naval, and Air Force academies. Some institutions found a financially beneficial increase in size conveniently linked to "going coed." The possibility of women's colleges also becoming coeducational provoked high controversy, with arguments that women were deprived of leadership experience in mixed-gender environments and that different approaches to social and intellectual problems could be explored in a women's college. Vassar in 1968 shifted to coeducation. Despite negative publicity about the results (a male transvestite was elected student body president shortly after the change), other women's colleges followed suit, some because their enrollments were slipping. A highly endowed women's college like Wellesley, however, could remain single-sex, and did so. The tradition of male heads of women's colleges (never one Wellesley had followed) ended abruptly.

Encouraged by the taboo-breaking counterculture, students began to attack the in loco parentis rationale for supervision of undergraduate behavior. Why should chapel be required? Why should dress be regulated? Why should opposite-sex visits to student rooms be limited? The rules in question and the timing varied from campus to campus, but by 1975 so many rules had simply been swept away that it was hard to recall why they had once seemed important. After a somewhat anarchic period in the early seventies, new systems of dormitory self-governance, peer counseling, and resident counselors developed. Probably the change in sexual mores and technological advances in contraception played a major part in the shift. During the 1970s, lesbian and gay student organizations emerged, overcame efforts to bar them from campus, and found the rationale of "diversity" adaptable to their claims for inclusion.

As American troops left Vietnam and as hopes for rapid achievement of full racial equality faded, most student protest dwindled, but divestment of stock in corporations doing business in South Africa emerged as a new cause. With the object of reform thousands of miles away, whites could join blacks in a struggle which carried little threat to white privilege in the United States. Pressing trustees rather than administrators, students showed they had learned something about the importance of financial control. Despite initial reluctance, Boston University, Brandeis, and Yale all made major divestments in 1979, and others followed.

Student life by the eighties had taken on a good deal of luxuriousness. Designer jeans replaced their ragged predecessors. Complaints about housing, food, and space for entertainment indicated that students did not look on their college years as a time set apart from middle-class comforts. Since institutional income was rising during the 1980s, especially endowment income, officials could meet some of these demands for more amenities. Perhaps because of the new openness and prosperity, theft, assault, rape, and murder on campuses increased. Authorities publicized as warnings incidents once hushed up, tightened security forces, and often ordered dormitories locked at all times.

As early as the mid-seventies, observers found evidence among college students to fit generalizations about the "me generation." From 1970 to 1987, entering freshman who embraced the value of "being very well-off financially," rose from 39.1 to 75.6 percent, during a period when the desire to develop "a meaningful philosophy of life" was declining. These opposite trends reached their extremes in 1987, then began to reverse direction. The late eighties brought a noticeable return to teaching as a preferred vocation, and gradually students began to find internships and even careers in consumers' rights, environmental protection, and community organizing, avenues kept open in considerable part by Ralph Nader's Public Interest Research Group and its local chapters. Perhaps because of its brevity, the Gulf War of 1991 inspired relatively minor campus peace activism, but student protests flared after inner city conditions were dramatized by the Los Angeles riots of 1992.

Diversity, the new admissions ideal, soon became a desideratum in selecting faculty, and slowly the proportion of women and minority group members holding faculty positions increased. Still, in the fall of 1987, of all full-time regular instructional faculty, 73 percent were male, and 90 percent were non-Hispanic white. Two extraneous developments hampered efforts to diversify the gender and ethnic composition of faculties. A shortage of openings appeared in the early 1970s, persisting in some fields for over a decade, and graduate schools reduced their enrollment in response. New federal laws removing any mandatory retirement age, though not in full effect till 1994, also narrowed opportunities for diversifying faculties.

In a buyer's market average faculty salaries dropped 17 percent (in constant dollars) between 1972 and 1981, and it was slight consolation that they rose by the same percentage in the next decade. Protesting the downward drift, faculties turned to unionization. The American Federation of Teachers had long sought this development, and now both the National Education Association and the once staidly professional AAUP joined it in competition for faculty selection as bargaining agent. Only 1 percent of institutions had had faculty collective bargaining agents in 1967. By 1976, 12 percent did, although the Supreme Court in the *Yeshiva* case (1980) declared faculty at private institutions to be managerial personnel not eligible for federal protection of unions.

As academic leadership ceased to be a white male preserve, news columns were peppered with announcements of "firsts." An African American, Clifton Wharton, Jr., president of Michigan State University since 1970, left in 1978 for the chancellorship of the State University of New York, and a woman, Hanna Holborn Gray, left the acting presidency of Yale to head the University of Chicago from 1978 to 1993. Women also headed the state university systems of California and Florida, and in 1992, 12 percent of institutional presidents were women, more than doubling the figure from 1975. In 1990, an Asian American, Chang-Lin Tien, became chancellor of the University of California at Berkeley.

Faculty members saw the president's activities grow more managerial and extramural, while their own teaching and research concerns were addressed by new administrative officers. Academia became more and more rule-bound, often in an effort to meet new federal regulations, but sometimes because faculties tended to challenge the fairness of casual procedures that permitted favoritism and old-boy networking. For their part, presidents often felt they had lost power, as they waited for committee reports, advice of legal counsel, votes of legislatures and trustees, or decisions of individual donors and foundations. The nonacademic staffs had long been a bulwark of security for administrators. This too changed, as staffs unionized, voiced demands, and (notably at Yale in 1984) went on strike. Staff activists tended to be women, no mere coincidence in an era of feminist awakening.

The turmoil of the sixties had included charges of "irrelevancy" in the curriculum. In response, new courses (and even majors) began to treat such untraditional themes as ethnicity, popular culture, nuclear weaponry, and environmentalism. With multiculturalism gaining favor, bachelor degree programs at Mount Holyoke College and elsewhere required at least one course treating American minorities or "Third World cultures." With the abolition of many other requirements, students were freer to select their courses. If they sometimes chose the easy, the superficial, the trendy, perhaps they learned from their mistakes—so supporters of the new curricular liberty argued. In the face of loosened requirements and other changes, such as pass-fail options and easier grading, bitter allegations arose of lowered academic quality. Pundits wrote books and columns about declining standards, and alumni urged alma mater to restore the sterner regime they recollected. Allan Bloom's *The Closing of the American Mind,* a bestseller in 1987, inspired a series of similar attacks on academic relativism and mediocrity.

Amid these alterations, however, the central distinction within the enterprise remained that between student and teacher. Teachers might say, "I learn so much from my students," enjoy being called by their given names, and show more sensitivity to varied backgrounds among those they taught. Most colleagues, nevertheless, came quickly to attention when the touchstone of professionalism was applied to their academic decisions, and the phrase "my own work" continued to refer to research, not teaching.

The American scientists who carried off the lion's share of Nobel prizes were mostly academics. Biomedical research, with its direct appeal to quality and length of life, had taken huge strides, with advances in molecular biology only the most spectacular. Regional developers saw universities as critical to prosperity, especially where high-tech centers grew up, as near Route 1 in New Jersey, Route 128 in Massachusetts, and Research Triangle Park in North Carolina. Worries recurred, however, about the decline in basic research as business and government increasingly supported applied programs, and as universities

themselves began to benefit financially from sharing in patent rights. Where was the proper balance between economic realism and intellectual values?

## AN ESSENTIAL INSTITUTION UNDER STRAIN

The tripartite mission of teaching, research, and public service, firmly in place by the 1890s, still dominated American higher education a century later. The American university had increased in complexity, but had not changed its essential identity: a four-year liberal arts college as the foundation for graduate and professional schools, and a faculty committed to research. Separate four-year colleges continued, some throve, but most lived in the shadow of the universities, recruiting Ph.D.-holders for their faculties and ever less likely to be the last stage in their students' formal education. Institutions unknown in 1900, the community colleges, had emerged and flourished, while the normal schools, having first elevated themselves into teachers colleges, had, with few exceptions, lost that identity by embracing more general functions. Like much of society, higher education had taken on an elaborately bureaucratized structure, with rules and specialized administrators, well-defined faculty ranks and promotion schedules. The earlier world of traditional norms and benevolent patriarchy had been largely displaced by formal rights and duties, subject to legal enforcement.

The twentieth century opened with colleges and universities stressing growth in student numbers, but as early as the 1920s, some institutions began to take pride in limiting their size and exercising selectivity. Gradually, an additional admission standard—diversity—gained prominence, a standard ratified in the *Bakke* decision. The most striking change of the century, however, was the growth to 14 million students a year, with 60 percent of all high school graduates entering college, the highest figures of any nation.

Institutions' external power relationships had shifted. Autonomy and local authority, highly valued in the late nineteenth century, had yielded to voluntary regional and national coordination, with mutual credentialing. In addition, by the 1990s, the widespread acceptance of federal money had brought with it a significant degree of federal intervention. While by no means highly centralized by European standards, American colleges and universities faced national requirements that would have appalled earlier academic leaders.

Entering the last decade of the twentieth century,

colleges and universities found the indicators of their institutional health strangely mixed. Endowments were at new highs, but budget deficits were appearing. There was wide acknowledgment that the nation's economic well-being must rest on a trained population, and academic credentials were highly valued, but when state budgets came under severe pressure beginning in 1989, appropriations for public higher education suffered drastic cuts. "Everyone" knew that a college degree greatly increased lifetime earnings, but there were bitter complaints as average costs for tuition, room, and board rose (between 1964 and 1989, in constant dollars) from $8,000 to $13,000 at private institutions and from $4,000 to $5,000 at public. Often presented without adjustment for inflation, such figures deepened resentments and led even well-to-do families to reassess the attractiveness of public institutions over private.

As academic scandals and campus crime appeared on the evening news, these institutions seemed no better than the rest of the society—possibly, with their many privileges, more given to corruption. In 1992, 25 percent of Americans responded to a Louis Harris survey that they had "a great deal of confidence" in those running universities, a significant drop from the 61 percent who had so responded in 1966. Still, every spring, when commencement exercises were held with festive reminders of work and play, with tradition and youth enriching each other, with honorary degrees awarding the closest thing the nation had to titles of nobility, with the hopes of one generation for the next brought almost painfully to light, there seemed little doubt that whatever new travails they faced, these institutions of learning would persist.

SEE ALSO Elementary and Secondary Education (in this volume); The Professions (volume III).

## BIBLIOGRAPHY

Two surveys of American higher education whose concluding chapters treat the first part of the twentieth century are Frederick Rudolph, *The American College and University: A History* (1962); and John S. Brubacher and Willis Rudy, *Higher Education in Transition: A History of American Colleges and Universities, 1636–1968* (1968). For a volume that meshes policy recommendations with historical insights, see Christopher Jencks and David Riesman, *The Academic Revolution* (1968). Richard M. Freeland links national trends to eight varied institutions, treated in depth, in his *Academia's Golden Age: Universities in Massachusetts, 1945–1970* (1992), with considerable coverage of the period before World War II. Hugh Hawkins uses the drive toward centralization and standardization to organize *Banding Together: The Rise of National Associations in American Higher Education, 1887–1950* (1992). Three works whose seemingly narrow subjects reveal a good deal of academic history are Richard Nelson Current, *Phi Beta Kappa in American Life: The First Two Hundred Years* (1990); Michael McGiffert, *The Higher Learning in Colorado: An Historical Study, 1860–1940* (1964); and David S. Webster, *Academic Quality Rankings of American Colleges and Universities* (1986). William Clyde De-Vane, *Higher Education in Twentieth-Century America* (1965), and David D. Henry, *Challenges Past, Challenges Present: An Analysis of American Higher Education since 1930* (1975), are brief but useful.

Long thought of as the crown of American academic life, the complex institutions now usually designated research universities are elucidated in Laurence R. Veysey, *The Emergence of the American University* (1965), which, though ending about 1910, ranks as an important paradigmatic work. Further developments are skillfully traced in Roger L. Geiger, *To Advance Knowledge: The Growth of American Research Universities, 1900–1940* (1986), and the same author's *Research and Relevant Knowledge: American Research Universities since World War II* (1993). Among Walter P. Metzger's trenchant writings, his *Academic Freedom in the Age of the University* (1961) treats the origins of the AAUP. For a view of the university among other institutions devoted to learning, see Alexandra Oleson and John Voss, eds., *The Organization of Knowledge in Modern America, 1860–1920* (1979).

The distinction between public and private universities has come to seem less and less significant; still, some important differences are observable in Allan Nevins, *The State Universities and Democracy* (1962). On Morrill land-grant universities, Roger L.

Williams, *The Origins of Federal Support for Higher Education: George W. Atherton and the Land-Grant College Movement* (1991), treats pattern-setting developments at the turn of the century; many are traceable in Edward Danforth Eddy, Jr., *Colleges for Our Land and Time: The Land-Grant Idea in American Education* (1957).

The myriad of books on liberal arts colleges are rarely historically organized. A valuable recent exception is David O. Levine, *The American College and the Culture of Aspiration, 1915–1940* (1986). Two books selecting a few colleges for close examination are Burton R. Clark, *The Distinctive College: Antioch, Reed and Swarthmore* (1970); and W. Bruce Leslie, *Gentlemen and Scholars: College and Community in the "Age of the University," 1865–1917* (1992). Some of the complexities of Catholic institutions are traceable in the works of Philip Gleason, notably his chapter in Robert Hassenger, ed., *The Shape of Catholic Higher Education* (1967); as well as William P. Leahy, *Adapting to America: Catholics, Jesuits, and Higher Education in the Twentieth Century* (1991). James D. Anderson, *The Education of Blacks in the South, 1860–1935* (1988), includes higher education; and Raymond Wolters, *The New Negro on Campus: Black College Rebellions of the 1920s* (1975), treats more than a single decade. For later developments, see Frank Bowles and Frank A. DeCosta, *Between Two Worlds: A Profile of Negro Higher Education* (1971).

Women's higher education has become one of the most fruitful sections of academic history. Good places to start that treat women in coeducational as well as single-sex colleges are Barbara Miller Solomon, *In the Company of Educated Women: A History of Women and Higher Education in America* (1985); and Lynn Gordon, *Gender and Higher Education in the Progressive Era* (1990).

A strongly interpretive work on junior and community colleges is Steven Brint and Jerome Karabel, *The Diverted Dream: Community Colleges and the Promise of Educational Opportunity in America, 1900–1985* (1989), usefully supplemented by Thomas Diener, ed., *Growth of an American Invention: A Documentary History of the Junior and Community College Movement* (1986).

General studies of professional schools have begun to appear, often based on calls for reform. Works of distinction include Kenneth M. Ludmerer, *Learning to Heal: The Development of American Medical Education* (1985); Robert Bocking Stevens, *Law School: Legal Education in America from the 1850s to the 1980s* (1983); David F. Noble, *America by Design: Science, Technology, and the Rise of Corporate Capitalism* (1977)

(for engineering); and Geraldine Joncich Clifford and James W. Guthrie, *Ed School: A Brief for Professional Education* (1988).

Religion's loss of centrality in the academic enterprise sets the theme of George M. Marsden and Bradley J. Longfield, eds., *The Secularization of the Academy* (1992); and William C. Ringenberg, *The Christian College: A History of Protestant Higher Education in America* (1984). An able study of institutions slow to achieve postsecondary status is Virginia Lieson Brereton, *Training God's Army: The American Bible School, 1880–1940* (1990).

Admissions history has been meticulously researched in Marcia Graham Synnott, *The Half-Opened Door: Discrimination and Admissions at Harvard, Yale, and Princeton, 1900–1970* (1979); and Harold S. Wechsler, *The Qualified Student: A History of Selective College Admission in America* (1977). Although past discrimination sets their theme, much can be learned from these volumes about other aspects of admissions policies.

Frederick Rudolph's delightfully readable *Curriculum: A History of the American Undergraduate Course of Study since 1636* (1977), a major summatory work, is usefully supplemented by Gary E. Miller, *The Meaning of General Education: The Emergence of a Curriculum Paradigm* (1988); and Russell Thomas, *The Search for a Common Learning: General Education, 1800–1960* (1962).

No full-scale account of relations with the federal government exists, but valuable studies, especially on financial aspects, include Alice M. Rivlin, *The Role of the Federal Government in Financing Higher Education* (1961); and Homer D. Babbidge, Jr., and Robert M. Rosenzweig, *The Federal Interest in Higher Education* (1962). Valuable historical sections appear in Harold Orlans, *Private Accreditation and Public Eligibility* (1975). War's heightening of federal influence is treated in two excellent histories: Carol S. Gruber, *Mars and Minerva: World War I and the Uses of the Higher Learning in America* (1975); and Keith W. Olson, *The G.I. Bill, the Veterans, and the Colleges* (1974). For the Cold War, see Ellen W. Schrecker, *No Ivory Tower: McCarthyism and the Universities* (1986); and Stuart W. Leslie, *The Cold War and American Science: The Military-Industrial-Academic Complex at M.I.T. and Stanford* (1993).

Very much a twentieth-century phenomenon, foundation support for academia (with the strings attached) comes under examination in two works by Ellen Condliffe Lagemann: *Private Power for the Public Good: A History of the Carnegie Foundation for the Advancement of Teaching* (1983), and *The Politics of*

*Knowledge: The Carnegie Corporation, Philanthropy, and Public Policy* (1989); and in Steven C. Wheatley, *The Politics of Philanthropy: Abraham Flexner and Medical Education* (1988). A pioneering work, Merle Curti and Roderick Nash, *Philanthropy and the Shaping of American Higher Education* (1965), remains useful. Clyde W. Barrow, *Universities and the Capitalist State: Corporate Liberalism and the Reconstruction of American Higher Education, 1894–1928* (1990), also treats modes of business influence.

Increasingly, studies of specific disciplines seriously explore their academic settings. Three outstanding examples are Gerald Graff, *Professing Literature: An Institutional History* (1987); Peter Novick, *That Noble Dream: The "Objectivity Question" and the American Historical Profession* (1988); and John W. Servos, *Physical Chemistry from Ostwald to Pauling: The Making of a Science in America* (1990).

Books on student life have often yielded to the calls of nostalgia or titillation. Superior works which resist those temptations include Philip G. Altbach, *Student Politics in America: A Historical Analysis* (1974); Paula S. Fass, *The Damned and the Beautiful: American Youth in the 1920's* (1977); Helen Lefkowitz Horowitz, *Campus Life: Undergraduate Cultures from the End of the Eighteenth Century to the Present* (1987); and David L. Westby, *The Clouded Vision: The Student Movement in the United States in the 1960s* (1976). College athletics receives serious attention in Jack Falla, *NCAA: The Voice of College Sports: A Diamond Anniversary History, 1906–1981*; and Ronald A. Smith, *Sports and Freedom: The Rise of Big-Time College Athletics* (1988).

The innumerable academic autobiographies, biographies, and institutional histories vary widely in quality. Examples of each at its most useful would include James B. Conant, *My Several Lives: Memoirs of a Social Inventor* (1970); Mary Ann Dzuback, *Robert M. Hutchins: Portrait of an Educator* (1991); and Stow Persons, *The University of Iowa in the Twentieth Century: An Institutional History* (1990).

For comparative treatments, in part historical, consult Burton R. Clark, ed., *The Academic Profession: National, Disciplinary, and Institutional Settings* (1987); Roger L. Geiger, *Private Sectors in Higher Education: Structure, Function, and Change in Eight Countries* (1986); and Konrad H. Jarausch, ed., *The Transformation of Higher Learning, 1860–1930: Expansion, Diversification, Social Opening, and Professionalization in England, Germany, Russia, and the United States* (1983).

# CONTRIBUTORS

**Joel D. Aberbach** is Professor of Political Science and director of the Center for American Politics and Public Policy at the University of California, Los Angeles. He studies executive and legislative politics in the United States and abroad. He is cochair of the International Political Science Association's Research Committee on Structure and Organization of Government and has been a senior fellow at the Brookings Institution in Washington, D.C., and a fellow at the Center for Advanced Study in the Behavioral Sciences. He is the author of *Keeping a Watchful Eye: The Politics of Congressional Oversight* (1990), and coauthor of *Race in the City* (1973), *Bureaucrats and Politicians in Western Democracies* (1981), and *The Administrative State in Industrialized Democracies* (1985). His service as a consultant includes work with the Commission on the Operation of the Senate, the General Accounting Office, the American Enterprise Institute–Brookings Institution Project on Congressional Renewal, and the Carnegie Institution Project on Science, Technology, and Government. CONGRESS

**Catherine L. Albanese** is Professor of Religious Studies at the University of California, Santa Barbara. A scholar of American religious history with a specialty in New England transcendentalism and related aspects of antebellum religion and culture, she has also ranged widely, as the author of a major textbook in the field, from colonial times to the present. In addition to *America: Religions and Religion,* 2d ed. (1992), she is the author of *Sons of the Fathers: The Civil Religion of the American Revolution* (1976), *Corresponding Motion: Transcendental Religion and the New America* (1977), *The Spirituality of the American Transcendentalists: Selected Writings of Ralph Waldo Emerson, Amos Bronson Alcott, Theodore Parker, and Henry David Thoreau* (1988), and *Nature Religion in America: From the Algonkian Indians to the New Age* (1990). NONTRADITIONAL RELIGIONS

**Michal R. Belknap** is Professor of Law at California Western School of Law and Adjunct Professor of History at the University of California, San Diego. He specializes in American legal and constitutional history, constitutional law, and criminal law. Richard J. Hughes Distinguished Visiting Professor of Consti-

tutional and Public Law and Policy at the Seton Hall University School of Law in 1984–1985, he is an editor for *American National Biography.* He is the author of *Cold War Political Justice: The Smith Act, the Communist Party, and American Civil Liberties* (1977), *Federal Law and Southern Order: Racial Violence and Constitutional Conflict in the Post-Brown South* (1987), and *To Improve the Administration of Justice: A History of the American Judicature Society* (1992), and editor of *Civil Rights, the White House, and the Justice Department, 1945–1968* (1991). THE CONSTITUTION

**Herman Belz** is Professor of History at the University of Maryland at College Park, where he teaches American constitutional and legal history. He is the author of *Equality Transformed: A Quarter Century of Affirmative Action* (1991), *Reconstructing the Union: Theory and Policy during the Civil War* (1969), "Constitutionalism and Bureaucracy in the 1980s: Some Bicentennial Reflections," *News for Teachers of Political Science* 41 (Spring 1984), and "The Separations of Powers," *Encyclopedia of American Political History* (1984), and coauthor of *The American Constitution,* 7th ed. (1991). BUREAUCRACY

**Edward D. Berkowitz** is chair of the Department of History at George Washington University. He has served as a policy analyst for the Department of Health, Education, and Welfare, as senior staff member of the President's Commission for a National Agenda for the Eighties, and as a Robert Wood Johnson Foundation faculty fellow in Health Care Finance. As a historian of social welfare, he concentrates on social policy in the twentieth century. He is the author of *Disabled Policy* (1987) and *America's Welfare State* (1991), and coauthor of *Group Health Association: A Portrait of a Health Maintenance Organization* (1988), *Creating the Welfare State,* rev. ed. (1992), and *Social Security and Medicare: A Policy Primer* (1993). SOCIAL WELFARE

**Michael A. Bernstein** is chair of the Department of History and associated faculty member in the Department of Economics at the University of California, San Diego. A member of the editorial board of the *Journal of Economic History,* he is a specialist on the economic and political history of the United

States. He is the author of a number of works, including *The Great Depression: Delayed Recovery and Economic Change in America, 1929–1939* (1988), and "The Contemporary American Banking Crisis in Historical Perspective," *Journal of American History* (March 1994), and coeditor of *Understanding American Economic Decline* (1994). He is currently working on a new monograph, "American Economics in the American Century: The State and Modern Economic Thought." DEPRESSIONS AND RECESSIONS: THE BUSINESS CYCLE

**Roger E. Bilstein** is Professor of History at the University of Houston, Clear Lake. He is also a research collaborator at the National Air and Space Museum, Smithsonian Institution. As a historian of the United States in the twentieth century, he teaches courses in social and cultural history, and the history of technology, specializing in aviation and aerospace history, including both civil and military. He prepared the annual "Aerospace" section for *Collier's Encyclopedia Year Book* for fifteen years, and has served as a historical consultant to NASA, the United States Air Force, and museums. He is the author of *Stages to Saturn: A Technological History of the Apollo-Saturn Launch Vehicles* (1980), *Flight Patterns: Trends of Aeronautical Development in the United States, 1918–1929* (1983), and *Flight in America: From the Wrights to the Astronauts,* 2d ed. (1994), and coauthor of *Orders of Magnitude: A History of NACA and NASA, 1915–1990* (1990). AEROSPACE TECHNOLOGY

**Howard Brick** is Associate Professor of History at the University of Oregon. As an intellectual historian, he specializes in the history of twentieth-century social theory in the United States. He is the author of *Daniel Bell and the Decline of Intellectual Radicalism: Social Theory and Political Reconciliation in the 1940s* (1986) and a number of articles, including "The Reformist Dimension of Talcott Parsons's Early Social Theory," in Thomas L. Haskell and Richard F. Techgraeber III, eds., *The Culture of the Market: Historical Essays* (1993), and "Optimism of the Mind: Imagining Postindustrial Society in the 1960s and 1970s," *American Quarterly* (September 1992). His book, *Age of Contradiction: American Thought and Culture in the 1960s,* is forthcoming, and he is preparing a study of the role played by the concept of capitalism in American social science from 1920 to 1970. SOCIETY

**W. Elliot Brownlee** is Professor of History at the University of California, Santa Barbara. An economic historian, he specializes in the history of public finance in the United States. He has been awarded fellowships by the Charles Warren Center and the Woodrow Wilson International Center for Scholars. He has been a visiting professor at Princeton, and in 1989 was bicentennial lecturer at the U.S. Department of the Treasury. He is the author of *Progressivism and Economic Growth: The Wisconsin Income Tax, 1911–1929* (1974) and *Dynamics of Ascent: A History of the American Economy,* 2d ed. (1979), and coauthor of *Women in the American Economy: A Documentary History, 1675–1929* (1976), *The Essentials of American History,* 4th ed. (1986), and *America's History,* 2d ed. (1993). His current projects include a history of the financing of World War I. TAXATION

**Patrick W. Carey** is Associate Professor of Theology at Marquette University. He is a former member of the advisory council of the American Catholic Historical Society. He specializes in the history of American Protestant and Catholic life and thought, and has published in a number of historical journals, including *Church History, Catholic Historical Review, Journal of the Early American Republic,* and *Archivum Historiae Pontificiae.* He is the author of *An Immigrant Bishop: John England's Adaptation of Irish Catholicism to American Republicanism* (1982), *People, Priests, and Prelates: Ecclesiastical Democracy and the Tension of Trusteeism* (1987), and *The Roman Catholics* (1993), and editor of *American Catholic Religious Thought* (1987) and *Orestes A. Brownson* (1991). CATHOLICISM

**Alfred D. Chandler, Jr.,** is Straus Professor of Business History emeritus at the Harvard University Graduate School of Business Administration. As a business historian, he has traced the creation and development of organizational structures of modern business enterprise and the rise and evolution of such enterprises in the United States and Europe. He is the author of *Strategy and Structure* (1962), *The Visible Hand* (1977; Pulitzer and Bancroft prizes), and *Scale and Scope* (1990; Leo Melamed Prize and Association of American Publishers award), and coauthor of *Pierre S. Du Pont and the Making of the Modern Corporation* (1971) among other works. He has served as a consultant to Du Pont, Alcoa, British Petroleum, Citibank, TRW, and the Atomic Energy Commission on historical projects. INDUSTRIAL PRODUCTION

**William R. Childs** is Associate Professor of American History at Ohio State University. He teaches and does research on topics in modern American history, business history, and American business-government relations. He specializes in the history of regulation, giving particular attention to the intersection of economic, institutional, and cultural forces. He became editor of *Essays in Economic and Business History* in 1994. He is the author of *Trucking and the Public Interest: The Emergence of Federal Regulation, 1914–1940* (1985) and articles on the Railroad Commission of Texas for *Business History Review* and *Journal of Policy History.* INFRASTRUCTURE

**Lizabeth Cohen** is Associate Professor of History at New York University. A specialist in twentieth-century social, political, and cultural history, she studies how the social and cultural experiences of ordinary people—of various classes, ethnicities, races, and genders—shaped their own political orientations and influenced the nation as a whole. She is the author of *Making a New Deal: Industrial Workers in Chicago, 1919–1939* (1990) and "The Class Experience of Mass Consumption: Workers as Consumers in Interwar America," in Richard Wightman Fox and T. Jackson Lears, eds., *The Power of Culture* (1993) among other works. She is working on a new book, *A Consumer's Republic: The Politics of Consumption in Postwar America.* GENDER ISSUES

**Jon Coleman,** a recent graduate of the University of Colorado, is a historian of the American West. THE WEST

**Richard Crawford** is Professor of Music, director of the American Music Institute, and a faculty associate in the American Culture program at the University of Michigan. He also serves as editor in chief of *Music of the United States of America,* a national series of scholarly editions sponsored by the National Endowment for the Humanities and the American Musicological Society. A historical musicologist, he specializes in the history of American music and has written widely on eighteenth- and early-nineteenth-century topics. He is the author of *The American Musical Landscape* (1993), coauthor of *Jazz Standards on Record, 1900–1942* (1992), and coeditor of *A Celebration of American Music* (1990) among other works. *A History of Music in the U.S.A.* is forthcoming. MUSIC

**David J. Depew** is Professor of Philosophy at California State University, Fullerton. A historian of philosophy, he is especially concerned with how social and political philosophy intersect with biological theories in such authors as Aristotle, Darwin, and John Dewey. He is the coauthor of *Darwinism Evolving: Systems Dynamics and the Genealogy of Natural Selection* (forthcoming), and coeditor of *The Greeks and the Good Life* (1981), *Evolution at a Crossroads: The New Biology and the New Philosophy of Science* (1985), *Infor-*

*mation, Evolution, and Entropy* (1987), and *Pragmatism from Progressivism to Postmodernism* (forthcoming). PHILOSOPHY

**Mary L. Dudziak** is Professor of Law at the University of Iowa, where she teaches constitutional law, American legal history, and immigration law. Her articles on twentieth-century American legal history and civil rights history have appeared in such journals as the *Stanford Law Review, Journal of American History,* and *Law and History Review.* She is writing a book on the impact of foreign affairs on domestic civil rights policy after World War II. THE COURTS

**Richard Wightman Fox** is Professor of History and director of American Studies at Boston University, where he also edits the *Intellectual History Newsletter.* His area of specialty is the intellectual and cultural history of the United States since the Civil War. He is the author of *Reinhold Niebuhr: A Biography* (1985) and "The Culture of Liberal Protestant Progressivism, 1875–1925," *Journal of Interdisciplinary History* 23 (Winter 1993), and coeditor of *The Power of Culture* (1993), which includes his essay, "Intimacy on Trial: Cultural Meanings of the Beecher-Tilton Affair." He is writing a history of liberal Protestantism in America. PROTESTANTISM

**Jeffry A. Frieden** is Professor of Political Science at the University of California, Los Angeles. He specializes in the politics of international monetary and financial relations. He is the author of *Banking on the World: The Politics of American International Finance* (1987) and *Debt, Development, and Democracy: Modern Political Economy and Latin America, 1965–1985* (1991), coauthor of *International Political Economy: Perspectives on Global Power and Wealth,* 3d ed. (1994), and coeditor of *The Political Economy of European Monetary Unification* (1994). He has written for a wide variety of scholarly journals on the politics of international economic relations. AMERICA AND THE WORLD ECONOMY

**Vanessa Northington Gamble** is Associate Professor in the Department of History of Medicine and the Department of Family Medicine at the University of Wisconsin School of Medicine. Her research interests include the history of race and American medicine, the history of American hospitals, and the history of American health policy. She is the author of *The Black Community Hospital* (1989) and *Making a Place for Ourselves: The Black Hospital Movement, 1920–1945* (1995), and editor of *Germs Have No Color Line: Blacks and American Medicine, 1900–1945* (1989). HEALTH-CARE DELIVERY

**David R. Goldfield** is Robert Lee Bailey Professor of History at the University of North Carolina, Charlotte. His area of interest is the twentieth-century South, with special emphasis on urbanization and race relations. The editor of the *Journal of Urban History*, he also serves as consultant to history museums and state humanities councils throughout the South, and as an expert witness in voting rights cases. He is the author of ten books, including two Mayflower award–winning works, *Cotton Fields and Skyscrapers: Southern City and Region, 1607–1980* (1982) and *Black, White, and Southern: Race Relations and Southern Culture, 1940 to the Present* (1990). THE SOUTH

**David C. Hammack** is Professor of History at Case Western Reserve University, where he directs the Social Policy History Ph.D. program. He has held a Guggenheim fellowship, has been a resident fellow at the Russell Sage Foundation, and has participated in several comparative, collaborative studies of urban development in the United States and central Europe. He is the author of *Power and Society: Greater New York at the Turn of the Century* (1982), and of many articles, including "Problems in the Historical Study of Power in the Cities and Towns of the United States, 1800–1960," *American Historical Review* (1978), and "Urban Politics and Social History in National Historical Perspective: The Development of Budapest and New York, 1870–1940," in *Papers of the 17th International Congress of Historical Sciences* (1992), and is coeditor of *Nonprofit Organizations in a Market Economy* (1993). THE EAST

**Hugh Hawkins** is Anson D. Morse Professor of History and American Studies at Amherst College. A social and intellectual historian, he specializes in the history of American higher education. Other research interests include African American history and academic relations between Germany and the United States. He is the author of *Pioneer: A History of the Johns Hopkins University, 1874–1889* (1960), *Between Harvard and America: The Educational Leadership of Charles W. Eliot* (1972), and *Banding Together: The Rise of National Associations in American Higher Education, 1887–1950* (1992), coauthor of *Education at Amherst Reconsidered: The Liberal Studies Program* (1978), and editor of *The Emerging University and Industrial America,* 2d ed. (1985). THE UNIVERSITY

**Ellis W. Hawley** is Professor of History Emeritus at the University of Iowa. His most recent work includes *Federal Social Policy: The Historical Dimension* (1988) and *Poverty and Public Policy in Modern America*

(1989), both edited with Donald T. Critchlow; *Herbert Hoover and the Historians* (1989); *The Great War and the Search for a Modern Order: A History of the American People and Their Institutions,* 2d ed. (1992); and *The New Deal and the Problem of Monopoly,* rev. ed. (1995). ECONOMIC POLICIES

**George C. Herring** is Alumni Professor of History at the University of Kentucky. A historian of U.S. foreign relations, he has written extensively on the era of the Cold War and on American involvement in Vietnam. He is the author of *America's Longest War: The United States and Vietnam, 1950–1975,* 2d ed. (1986), *The Secret Diplomacy of the Vietnam War* (1983), and *LBJ and Vietnam: "A Different Kind of War"* (1994). He is a former editor of the journal *Diplomatic History* and was president of the Society for Historians of American Foreign Relations (1990). He has been a Fulbright scholar in New Zealand and a visiting professor at the United States Military Academy. LIMITED WARS

**Jack High** lives in Annandale, Virginia. An economic historian, he is the author of *Minimizing, Action, and Market Adjustment: An Inquiry into the Theory of Market Equilibrium* (1990) and the editor of *Regulation: Economic Theory and History* (1991). He is also the coeditor, with Richard H. Fink, of *A Nation in Debt: Economists Debate the Federal Budget Deficit* (1987) and, with Wayne E. Gable, of *A Century of the Sherman Act: American Economic Opinion, 1890–1990* (1992). ECONOMIC THOUGHT

**David A. Hollinger** is Professor of History at the University of California, Berkeley. He specializes in the study of American academic and literary intellectuals. He is the author of *Morris R. Cohen and the Scientific Ideal* (1975) and *In the American Province: Studies in the History and Historiography of Ideas* (1985), coeditor of *The American Intellectual Tradition,* 2 vols., 2d ed. (1993), senior editor of the *American National Biography* (forthcoming), and a regular contributor to *New Literary History, American Quarterly, American Historical Review,* and other journals of literary and intellectual history. He has been a Guggenheim fellow, a fellow of the Center for Advanced Study in the Behavioral Sciences (Stanford), and a member of the Institute for Advanced Study. LITERATURE

**David A. Hounshell** is Henry R. Luce Professor of Technology and Social Change at Carnegie Mellon University in Pittsburgh, where he is a member of the Department of History as well as the Department of Social and Decision Sciences. His research focuses on the relationship of science, technology, and business and social change. He is the author of *From the American System to Mass Production* (1984), "Du Pont and the Management of Large-Scale Research and Development," in Peter Galison and Bruce Hevly, eds., *Big Science* (1992), "Planning and Executing 'Automation' at Ford Motor Company, 1945–1965: The Cleveland Engine Plant and Its Consequences," in Haruhito Shiomi and Kazuo Wada, eds., *Fordism Transformed* (1995), and coauthor of *Science and Corporate Strategy: Du Pont R&D, 1902–1980* (1988; Newcomen book award). He is also recipient of the Institute of Electrical and Electronics Engineers' Browder J. Thompson award for 1978 and the Business History Society's Harold Williamson medal for 1992. INDUSTRIAL RESEARCH AND MANUFACTURING TECHNOLOGY

**Akira Iriye** is Professor of History at Harvard University. His most recent works include *The Origins of the Second World War in Asia and the Pacific* (1987), *China and Japan in the Global Setting* (1992), *Across the Pacific: An Inner History of American–East Asian Relations,* rev. ed (1992), *The Cambridge History of American Foreign Relations, Vol. 3: The Globalizing of America, 1913–1945* (1993). WORLD REGIONS

**Carl F. Kaestle** is William F. Vilas Professor of Educational Policy Studies and History at the University of Wisconsin–Madison. He is currently the president of the National Academy of Education. He has been a visiting fellow at the Charles Warren Center for Studies in American History (Harvard), the Shelby Cullom Davis Center for Historical Studies (Princeton), and the Center for Advanced Study in the Behavioral Sciences (Stanford). He is the author of several works on the history of American education in the nineteenth century, including *Pillars of the Republic: Common Schools and American Society, 1780–1860* (1983), and on the history of literacy and the history of the federal role in education in the twentieth century, including *Literacy in the United States* (1991) and, as coauthor, "The Federal Role in Elementary and Secondary Education, 1940–1980," *Harvard Educational Review* (Fall 1982). ELEMENTARY AND SECONDARY EDUCATION

**Barry D. Karl** is Norman and Edna Freehling Professor of History at the University of Chicago. A political historian of the twentieth century, he has focused on the history of the United States presidency, public administration and bureaucracy, the social sciences, and the role of philanthropy and private foundations in the development of American public policy. He is the author of *Administrative Reorganization and Reform in the New Deal* (1963), *Charles E. Merriam and the Study of Politics* (1973), and *The Uneasy State* (1983). FOUNDATIONS AND PUBLIC POLICY

**David M. Kennedy** is the Donald J. McLachlan Professor of History and Chairman of the Department of History at Stanford University. His teaching and research focus is on the political, social, and economic history of the United States in the twentieth century. He is the author of *Birth Control in America: The Career of Margaret Sanger* (1970) and *Over Here: The First World War and American Society* (1980), and coauthor of *The American Pageant: A History of the Republic,* 10th ed. (1994). He is at work on a volume in *The Oxford History of the United States* covering the period from 1938 to 1945. THE WORLD WARS

**James T. Kloppenberg** is Associate Professor of History at Brandeis University, where he teaches American and European intellectual history and political theory. He has held Danforth, Whiting, American Council of Learned Societies, and Guggenheim fellowships, has served as visiting professor at the École des Hautes Études en Sciences Sociales in Paris, and has been elected a fellow of the Stanford Center for Research in the Behavioral Sciences. His first book, *Uncertain Victory: Social Democracy and Progressivism in European and American Thought, 1870–1920* (1986), received the Merle Curti award from the Organization of American Historians. He is coeditor of *A Companion to American Thought* (1995) and is currently working on a study of democracy in America and Europe since the seventeenth century. POLITICAL IDEAS AND MOVEMENTS

**Susan E. Lederer** is Associate Professor of Humanities at Penn State University College of Medicine. Her work focuses extensively on the history of human and animal experimentation in the United States. She is the author of *Subjected to Science: Human Experimentation in America before the Second World War* (1995). In 1994, she was appointed by President Bill Clinton to serve on the Advisory Committee on Human Radiation Experiments. MEDICAL SCIENCE AND TECHNOLOGY

**Peter Levine** is Professor of History at Michigan State University. He specializes in nineteenth-century American social history, including sport history. He is the former editor of *Baseball History* and coeditor of a series on sport and history for Oxford University Press. He is the author of *A. G. Spalding and the Rise of Baseball: The Promise of American Sport* (1985), *American Sport: A Documentary History* (1989), and *Ellis Island to Ebbets Field: Sport and the American Jewish Experience* (1992). SPORTS

**Earl Lewis** is Associate Professor of History and Afroamerican and African Studies at the University of Michigan, Ann Arbor. He is the author of *In Their Own Interests* (1991), as well as essays on African American migration and family patterns, including "Invoking Concepts, Problematizing Identities," *Labor History* (Spring–Summer 1993). He is currently at work on a collection of essays on race in the twentieth century, *All Because of the Color of Your Skin*. RACE

**Patricia Nelson Limerick** is Professor of History at the University of Colorado. She specializes in the history of the American West. She is the author of *Desert Passages: Encounters with American Deserts* (1985) and *The Legacy of Conquest: The Unbroken Past of the American West* (1987). THE WEST

**Kenneth J. Lipartito** is Associate Professor of History at the University of Houston. An economic and business historian, he specializes in the telecommunications and information industries. He is the author of *The Bell System and Regional Business: The Telephone in the South, 1877–1920* (1989), "What Have Lawyers Done for American Business?" *Business History Review* (1990), and "When Women were Switches: Technology, Work, and Gender in the Telephone Industry, 1890–1920," *American Historical Review* (1994), coauthor of a history of a major Houston law firm, *Baker & Botts and the History of Modern Houston* (1991), and editor of Twayne Publishers' series The Evolution of Modern Business. He is working on a study of the history of telecommunications technology, business, and public policy in the United States and Europe. THE PROFESSIONS

**Mark M. Lowenthal** is the senior specialist in U.S. Foreign Policy at the Congressional Research Service, Library of Congress. His current research focuses on the conceptualization and making of U.S. foreign policy. He earlier served in the State Department's Bureau of Intelligence and Research, first as Director of the Office of Strategic Forces Analysis, and the as deputy assistant secretary for functional analysis. He is the author of *Crispin Magicker* (a novel, 1979), *Leadership and Indecision: American War Planning and Policy Process, 1937–1942* (1988), and *U.S. Intelligence: Evolution and Anatomy*, 2d ed. (1992), and of over seventy articles and congressional studies on

a variety of national security issues, and coauthor of *Secrets of the JEOPARDY! Champions*. He was the 1988 grand champion on the TV game show *Jeopardy!* THE NATIONAL-SECURITY STATE

**James H. Madison** is Professor and chair of the Department of History, Indiana University, Bloomington. From 1976 to 1993 he served as editor of the *Indiana Magazine of History*. He is the author of *The Indiana Way: A State History* (1986), and *Eli Lilly: A Life, 1885–1977* (1989), editor of *Heartland: Comparative Histories of the Midwestern States* (1988) and *Wendell Willkie: Hoosier Internationalist* (1992), and coeditor of Midwestern History and Culture, a series of books on the region published by Indiana University Press. THE MIDWEST

**Kathleen D. McCarthy** is Professor of History at the Graduate School and University Center of the City University of New York, where she is also the director of the Center for the Study of Philanthropy. A social historian, she specializes in the history of giving, voluntarism, social reform, women's history, and American culture. She is the president-elect of the Association of Researchers on Nonprofit Organizations and Voluntary Action, and chairperson of the Nonprofit Academic Centers Council. She has served as a consultant to the Ford Foundation, IBM, and other grantmaking organizations, and is a former visiting research fellow of the Rockefeller Foundation. She is the author of *Noblesse Oblige: Charity and Cultural Philanthropy in Chicago, 1849–1929* (1982), and *Women's Culture: American Philanthropy and Art, 1830–1930* (1991), and editor and coauthor of *Lady Bountiful Revisited: Women, Philanthropy, and Power* (1990). PATRONAGE OF THE ARTS

**Stuart McConnell** is Associate Professor of History at Pitzer College, Claremont, California. Primarily a social and cultural historian, he is also interested in historical memory and in the intellectual history of American nationalism, especially in the period 1865 to 1920. He is the author of *Glorious Contentment: The Grand Army of the Republic, 1865–1900* (1992), and "The Gilded Age, the Era of Incorporations, and Populism," in *Encyclopedia of American Social History* (1992), and he edited a special issue of the Organization of American Historians' *Magazine of History* on the Civil War and memory (1993). NATIONALISM

**Arthur F. McEvoy** is Professor of Law and History at the University of Wisconsin–Madison. Previously he held appointments as Associate Professor of History at Northwestern University and a Research Fellow at the American Bar Foundation. He is the author of *The Fisherman's Problem: Ecology and Law in the California Fisheries, 1850–1980* (1990). He is currently at work on a history of industrial safety law in the United States. CONSERVATION AND THE ENVIRONMENT

**Richard A. Meckel** is Associate Professor of American Civilization and an associate of the Population and Training Center, Brown University. Much of his scholarship centers on patterns of morbidity and public health policy in the United States during the nineteenth and twentieth centuries. He is the author of *Save the Babies: American Public Health Reform and the Prevention of Infant Mortality, 1850–1929* (1990) and is at work on a study tracing the use of the public schools to promote child health in the United States since 1870. HEALTH AND DISEASE

**Steven Mintz** is Professor of History at the University of Houston. A specialist in the history of the family, he is the author of *A Prison of Expectations: The Family in Victorian Culture* (1983), coauthor of *Domestic Revolutions: A Social History of American Family Life* (1988) and *America and Its People,* 2d ed. (1993), editor of *African American Voices: The Life Cycle of Slavery* (1993), and coeditor of *Hollywood's America: United States History through Its Films* (1993). He has been a visiting scholar at Harvard University's Center for European Studies as well as a guest professor at Universität-Gesamthochschule Siegen, Germany. He is an editor of New York University Press's American Social Experience series, and has served as a consultant in family history to the National Museum of American History and other museums and historical societies. FAMILY

**Paul J. Miranti** is Associate Professor of Accounting at the School of Business of Rutgers University in New Brunswick, New Jersey. A historian of business, he specializes both in the professionalization of accountancy and finance as well as in the application of measurement methodologies to governmental processes. In addition to numerous articles on these topics, he is the author of *Accountancy Comes of Age: The Development of an American Profession, 1886–1940* (1990). THE PROFESSIONS

**Gregg A. Mitman** is Assistant Professor in the Department of the History of Science at the University of Oklahoma. His work centers on the social, ethical, and political dimensions of biology, and, in particular, ecology and animal behavior, within twentieth-century American culture. He is the author of *The State of Nature: Ecology, Community, and American Social Thought, 1900–1950* (1992), which won the 1994 Gustav Arit Award in the Humanities from the Council of Graduate Schools. He is at work on *Cinematic Nature: Hollywood Technology, Popular Culture, and the Science of Animal Behavior,* which explores the intersection of art, science, and entertainment through a focus on the history of nature films. EVOLUTIONARY THEORY

**Deborah Dash Moore** is Professor of Religion at Vassar College and director of its American Culture program. In 1988–1989 she served as research director of the YIVO Institute for Jewish Research and dean of the Max Weinreich Center for Advanced Jewish Studies. A historian of American Jews, she specializes in twentieth-century urban Jewish history. She edits the *YIVO Annual,* an interdisciplinary journal of contemporary Jewish studies. She is the author of *At Home in America: Second Generation New York Jews* (1981), *B'nai B'rith and the Challenge of Ethnic Leadership* (1981), and *To the Golden Cities: Pursuing the American Jewish Dream in Miami and L.A.* (1994), editor of *East European Jews in Two Worlds* (1989), and coeditor of *Jewish Settlement and Community in the Modern Western World* (1990). JUDAISM AND JEWISH CULTURE

**Jill G. Morawski** is Professor of Psychology at Wesleyan University and is affiliated with Wesleyan's Women's Studies program. She has served as president of the Division on the History of Psychology of the American Psychological Association and serves on the editorial board of *Theory and Psychology.* She specializes in the psychology of gender and the history of psychology. She is the author of "The Troubled Quest for Masculinity, Femininity, and Androgyny," in *Review of Personality and Social Psychology* (1987), "Toward the Unimagined: Feminism and Epistemology in Psychology," in Roy Hare-Mustin and J. Maracek, eds., *Making a Difference: Psychology and the Construction of Gender* (1990), and *Practicing Feminism, Reconstructing Psychology: Notes on a Liminal Science* (1994), and editor of *The Rise of Experimentation in American Psychology* (1988). GENDER THEORIES

**Ronald L. Numbers** is the William Coleman Professor of the History of Science and Medicine at the University of Wisconsin–Madison, where for over two decades he has taught the history of American science and medicine. He is the author or editor of fourteen books, including *The Creationists* (1992), which won the Albert C. Outler Prize from the American Society of Church History. He has received fellowships from the Josiah Macy, Jr., Foundation and the John Simon Guggenheim Foundation and a scholar's award from the National Science Foundation. From 1989 to 1993 he edited *Isis,* the journal of the History of Science Society. He is currently writing a history of science in America for the Cambridge History of Science series and coediting an eight-volume *Cambridge History of Science.* EVOLUTIONARY THEORY

**David S. Patterson** is chief of the Arms Control and Economics Division, Office of the Historian, U.S. Department of State. A diplomatic historian, he specializes in the arms control, national security, and foreign economic policies of the United States. He has edited several volumes in these subject areas covering the 1950s and 1960s for the *Foreign Relations of the United States* series, the official record of U.S. foreign policy. He is the author of *Toward a Warless World: The Travail of the American Peace Movement, 1887–1914* (1976), essays in Charles Chatfield and Peter van den Dungen, eds., *Peace Movements and Political Cultures* (1988) and Gregg Walker et al., eds., *The Military-Industrial Complex: Eisenhower's Warning Three Decades Later* (1992), and articles on national security and arms control issues during the Cold War in *Diplomatic History, Peace and Change,* and other journals. PACIFISM AND ARMS LIMITATION

**James T. Patterson** is Ford Foundation Professor of History at Brown University, where he teaches and writes on aspects of twentieth-century U.S. social, economic, political, and medical history. He also teaches courses concerning race relations in American history. He has been Harmsworth Professor of American History at the University of Oxford and John Adams Professor of American Civilization at the University of Amsterdam. He is the author of *The New Deal and the States: Federalism in Transition* (1969), *Mr. Republican: A Biography of Robert A. Taft* (1972), *The Dread Disease: Cancer and Modern American Culture* (1987), *America in the Twentieth Century: A History,* 4th ed. (1993), and *America's Struggle against Poverty, 1900–1994,* 3d ed. (1994). WEALTH AND POVERTY

**Nancy Rexford** has a B.A. from Vassar College and an M.A. from the University of Iowa. Since 1975 she has worked with museum costume collections as both a curator and a consultant. She has written articles on approaches to studying costume history, on using shoes as historical evidence, and on dating early-nineteenth-century portraits, as well as the entry on clothing in the *Encyclopedia of American Social History.* Her illustrations appear in *Everyday Dress of Rural America, 1793–1800.* She is currently writing and illustrating a multivolume reference work, *Women's Clothing in America, 1795–1930.* CLOTHING AND APPEARANCE

**Jon H. Roberts** is Associate Professor of History at the University of Wisconsin–Stevens Point. An intellectual historian, he has focused most of his research on the cultural impact of modern science in the United States. He is an advisory editor for *Isis* and a member of the Council of the American Society of Church History. He is the author of *Darwinism and the Divine in America: Protestant Intellectuals and Organic Evolution, 1859–1900* (1988). The manuscript for that book was awarded the Brewer Prize by the American Society of Church History. THE HUMAN MIND AND PERSONALITY

**Randy Roberts** is Professor of History at Purdue University. A specialist in the history of popular culture and sport history, he is the author of *Jack Dempsey: The Manassa Mauler* (1979), *Papa Jack: Jack Johnson and the Era of White Hopes* (1983), and *Where the Domino Fell: America and Vietnam, 1945–1990* (1991), and coauthor of *Winning Is the Only Thing: Sports in America since 1945* (1989) and *Heavy Justice: The State of Indiana v. Mike Tyson* (1994). He is the coeditor of Sport and Society, a University of Illinois Press series. LEISURE AND RECREATION

**Bert A. Rockman** is the University Professor of Political Science at the University of Pittsburgh, where he is also research professor at the Center for International Studies, professor in its graduate school of Public and International Affairs, and director of its Center for American Politics in Society. He is also nonresident senior fellow in the Governmental Studies program of the Brookings Institution in Washington, D.C. His work focuses on U.S. and comparative political institutions and leadership, especially executive politics. He has served as president of the Organized Section for Presidency Research of the American Political Science Association. He is the author of *The Leadership Question: The Presidency and the American System* (1984; winner of the 1985 Richard E. Neustadt Award), and coeditor of *The Bush Presidency: First Appraisals* (1991) and *Researching the Presidency: Vital Questions, New Approaches* (1993). THE PRESIDENCY

**George H. Roeder, Jr.,** is chair of the Undergraduate Division and Professor of Liberal Arts at the School of the Art Institute of Chicago. He is also a lecturer at Northwestern University. A cultural and intellectual historian, he specializes in the history of the American visual environment, with emphasis on the twentieth century. He is the author of *Forum of Uncertainty: Confrontations with Modern Painting in Twentieth-Century American Thought* (1981) and *The Censored War: American Visual Experience during World War II* (1993). He has been awarded an National Endowment for the Humanities Fellowship for College Teachers and Independent Scholars (1987–1988), served as principal historical consultant for a filmstrip on Vietnam that won a gold medal at the New York International Film and Video Festival, and spoken on American visual experience on CNN and public television and radio. THE VISUAL ARTS

**Emily S. Rosenberg** is DeWitt Wallace Professor of History at Macalester College. A historian of U.S. foreign relations in the twentieth century, she has specialized in both economic and cultural interactions. She serves on the executive board of the Organization of American Historians, the Council of the Society for Historians of American Foreign Relations, and the U.S. State Department's Advisory Committee on Historical Diplomatic Documentation. She is the author of *Spreading the American Dream: American Economic and Cultural Expansion, 1890–1945* (1982) and coauthor of *In Our Times: America since World War II,* 5th ed. (1995). CULTURAL INTERACTIONS

**Harry N. Scheiber** is the Stefan Reisenfeld Chair Professor of Law and History at the Boalt Hall School of Law, University of California, Berkeley. His special fields of research include constitutional law and history, ocean law and policy, and economic history. He has served as distinguished Fulbright senior lecturer in Australia, and has held Guggenheim, American Council of Learned Societies, and Center for Advanced Study in the Behavioral Sciences fellowships. He is the author of *Ohio Canal Era: A Case Study of State Government and the Economy,* 2d ed. (1987) and *American Law and the Constitutional Order,* 2d ed. (1988), editor of *Federalism: Studies in History, Law, and Policy* (1988) and *Federalism and the Judicial Mind* (1992), and a contributor to *Ambivalent Legacy: A Legal History of the South* (1984), *The U.S. Constitution: Roots, Rights, and Responsibilities* (1992), and numerous other collaborative studies in legal history. FEDERALISM AND THE STATES

**Melvin Small** is Professor of History at Wayne State University. A former president of the Council on Peace Research in History, he specializes in American foreign relations with an emphasis on questions dealing with the causes of war and the impact of opinion on policy. He is the author of *Was War Necessary? National Security and American Entry into War, 1812–1950* (1980), *Johnson, Nixon, and the Doves* (1988), *Covering Dissent: The Media and the Vietnam Antiwar Movement* (1994), editor of *Public Opinion and Historians* (1970), and coeditor of *International War* (1988) and *Give Peace a Chance: Exploring the Vietnam Antiwar Movement* (1992). FOREIGN POLICY

**George David Smith** is president of the Winthrop Group, Inc., and also serves as Clinical Professor of Economics at the Stern School of Business of New York University. His research interests span the history of business strategy and structure, technology, and entrepreneurship. He is the author of *Anatomy of a Business Strategy* (1985) and *From Monopoly to Competition* (1988), and coauthor of *The Transformation of Financial Capitalism* (1993). He has served as a consultant to AT&T, ALCOA, General Electric, and Shell Oil, among others. CAPITAL MARKETS

**Robert W. Smith** is a historian at the Smithsonian Institution's National Air and Space Museum. He also teaches the history of science at Johns Hopkins University. He specializes in the history of science and technology in the United States in the nineteenth and twentieth centuries, and has a particular interest in the material culture of science. He is the author of *The Expanding Universe: Astronomy's "Great Debate," 1900–1931* (1982) and *The Space Telescope: A Study of NASA, Science, Technology, and Politics* (rev. ed., 1993), which was awarded the History of Science Society's Watson Davis Prize, selected as one of *Choice*'s top academic books, and one of the *New York Times*'s notable books of the year. LARGE-SCALE SCIENTIFIC ENTERPRISE

**Susan Strasser** is a research fellow at the German Historical Institute in Washington, D.C., its first American scholar of U.S. history. She was formerly director of the University Honors program at George Washington University and member of the faculty at Evergreen State College. Her work on nineteenth- and twentieth-century American daily life addresses issues in business history, women's history, labor history, and the history of technology. She is the author of *Never Done: A History of American Housework* (1982) and *Satisfaction Guaranteed: The Making of the American Mass Market* (1989). She has received fellowships from the John Simon Guggenheim Foundation, the Newcomen Society and the Harvard Business School, the American Council of Learned Societies, the Bunting Institute, the Smithsonian Institution, and the Woodrow Wilson Foundation. CONSUMPTION

**Richard Sylla** is Henry Kaufman Professor of the History of Financial Institutions and Markets and Professor of Economics at the Stern School of Business of New York University. He is also a research associate of the National Bureau of Economic Research. As an economic historian, he specializes in the economic and financial history of the United States, including both private and public finance. He is a former editor of the *Journal of Economic History,* and has served as consultant to Citibank and Chase Manhattan Bank on historical projects. He is the author of *The American Capital Market, 1846–1914* (1975), coauthor of *A History of Interest Rates,* 3d ed. (1991), and *The Evolution of the American Economy,* 2d ed. (1993), and coeditor of *Patterns of European Industrialization—the Nineteenth Century* (1991). CAPITAL MARKETS

**Jon C. Teaford** is Professor of History at Purdue University. An urban historian, he specializes in the development of American city government. He is the author of *City and Suburb: The Political Fragmentation of Metropolitan America, 1850–1970* (1979), *The Rough Road to Renaissance: Urban Revitalization in America, 1940–1985* (1990), *The Twentieth-Century American City* (rev. ed., 1993), and *Cities of the Heartland: The Rise and Fall of the Industrial Midwest* (1993). CITY AND SUBURB

**Mark Tebeau** is a Ph.D. candidate in American Social History at Carnegie Mellon University. His dissertation, "Eating Smoke: Masculinity, Technology, and the Politics of Urbanization," addresses issues of gender and technology and the study of systems of urban fire protection. GENDER ISSUES

**Richard S. Tedlow** is MBA Class of 1957 Professor of Business Administration and director of research at the Harvard University Graduate School of Business Administration. The focus of his research is the history of marketing. The former editor of *Business History Review,* he is the author of *Keeping the Corporate Image: Public Relations and Business, 1900–1950* (1979) and *New and Improved: The Story of Mass Marketing in America* (1990), and coauthor of *The Coming of Managerial Capitalism: A Casebook on the History of American Economic Institutions* (1985). He has served as a consultant to businesses and to government agencies. MARKETING

**John L. Thomas** is George L. Littlefield Professor of American History at Brown University. An intellectual and cultural historian of the United States, he specializes in nineteenth- and twentieth-century reform movements, most recently the programs and activities of regional planners and critics. He is the author of *The Liberator: William Lloyd Garrison* (1963) and *Alternative America: Henry George, Edward Bellamy, Henry Demarest Lloyd, and the Adversary Tradition* (1983), and of several essays on regionalism and regional planning, including "Lewis Mumford, Benton MacKaye, and the Regional Vision," in Thomas P. Hughes and Agatha P. Hughes, eds., *Lewis Mumford: Public Intellectual* (1990). REGIONALISM

**Robert Twombly** teaches U.S., Dutch, and modern French architecture in the Department of History at the City College of New York. He is the author of *Frank Lloyd Wright: His Life and His Architecture* (1979), *Louis Sullivan: His Life and Work* (1986), and *Louis Sullivan: The Public Papers* (1988), and coauthor of *Seeds of Democracy: Iconography, Social Thought, and the Drawings of Louis Sullivan* (forthcoming). He is at work on a biography of Henry Hobson Richardson. ARCHITECTURE

**Steven W. Usselman** is Associate Professor in the School of History, Technology, and Society at the Georgia Institute of Technology. His research focuses on the creation and regulation of complex technical systems in the United States since 1850. He has published numerous essays on the American railroad industry in journals such as *Business History Review* and *Technology and Culture* and is completing a book on that subject entitled *Regulating Innovation: The Management, Economics, and Politics of Technical Change on American Railroads, 1846–1914.* His studies of computing stem from a fourteen-month research project during which he had access to the corporate records of the IBM Corporation. His essay, "IBM and Its Imitators: Organizational Capabilities and the Emergence of the International Computer Industry," *Business and Economic History* (1993), won the Newcomen Prize of the Business History Conference. COMPUTER AND COMMUNICATIONS TECHNOLOGY

**Rudolph J. Vecoli** is Professor of History and director of the Immigration History Research Center, University of Minnesota. He has served as president of the American Italian Historical Association and the Immigration History Society as well as chairman of the history committee of the Statue of Liberty–Ellis Island Centennial commission. His writings have dealt with ethnic and immigration history and more specifically with various aspects of the Italian immigration to the United States. He is the author of "An Inter-ethnic Perspective on American Immigration History," *Mid-America* (April–July 1993), coauthor of *A Century of American Immigration, 1884–*

*1984* (1984) and "The Invention of Ethnicity: A Perspective from the USA," *Journal of American Ethnic History* (Fall 1992), and coeditor of *A Century of European Migrations, 1830–1930* (1991). ETHNICITY

**Richard H. K. Vietor** is the Senator Heinz Professor of Environmental Management at the Harvard University Graduate School of Business Administration. He serves on the editorial board of the *Business History Review*, and was president of the Business History Conference in 1993–1994. In his teaching and research, he specializes in the government's regulation of business in the twentieth century. He is the author of *Environmental Policy and the Coal Coalition* (1980), *Energy Policy in America since 1945* (1984), *Telecommunication in Transition* (1986), *Strategic Management in the Regulated Environment* (1989), and *Contrived Competition: Regulation and Deregulation in America* (1994). ECONOMIC PERFORMANCE

**Ronald G. Walters** is Professor of History at Johns Hopkins University, where he teaches U.S. social and cultural history. His research interests encompass American radical and reform movements and the study of popular culture. He is the author of *The Antislavery Appeal: American Abolitionism after 1830* (1976), *American Reformers: 1815–1860* (1978), and editor of *Primers for Prudery: Sexual Advice to Victorian America* (1974) and *A Black Woman's Odyssey: The Narrative of Nancy Prince* (1990), as well as a forthcoming study of twentieth-century American popular culture. THE MASS MEDIA AND POPULAR CULTURE

**Kenneth W. Warren** is Associate Professor of English and Humanities at the University of Chicago. He is the author of *Black and White Strangers: Race and American Literary Realism* (1993), and has also published articles on nineteenth- and twentieth-century American and African American writers, including William Dean Howells, Langston Hughes, and Leon Forrest. AFRICAN AMERICAN CULTURAL MOVEMENTS

**Mira Wilkins** is Professor of Economics at Florida International University, Miami. As an economic and business historian, she specializes in the history of foreign investment, and particularly the history of multinational enterprise. She is the author of, among other works, *The Emergence of Multinational Enterprise: American Business Abroad from the Colonial Era to 1914* (1970), *The Maturing of Multinational Enterprise: American Business Abroad from 1914 to 1970* (1974), and *The History of Foreign Investment in the United States to 1914* (1989). She has also published many scholarly articles in leading journals. She is on the editorial

board of *Business History Review* and *Business History* and was a past president of the Business History Conference. She has been the recipient of many awards, including a Guggenheim fellowship. FOREIGN TRADE AND INVESTMENT

**Graham K. Wilson** is Professor of Political Science at the University of Wisconsin–Madison, where he specializes in American and British politics. He has written numerous articles and books on interest groups in the United States and other democracies, including *Unions in American National Politics* (1979), *Interest Groups in the United States* (1981), and *Interest Groups* (1992). He has also written studies of policy making in the United States and Britain, including *Special Interests and Policymaking* (1977) and *The Politics of Safety and Health* (1985). He is editor of *Governance* and has served as editor of the *British Journal of Political Science*. He writes regularly on American elections for academic journals and comments on elections for both American and British media. PARTIES AND INTEREST GROUPS

**Gavin Wright** is Professor of Economics at Stanford University. A specialist in American economic history, he has written extensively on the economic development of the U.S. South, and more recently on the historical foundations of American economic performance. He is the author of *The Political Economy of the Cotton South* (1978), *Old South New South: Revolutions in the Southern Economy since the Civil War* (1986), and "The Origins of American Industrial Success, 1879–1940," *American Economic Review* (September 1990), and coauthor of "The Rise and Fall of American Technological Leadership," *Journal of Economic Literature* (December 1992). He was elected to the American Academy of Arts and Sciences in 1992. NATURAL RESOURCES

**Shoshana Zuboff** is the Benjamin and Lilian Hertsberg Professor of Business Administration at the Harvard University Graduate School of Business Administration. She is a specialist in the relationship between technology and the nature of work, both as it has developed historically and as it is unfolding in the emerging work place of the future. Her principal work in this area is *In the Age of the Smart Machine: The Future of Work and Power* (1988). WORK

**Olivier Zunz** is Professor of History at the University of Virginia and visiting directeur d'études at the École des Hautes Études en Sciences Sociales in Paris. A specialist in American social, urban, and cultural history, he is the author of *The Changing Face of Inequality: Urbanization, Industrial Development, and*

*Immigrants in Detroit, 1880–1920* (1990) and "Producers, Brokers, and Users of Knowledge: The Institutional Matrix," in Dorothy Ross, ed., *Modernist Impulses in the Human Sciences* (1994), editor and coauthor of *Reliving the Past: The Worlds of Social History* (1985), and coeditor of *The Landscape of Modernity:* *Essays on New York City, 1900–1940* (1992). His work has been supported by the National Science Foundation, the National Endowment for the Humanities, and the John Simon Guggenheim Memorial Foundation, among others. CLASS

# INDEX

Numbers in boldface refer to the main entry on the subject. Numbers in italic refer to photographs, illustrations, and maps. Numbers followed by tab refer to tables. Titles of films appear under "Films"; museums are listed under "Museums"; titles of musicals appear under "Musicals"; orchestras are listed under "Orchestras"; titles of radio programs appear under "Radio programs"; Supreme Court cases under "Legal cases"; and titles of television programs and series under "Television programs."

## A

AAA. *See* Agricultural Adjustment Act
Aaron, Daniel, 1443a
AARP. *See* American Association of Retired Persons (AARP)
AAUP. *See* American Association of University Professors (AAUP)
Abbey, Edward, 1378b
Abbott, Berenice, 1709b
Abbott, Edith, 121b, 922a
Abbott, Grace, 121b
Abbott, Shirley, 63a
ABC. *See* American Broadcasting Company (ABC)
ABC (American-British Conversation) Talks, 602a
ABC-1 agreement, 635b
Abelson, Philip, 754a
Aberbach, Joel D., *as contributor*, 355a–376b
Aberdeen Proving Ground, 810b
ABMA. *See* Army Ballistic Missile Agency
ABM Treaty. *See* Antiballistic Missile Systems (ABM) Treaty
Abortion
  Catholics, 1512a, 1528a, 1531a, 1532a–b
  feminists, 120b, 121a
  interest groups, 317a,b
  legislation, 448a
  Protestants, 1506a
  state laws, 240b
  Supreme Court appointments, 392a–b
  Supreme Court decisions, 421b
Abramovitz, Moses, 1184a
Abrams, Creighton, 662b
*Absalom, Absalom!* (Faulkner), 10a, 1445b
Absolutists, 556a
Abstract Expressionism, 1712a–1714a, 1715b
  Jews and, 1587a
Abundance
  divorce and, 215b
  middle class and, 199a,b
*Abyssinia*, 1596a
*Academic and Industrial Efficiency* (Cooke), 1409a
Academic community
  during Cold War, 687b
  and federal government, 605b
  foundations and, 498a

internationalization, 498a
  scholarly writing peer review, 1831a
Acadia Institute, 948b
Accommodationism, 1534a
Acconci, Vito, 1720a
*According to What* (Johns), 1718b
Accountancy
  accreditation, 1412a,b
  corporate auditors, 1219b, 1226b, 1411a–b
  evolution of profession, 1410a
  Great Depression, 1419a
  New Deal, 1420a
  restricted access to, 1416b
  standardization of practice, 1231a, 1420b
  stratification, 1413a
Accumulatorem Fabrik (Germany), 1138b
Acheson, Dean, 610b, 656b, 659b, 662b, 725b
Ackerman, Bruce, 388b
ACLU. *See* American Civil Liberties Union (ACLU)
Acquired Immunodeficiency Syndrome. *See* AIDS
Act Further to Promote the Defense of the United States. *See* Lend–Lease Act
Action intellectuals, 1832a
Act of 29 April 1943, 165a–b tab
Act of 14 June 1940, 165a–b tab
Act of 3 March 1875, 154a–b tab
Acton, Lord, 427b, 1506b
Adamic, Louis, 174a, 176a, 178b
Adams, Ansel, 1373a,b, 1709b, 1714b
Adams, Frederick Upham, 382a
Adams, Henry, 1669b, 1744a,b
Adams, Henry Carter, 919a, 1291b
Adams, John, 260a
Adams, John Taylor, *574b*
Adams, Roger, 837a
Adams, Thomas, 13a, 16b, 18a
Adams, Thomas S., 1315a, 1317b, 1321a, 1329a–b
Adamson Act (1916), 519b
*Adam's Rib* (Herschberger), 910a
Addams, Jane, 49b, 51b, 121b, 256b, 275a–b, 453b, *547a*, 697a, 1068b, 1495a, 1804b
  Dewey, John, and, 277b, 1641a
  on *The Melting Pot*, 1568b
  neutral mediation of World War I, 546b

on women's role, 102a
*Address Unknown* (Wright), 123a
Adelman, Morris A., 1050a, 1399b
ADL. *See* Anti–Defamation League (ADL)
Adler, Alfred, 234b
Adler, Celia, 1570b
Adler, Cyrus, 1574b
Adler, Felix, 1567b
Adler, Jacob, 1570a
Adler, Mortimer, 1648b
Adler, Samuel, 1567b
Adler and Sullivan, 1675b, 1676a,b
Administrative law, 521b
Administrative Procedure Act (1946), 333b, 525b, 526a, 528b–529a, 534b
Administrative state, 513a,b
  economic regulation, 1269b–1270a
  expansion under Johnson, 485b
  reasons for the creation, 517b–518a
  *See also* Bureaucracy
*Admirals, Generals, and American Foreign Policy, 1898–1914* (Challener), 594b
*Admirals Lobby, The* (Davis), 599a
Adolescence
  consumption, 1793b
  as defined stage of life, 226a
  teenage subculture, 230b
Adorno, Theodor W., 1485a–b, 1486a, 1584b, 1826a
ADP. *See* Automatic Data Processing (ADP)
Adrian, Gilbert, 1790a
*Adventures in Art* (Hartley), 1703a
*Adventures of Augie March, The* (Bellow), 1450a,b, 1450b, 1457a, 1587b
*Adventures of Huckleberry Finn, The* (Twain), 1438a, 1456a
*Advertisements for Myself* (Mailer), 34a
Advertising, 28a–b, 31a, 1017a–b, 1019b, 1022b–1023b, 1025b
  American cultural references, 714b
  cable television, 1032b
  consumption, 1021a, 1024b
  incorporated in paintings, 1702b
  industrial production, 1129b, 1131b
  liquor industry, 1132a
  movies stars, 1466b
  in politics, 116b
  radio, 807a,b–808b, 1059b, 1467a, 1474b
  specialists, 1411a
  suffragists, 117a

# INDEX

airlift, 782a
  blockade, 608b
  Kennedy and, 341b
  wall, 341b, 693a, 853a
Berlin, Irving, 1323b, 1581a, 1615a–b, 1619a, 1625b
Berman, Marshall, 1455a
Bernard, Luther L., 886b, 923a,b
Bernbach, William, 1064a
Bernstein, Leonard, 1586b, 1621a, 1625b
Bernstein, Richard J., 189a, 291b, 292a, 1658a
Berrigan, Daniel, 1529a
Berrigan, Philip, 1529a
Berry, Brian J. L., 18b
Berry, Chuck, 58b, 1625a
Berstein, Michael A., *as contributor,* 1183a–1207b
Berube, Allan, 104a
Bessemer steel process, 1134b–1135a
Best, Charles H., 944b
Bestor, Arthur, 1811b
Bether, Hans, 558b
Bethlehem Steel, 1135b
Betsy Ross House, 37a
Bettelheim, Bruno, 1584b
Bettercare, 1002a
Betts, Richard, 610b, 612a
Bevatron. *See* Particle accelerators
Beveridge, Albert, 255a
*Beyond Ethnicity* (Sollors), 190b
Beyond Freedom and Dignity (Skinner), 891b
*Beyond Separate Spheres* (Rosenberg), 904b, 922a
*Beyond the Melting Pot* (Glazer and Moynihan), 184a
B-52 Stratofortress, *783a–b*
Bhagwan Rajneesh, 1552b
Bhaktivedanta, A. C., Swami Prabhupada, 1552a
Bias, Len, 1776b
Bible
  Catholics, 1511a, 1533a–b
  fundamentalists, 1499a–b
  Judaism, 1566b
  liberal Protestants, 1495b
  Presbyterians, 1500a
Bible institutes, 1499a, 1503a–b
Bicentennial, 267b, 268a
Bickel, Alexander, 388b
Bidault, Georges, *582a–b*
Biddle, Francis, 176b, 1705a
Biddle, George, 1705a
  World War I, 1701b
Biddle, Livingston J., Jr., 1736b, 1738b
Biden, Joseph, 393a
"Bie Mir Bist Du Sheyn," 1571b
*Biennial Census of Manufacturers,* 1057b
Bierce, Ambrose, 1437b
Big bands, 1620b
Big Brother and the Holding Company, 1628b
*Big Daddy Paper Doll* (Stevens), 1720a
Bigelow, Maurice, 861b
Big Science, 739b, 763a–b, 846a, 849b, 852a
  critics, 751b–754a
  as term, 745a, 753b
  *See also* Large-scale science
*Big Sea, The* (Hughes), 1597b, 1601a

*Big Sleep, The* (Chandler), 1363a
Biker style, 1793a
Bilbo, Theodore, 66b
Bilingual Education Act (1968), 1812a–b tab, 1814a
Bilingualism, movement against, 187b
Billboards, 1023a
Billiards, 1747b
Bill of Rights, 435b–436a, 440a
  applicability to states, 414a–415a
*Billy the Kid* (Copland), 1581a, 1617b
Bilstein, Roger E., *as contributor,* 767a–797b
Biltmore, 1669a
Binet, Alfred, 881a
*Bintel brief* column, 1569a
Biograph, 1469a
Biological Sciences Curriculum Study, 871b
Biological weapons, 850a
  tests on American civilians, 950a
Biological Weapons Convention (1972), 563a
Biologics Control Act (1902), 996a–b tab
Biomedical research, 1836a
Biotechnology, 854a
  research, 852b
Birth control, 30a, 103b, 227b
  Catholics, 1512a, 1528b, 1531a–b
  funding of research, 228a, 946b
  growing public acceptance, 229a
  pill, 235a
  restricted access, 227b
  restricted information, 227a,b
  Sanger, Margaret, 226b
  *United States* v. *One Package of Japanese Pessaries,* 228a
Birth rate, 222b
Bishop, Isabel, 1704b, 1710b
Bishops, Roman Catholic, 1515b–1516a, 1522b
  "Discrimination and Christian Conscience" (1958), 1524b
  politics, 1532a–b
  on secularism, 1521a
Bismarck, Otto von, 990a
*Bitter Cry of the Children, The* (Spargo), 1804b
Bituminous Coal Conservation Act (1935), 380b
*Black, Brown, and Beige* (Ellington), 1602a, 1620b
Black, Charles, 388a
Black, Hugo L., 382b, 390a–b tab, 415a, 417a, 436a, 444a,b
Black, Joe, 1777b
Black Aesthetic, 1602b
*Black Aesthetic, The* (Gayle), 1603a,b
Black Arts movement, 1602a–1604a
Black Arts Repertory Theater and School, 1604a
"Black Boys and Native Sons" (Howe), 1601b
Black Catholic Clergy Caucus, 1529b
Black Community Development, 1604a
*Black Culture and Black Consciousness* (Levine), 1595b
*Black Fire* (Baraka and Neal), 1603a
*Black Hair* (Soto), 1456b
"Black Man Brings His Gifts, The" (Du Bois), 259b
*Black Metropolis* (Cayton and Drake), 213a–b, 925b

Black Mountain College, 1715b, 1827a
Blackmun, Harry A., 390a–b tab, 392a
Blackmur, R. P., 1447a, 1448a
Black Muslims, 266b, 287b
Black nationalism, 259b, 260a
Black Panthers, 180a, 266a, 288b
Black Political Convention, 1604a
Black Power, 180a, 266b, 1602b
Black pride style, 1793a
Blacks. *See* African Americans
Black separatism, 259b
*Black Skin, White Masks* (Fanon), 1603b
Black societies, 1514b, 1515a
Black Star Line, 259b, 1599a–b
Black studies, 1604a–1605a, 1831b
*Black Worker, The* (Harris and Spero), 929b
Blades, Rubén, 1632b
Blake, Peter, 1665b
Blakelock, Ralph, 1693b
Blakey, Art, 1624a
Blanshard, Paul, 1521b
Blashfield, Edwin, 1696a
Blatch, Harriot Stanton, 117b
Blatz distillery, 1132a
Blauner, Robert, 155b, 1113b, 1114a
Blaut, James, 252b
Blavatsky, Helena, 1540b, 1543b, 1554b
Blease, Cole, 66b
Bleier, Ruth, 913b
Bleriot, Louis, 770a
Blewett, John P., 750a
Blimps. *See* Airships
Bliss, Lillie P., 1684b, 1699a, 1705a
Bliss, Lizzie, 1728b
Bliss, William Dwight Porter, 275a
*Blitzkrieg,* 601a, 634b, 778a
Bloch, Erich, 852a
Bloch, Ernest, 1581a
Blonsky, Marshall, 714a
Bloom, Allan, 189b
  *Closing of the American Mind, The,* 1836a
Bloom, Hyman, 1714a, 1721b
Bloomgarden, Solomon, 1569b
Blue Army of Mary, 1518b
*Blue-Collar Marriage* (Komarovsky), 929a
Blue Cross, 486a, 993b, 994b, 1078a
Blue laws, 1749a
"Blueprint for Negro Writing" (Wright), 1600b
Blue Shield, 994b, 1078a
Blue-sky laws, 1224a–b
Blues music, 48a, 149b, 150a, 1597b
  African Americans, 1595b
  female singers, 1597b
  Southern origin, 67b
Bluestone industry, 27b
Bluford, Guion, 790b
Blumberg, 1648b
Blume, Peter, 1721b
  *Eternal City,* 1708b
Blumer, Herbert, 1484b
Bly, Carol, 59b
B'nai B'rith, 1566a, 1577a, 1583b
  Klutznick Museum, 1590a
  women, 1587b–1588a
Board for International Broadcasting, 614a
Boards of equalization, 1315a
Boas, Franz, 161a, 173b, 261a, 869b, 886b, 922a, 925a, 1567b, 1599a
Bobbitt, Franklin, 1806a
Bob Jones University, 1833a

Coal industry (*cont.*)
Gillette syndrome, 87b
Great Depression, 1161b
South, 63b
*Coal Question, The* (Jevons), 1387a–b
Coase, Ronald, 1301b
Coast and Geodetic Survey, 742b
Coast Survey, 741a
Coats, A. W., 1299a
Coca, Imogene, 1578b
Coca-Cola, 700b, 1059a
advertising material distributed in 1913,
1056a–b tab
distribution system, *1038a–b,* 1039a
market power, 1054a
mass marketing, 1045b, 1053a–b
penetration pricing, 1052a
product line in 1993, 1038a tab
product variety, 1040a
railroad and sales, 1051b–1052a
Code-breaking. *See* Cryptanalysis
Cody, Buffalo Bill, 83b, 697b
Coffin, Charles, 1137b
Coffin, James, 741a
Coffin, William Sloane, Jr., 1505b
Cogley, John, 1524a, 1525b
Cognitive psychologists, 892b–893a
Cohan, George M., 1614a
Cohen, Andy, 173a, 1766b
Cohen, Arthur A., 1589a,b
Cohen, Elliot, 1581b, 1586b
Cohen, Gerson, 1588b–1589a
Cohen, Lizabeth, 175a, 260b, 261b
*as contributor,* 101a–127b
*Making a New Deal,* 206a
Cohen, Morris R., 1579b, 1644b–1645a,
1652b
Cohen, "Nudie," 1792b
Cohen, Wesley, 852b
Cohen, Wilbur, 485a, 486a,b
Cohen, William, 397b
Cohn, Harry, 1580a, 1752b
COINTELPRO, 616b
Colander, David, 1306b
Cold War, 284a, 687a–688b
aircraft industry, 462b, 779b–784b, 796b
and American intellectual life, 501a
and the arts, 1713b, 1735b
Catholics, 1520a–1526b
civil liberties, 614b
consensus, 615b
corporatism, 687b
displacement of Fair Deal, 334b
dissolution of Jewish Left, 1586a
domestic policy, 687b
Eastern region economy, 28b
end of, 349b
foreign policy, 578b–584a, 589a
higher education, 1829a
immigrants and immigration, 178a,b
Korea, 654b
militarization, 612a, 688b–691a
National Defense Education Act
(NDEA), 615a
national highway system, 615a
national security state, 333a–b
research funding, 849a–851b, 850a–b,
1424b, 1425a
responsibility for, 607b
space program, 615a
strains on civil-military relations, 610b

traditional gender roles, 104b
United World Federalists' decline, 558b
and Vietnam War, 615b–616a
Cole, Leon J., 861b
Coleman, James S., 933b, 934b, 935a–b
Coleman, Jon, *as contributor,* 81a–99b
Coleman, Ornette, 1624a
*Collapse of Evolution* (Townsend), 861a
*Collected Poems* (Stevens), 1449b
Collective security, 679b
*College and University Finance* (Arnott),
1409b
College Equal Suffrage League, 1823a
College football, 1767a–b, 1768a
1929 Carnegie Report, 1768a, 1776a
games as entertainment, 1745b
1920s, *1767a–b*
Colleges
buildings, 36b
community colleges, 1827b, 1836b
Eastern region, 32a–b, 32b, 36b
land-grant. *See* Morrill land-grant
colleges
Negro colleges, 1824b
women, 1764b, 1824b, 1831b
*See also* Catholic colleges and universities;
Liberal arts colleges; Universities
"College Sport and Motherhood," 1765a
College sports
integrated teams, 1771b
unequal financial support for women,
1780b
at women's colleges, 1764b
*See also* College football
Collier, Jane, 933a
Collier, John, 92a, 1810b
*Collier's,* 703b, 1482b
Collins, Michael, 788b
Collins, Randall, 932a
Collyer, Joseph, 7a
Colonialism, 726a
Colonial musical culture, 1611a–b
Colorado Fuel and Iron Company, 86b
Colorado River, 91b
hydroelectric power, 85a
*Colored American,* 1594a, 1595a
*Color of a Great City, The* (Dreiser), 33b
COLOR plans, 595a
Coltrane, John, 1630b
Columbia, S.C., 118b
Columbia Basin Project, 1026a
hydroelectric power, 85a,b
Columbia Broadcasting System (CBS), 18a,
262a, 807a, 1472b, 1473a, 1475b,
1755a
cable television, 1480a
news, 1478a
radio shows, 1025a
revenues, 1474a
sports, 1774a, 1776b
television, 1476a
world news format, 1473b
Columbia Pictures, 1469a, 1754a
foreign ownership, 715a
Japanese investment, 1263a
television, 1476b
Columbia Records, 1471a
Columbia School of Mines, 1389b
Columbia University, 1821a
coeducation, 1824b–1825a
Dewey, John, move to, 1641a

general education courses, 1831a
law school, 31a
Office of Radio Research, 1485a
student violence, 1830b
Teachers College, 1574b
Columbus Platform, 1582b
Colwin, Laurie, 34
Colyer, W. T., 702a
Comedies
radio, 1473a
situation (sitcoms), 1477a
slapstick, 1462a
Comic books, 1481a, 1482a
censorship, 1468a, 1483b
publishing, 1483a
violence, 1483b
Comics Code Authority, 1483b
Comic strips, 708a
Cominform, 687b
*Coming Crisis of Western Sociology, The*
(Gouldner), 931a
*Coming of Age in Samoa* (Mead), 908b
*Coming of Post-industrial Society, The* (Bell),
208b
Comintern, 682a
Commander in Chief
Lincoln, 402b
president as, 326a
*Commentary,* 1586b
Commerce, Department of, 1250a, 1254a,
1280a, 1281a,b
under Hoover, 1275a
Industrial Economics Division, 1322a
Commerce Clause
congressional power under, 382a, 384b
and economic regulation, 379a
Supreme Court interpretation, 379a,
402a, 405b, 408b, 409b
Commercial banks
foreign branches, 1249a
and investment banking, 1222a, 1226a
and long-term securities, 1213b
Commercial broadcasting, 1478a
Commercial entertainment, 1461b–1463a
home, 1470b
Commercial insurance companies
group hospitalization insurance, 994b
health insurance, 999b
Commercial nationalism, 266a, 268a
Commercial power, 516a
Commission on Country Life, 51a
Commission on Immigration Reform, 189a
Commission on Industrial Relations,
1272b
Commission on Intergovernmental
Relations, 438b–439a
Commission on Law and Social Action,
1584a
Commission on Private Philanthropy and
Public Needs, 505b
Commission on the Humanities, 1736a
Commission on the Reorganization of the
Executive Branch. *See* Hoover
Commission
Commission to Study the Bases of a Just
and Durable Peace, 556b
Commission to Study the Organization of
Peace, 556b
Committee against the Extension of Race
Prejudice in the Church, 1517b
Committee for Cultural Freedom, 282b

# INDEX

world economy, 732a, 733b
DEC. *See* Digital Equipment Corporation
De Capite, Michael, 176a
De Casseres, Benjamin, 1705a
DeCastro, Edson, 1149a
*Decline and Resurgence of Congress, The* (Sundquist), 355b, 364a
*Declining Significance of Race, The* (W. J. Wilson), 214b
Decolonization, 1253b
"Deconstructing Europe" (Pocock), 268b
Deconstruction (architecture), 1689b
Deconstructionism, 268b
Deegan, Mary Jo, 929a
Deep Ecology, 1378b–1379a
*Deep South* (Davis, Gardner and Gardner), 925b
Deering, Christopher J., 360a
Defense, Department of, 333b, 526b, 609a, 687b, 1281a
  aviation, 779b
  contracts, 1201b
  nuclear research, 750b
  Research and Development Board, 755b
  research funding, 850a, 852b
  space programs, 787a–b
Defense Advanced Research Projects Administration (DARPA), 853a
Defense industry, 28b, 98b, 312a
  development under Reagan, 1201b
  government intervention, 311a
  South, 72a, 457a
  West, 81a, 85a
Defense spending, 1167b, 1174b, 1309a–b
  and federal budget deficit, 1202b
  increase during Cold War, 612b
  Midwest, 57b–58a, 59a
  as percentage of GNP, 1201b
  under Reagan, 1327a
  source of revenues for universities, 613b
  South, 75a
*Deficit Politics* (Kettl), 358a
Deficit spending, 1162b 1163a, 1164a, 1177a, 1321b–1322a,b, 1324a
DeForest, Lee, 803b, 804b, 1471a–b
Degas, Edgar, 1698b
Deindustrialization, 216b–217a, 1201b
  African American families, 112b
  and class mobility, 202a, 209b–210a
  labor market, 112a–b, 113a
  nativism and, 188a
Delacroix, Eugène, 1698b
Delany, Frank, 1524a
Delaware, 474b
Delaware and Lackawanna Railroad, 83b
DeLong, Bradford, 1217b
Delta Airlines, 795a
Deluge Geology Society, 868a
DeMille, Cecil B., 1473a
Democracy, 295a–b, 319a
  conflicts about authority, 321b
  continuity and quality, 296a–b
  Midwest, 49a, 53b
*Democracy in America* (Tocqueville), 196b, 295a, 1067a
"Democracy versus the Melting Pot" (Kallen), 171a, 258a
Democratic party
  African Americans, 331b, 342b
  alliance between South and Northern cities, 298a

blue-collar ethnics and, 175a
Congress, 366a–b, 371a–b tab, 372a
divided by Vietnam war, 616a
fiscal policy, 1315b, 1324b
fundraising, 307a
House of Representatives, 374a
labor unions, 314a
New Deal coalition, 175a, 182b, 300a–301a, 331b, 334b
nominating conventions, 298a
reforms, 307b
Roosevelt, Franklin, 331a, 332a
Senate, 305a
social reform, 300a
South, 64a, 74b, 429a
  *See also* Southern Democrats
tariffs, 1312b, 1314a
two-party system, 296b
Watergate, 313a
*Democratic Promise* (Goodwyn), 204b
Democratic statism, 1313a–1314a, 1317a–b
  abandoned, 1324b
  Roosevelt, F., and, 1320a
Demographic changes
  effect on poverty, 1087a
  income distribution, 1087a
Dempsey, Jack, 1768a
  appearance in vaudeville, 1463b
Demuth, Charles, 1697b, 1702a
  poster portrait of William Carlos Williams, 1702b
Denfeld, Louis, *611a–b,* 612a
Denison, Edward F., 1165b–1166a, 1173a
Denmark, 960b
Dennis, Michael, 746b
*Den of Thieves,* 1238b
Denton, Nancy, 214b
De Pauw, Gommar, 1533b
Depew, David J., *as contributor,* 1635a–1663b
Depolarization Project on Ethnic America, 182a
Depository Institutions Deregulation and Monetary Control Act (1980), 531b
Depression. *See* Great Depression
Depressions and recessions: the business cycle, **1183a–1207b**
De Priest, Oscar, 172b
Deregulation, 531a–533b, 1283b
  airlines, 794a–795a
De Roose, Frank, 252a
Derrida, Jacques, 291a, 1454a, 1658b
  influence on architecture, 1689b
*Descent of Man, The* (Darwin), 859a
  racist application, 134a–b
Deserts, 81a, 91b
Desert Storm. *See* Operation Desert Storm
de Stijl movement, 1682a
*Destiny of a Continent* (Ugarte), 702a
Destroyer-for-bases agreement (1940), 577a, 601b, 635a
*Destruction of European Jews, The* (Hilberg), 1589b
Détente, 616a
Detergents, 1372a
Detroit, 451b
  financial crisis, 464b
  suburbs, 459b–460a, 467a
  working class evolution in, 205b
Detzer, Dorothy, 554b
Devanter, Willis Van, 381b, 382b, 390a–b tab

*Device* (Johns), 1718b
DeVoto, Bernard, 10b
De Vries, Hugo, 860b
Dew, Thomas, 134a
Dewes Act (1887), 92a
Dewey, Alice, 1641a, 1805a
Dewey, Evelyn, 1808a
Dewey, Jane M., 277b
Dewey, John, 196a–b, 257b–258a,b, 264a, 276a, 277b–278a, 280a–b, 282b, 292a–b, 878b, 880b, 887a, 888a, 1496b, 1501b, 1502a, 1521b, 1574b, 1639a–1641a, 1644b, 1651a, 1807a
  and Addams, Jane, 277b, 1641a
  "Americanism and Localism," 257b
  *Child and the Curriculum, The,* 1805a
  China's education system, 697a
  "Christianity and Democracy," 277b
  Committee of One Hundred Thousand, 281b
  *Common Faith, A,* 277b
  in *Contemporary American Philosophy,* 1640b
  *Essays on Experimental Logic,* 1642b
  *Ethics of Democracy, The,* 278a
  *Experience and Nature,* 1644b
  *Freedom and Culture,* 282b
  *Individualism,* 197b
  *Individualism Old and New,* 281a
  laboratory school, 1805a
  *Liberalism and Social Action,* 277b, 282b
  *Public and Its Problems, The,* 197b, 280a–b, 287a
  *Quest for Certainty, The,* 281a
  *Reconstruction in Philosophy,* 281a, 284b, 1639a, 1651a
  response to new realists, 1642b
  *School and Society, The,* 201a, 1805a
  *Schools of Tomorrow,* 1808a
  "Shortcut to Realism Examined, The," 1642b
  "Theory of Valuation," 1651a
Dewey, Thomas E., 334b, 578a–b, 580a, 1828a
  presidential elections, 335a–b tab
DeWitt, John, 385b
Dewson, Molly, 122a
"Diagnosis by Dream" (*Good Housekeeping*), 200a
*Dial,* 257b
*Dialectic of Sex, The* (Firestone), 913a
Diarrhea and enteritis, 960a, 961a
  leading cause of death in 1900, 968a
Dichter, Ernest, 1052b
Dick, A. B., 822a
Dick Act (1903), 595b–596a
Dickens, Charles, 1067a, 1436a, 1746b
Dickinson, Preston, 1702a
Dickinson, Robert Lou, 227b
Dickson, William K. L., 1752b
*Dictionary of Races and Peoples, A,* 163b
Di Donato, Pietro, 176a
Didrikson, Mildred "Babe," 1764b
Diebenkorn, Richard, 1714b
Dien Bien Phu, 664b
Dies, Martin, 1731a
Diet
  change in the end of the century, 1367a
  as obsession, 1798a
Dietrich, Marlene, 700a, 1795a
Dietz, Peter, 1515b, 1517b

*Different Mirror, A* (Takaki), 190b
DiGiorgio Corporation, 91a
Digital Equipment Corporation (DEC),
   821b–822a, 1149a
Digitized data, 799a, 826a
*Dignitatis Humanae,* 1522b
Dignity, 1531b
*Di Inzikhistn* (The introspectivists), 1570a
Dillingham Commission (1907-1911),
   163a
DiMaggio, Paul, 1462b
Dine, Jim, 1587a
Dine, Thomas, 1590a
Dingell, John D., 997a
Dingley Tariff (1897), 1246b, 1269a
Dinnerstein, Dorothy, 913a
Dinnerstein, Leonard, 138a
Dionne, E. J., 292a
Dior, Christian, 1790a,b
Diphteria, 960a, 968a,b
   antitoxin, 974a, 977a
Diplomatic power, 720a–b
*Directive No. 15: Race and Ethnic Standards for
   Federal Statistics and Administrative
   Reporting* (OMB), 180b
Directors of Industrial Research, 842a,
   847b
Direct taxation, 1310b
Dirigibles. *See* Airships
Disabilities Act, 447b
Disability insurance, 485a–b, 1076a
Disarmament Conference in Geneva (1933),
   633a
*Disaster by Decree* (Graglia), 388a
Disciples of Christ
   liberalism, 1500b
   population percentages, 1492b, 1493a
   schism, 1493a–b
Discrimination, 95a, 96a, 97b
   in art institutions, 1703b
   housing, 95b
   Judaism, 1578b
   *See also* Anti-Semitism
Disease
   chronic, 967b, 970a
   cultural and behavioral determinants,
      972a
   degenerative, 967b
   ecobiologic determinants, 972a
   health and, 957a–986b
   medical, public health and political
      determinants, 972a
   standard of living determinants, 972a–b
   *See also* specific diseases
Disney, Walt, 59b, 707a, 1030a, 1468a,
   1476b
Disney Studios, 703a, 1030a
   animation, 1466a
Dispensationalism, 1499b
Displaced Persons Act (1948), 165a–b tab,
   178b
Displaced Persons Act (1950), 178b
Disposable diapers, 1034a
*Dissent,* 209b, 1831b
Distillers Securities, 1132a
*Distribution of Wealth, The* (Clark), 1290a–b
*Distribution of Wealth, The* (Commons),
   1296a–b
Distribution organizations, 1129b–1130a,
   1131a
District of Columbia rent control law, 407b

*Disuniting of America, The* (Schlesinger),
   189b
Divided government, 302b–303a, 304a–b
   tab, 305a–b tab, 323a, 349b, 360a
   Bush and, 351a
   Eisenhower and, 349b
   Nixon and, 349b
   Reagan and, 349b
Divine, Father, 1600a
Divine Light Mission, 1552b
Divine Science, 1545b, 1546a
Divorce, 105a
   and abundance, 215b
   child poverty, 237a–b
   at end of nineteenth century, 222a
   feminization of poverty, 123a
   impact on children, 236b–237a
   law reform, 105b, 123a, 227a–b, 241a
   mutual consent, 227a, 241a
   and politicians, 233a
   rates in mid-1960s, 233a
Dixiecrat movement, 436b
Dixon, A. C., 861a
Dixon, Thomas, 150b, 1593a
*Di Yunge,* 1570a
DNA, 763b
Dobie, J. Frank, 10b
Dobrynin, Anatoliy, 561b
Doby, Larry, 1778a
Dobzhansky, Theodosius, 869a–870a,b
"Doctors, Economists, and the Depression"
   (Taussig), 1298b–1299a
Dodd, Lawrence, 357a–b, 360a, 371a–b
   "Congress and the Quest for Power,"
   356b
Dodd, Thomas J., 1479a
Dodge, Charles, 1630a
Dodge, Mabel. *See* Luhan, Mabel Dodge
Dodgers, 462a
*Dodsworth* (Lewis), 1027a
*Doggie Bob* (Arneson), 1720a
Dole, Robert, 306a, 350a, 488b
   presidential elections, 336a–b tab
Dollar, 1253a
   devaluation, 313a, 730a,b, 1162b, 1199b,
      1235b, 1250b, 1257b, 1262a
   foreign investments, 1245a, 1265a
   and international monetary system, 728a
   loss of confidence in, 728a–729b
   valuation, 728b–729a,b, 731b, 732a–b,
      1164b, 1166b, 1169b, 1176b, *1177a–b,*
      1256a, 1257a
Dollard, John, 927a
Dollar Diplomacy, 721a
Domestic economy, 1264a
   foreign trade, 1262b
   government, 1167a
   investments, 1176a
Domestic policy
   versus foreign policy, 569b, 577b, 590b
   national-security, 334a–b
   presidency, 336a
   world economy, 723b, 731a, 732b
Domestic Policy Council, 529b–530a
Domestic relations courts, 395b
Domestic science, 226b
Domestic violence, 237b–238a
Domhoff, G. William, 208a,b
Dominican Republic, 679b, 682b
Dominicans, 1511b
Donagan, Alan, 1655a

Donald Duck, 1323b
Dondero, George, 1713b
Donnellan, Keith, 1659a
Donor's Forum of Chicago, 506b
Donovan, William J., *604b,* 604b
Dooley, Tom, 1524a
Doolittle, James, 641a
Doolittle Commission, 581a
Doors, 1628b
Dorfman, Ariel, 710a
Dorrance family, 1131b
Dorsey, Tommy (Thomas A.), 149b, 1621a
Dos Passos, John, 33b, 262a
Dostoyevsky, Fyodor, 1446a
Dott, Robert H., Jr., 874a
Doubleday, Abner, 1762b
*Double Dealer,* 67b
Douglas, Paul, 1832a
Douglas, William O., 382b, 390a–b tab
Douglas Aircraft, 773b, 795b
   Douglas DC-3, *774a–b*
   *See also* McDonnell Douglas Corporation
Douglass, Frederick, 143a, 145a, 1595a
   abolitionism, 133b, 134a
Douglass, Harlan Paul, 460a
Dove, Arthur, 1697b, 1698a, 1704b
Dow, Arthur Wesley, 1704a
Dow, Herbert, 1139a
Dow Chemical, 1139a, 1143a, 1145b,
   1146a,b–1147a
   research, 835a
Dow-Jones Industrial Average, 1261b
*Down Beat,* 1624a
Downs, Anthony, 1302a
Drachsler, Julius, 1577b
Drake, Edwin, 1396b
Drake, St. Clair, 213a, 925b, 929b
Draper, Mrs. Henry, 741b
*Dreadnought,* 594a
Dreier, Katherine, 1700a
Dreiser, Theodore, 33b, 52a, 1437b, 1438b
   *American Tragedy, An,* 1359a
   *Sister Carrie,* 1437b
Dresser, Annetta, 1545b
Dresser, Julius, 1545b
Drew, Charles Richard, 948a
Drexel, Burnham, Lambert, 1211a, 1236a
Drexel Institute of Technology, 32b
Dreyfus, Hubert, 1658a
*Drift and Mastery* (Lippmann), 196a–b,
   256a–b, 274a, 277a
Drinking. *See also* Prohibition
   New Deal laws, 122a
   Progressive Era laws, 122a
Dropkin, Celia, 1570a
Dropsie College for Hebrew and Cognate
   Learning, 1566b
Droughts, 44a, 53a
Droz, Rick, 1721b
Drucker, Peter, 1101a
Drug manufacturers. *See* Pharmaceutical
   industry
Dubnov, Simon, 1569a
Dubois, Rachel Davis, 174a, 183b
Du Bois, W. E. B., 129a, 144a,b, 145a,
   155b, 287a–b, 1087b, 1644b
   "Black Man Brings His Gifts, The," 259b
   black sacred culture, 1594b, 1595b
   "Conservation of Races, The," 1595a
   "Criteria of Negro Art, The," 1593a,b
   criticism of Booker T. Washington, 145b

editor of *Crisis,* 1597a
education, 1810a
Niagara Movement, 146a
*Philadelphia Negro, The,* 922a
*Souls of Black Folk, The,* 259a, 276b,
1456a, 1594b
on William James, 276b
Duchamp, Marcel, 1699b, 1701b, 1715a
*Nude Descending the Staircase,* 1699b
Dudgeon, Richard B., 1807a
Dudley, Charles B., 832b–833a
Dudziak, Mary L., *as contributor,* 377a–399b
Duffy, Francis, 1519b
Duisberg, Carl, 835a, 838a
Dukakis, Michael, 185a, 350a, 589b
presidential elections, 336a–b tab
Duke, James B., 1042b, 1131a,b
Duke University, 75b, 506b
Dulles, Allen, 581a, *581b*
Dulles, John Foster, 560a, 581a, *582a–b,*
614b, 754b
television, 1478b
Dumbarton Oaks conference (1944),
557a
Dummer, Ethel, 236b
DuMont Laboratories, 1475b
Dunbar, Charles, 1289a, 1291a
Dunbar, Paul Laurence, 1594b
writing in dialect, 1596a,b
Duncan, Isadora, 1704b
Duncan, Robert Kennedy, 839a, 842b
Dunlop, 1249b
Dunlop, John, 1110a
Dunn, Leslie C., 870a
Dunnigan, Alice, 148a
Dupee, F. W., 1444a
du Pont, Irénée, 1414a
Du Pont de Nemours, E. I., Company,
840a, 846a, 850b, 1139a, 1143a–b,
1416b
antitrust actions, 838a, 847a–b, 849a
arts patronage, 1737a
Experimental Station, 837a,b
explosives industry, 837b–838a
fellowships, 842b
General Experimental Laboratory,
837b–838a
grants, 852a
industrial research, 837a
neoprene, 845b
nuclear research, 849b
nylon, 845b–846a, 848a–b
Patent and Process Agreement, 1145b
polymers, 845a–846a, 1146a, 1147a
research, 835b, 847a–b, 851a
Durkheim, Émile, 924b, 926b
Durr, Virginia, 71b
Dushkin, Alexander, 1576a
Dust Bowl, 84b, 88a, 1366b, 1368a–b
Dust storm, *53a–b*
*Dutchman* (Baraka), 1604a
Duveneck, Frank, 1694b
Dwight, John Sullivan, 1611b
Dworkin, Gerald, 1655a
Dworkin, Ronald, 423a
*Dybbuk, The* (Ansky), 1570b
Dyestuff industry, 840a
Dylan, Bob, 1627a,b, 1628a
*Dynamic Sociology* (Ward), 919b
*Dynamics of Prejudice* (Bettelheim &
Janowitz), 1584b

# E

Eakins, Thomas, 1694a, 1697b
Early music revival, 1629a
Earth Day (22 April 1970), 1371b, 1377a,
1380b
Earth First!, 88a, 1378b, 1560b
Earth from space, *1379a–b*
Earthquakes, 98b
EarthSave, 1560b
East, E. M., 869a
East, The, **25a–40b,** *26a–b*
East Coast Edison Trust, 83b
Easterlin, Richard, 1184a
Eastern Europe
after World War I, 683a
American firms in, 1205a
Eastern Liberalism, 30a
East European Jews, 1565b, 1566b, 1567a,
1572a, 1574b, 1575a,b, 1577a, 1586a
second-generation, 1578a, 1580b
Eastman, Crystal, 476a, 547b, 549b
Eastman, George, 838a–b, 1752b
Eastman, Max, 282a, 1439b
Eastman, R. O., company, 1024b
Eastman Kodak, 28a, 822a, 840a, 1021a,
1030a, 1411a, 1469a
industrial research in Japan, 854a
reliance on German chemical industry,
838a
research, 835b, 838a–b, 848b, 851a
Eastman School of Rochester, 33a
*East-West Journal,* 1558a
Eaton, Fred, 1362b
Eberstadt, Ferdinand, 608b
Eccles, Marriner, 1277b, 1321b
Echo Park, 1373a
Eckert, Wallace, 847a
Eco, Umberto, 1484a
*Eco-Defense* (Foreman), 1378b
Ecofeminism, 1560b
École des Beaux Arts (Paris), 1669a, 1679a
Ecology
artists and, 1720a
disasters, 1376b
industrial chemistry, 1372a
philosophy of the commons, 21b
regionalism and, 21a–b
*Econometrica,* 1299a, 1300a, 1304a
Econometrics, 1299a
Econometric Society, 1299a
*Economic Analysis of Law* (Posner), 1302a
*Economic Approach to Human Behavior, The*
(Becker), 934b
Economic blocs, 733a–b
*Economic Cycles* (Moore), 1293b
Economic history, 1302b
Economic inequality, 1353a
ethnic antagonisms, 191b
racial antagonisms, 191b
Economic interdependence, 1187b, 1204b
*Economic Interpretation of History, The*
(Seligman), 920a, 1186b
*Economic Interpretation of the Constitution, An*
(Beard), 920a
*Economic Justice for All* (1986), 1529b
Economic leadership
after World War II, 1197a–1199a
loss in the 1970s, 1199a
Economic opportunity

popular belief in, 1072a
Economic output
during Great Depression, *1162a–b*
per sector, 1900-1913, *1160a*
Economic performance, **1155a–1181b**
Economic policies, 1249b, **1267a–1287b**
banking, 1295a,b
controversy about, 1289a–b
science and, 1289b
trusts, 1295a
*Economic Principles* (Fetter), 1292a
Economic Recovery Tax Act (1981),
1174a–b, 1204a–b, 1327a
Economics
consumption, 1025b
demand management, 1167b, 1203a
game theory, 1304b–1305a
general equilibrium theory, 1299b, 1302b
institutionalism, 1290b, 1294a, 1296a–b,
1303b
Keynesian, 311a, 437a, 1026a, 1299a,
1300a–b, 1302b, 1304b
marginal productivity theory, 1290a
Marxism, 1304a
mathematical, 1299a
neoclassical, 316a
Nobel prizes, 1299a
Phillips curve, 1300b, 1302b–1303a
scientific method, 1305a
utility theory, 1290a
*Economics and Philosophy,* 1305a
*Economics of Discrimination, The* (Becker),
934b
*Economics of Enterprise* (Davenport), 1292a
"Economics of Exhaustible Resources, The"
(Hotelling), 1383b
*Economics of Higher Education* (1962), 1829b
Economic Stabilization Act (1970), 528a
*Economic Theory of Democracy, An* (Downs),
1302a
Economic thought, **1289a–1307b**
Economies of scale, 1137b, 1140a, 1147a,
1166a, 1255a
Economies of scope, 1137b, 1140a
*Economist,* 709b
Economists
as celebrities, 1305b
Chicago school, 1174a
Keynesianism, 1322a
New Deal and, 1420b–1421a
taxation, 1315a, 1323a
Economy
compositional changes, 1186b–1187b
Congress, 356a
Eastern region, 26a–28b, 38b
effect of rise of new industries, 1187a
foreign policy, 569b, 575b, 589b–590a
instability, 1188a
post-World War II, 1198a
private-sector agencies, 1281b
racism, 95b
regulation, 436a
secular transitions in development,
1186b–1187b
service expansion, 1422b–1423a
South, 69b, 75a–77a
structural changes, 1186b–1187b
structure, 1116a–1124b, *1157a–b*
West, 83a
*Economy and Society* (Weber), 199b
Ecumenical councils, 1511a, 1520b

# INDEX

# INDEX

fees, 1221a
influence over corporate strategy and
 policy, 1219a
merchants as, 1213a–b
private, 1213b–1214a
and railroad companies, 1215a
Second Bank of the United States, 1213a
separation from commercial banking,
 1226a
Investment behavior
accelerator model, 1184a–b
and Great Depression, 1196a
post–World War II, 1198a
Investment Company Act (1940), 1227a–b
 tab, 1228b
Investments, 1164a, 1167a, 1174b
broadening of demographic base, 1222b
Great Depression, 1161a, *1162a–b*, 1163a
international position, 1970–1990,
 *1179a–b*
telephones, 802a
trusts, 1223a
underwriting syndicates, 1216b
*See also* Institutional investors; Savings and
 investments
*Invisible Man* (Ellison), 34a, 154a,
 1450b–1451a, 1601a–b
IPA. *See* Institute for Public Administration
 (IPA)
"I Paid My Income Tax Today" (Berlin),
 1323b
Ipana Troubadours, 1024b
IQ tests. *See* Mental testing
Iran, 689b
foreign policy, 588b, 589a
revolution of 1979, 692b
Iran-Contra affair, 533b, 589a, 617a
Iranian Jews, 1566a
Iran-Iraq War, 1258a
Iraq, 689b, 690a
Ireland, John, 1514a
IRI. *See* Industrial Research Institute
Irish American Gaelic Athletic Association,
 1748a
Irish Americans, 570b
foreign policy, 574a
politics, 169a
popular culture, 1462a
*Irish Melodies* (Moore), 1462b
Iriye, Akira, *as contributor,* 675a–694b
Ironmaking, 1092b
Iron ore, 1387b, 1392b, 1393b–1394a
world iron-ore reserves by continent
 (estimated), 1910, 1955, 1985, *1394a–b*
*Irony of American History, The* (Niebuhr),
 284a
Irrigation, 1164b
IRS. *See* Internal Revenue Service (IRS)
Irving, Washington, 1436b, 1744b
Isaacs, Susan, 34a
*Is America Safe for Democracy?* (McDougall),
 885b
*Is Curly Jewish?* (Jacobs), 1586b
Iseman, M. S., 137a, 138a
"Is Female to Male as Culture Is to
 Nature?" (Ortner), 912a
Isham, Samuel, 1693b
Islam, 1547b–1550a
Ahmadiyya Movement in Islam, 1548a
Islamic Center (D.C.), 1549b
Islamic Conference in America, 1549b

Islamic fundamentalism, 692b
reaction to American culture, 712b
Islamic Society of North America, 1549b
*Island Within, The* (Lewisohn), 1581b
*Isolated State, The* (Thünen), 16b
Isolationism, 554a, 555a, 575a, 633a,
 1249b–1250a, 1251b
Catholics, 1520a, 1524a
foreign policy, 578b
during Great Depression, 684a
Midwest, 55b
post–World War I, 722b, 723b
post–World War II, 725a
Israel, 690a
American Jewish support, 1584a, 1586a,
 1587b, 1590b
Israeli Jews, 1566a
recognition, 579b
War for Independence, 580a
Israel, Paul, 833b
Italian Americans, 137b
anti-Italian violence, 138a–b
fascism, 175b
foreign policy, 576b
popular culture, 1462a
World War II, 176b
Italy, 960b
film agreement with, 707a
nuclear electric power, 1353a
radio and television, 712b
ITO. *See* International Trade Organization
 (ITO)
Ives, Burl, *1627a–b*
Ives, Charles, 1610b, 1612b, *1613a,* 1617a,
 1622b
Ivy League, 32a,b
"I Want to Hear a Yankee Doodle Tune"
 (Cohan), 1614a
"I Was Marching" (Le Sueur), 1443a
Iwo Jima, 642a
I.W.W.. *See* Industrial Workers of the World
Izaak Walton League, 58b, 1370b, 1371a


# J

J. M. Kaplan Fund, 504a
J. Paul Getty Trust, 1737b
Jack, Homer, 559a
Jackson, Andrew, 324a, 402a
Jackson, Carol, 1523b
Jackson, Jack, 1484a
Jackson, Kenneth, 31a
Jackson, Mahalia, 149b, 1624b
Jackson, Michael, 1631a,b
Jackson, Robert, 526a
Jackson, Robert H., 382b, 390a–b tab
 *Korematsu* v. *United States* (1944), dissent
 in, 385b, 387a
 *West Virginia State Board of Education* v.
 *Barnette* (1943), opinion in, 386a
Jackson State University, 1830b
Jackson-Vanik Amendment (1974), 585a
Jacobs, Aletta, 547a
Jacobs, Jane, 179a
Jacobs, Paul, 1586b
Jacobson, Eddie, 579b
Jacobson, Gary C., 324b
Jacoby, Sanford, 1103b
Jahn, Helmut, 1688a

Jahoda, Marie, 200a
Jamaica, 1395a
James, Charles, 1790b
James, D. Cleighton, 663a
James, Henry, 163a, 1439a,b, 1455a, 1744a
 *Ambassadors, The,* 1439b
 *American Scene, The,* 1439b
 *Golden Bowl, The,* 1439b
 *Wings of the Dove,* 1439b
James, William, 258a, 276a, 878b, 1439a,
 1455a, 1635b, 1636b, 1637a,b–1638b
 Dewey, John, on, 1640b
 *Pragmatism,* 1638b
 *Principles of Psychology,* 1638a
 review of *Studies in Logical Theory,* 1641a
*Jane Fonda's Workout Book,* 1798b
*Janitor* (Hanson), 1716b
Janowitz, Morris, 1584b
Janowitz, Tama, 34a
Japan, 325a–b, 678a, 688b, 690b, 691b, 960b
air warfare, 778a–779a
armament, 684a
automobile industry, 58a, 731b–732a
competition from, 1084b
cooperative role of banks, 1217a
cultural protectionism, 702b
defense spending, 1202a
East Asian sphere of influence, 732b
economy, 693b, 729b, 1200a, 1284a
employers' groups, 310b
exports, *1166b*
film industry, 707b
five industrial countries compared, 1990,
 1332a–b tab
foreign policy, 589a–b
high-speed passenger trains, 1353b
industrial research, 853b, 854a–b
labor productivity, *1156a–b*
manufacturing productivity, 1202a
nuclear electric power, 1353a
peace treaty with, 688b
real GDP per person, *1156a–b*
reconstruction, 726b
as threat, 595a
withdrawal from the League of Nations,
 632b
world economy, 726a
*Japan as Number One* (Vogel), 1259a
Japanese Americans, 135a
internment during World War II, 152b,
 176b–177a, 231a, 263a–b, 385b, 605b
segregation, 572a
West, 96a
Jarrell, Randall, 1449b
Jaspers, Karl, 926b
Jastrow, Joseph, 880a, 903b–904a
Javits, Jacob, 30a, 307b, 951a, 1735a
Jazz, 149b, 150a, 1601b–1602a,
 1615b–1616a, 1623b, 1630b
cultural export, 701b, 706b
important art form, 1630b–1631a
Southern origin, 67b
*Jazz Review, The,* 1624a
Jeanes Fund, 1803b
Jeans, 1792b, 1795a
Jefferson, Thomas, 324a, 1332a
 Southerners versus Northerners, 61b
Jeffries, Jim, 143a,b, 1770a
Jehovah's Witnesses, 1498b, 1501b
absolutists, 556a
and freedom of expression, 417b, 419b

# INDEX

# INDEX

Mining Law of 1872, 1388b–1389a
Ministerial Association of Greater Houston, 1526a
Ministry, 1415b
Minkoff, N. B., 1570a
Minneapolis-Saint Paul
  Census Bureau study (1940), 109a
  Eastern rite Catholics, 1514a
Minnesota Committee on Public Safety, 171a
Minnesota Council on Foundations, 506b
Minnesota Mining and Manufacturing Company, 822a, 1028a
Minnow, Newton, 1479b, 1480b
Minorities
  protection though freedom of religion, 418a
  in service sector, 1201a
Minstrel shows, 134a, 1461b, 1462a
  African Americans, 1594a, 1595b
Minton, Sherman, 390a–b tab
Mintz, Steven, *as contributor,* 221a–243b
Mirabal, Nancy, 138a
Miranti, Paul J., Jr., *as contributor,* 1407a–1430b
*Mirele Efros* (Jewish Queen Lear), 1570a–b
Mises, Ludwig von, 924b, 1299a, 1304a, 1305b, 1306a
Mishkin, *1612a*
Miss, Mary, 1721a
Missiles, 778b, 783b–784b, 786b, 787b, 850b, 1145a
  Atlas, 788a
  nuclear, 787b
  Titan, 788a
Missionaries
  Catholics, 1520b, 1523b–1524a
  liberal Protestants, 1495a–b
  social reform, 696b
Mission to Planet Earth, 739b
Mississippi River, 41b
  transportation, 45a, 56b
Missouri, 473a
Missouri River, 41b
  transportation, 45a
*Missouri* (ship), 647b
Miss Porter's School, 1808b
MIT. *See* Massachusetts Institute of Technology (MIT)
Mitchell, Arthur, 1738a
Mitchell, Charles, 1225b
Mitchell, Joan, 1714a
Mitchell, Lucy Sprague, 276a
Mitchell, Wesley C., 279a, 1293b–1294a, 1296a, 1298a
Mitchell, William (Billy), 776b, 776b–777a
Mitman, Gregg A., *as contributor,* 859a–876b
Mitterand, François, 352a
Mix, Tom, 84a
Mixter, Russell L., 868a
Mlakar, Frank, 176a
Mobil Corporation, 1737a
Mobility
  geographical, 206b
  as illusion of class advancement, 207a
  upward intergenerational, 199b
Mobilization Committee, 562b
*Moby Dick* (Melville), 1440a
Model Cities program, 466a, 1081b
Model T Ford, 46a–b, 48a, 455b, 1021b–1022a, 1057b–1058a, 1059a, 1140a, 1751a

*Modern Age,* 1525a
Modern Architecture-International Exhibition (Museum of Modern Art, 1932), 1683b–1684a
*Modern Corporation and Private Property, The* (Berle and Means), 1233a, 1296b
Moderne style, 1681a
Modernism (architecture), 1680a
  neo- or late, 1689a
Modernism (literature), 1441a–b
  African American writers, 1450b
  defined, 1447b–1448a
Modernist art, 1698b–1699a
  influence on cultural values, 1703b
Modern Language Association, 1458a, 1831a
*Modern Maturity,* 1483a
*Modern Music,* 1617b
*Modern Schoolman,* 1517a
*Modern Temper, The* (Krutch), 1501a
*Modern Tradition, The* (Ellman and Feidelson), 1453a
*Modern Woman* (Farnham and Lundberg), 110a, 288b
Modigliani, Franco, 1299a
Moelin distillery, 1132a
Mohole project, 757a–758a
Moholy-Nagy, Lazlo, 1710a
Mohorovicic Discontinuity, 757a
Molloy, John T., 1794a, 1797a
  *Woman's Dress for Success Book, The,* 1785b, 1796a
Molnar, Thomas, 1525a
Molodovsky, Kadia, 1570a
Molotov, Vyacheslav, 685b
MoMA. *See* Museums: Museum of Modern Art
Momaday, N. Scott, 1456a
*Moment,* 1587a
*Mona* (Parker), 1612b
Mondale, Walter, 307b
Mondale, Walter F., 951a
  presidential elections, 336a–b tab
Mondrian, Piet, 1712b
*Monetary History of the United States* (Friedman and Schwarz), 1301b
Monetary policy
  anti-inflationary under Reagan, 1204b
  as countercyclical policy, 1187b–1188a, 1203a
  effect on international trade, 1187b
  reform, 1271b
Monetary theory
  bimetallism, 1291a
  in economic thought, 1292a–1293a
*Money,* 1481b
Money Machine, The, 1238a
Money Trust, 1216b
  and Pujo committee, 1220a
Monk, Meredith, 1581a
Monk, Thelonious, 1630b
*Monkey-Wrench Gang, The* (Abbey), 1378b
Monopolies
  entertainment, 1465b, 1472b
  media, 1488a
*Monopolies and Trusts* (Ely), 1295a
Monopoly Capital (Baran and Sweezy), 1304a
Monroe, Hornet, 1678a
Monroe, James, 402a
Monroe Doctrine, 675b

preserved by the United Nations, 557b
  Roosevelt Corollary, 721a
Monsanto, 1143b, 1146a, 1147a
  research, 852a
Monsky, Henry, 1583b
Montagu, M. F. Ashley, 263a, 869b, 870a
Montague, William Pepperell, 1641b
Montevideo (1933), 685a
Montgomery, David, 107a, 166b–167a, 1093a
  *Fall of the House of Labor, The,* 205b
  *Workers' Control in America,* 205b
Montgomery Ward, 452a, 700b, 1022b, 1030b, 1051a
  catalog, 48b, 1019a
  1955 proxy war, 1233b
*Monthly Review,* 1304a–b
*Mood Indigo* (Ellington), 1620b
Moody, 1231a
Moody, Dwight, 1498a
Moody, William H., 390a–b tab
Moody Bible Institute, 1499a, 1503a,b
Moore, Barrington, Jr., 932b
Moore, Charles, 1689b
Moore, Deborah Dash, *as contributor,* 1565a–1592b
Moore, G. E., 1642b, 1653b
Moore, Harry Estill, 13b
Moore, Henry L., 1293b, 1299a
Moore, Joan, 210b
Moore, John Bassett, 550b
Moore, Marianne, 1458a
Moore, Michael, 57b
Moore, Thomas, 1462b
Moqui tribe, 93a
*Moral Equivalent of War, The* (W. James), 258a
Moral Majority, 182b, 184b, 309a, 1492a, 1507a
*Moral Man and Immoral Society* (Niebuhr), 282b, 287b, 1502a
Morawska, Ewa, 168a
Morawski, Jill, *as contributor,* 899a–915b
*Morbidity and Mortality Weekly Report,* 983b
Morbidity increase, 979b
Moreland, Bob, 1625b
Morgan, Arthur E., 15b
Morgan, Barbara, 1710a
Morgan, H. Wayne, 1695b
Morgan, J. P., & Company, 1214a, 1216b, 1217b, 1218a
  on concentration of banks in New York, 1220b
  creation of U.S. Steel, 1218b
  Glass-Steagall Act, 1226a
  international loans to Europe, 723a
  World War I loans, 722a
Morgan, Jay, 1672b
Morgan, John Pierpont, 802a, 1135b, 1193b, 1214a, 1215a, 1218b, 1219b, 1727a, 1730b
  on corporate disclosures, 1223b
  Pujo committee, 1220a
Morgan, Lewis Henry, 918b
Morgan, Thomas Hunt, 865a, 869a
Morgan Library, 33a, 1726a
Morgan Stanley investment bank, 1226a
Morgenstern, Oskar, 1304b
Morgenthau, Henry, Jr., 603a, 637a, 1252a, 1277b, 1320a–b, 1322b, 1583b
*Morgen Zhurnal,* 1569a,b

Schindler, Rudolph, 1680a, 1682b
Schlafly, Phyllis, 121a
Schlesinger, Arthur M., Jr., 189b, 1739b
  and Americans for Democratic Action, 285a
  *Vital Center, The,* 285a
Schlick, Moritz, 1647a
Schlink, F. J., 1027a
Schlipp, Paul Arthur, 277b
Schlitz distillery, 1132a
Schmeling, Max, 1772b
Schmetz, Joseph, 260b
Schmidt, Walter S., 459a
Schnabel, Julian, 1587a
Schneerson, Menachem Mendel, 1585a
Schneider, Susan Weidman, 1587a
Schneiderman, Rose, 1574a
Schoenberg, Arnold, 1617a, 1621a, 1630a
*School and Society, The* (Dewey), 201a, 1805a
School desegregation
  busing, 387a, 388b–389a
  integration, 1813a
  resegregation, 1815b
  Supreme Court and, 386b–387b
Schoolman, Albert, 1576a
Schools
  centralization v. decentralization, 1815b
  desegregation. *See* School desegregation
  health programs, 974b, 975a
  one-room, 51a, 56b
  prayer, 306b
*Schools of Tomorrow* (Dewey and Dewey), 1808a
Schroeder, John P., 460b
Schulman, Bruce J., 68b
Schulman, Grace, 1587a
Schuman, William, 1622a
Schumpeter, Joseph, 1289a, 1290b, 1295a, 1299a, 1300b–1301a, 1416b
Schutz, Alfred, 928b
Schuyler, George, 153a
Schuyler, Montgomery, 453b, 1669a, 1675b
Schwartz, Abe, 1571a
Schwartz, Anna, 1162a
Schwartz, Delmore, 1445a, 1581a
Schwartz, I. J., 1569b
Schwartz, Maurice, 1570b
Schwarz, Anna, 1301a
Schwarzenegger, Arnold, 1798b
Schweiker, Richard, 30a
Schwerner, Michael, 153b
Schwimmer, Rosika, 546b
*Science,* 866b
Science
  industrial processes, 1142b, 1144a
  as justification of racism, 134a–b, 136b
  liberal Protestantism, 1495b–1496b, 1496b, 1497a, 1502a
  linear model, 846b, 847b, 848b, 851a, 854b
Science Advisory Committee, 755b, 759a
*Science and Creationism,* 873b
*Science and Health* (Eddy), 1544b, 1545a,b
*Science and Human Behavior* (Skinner), 891b
*Science* (Bush), 1828b
*Science—The Endless Frontier* (Bush), 846b, 847b, 851b
*Scientific American,* 1475a
*Scientific Creationism* (Morris), 873a
Scientific equipment industry, 28a
Scientific management

managerial authority, 1103a
  and mass production, 1092a–1096a
  offices, 1106a
Scientists
  and federal government, 605b
  versus inventors, 832b
*Scientists against Time* (Baxter), 846b
Scientology, 1557b
SCLC. *See* Southern Christian Leadership Conference (SCLC)
Scofield, Cyrus, 1499a–b
*Scofield Reference Bible,* 1499b, 1500a
  gap creation theory, 861b
Scopes, John Thomas, 866a, *867a–b,* 1415b
Scopes trial, 866a, *867a–b,* 1497b, 1500b, 1501b, 1503a, 1516b, 1825b
  radio broadcast, 805b
Scorsese, Martin, 1458a
Scott, James, 147a
Scott, James Brown, 545a, 550b
Scott, Kerr, 72b
Scott, Lawrence, 559a
Scott, Nathan A., Jr., 1456a
Scottish American Celodonian clubs, 1748a
*Screen* (Miss), 1721a
Scripps Foundation, 228a
Sculptors, 1694b, 1729b, 1730a, 1733a
SDS. *See* Students for a Democratic Society (SDS)
Seager, Henry, 1292a
Seagram Building (New York), 1685a, 1685b
Searle, John, 1658a
Searle Company, 946b
Sears, Roebuck, 55b, 452a, 1018a, 1022b, 1030b, 1051a
  catalog, 48b, 51b, 1019a, 1064a
Sears Tower (Chicago), 464a, 1686a
SEATO. *See* Southeast Asian Treaty Organization (SEATO)
Seattle, revitalization, 1346a
Seavey, Jane, 1104a
SEC. *See* Securities and Exchange Commission (SEC)
Secondary (trading) markets, 1209a
  formed after assumption of the states' debts, 1211b
Second Bank of the United States, 1212b
  investment banking functions, 1213a
  rechartering vetoed by Jackson, Andrew, 1213a
Second Hague Peace Conference (1907), 543b, 544b, 599a
*Second Industrial Divide* (Piore and Sabel), 855b
Sectionalism, 7a, 8b
Secularism, 1517a
  Catholics, 1520b–1521b, 1526a
Secular Jews, 1573a
Secunda, Brant, 1561a
Securities
  analysis, 1231a
  corporate, 1230a
  government, 731a, 1214b, 1230a, 1244b, 1245a, 1254a, 1255b
  rating, 1231a
Securities Act (1933), 1226a, 1227a–b tab, 1420a
Securities Act Amendments (1964), 1227a–b tab
Securities and Exchange Commission

(SEC), 524b, 1226a, 1227a–b tab, 1420a
Securities Exchange Act (1934), 1226b, 1227a–b tab, 1420a
Securities-industry regulatory legislation, 1227a–b tab
Securities Investor Protection Act (1970), 1227a–b tab
Securities Investor Protection Corporation (SPIC), 1227a–b tab, 1232b
Securities markets
  democratization, 1222b
  investment trusts, 1223a
  mass marketing of commercial banks, 1222b
  over-the-counter market, 1228a
  public utility holding companies, 1223a
Securities Reform Act (1975), 1227a–b tab, 1233a
Sedition Act (1918), 171b, 257a, 416a, 626a
*Seduction of the Innocent* (Wertham), 1483b
*Seedbed* (Acconci), 1720a
Seeger, Pete, 1627a
Segal, Daniel, 252b, 253b, 255b
Segal, George, 1587a, 1717a
  *Gay Liberation, 1718a*
Segal, Lore, 1589b
Segmented market, 1059a–1061b
Segré, Emilio, 750a
Segregation, 95a, 97b, 142a, 436b, 437b, 439b, 440b
  housing, 50b, 58b
  increase at turn of the century, 163a
  Jim Crow system, 255b
  in poor houses, 473a
  residential, 97b, 1086a
  separate-but-equal doctrine, 386b
  South, 65b, 66a–b, 71a–b, 73a, 74a–b
  State government, 428b
Seidel, Emil, 335a–b tab
Seidel, Robert, 746a,b, 751a, 849a
Seismology, 743b
Select Commission on Immigration and Refugee Policy (1979), 185b
*Selective Draft Law* cases (1918), 407b
Selective Service Act (1917), 523a, 549a, 596b
Selective service lottery, *576a*
Selective Training and Service Act (1940), 525b, 555b, 601b
  effect on number of marriages, 230a
Self-determination, 679b
Self-realization, 234b
Self-Realization Fellowship, 1550a, 1551a–b
Selig Company, 1465b
Seligman, Edwin R. A., 274b, 920a, 1291a, 1292a, 1315a
Seligman, Isaac, 1214a, 1218b
Sellars, Roy Wood, 1643a
  in *Contemporary American Philosophy,* 1643b
  *Critical Realism,* 1643b
  *Evolutionary Naturalism,* 1643b
Sellars, Wilfrid, 1653a
Sellers, James, 61b
Selma civil rights march (1965), 74a, 1524b
Sematech, 852b
Semel, Bernard, 1567a, 1573a
Semi-Automatic Ground Environment (SAGE), 812a
Semiskilled workers, 166a, 205b, 1107a

# INDEX

West, 83b, 88b
world trade, 1166b
Transportation Act (1920), 519b
Transportation Act (1940), 1341a
Transportation Workers Association, 148b
Trans World Airlines, 1030a
Travel
democratization, 1750b–1752a
middle class, 1746a
upper class, 1744a
Travelers' Aid societies, 223b
Traveling exhibitions, 1465a
Treasury, Department of the, 358a,b, 1254a,
1316a–1317a, 1323b
under Mellon, 1318a
plan for "Modernizing the Financial
System" (1991), 1238b
Section on Painting and Sculpture, 1730a
Treasury Relief Art Project, 1705b
Treaty of Brest-Litovsk (1918), 628a
Treaty of Guadalupe Hidalgo (1848), 140a
Treaty of Portsmouth (1905), 678a
Treaty of Rome (1957), 726b, 853b, 1253b
Treaty of Versailles, 551a, 574a, 722b, 1249b
and stability of world finances, 1193a
Treaty of Washington (1922). *See* Five-
power Naval Limitation Treaty (1922)
Treaty on conventional arms forces in
Europe (CFE) (1990), 564b
Treaty on Open Skies, 564b
Treaty on the Elimination of Intermediate-
Range and Shorter-Range Missiles
(1978), 566a–b tab
Tree farming, 1403a
*Tree Grows in Brooklyn, A* (B. Smith), 34a
*Treemonisha* (Joplin), 1596a, 1615a
*Trends in American Economic Growth*
(Denison), 1165b
*Trial, The* (Reisman), 1714a
Tribune Tower, *1680b,* 1681a
competition for, 1680a
Trigere, Pauline, 1790b
Trilling, Lionel, 1443b, 1444a, 1448a,
1581b
"On the Teaching of Modern Literature,"
1448b–1449a, 1452b
TRIMS. *See* Trade-related investment
matters
Trine, Ralph Waldo, 1496a, 1546a
Trinity Church (New York), 36b
Tripartite Agreement (1936), 724a
Tri-Partite Pact, 637b
TRIPS. *See* Trade-related intellectual
property rights
Trist, Eric, 1119a
Trost and Trost, 1681a
Trotsky, Leon, 1443a
Trotter, Monroe, 145b, 146a
Trow, James, 934b
Trucking industry, 1160b
cartel-like regulation, 1341a
deregulation, 1283b
South, 72a
World War II, 1344b
"True Americanism" (Brandeis), 258a
Trueblood, Benjamin F., 543a,b
*Truly Disadvantaged, The* (W. J. Wilson),
210a
Truman, Harry S., 284b, 321a, 322b, *333a,*
337b, 577b, *647a,* 1278b, 1279a, 1280a
arts patronage, 1735a

blue-collar vote, 300a
Campaign of truth, 705a
civil rights, 73a, 436b, 437a
demobilization, 607a
draft violators, 556a
foreign policy, 579a–580b, 725b
Graham, Billy, 1504a
health legislation, 997b
and Hoover Commission report, 526b
industrial research, 847a, 849a
limited war, 662b
national security state, 333b, 334a
nuclear weapons, 750b
presidential elections, 334b, 335a–b tab
public approval, 336b
Special Committee to Investigate the
National Defense Program, 606a
steel mills seizure, 386a, 412a
Supreme Court appointments, 389b
vetoes, 347a tab
Truman Doctrine, 579b, 608a, 725b, 849b
Trust Indenture Act (1939), 1227a–b tab,
1228a
*Trust Problem, The* (Jenks), 1295a
Trusts, 1132b, 1188b, 1215b
growing influence, 1291a–b
Truth in Lending Act (1968), 527b
TRW, 849b, 1145a, 1150b
work reform, 1119b
Tschumi, Bernard, 1689b
Tsiolkowsky, Konstantin, 785b
*Tsukunft,* 1569a
Tuberculosis, 959b, 960b, 977a
drug-resistant strains, 970a
government health care, 989b
leading cause of death in 1900, 968a
tuberculin skin test, 973b
Tucker, Richard, 1578b
Tucker, Sophie, 1464a, 1579b
Tufts, James Hayden, 1640b
in *Contemporary American Philosophy,*
1641a
Tugwell, Rexford G., 281b, 1296a, 1298b,
1305b, 1369b
Greenbelt program, 460b
Tulane University, 1824b
Tulis, Jeffrey, 328a
Tullock, Gordon, 1302a
Tunney, Jim, 1768a
Turkey, 608a, 679a, 682b, 689b
Turner, Frederick Jackson, 7a, 8a–9b, 17a,
42a, 49a, 55a, 83a, 846b, 864b, 1380a
"Significance of the Frontier in American
History, The," 1357b
Turner, Ted, 1478a
Turner, Thomas Wyatt, 1517b
Turner Broadcasting Network, 1032b
Turrell, James, 1718b
Tuskegee Institute, 1595a, 1598b, 1809b
Tussman, Malka Heifetz, 1570a
Tuve, Merle, 752a–b, 753a–b, 763a
TVA. *See* Tennessee Valley Authority
*TVA: Democracy on the March* (Lilienthal),
10a
*TVA* (Lilienthal), 748b
*TV Guide,* 1482b
Twain, Mark, 33b, 274a, 1437a–b, 1438a,
1746b
*Adventures of Huckleberry Finn, The,* 1438a,
1456a
on baseball, 1745a

*Connecticut Yankee in King Arthur's Court,
A,* 1438a
*Innocents Abroad, The,* 1746a
"Mysterious Stranger, The," 1438a
Twachtman, John H., 1695b
Twentieth Century Fox, 1466b, 1754a
foreign ownership, 715a
Twentieth Century Fund, 18b, 1735b
*Twenty Years at Hull-House* (Addams), 275a
*Two Cultures, The* (Snow), 1453a
"Two Dogmas of Empiricism" (Quine),
1649b–1650a
Twombly, Robert, *1666a, 1670a, 1674b,
1678a–b, 1683a–b, 1690a–b, 1691a–b*
as contributor, 1665a–1692b
Two-party politics, 296b
Tyack, David, 1806b
Tydings-McDuffie Act (1934), 97a
Typhoid, 959b, 960b, 968a
Typhus, 942b
Typographical Union, 1749b
Tyson, Mike, 397b

# U

U-boats. *See* Submarines
Udall, Morris, 301a
UFO cults, 1557b
Ugarte, Manuel, 702a
Ukraine, 565b
Ullman, Al, 1326b
Ullman, Edward L., 18a
Ulysses solar polar mission, 790a
Un-American Activities Committee
(House), 178a, 265a, 1469b
artists depiction of, 1714a
Hollywood investigation, 1467a–1468b,
1754b
student protest against hearings, 1830a
television coverage, 1478a
Writers and Theater Projects
investigation, 1731a
*Unanswered Question, The* (Ives), 1613b
*Uncle Tom's Children* (Wright), 1601a
Underclass, 209a–210b
family dissolution, 236a–b
*Underclass, The* (Auletta), 210a
*"Underclass" Debate, The* (Katz), 210b
*Under Fire* (North), 589a
*Under God* (Wills), 1497b
Underwood, Oscar, 599a
Underwood Tariff (1913), 721b, 1271b,
1314b
Undistributed profits tax, 1320b–1321a
Unemployment, 1169a
aggregate, (in percent), 1929-1940, *1194a*
compensation, 433a, 439b, 1075b
consumption, 1024a
Great Depression, 1073a, 1161a, *1162a–b,*
1163a
insurance cuts under Reagan, 1204a
Midwest, 57b
nineteenth century, 1068b
structural in the 1930s, 1197b
UNESCO. *See* United Nations Economic
and Social Council (UNESCO)
UNIA. *See* Universal Negro Improvement
Association (UNIA)
Uniates, 1547b

White House Domestic Policy Council, 532b
Whiteman, Paul, 1615b, 1616a, 1619a
White Motor, 1140b
White privilege, 97b
White Sands, N.M., 786b
Whites as minority, 156b
White Slave Traffic Act. *See* Mann Act
White supremacy, 64a, 65b, 67b, 68b, 71b, 74a–b
  replaced by consensus politics, 72b
  Republican party and, 77a
  use of educational reform, 64b
  *See also* Racism
Whitford, Albert, 745a
Whitman, Charles Otis, 863a
Whitman, Ruth, 1587a
Whitman, Walt, 204a, 427b, 1436b, 1449a
  Mumford and, 11a–b
Whitney, Dudley Joseph, 867b, 868a
Whitney, Gertrude Vanderbilt, 1706b, 1728b
Whitney, Richard, 1419b
  and Gray-Pecora investigation, 1225b
Whitney, William C., 1669b
Whitney, Willis R., 836a–b, 838b, 840b, 841b, 842a, 843b, 1138a
Whittaker, Charles E., 390a–b tab
Whittaker and Baxter, 998a
Whittier, John Greenleaf, 1436b
Whittle, Frank, 781a
*Whole Earth Catalog,* 1031b
Whole Life Expo, 1562a
Wholesalers, 1130b, 1131b, 1137a
Whooping cough, 960a, 968a,b
*Who Rules America?* (Domhoff), 208a,b
*Whose Justice? Which Rationality?* (MacIntyre), 291a
*Why Americans Hate Politics* (Dionne), 292a
"Why Is Economics Not an Evolutionary Science?" (Veblen), 1290b
"Why Is There No Socialism in the United States?" (Sombart), 203a
"Why Modernism Still Matters" (Berman), 1455a
Whyte, William H., 21a, 198b, 265b, 340a
  *Organization Man, The,* 1111a–b
*Why We Fought* (Grattan), 633a
Wickard, Claude P., 384b
Wicksell, Knut, 1290b
Wicksteed, Philip, 1290b
Wiener, Norbert, 751b
Wiesel, Elie, 1589a,b
*Wife-Dressing* (Fogarty), 1790b
Wilberforce University, 1819b
Wilcock, Richard, 112b
Wild and Scenic Rivers Act (1968), 1373b
Wilde, Oscar, 1448b, 1746b
Wilder, Laura Ingalls, 55a
Wilderness Act (1964), 1373b
Wilderness Society, 1370a,b, 1371a
  Echo Park, 1373a
Wildlife, 1384a
  conservationism and, 1361a
Wildman, Donald, 1740b
Wild West shows, 83b, *697a–b,* 697b, 698a, 1461b, 1462a, 1463a
Wiley, Harvey, 943a
Wiley, Maude, 155b
Wilhelmsen, Frederick, 1525a
Wilkes, Charles, 740a

Wilkes Expedition, 740a–b
Wilkins, Mira, *as contributor,* 1243a–1266b
Wilkins, Roy, 152a
Will, George, 189b
Willard, Jess, 1772a
William and Mary College, 1819a
Williams, Bert, 1464a, 1596a,b
Williams, Francis, 709b
Williams, Hank, 1626b
Williams, Joan, 289a, 291b
Williams, John, 487b
Williams, Marion, 1624b
Williams, Martin, 1625b
Williams, Raymond, 917a, 932a
Williams, William Carlos, 1448a, 1449b, 1701b
  *Paterson,* 1449b
Williams Act (1968), 1227a–b tab, 1238a
Williams College, 32a
Williamson, Joel, 142b
  *New People,* 212b
Williamson, Oliver, 1296b
*William Styron's Nat Turner: Ten Black Writers Respond,* 1603a
Willis, Henry Parker, 1293a
  banking reform, 1295b
Willkie, Wendell, 264b, 577a, 635a
  *One World,* 556b
  presidential elections, 335a–b tab
Willowbrook State School, 950b
Wills, Garry, 1497b
Wilson, Charles E., 1280a
Wilson, Edmund, 33b, 262a, 1442a–b, 1446a, 1448b
  *Axel's Castle,* 1442a, 1446a, 1448b
  *To the Finland Station,* 1442a–b
Wilson, Edmund Beecher, 860a–b
Wilson, Edward O., 871a, 894a
Wilson, Graham K, *as contributor,* 295a–320b
Wilson, James Q., 361a
Wilson, Pete, 189a
Wilson, Robert, 760b, 762b
Wilson, Samuel, 257b
Wilson, Sloan, 179b
Wilson, William Julius, 239b, 488a, 930b
  *Declining Significance of Race, The,* 214b
  *Truly Disadvantaged, The,* 210a
Wilson, Woodrow, 322a–b, 326a, 327a, 327b, 328a, 332b, 380a, 430a–b, 521a, 523a, *598a–b,* 623b–624a, 721b, 722b, 1271a,b
  on *Birth of a Nation,* 1593a
  *Congressional Government,* 355b, 360b–361a
  *Constitutional Government in the United States,* 428a
  Dewey, John, on, 278a
  fiscal policy, 1315b, 1316a–1317b
  foreign policy, 572a–574b
  Fourteen Points, 550b, 551b, 627b, 679a
  Lippmann, Walter, and, 279b
  neutrality, 621a
  peace, 543b, 547b, 630a
  preparedness, 596a
  presidential elections, 335a–b tab
  presidential power, 406b, 407a, 522a
  Progressivism, 1314b
  radio broadcasts, 807a
  segregation, 255b
  and separation of powers, 522a–b
  and Southern politicians, 67b

  tariff policy, 1246b, 1314a
  U.S. Railroad Administration, 519b
  in Versailles, 597a–b
  vetoes, 347a tab
  World War I, 494a, 596a, 678b
Wilson-Gorman Tariff (1894), 1313b
  overruled by Supreme Court, 1314a
*Wilson the Diplomatist* (Link), 596b, 597b
Wind tunnels, 772b, 841b
*Winesburg, Ohio* (Anderson), 1440a, 1702a
*Wings of the Dove* (H. James), 1439b
Winkler, Allan M., 605a
Winston, Ellen, 484b
*Winters* decision (1908), 92b
Winterthur, 33a
Wireless. *See* Telegraph
Wireless communications, 803a–b
Wireless hook-ups, 799a
Wirsum, Karl, 1719a
Wirt, William, 1807b
Wisconsin
  bureaucracy, 1270b
  income tax, 1315a
Wisconsin Alumni Research Foundation, 945a
Wisconsin Cutover District, *1361a–b*
Wisconsin Idea, 49a
Wise, George, 840b
Wise, Isaac Mayer, 1566b
Wise, Stephen, 1567a, 1576b, 1579a, 1583a, 1584a
Wister, Owen, 83b
Witmer, Lightner, 880b
Wittgenstein, Ludwig, 1646a, 1647b, 1653b
  *Tractatus Logico-Philosophicus,* 1646b
Wobblies. *See* Industrial Workers of the World
Wofford, Harris, 987a
Wohlstetter, Albert, 613a
Wohlstetter, Roberta, 602b
Wolf, Eric, 917b, 937b
Wolf, Naomi, 1797a
Wolfe, Catherine Lorillard, 1728a
Wolfe, Thomas, 68a
Wolfe, Tom, 34a, 1238b
Wolfson, Harry, 1579a
Wolfson, Louis, 1233b
Wolven, E. L., 1765a–b
*Woman Movement from the Point of View of Social Consciousness, The* (Taft), 276a
*Woman's Dress for Success Book, The* (Molloy), 1785b, 1796a
Woman's Peace Party, 546b, 548b
*Woman Warrior, The* (Kingston), 1456b
Women
  access to health care, 1005b
  arts patronage, 1728a,b
  aviation, 770a, 779b
  career vs. domesticity, 102a
  clerical work, 1104b
  clothing, 1789a, 1794a–1795b
  Congress, 365a–b, 367a–b tab
  consciousness-raising, 120a
  Conservative Judaism, 1575a
  as consumers, 115a
  economic contribution to family, 107b
  education, 102a, 1021a, 1809a
  employment, 1173a
  at end of nineteenth century, 223a
  ethnicity and work, 107b

# INDEX

Yamamoto, Isoruku, 639b, 640b–641a
Yamasaki, Minoru, 1689a
   Pruitt-Igoe Houses (Saint Louis), 1689a
   World Trade Center (New York), 1686a
*Yankee City* studies (Warner), 199b
Yankee ethnicity, 162b
Yankee Stadium, 1775b
Yannacone, Victor, 1373b–1374a
Yardley, Herbert O., 599b
Yates, JoAnne, 1104b
Yates, Peter, 1622b
Yeager, Chuck, 781b
Yeats, William Butler, 1442a, 1448b
Yehoash. *See* Bloomgarden, Solomon
Yehoshua, A. B., 1588a
Yellow fever, 942b, 959b
   Yellow Fever Board, 942a
Yellow peril, 96b
Yellowstone National Park, 84b
*Yellow Wall-Paper, The* (Gilman), 1438b,
   1458a
Yen bonds, 1262a
Yerkes, Robert M., 879a, 881a, 885b,
   1806b
Yerkes, T. C., 743b
Yeshiva College, 1575a,b
   *See also* Yeshiva University
Yeshiva Metivta Tiffereth Jerusalem, 1585a
Yeshivas, 1572a, 1575b, 1585a
Yeshiva University, 32a, 1576a, 1585b,
   1586a
   *See also* Yeshiva College
Yezierska, Anzia, 397a, 1578a
Yiddish Art Theater, 1570b
Yiddish culture, 1568a–b, 1569a,
   1570a–1571b, 1573a, 1580a
   films, 1570b
   literature translated into English, 1588a
   music, 1571a,b
   newspapers, 1569a
   radio, 1571a
   theater, 1570a–b, 1574a
   Yiddish press, 1569a–b
YIVO Institute for Jewish Research, 1584b
YMCA. *See* Young Men's Christian
   Association
YMHA. *See* Young Men's Hebrew
   Association

Yntema, Theodore, 1298a
Yoga, 1550a, 1551a
   Integral Yoga, 1552b
   Siddha Yoga, 1552b
Yogananda, Paramahansa, 1550a, 1551a–b
"Yom Kippur 1984" (Rich), 1587a
Yom Kippur War (1973), 587b, 1199a
*Yosemite and The Range of Light* (Adams),
   1373b
*Yoshe Kalb,* 1570b
Yoshida, Ray, 1714b
Yost, Fielding "Hurry-Up," 1767b
Young, Allyn, 1305b
Young, Andrew, 75a
Young, Brigham, 1542a
Young, Coleman, 58b
Young, Ella Flagg, 1810a
Young, Owen D., 700a, 843a
Young, Robert, 232b
Young, Shirley, 1052b
Young, Stark, 14a,b
Young Israel, 1575b
*Young Lonigan* (Farrell), 1443a
*Young Manhood of Studs Lonigan, The*
   (Farrell), 1443a
Young Men's Christian Association
   immigrants and sports, 1766a
   Student Volunteer Movement, 696a
Young Men's Hebrew Association (YMHA),
   1566a, 1576a, 1579a, 1582b
Young Plan (1929), 632a, 723a,
   1249b–1250a
Young Socialist Alliance, 1827a
Young Women's Christian Association
   (YMCA), 65b
Young Women's Christian Association
   (YWCA)
   Equal Rights Amendment, 120b
Young Women's Hebrew Association
   (YWHA), 1572b, 1576a
*Your Money's Worth* (Chase and Schlink),
   1027a
Youth
   automobiles and, 1751b
   concerts, 1586b
   new identity in 1950s, 233a
   as separate culture, 1793a
Yugoslavia, 679a

YWCA. *See* Young Women's Christian
   Association
YWHA. *See* Young Women's Hebrew
   Assocation

## Z

Zabel, Morton Dauwen, 1447b, 1448a
Zahm, John, 859b
Zahniser, Howard, 1369b, 1373a
Zanesville, Ohio, 1019a, 1020a, 1024b
Zangwill, Israel, 163b, 1568b
Zaretsky, Eli, 923a
Zayas, Marius de, 1698a
Z Budapest, 1557b
Zemach, Benjamin, 1579a
Zen Buddhism, 1553b, 1555a–b
Zevin, Robert, 464b
Zhitlowsky, Hayim, 1567a, 1568b
Zhongshan Hot Springs Golf Club, 712a
Ziegler, Karl, 1146a
Zimmerman, Carle, 924a
Zimmermann, Arthur
   Zimmermann telegram, 624b
Zinc, 1387b, 1392b
Zionism, 578b, 1568a–1569a, 1569a,
   1573a–1574a, 1577a, 1578b, 1582a–b,
   1583a, 1586a
   division, 1573b
   revisionists, 1583b
Zionist Organization of America, 1573b
Znaniecki, Florian, 922b
Zola, Émile, 1437b
Zoot suit, 1792a–b
   riots during World War II, 1792b
Zorach, Marguerite, 1704a
Zoroastrianism, 1550a
Zuboff, Shoshana, *as contributor,*
   1091a–1126b
Zukofsky, Louis, 1580b
Zukor, Adolph, 1580a, 1752b
Zunz, Olivier, 107b, 1101b
   *Changing Face of Inequality, The,* 206a
   *as contributor,* 195a–220b
Zweig, Paul, 1587a
Zworykin, Vladimir, 815a
*Zygon: Journal of Religion and Science,* 871a